FROM PRIMITIVES TO ZEN

Mircea Eliade, the recognised pioneer in the systematic study of the world's religions, was born in Bucharest in 1907. After graduating from Calcutta University, he spent a further two years in India. In 1933 he returned to Rumania to take up his first academic appointment as Lecturer in the History of Religions and Metaphysics at the University of Bucharest. After the war he made his home in Paris, visiting many of the universities of Europe and America to teach and to attend conferences. In 1956 he was appointed visiting professor and Heskell Lecturer at the University of Chicago; he is now Sewell L. Avery Distinguished Service Professor of the History of Religions at that university.

By the same author

THE MYTH OF THE ETERNAL RETURN
PATTERNS IN COMPARATIVE RELIGION
THE SACRED AND THE PROFANE
YOGA: IMMORTALITY AND FREEDOM
BIRTH AND REBIRTH
MYTHS, DREAMS AND MYSTERIES
IMAGES AND SYMBOLS
THE FORGE AND THE CRUCIBLE
MYTH AND REALITY
SHAMANISM: ARCHAIC TECHNIQUES OF ECSTASY
THE TWO AND THE ONE
THE QUEST
ZALMOXIS: THE VANISHING GOD
AUSTRALIAN RELIGIONS: AN INTRODUCTION
NO SOUVENIRS

FROM PRIMITIVES TO ZEN

A Thematic Sourcebook of the
History of Religions

Mircea Eliade

COLLINS
FOUNT PAPERBACKS

First published by William Collins Sons & Co. Ltd,
London 1967
First issued in Fount Paperbacks 1977

Copyright © 1967 by Mircea Eliade

Made and printed in Great Britain by
Richard Clay (The Chaucer Press) Ltd,
Bungay, Suffolk

Preface

The instigation for this anthology of religious texts came during my first years of teaching History of Religions at the University of Chicago. In discussing a specific problem, I expected my students to read at least some of the basic original sources; but I soon discovered that I was unable to recommend to them any single work where one might find a number of essential texts regarding, for example, high gods, cosmogonic myths, conceptions of death and the afterlife, etc. Although we have many source books, some of them excellent, for the most important religions, there are no comprehensive anthologies in English presenting religious documents according to themes and topics. It seems to me that only by reading a certain number of religious texts related to the same subject (cosmogony, initiation, myths on the origin of death, etc.) is a student able to grasp their structural similarities and their differences.

Any thematic classification of religious documents implies a certain amount of arbitrariness. For example, some of the texts located in the chapter on divine beings could just as well have been integrated into the chapters on cosmogony or religious speculations. But this source book is designed to be *read* first, from beginning to end, and only afterward to be *consulted*. A cross-reference index will help the reader, if he so wishes, to examine consecutively all the documents related to a specific religion or a particular cultural-geographic area such as Mespotamia, Ancient Greece, India (or again just one segment of Indian religion: Vedism, Brahmanism, Buddhism, etc.), or the 'primitives' (but also just Australia, Oceania, Africa, Asia, North or South America).

A disturbing problem was raised by the respective proportions to be allotted to the documents representing the different religions and cultural-geographic areas. I was understandably eager to include the most representative religious texts; on the other hand, the thematic classification compelled me to illustrate all the important religious beliefs, conceptions, rituals, and institutions, Thus, for example, because I selected copiously from the *Tao Tê Ching*, the Vedic hymns and the *Upanishads*, I was compelled to be sparing with Chinese and Indian rituals.

For obvious reasons, only a limited number of documents could be reprinted *in toto*. Omissions in the body of the text are indicated by ellipsis points. In the case of long documents (e.g., *Enuma elish* and the *Gilgamesh Epic*), portions omitted are summarized. In rare cases, when the text was unusually long (e.g., Radlov's classic description of the Altaic horse sacrifice and the shaman's ascent to heaven, which fills more than fifty printed pages), I gave a résumé with long quotations. In considering yoga techniques, I thought it pertinent to present a systematic *exposé* with numerous quotations from the original texts rather than to reprint fragments from the *Yoga-sūtra*, a text difficult to understand even when accompanied by classic Indian commentary. Explanatory notes are restricted to bare essentials; in many instances, I made use of or adapted the translator's notes. When it seemed necessary, I introduced a document or a group of documents with a brief comment (e.g., initiation, shamanism, myths of the origin of death). My own comments are printed in italics. Commentaries by others are printed in the same type as the documents they accompany; credit is given in the source line for the document. The use of parentheses and brackets within the documents reprinted follows the style of the book from which the particular selection was taken.

I have tried to avoid using materials from books and periodicals that are rare or hard to get. Thus the reader interested in a specific topic can find additional documents in rather easily accessible publications. The selective bibliography at the end of the volume was prepared with the same end in view: only the most useful and important books are listed. Whenever I could cite a recent monograph on a specific subject containing a rich and well-organized bibliography, I thought it unnecessary to quote other works.

I have made use only of existing English translations of sacred texts. In the case of Ancient Near Eastern, Indian, Greek, Chinese, and Japanese texts, I chose from all the competent translations available, in order to convey to the reader the various possibilities for rendering such abstruse and nonfamiliar texts. In selecting documents related to the 'primitive,' pre-literate societies, I followed the same principle: I limited my choice to works written in, or translated into, English. I hasten to add that although the term 'primitive' is misleading, and should be replaced by 'pre-literate' or 'archaic,' I have kept it, with the majority of authors, for reasons of convenience.

I have tried to include documents from almost all the important religious traditions, from primitive religion to the Ancient Near East to Islam, late Buddhism, and Zen. I have not included Hittite and Ugaritic texts, however, because their fragmentary condition would have demanded too extensive a commentary; furthermore, there are many readily available and competent translations of such texts. A more serious omission it that of Judaism and Christianity. But one cannot present these religions without quoting extensively from the Old and New Testaments, and it seemed unwise to increase the bulk and price of this source book considerably by reproducing such well-known texts. However, a companion volume presenting the Judaic and Christian documents on a somewhat similar thematic basis would be timely. For the moment, the omission of Judaism and Christianity may give the reader a rather inexact idea of the novelty and uniqueness of Muhammad's prophetic experience and of Islamic mystical and theological speculations on the One God. But of course I am assuming that the majority of readers will know something of the other two older monotheistic traditions.

No author of such anthology can hope to satisfy all of his colleagues or, even less so, all of his readers. No matter how 'objective' an author may be in collecting, classifying, and presenting religious documents, his choice is ultimately a personal one. But I should like to point out that this book must be judged as a whole, and not from the particular viewpoint of the anthropologist, or the classical scholar, or the orientalist. As I have already said, the book was conceived as one to be read from beginning to end, and not merely consulted. For the same reason I have tried to limit the scientific apparatus to a minimum. I have not intended to bring out another scholarly work for the exclusive use of the scholar, but a simple and readable book accessible to any *honnête homme* curious about the religious beliefs of his fellow men.

I have to thank my friend and colleague Professor Joseph Kitagawa for helping me in the selection of Japanese materials, Mrs. Rehova Arthur for carefully typing a great portion of the manuscript, Mr. Alan Miller for reading a number of Islamic texts, and Mr. David Knipe for editing and providing notes (not otherwise credited) to the Indian and Scandinavian materials. I am grateful to Miss Nancy Auer for typing and editing most of the Mesopotamian documents, for helping me at various stages of the work, and also for reading and correcting the proofs. Finally, I am thankful to my wife not only for typing a certain number of texts, but especially for encouraging me to continue and complete this work, which has kept me intermittently busy for the past five years. Of course, had I known that so much work would be involved, I would not have dared to embark on such a project. My one consolation for the time and energy consumed is that such a source book will help the student and the interested reader to confront and understand the religious life of ancient and non-Western man.

Mircea Eliade

University of Chicago
January 1966

Contents

Contents

Contents

CHAPTER II

MYTHS OF CREATON AND OF ORIGIN

Contents

Contents

CHAPTER III

MAN AND THE SACRED

Contents

Contents

Contents

Contents

CHAPTER IV

DEATH, AFTERLIFE, ESCHATOLOGY

Contents

Contents

CHAPTER V

SPECIALISTS OF THE SACRED: FROM MEDICINE MEN TO MYSTICS AND FOUNDERS OF RELIGIONS

Contents

Contents

Contents

CHAPTER VI

SPECULATIONS ON MAN AND GOD

Contents

Contents

Contents

CHAPTER I

Gods, Goddesses and Supernatural Beings

A. DIVINITIES OF PRIMITIVES
(PRE-LITERATE SOCIETIES)

1. AUSTRALIAN SUPERNATURAL BEINGS

Beliefs of tribes of Southeast Australia.

The following are the beliefs of the Kulin as they appear in their legends, and from the statements of surviving Wurunjerri to me. *Bunjil*, as represented by them, seems to be an old man, the benign *Ngurungaeta* or Headman of the tribe, with his two wives, who were *Ganawarra* (Black Swan), and his son *Binbeal*, the rainbow, whose wife was the second rainbow which is sometimes visible. *Bunjil* taught the Kulin the arts of life, and one legend states that in that time the Kulin married without any regard for kinship. Two medicine-men *(Wirrarap)* went up to him in the *Tharangalk-bek*, and he said in reply to their request that the Kulin should divide themselves into two parts—'Bunjil on this side and *Waang* on that side, and *Bunjil* should marry *Waang* and *Waang* marry *Bunjil*.'

Another legend relates that he [*Bunjil*] finally went up to the skyland with all his people (the legend says his 'sons') in a whirlwind, which Bellin-bellin (the Musk-crow) let out of his skin bag at his order. There, as the old men instructed the boys, he still remains, looking down on the Kulin. A significant instance of this belief is that Berak, when a boy, 'before his whiskers grew,' was taken by his *Kangun* (mother's brother) out of the camp at night, who, pointing to the star Altair with his spear-thrower, said: 'See! that one is *Bunjil*; you see him, and he sees you.' This was before Batman settled on the banks of the Yarra River, and is conclusive as to the primitive character of this belief. . . .

Usually *Bunjil* was spoken of as *Mami-ngata*, that is 'Our Father,' instead of by the other name *Bunjil*.

It is a striking phase in the legends about him that the human element preponderates over the animal element. In fact, I cannot see any trace of the latter in him, for he is in all cases the old black-fellow, and not the eagle-hawk, which his name denotes; while another actor

3

may be the kangaroo, the spiny ant-eater, or the crane, and as much animal as human. . . .

Among the Kurnai, under the influence of the initiation ceremonies, the knowledge of the being who is the equivalent of *Bunjil* is almost entirely restricted to the initiated men. The old women know that there is a supernatural being in the sky, but only as *Mungan-ngaua*, 'our father.' It is only at the last and the most secret part of the ceremonies that the novices are made aware of the teachings as to *Mungan-ngaua*, and this is the only name for this being used by the Kurnai. . . .

The conception of *Baiame* may be seen from Ridley's statements, and so far as I now quote them, may be accepted as sufficiently accurate. I have omitted the colouring which appears to be derived from his mental bias as a missionary to blacks. He says that *Baiame* is the name in Kamilaroi of the maker (from *Biai*, 'to make or build') who created and preserves all things. Generally invisible, he has, they believe, appeared in human form, and has bestowed on their race various gifts.

The following is the statement of one of the early settlers in the Kamilaroi country, and, I think, gives the aboriginal idea of *Baiame* free from any tinge derived from our beliefs. If you ask a Kamilaroi man 'Who made that?' referring to something, he replies, 'Baiame deah,' that is 'Baiame, I suppose.' It is said that Baiame came from the westward long ago to Golarinbri on the Barwon, and stayed there four or five days, when he went away to the eastward with his two wives. They believe that some time he will return again. . . .

The belief in *Daramulun*, the 'father,' and *Biamban*, or 'master,' is common to all of the tribes who attend the *Yuin Kuringal*. I have described them at length in chapter IX, and may now summarize the teachings of the ceremonies. Long ago *Daramulun* lived on the earth with his mother *Ngalalbal*. Originally the earth was bare 'like the sky, as hard as a stone,' and the land extended far out where the sea is now. There were no men or women, but only animals, birds, and reptiles. He placed trees on the earth. After Kaboka, the thrush, had caused a great flood on the earth, which covered all the coast country, there were no people left, excepting some who crawled out of the water on to Mount Dromedary. Then *Daramulun* went up to the sky, where he lives and watches the actions of men. It was he who first made the *Kuringal* and the bull-roarer, the sound of which represents his voice. He told the Yuin what to do, and he gave them the laws which the old people have handed down from father to son to this time. He gives the *Gommeras* their power to use the *Joias*, and other magic. When a man dies and his *Tulugal* (spirit) goes away, it is *Daramulun* who meets it and takes care of it. It is a man's shadow which goes up to *Daramulun*. . . .

It seems quite clear that *Nurrundere, Nurelli, Bunjil, Mungan-ngaua, Daramulun,* and *Baiame* all represent the same being under different names. To this may be reasonably added *Koin* of the Lake Macquarie tribes, *Maamba, Birral,* and *Kohin* of those on the Herbert River, thus extending the range of this belief certainly over the whole of Victoria and of New South Wales, up to the eastern boundaries of the tribes of the Darling River. If the Queensland coast tribes are included, then the western bounds might be indicated by a line drawn from the mouth of the Murray River to Cardwell, including the Great Dividing Range, with some of the fall inland in New South Wales. This would define the part of Australia in which a belief exists in an anthropomorphic supernatural being, who lives in the sky, and who is supposed to have some kind of influence on the morals of the natives. No such belief seems to obtain in the remainder of Australia, although there are indications of a belief in anthropomorphic beings inhabiting the sky-land. . . .

This supernatural being, by whatever name he is known, is represented as having at one time dwelt on the earth, but afterwards to have ascended to a land beyond the sky, where he still remains, observing mankind. As *Daramulun,* he is said to be able to 'go anywhere and do anything.' He can be invisible; but when he makes himself visible, it is in the form of an old man of the Australian race. He is evidently everlasting, for he existed from the beginning of all things, and he still lives. But in being so, he is merely in that state in which, these aborigines believe, every one would be if not prematurely killed by evil magic.

A. W. Howitt, *The Native Tribes of South-East Australia* (London, 1904), pp. 491-500

See also no. 142

AFRICAN HIGH GODS

Like many celestial Supreme Beings of 'primitive' peoples, the High Gods of a great number of African ethnic groups are regarded as creators, all-powerful, benevolent, and so forth; but they play a rather insignificant part in the religious life. Being either too distant or too good to need a real cult, they are invoked only in cases of great crisis. (Cf. M. Eliade, 'Patterns in Comparative Religion,' trans. Rosemary Sheed [New York: Sheed and Ward, 1958], pp. 47-50; cf. also Bibliography below, p. 635.)

2. NZAMBI, THE HIGH GOD OF THE BAKONGO

The Bakongo tribe is native to the lower Congo River area.

Nzambi Mpungu is a being, invisible, but very powerful, who has made all, men and things, even fetishes which he has given to men for their good. 'If he had not given us our fetishes, we should all be dead long ago.' He intervenes in the creation of every child, he punishes those who violate his prohibitions. They render him no worship, for he has need of none and is inaccessible. On earth man lives with his incessant needs to satisfy; the aged have there a privileged position. Above all is Nzambi, the sovereign Master, unapproachable, who has placed man here below to take him away some day, at the hour of death. He watches man, searches him out everywhere and takes him away, inexorably, young or old. . . . Among the laws there are *nkondo mi Nzambi*, 'God's prohibitions,' the violation of which constitutes a *sumu ku Nzambi* [a sin against Nzambi], and an ordinary sanction of this is *lufwa lumbi* 'a bad death.'

> Van Wing, *Études Bakongo* (Brussels, 1921; pp. 170 ff.) as translated by Edwin W. Smith in Smith (ed.), *African Ideas of God: A Symposium* (2nd ed.; London, 1950), p. 159

3. THE SUPREME BEING OF THE ISOKO (SOUTHERN NIGERIA)

Isoko religion begins with Cghene the Supreme Being, who is believed to have created the world and all peoples, including the Isoko. He lives in the sky which is a part of him, sends rain and sunshine, and shows his anger through thunder. Cghene is entirely beyond human comprehension, has never been seen, is sexless, and is only known by his actions, which have led men to speak of Cghene as 'him,' because he is thought of as the creator and therefore father of all the Isokos. He is spoken of as Our Father never as My Father. Cghene always punishes evil and rewards good, a belief that leads the Isokos to blame witchcraft for any evil which may happen to a good man. As however Cghene is so distant and unknowable, he has no temples or priests, and no prayers or sacrifices are offered to him direct. To bridge the gulf between himself and man, Cghene appointed an intermediary, called *oyise*, which is referred to as *uko Cghene* or 'messenger of Cghene.' This *oyise* is a pole about eight feet long made from the *oyise* tree, erected after a seven-fold offering to Cghene, in the compound of the oldest member of the family, and only in his. Before this pole the family elder throws his used chewing stick each morning and offers prayer for the family and town. Through *oyise*, Cghene can be invoked in case of calamity or need.

James W. Telch, 'The Isoko Tribe,' *Africa*, VII (1934), pp. 160-73; quotation from p. 163

4. NGAI, THE HIGH GOD OF THE KIKUYU

The Kikuyu are a Bantu-speaking tribe of East Africa.

First we have Gothaithaya Ngai, which means 'to beseech Ngai,' or 'to worship Ngai.' Ngai is a name of the High God. The difference between deity worship and ancestor worship is demonstrated by the fact that Gothaithaya is never used in connection with ancestral spirits.

The Conception of a Deity. The Kikuyu believes in one God, Ngai, the Creator and giver of all things. He has no father, mother, or companion of any kind. He loves or hates people according to their behaviour. The Creator lives in the sky, but has temporary homes on earth, situated on mountains, where he may rest during his visits. The visits are made with a view to his carrying out a kind of 'general inspection,' *Koroora thi*, and to bring blessings and punishments to the people. . . . Ngai cannot be seen by mortal eyes. He is a distant being and takes but little interest in individuals in their daily walks of life. Yet at the crises of their lives he is called upon. At the birth, initiation, marriage and death of every Kikuyu, communication is

7

established on his behalf with Ngai. The ceremonies for these four events leave no doubt as to the importance of the spiritual assistance which is essential to them. . . . In the ordinary way of everyday life, there are no prayers or religious ceremonies, such as 'morning and evening prayers.' So long as people and things go well and prosper, it is taken for granted that God is pleased with the general behaviour of the people and the welfare of the country. In this happy state there is no need for prayers. Indeed they are inadvisable, for Ngai must not needlessly be bothered. It is only when humans are in real need that they must approach him without fear of disturbing him and incurring his wrath. But when people meet to discuss public affairs or decide a case, or at public dances, they offer prayers for protection and guidance. When a man is stricken by lightning it is said: 'He has been smashed to smithereens for seeing Ngai in the act of cracking his joints in readiness to go to smash and chase away his enemies.'

It is said that lightning is a visible representation of some of God's weapons which he uses on ahead to warn people of his coming and to prepare and clear the way. His approach is foretold only by the sounds of his own preparations. Thunder is the cracking of his joints, as a warrior limbering up for action.

Jomo Kenyatta, 'Kikuyu Religion, Ancestor-Worship, and Sacrificial Practices,' *Africa*, x (1937), pp. 308-28; quotation from pp. 308-9

5. LEZA, THE HIGH GOD OF THE BA-ILA OF NORTHERN RHODESIA

Long ago the Ba-ila did not know Leza as regards his affairs—no, all that they knew about him, was that he created us, and also his unweariedness in doing things. As at present when the rainy season is annoying and he does not fall, when then they ask of Leza different things: they say now: 'Leza annoys by not falling': then later when he falls heavily they say: 'Leza falls too much.' If there is cold they say 'Leza makes it cold,' and if it is not they say, 'Leza is much too hot, let it be overclouded.' All the same, Leza as he is the Compassionate, that is to say, as he is Merciful, he does not get angry, he doesn't give up falling, he doesn't give up doing them all good—no, whether they curse, whether they mock him, whether they grumble at him, he does good to all at all times, that is how they trust him always. But as for seeing always his affairs, no, the Ba-ila do not know, all they say is: Leza is the good-natured one; he is one from whom you beg different things. We Ba-ila have no more that we know.

Edwin W. Smith and A. M. Dale, *The Ila-speaking People of Northern Rhodesia*, II (London, 1920), p. 199

6. THE SUPREME BEING OF THE HERERO

The Herero are a Bantu tribe of South-West Africa.

'The Hereros know a supreme being whom they call by two names: Ndjambi Karunga. The name Karunga has an Ovambo derivation and is only known intimately to those Hereros, who have been in contact with the Ovambo in former times. . . . Ndjambi is the Heavenly God. He lives in Heaven, yet is omnipresent. His most striking characteristic is kindness. Human life is due to and dependent on him and all blessings ultimately come from him. He who dies a natural death is carried away by Ndjambi. As his essence is kindness people cherish no fear but a veneration for him. As his blessings are the gifts of his kindness without any moral claims, the belief in Ndjambi has no moral strength, nor has the worship of Ndjambi become a cult. At best his name is invoked only in thanksgiving after some unexpected luck or they pray to him when all other means of help fail. For the rest, the utterance of his name is not allowed. In reply to a question I put to a Tjimba woman in the Kaokoveld as to the abode of Ndjambi Karunga, she said: 'He stays in the clouds because, when the clouds rise, his voice is clearly heard,' and further research has brought to light that the Tjimba look upon Ndjambi as the giver of rain.' (H. Vedder, *The Native Tribes of South-West Africa*, Capetown, 1928, p. 164.)

Dr. Vedder's statement that the sacred name should not be uttered is significant. It explains partly, if not wholly, why the missionaries who had lived in close contact with the Herero since 1844 heard his name for the first time only in 1871.

Dr. H. Vedder, as quoted and commented on by Edwin W. Smith (ed.), *African Ideas of God: A Symposium* (2nd ed.; London, 1950), pp. 132-3

Gods, Goddesses and Supernatural Beings

7. RALUVHIMBA, THE HIGH GOD OF THE VENDA

The Venda are a Bantu tribe of the northern Transvaal.

The name is composed of the prefix *Ra-*, which is honorific and perhaps connected with the idea of 'Father'; *luvhimba* is the eagle, the bird that soars aloft. It symbolizes the great power which travels through the cosmos, using the heavenly phenomena as its instruments.

'Raluvhimba is connected with the beginning of the world and is supposed to live somewhere in the heavens and to be connected with all astronomical and physical phenomena. . . . A shooting star is Raluvhimba travelling; his voice is heard in the thunder; comets, lightning, meteors, earthquakes, prolonged drought, floods, pests, and epidemics—in fact, all the natural phenomena which affect the people as a whole—are revelations of the great god. In thunderstorms he appears as a great fire near the chief's kraal, whence he booms his desires to the chief in a voice of thunder; this fire always disappears before any person can reach it. At these visitations the chief enters his hut and, addressing Raluvhimba as *Makhulu* [Grandfather], converses with him, the voice of the god replying either from the thatch of the hut or from a tree nearby; Raluvhimba then passes on in a further clap of thunder. Occasionally he is angry with the chief and takes revenge on the people by sending them a drought or a flood, or possibly by opening an enormous cage in the heavens and letting loose a swarm of locusts on the land.'

(H. A. Stayt, *The Bavenda*, Oxford, 1931, p. 236)

Raluvhimba, it is said, was wont to manifest himself by appearing from time to time as a great flame on a platform of rock above a certain cave. With the flame there came a sound as of clanking irons, on hearing which the people shouted with joy and their cries passed on throughout the country. The Chief mounted to the platform where he called upon Raluvhimba, thanked him for revealing himself and prayed on behalf of his people for rain, felicity and peace.

He is at times greeted spontaneously by the whole people in a way that is most unusual among the southern Bantu. The Rev. G. Westphal of the Berlin Mission relates that in 1917 a meteor burst in the middle of the day making a strange humming sound followed by a thunder-like crash. This portent was greeted by the people, not with terror but with cries of joy. Another missionary, the Rev. McDonald, tells how after a slight tremor of the earth there was an extraordinary clamour among the people, the lululuing of women, clapping of hands and shouting. 'The whole tribe was greeting Raluvhimba who was passing through the country.' People say that during an earthquake they hear a noise in the sky similar to thunder. Then they clap their hands to welcome the mysterious god and pray: 'Give us rain! Give us health!'

Dr. H. A. Junod says that Raluvhimba is regarded as the maker and former of everything and as the rain-giver. If rain is scarce and starvation threatens, people complain: 'Raluvhimba wants to destroy us.' They say the same if floods spoil their fields. Prayers and sacrifices are offered in times of drought. There is some notion of Raluvhimba as Providence. He takes care not only of the tribe as a whole but of individual members. When a man has narrowly escaped drowning he will say: 'I have been saved by Raluvhimba, Mudzimu.'

Raluvhimba is identified with Mwari (or Nwali) whose earthly abode (like Yahwe's on Mount Sinai) is in the Matopo Hills of Southern Rhodesia. Every year the Venda used to send a special messenger (whose office was hereditary) with a black ox and a piece of black cloth as an offering to Mwari. The black ox was set free in a forest to join the god's large herd which had accumulated there.

Edwin W. Smith, 'The Idea of God among South African Tribes' in Smith (ed.), *African Ideas of God: A Symposium* (2nd ed.; London, 1950), pp. 124-6

See also nos. 51, 67, 91, 126, 127, 299

NORTH AMERICAN INDIANS

8. WAKAN TANKA, THE SUPREME DEITY OF THE DAKOTA

Following are the words of Sword, an Oglala of the Teton division of the Dakota Indians, as recorded by J. R. Walker.

Every object in the world has a spirit and that spirit is *wakan*. Thus the spirits of the tree or things of that kind, while not like the spirit of man, are also *wakan*. *Wakan* comes from the *wakan* beings. These *wakan* beings are greater than mankind in the same way that mankind is greater than animals. They are never born and never die. They can do many things that mankind cannot do. Mankind can pray to the *wakan* beings for help. There are many of these beings but all are of four kinds. The word *Wakan Tanka* means all of the *wakan* beings because they are all as if one. *Wakan Tanka Kin* signifies the chief or leading *Wakan* being which is the Sun. However, the most powerful of the *Wakan* beings is *Nagi Tanka*, the Great Spirit who is also *Taku Skanskan. Taku Skanskan* signifies the Blue, in other words, the Sky. . . . Mankind is permitted to pray to the *Wakan* beings. If their prayer is directed to all the good *Wakan* beings, they should pray to *Wakan Tanka*; but if the prayer is offered to only one of these beings, then the one addressed should be named. . . . *Wakan Tanka* is like sixteen different persons; but each person is *kan*. Therefore, they are only the same as one.

J. R. Walker, *The Sun Dance and Other Ceremonies of the Oglala Division of the Teton Dakota* (American Museum of Natural History, Anthropological Papers, vol. XVI, part II (1917), pp. 152-3)

9. THE 'GREAT SPIRIT' OF THE LENAPE

The Lenape (or Delaware) Indians, an important Algonquian tribe, occupied a large area from Ontario southward into the middle Atlantic region, and westward principally in Oklahoma.

All the Lenape so far questioned, whether followers of the native or of the Christian religion, unite in saying that their people have always believed in a chief *Mani 'to*, a leader of all the gods, in short, in a Great Spirit or Supreme Being, the other *mani 'towuk* for the greater part being merely agents appointed by him. His name, according to present Unami usage is *Gicelĕmû 'kaong*, usually translated 'great spirit,' but meaning literally, 'creator.' Directly, or through the *mani-'towuk* his agents, he created the earth and eveything in it, and gave to the Lenape all they possessed, 'the trees, the waters, the fire that springs from flint,—everything.' To him the people pray in their greatest ceremonies, and give thanks for the benefits he has given them. Most of their direct worship, however, is addressed to the *mani 'towuk* his agents, to whom he has given charge of the elements, and with whom the people feel they have a closer personal relation, as their actions are seen in every sunrise and thunderstorm, and felt in every wind that blows across woodland and prairie. Moreover, as the Creator lives in the twelfth or highest heaven above the earth, it takes twelve shouts or cries to reach his ear.

M. R. Harrington, *Religion and Ceremonies of the Lenape* (New York, 1921), pp. 18-19

10. TIRAWA, THE SUPREME GOD OF THE PAWNEE

Once among the strongest tribes of the Plains Indians, the Pawnee were found from the shores of the Platte River in Nebraska south to the Arkansas River. Today they live mostly in Oklahoma.

'The white man,' said the Kurahus, 'speaks of a heavenly Father; we say Tirawa atius, the Father above, but we do not think of Tirawa as a person. We think of Tirawa as in everything, as the Power which has arranged and thrown down from above everything that man needs. What the Power above, Tirawa atius, is like, no one knows; no one has been there.'

When Kawas explains to the Kurahus the meaning of the signs in the East, 'she tells him that Tirawa atius there moves upon Darkness, the Night, and causes her to bring forth the Dawn. It is the breath of the new-born Dawn, the child of Night and Tirawa atius, which is felt by all the powers and all things above and below and which gives them new life for the new day. . . .'

H. B. Alexander, *The World's Rim* (Lincoln, Neb.: University of Nebraska Press, 1953), p. 132; quoting and summarizing Alice C. Fletcher, *The Hako: A Pawnee Ceremony* (Bureau of American Ethnology, Twenty-second Annual Report, part 2, 1904)

See also nos. 44, 45

POLYNESIA, COLOMBIA, LABRADOR, NEW GUINEA

11. THE MAORI SUPREME BEING (POLYNESIA)

The core of the esoteric theology of the Maori was the concept of the Supreme Io which remained wholly unrevealed to foreign enquirers for many decades after the first contact of Europeans and Maori. I cannot help feeling that our lack of knowledge of such a supreme god in other island groups is due largely to the fact that the knowledge was limited to the ancient priesthood, whose rules would have compelled them to conceal from outsiders the most sacred of the lore; while personal instinct would at the same time have led them to shelter their hallowed belief from strangers with the attitude typical of practically all the early enquirers. With the ancient priesthoods, the knowledge of the great body of the most sacred Polynesian lore died. The following pictures well the attitude of Maori priests towards the indiscreetly inquisitive and disrespectful. Tregear writes:

'C. O. Davis mentions that when attempting to question an old priest on the subject of the ancient Maori worship of the Supreme Being he was refused information, and politely referred to another priest 100 miles away. Probably that priest would have referred him again to someone else and so on. Each initiate into the sacred mysteries considered his knowledge as a trust to be guarded against the outer world, and it is only under most exceptional circumstances that information could be acquired. Some gods could only be named in the Whare Kura and Wharewanagna (temples) of the tribe. To utter "the ineffable name" (Io) under a roof of any kind was to blaspheme most frightfully, and would be a sacrilege that only an ignorant person (religiously ignorant) like a European would have the depravity to attempt. Even the names of ancestors, as god-descended, would not be regarded as treated with due respect if mentioned at certain times or in unsuitable localities. A European student of Maori lore once ventured to speak to an old priest whom he met in a country store (shop) and asked him some question about ancient history. The Maori turned round with a disgusted look and remarked, "This is no place in which to speak of solemn things," . . . Only one who loved the enquirer and dared unknown terrors for the sake of that love would answer such questions (about sacred things) or repeat the consecrated hymns for him. It is not unusual for a priest after going a certain length to say, "If I tell you any more death will overtake me," or "I must not repeat what follows, because there is now no priest alive sacred enough to perform the ceremonies necessary to purify me from such sacrilege." Another has been known to say, "The presence of the Christian God has silenced the Maori gods, but the gods of the Maori still hold us in their power, and if I break their laws they will punish me with death." '

The mere fact of the existence of Io was unknown to most Maoris. Best writes that:

'The number of men initiated into the cult of Io was but small; only members of the higher grade of priestly experts and men of high-class families, were allowed to learn the ritual pertaining to it. The common folk apparently had no part in it and it is doubtful if they were even allowed to know the name of the Supreme Being. This cult of Io was an esoteric one; that of the lower tribal gods may be termed exoteric. All ritual and ceremonial pertaining to Io was retained in the hands of the superior priesthood, by no means a numerous body. It may be described as an aristocratic cultus, known only to such experts and the more important chiefs. It is quite probable, indeed, that this superior creed may have been too exalted for ordinary minds, that such would prefer to depend on more accessible and less moral deities.

'It is interesting to note that no form of offering or sacrifice was made to Io, that no image of him was ever made, and that he had no *aria*, or form of incarnation, such as inferior gods had.'

E. S. Craighill Handy, *Polynesian Religion*, Bernice P. Bishop Museum Bulletin 34 (Honolulu, 1927), pp. 95-6; quoting Edward Tregear, *The Maori Race* (Wanganui, 1904), pp. 450-2, and Elsdon Best, *Some Aspects of Maori Myth and Religion* (Dominion Museum Monograph no. 1, Wellington, 1922), p. 20

See also no. 47

12. THE UNIVERSAL MOTHER AND SUPREME DEITY

The following comes from the Kagaba people of Colombia in South America.

'The mother of our songs, the mother of all our seed, bore us in the the beginning of things and so she is the mother of all types of men, the mother of all nations. She is the mother of the thunder, the mother of the streams, the mother of trees and of all things. She is the mother of the world and of the older brothers, the stone-people. She is the mother of the fruits of the earth and of all things. She is the mother of our youngest brothers, the French and the strangers. She is the mother of our dance paraphernalia, of all our temples and she is the only mother we possess. She alone is the mother of the fire and the Sun and the Milky Way. . . . She is the mother of the rain and the only mother we possess. And she has left us a token in all the temples . . . a token in the form of songs and dances.'

She has no cult, and no prayers are really directed to her, but when the fields are sown and the priests chant their incantations the Kagaba say, 'And then we think of the one and only mother of the growing things, of the mother of all things.' One prayer was recorded. 'Our mother of the growing fields, our mother of the streams, will have pity upon us. For whom do we belong? Whose seeds are we? To our mother alone do we belong.'

Paul Radin, *Monotheism among Primitive Peoples* New York, p. 15; translating and quoting K. T. Preuss

13. A SOUTH AMERICAN EPIPHANY OF THE SUN GOD

The Apinayé, one of the Gé tribes of eastern Brazilia, regard the Sun as creator and father of men. They address the Sun God as 'my father' and he calls men his children. The following experience was told to the anthropologist Curt Nimuendaju by an Apinayé village chief.

'I was hunting near the sources of the Botica creek. All along the journey there I had been agitated and was constantly startled without knowing why.

'Suddenly I saw him standing under the drooping branches of a big steppe tree. He was standing there erect. His club was braced against the ground beside him, his hand he held on the hilt. He was tall and light-skinned, and his hair nearly descended to the ground behind him. His whole body was painted, and on the outer side of his legs were broad red stripes. His eyes were exactly like two stars. He was very handsome.

'I recognized at once that it was he. Then I lost all courage. My hair stood on end, and my knees were trembling. I put my gun aside, for I thought to myself that I should have to address him, but I could not utter a sound because he was looking at me unwaveringly. Then I lowered my head in order to get hold of myself and stood thus for a long time. When I had grown somewhat calmer, I raised my head. He was still standing and looking at me. Then I pulled myself together and walked several steps toward him, then I could not go any further for my knees gave way. I again remained standing for a long time, then lowered my head, and tried again to regain composure. When I raised my eyes again, he had already turned away and was slowly walking through the steppe.

'Then I grew very sad. I kept standing there for a long time after he had vanished, then I walked under the tree where he had stood. I saw his footprints, painted red with urucú at the edges; beside them was the print of his clubhead. I picked up my gun and returned to the village. On the way I managed to kill two deer, which approached me without the least shyness. At home I told my father everything. Then all scolded me for not having had the courage to talk to him.

'At night while I was asleep he reappeared to me. I addressed him, and he said he had been waiting for me in the steppe to talk to me, but since I had not approached he had gone away. He led me some distance behind the house and there showed me a spot on the ground where, he said, something was lying in storage for me. Then he vanished.

'The next morning I immediately went there and touched the ground with the tip of my foot, perceiving something hard buried there. But others came to call me to go hunting. I was ashamed to stay behind and joined them. When we returned, I at once went back to the site he had shown me, but did not find anything any more.

'Today I know that I was very stupid then. I should certainly have received from him great self-assurance (segurança) if I had been able to talk to him. But I was still very young then; today I should act quite differently.'

Curt Nimuendaju, *The Apinayé* (Washington, D.C., 1939), 136-7

14. THE MASTER OF THE CARIBOU

A belief of the Naskapi Indians of the Labrador Peninsula.

In the interior between Ungava Bay and Hudson's Bay is a distant country where no Indians will go under any consideration for the following reason. There is a range of big mountains pure white in colour formed neither of snow, ice, nor white rock, but of caribou hair. They are shaped like a house and so they are known as Caribou House. One man of the Petisigabau band says there are two houses. In this enormous cavity live thousands upon thousands of caribou under the overlordship of a human being who is white and dressed in black. Some say there are several of them and they have beards. He is master of the caribou and will not permit anyone to come within some one hundred and fifty miles of his abode, the punishment being death. Within his realm the various animals are two or three times their ordinary size. The few Indians who have approached the region say that the caribou enter and leave their kingdom each year, passing through a valley between two high mountains about fifteen miles apart. And it is also asserted that the deer hair on the ground here is several feet in depth, that for miles around the cast-off antlers on the ground form a layer waist deep, that the caribou paths leading back and forth there are so deep as to reach a man's waist, and that a young caribou going along in one would be visible only by its head.

F. G. Speck, *Naskapi, The Savage Hunters of the Labrador Peninsula* (Norman, Okla.: University of Oklahoma Press, 1935), p. 84

15. HAINUWELE AND THE 'CREATIVE MURDER' (CERAM, NEW GUINEA)

The Marind-anim apply the term *dema* to the divine creators and primordial beings who existed in mythical times. The *dema* are described sometimes in human form, sometimes in the form of animals and plants. The central myth narrates the slaying of the *dema*-divinity by the *dema*-men of the primordial time. Especially famous is the myth of the girl Hainuwele, recorded by A. E. Jensen in Ceram, one of the islands of the New Guinea Archipelago. In substance it runs:

In mythical Times, a man named Ameta, out hunting, came on a wild boar. Trying to escape, the boar was drowned in a lake. On its tusk Ameta found a coconut. That night he dreamed of the coconut and was commanded to plant it, which he did the next morning. In three days a coconut palm sprang up, and three days later it flowered. Ameta climbed it to cut some flowers and make a drink from them. But he cut his finger and the blood dropped on a flower. Nine days later he found a girl-child on the flower. Ameta took her and wrapped her in coconut fronds. In three days the child became a marriageable girl, and he named her Hainuwele ('coconut branch'). During the great Maro festival Hainuwele stood in the middle of the dancing place and for nine nights distributed gifts to the dancers. But on the ninth day the men dug a grave in the middle of the dancing place and threw Hainuwele into it during the dance. The grave was filled in and men danced on it.

The next morning, seeing that Hainuwele did not come home, Ameta divined that she had been murdered. He found the body, disinterred it, and cut it into pieces, which he buried in various places, except the arms. The buried pieces gave birth to plants previously unknown, especially to tubers, which since then are the chief food of human beings. Ameta took Hainuwele's arms to another *dema*-divinity, Satene. Satene drew a spiral with nine turns on a dancing ground and placed herself at the centre of it. From Hainuwele's arms she made a door, and summoned the dancers. 'Since you have killed,' she said, 'I will no longer live here. I shall leave this very day. Now you will have to come to me through this door.' Those who were able to pass through it remained human beings. The others were changed into animals (pigs, birds, fish) or spirits. Satene announced that after her going men would meet her only after their death, and she vanished from the surface of the Earth.

A. E. Jensen has shown the importance of this myth for an understanding of the religion and world image of the paleocultivators. The murder of a *dema* divinity by the *dema*, the ancestors of present humanity, ends an epoch (which cannot be considered 'paradisal') and opens that in which we live today. The *dema* became men, that is, sexed and mortal beings. As for the murdered *dema*-divinity, she survives both in her own 'creations' (food, plants, animals, etc.) and in the house of the dead into which she was changed, or in the 'mode of being of death,' which she established by her own demise.

M. Eliade, *Myth and Reality* (New York, 1963), pp. 104-5; translated and abridged from A. E. Jensen, *Das religiöse Weltbild einer frühen Kultur* (Stuttgart, 1948), pp. 35-8

B. GODS OF THE ANCIENT NEAR EAST, ANCIENT INDIA, AND JAPAN

16. ENKI, A SUMERIAN HIGH GOD

'Enki and the World Order' is one of the longest and best preserved of the extant Sumerian narrative poems. The poem begins with a hymn of praise addressed to Enki; some of it is destroyed and unintelligible, but generally speaking, it seems to exalt Enki as the god who watches over the universe and is responsible for the fertility of field and farm, flock and herd. It continues to follow the same motif at some length, with Enki now praising himself, now being praised by the gods. Next, a badly damaged passage seems to describe the various rites and rituals performed by some of the more important priests and spiritual leaders of Sumer in Enki's Abzu-shrine. The scene shifts again to reveal Enki in his boat, passing from city to city to 'decree the fates' and render proper exaltation to each. Two inimical lands are not so fortunate; he destroys them and carries off their wealth.

Enki now turns from the fates of the various lands which made up the Sumerian inhabited world and performs a whole series of acts vital to the earth's fertility and productiveness. He fills the Tigris with life-giving water, then appoints the god Enbilulu, the 'canal inspector,' to make sure that the Tigris and Euphrates function properly. He 'calls' the marshland and the canebrake, supplies them with fish and reeds, and again appoints a deity for them. He erects his own shrine by the sea and places the goddess Nanshe in charge of it. Similarly, he 'calls' the earth's plow, yoke, and furrow, the cultivated field, the pickaxe, and brick mould; he turns to the high plain, covers it with vegetation and cattle, stall and sheepfolds; he fixes the borders and cities and states; finally he attends to 'woman's task,' particularly the weaving of cloth. For each realm a deity is appointed.

The poem comes to an end in yet another key as the ambitious and aggressive Inanna complains that she has been slighted and left without any special powers and perogatives. Enki reassures her with a recitation of her own insignia and provinces.

Gods, Goddesses and Supernatural Beings

Enki, the king of the Abzu, overpowering in his majesty, speaks up with authority:

'My father, the king of the universe,
Brought me into existence in the universe,
My ancestor, the king of all the lands,
Gathered together all the me's, placed the me's in my hand.
From the Ekur, the house of Enlil,
I brought craftsmanship to my Abzu of Eridu.
I am the fecund seed, engendered by the great wild ox, I am the first born son of An,
I am the "great storm" who goes forth out of the "great below," I am the lord of the Land,
I am the gugal of the chieftains, I am the father of all the lands,
I am the "big brother" of the gods, I am he who brings full prosperity,
I am the record keeper of heaven and earth,
I am the ear and the mind of all the lands,
I am he who directs justice with the king An on An's dais,
I am he who decrees the fates with Enlil in the "mountain of wisdom,"
He placed in my hand the decreeing of the fates of the "place where the sun rises,"
I am he to whom Nintu pays due homage,
I am he who has been called a good name by Ninhursag,
I am the leader of the Anunnaki,
I am he who has been born as the first son of the holy An.'

After the lord had uttered (his) exaltedness,
After the great prince had himself pronounced his praise,
The Anunnaki came before him in prayer and supplication:
'Lord who directs craftsmanship,
Who makes decisions, the glorified; Enki, praise!'

For a second time, because of his great joy,
Enki, the king of the Abzu, in his majesty, speaks up with authority:
'I am the lord, I am one whose command is unquestioned, I am the foremost in all things,
At my command the stalls have been built, the sheepfolds have been enclosed,
When I approached heaven a rain of prosperity poured down from heaven,
When I approached the earth, there was a high flood,
When I approached its green meadows,
The heaps and mounds were piled up at my word.

....

[After the almost unintelligible description of Enki's rites, Enki proceeds
to decree the fates of a number of cities. Ur is one example.]

He proceeded to the shrine Ur,
Enki, the king of the Abzu decrees its fate:
'City possessing all that is appropriate, water-washed, firm-standing ox,
Dais of abundance of the highland, knees open, green like a mountain,
Hashur-grove, wide of shade—he who is lordly because of his might
Has directed your perfect me's,
Enlil, the "great mountain," has pronounced your lofty name in the
  universe.
City whose fate has been decreed by Enlil,
Shrine Ur, may you rise heaven high.'

....

[Enki next stocks the land with various items of prosperity: A deity
is placed in charge of each. For example:]

He directed the plow and the . . . yoke,
The great prince Enki put the 'horned oxen' in the . . .
Opened the holy furrows,
Made grow the grain in the cultivated field.
The lord who dons the diadem, the ornament of the high plain,
The robust, the farmer of Enlil,
Enkimdu, the man of the ditch and dike,
Enki placed in charge of them.

The lord called the cultivated field, put there the checkered grain,
Heaped up its . . . grain, the checkered grain, the innuba-grain into
  piles,
Enki multiplied the heaps and mounds,
With Enlil he spread wide the abundance in the Land,
Her whose head and side are dappled, whose face is honey-covered,
The Lady, the procreatress, the vigour of the Land, the 'life' of the
  black-heads,
Ashnan, the nourishing bread, the bread of all,
Enki placed in charge of them.

....

He built stalls, directed the purification rites,
Erected sheepfolds, put there the best fat and milk,
Brought joy to the dining halls of the gods,

23

In the vegetation-like plain he made prosperity prevail.
....

He filled the Ekur, the house of Enlil, with possessions,
Enlil rejoiced with Enki, Nippur was joyous,
He fixed the borders, demarcated them with boundary stones,
Enki, for the Anunnaki,
Erected dwelling places in the cities,
Set up fields for them in the countryside,
The hero, the bull who comes forth out of the hashur (forest), who
    roars lion-like,
The valiant Utu, the bull who stands secure, who proudly displays
    his power,
The father of the great city, the place where the sun rises, the great
    herald of holy An,
The judge, the decision-maker of the gods,
Who wears a lapis lazuli beard, who comes forth from the holy heaven,
    the . . . heaven,
Utu, the son born of Ningal,
Enki placed in charge of the entire universe.

[The remainder of the extant text is devoted to Inanna's challenge
and Enki's response.]

> Translation by Samuel Noah Kramer, in his The
> Sumerians. Their History, Culture and Character
> (Chicago: University of Chicago Press, 1963), pp. 174-
> 83; introductory material paraphrased and summarized
> by M. Eliade from Kramer, op. cit., pp. 171-4

See also no. 133

17. THE EGYPTIAN HIGH GOD IN THE AGE OF THE COFFIN TEXTS

('Coffin Texts,' 714)

The so-called 'Coffin Texts,' inscribed on the interior of coffins, belong
to the Middle Kingdom (2250-1580 B.C.).

I was [the spirit in?] the Primeval Waters,
he who had no companion when my name came into existence.
The most ancient form in which I came into existence was as a drowned
    one.

I was [also] he who came into existence as a circle,
he who was the dweller in his egg.
I was the one who began [everything], the dweller in the Primeval
  Waters.
First Hahu[1] emerged for me
and then I began to move.
I created my limbs in my 'glory.'
I was the maker of myself, in that I formed myself according to my
  desire and in accord with my heart.

Note

1 Hahu, the wind which began the separation of the waters and raised the sky.

Translated by R. T. Rundle Clark, in his *Myth and
Symbol in Ancient Egypt* (London, 1959), p. 74

18. ATUM, A BISEXUAL HIGH GOD

('*Coffin Texts*,' I, 161 ff.)

I am Atum, the creator of the Eldest Gods,
I am he who gave birth to Shu,
I am that great He-She,
I am he who did what seemed good to him,
I took my space in the place of my will,
Mine is the space of those who move along
like those two serpentine circles.

Translated by R. T. Rundle Clark, in his *Myth and
Symbol in Ancient Egypt* (London, 1959), p. 80

19. DEBATE BETWEEN OSIRIS AND THE HIGH GOD

('*Book of the Dead*,' Chapter 175)

After his death Osiris finds himself in a cheerless underworld and
laments his lot.

OSIRIS O Atum! What is this desert place into which I have come?
  It has no water, it has no air,

25

it is depth unfathomable, it is black as the blackest night.
I wander helplessly herein.
One cannot live here in peace of heart, nor may the longings
of love be satisfied herein.

ATUM *You may live in peace of heart, I have provided illumination*
in place of water and air, and satisfaction and quiet in the
place of bread and beer. Thus spoke Atum.

OSIRIS *But shall I behold your face?*

ATUM *I will not allow you to suffer sorrow.*

OSIRIS *But every other god has his place in the Boat of Millions of*
Years.

ATUM *Your place now belongs to your son Horus. Thus spoke Atum.*

OSIRIS *But will he be allowed to dispatch the Great Ones?*

ATUM *I have allowed him to dispatch the Great Ones, for he will*
inherit your throne on the Isle of Fire.

OSIRIS *How good would it be if one god could see another!*

ATUM *My face will look upon your face.*

OSIRIS *But how long shall I live? says Osiris.*

ATUM *You will live more than millions of years, an era of millions,*
but in the end I will destroy everything that I have created,
the earth will become again part of the Primeval Ocean,
like the Abyss of waters in their original state.
Then I will be what will remain, just I and Osiris,
when I will have changed myself back into the Old Serpent
who knew no man and saw no god.

How fair is that which I have done for Osiris, a fate different
from that of all the other gods!
I have given him the region of the dead while I have put his
son Horus as heir upon his throne in the Isle of Fire;
I have thus made his place for him in the Boat of Millions of
Years, in that Horus remains on his throne to carry on his
work.

OSIRIS *But will not also the soul of Seth be sent to the West—a fate*
different from that of all other gods?

ATUM *I shall hold his soul captive in the Boat of the Sun—such is*
my will—
so that he will no longer terrorize the Divine Company.

Translation and introductory note by R. T. Rundle
Clark, in his *Myth and Symbol in Ancient Egypt*
(London, 1959), pp. 139-40

20. AMENHOTEP IV AND THE HYMN TO ATEN

At the time when Egypt was at the height of her career as a world power during the New Kingdom, the land was shaken by a revolutionary religious doctrine which threatened to sweep away the theological dogmas of centuries. The key figure in this iconoclastic movement was the Pharaoh Amenhotep IV who came to the throne *c.* 1370 B.C. to reign as co-regent with his father Amenhotep III (*c.* 1397-1360 B.C.). This youth, frail of body, with the temperament of a dreamer and the fanatical zeal of a reformer, inspired the somewhat extravagant description of him as 'the first individual in human history' (J. H. Breasted). So romantic a figure has he appeared to historians, that many have credited him with originating the worship of the god Aten and establishing the first monotheistic faith.

There is, however, a continually increasing body of evidence which points to the fact that the cult of Aten had developed before the time of Amenhotep IV, indeed probably as early as the reign of Thutmose IV (*c.* 1411-1397 B.C.). It is likely that the worship of Aten developed from the ancient cult of the Helopolitan sun-god Re. In the course of time the syncretistic character of Egyptian religious thinking had led to the fusion of the god Re with many other deities such as Atum, Horus, and Amun, with the consequent assimilation of their characteristics and functions. The new cult paid homage to the physical orb of the sun (for which the Egyptian word was *aten*), stripped of its mythological accretions. Hence, except in the earliest period, no images or other representations of Aten were employed other than the figure of the sun disc with its rays extending towards the earth, each ending with a hand beneficently proffering the hieroglyphic symbol for life. . . . Central to the new faith was the idea of 'living on *ma 'at.*' This important term *ma 'at*, variously translated 'righteousness,' 'justice,' or 'truth,' meant basically the divinely ordained cosmic order. By the Middle Kingdom it had acquired the overtones of social justice. But Akhenaten's use of it emphasized the aspect of truth, by which he meant the subjective truth of the senses rather than the traditional objective, universal truth. This is consonant with the further observation that the Atenist faith was an intellectual rather than an ethical one, a fact which is apparent in the Aten Hymn. . . .

Noble though this doctrine may have been in many ways, it failed to win the approval or support of any but Akhenaten's circle of courtiers and adherents. To the people, as from time immemorial in

Egypt, the Pharaoh was himself a god, and Akhenaten did not seek to alter this. Only he and his family were privileged to offer worship directly to Aten; the people directed their prayers to the king, and through him the blessings of Aten were vouchsafed to them. It was inevitable that a doctrine of so contemplative and intellectual a nature would be incomprehensible to the common folk who either ignored it or adopted a hostile attitude towards it. This fact, combined with the lack of a spirit of compromise, so essential to the syncretistical-minded Egyptian, spelled disaster for Atenism. Under Akhenaten's co-regent and successor Smenkhkare, perhaps even before the former's death, a movement for reconciliation with the Amon-Re cult began. Before many years had passed, Atenism was forgotten, and the heretic King Akhenaten was anathematized by later generations. . . .

The first strophe extols the splendour of Aten as he rises in the heaven. Re, the sun-god of Heliopolis, is identified with Aten in line 7, . . . The next two strophes describe the terrors of darkness, when Aten is absent from the sky, as contrasted with the joys of day, when he has returned to pour his beneficent rays on the earth. . . . The fourth strophe speaks of Aten's life-giving powers in the world of nature. . . . The fifth and sixth strophes laud Aten as creator of the Universe. . . . In the seventh strophe Aten is hailed as a universal god, creating and sustaining all people. . . . The eighth strophe tells of Aten's concern for foreign lands. . . . Aten is viewed as the creator of the seasons in the next strophe.

1. Thou dost appear beautiful on the horizon of heaven,
     O living Aten, thou who wast the first to live.
   When thou hast risen on the eastern horizon,
     Thou hast filled every land with thy beauty.
5. Thou art fair, great, dazzling, high above every land;
     Thy rays encompass the lands to the very limit of all thou
       hast made.
   Being Re, thou dost reach to their limit
     And curb them [for] thy beloved son;
   Though thou art distant, they rays are upon the earth;
10. Thou art in their faces, yet thy movements are unknown(?).

   When thou dost set on the western horizon,
     The earth is in darkness, resembling death.
   Men sleep in the bed-chamber with their heads covered,
     Nor does one eye behold the other.
15. Were all their goods stolen which are beneath their heads,

They would not be aware of it.
Every lion has come forth from his den,
   All the snakes bite.
Darkness prevails, and the earth is in silence,
20.   Since he who made them is resting in his horizon.

At daybreak, when thou dost rise on the horizon,
   Dost shine as Aten by day,
Thou dost dispel the darkness
   And shed thy rays.
25. The two Lands are in a festive mood,
   Awake, and standing on (their) feet,
For thou hast raised them up;
   They cleanse their bodies and take (their) garments;
   Their arms are (lifted) in adoration at thine appearing;
30.   The whole land performs its labour.

All beasts are satisfied with their pasture;
   Trees and plants are verdant.
The birds which fly from their nests, their wings are (spread)
   in adoration to thy soul;
   All flocks skip with (their) feet;
35. All that fly up and alight
   Live when thou has risen [for] them.
Ships sail upstream and downstream alike,
   For every route is open at thine appearing.
The fish in the river leap before thee,
40.   For thy rays are in the midst of the sea.

Thou creator of issue in woman, who makest semen into mankind,
   And dost sustain the son in mother's womb,
Who dost soothe him with that which stills his tears,
   Thou nurse in the very womb, giving breath to sustain all
   thou dost make!
45. When he issues from the womb to breathe on the day of his birth,
   Thou dost open his mouth completely and supply his needs.
When the chick in the egg cheeps inside the shell,
   Thou givest it breath within it to sustain it.
Thou hast set it its appointed time in the egg to break it,
50.   That it may emerge from the egg to cheep at its appointed time;
   That it may walk with its feet when it emerges from it.

How manifold is that which thou hast made, hidden from view!

Thou sole god, there is no other like thee!
Thou didst create the earth according to thy will, being alone:
55.   Mankind, cattle, all flocks,
Everything on earth which walks with (its) feet,
And what are on high, flying with their wings.

The foreign lands of Hurru and Nubia, the land of Egypt—
Thou dost set each man in his place and supply his needs;
60. Each one has his food, and his lifetime is reckoned.
Their tongues are diverse in speech and their natures likewise;
Their skins are varied, for thou dost vary the foreigners.
Thou dost make the Nile in the underworld,
And bringest it forth as thou desirest to sustain the people
65 As thou dost make them for thyself,
Lord of them all, who dost weary thyself with them,
Lord of every land, who dost rise for them,
Thou Aten of the day, great in majesty.

As for all distant foreign lands, thou makest their life,
70.   For thou hast set a Nile in the sky,
That it may descend for them,
That it may make waves on the mountains like the sea,
To water their fields amongst their towns.
How excellent are thy plans, thou lord of eternity!
75.   The Nile in the sky is for the foreign peoples,
For the flocks of every foreign land that walk with (their) feet,
While the (true) Nile comes forth from the underworld for
Egypt.

Thy rays suckle every field;
When thou dost rise, they live and thrive for thee.
80. Thou makest the seasons to nourish all that thou hast made:
The winter to cool them; the heat that they (?) may taste thee.
Thou didst make the distant sky to rise in it,
To see all that thou hast made.
Being alone, and risen in thy form as the living Aten,
85. Whether appearing, shining, distant, or near,
Thou makest millions of forms from thyself alone:
Cities, towns, fields, road, and river. . . .

There is no other that knows thee,
95. Save thy son Akhenaten,
For thou hast made him skilled in thy plans and thy might.

The earth came into being by thy hand,
 Just as thou didst make them (i.e. mankind).

When thou hast risen, they live;
100.   When thou dost set, they die.
 For thou art lifetime thyself; one lives through thee;
 Eyes are upon (thy) beauty until thou dost set.
 All labour is put aside when thou dost set in the west;
 When [thou] risest [thou] makest . . . flourish for the king.
105. As for all who hasten on foot,
 Ever since thou didst fashion the earth,
 Thou dost raise them up for thy son who came forth from thyself,
 The King of Upper and Lower Egypt, Akhenaten.

Introduction and translation by R. J. Williams, in
D. Winton Thomas (ed.), *Documents from Old Testament Times* (London: Thomas Nelson, 1958)

See also nos. 54, 133, 272, 273

21. VARUNA, THE ALL-KNOWING GOD

'He knows the pathway of the wind . . .'

('Rig Veda,' I, 25, 1-3, 7-14)

1. Whatever law of thine, O god, O Varuna, as we are men,
  Day after day we violate,
2. Give us not as a prey to death, to be destroyed by thee in wrath,
  To thy fierce anger when displeased.
3. To gain thy mercy, Varuna, with hymns we bind thy heart,
    as binds
  The charioteer his tethered horse. . . .
7. He knows the path of birds that fly through heaven, and,
    sovereign of the sea,
  He knows the ships that are thereon.
8. True to his holy law, he knows the twelve moons with their
    progeny:
  He knows the moon of later birth.[1]

The notes to this text are on p. 32.

9. He knows the pathway of the wind, the spreading, high and
   mighty wind;
   He knows the gods who dwell above.

10. Varuna, true to holy law, sits down among his people; he,
    Most wise, sits there to govern all.

11. From thence perceiving he beholds all wondrous things, both
    what hath been,
    And what hereafter will be done.

12. May that Adyita very wise, make fair paths for us all our days;
    May he prolong our lives for us,

13. Varuna, wearing golden mail, hath clad him in a shining robe;
    His spies[2] are seated round about.

17. The god whom enemies threaten not, nor those who tyrannize
    o'er men,
    Nor those whose minds are bent on wrong.

Notes

1 Twelve months have days as the progeny; 'the moon of later birth' is perhaps
an intercalary 'thirteenth' month. Thus is there no 'time' to which Varuna is
not a witness.
2 Perhaps the other Adityas (cf. *Rigveda*, VIII, 47, 11).

Translation by Ralph T. H. Griffith, in his *The Hymns
of the Rigveda*, I (Benares, 1889), pp. 42-3

22. 'KING VARUNA IS THERE . . .'

('Atharva Veda,' IV, 16, 1-6)

1. The great guardian among these (gods) sees as if from anear. He
that thinketh he is moving stealthily—all this the gods know.

2. If a man stands, walks, or sneaks about, if he goes slinking away,
if he goes into his hiding-place; if two persons sit together and scheme,
King Varuna is there as a third, and knows it.

3. Both this earth here belongs to King Varuna, and also yonder
broad sky whose boundaries are far away. Moreover these two oceans
are the loins of Varuna; yea, he is hidden in this small (drop of) water.

4. He that should flee beyond the heaven far away would not be free
from King Varuna. His spies[1] comes hither (to the earth) from heaven,
with a thousand eyes do they watch over the earth.

The notes to this text are on p. 33.

5. King Varuna sees through all that is between heaven and earth, and all that is beyond. He has counted the winkings of men's eyes. As a (winning) gamester puts down his dice, thus does he establish these (laws).[2]

6. May all thy fateful toils which, seven by seven, threefold, lie spread out, ensnare him that speaks falsehood; him that speaks the truth they shall let go!

Notes

1 Varuna's spies are the stars 'The eyes of the night' (R V, X, 127, 1) the beholders of men' (A V, XIX, 47, 3 ff.)
2 As the player plants down these (successful dice) thus does Varuna establish these laws.

> Translation by Maurice Bloomfield, *Hymns of the Atharva-Veda*, in *Sacred Books of the East*, XLII (Oxford, 1897), pp. 88-9

23. VARUNA AND INDRA

('Rig Veda,' IV, 42, 1-7, 10)

1. *I am the royal ruler, mine is empire, as mine who
    sway all life are all the immortals.*
   *Varuna's will the gods obey and follow. I am the
    king o'er folk of sphere sublimest.*
2. *I am king Varuna. To me was given these first
    existing high celestial powers.*[1]
   *Varuna's will the gods obey and follow. I am the
    king o'er the folk of the sphere sublimest.*
3. *I Varuna am Indra: in their greatness, these the
    two wide deep fairly-fashioned regions,*
   These the two world-halves have I, even as Tvashtar,[2]
    knowing all beings, joined and held together.
4. *I made to flow the moisture-shedding waters, and set
    the heaven firm in the seat of Order.*[3]
   By Law, the son of Aditi,[4] *Law-observer, hath spread
    abroad the world in three fold measure.*

The notes to this text are on p. 34.

5. Heroes with noble horses, fain for battle, selected
   warriors, call on me in combat.
   I, Indra Maghavan,[5] excite the conflict; I stir the
   dust, lord of surpassing vigour.
6. All this I did. The gods' own conquering power
   never impedeth me to whom none opposeth.
   When lauds and Soma-juice have made me joyful,
   both the unbounded regions are affrighted.
7. All beings know these deeds of thine: thou tellest
   this unto Varuna, thou great disposer!
   Thou art renowned as having slain the Vritras. Thou
   madest flow the floods that were obstructed. . . .
10. May we, possessing much, delight in riches, gods in
    oblations and the kine in pasture;
    And that milch-cow[6] who shrinks not from the milking
    O Indra Varuna, give to us daily.

Notes

1 Varuna speaks in stanzas 1 to 4, stressing that celestial sovereignty which is rightfully his as creator of the universe and maintainer of the cosmic order (rita).
2 Varuna, master of *māyā (māyin)*, here identifies himself with the divine articifer, Tvashtar, who is significantly, the father of Indra and of Vritrain the later Samhitās).
3 *Rita.*
4 Varuna, son of Aditi.
5 Indra, the 'Bountiful One,' now replies in stanzas 5 and 6. His boasts of physical power, of his exploits in battle and of the 'surpassing vigour' of his generative strength, illustrate how 'might makes right' for this warrior god. He is king by force and in the following stanza (7) the poet is duly impressed with the fact that Indra has successfully challenged the sovereign lordship of Varuna.
6 I.e., wealth.

> Translation by Ralph T. H. Griffith, in his *The Hymns of the Rigveda*, II (Benares, 1890), pp. 163-5

24. 'WHAT GOD SHALL WE ADORE WITH OUR OBLATION?'

('Rig Veda,' X, 121, 1-10)

1. In the beginning rose Hiranyagarbha,[1] born only lord of all created beings.

The notes to this text are on pp. 35-6.

He fixed and holdeth up this earth and heaven.
What god shall we adore with our oblation?

2. Giver of vital breath, of power and vigour, he whose commandments
all the gods acknowledge;
Whose shade is death, whose lustre makes immortal.
What god shall we adore with our oblation?

3. Who by his grandeur hath become sole ruler of all the moving
world that breathes and slumbers;
He who is lord of men and lord of cattle.
What god shall we adore with our oblation?

4. His, through his might, are these snow-covered mountains, and
men call sea and Rasā[2] his possession;
His arms are these, his are these heavenly regions.
What god shall we adore with our oblation?

5. By him the heavens are strong and earth is steadfast, by him light's
realm and sky-vault are supported;[3]
By him the regions in mid-air were measured.
What god shall we adore with our oblation?

6. To him, supported by his help, two armies embattled look while
trembling in their spirit,
When over them the risen sun is shining.
What god shall we adore with our oblation?

7. What time the mighty waters[4] came, containing the universal
germ, producing Agni,
Thence sprang the gods' one spirit[5] into being.
What god shall we adore with our oblation?

8. He in his might surveyed the floods containing productive force
and generating worship.[6]
He is the god of gods, and none beside him.
What god shall we adore with our oblation?

9. Ne'er may he harm us who is earth's begetter, nor he whose laws
are sure, the heavens' creator,
He who brought forth the great and lucid waters.
What god shall we adore with our oblation?

10. Prajāpati![7] thou only comprehendest all these created things, and
none beside thee.
Grant us our hearts' desire when we invoke thee;
may we have store in riches in possession.

Notes

: The 'golden germ (garbha).' Compare the 'primal seed' (retas, semen virile) of

X, 12, 4. The refrain concluding each stanza asks, 'Who is the god whom I should worship?' The poet in this creation hymn seeks to *name* That One who is the true source of being. Later reciters, confused by the recurrent interrogative, posited a deity named 'Ka' ('Who?') to whom this hymn was thenceforth addressed.

2 The mythological river which encompasses the earth and the atmosphere.

3 As Varuna, in his work of creation (see VII, 86, 1) propped apart heaven and earth, so here does Hiranyagarbha perform the same divisive operation, creating a mid-space (*antariksha*) in the process.

4 Again, as in X, 129, it is the primordial waters which bear creation's germ. Here the solar germ and the fire forms of Agni are generated from the waters. Hiranyagarbha and Agni are both golden sons of the waters; they portray that unique coincidence of creation-in-chaos where the bright fire glows in the lap of dark chaotic waters.

5 The living spirit (*asu*) of all the gods is manifest uniquely when Hiranygarbha comes with the flooding waters.

6 Or, generating sacrifice.

7 Lord of creatures, the answer to the interrogative refrain. This is an important text for the later Brāhmanas, where Prajāpati is identical with the sacrifice and 'creates the all out of himself.'

Translation by Ralph T. H. Griffith, in his *The Hymns of the Rigveda*, IV (Benares, 1892), pp. 355-6

25. 'INDRA—WHO AS SOON AS BORN SURPASSED THE GODS IN POWER'

('Rig Veda,' II, 12, 1-5, 13)

1. The chief wise god who as soon as born
    surpassed the gods in power;
   Before whose vehemence the two worlds trembled by reason
    of the greatness of his valour: he, O men, is, Indra.[1]
2. Who made firm the quaking earth,
    who set at rest the agitated mountains;
   Who measures out the air more widely,
    who supported heaven: he, O men, is Indra.
3. Who having slain the serpent released the seven streams,
    who drove out the cows by the unclosing of Vala,
   Who between two rocks has produced fire,
    victor in battles: he, O men, is Indra.[2]
4. By whom all things here have been made unstable,[3]

The notes to this text are on p. 37.

who has made subject the Dāsa colour[4] and has made it
    disappear;
Who, like a sinning gambler the stake,
    has taken the possessions of the foe: he, O men, is Indra.
5. The terrible one of whom they ask 'where is he,'
    of whom they also say 'he is not';
He diminishes the possessions of the foe like the stakes of
    gamblers. Believe in him: he, O men, is Indra. . . .
13. Even Heaven and Earth bow down before him;[5]
    before his vehemence even the mountains are afraid.
Who is known as the Soma-drinker, holding the bolt in his arm,
    who holds the bolt in his hand: he, O men, is Indra.[6]

Notes

1 In contrast with Varuna and the *asuras*, another group of gods, the *devas*, is led by Indra, the warrior god, who is king (*svarāj*) not like Varuna through the evolving cosmic order, but rather by virtue of his own dynamic being.

2 Here the famous exploits of Indra are recalled: the slaying of the serpent Vritra, who encompassed the cosmic waters, released for men the seven rivers (see *Rig Veda* I, 32); Vala, another demon and the brother of Vritra, was also slain by Indra; and Agni as lightning was generated by Indra from the clouds, as fire is struck from flint. All of Indra's effusive deeds are the result of his generative bull-like nature.

3 *Cyavanā*, 'shaking'; the advent of Indra's power has calmed earthquakes (stanza 2) but has agitated and made transient all worldly phenomena.

4 The non-Aryan population.

5 Gradually in the *Rig Veda* Indra takes over those roles which formerly had been Varuna's, until eventually Indra too achieves sovereignty. (cf. *Rig Veda* IV, 42 and X, 124.)

6 Indra is the greatest drinker of intoxicating *soma*. The *vajra*, his thunderbolt, is in constant use against his foes.

Translation by A. A. Macdonell, in his *A Vedic Reader for Students* (Oxford: Clarendon Press, 1917), pp. 45-54, *passim* (slightly modified)

See also nos. 56, 101, 115, 134-7

26. A VEDIC HYMN TO THE GODDESS EARTH

('Atharva Veda,' XII, 1, selections)

1. Truth, greatness, universal order (*rita*), strength, consecration, creative fervour (*tapas*), spiritual exaltation (*brahman*), the sacrifice,

support the earth. May this earth, the mistress of that which was and shall be, prepare for us a broad domain!

2. The earth that has heights, and slopes, and great plains, that supports the plants of manifold virtue, free from the pressure that comes from the midst of men, she shall spread out for us, and fit herself for us!

3. The earth upon which the sea, and the rivers and the waters, upon which food and the tribes of men have arisen, upon which this breathing, moving life exists, shall afford us precedence in drinking!

4. The earth whose are the four regions of space upon which food and the tribes of men have arisen, which supports the manifold breathing, moving things, shall afford us cattle and other possessions also!

5. The earth upon which of old the first men[1] unfolded themselves, upon which the gods overcame the Asuras,[2] shall procure for us (all) kinds of cattle, horses, and fowls, good fortune, and glory!

6. The earth that supports all, furnishes wealth, the foundation, the golden breasted resting-place of all living creatures, she that supports Agni Vaishvānara,[3] and mates with Indra, the bull,[4] shall furnish us with property!

7. The broad earth, which the sleepless gods ever attentively guard, shall milk for us precious honey, and, moreover, besprinkle us with glory!

8. That earth which formerly was water upon the ocean (of space), which the wise (seers) found out by their skilful devices;[5] whose heart is in the highest heaven, immortal, surrounded by truth, shall bestow upon us brilliancy and strength, (and place us) in supreme sovereignty! . . .

10. The earth which the Ashvins[6] have measured, upon which Vishnu[7] has stepped out, which Indra, the lord of might, has made friendly to himself; she, the mother, shall pour forth milk for me, the son!

11. Thy snowy mountain heights, and thy forests, O earth, shall be kind to us! The brown, the black, the red, the multi-coloured, the firm earth, that is protected by Indra, I have settled upon, not suppressed, not slain, not wounded.

12. Into thy middle set us, O earth, and into thy navel, into the nourishing strength that has grown up from thy body; purify thyself for us! The earth is the mother, and I the son of the earth: Parjanya[8] is the father; he, too, shall save us!

The notes to this text are on p. 40.

13. The earth upon which they (the priests) inclose the altar *(vedi)*, upon which they, devoted to all (holy) works, unfold the sacrifice, upon which are set up, in front of the sacrifice, the sacrificial posts, erect and brilliant, that earth shall prosper us, herself prospering!

14. Him that hates us, O earth, him that battles against us, him that is hostile towards us with his mind and his weapons, do thou subject to us, anticipating (our wish) by deed!

15. The mortals born of thee live on thee, thou supportest both bipeds and quadrupeds. Thine, O earth, are these five races of men, the mortals, upon whom the rising sun sheds undying light with his rays. . . .

22. Upon the earth men give to the gods the sacrifice, the prepared oblation: upon the earth mortal men live pleasantly by food. May this earth give us breath and life, may she cause me to reach old age!

23. The fragrance, O earth, that has arisen upon thee, which the plants and the waters hold, which the Gandharvas and the Apsaras⁹ have partaken of, with that make me fragrant: not any one shall hate us! . . .

40. May this earth point out to us the wealth that we crave: may Bhaga (fortune) add his help, may Indra come here as (our) champion!

41. The earth upon whom the noisy mortals sing and dance, upon whom they fight, upon whom resounds the roaring drum, shall drive forth our enemies, shall make us free from rivals!

42. To the earth upon whom are food, and rice and barley, upon whom live these five races of men, to the earth, the wife of Parjanya, that is fattened by rain, be reverence!

43. The earth upon whose ground the citadels constructed by the gods unfold themselves, every region of her that is the womb of all, Prajāpati¹⁰ shall make pleasant for us! . . .

45. The earth that holds people of manifold varied speech, of different customs, according to their habitations, as a reliable milch-cow that does not kick, shall she milk for me a thousand streams of wealth!

46. The serpent, the scorpion with thirsty fangs, that hibernating torpidly lies upon thee; the worm, and whatever living thing, O earth, moves in the rainy season, shall, when it creeps not creep upon us; with what is auspicious (on thee) be gracious to us! . . .

48. The earth holds the fool and holds the wise, endures that good and bad dwell (upon her); she keeps company with the boar, gives herself up to the wild hog. . . .

52. The earth upon whom day and night jointly, black and bright,

have been decreed, the broad earth covered and enveloped with rain, shall kindly place us into every pleasant abode!

53. Heaven, and earth, and air have here given me expanse: Agni, Sūrya,[11] the waters, and all the gods together have given me wisdom. . . .

63. O mother earth, kindly set me down upon a well-founded place! With (father) heaven cooperating, O thou wise one, do thou place me into happiness and prosperity![12]

Notes

1 *Pūrvajana*, 'men of former times.'

2 By the time of the composition of the Atharvaveda, as in the late *Rigveda*, the *asuras*, sovereign gods under Varuna's command, have become demons; the *devas* were the gods who 'overcame' them.

3 *Vaishvānara*, 'belonging to all men,' is a frequent epithet of Agni, the fire, and refers to his omnipresence.

4 Indra's fecund powers are often characterized by his bull form: here, 'the earth (*bhūmi*) whose bull is Indra.'

5 *Māyā*.

6 The divine twins, beautiful and amiable physicians among the gods, whose golden chariot traverses heaven and earth in a day.

7 Vishnu, still a minor god in the Atharvaveda, is celebrated for his three great strides: already the first of these covered the broad span of earth, the second then limited the sky, and the third encompassed transcendent space.

8 A lesser deity associated with the rain clouds and terrestrial fertility. Verse 42 calls earth his wife.

9 The Gandharvas are a class of celestial beings sometimes described as dwelling with their Apsaras nymphs in the waters on earth. [*See below, selection no. 116, the story of Purūravas, Urvashī and the lotus lake. M.E.*]

10 Lord of creatures and protector of generation.

11 The sun.

12 Vaitāna-sūtra 27.8 prescribes this verse for recitation upon descending from the sacrificial post (W. D. Whitney [trans.], *Atharva-Veda Samhitā* [ed. by C. R. Lanman], Cambridge, Mass.: Harvard University, 1905, p. 672). The hymn itself is one of the few examples of freshly inspired poetry in the Atharvaveda. 'Its chief use is at the *āgrahāyani*-ceremonies, the concluding ceremonies of the rites devoted to serpents, undertaken on the full-moon day of the month Mārgashīrsha.' It is also connected with rites that firmly establish the house, homestead, or village. (Bloomfield, pp. 639-40.)

Translation by Maurice Bloomfield, *Hymns of the Atharva-Veda*, in *The Sacred Books of the East*, XLII (Oxford, 1891), pp. 199-207

See also no. 163

27. VISHNU, THE COSMIC GOD

('Vishnu Purāna,' 3, 17, 14-34)

You are everything, earth, water, fire, air, and space,
the subtle world, the Nature-of-All (pradhāna),
and the Person (pums) who stands forever aloof.

O Self of all beings!
From the Creator (Brahmā) to the blade of grass
all is your body, visible and invisible,
divided by space and time.

We worship you as Brahmā, the Immense Being, the first shape,
who sprang from the lotus of your navel to create the worlds.

We, the gods, worship you in our selves,
we, the King of Heaven, the Sun, the Lord of Tears,
the Indweller, the twin gods of agriculture,
the Lord of Wind, the Offering, who all are your shapes
while you are our Selves.

We worship you in your demonic shapes, deceitful and stupid,
wild in their passions, suspicious of wisdom.

We worship you in the genii, the yakshas,
with their narrow minds obdurate to knowledge,
their blunt faculties covetous of the objects of words.

O Supreme Man! We bow to your fearful evil shapes
which wander at night, cruel and deceitful.

O Giver-of-Rewards (Junārdana)!
We worship you as the Eternal Law
whence virtuous men, who dwell in the heaven,
obtain the blissful fruit of their just deeds.
We bow to the Realized (Siddhas) who are your shapes of joy;
free from contacts, they enter and move within all things.

O Remover-of-Sorrow (Hari)! We bow to you the serpent shapes,
lustful and cruel, whose forked tongues know no mercy.

O Pervader! We worship you as knowledge
in the peaceful form of the seers,
faultless, free from sin.

Gods, Goddesses and Supernatural Beings

O Dweller in the lotus of the Heart! We bow to you
as the self of Time which, at the end of the ages,
infallibly devours all beings.

We worship you as the Lord of Tears,
who dances at the time of destruction,
having devoured gods and men alike.

O Giver of Rewards! We worship your human shape
bound by the twenty-eight incapacities (badha),
ruled by the powers of darkness.

We bow to you as vegetal life (mukhya rūpa),
by which the world subsists and which—six in kind,
trees, [creepers, bushes, plants, herbs, and bamboo]—
supports the sacrificial rites.

O Universal Self! We bow to you under that elemental shape
from which beasts and men have sprung,
gods and living beings, ether and the elements,
sound and all the qualities.

O Transcendent Self! We bow to you as the Cause of causes,
the Principal shape beyond compare,
beyond Nature (pradhāna) and Intellect.

O All-powerful (Bhagavān)! We bow to your shape
which the seers alone perceive and in which is found
no white nor other colour, no length nor other dimension,
no density nor other quality.

Purer than purity it stands
beyond the sphere of quality.

We bow to you, the birthless, the indestructible,
outside whom there is but nothingness.

You are the ever-present within all things,
as the intrinsic principle of all.

We bow to you, resplendent Indweller (Vāsudeva)! the seed of all
that is!
You stand changeless, unsullied.

The Supreme stage is your core, the Universe your shape.
You are the unborn, Eternal.

Translation by Alain Daniélou, in his *Hindu Polytheism* (New York: Bollingen Series LXXIII, 1964),
pp. 367-8

42

28. KRISHNA'S EPIPHANY

(Bhagavad Gītā, XI, selections)

3. Thus it is, as Thou declarest
   Thyself, O Supreme Lord.
   I desire to see Thy form
   As God, O Supreme Spirit!

4. If Thou thinkest that it can
   Be seen by me, O Lord,
   Prince of mystic power, then do Thou to me
   Reveal Thine immortal Self.

   The Blessed One said:
5. Behold My forms, son of Prtha,
   By hundreds and by thousands,
   Of various sorts, marvelous,
   Of various colours and shapes. . . .

8. But thou canst not see Me
   With this same eye of thine own;
   I give thee a supernatural eye:
   Behold My mystic power as God!

   Samjaya said:
9. Thus speaking then, O king,
   Hari (Visnu), the great Lord of Mystic Power,
   Showed unto the son of Prtha
   His supernal form as God: . . .

12. Of a thousand suns in the sky
    If suddenly should burst forth
    The light, it would be like
    Unto the light of that exalted one. . . .

14. Then filled with amazement,
    His hair standing upright, Dhanamjaya
    Bowed with his head to the God,
    And said with a gesture of reverence:

    Arjuna said:
15. I see the gods in Thy body, O God,
    All of them, and the hosts of various kinds of beings too,
    Lord Brahma sitting on the lotus-seat,
    And the seers all, and the divine serpents.

16. With many arms, bellies, mouths, and eyes,
    I see Thee, infinite in form on all sides;
    No end nor middle nor yet beginning of Thee
    Do I see, O All-God, All-formed!

17. With diadem, club, and disc,
    A mass of radiance, glowing on all sides,
    I see Thee, hard to look at, on every side
    With the glory of flaming fire and sun, immeasurable.

18. Thou art the Imperishable, the supreme Object of Knowledge;
    Thou art the ultimate resting-place of this universe;
    Thou are the immortal guardian of the eternal right.
    Thou art the everlasting Spirit, I hold.

19. Without beginning, middle, or end, of infinite power,
    Of infinite arms, whose eyes are the moon and sun,
    I see Thee, whose face is flaming fire,
    Burning this whole universe with Thy radiance.

20. For this region between heaven and earth
    Is pervaded by Thee alone, and all the directions;
    Seeing this Thy wondrous, terrible form,
    The triple world trembles, O exalted one!

21. For into Thee are entering yonder throngs of gods;
    Some, affrighted, praise Thee with reverent gestures;
    Crying 'Hail!' the throngs of the great seers and perfected ones
    Praise Thee with abundant laudations. . . .

24. Touching the sky, aflame, of many colours,
    With yawning mouths and flaming enormous eyes,
    Verily seeing Thee (so), my inmost soul is shaken,
    And I find no steadiness nor peace, O Visnu!

25. And Thy mouths, terrible with great tusks,
    No sooner do I see them, like the fire of dissolution (of the world),
    Than I know not the directions of the sky, and I find no refuge;
    Have mercy, Lord of Gods, Thou in whom the world dwells! . . .

31. Tell me, who art Thou, of awful form?
    Homage be to Thee: Best of Gods, be merciful!
    I desire to understand Thee, the primal one;
    For I do not comprehend what Thou hast set out to do.

The Blessed One said:

32. I am Time (Death), cause of destruction of the worlds, matured
    And set out to gather in the worlds here.
    Even without thee (thy action), all shall cease to exist,
    The warriors that are drawn up in the opposing ranks.

33. Therefore arise thou, win glory,
    Conquer thine enemies and enjoy prospered kingship;
    By Me Myself they have already been slain long ago;
    Be thou the mere instrument, left-handed archer!

34. Drona and Bhisma and Jayadratha,
    Karna too, and the other warrior-heroes as well,
    Do thou slay, (since) they are already slain by Me; do not hesitate!
    Fight! Thou shalt conquer thy rivals in battle. . . .

Arjuna said:

36. It is in place, Hrsikesa, that at Thy praise
    The world rejoices and is exceeding glad;
    Ogres fly in terror in all directions,
    And all the hosts of perfected ones pay homage.

37. And why should they not pay homage to Thee, Exalted One?
    Thou art greater even than Brahman; Thou art the First Creator;
    O infinite Lord of Gods, in whom the world dwells,
    Thou the imperishable, existent, non-existent, and beyond both!

38. Thou art the Primal God, the Ancient Spirit,
    Thou art the supreme resting-place of this universe;
    Thou art the knower, the object of knowledge, and the highest
        station,
    By Thee the universe is pervaded, Thou of infinite form! . . .

42. And if I treated thee disrespectfully to make sport of Thee,
    In the course of amusement, resting, sitting, or eating,
    Either since, O unshaken one, or in the presence of those (others),
    For that I beg forgiveness of Thee, the immeasurable one.

43. Thou art the father of the world of things that move and move not,
    And thou art its revered, most venerable Guru;
    There is no other like Thee—how then a greater?—
    Even in the three worlds, O Thou of matchless greatness!

44. Therefore, bowing and prostrating my body,
    I beg grace of Thee, the Lord to be revered:
    As a father to his son, as a friend to his friend,
    As a lover to his beloved, be pleased to show mercy, O God!

45. Having seen what was never seen before, I am thrilled,
   And (at the same time) my heart is shaken with fear;
   Show me, O God, that same form of Thine (as before)!
   Be merciful, Lord of Gods, Abode of the World!

Translation by Franklin Edgerton, in Edgerton *Bhagavad Gītā*, Vol. I, Harvard Oriental Series, Vol. 38 (Cambridge, Harvard University Press, 1944)

29. TO EACH GENERATION THE TATHĀGATA ANNOUNCES HIS NAME AND DECLARES THAT HE HAS ENTERED NIRVĀNA

('Saddharmapundarika,' XV, 268-72)

The Buddha, considered as a spiritual principle and not as a historical person, is called 'Tathāgata.' The original meaning of the term is no longer known.

The Lord said: As a result of my sustaining power this world, with its Gods, men and Asuras, forms the notion that recently the Lord Shakyamuni, after going forth from his home among the Shakyas, has awoken to full enlightenment, on the terrace of enlightenment, by the town of Gayā.

But one should not see it thus, sons of good family. In fact it is many hundreds of thousands of myriads of Kotis of aeons ago that I have awoken to full enlightenment. . . . Ever since, during all that time I have demonstrated Dharma to beings in this Saha world system, and also in hundreds of thousands of Nayutas of Kotis of other world systems. But when I have spoken of other Tathāgatas, beginning with the Tathāgata Dīpankara, and of the Nirvāna of these Tathāgatas, then that has just been conjured up by me as an emission of the skill in means by which I demonstrate Dharma.

Moreover, the Tathāgata surveys the diversity in the faculties and vigour of successive generations of beings. To each generation he announces his name, declares that he has entered Nirvāna, and brings peace to beings by various discourses on Dharma. To beings who are of low disposition, whose store of merit is small, and whose depravities are many, he says in that case: 'I am young in years, monks, I have left the home of my family, and but lately have I won full enlightenment.' But when the Tathāgata, although fully enlightened for so long, declares that he has been fully enlightened but recently, then such discourses on Dharma have been spoken for no other reason than to bring beings to maturity and to save them. All these discourses on Dharma have been taught by the Tathāgata in order to discipline beings.

And whatever the Tathāgata says to educate beings, and whatever the Tathāgata utters,—whether he appears as himself or as another, whether under his own authority or another,—all these discourses on Dharma are taught as factually true by the Tathāgata, and there is no false speech in them on the part of the Tathāgata. For the Tathāgata has seen the triple world as it really is: It is not born, it dies not; there is no decease or rebirth, no Samsāra or Nirvāna; it is not real, or unreal, not existent, or non-existent, not such, or otherwise, not false or not-false. Not in such a way has the Tathāgata seen the triple world as the foolish common people see it. The Tathāgata is face to face with the reality of dharmas; he can therefore be under no delusion about them. Whatever words the Tathāgata may utter with regard to them, they are true, not false, not otherwise.

He utters, however, different discourses on Dharma, which differ in their objective basis, to beings who differ in their mode of life and their intentions, and who wander amidst discriminations and perceptions, in order to generate the roots of good in them. For a Tathāgata performs a Tathāgata's work. Fully enlightened for ever so long, the Tathāgata has an endless span of life, he lasts for ever. Although the Tathāgata has not entered Nirvāna, he makes a show of entering Nirvāna, for the sake of those who have to be educated. And even today my ancient course as a Bodhisattva is still incomplete, and my life-span is not yet ended. From today onwards still twice as many hundreds of thousands of Nayutas of Kotis of aeons must elapse before my life-span is complete. Although therefore I do not at present enter into Nirvāna (or extinction), nevertheless I announce my Nirvāna. For by this method I bring beings to maturity. Because it might be that, if I stayed here too long and could be seen too often, beings who have performed no meritorious actions, who are without merit, a poorly lot, eager for sensuous pleasures, blind, and wrapped in the net of false views, would, in the knowledge that the Tathāgata stays (here all the time), get the notion that life is a mere sport, and would not conceive the notion that the (sight of the) Tathāgata is hard to obtain. In the conviction that the Tathāgata is always at hand they would not exert their vigour for the purpose of escaping from the triple world, and they would not conceive of the Tathāgata as hard to obtain.

Translation by Edward Conze, in Conze, *et al.*, *Buddhist Texts through the Ages* (Oxford: Bruno Cassirer, 1954)

30. THE BODHISATTVA'S INFINITE COMPASSION

('Shikshāsamuccaya,' 280-2 *['Vajradhvaha-sūtra']*)

A Bodhisattva resolves: I take upon myself the burden of all suffering. I am resolved to do so, I will endure it. I do not turn or run away, do not tremble, am not terrified, nor afraid, do not turn back or despond.

And why? At all costs I must bear the burdens of all beings. In that I do not follow my own inclinations. I have made the vow to save all beings. All beings I must set free. The whole world of living beings I must rescue, from the terrors of birth, of old age, of sickness, of death and rebirth, of all kinds of moral offence, of all states of woe, of the whole cycle of birth-and-death, of the jungle of false views, of the loss of wholesome dharmas, of the concomitants of ignorance,— from all these terrors I must rescue all beings. . . . I walk so that the kingdom of unsurpassed cognition is built up for all beings. My endeavours do not merely aim at my own deliverance. For with the help of the boat of the thought of all-knowledge, I must rescue all these beings from the stream of Samsāra, which is so difficult to cross, I must pull them back from the great precipice, I must free them from all calamities, I must ferry them across the stream of Samsāra. I myself must grapple with the whole mass of suffering of all beings. To the limit of my endurance I will experience in all the states of woe, found in any world system, all the abodes of suffering. And I must not cheat all beings out of my store of merit, I am resolved to abide in each single state of woe for numberless aeons; and so I will help all beings to freedom, in all the states of woe that may be found in any world system whatsoever.

And why? Because it is surely better that I alone should be in pain than that all these beings should fall into the states of woe. There I must give myself away as a pawn through which the whole world is redeemed from the terrors of the hells, of animal birth, of the world of Yama, and with this my own body I must experience, for the sake of all beings, the whole mass of all painful feelings. And on behalf of all beings I give surety for all beings, and in doing so I speak truthfully, am trustworthy, and do not go back on my word. I must not abandon all beings.

And why? There has arisen in me the will to win all-knowledge, with all beings for its object, that is to say, for the purpose of setting free the entire world of beings. And I have not set out for the supreme enlightenment from a desire for delights, not because I hope to experience the delights of the five-sense qualities, or because I wish to indulge in the pleasures of the senses. And I do not pursue the course of a Bodhisattva in order to achieve the array of delights that can be found in the various worlds of sense-desire.

And why? Truly no delights are all these delights of the world. All this indulging in the pleasures of the senses belongs to the sphere of Māra.

> Translation by Edward Conze, in Conze, *et al.*, *Buddhist Texts through the Ages* (Oxford: Bruno Cassirer, 1954)

31. THE SUN GODDESS AMATERASU AND THE STORM GOD SUSA-NO-O

('Nihongi,' I, 40-5)

In Japanese tradition, Amaterasu and Susa-no-o were the two most important among many offspring of the primordial pair, Izanagi and Izanami.

After this Susa-no-o Mikoto's behaviour was exceedingly rude. In what way? Amaterasu [the Heaven-shining Deity] had made august rice fields of Heavenly narrow rice fields and Heavenly long rice fields. Then Susa-no-o, when the seed was sown in spring, broke down the divisions between the plots of rice, and in autumn let loose the Heavenly piebald colts, and made them lie down in the midst of the rice fields. Again, when he saw that Amaterasu was about to celebrate the feast of first-fruits, he secretly voided excrement in the New Palace. Moreover, when he saw that Amaterasu was in her sacred weaving hall, engaged in weaving garments of the Gods, he flayed a piebald colt of Heaven, and breaking a hole in the roof-tiles of the hall, flung it in. Then Amaterasu started with alarm, and wounded herself with the shuttle. Indignant of this, she straightway entered the Rock-cave of Heaven, and having fastened the Rock-door, dwelt there in seclusion. Therefore constant darkness prevailed on all sides, and the alternation of night and day was unknown.

Then the eighty myriads of Gods met on the bank of the Tranquil River of Heaven, and considered in what manner they should supplicate her. Accordingly Omoi-kane[1] no Kami, with profound device and far-reaching thought, at length gathered long-singing birds[2] of the Eternal Land and made them utter their prolonged cry to one another. Moreover he made Ta-jikara-o[3] to stand beside the Rock door. Then Ame no Koyane no Mikoto, ancestor of the Nakatomi Deity Chieftains, and Futo-dama no Mikoto, ancester of the Imibe Chieftains, dug up a five-hundred branched True Sakaki tree of the Heavenly Mt. Kagu. On its upper branches they hung an august five-hundred string of Yasaka jewels. On the middle branches they hung an eight-hand mirror.[4] . . .

On its lower branches they hung blue soft offerings and white soft offerings. Then they recited their liturgy together.

Moreover Ama no Uzume[5] no Mikoto, ancestress of the Sarume[6] Chieftain, took in her hand a spear wreathed with Eulalia grass, and standing before the door of the Rock-cave of Heaven, skilfully performed a mimic dance.[7] She took, moreover, the true Sakaki tree of the Heavenly Mount Kagu, and made of it a head-dress, she took club-moss and made of it braces, she kindled fires, she placed a tub bottom upwards,[8] and gave forth a divinely-inspired utterance.

Now Amaterasu heard this, and said: 'Since I have shut myself up in the Rock-cave, there ought surely to be continual night in the Central Land of fertile reed-plains. How then can Ama no Uzume no Mikoto be so jolly?' So with her august hand, she opened for a narrow space the Rock-door and peeped out. Then Ta-jikara-o no Kami forthwith took Amaterasu by the hand and led her out. Upon this the Gods Nakatomi no Kami and Imibe no Kami at once drew a limit by means of a bottom-tied rope[9] (also called a left-hand rope) and begged her not to return again [into the cave].

After this all the Gods put the blame on Susa-no-o, and imposed on him a fine of one thousand tables,[10] and so at length chastised him. They also had his hair plucked out, and made him therewith expiate his guilt.

The notes to this text are on p. 51.

Notes

1 Thought-combining or thought including.
2 The cock is meant.
3 Hand-strength-male.
4 It is said to be this mirror which is worshipped at Ise as an emblem of the Sun Goddess.
5 Terrible female of Heaven.
6 Monkey-female.
7 This is said to be the origin of the kagura or pantomime dance performed at Shinto festivals.
8 The *Nihongi* strangely omits to say that, as we learn from the *Kojiki*, she danced on this and made it give out a sound.
9 A rope made of straw of rice which has been pulled up by the roots.
10 By tables are meant tables of offerings.

Adapted from Aston's translation of *Nihongi* by Wm. Theodore de Bary (ed.), *Sources of Japanese Tradition* (New York: Columbia University Press, 1958), pp. 29-31; notes by de Bary

C. GREEK GODS AND HEROES, AND THE IRANIAN SUPREME BEING, AHURA-MAZDA

32. TO PYTHIAN APOLLO

('The Homeric Hymns,' III, 179 ff.)

O Lord, Lycia is yours and lovely Maeonia and Miletus, charming city by the sea, but over Delos you greatly reign your own self.

Leto's all-glorious son goes to rocky Pytho, playing upon his hollow lyre, clad in divine, perfumed garments; and at the touch of the golden key his lyre sings sweet. Thence, swift as thought, he speeds from earth to Olympus, to the house of Zeus, to join the gathering of the other gods: then straightway the undying gods think only of the lyre and song, and all the Muses together, voice sweetly answering voice, hymn the unending gifts the gods enjoy and the sufferings of men, all that they endure at the hands of the deathless gods, and how they live witless and helpless and cannot find healing for death or defence against old age. Meanwhile the rich-tressed races and cheerful Seasons dance with Harmonia and Hebe and Aphrodite, daughter of Zeus, holding each other by the wrist. And among them sings one, not mean nor puny, but tall to look upon and enviable in mien, Artemis who delights in arrows, sister of Apollo. Among them sport Ares and the keen-eyed Slayer of Argus, while Apollo plays his lyre stepping high and featly and a radiance shines around him, the gleaming of his feet and close-woven vest. And they, even gold-tressed Leto, and wise Zeus, rejoice in their great hearts as they watch their dear son playing among the undying gods.

How then shall I sing of you—though in all ways you are a worthy theme for song? Shall I sing of you as wooer and in the fields of love, how you went wooing the daughter of Azan along with god-like Ischys the son of well-horsed Elatius, or with Phorbas sprung from Triops, or with Ereutheus, or with Leucippus and the wife of Leucippus . . . you on foot, he with his chariot, yet he fell not short of Triops. Or shall I sing how at the first you went about the earth seeking a place of oracle for men, O far-shooting Apollo? To Pieria first you went down from Olympus and passed by sandy Lectus and Enienae and through the land of the Perrhaebi. Soon you came to Iolcus and set foot on Cenaeum in Euboea, famed for ships: you stood in the Lelantine plain, but it pleased not your heart to make a temple there and wooded groves. . . .

And further still you went, O far-shooting Apollo, and came to Onchestus, Poseidon's bright grove: there the new-broken colt distressed with drawing the trim chariot gets spirit again, and the skilled driver springs from his car and goes on his way. . . .

Then you went towards Telphusa: and there the pleasant place seemed fit for making a temple and wooded grove. You came very near and spoke to her: 'Telphusa, here I am minded to make a glorious temple, and oracle for men, and hither they will always bring perfect hecatombs, both those who live in rich Peloponnesus and those of Europe all the wave-washed isles, coming to seek oracles. And I will deliver to them all counsel that cannot fail, giving answer in my rich temple.'

So said Phoebus Apollo, and laid out all the foundations throughout, wide and very long. But when Telphusa saw this, she was angry in heart and spoke, saying: 'Lord Phoebus, worker from afar, I will speak a word of counsel to your heart, since you are minded to make here a glorious temple to be an oracle for men who will always bring hither perfect hecatombs for you; yet I will speak out, and do you lay up my words in your heart. The trampling of swift horses and the sound of mules watering at my sacred springs will always irk you, and men like better to gaze at the well-made chariots and stamping, swift-footed horses than at your great temple and the many treasures that are within. But if you will be moved by me—for you, lord, are stronger and mightier than I, and your strength is very great—build at Crisa below the glades of Parnassus: there no bright chariot will clash, and there will be no noise of swift-footed horses near your well-built altar. But so the glorious tribes of men will bring gifts to you as Iepaeon ("Hail-Healer"), and you will receive with delight rich sacrifices from the people dwelling round about.' So said Telphusa, that she alone, and not the Far-Shooter, should have renown there; and she persuaded the Far-Shooter.

Further yet you went, far-shooting Apollo, until you came to the town of the presumptous Phlegyae who dwell on this earth in a lovely glade near the Cephisian lake, caring not for Zeus. And thence you went . . . to Crisa beneath snowy Parnassus, a foothill turned towards the west: a cliff hangs over it from above, and a hollow, rugged glade runs under. There the lord Phoebus Apollo resolved to make his lovely temple, and thus he said:

'In this place I am minded to build a glorious temple to be an oracle for men, and here they will always bring perfect hecatombs, both they who dwell in rich Peloponnesus and the men of Europe and from all the wave-washed isles, coming to question me. And I will deliver to them all counsel that cannot fail, answering them in my rich temple.'

When he had said this, Phoebus Apollo laid out all the foundations throughout, wide and very long; and upon these the sons of Erginus, Trophonius and Agamedes, dear to the deathless gods, laid a footing of stone. And the countless tribes of men built the whole temple of wrought stones, to be sung of for ever.

But near by was a sweet flowing spring, and there with his strong bow the lord, the son of Zeus, killed the bloated, great-she-dragon, a fierce monster wont to do great mischief to men upon earth, to men themselves and to their thin-shanked sheep; for she was a very bloody plague. She it was who once received from gold-throned Hera and brought up fell, cruel Typhaon to be a plague to men. Once on a time Hera bare him because she was angry with father Zeus, when the son of Cronos bare all-glorious Athena in his head. . . .

And this Typhaon used to work great mischief among the famous tribes of men. Whosoever met the dragoness, the day of doom would sweep him away, until the lord Apollo, who deals death from afar, shot a strong arrow at her. Then she, rent with bitter pangs, lay drawing great gasps for breath and rolling about that place. An awful noise swelled up unspeakable as she writhed continually this way and that amid the wood: and so she left her life, breathing it forth in blood. Then Phoebus Apollo boasted over her:

'Now rot here upon the soil that feeds man! You at least shall live no more to be a fell bane to men who eat the fruit of the all-nourishing earth, and who will bring hither perfect hecatombs. Against cruel death neither Typhoeus shall avail you nor ill-famed Chimera, but here shall the Earth and shining Hyperion make you rot.'

Thus said Phoebus, exulting over her: and darkness covered her eyes. And the holy strength of Helios made her rot away there: wherefore the place is now called Pytho, and men call the lord Apollo by another name, Pythian; because on that spot the power of piercing Helios made the monster rot away.

Then Phoebus Apollo saw that the sweet-flowing spring had beguiled him, and he started out in anger against Telphusa; and soon coming to her, he stood close by and spoke to her:

'Telphusa, you were not, after all, to keep to yourself this lovely place by deceiving my mind, and pour forth your clear flowing water: here my renown shall also be and not yours alone.'

Thus spoke the lord, far-working Apollo, and pushed over upon her a crag with a shower of rocks, hiding her streams: and he made himself an altar in a wooded grove very near the clear-flowing stream. In that place all men pray to the great one by the name Telphusian, because he humbled the stream of holy Telphusa.

Translation by Hugh G. Evelyn-White, in the Loeb Classical Library (New York, 1914), pp. 337 *ff*.

See also nos. 139, 304

33. THE EARTH, MOTHER OF ALL

(*'The Homeric Hymns,'* xxx)

I will sing of well-founded Earth, mother of all, eldest of all beings. She feeds all creatures that are in the world, all that go upon the goodly land, and all that are in the paths of the seas, and all that fly: all these are fed of her store. Through you, O queen, men are blessed in their children and blessed in their harvests, and to you it belongs to give means of life to mortal men and to take it away. Happy is the man whom you delight to honour! He has all things abundantly: his fruitful land is laden with corn, his pastures are covered with cattle, and his house is filled with good things. Such men rule orderly in their cities of fair women: great riches and wealth follow them: their sons exult with everfresh delight, and their daughters with flower-laden hands play and skip merrily over the soft flowers of the field. Thus it is with those whom you honour O holy goddess, bountiful spirit.

Hail, Mother of the gods, wife of starry Heaven; freely bestow upon me for this my song substance that cheers the heart! And now I will remember you and another song also.

Translation by Hugh G. Evelyn-White, in the Loeb Classical Library (New York, 1914), p. 456

See also nos. 59, 148

34. HERCULES: HIS LABOURS, HIS DEATH, HIS APOTHEOSIS

(Apollodorus, 'The Library,' II; IV, 8—VII, 7)

. . . But before Amphitryon reached Thebes, Zeus came by night and prolonging the one night threefold he assumed the likeness of Amphitryon and bedded with Alcmena and related what had happened concerning the Teleboans. But when Amphitryon arrived and saw that he was not welcomed by his wife, he inquired the cause; and when she told him that he had come the night before and slept with her, he learned from Tiresias how Zeus had enjoyed her. And Alcmena bore two sons, to wit, Hercules, whom she had by Zeus and who was the elder by one night, and Iphicles, whom she had by Amphitryon. When the child was eight months old, Hera desired the destruction of the babe and sent two huge serpents to the bed. Alcmena called Amphitryon to her help, but Hercules arose and killed the serpents by strangling them with both his hands. However, Pherecydes says that it was Amphitryon who put the serpents in the bed, because he would know which of the two children was his, and that when Iphicles fled, and Hercules stood his ground, he knew that Iphicles was begotten of his body.

Hercules was taught to drive a chariot by Amphitryon, to wrestle by Autolycus, to shoot with the bow by Eurytus, to fence by Castor, and to play the lyre by Linus. This Linus was a brother of Orpheus; he came to Thebes and became a Theban, but was killed by Hercules with a blow of the lyre; for being struck by him, Hercules flew into a rage and slew him. When he was tried for murder, Hercules quoted a law of Rhadamanthys, who laid it down that whoever defends himself against a wrongful aggressor shall go free, and so he was acquitted. But fearing he might do the like again, Amphitryon sent him to the cattle farm; and there he was nurtured and outdid all in stature and strength. Even by the look of him it was plain that he was a son of Zeus; for his body measured four cubits, and he flashed a gleam of fire from his eyes; and he did not miss, neither with the bow nor with the javelin.

While he was with the herds and had reached his eighteenth year he slew the lion of Cithaeron, for that animal, sallying from Cithaeron, harried the kine of Amphitryon and of Thespius. Now this Thespius was king of Thespiae, and Hercules went to him when he wished to catch the lion. The king entertained him for fifty days, and each night, as Hercules went forth to the hunt, Thespius bedded one of his daughters with him (fifty daughters having been borne to him by Megamede, daughter of Arneus); for he was anxious that all of them should have children by Hercules. Thus Hercules, though he thought that his bedfellow was always the same, had intercourse with them all. And having vanquished the lion, he dressed himself in the skin and wore the scalp as a helmet. . . .

Having first learned from Eurytus the art of archery, Hercules received a sword from Hermes, a bow and arrows from Apollo, a golden breastplate from Hephaestus, and a robe from Athena; for he had himself cut a club at Nemea.

Now it came to pass that after the battle with the Minyans Hercules was driven mad through the jealousy of Hera and flung his own children, whom he had by Megara, and two children of Iphicles into the fire; wherefore he condemned himself to exile, and was purified by Thespius, and repairing to Delphi he inquired to the god where he should dwell. The Pythian priestess then first called him Hercules, for hitherto he was called Alcides. And she told him to dwell in Tiryns, serving Eurystheus for twelve years and to perform the ten labours imposed on him, and so, she said, when the tasks were accomplished, he would be immortal.

When Hercules heard that, he went to Tiryns and did as he was bid by Eurystheus. First, Eurystheus ordered him to bring the skin of the Nemean lion; now that was an invulnerable beast begotten by Typhon. . . . And having come to Nemea and tracked the lion, he first shot an arrow at him, but when he perceived that the beast was invulnerable, he heaved up his club and made after him. And when the lion took refuge in a cave with two mouths, Hercules built up the one entrance and came in upon the beast through the other, and putting his arm round its neck held it tight till he had choked it; so laying it on his shoulders he carried it to Cleonae. . . .

As a second labour he ordered him to kill the Lernaean hydra. That creature, bred in the swamp of Lerna, used to go forth into the plain and ravage both the cattle and the country. Now the hydra had a huge body, with nine heads, eight mortal, but the middle one immortal. So mounting a chariot driven by Iolaus, he came to Lerna, and having halted his horses, he discovered the hydra on a hill beside the springs of the Amymone, where was its den. By pelting it with fiery shafts he forced it to come out, and in the act of doing so he seized and held it fast. But the hydra wound itself about one of his feet and clung to him. Nor could he effect anything by smashing its heads with his club, for as fast as one head was smashed there grew up two. A huge crab also came to the help of the hydra by biting his foot. So he killed it, and in his turn called for help on Iolaus who, by setting fire to a piece of the neighbouring wood and burning the roots of the heads with the brands, prevented them from sprouting. Having thus got the better of the sprouting heads, he chopped off the immortal head, and buried it, and put a heavy rock on it, beside the road that leads through Lerna to Elaeus. But the body of the hydra he slit up and dipped his arrows in the gall. However, Eurystheus said that this labour should not be reckoned among the ten because he had not got the better of the hydra by himself, but with the help of Iolaus.

As a third labour he ordered him to bring the Cerynitian hind alive to Mycenae. Now the hind was at Oenoe; it had golden horns and was sacred to Artemis; so wishing neither to kill nor wound it, Hercules hunted it for a whole year. But when, weary with the chase, the beast took refuge on the mountain called Artemisius, and thence passed to the river Ladon, Hercules shot it just as it was about to cross the stream, and catching it put it on his shoulders and hastened through Arcadia. But Artemis with Apollo met him, and would have wrestled the hind from him, and rebuked him for attempting to kill her sacred animal. Howbeit, by pleading necessity and laying the blame on Eurystheus, he appeased the anger of the goddess and carried the beast alive to Mycenae.

As a fourth labour he ordered him to bring the Erymanthian boar alive; now that animal ravaged Psophis, sallying from a mountain which they call Erymanthus. . . .

The fifth labour he laid on him was to carry out the dung of the cattle of Augeas in a single day. Now Augeas was king of Elis; some say that he was a son of the Sun, others that he was a son of Poseidon, and others that he was a son of Phorbas; and he had many herds of cattle. Hercules accosted him, and without revealing the command of Eurystheus, said that he would carry out the dung in one day, if Augeas would give him the tithe of the cattle. Augeas was incredulous, but promised. Having taken Augeas's son Phyleus to witness, Hercules made a breach in the foundations of the cattle-yard, and then, diverting the courses of the Alpheus and Peneus, which flowed near each other, he turned them into the yard, having first made an outlet for the water through another opening. . . .

The sixth labour he enjoined on him was to chase away the Stymphalian birds. Now at the city of Stymphalus in Arcadia was the

lake called Stymphalian, embosomed in a deep wood. To it countless
birds had flocked for refuge, fearing to be preyed upon by the wolves.
So when Hercules was at a loss how to drive the birds from the wood,
Athena gave him brazen castanets, which she had received from
Hephaestus. By clashing these on a certain mountain that overhung
the lake, he scared the birds. They could not abide the sound, but
fluttered up in a fright, and in that way Hercules shot them.

The seventh labour he enjoined on him was to bring the Cretan Bull.
Acusilaus says that this was the bull that ferried across Europa for
Zeus; but some say it was the bull that Poseidon sent up from the sea
when Minos promised to sacrifice to Poseidon what should appear out
of the sea. And they say that when he saw the beauty of the bull he
sent it away to the herds and sacrificed another to Poseidon; at which
the god was angry and made the bull savage. To attack this bull
Hercules came to Crete, and when, in reply to his request for aid,
Minos told him to fight and catch the bull for himself, he caught it
and brought it to Eurystheus, and having shown it to him he let it
afterwards go free. But the bull roamed to Sparta and all Arcadia, and
traversing the Isthmus arrived at Marathon in Attica and harried the
inhabitants.

The eighth labour he enjoined on him was to bring the mares of
Diomedes the Thracian to Mycenae. . . .

The ninth labour he enjoined on Hercules was to bring the belt of
Hippolyte. She was queen of the Amazons, who dwelt about the river
Thermodon, a people great in war; for they cultivated the manly
virtues, and if ever they gave birth to children through intercourse
with the other sex, they reared the females; and they pinched off the
right breasts that they might not be trammelled by them in throwing
the javelin, but they kept the left breasts, that they might suckle.
Now Hippolyte had the belt of Ares in token of her superiority to
all the rest. Hercules was sent to fetch this belt because Admete,
daughter of Eurystheus, desired to get it. So taking with him a band
of volunteer comrades in a single ship he set sail and put it to the
island of Paros, which was inhabited by the sons of Minos, to wit,
Eurymedon, Chryses, Nephalion, and Philolaus. . . .

Having put in at the harbour of Themiscyra, he received a visit
from Hippolyte, who inquired why he was come, and promised to
give him the belt. But Hera in the likeness of an Amazon went up
and down the multitude saying that the strangers who had arrived
were carrying off the queen. So the Amazons in arms charged on
horseback down on the ship. But when Hercules saw them in arms,

he suspected treachery, and killing Hippolyte stripped her of her belt. And after fighting the rest he sailed away and touched at Troy. . . .

As a tenth labour he was ordered to fetch the kine of Geryon from Erythia. Now Erythia was an island near the ocean; it is now called Gadira. This island was inhabited by Geryon, son of Chrysaor by Callirrhoe, daughter of Ocean. He had the body of three men grown together and joined in one at the waist, but parted in three from the flanks and thighs. He owned red kine, of which Eurytion was the herdsman and Orthus, the two-headed hound, begotten by Typhon on Echidna, was the watch-dog. So journeying through Europe to fetch the kine of Geryon he destroyed many wild beasts and set foot in Libya, and proceeding to Tartessus he erected as tokens of his journey two pillars over against each other at the boundaries of Europe and Libya. But being heated by the Sun on his journey, he bent his bow at the god, who in admiration of his hardihood, gave him a golden goblet in which he crossed the ocean. And having reached Erythia he lodged on Mount Abas. However the dog, perceiving him, rushed at him; but he smote it with his club, and when the herdsman Eurytion came to the help of the dog, Hercules killed him also. But Menoetes, who was there pasturing the kine of Hades, reported to Geryon what had occurred, and he, coming up with Hercules besides the river Anthemus, as he was driving away the kine, joined battle with him and was shot dead. And Hercules, embarking the kine in the goblet and sailing across to Tartessus, gave back the goblet to the Sun. . . .

When the labours had been performed in eight years and a month, Eurystheus ordered Hercules, as an eleventh labour, to fetch golden apples from the Hesperides, for he did not acknowledge the labour of the cattle of Augeas nor that of the hydra. These apples were not, as some have said, in Libya, but on Atlas among the Hyperboreans. They were presented by Earth to Zeus after his marriage with Hera, and guarded by an immortal dragon with a hundred heads, offspring of Typhon and Echidna, which spoke with many and divers sorts of voices. With it the Hesperides also were on guard, to wit, Aegle, Erythia, Hesperia, and Arethusa. . . .

And passing by Arabia he slew Emathion, son of Tithonus, and journeying through Libya to the outer sea he received the goblet from the Sun. And having crossed to the opposite mainland he shot on the Caucasus the eagle, offspring of Echidna and Typhon, that was devouring the liver of Prometheus, and he released Prometheus, after choosing for himself the bond of olive, and to Zeus he presented Chiron who, though immortal, consented to die in his stead.

Now Prometheus had told Hercules not to go himself after the apples but to send Atlas, first relieving him of the burden of the sphere; so when he was come to Atlas in the land of the Hyperboreans, he took the advice and relieved Atlas. But when Atlas had received three apples from the Hesperides, he came to Hercules, and not wishing to support the sphere he said that he would himself carry the apples to Eurystheus, and bade Hercules hold up the sky in his stead. Hercules promised to do so, but succeeded by craft in putting it on Atlas instead. For at the advice of Prometheus he begged Atlas to hold up the sky till he should put a pad on his head. When Atlas heard that, he laid the apples down on the ground and took the sphere from Hercules. And so Hercules picked up the apples and departed. But some say that he did not get them from Atlas, but that he plucked the apples himself after killing the guardian snake. And having brought the apples he gave them to Eurystheus. But he, on receiving them, bestowed them on Hercules, from whom Athena got them and conveyed them back again; for it was not lawful that they should be laid down anywhere.

A twelfth labour imposed on Hercules was to bring Cerberus from Hades. Now this Cerberus had three heads of dogs, the tail of a dragon, and on his back the heads of all sorts of snakes. When Hercules was about to depart to fetch him, he went to Eumolpus at Eleusis, wishing to be initiated. However it was not then lawful for foreigners to be initiated, since he proposed to be initiated as the adoptive son of Pylius. But not being able to see the mysteries because he had not been cleansed of the slaughter of the centaurs, he was cleansed by Eumolpus and then initiated. And having come to Taenarum in Laconia, where is the mouth of the descent to Hades, he descended through it. But when the souls saw him, they fled, save Meleager and the Gorgon Medusa. And Hercules drew his sword against the Gorgon, as if she were alive, but he learned from Hermes that she was an empty phantom. And being come near to the gates of Hades he found Theseus and Pirithous, him who wooed Persephone in wedlock and was therefore bound fast. And when they beheld Hercules, they stretched out their hands as if they should be raised from the dead by his might. And Theseus, indeed, he took by the hand and raised up, but when he would have brought up Pirithous, the earth quaked and he let go. And he rolled away also the stone of Ascalaphus. And wishing to provide the souls with blood, he slaughtered one of the kine of

Hades. But Menoetes, son of Ceuthonymus, who tended the kine, challenged Hercules to wrestle, and, being seized round the middle, had his ribs broken; howbeit, he was let off at the request of Persephone. When Hercules asked Pluto for Cerberus, Pluto ordered him to take the animal provided he mastered him without the use of the weapons which he carried. Hercules found him at the gates of Acheron, and, cased in his cuirass and covered by the lion's skin, he flung his arms round the head of the brute, and though the dragon in its tail bit him, he never relaxed his grip and pressure till it yielded. So he carried it off and ascended through Troezen. But Demeter turned Ascalaphus into a short-eared owl, and Hercules, after showing Cerberus to Eurystheus, carried him back to Hades. . . .

. . . And having come to Calydon, Hercules wooed Deianira, daughter of Oeneus. He wrestled for her hand with Achelous, who assumed the likeness of a bull; but Hercules broke off one of his horns. So Hercules married Deianira. . . . And taking Deianira with him, he came to the river Evenus, at which the centaur Nessus sat and ferried passengers across for hire, alleging that he had received the ferry from the gods for his righteousness. So Hercules crossed the river by himself, but on being asked to pay the fare he entrusted Deianira to Nessus to carry over. But he, in ferrying her across, attempted to violate her. She cried out, Hercules heard her, and shot Nessus to the heart when he emerged from the river. Being at the point of death, Nessus called Deianira to him and said that if she would have a love-charm to operate on Hercules she should mix the seed he had dropped on the ground with the blood that flowed from the wound inflicted by the barb. She did so and kept it by her. . . .

On his arrival at Trachis he mustered an army to attack Oechalia, wishing to punish Eurytus. Being joined by Arcadians, Melians from Trachis, and Epienemidian Locrians, he slew Eurytus and his sons and took the city. After burying those of his own side who had fallen, to wit, Hippasus, son of Ceyx, and Argius and Melas, the sons of Licymnius, he pillaged the city and led Iole captive. And having put in at Cenaeum, a headland of Euboea, he built an altar of Cenaean Zeus. Intending to offer sacrifice, he sent the herald Lichas to Trachis to fetch fine raiment. From him Deianira learned about Iole, and fearing that Hercules might love that damsel more than herself, she supposed that the spilt blood of Nessus was in truth a love-charm, and with it she smeared the tunic. So Hercules put it on and proceeded to offer sacrifice. But no sooner was the tunic warmed than the poison of the hydra began to corrode his skin; and on that he lifted

Lichas by the feet, hurled him down from the headland, and tore off the tunic, which clung to his body, so that his flesh was torn away with it. In such a sad plight he was carried on shipboard to Trachis: and Deianira, on learning what had happened, hanged herself. But Hercules, after charging Hyllus his elder son by Deianira, to marry Iole when he came of age, proceeded to Mount Oeta, in the Trachinian territory, and there constructed a pyre, mounted it, and gave orders to kindle it. When no one would do so, Poeas, passing by to look for his flocks, set a light to it. On him Hercules bestowed his bow. While the pyre was burning, it is said that a cloud passed under Hercules and with a peal of thunder wafted him up to heaven. Thereafter he obtained immortality, and being reconciled to Hera he married her daughter Hebe, by whom he had sons, Alexiares and Anicetus.

Translation by Sir James George Frazer, in the Loeb Classical Library, vol. I (New York, 1921), pp. 173-237, 257-73

35. DEMETER AND THE FOUNDING OF THE ELEUSINIAN MYSTERIES

('The Homeric Hymns': To Demeter, II, 185-299)

Hades has carried off Demeter's daughter, Kore. After vainly searching for her, Demeter comes to Eleusis, in disguise as an old woman, and there is received into the house of King Celeus.

Soon they came to the house of heaven-nurtured Celeus and went through the portico to where their queenly mother sat by a pillar of the close-fitted roof, holding her son, a tender scion, in her bosom. And the girls ran to her. But the goddess walked to the threshold: and her head reached the roof and she filled the doorway with a heavenly radiance. Then awe and reverence and pale fear took hold of Metaneira, and she rose up from her couch before Demeter, and bade her be seated. But Demeter, bringer of seasons and giver of perfect gifts, would not sit upon the bright couch, but stayed silent with lovely eyes cast down until careful Iambe placed a jointed seat for her and threw over it a silvery fleece. Then she sat down and held her veil in her hands before her face. A long time she sat upon the stool[1] without speaking because of her sorrow, and greeted no one by word or by sign, but rested, never smiling, and tasting neither food nor drink, because she pined with longing for her deep-bosomed daughter, until careful Iambe—who pleased her moods in aftertime also—moved the holy lady with many a quip and jest to smile and laugh and cheer her heart. Then Metaneira filled a cup with sweet wine and offered it to her; but she refused it, for she said it was not lawful for her to drink red wine, but bade them mix meal and water with soft mint and give her to drink. And Metaneira mixed the draught and gave it to the goddess as she bade. So the great queen Deo received it to observe the sacrament.[2]

And of them all, well-girded Metaneira first began to speak: 'Hail, lady! For I think you are not meanly but nobly born; truly dignity and grace are conspicuous upon your eyes as in the eyes of kings that deal justice. Yet we mortals bear perforce what the gods send us, though we be grieved; for a yoke is set upon our necks. But now, since you are come here, you shall have what I can bestow: and nurse me this child whom the gods gave me in my old age and beyond my hope, a son much prayed for. If you should bring him up until he reach the full measure of youth, any one of womankind that sees you will straightway envy you, so great reward would I give for his upbringing.'

Then rich-haired Demeter answered her: 'And to you, also, lady, all hail, and may the gods give you good! Gladly will I take the boy to my breast, as you bid me, and will nurse him. Never, I ween, through any heedlessness of his nurse shall witchcraft hurt him nor yet the Undercutter: for I know a charm far stronger than the Woodcutter, and I know an excellent safeguard against woeful witchcraft.'

When she had so spoken, she took the child in her fragrant bosom with her divine hands: and his mother was glad in her heart. So the goddess nursed in the place Demophoon, wise Celeus' goodly son whom well-girded Metaneira bare. And the child grew like some immortal being, not fed with food nor nourished at the breast: for by day rich-crowned Demeter would anoint him with ambrosia as if he were the offspring of a god and breathe sweetly upon him as she held him in her bosom. But at night she would hide him like a brand in the heart of the fire, unknown to his dear parents. And it wrought great wonder in these that he grew beyond his age; for he was like the gods face to face. And she would have made him deathless and unaging,

The notes to this text are on p. 66.

had not well-girded Metaneira in her heedlessness kept watch by night from her sweet-smelling chamber and spied. But she wailed and smote her two hips, because she feared for her son and was greatly distraught in her heart, so she lamented and uttered winged words:

'Demophoon, my son, the strange woman buries you deep in fire and works grief and bitter sorrow for me.'

Thus she spoke, mourning. And the bright goddess, lovely-crowned Demeter, heard her, and was wroth with her. So with her divine hands she snatched from the fire the dear son whom Metaneira had borne unhoped-for in the palace, and cast him from her to the ground, for she was terribly angry in her heart. Forthwith she said to well-girded Metaneira:

'Witless are you mortals and dull to foresee your lot, whether of good or of evil, that comes upon you. For now in your heedlessness you have wrought folly past healing; for—be witness the oath of the gods, the relentless water of Styx—I would have made your dear son death-less and unaging all his days and would have bestowed on him ever-lasting honour, but now he can in no way escape death and the fates. Yet shall unfailing honour always rest upon him, because he lay upon my knees and slept in my arms. But, as the years move round and when he is in his prime, the sons of the Eleusinians shall ever wage war and dread strife with one another continually. Lo! I am that Demeter who has share of honour and is the greatest help and cause of joy to the undying gods and mortal men. But now, let all the people build me a great temple and an altar below it and beneath the city and its sheer wall upon a rising hillock above Callichorus. And I myself will teach my rites, that hereafter you may reverently perform them and so win the favour of my heart.'

When she had so said, the goddess changed her stature and her looks, thrusting old age away from her: beauty spread round about her and a lovely fragrance was wafted from her sweet-smelling robes, and from the divine body of the goddess a light shone afar, while golden tresses spread down over her shoulders, so that the strong house was filled with brightness as with lightning. And so she went out from the palace.

And straightway Metaneira's knees were loosed and she remained speechless for a long while and did not remember to take up her late-born son from the ground. But his sisters heard his pitiful wailing and sprang down from their well-spread beds; one of them took up the child in her arms and laid him in her bosom, while another revived the fire, and a third rushed with soft feet to bring their mother from her fragrant chamber. And they gathered about the struggling child and washed him, embracing him lovingly; but he was not comforted, because nurses and handmaids much less skilful were holding him now.

All night long they sought to appease the glorious goddess, quaking with fear. But, as dawn began to show, they told powerful Celeus all things without fail, as the lovely-crowned goddess Demeter charged them. So Celeus called the countless people to an assembly and bade them make a goodly temple for rich-haired Demeter and an altar upon the rising hillock. And they obeyed him right speedily and harkened to his voice, doing as he commanded. As for the child, he grew like an immortal being.

Notes

1 Demeter chooses the lowlier seat, supposedly as being more suitable to her assumed condition, but really because in her sorrow she refuses all comforts.
2 An act of communion—the drinking of the potion (*kykeon*) here described—was one of the most important pieces of ritual in the Eleusinian mysteries, as commemorating the sorrow of the goddess.

Translation by Hugh G. Evelyn-White, in the Loeb Classical Library (New York, 1936)

See also nos. 148, 150, 155

36. ZALMOXIS, THE GOD OF THE GETAE

(Herodotus, 'History,' IV, 93-6)

Zalmoxis (Salmoxis) was the Supreme God of the Getae (or Dacians), a Thracian people inhabiting a territory including today's Romania, but also extending farther east and northeast. Our only important information concerning this rather enigmatic deity is the text of Herodotus quoted below. The scholars have interpreted Zalmoxis as a Sky-god, a god of the dead, a Mystery-god, etc.

93. But before he came to the Ister, he first subdued the Getae, who pretend to be immortal. The Thracians of Salmydessus and of the country above the towns of Appolonia and Mesambria, who are called

Cyrmaianae and Nipsaei, surrendered themselves unresisting to Darius; but the Getae, who are the bravest and most law-abiding of all Thracians, resisted with obstinacy, and were enslaved forthwith.

94. As to their claim to be immortal, this is how they show it: they believe that they do not die, but that he who perishes goes to the god Salmoxis of Gebelexis, as some of them call him. Once in every five years they choose by lot one of their people and send him as a messenger to Salmoxis, charged to tell of their needs; and this is their manner of sending: Three lances are held by men thereto appointed; others seize the messenger to Salmoxis by his hands and feet, and swing and hurl him aloft on to the spear-point. If he be killed by the cast, they believe that the gods regard them with favour; but if he be not killed, they blame the messenger himself, deeming him a bad man, and send another messenger in place of him whom they blame. It is while the man yet lives that they charge him with the message. Moreover when there is thunder and lightning these same Thracians shoot arrows skyward as a threat to the god, believing in no other god but their own.

95. For myself, I have been told by the Greeks who dwell beside the Hellespont and Pontus that this Salmoxis was a man who was once a slave in Samos, his master being Pythagoras, son of Mnesarchus; presently, after being freed and gaining great wealth, he returned to his own country. Now the Thracians were a meanly-living and simple-witted folk, but this Salmoxis knew Ionian usages and a fuller way of life than the Thracian; for he had consorted with Greeks, and more-over with one of the greatest Greek teachers, Pythagoras; wherefore he made himself a hall, where he entertained and feasted the chief among his countrymen, and taught them that neither he nor his guests nor any of their descendants should ever die, but that they should go to a place where they would live for ever and have all good things. While he was doing as I have said and teaching this doctrine, he was all the while making him an underground chamber. When this was finished, he vanished from the sight of the Thracians, and descended into the underground chamber, where he lived for three years, the Thracians wishing him back and mourning him for dead; then in the fourth year he appeared to the Thracians, and thus they came to believe what Salmoxis had told them. Such is the Greek story about him.

96. For myself, I neither disbelieve nor fully believe the tale about Salmoxis and his underground chamber; but I think that he lived many years before Pythagoras; and whether there was a man called Salmoxis,

or this be the name among the Getae for a god of their country, I have done with him.

Translation by A. D. Godley, in the Loeb Classical Library, vol. II (New York, 1938)

37. ZARATHUSTRA PRESENTS A 'SUMMARY OF THE DOCTRINE'

('Gāthā:Yasna' 45)

This *Gāthā:Yasna* 45 is addressed to the 'great public,' or at least to an unaccustomed audience. As always, the cosmogony is explained in accordance with the eschatology which is its fount and origin. Thus the opening stanza already contains a reference to the 'second existence,' the renewed existence.

1. I will speak; hear now and attend,
   You who from nearby or from afar come for instruction,
   Do you all make your wisdom of him, for he is manifest.
   May the false teacher not destroy the second existence.
   Who for his evil choice has been reckoned wicked, through the tongue.

2. I will speak of the two spirits
   Of whom the holier said unto the destroyer at the beginning of existence:
   'Neither our thoughts nor our doctrines nor our minds' forces,
   Neither our choices nor our words nor our deeds,
   Neither our consciences nor our souls agree.'

3. I will speak of the beginnings of this existence,
   Of the things which the Wise Lord has told me, he who knows.
   Those of you who do not carry out the word
   As I shall think it and speak it,
   For them the end of existence shall be 'Woe!'

4. I will speak of the things which are best in this existence.
   He who created it according to Righteousness,
   I know, O Wise One, he is the father of the active Good Mind,
   Whose daughter is beneficent Devotion.
   Not to be deceived is the all-divining Lord.

5. I will speak of the word which the Most Holy Wise Lord
   Has told me as the best for mankind to hear:
   'Those who for me shall give heed and obedience to him,
   Shall attain integrity and Immortality through the deeds of Good
      Mind.'

6. I will speak of the greatest of all,
   Praising him as Righteousness, who is benevolent towards the
      living.
   Let the Wise lord hear, as the Holy Spirit,
   Whom I have praised when I took counsel with the Good Mind!
   By his mind's force may he teach me the supreme good,

7. He who gives salvation or perdition
   To those who are living or have been or shall be:
   The soul of the righteous rewarded with Immortality,
   Everlasting torments for the wicked.
   (Of these torments also is the Wise Lord the creator, through his
      Dominion.)

   (Listeners:)
8. 'Seek to win him for us by praises of veneration
   —For I have now beheld this with mine eye,
   Knowing the Wise Lord by the Righteousness of his Good Spirit,
   Of his good deed and his good word—
   And may we offer him hymns of praise in the house of song!

9. 'Seek to propitiate him for us with the Good Mind,
   Him who gives us fortune and misfortune at will.
   May the Wise Lord through his Dominion over the village,
   Through the intimacy of the Good Mind with Righteousness,
   Prosper our cattle and our men!

10. 'Seek to glorify him for us with hymns of Devotion,
    Him who is beheld in the soul as the Wise Lord,
    Because he has promised with his Righteousness and his Good
       Mind
    That Integrity and Immortality shall be ours in his Dominion,
    Strength and endurance in his house!'

    (Zarathustra:)
11. Whoever (?therefore?) shall henceforth bear ill-will to the false
       gods
    And to those who bear ill-will to the saviour

(That is, to those who shall not submit themselves to him),
To him shall the holy conscience of the coming saviour, the master
of his house,
Stand in stead of sworn friend, of brother or father, O Wise Lord!

Translation and introductory note by Jacques
Duchesne-Guillemin, in his *The Hymns of Zarathustra*
(London, 1952), pp 90-7

See also nos. 60, 290, 303

38. GĀTHĀ OF THE CHOICE: ZARATHUSTRA REVEALS THE EXEMPLARY CHOICE WHICH TOOK PLACE AT THE BEGINNING OF THE WORLD

('Gāthā:Yasna' 30)

Yasna 30 is one of the clearest and most frequently quoted Gāthās. Zarathustra manifests his powerful originality by reducing the history of the origins to that of a choice. . . . Better still, in Zoroaster's poem this tale of the original choice is balanced by an announcement of the final things, choice and rewards being closely interdependent. The whole human drama, reduced to its essential structure, is contained in a few stanzas.

1. Now will I *speak* to those who will hear
   Of the things which the initiate should remember;
   The praises and prayer of the Good Mind to the Lord
   And the joy which he shall see in the light who has remembered
   them well.

2. Hear with your ears that which is the sovereign good;
   With a clear mind look upon the two sides
   Between which each man must choose for himself,
   Watchful beforehand that the great test may be accomplished in
   our favour.

3. Now at the beginning the twin spirits have declared their nature,
   The better and the evil,
   In thought and word and deed. And between the two
   The wise ones choose well, not so the foolish.

4. And when these two spirits came together,
   In the beginning they established life and non-life,

And that at the last the worst experience should be for the wicked,
But for the righteous one the Best Mind.

5. Of these two spirits, the evil one chose to do the worst things;
But the most Holy Spirit, clothed in the most steadfast heavens,
Joined himself unto Righteousness;
And thus did all those who delight to please the Wise Lord by
honest deeds.

6. Between the two, the false gods also did not choose rightly,
For while they pondered they were beset by error,
So that they chose the Worst Mind.
Then did they hasten to join themselves unto Fury,
That they might by it deprave the existence of man.

7. And to him came Devotion, together with Dominion, Good Mind
and Righteousness;
She gave perpetuity of body and the breath of life,
That he may be thine apart from them,
As the first by the retributions through the metal.

8. And when their punishment shall come to these sinners,
Then, O Wise One, shall thy Dominion, with the Good Mind,
Be granted to those who have delivered Evil into the hands of
Righteousness, O Lord!

9. And may we be those that renew this existence!
O Wise One, and you other Lords, and Righteousness, bring
your alliance,
That thoughts may gather where wisdom is faint.

10. Then shall Evil cease to flourish,
While those who have acquired good fame
Shall reap the promised reward
In the blessed dwelling of the Good Mind, of the Wise One, and of
Righteousness.

11. If you, O men, understand the commandments which the Wise
One has given,
Well-being and suffering—long torment for the wicked and
salvation for the righteous—
All shall hereafter be for the best.

Translation and introductory note by Jacques
Duchesne-Guillemin, in his *The Hymns of Zarathustra*
(London, 1952), pp. 102-7

39. THE SECOND GĀTHĀ OF THE CHOICE

('Gāthā:Yasna' 31)

Yasna 31 is closely connected with the preceding one, Yasna 30. It adds supplementary words which are meant for the faithful and which were judged necessary because the choice to be made did not yet appear clearly enough.

7. He who first through the mind filled the blessed spaces with light,
He it is who by his will created Righteousness,
Whereby he upholds the Best Mind.
This thou hast increased, O Wise One, by the Spirit
Which is even now one with thee, O Lord!

8. Through the mind, O Wise One, have I known thee as the first and the last,
As the father of the Good Mind,
When I perceived thee with mine eyes as the true creator of Righteousness,
As the Lord in the deeds of existence. . . .

11. Since thou, O Wise One, at the first didst create for us by thy mind
Beings and consciences and wills,
Since thou didst give a body to the soul of life,
Since thou didst create deeds and words, that man may decide freely,

12. Since then does the man of false words lift up his voice as well as the man of true words,
The initiate as well as the non-initiate, each according to his heart and his mind.
May devotion put to the proof, one after the other, the spirits where there is bewilderment!. . .

17. Is it righteous, or is it the wicked one that takes to himself the greater part?
Let him that knows speak knowledge; let the unlearned cease to deceive!
O wise Lord, be thou our teacher in Good Mind! . . .

20. Whoever stands by the righteous man, to him shall future glory appear,

Long-lasting darkness, ill food, and wailing—
To such an existence shall your conscience
Lead you by your own deeds, O wicked ones.

Translation and introductory note by Jacques
Duchesne-Guillemin, in his *The Hymns of Zarathustra*
(London, 1952), pp. 108-17

D. ISLAM: ALLAH AND HIS PROPHET

40. MUHAMMAD SPEAKS OF ALLAH:
'THERE IS NO GOD BUT HE . . .'

('Koran,' II, 256-9; VI, 102-3)

God
there is no god but He, the
Living, the Everlasting.
Slumber seizes Him not, neither sleep;
   to Him belongs
all that is in the heavens and the earth
Who is there that shall intercede with Him
   save by His leave?
He knows what lies before them
   and what is after them,
and they comprehend not anything of His knowledge
   save such as He wills.
His Throne comprises the heavens and earth;
   the preserving of them oppresses Him not;
He is the All-high, the All-glorious.

No compulsion is there in religion.
Rectitude has become clear from error.
So whosoever disbelieves in idols
and believes in God, has laid hold of
the most firm handle, unbreaking; God is
   All-hearing, All-knowing.
God is the protector of the believers;
He brings them forth from the shadows
   into the light.
And the unbelievers—their protectors are
idols, that bring them forth from the light
   into the shadows;
those are the inhabitants of the Fire,
   therein dwelling forever. (II, 256-9)

That then is God your Lord;
there is no god but He,
the Creator of everything.
So serve Him,
for He is Guardian over everything.
The eyes attain Him not, but He attains the eyes;
He is the All-subtle, the All-aware. (VI, 102-3.)

Translation by A. J. Arberry

41. ALLAH IS ALL-KNOWING, ALL-POWERFUL— THE CREATOR!

('Koran,' XXVII, 61-5; XXX, 47-54; XXXV, 36-9)

He who created the heavens and earth, and sent down for you
out of heaven water;
and We caused to grow therewith gardens full of loveliness
whose trees you could never grow.
Is there a god with God?
Nay, but they are a people who assign to Him equals!

He who made the earth a fixed place
and set amidst it rivers
and appointed it firm mountains
and placed a partition between the two seas.
Is there a god with God?
Nay, but the most of them have no knowledge.

He who answers the constrained, when he calls unto Him,
and removes the evil
and appoints you to be successors in the earth.
Is there a god with God?
Little indeed do you remember.

He who guides you in the shadows of the land and the sea
and looses the winds,
bearing goods tidings before His mercy.
Is there a god with God?
High exalted be God, above that which they associate!

Who originates creation, then brings it back again,
and provides you out of heaven and earth.
        Is there a god with God? (XXVII, 61-5.)

God is He that looses the winds, that stirs up clouds,
and He spreads them in heaven how He will, and shatters them;
then thou seest the rain issuing out of the midst of them,
and when he smites with it whomsoever of His servants
            He will, lo, they rejoice,
although before it was sent down on them before that
            they had been in despair.

        So behold the marks of God's mercy,
        how He quickens the earth after it
        was dead; surely He is the quickener
        of the dead, and He is powerful
            over everything.
But if We loose a wind, and they see it growing yellow,
        they remain after that unbelievers.

        Thou shalt not make the dead to hear,
    neither shalt thou make the deaf to hear the call
        when they turn about, retreating.
    Thou shalt not guide the blind out of their error
        neither shalt thou make any to hear
except for such as believe in Our signs, and so surrender.

God is He that created you of weakness, then He appointed
after weakness strength, then after strength He appointed
weakness and grey hairs; He creates what He will, and
        He is the All-knowing, the All-powerful. (XXX, 47-54.)

God knows the Unseen in the heavens and the earth;
    He knows the thoughts within the breasts.
It is He who appointed you viceroys in the earth.
So whosoever disbelieves, his unbelief shall be
charged against him; their unbelief increases
the disbelievers only in hate in God's sight;
their unbelief increases the disbelievers only in loss.
Say: 'Have you considered your associates on whom
you call, apart from God? Show what they have
created in the earth; or have they a partnership
in the heavens?' Or have We given them a Book,
so that they are upon a clear sign from it?

Nay, but the evildoers promise one another
    naught but delusion.

God holds the heavens and the earth, lest they remove;
did they remove, none would hold them after Him
    Surely He is All-clement, All-forgiving. (XXXV, 36-9.)

Translation by A. J. Arberry

42. ALLAH 'IS THE FIRST AND THE LAST,' THE CREATOR,
MAKER, AND SHAPER ... HE HAS KNOWLEDGE OF
EVERYTHING

('Koran,' LVII, 1-5; LVIII, 7-8; LIX, 23-5)

In the Name of God, the Merciful, the Compassionate

All that is in the heavens and the earth magnifies God;
    He is the All-mighty, the All-wise.
To Him belongs the Kingdom of the heavens and the earth;
He gives life, and He makes to die, and He is powerful
    Over everything.
He is the First and the Last, the Outward and the Inward;
    He has knowledge of everything.
    It is He that created the heavens and the earth
    in six days
    then seated Himself upon the Throne.
    He knows what penetrates into the earth
    and what comes forth from it,
what comes down from heaven, and what goes up into it.
    He is with you wherever you are; and God sees
    the things you do.
To Him belongs the Kingdom of the heavens and the earth;
    and unto Him all matters are returned,
    He makes the night to enter into the day
    and makes the day to enter into the night.
    He knows the thoughts within the breasts. (LVII, 1-5.)

Hast thou not seen that God knows whatsoever is in
the heavens, and whatsoever is in the earth? Three

men conspire not secretly together, but He is the
fourth of them, neither five men, but He is the
sixth of them, neither fewer than that, neither
more, but He is with them, wherever they may be;
then He shall tell them what they have done, on the
Day of Resurrection. Surely God has knowledge
of everything. (LIV, 7-8.)

He is God;
There is no god but He.
He is the knower of the Unseen and the Visible;
He is the All-merciful, the All-compassionate.

He is God;
There is no god but He.
He is the King, the All-holy, the All-peaceable,
the All-faithful, the All-preserver,
the All-mighty, the All-compeller,
the All-sublime.
Glory be to God, above that they associate!

He is God;
the Creator, the Maker, the Shaper.
To Him belong the Names Most Beautiful.
All that is in the heavens and the earth magnifies Him;
He is the All-mighty, the All-wise. (LIX, 23-5.)

Translation by A. J. Arberry

43. ALLAH IS LIGHT . . .

('Koran,' XXIV, 33-44)

Now We have sent down to you signs
making all clear, and an example
of those who passed away before you,
and an admonition for the godfearing.

God is the Light of the heavens and the earth;
the likeness of His Light is as a niche
wherein is a lamp
(the lamp is a glass,

the glass as it were a glittering star)
    kindled from a Blessed Tree,
  an olive that is neither of the East nor of the West
whose oil wellnigh would shine, even if no fire touched it;
    Light upon Light;
  (God guides to His Light whom He will.)
  (And God strikes similitudes for men,
  and God has knowledge of everything.)
  in temples God has allowed to be raised up,
  and His name to be commemorated therein;
therein glorifying Him, in the mornings and the evenings,
  are men whom neither commerce nor trafficking
    diverts from the remembrance of God
  and to perform the prayer, and to pay the alms,
fearing a day when hearts and eyes shall be turned about,
that God may recompense them for their fairest works
    and give them increase of His bounty;
and God provides whomsoever He will, without reckoning.
    And as for the unbelievers,
their works are as a mirage in a spacious plain
  which the man athirst supposes to be water
    till, when he comes to it, he finds it is nothing;
    there indeed he finds God,
and He pays him his account in full; (And God is swift
    at the reckoning.)
  or they are as shadows upon a sea obscure
    covered by a billow
    above which is a billow
    above which are clouds,
    shadows piled one upon another;
when he puts forth his hand, wellnigh he cannot see it.
  And to whomsoever God assigns no light,
    no light has he.
Hast thou not seen how that whatsoever is in the heavens
    and in the earth extols God,
    and the birds spreading their wings?
Each—He knows its prayer and its extolling; and God knows
    the things they do.
To God belongs the Kingdom of the heavens and the earth,
    and to Him is the homecoming.
Hast thou not seen how God drives the clouds, then composes them,

then converts them into a mass,
then thou seest the rain issuing out of the midst of them?
And He sends down out of heaven mountains, wherein is hail,
so that He smites whom He will with it, and turns it aside
        from whom He will;
wellnigh the gleam of His lightning snatches away at the sight.
    God turns about the day and the night;
    surely in that is a lesson for those who have eyes.
    God has created every beast of water,
        And some of them go upon their bellies,
        and some of them go upon two feet,
        and some of them go upon four; God
        creates whatever He will; God is powerful
        over everything.

Translation by A. J. Arberry

See also nos. 231-7, 252, 268-9

CHAPTER II

Myths of Creation
and of Origin

A. MYTHS OF THE CREATION OF THE WORLD

There is a great variety of cosmogonic myths. However, they can be classified as follows: 1. creation ex nihilo (a High Being creates the world by thought, by word, or by heating himself in a steam-hut, and so forth); 2. The Earth Diver Motif (a God sends aquatic birds or amphibious animals, or dives, himself, to the bottom of the primordial ocean to bring up a particle of earth from which the entire world grows); 3. creation by dividing in two a primordial unity (one can distinguish three variants: a. separation of Heaven and Earth, that is to say of the World-Parents; b. separation of an original amorphous mass, the 'Chaos'; c. the cutting in two of a cosmogenic egg); 4. creation by dismemberment of a primordial Being, either a voluntary, anthropomorphic victim (Ymir of the Scandinavian mythology, the Vedic Indian Purusha, the Chinese P'an-ku) or an aquatic monster conquered after a terrific battle (the Babylonian Tiamat). The texts reprinted below cover almost all of these types and variants. We have added some examples of Indian speculative cosmogonic texts.

44. CREATION BY THOUGHT

An account by a Winnebago Indian of Wisconsin, recorded by Paul Radin.

'What it was our father lay on when he came to consciousness we do not know. He moved his right arm and then his left arm, his right leg and then his left leg. He began to think of what he should do and finally he began to cry and tears began to flow from his eyes and fall down below him. After a while he looked down below him and saw something bright. The bright objects were his tears that had flowed below and formed the present waters. . . . Earthmaker began to think again. He thought: "It is thus, If I wish anything it will become as I wish, just as my tears have become seas." Thus he thought. So he wished for light and it became light. Then he thought: "It is as I supposed; the things that I have wished for have come into existence as I desired." Then he again thought and wished for the earth and this earth came into existence. Earthmaker looked at the earth and he liked it but it was not quiet. . . . (After the earth had become quiet) he thought again of how things came into existence just as he desired. Then he first began to talk. He said, "As things are just as I wish them I shall make one being like myself." So he took a piece of earth and made it like himself. Then he talked to what he had created but it did not answer. He looked upon it and he saw that it had no mind or thought. So he made a mind for it. Again he talked to it, but it did not answer. So he looked upon it again and saw that it had no tongue. Then he made it a tongue. Then he talked to it again but it did not answer. So he looked upon it again and saw that it had no soul. So he made it a soul. He talked to it again and it very nearly said something. But it did not make itself intelligible. So Earthmaker breathed into its mouth and talked to it and it answered.'

Paul Radin, 'The Winnebago Indians,' in *Thirty-seventh Annual Report*, Bureau of American Ethnology (Washington, D.C., 1923), pp. 212-13

45. OMAHA COSMOGONY: AT THE BEGINNING THE WORLD WAS IN GOD'S MIND

An Omaha Indian explains the Omaha belief about the creation of the world as recorded by Fletcher and La Flesche.

'At the beginning,' said the Omaha, 'all things were in the mind of Wakonda. All creatures, including man, were spirits. They moved about in space between the earth and the stars (the heavens). They were seeking a place where they could come into bodily existence. They ascended to the sun, but the sun was not fitted for their abode. They moved on to the moon and found that it also was not good for their home. Then they descended to the earth. They saw it was covered with water. They floated through the air to the north, the east, the south, and the west, and found no dry land. They were sorely grieved. Suddenly from the midst of the water uprose a great rock. It burst into flames and the waters floated into the air in clouds. Dry land appeared; the grasses and the trees grew. The hosts of the spirits descended and became flesh and blood. They fed on the seeds of the grasses and the fruits of the trees, and the land vibrated with their expressions of joy and gratitude to Wakonda, the maker of all things.'

Fletcher and La Flesche, 'The Omaha Tribe,' in *Twenty-seventh Annual Report*, Bureau of American Ethnology, (Washington, D.C., 1911), pp. 570-1.

See also nos. 8, 9, 10

46. CREATION FROM MERE APPEARANCE

A belief of the Uitoto of Colombia, South America.

In the beginning there was nothing but mere appearance, nothing really existed. It was a phantasm, an illusion that our father touched; something mysterious it was that he grasped. Nothing existed. Through the agency of a dream our father, He-who-is-appearance-only, Nainema, pressed the phantasm to his breast and then was sunk in thought.

Not even a tree existed that might have supported this phantasm and only through his breath did Nainema hold this illusion attached to the thread of a dream. He tried to discover what was at the bottom of it, but he found nothing. 'I have attached that which was non-existent,' he said. There was nothing.

Then our father tried again and investigated the bottom of this something and his fingers sought the empty phantasm. He tied the emptiness to the dream-thread and pressed the magical glue-substance upon it. Thus by means of his dream did he hold it like the fluff of raw cotton.

He seized the bottom of the phantasm and stamped upon it repeatedly, allowing himself finally to rest upon the earth of which he had dreamt.

The earth-phantasm was now his. Then he spat out saliva repeatedly so that the forests might arise. He lay upon the earth and set the covering of heaven above it. He drew from the earth the blue and white heavens and placed them above.

Paul Radin, *Monotheism among Primitive Peoples* (Basel, 1954), pp. 13-14; paraphrasing and summarizing K. T. Preuss, *Religion und Mythologie der Uitoto*, I (Göttingen, 1921), pp. 166-8

47. IO AND THE MAORI COSMOGONY

Io (Iho), the Supreme Being of the Maori of New Zealand, is regarded as eternal, omniscient, and the creator of the universe, of the gods, and of man. As will be seen from the following text, the cosmogonic myth constitutes, for the Maori, a paradigmatic model for every kind of 'creation': the procreation of a child, the inspiration of a poet, and the like. (Cf. M. Eliade, 'Myth and Reality' [New York: Harper & Row, 1963], pp. 30 ff.)

> Io dwelt within the breathing-space of immensity.
> The Universe was in darkness, with water everywhere.
> There was no glimmer of dawn, no clearness, no light.
> And he began by saying these words,—
> That He might cease remaining inactive:
>   'Darkness become a light-possessing darkness.'
> And at once light appeared.
> (He) then repeated those self-same words in this manner.
> That He might cease remaining inactive:
>   'Light, become a darkness-possessing light.'
> And again an intense darkness supervened.
> Then a third time He spake saying:
>   'Let there be one darkness above,
>   Let there be one darkness below.
>   . . . .
>   Let there be one light above,
>   Let there be one light below,
>   . . . .
>   A dominion of light,
>   A bright light.'
> And now a great light prevailed.
> (Io) then looked to the waters which compassed him about,
>   and spake a fourth time, saying:
>   'Ye waters of Tai-kama, be ye separate.
>   Heaven, be formed.' Then the sky became suspended.
>   'Bring forth thou Tupua-horo-nuku.'
> And at once the moving earth lay stretched abroad.

Those words (of Io) (the supreme god) became impressed on the minds of our ancestors, and by them were they transmitted down through generations, our priest joyously referred to them as being:

The Creation of the World

The ancient and original sayings.
The ancient and original words.
The ancient and original cosmological wisdom (wananga).
Which caused growth from the void.
The limitless space-filling void,
As witness the tidal-waters,
The evolved heaven,
The birth-given evolved earth.

And now, my friends, there are three very important applications of those original sayings, as used in our sacred rituals. The first occurs in the ritual for planting a child in the barren womb.

The next occurs in the ritual for enlightening both the mind and body. The third and last occurs in the ritual on the solemn subject of death, and of war, of baptism, of genealogical recitals and such like important subjects, as the priests most particularly concerned themselves in.

The words by which Io fashioned the Universe—that is to say, by which it was implanted and caused to produce a world of light—the same words are used in the ritual for implanting a child in a barren womb. The words by which Io caused light to shine in the darkness are used in the rituals for cheering a gloomy and despondent heart, the feeble aged, the decrepit; for shedding light into secret places and matters, for inspiration in song-composing, and in many other affairs, affecting man to despair in times of adverse war. For all such the ritual to enlighten and cheer includes the words (used by Io) to overcome and dispel darkness. Thirdly, there is the preparatory ritual which treats of successive formations within the universe, and the genealogical history of man himself.

Hare Hongi, 'A Maori Cosmogony,' *Journal of the Polynesian Society*, XVI (1907), pp. 113-14

See also no. 11

48. POLYNESIAN THEOGONY AND COSMOGONY
(SOCIETY ISLANDS)

Ta'aroa (Tangararoa) is the Supreme Being, the noncreated Creator of the universe. He came forth from a shell (Rumia), which later became the world.

Ta'aroa was the ancestor of all the gods; he made everything. From time immemorial was the great Ta'aroa, Tahi-tumu (The-origin). Ta'aroa developed himself in solitude; he was his own parent, having no father or mother. . . .

Ta'aroa sat in his shell in darkness from eternity. The shell was like an egg revolving in endless space, with no sky, no land, no sea, no moon, no sun, no stars. All was darkness, it was continuous thick darkness. . . . The record then proceeds to describe Ta'aroa's breaking his shell, which became the sky, his swimming in empty space and retirement into a new shell which, after he had again emerged, . . . he took . . . for the great foundation of the world, for stratum rock and for soil for the world.

And the shell Rumia that he opened first, became his house, the dome of the gods' sky, which was a confined sky, enclosing the world then forming.

E. S. Craighill Handy, *Polynesian Religion*, Bernice P. Bishop Museum Bulletin 34 (Honolulu, 1927), pp. 11-12

49. AN EARTH-DIVER CREATION MYTH

Beliefs of the Maidu Indians of California.

In the beginning there was no sun, no moon, no stars. All was dark, and everywhere there was only water. A raft came floating on the water. It came from the north, and in it were two persons,—Turtle (A'nōshma) and Father-of-the-Secret-Society (Pehē'ipe). The stream flowed very rapidly. Then from the sky a rope of feathers, called Pō'kelma, was let down, and down it came Earth-Initiate. When he reached the end of the rope, he tied it to the bow of the raft, and stepped in. His face was covered and was never seen, but his body shone like the sun. He sat down, and for a long time said nothing. At last Turtle said, 'Where do you come from?' and Earth-Initiate answered, 'I come from above.' Then Turtle said, 'Brother, can you not make for me some good dry land, so that I may sometimes come up out of the water?' Then he asked another time, 'Are there going to be any people in the world?' Earth-Initiate thought awhile, then said, 'Yes.' Turtle asked, 'How long before you are going to make people?' Earth-Initiate replied, 'I don't know. You want to have some dry land: well, how am I going to get any earth to make it of?' Turtle answered, 'If you will tie a rock about my left arm, I'll dive for some.' Earth-Initiate did as Turtle asked, and then, reaching around, took the end of a rope from somewhere, and tied it to Turtle. When Earth-Initiate came to the raft, there was no rope there: he just reached out and found one. Turtle said, 'If the rope is not long enough, I'll jerk it once, and you must haul me up; if it is long enough, I'll give two jerks, and then you must pull me up quickly, as I shall have all the earth that I can carry.' Just as Turtle went over the side of the boat, Father-of-the-Secret-Society began to shout loudly.

Turtle was gone a long time. He was gone six years; and when he came up, he was covered with green slime, he had been down so long. When he reached the top of the water, the only earth he had was a very little under his nails; the rest had all washed away. Earth-Initiate took with his right hand a stone knife from under his left armpit, and carefully scraped the earth out from under Turtle's nails. He put the earth in the palm of his hand, and rolled it about till it was round; it was as large as a small pebble. He laid it on the stern of the raft. By and by he went to look at it; it had not grown at all. The third time he went to look at it, it had grown so that it could be spanned by the arms. The fourth time he looked, it was as big as the world, the raft was aground, and all around were mountains as far as he could see. The raft came ashore at Tadoikö and the place can be seen today.

When the raft had come to land, Turtle said, 'I can't stay in the dark all the time. Can't you make a light, so that I can see?' Earth-Initiate replied, 'Let us get out of the raft, and then we will see what we can do.' So all three got out. Then, Earth-Initiate said, 'Look that way, to the east! I am going to tell my sister to come up. Then it began to grow light, and day began to break; then Father-of-the-Secret-Society began to shout loudly, and the sun came up. Turtle said 'Which way is the sun going to travel?' Earth-Initiate answered, 'I'll tell her to go this way, and go down there.' After the sun went down, Father-of-the-Secret-Society began to cry and shout again, and it grew very dark. Earth-Initiate asked Turtle and Father-of-the-Secret-Society, 'How do you like it?' and they both answered, 'It is very good.' Then Turtle asked, 'Is that all you are going to do for us?' and Earth-Initiate answered, 'No, I am going to do more yet.' Then he called the stars each by its name, and they came out. When this was done,

Turtle asked, 'Now what shall we do?' Earth-Initiate replied, 'Wait, and I'll show you.' Then he made a tree grow at Ta'doikö,—the tree called Hu'kimsta and Earth-Initiate and Turtle and Father-of-the-Secret-Society sat in its shade for two days. The tree was very large, and had twelve different kinds of acorns growing on it.

Roland B. Dixon, *Maidu Myths*, Bulletin of the American Museum of Natural History, XVII, no. 2 (1902-7) pp. 33-118; quotation from pp. 39 *ff*.

50. THE BEGINNING OF THE WORLD

A myth from the Yauelmani Yokuts of California.

At first there was water everywhere. A piece of wood (wicket, stick, wood, tree) grew up out of the water to the sky. On the tree there was a nest. Those who were inside did not see any earth. There was only water to be seen. The eagle was the chief of them. With him were the wolf, Coyote, the panther, the prairie falcon, the hawk called *po'yon*, and the condor. The eagle wanted to make the earth. He thought, 'We will have to have land.' Then he called *k'uik'ui*, a small duck. He said to it: 'Dive down and bring up earth.' The duck dived, but did not reach the bottom. It died. The eagle called another kind of duck. He told it to dive. This duck went far down. It finally reached the bottom. Just as it touched the mud there it died. Then it came up again. Then the eagle and the other six saw a little dirt under its finger nail. When the eagle saw this he took the dirt from its nail. He mixed it with *telis* and *pele* seeds and ground them up. He put water with the mixture and made dough. This was in the morning. Then he set it in the water and it swelled and spread everywhere, going out from the middle. (These seeds when ground and mixed with water swell.) In the evening the eagle told his companions: 'Take some earth.' They went down and took a little earth up in the tree with them. Early in the morning, when the morning star came, the eagle said to the wolf: 'Shout.' The wolf shouted and the earth disappeared, and all was water again. The eagle said: 'We will make it again,' for it was for this purpose that they had taken some earth with them into the nest. Then they took *telis* and *pele* seeds again, and ground them with the earth, and put the mixture into the water, and it swelled out again. Then early next morning, when the morning star appeared, the eagle told the wolf again: 'Shout!' and he shouted three times. The earth was shaken by the earthquake, but it stood. Then Coyote said: 'I must shout too.' He shouted and the earth shook a very little. Now it was good. Then they came out of the tree on the ground. Close to where this tree stood there was a lake. The eagle said: 'We will live here.' Then they had a house there and lived there.

A. L. Kroeber, *Indian Myths of South Central California*, University of California Publications, American Archeology and Ethnology, IV, no. 4 (1906-7), pp. 229-31

51. AN AFRICAN COSMOGONY

An account from the Boshongo, a Central Bantu Tribe of the Lunda Cluster

In the beginning, in the dark, there was nothing but water. And Bumba was alone.

One day Bumba was in terrible pain. He retched and strained and vomited up the sun. After that light spread over everything. The heat of the sun dried up the water until the black edges of the world began to show. Black sandbanks and reefs could be seen. But there were no living things.

Bumba vomited up the moon and then the stars, and after that the night had its light also.

Still Bumba was in pain. He strained again and nine living creatures came forth; the leopard named Koy Bumba, and Pongo Bumba the crested eagle, the crocodile, Ganda Bumba, and one little fish named Yo; next, old Kono Bumba, the tortoise, and Tsetse, the lightning, swift, deadly, beautiful like the leopard, then the white heron, Nyanyi Bumba, also one beetle, and the goat named Budi.

Last of all came forth men. There were many men, but only one was white like Bumba. His name was Loko Yima.

The creatures themselves then created all the creatures. The heron created all the birds of the air except the kite. He did not make the kite. The crocodile made serpents and the iguana. The goat produced every beast with horns. Yo, the small fish, brought forth all the fish of all the seas and waters. The beetle created insects.

Then the serpents in their turn made grasshoppers, and the iguana made the creatures without horns.

Then the three sons of Bumba said they would finish the world. The first, Nyonye Ngana, made the white ants; but he was not equal to the task, and died of it. The ants, however, thankful for life and being, went searching for black earth in the depths of the world and covered the barren sands to bury and honour their creator.

Chonganda, the second son, brought forth a marvellous living plant from which all the trees and grasses and flowers and plants in the world have sprung. The third son, Chedi Bumba, wanted something different, but for all his trying made only the bird called the kite.

Of all the creatures, Tsetse, lightning, was the only trouble-maker. She stirred up so much trouble that Bumba chased her into the sky. Then mankind was without fire until Bumba showed the people how to draw fire out of trees. 'There is fire in every tree,' he told them, and showed them how to make the firedrill and liberate it. Sometimes today Tsetse still leaps down and strikes the earth and causes damage.

When at last the work of creation was finished, Bumba walked through the peaceful villages and said to the people, 'Behold these wonders. They belong to you.' Thus from Bumba, the Creator, the First Ancestor, came forth all the wonders that we see and hold and use, and all the brotherhood of beasts and man.

Maria Leach, *The Beginning* (New York, 1956), pp. 145-6; translated and adapted from E. Torday and J. A. Joyce, *Les Boshongo*, pp. 20 f.

52. THE MAYA-QUICHÉ GENESIS

('Popol Vuh,' chapter 1)

The 'Popol Vuh' is the most important surviving work of Mayan literature. It was first written down after the introduction of Christianity.

Admirable is the account—so the narrative opens—admirable is the account of the time in which it came to pass that all was formed in heaven and upon earth, the quartering of their signs, their measure and alignment, and the establishment of parallels to the skies and upon the earth to the four quarters thereof, as was spoken by the Creator and Maker, the Mother, the Father of life and of all existence, that one by whom all move and breathe, father and sustainer of the peace of peoples, by whose wisdom was premediated the excellence of all that doth exist in the heavens, upon the earth, in lake and sea.

Lo, all was in suspense, all was calm and silent; all was motionless, all was quiet, and wide was the immensity of the skies.

Lo, the first word and the first discourse. There was not yet a man, not an animal; there were no birds nor fish nor crayfish; there was no wood, no stone, no bog, no ravine, neither vegetation nor marsh; only the sky existed.

The face of the earth was not yet to be seen; only the peaceful sea and the expanse of the heavens.

Nothing was yet formed into a body; nothing was joined to another thing; naught held itself poised; there was not a rustle, not a sound beneath the sky. There was naught that stood upright; there were only the quiet waters of the sea, solitary within its bounds; for as yet naught existed.

There were only immobility and silence in the darkness and in the night. Alone was the Creator, the Maker, Tepeu, the Lord, and Gucumatz, the Plumed Serpent, those who engender, those who give being, alone upon the waters like a growing light.

They are enveloped in green and azure, whence is the name Gucumatz, and their being is great wisdom. Lo, how the sky existeth, how the Heart of the Sky existeth—for such is the name of God, as He doth name Himself!

It is then that the word came to Tepeu and to Gucumatz, in the shadows and in the night, and spake with Tepeu and with Gucumatz. And they spake and consulted and meditated, and they joined their words and their counsels.

Then light came while they consulted together; and at the moment of dawn man appeared while they planned concerning the production and increase of the groves and of the climbing vines, there in the shade and in the night, through that one who is the Heart of the Sky, whose name is Hurakan.

The Lightning is the first sign of Hurakan; the second is the Streak of Lightning; the third is the Thunderbolt which striketh; and these three are the Heart of the Sky.

Then they came to Tepeu, the Gucumatz, and held counsel touching civilized life; how seed should be formed, how light should be produced, how the sustainer and nourisher of all.

'Let it be thus done. Let the waters retire and cease to obstruct, to

the end that earth exist here, that it harden itself and show its surface, to the end that it be sown, and that the light of day shine in
the heavens and upon the earth; for we shall receive neither glory nor
honour from all that we have created and formed until human beings
exist, endowed with sentience.' Thus they spake while the earth was
formed by them. It is thus, veritably, that creation took place, and the
earth existed. 'Earth,' they said, and immediately it was formed.

Like a fog or a cloud was its formation into the material state,
when, like great lobsters, the mountains appeared upon the waters,
and in an instant there were great mountains. Only by marvellous
power could have been achieved this their resolution when the mountains and the valleys instantly appeared, with groves of cypress and
pine upon them.

Then was Gucumatz filled with joy. 'Thou art welcome, O Heart of
the Sky, O Hurakan, O Streak of Lightning, O Thunderbolt!'

'This that we have created and shaped will have its end,' they replied.

Translation by H. B. Alexander in his *Latin-American
Mythology* (Boston, 1920); pp. 160-2

53. JAPANESE COSMOGONY

('Nihongi' and 'Ko-ji-ki')

*At the beginning of the eighth century A.D., the early Japanese myths
were gathered together in two collections: 'Nihongi' ('Chronicles of
Japan') and 'Ko-ji-ki' ('Records of Ancient Matters').*

Of old, Heaven and Earth were not yet separated, and the In and Yo
not yet divided. They formed a chaotic mass like an egg, which was of
obscurely defined limits, and contained germs. The purer and clearer
part was thinly diffused and formed Heaven, while the heavier and
grosser element settled down and became Earth. The finer element
easily became a united body, but the consolidation of the heavy and
gross element was accomplished with difficulty. Heaven was therefore
formed first, and Earth established subsequently. Thereafter divine
beings were produced between them. (*Nihongi*, pp. 1-2.)

We have next what is called 'the seven generations of Gods,' ending with the creator-deities, Izanagi, the Male-Who-Invites, and his sister, Izanami, the Female-Who-Invites.

Hereupon all the Heavenly Deities commanded the two Deities His Augustness the Male-Who-Invites and Her Augustness the Female-Who-Invites, ordering them to 'Make, consolidate and give birth to this drifting land.' Granting to them an heavenly jewelled spear, they (thus) deigned to charge them. So the two Deities, standing upon the Floating Bridge of Heaven, pushed down the jewelled spear and stirred with it, whereupon, when they had stirred the brine till it went curdlecurdle, and drew (the spear) up, the brine that dripped down from the end of the spear was piled up and became an island. This is the Island of Onogoro. (*Ko-ji-ki*, p. 19.)

The two Deities having descended on Onogoro-jima erected there an eight fathom house with an august central pillar. Then Izanagi addressed Izanami, saying: 'How is thy body formed?' Izanami replied, 'My body is completely formed except one part which is incomplete.' Then Izanagi said, 'My body is completely formed and there is one part which is superfluous. Suppose that we supplement that which is incomplete in thee with that which is superfluous in me, and thereby procreate lands.' Izanami replied, 'It is well.' Then Izanagi said, 'Let me and thee go round the heavenly august pillar, and having met at the other side, let us become united in wedlock.' This being agreed to, he said, 'Do thou go round from the left, and I will go round from the right.' When they had gone round, Izanami spoke and exclaimed, 'How delightful! I have met a lovely youth.' Izanagi then said, 'How delightful! I have met a lovely maiden.' Afterwards he said, 'It was unlucky for the woman to speak first.' The child which was the first offspring of their union was the Hiruko (leech-child), which at the age of three was still unable to stand upright, and was therefore placed in a reed-boat and sent adrift. (*Nihongi*, p. 13; cf. *Ko-ji-ki*, pp. 20-1.)

The two deities next give birth to the islands of Japan and a number of deities. The last deity to be produced is the God of Fire. But in giving birth to him Izanami is mortally burned. After death, she descends beneath the earth. Izanagi goes in search of her, like Orpheus descending into the Shades to recover Eurydice. Under the earth it is very dark; but Izanagi finally meets his wife and offers to bring her back with him. Izanami begs him to wait at the door of the subterranean palace, and not to show a light. But the husband loses patience; he lights a tooth of his comb and enters the palace where, by the flame of this torch, he perceives Izanami in process of decomposition; seized with panic, he flees. His dead wife pursues him but Izanagi, managing to escape by the same way that he had gone down under the earth, casts a great rock over the aperture. Husband and wife talk together for the last time, separated from each other by this rock. Izanagi pronounces the sacramental formula for separation between them, and then goes up to heaven; while Izanami goes down forever into subterranean regions. She becomes the Goddess of the dead, as is generally the case with chthonian and agricultural goddesses, who are divinities of fecundity and, at the same time, of death, of birth, and of re-entry into the maternal bosom.

Nihongi translated by W. G. Aston (London, 1924).
Ko-ji-ki translated by B. H. Chamberlain (Tokyo: Asiatic Society of Japan, 1906)

54. EGYPTIAN COSMOGONY AND THEOGONY

('The Book of Overthrowing Apophis')

The following text is from 'The Book of Overthrowing Apophis,' a late work, but one which conserves basic material from a relatively early period.

The Lord of All, after having come into being, says: I am he who came into being as Khepri (i.e., the Becoming One). When I came into being, the beings came into being, all the beings came into being after I became. Numerous are those who became, who came out of my mouth, before heaven ever existed, nor earth came into being, nor the worms, nor snakes were created in this place. I, being in weariness, was bound to them in the Watery Abyss. I found no place to stand. I thought in my heart, I planned in myself, I made all forms being alone, before I ejected Shu, before I spat out Tefnut,[1] before any other who was in me had become. Then I planned in my own heart, and many forms of beings came into being as forms of children, as forms of their children. I conceived by my hand, I united myself with my hand, I poured out of my own mouth. I ejected Shu, I spat out

The notes to this text are on p. 97.

The Creation of the World

Tefnut. It was my father the Watery Abyss who brought them up, and my eye followed them (?) while they became far from me. After having become one god, there were (now) three gods in me. When I came into being in this land, Shu and Tefnut jubilated in the Watery Abyss in which they were. Then they brought with them my eye. After I had joined together my members, I wept over them, and men came into being out of the tears which came out of my eyes.[2] Then she (the eye) became enraged[3] after she came back and had found that I had placed another in her place, that she had been replaced by the Brilliant One. Then I found a higher place for her on my brow,[4] and when she began to rule over the whole land her fury fell down on the flowering (?) and I replaced what she had ravished. I came out of the flowering (?), I created all snakes, and all that came into being with them. Shu and Tefnut produced Geb and Nut; Geb and Nut produced out of a single body Osiris, Horus the Eyeless One,[5] Seth, Isis, and Nephthys, one after the other among them. Their children are numerous in this land.

Notes

1 Shu the air, Tefnut the moist.
2 Same myth in the *Book of Gates*, division 4 (*The Tomb of Ramesses* VI, p. 169).
3 An allusion to the myth of the Eye of the sun god which departs into a foreign land and is brought back by Shu and Tefnut. Another aspect of this myth is to be found in the *Book of the Divine Cow*.
4 The fire-spitting snake, the uraeus on the head of the god.
5 The Elder Horus of Letopolis.

Translation and notes by Alexandre Piankoff, in his *The Shrines of Tut-ankh-amon* (New York, 1955), p. 24. Cf. the translation by John A. Wilson, in ANET, pp. 6-7

See also no. 17

55. MESOPOTAMIAN COSMOGONY

('Enuma elish')

The long Babylonian creation epic 'Enuma elish' ('When on high'), so called from the first two words of the poem, narrates a chain of events beginning with the very first separation of order out of chaos and culminating in the creation of the specific cosmos known to the ancient Babylonians. As the gods are born within the commingled waters of their primeval parents, Apsu and Tiamat, their restlessness disturbs Apsu. Over Tiamat's protests, he plans to kill them; but the clever Ea learns of his plan and kills Apsu instead. Now Tiamat is furious; she produces an army of monsters to avenge her husband and to wrest lordship from the younger generation. The terrified gods turn to Ea's son Marduk for help. Marduk agrees to face Tiamat, but demands supremacy over them as compensation. They promptly assemble, declare him king, and send him forth, armed with his winds and storms. The battle is short; the winds inflate Tiamat's body like a balloon and Marduk sends an arrow through her gaping mouth into her heart. He then splits her body, forming heaven and earth with the two halves. After putting the heavens in order, he turns to Ea for help in creating, out of the blood of Tiamat's demon-commander Kingu, the black-haired men of Mesopotamia. The poem concludes as the gods build a temple for Marduk and gather in it to celebrate his mighty deeds. Enuma elish was probably composed in the early part of the second millennium B.C.

When on high the heaven had not been named,
Firm ground below had not been called by name,
Naught but primordial Apsu,[1] their begetter,
(And) Mummu[2]-Tiamat,[3] she who bore them all,
Their waters[4] commingling as a single body;
No reed hut had been matted, no marsh land had appeared,
When no gods whatever had been brought into being,
Uncalled by name, their destinies undetermined—
Then it was that the gods were formed within them.[5]
Lahmu and Lahamu[6] were brought forth, by name they were called.
For aeons they grew in age and stature.
Anshar and Kishar[7] were formed, surpassing the others.
They prolonged the days, added on the years.
Anu[8] was their son, of his fathers the rival;
Yea, Anshar's first-born, Anu, was his equal.
Anu begot in his image Nudimmud.[9]
This Nudimmud was of his fathers the master;
Of broad wisdom, understanding, mighty in strength,

The Creation of the World

Mightier by far than his grandfather, Anshar.
He had no rival among the gods, his brothers.
The divine brothers banded together,
They disturbed Tiamat as they surged back and forth,
Yea, they troubled the mood of Tiamat
By their hilarity in the Abode of Heaven.
Apsu could not lessen their clamour
And Tiamat was speechless at their ways.
Their doings were loathsome unto [. . .].
Unsavoury were their ways; they were overbearing.
Then Apsu, the begetter of the great gods,
Cried out, addressing Mummu, his vizier:
'O Mummu, my vizier, who rejoicest my spirit,
Come hither and let us go to Tiamat!'
They went and sat down before Tiamat,
Exchanging counsel about the gods, their first-born.
Apsu, opening his mouth,
Said unto resplendent Tiamat:
'Their ways are verily loathsome unto me.
By day I find no relief, nor repose by night.
I will destroy, I will wreck their ways,
That quiet may be restored. Let us have rest!'
As soon as Tiamat heard this,
She was wroth and called out to her husband.
She cried out aggrieved, as she raged all alone,
Injecting woe into her mood:
What? Should we destroy that which we have built?
Their ways are indeed troublesome, but let us attend kindly!'
Then answered Mummu, giving counsel to Apsu;
Ill-wishing and ungracious was Mummu's advice:
'Do destroy, my father, the mutinous ways.
Then shalt thou have relief by day and rest by night!'
When Apsu heard this, his face grew radiant
Because of the evil he planned against the gods, his sons.
As for Mummu, by the neck he embraced him
As (that one) sat down on his knees to kiss him.
(Now) whatever they had plotted between them
Was repeated unto the gods, their first born.
When the gods heard (this), they were astir,
(Then) lapsed into silence and remained speechless.
Surpassing in wisdom, accomplished, resourceful,

Ea,[10] the all-wise, saw through their[11] scheme.
A master design against it he devised and set up,
Made artful his spell against it, surpassing and holy.
He recited it and made is subsist in the deep,[12]
As he poured sleep upon him. Sound asleep he lay.
When Apsu he had made prone, drenched with sleep,
Mummu, the adviser, was impotent to move.
He loosened his band, tore off his tiara,
Removed his halo (and) put it on himself.
Having fettered Apsu, he slew him.
Mummu he bound and left behind lock.
Having thus upon Apsu established his dwelling,
He laid hold on Mummu, holding him by the nose-rope.
After he had vanquished and trodden down his foes,
Ea, his triumph over his enemies secured,
In his sacred chamber in profound peace he rested.
He named it 'Apsu,'[13] for shrines he assigned (it).
In that same place his cult hut he founded.
Ea and Damkina, his wife, dwelled (there) in splendour.
In the chamber of fates, the abode of destinies,
A god was engendered, most potent and wisest of gods.
In the heart of Apsu[14] was Marduk created,
In the heart of holy Apsu was Marduk created.
He who begot him was Ea, his father;
She who conceived him was Damkina, his mother.
The breast of goddessess did she suck.
The nurse that nursed him filled him with awsomeness.
Alluring was his figure, sparkling the lift in his eyes.
Lordly was his gait, commanding from of old.
When Ea saw him, the father who begot him,
He exulted and glowed, his heart filled with gladness.
He rendered him perfect and endowed him with a double godhead.
Greatly exalted was he above them, exceeding throughout.
Perfect were his members beyond comprehension,
Unsuited for understanding, difficult to perceive.
Four were his eyes, four were his ears;[15]
When he moved his lips, fire blazed forth.
Large were all hearing organs,
And the eyes, in like number, scanned all things.
He was the loftiest of the gods, surpassing was his stature;
His members were enormous, he was exceeding tall.

The Creation of the World

'My little son, my little son!'
My son, the Sun! Sun of the heavens!'
Clothed with the halo of ten gods, he was strong to the utmost,
As their awesome flashes were heaped upon him.

....

Disturbed was Tiamat, astir night and day.
The gods, in malice, contributed to the storm.
Their insides having plotted evil,
To Tiamat these brothers said:
'When they slew Apsu, thy consort,
Thou didst not aid him but remaindest still.
Although he fashioned the awesome Saw,[16]
Thy insides are diluted and so we can have no rest.
Let Apsu, thy consort, be in thy mind
And Mummu, who has been vanquished! Thou art left alone.

....

[Several of the preceding lines are fragmentary. The gods incite
Tiamat to avenge Apsu and Mummu. She is pleased and proposes to do
battle against the offending gods. But first she bears a horrible brood
of helpers—eleven monsters, 'Sharp of tooth, unsparing of fang/ With
venom for blood she has filled their bodies.']

From among the gods,[17] her first-born, who formed her Assembly,
She elevated Kingu, made him chief among them.
The leading of the ranks, command of the Assembly,
The raising weapons for the encounter, advancing to combat,
In battle the command-in-chief—
These to his hand she entrusted as she seated him in the Council:
'I have cast for thee the spell, exalting thee in the Assembly of the gods.
To counsel all the gods I have given thee full power.
Verily, thou art supreme, my only consort art thou!
Thy utterance shall prevail over all the Anunnaki!'[18]
She gave him the Tablets of Fate, fastened on his breast:
'As for thee, thy command shall be unchangeable, Thy word shall
    endure!'
As soon as Kingu was elevated, possessed of the rank of Anu,
For the gods, her sons, they[19] decreed the fate:
'Your word shall make the fire subside,
Shall humble the 'Power-Weapon,' so potent in (its) sweep!'

[Ea again learns of the plot; but this time he has no ready response for it. He goes to his grandfather Anshar and repeats the entire story of Tiamat's fury and her preparations for battle. Anshar is profoundly disturbed. Finally he dispatches Anu, saying, 'Go and stand thou up to Tiamat,/ that her mood be calmed, that her heart expand.' But when Anu sees the hosts of Tiamat, he loses his nerve and returns to Anshar.]

He came abjectly to his father, Anshar.
As though he were Tiamat thus he addressed him:
'My hand suffices not for me to subdue thee.'
Speechless was Anshar as he stared at the ground,
Frowning and shaking his head at Ea.
All the Anunnaki gathered at that place;
Their lips closed tight, they sat in silence.
'No god' (thought they) 'can go to battle and,
Facing Tiamat, escape with his life.'
Lord Anshar, father of the gods, rose up in grandeur,
And having pondered in his heart, he said to the Anunnaki:
'He whose strength is potent shall be our avenger,
He who is keen in battle, Marduk, the hero!'

[Ea warns Marduk of Anshar's plan and advises him to go before Anshar boldly. Marduk obeys and Anshar, seeing the hero, is instantly calmed.]

'Anshar, be not muted; open wide thy lips.
I will go and attain thy heart's desire. . . .
What male is it who has pressed his fight against thee?
It is but Tiamat, a woman, that opposes thee with weapons!
O my father-creator, be glad and rejoice;
The neck of Tiamat thou shalt soon tread upon!
. . . .
My son, (thou) who knowest all wisdom,
Calm Tiamat with thy holy spell.
On the storm-chariot proceed with all speed.
From her presence they shall not drive (thee)! Turn them back!'
The lord rejoiced at the word of his father.
His heart exulting, he said to his father:
'Creator of the gods, destiny of the great gods,
If I indeed, as your avenger,
Am to vanquish Tiamat and save your lives,
Set up the Assembly, proclaim supreme my destiny!
When jointly in Ubshukinna[20] you have sat down rejoicing,

The Creation of the World

Let my word, instead of you, determine the fates.
Unalterable shall be what I may bring into being;
Neither recalled nor changed shall be the command of my lips.'

[*Anshar is prepared to accept Marduk's terms. He sends his vizier Gaga to a still older generation of gods, Lahmu and Lahamu. Gaga is instructed to repeat the entire story to them, and to invite the gods to assemble at a banquet for fixing Marduk's decrees.*]

When Lahmu and Lahamu heard this, they cried out aloud,
All the Igigi[21] wailed in distress:
'How strange that they should have made this decision!
We cannot fathom the doings of Tiamat!'
They made ready to leave on their journey,
All the great gods who decree the fates.
They entered before Anshar, filling Ubshukinna.
They kissed one another in the Assembly.
They held converse as they sat down to the banquet.
They ate festive bread, partook of the wine,
They wetted their drinking tubes with sweet intoxicant.
As they drank the strong drink their bodies swelled.
They became very languid as their spirits rose.
For Marduk, their avenger, they fixed the decrees.
They erected for him a princely throne.
Facing his fathers, he sat down, presiding.
'Thou art the most honoured of the great gods,
Thy decree is unrivalled, thy command is Anu.[22]
Thou, Marduk, art the most honoured of the great gods.
....
We have granted thee Kingship over the universe entire.
When in the Assembly thou sittest, thy word shall be supreme.
Thy weapons shall not fail; they shall smash thy foes!
O lord, spare the life of him who trusts thee,
But pour out the life of the god who seized evil.'
Having placed in their midst a piece of cloth,
They addressed themselves to Marduk, their first-born:
'Lord, truly thy decree is first among gods.
Say but to wreck or create; it shall be.
Open thy mouth: the cloth will vanish!
Speak again, and the cloth shall be whole!'
At the word of his mouth the cloth vanished.
He spoke again, and the cloth was restored.

When the gods, his fathers, saw the fruit of his word,
Joyfully they did him homage: 'Marduk is king!'
They conferred on him sceptre, throne, and palū;
They gave him matchless weapons that ward off the foes:
Bel's[23] destiny thus fixed, the gods, his fathers,
Caused him to go the way of success and attainment.
He constructed a bow, marked it as his weapon,
Attached thereto the arrow, fixed its bow-cord.
He raised the mace, made his right hand grasp it;
Bow and quiver he hung at his side.
In front of him he set the lightning,
With a blazing flame he filled his body.
He then made a net to enfold Tiamat therein.
The four winds he stationed that nothing of her might escape,
The South Wind, the North Wind, the East Wind, the West Wind.
Close to his side he held the net, the gift of his father, Anu.
He brought forth Imhullu, 'the Evil Wind,' the Whirlwind, the
   Hurricane,
The Fourfold Wind, the Sevenfold Wind, the Cyclone, the Matchless
   Wind;
Then he sent forth the winds he had brought forth, the seven of them.
To stir up the inside of Tiamat they rose up behind him.
Then the lord raised up the flood-storm, his mighty weapon.
He mounted the storm-chariot irresistible and terrifying.
He harnessed (and) yoked to it a team-of-four,
The Killer, the Relentless, the Trampler, the Swift.
Sharp were their teeth, bearing poison.
They were versed in ravage, in destruction skilled.
....

With his fearsome halo his head was turbaned,
The lord went forth and followed his course,
Towards the raging Tiamat he set his face.
In his lips he held [a . . .] of red paste;[24]
A plant to put out poison was grasped in his hand.
Then they milled about him, the gods milled about him.
The lord approached to scan the inside of Tiamat,
(And) of Kingu, her consort, the scheme to perceive.
As he looks on, his[25] course becomes upset,
His will is distracted and his doings are confused.
And when the gods, his helpers, who marched at his side,
Saw the valiant hero, blurred became their vision.

Tiamat uttered a cry, without turning her neck,
Framing savage defiance in her lips:
'Too important art thou for the lord of the gods to rise up against thee!
Is it in their place that they have gathered, (or) in thy place?'
Thereupon the lord having raised the flood-storm, his mighty weapon,
To enraged Tiamat he sent word as follows:
'Mightily art thou risen, art haughtily exalted;
Thou hast charged thine own heart to stir up conflict,
So that sons reject their own fathers,
And thou who hast borne them, dost hate [. . .]!
Thou hast aggrandized Kingu to be (thy) consort;
A rule, not rightfully his, thou hast substituted for the rule of Anu.
Against Anshar, king of the gods, thou seekest evil;
Against the gods, my fathers, thou hast confirmed thy wickedness.
Though drawn up be thy forces, girded on thy weapons,
Stand thou up, that I and thou meet in single combat!'
When Tiamat heard this,
She was like one possessed; she took leave of her senses.
In fury Tiamat cried out aloud.
To the roots her legs shook both together.
She recited a charm, keeps casting her spell,
While the gods of battle sharpen their weapons.
Then joined issue Tiamat and Marduk, wisest of gods,
They swayed in single combat, locked in battle.
The lord spread out his net to enfold her,
The Evil Wind, which followed behind, he let loose in her face.
When Tiamat opened her mouth to consume him,
He drove in the Evil Wind that she close not her lips.
As the fierce winds charged her belly,
Her body was distended and her mouth was wide open.
He released the arrow, it tore her belly,
It cut through her insides, splitting the heart.
Having thus subdued her, he extinguished her life.
He cast down her carcass to stand upon it.
After he had slain Tiamat, the leader,
Her band was shattered, her troupe broken up.

[Tiamat's helpers panic and run, but Marduk captures and fetters all of them.]

And Kingu, who had been made chief among them,
He bound and accounted him to Uggae.[26]

He took from him the Tablets of Fate, not rightfully his,
Sealed (them) with a seal[27] and fastened (them) on his breast.
When he had vanquished and subdued his adversaries,
. . . .
And turned back to Tiamat whom he had bound.
The lord trod on the legs of Tiamat,
With his unsparing mace he crushed her skull.
When the arteries of her blood he had severed,
The North Wind bore (it) to places undisclosed.
On seeing this, his fathers were joyful and jubilant,
They brought gifts of homage, they to him.
Then the lord paused to view her dead body,
That he might divide the monster and do artful works.
He split her like a shellfish into two parts:
Half of her he set up and ceiled as sky,
Pulled down the bar and posted guards.
He bade them to allow not her waters to escape.
He crossed the heavens and surveyed (its) regions.
He squared Apsu's quarter, the abode of Nudimmud,
As the lord measured the dimensions of Apsu.
The Great Abode, its likeness, he fixed as Esharra,
The Great Abode, Esharra, which he made as the firmament.
Anu, Enlil,[28] and Ea he made occupy their places.

[Much of Tablet V is broken. Marduk puts the heavens in order,
establishing the zodiac and telling the moon how to shine.]

When Marduk hears the words of the gods,
His heart prompts (him) to fashion artful works.
Opening his mouth, he addresses Ea
To impart the plan he addresses Ea
To impart the plan he had conceived in his heart:
'Blood I will mass and cause bones to be.
I will establish a savage, "man" shall be his name.
Verily, savage-man I will create.
He shall be charged with the service of the gods
    That they might be at ease!
The ways of the gods I will artfully alter.
Though alike revered, into two (groups) they shall be divided.'
Ea answered him, speaking a word to him,
To relate to him a scheme for the relief of the gods:
'Let but one of their brothers be handed over;

He alone shall perish that mankind may be fashioned.[29]
Let the great gods be here in Assembly,
Let the guilty be handed over that they may endure.'
Marduk summoned the great gods to Assembly;
Presiding graciously, he issued instructions.
To his utterance the gods pay heed.
The king addresses a word to the Anunnaki:
'If your former statement was true,
Do (now) the truth on oath by me declare!
Who was it that contrived the uprising,
And made Tiamat rebel, and joined battle?
Let him be handed over who contrived the uprising.
His guilt I will make him bear that you may dwell in peace!'
The Igigi, the great gods, replied to him,
To Lugaldimmerankia,[30] counsellor of the gods, their lord:
'It was Kingu who contrived the uprising,
And made Tiamat rebel, and joined battle.'
They bound him, holding him before Ea.
They imposed on him his guilt and severed his blood (vessels).
Out of his blood they fashioned mankind.
He[31] imposed the service and let free the gods.

[After the creation of mankind, Marduk divides the Anunnaki and assigns them to their proper stations, three hundred in heaven, three hundred on the earth.]

After he had ordered all the instructions,
To the Anunnaki of heaven and earth had allotted their portions,
The Anunnaki opened their mouths
And said to Marduk, their lord:
'Now, O lord, thou who hast caused our deliverance,
What shall be our homage to thee?
Let us build a shrine to thee whose name shall be called
'Lo, a chamber for our nightly rest'; let us repose in it!
Let us build a shrine, a recess for his abode!
On the day that we arrive[32] we shall repose in it.'
When Marduk heard this,
Brightly glowed his features, like the day:
'Like that of lofty Babylon, whose building you have requested,
Let its brickwork be fashioned. You shall name it "The Sanctuary."'
The Anunnaki applied the implement;
For one whole year they moulded bricks.

When the second year arrived,
They raised high the head of Esagila[33] equaling Apsu.[34]
Having built a stage-tower as high as Apsu,
They set up in it an abode for Marduk, Enlil, (and) Ea.
In their presence he adorned (it) in grandeur.
To the base of Esharra its horns look down.
After they had achieved the building of Esagila,
The Anunnaki themselves erected their shrines.
[. . .] all of them gathered,
[. . .] they had built as his dwelling.
The gods, his fathers, at his banquet he seated:
'This is Babylon, the place that is your home!
Make merry in its precincts, occupy its broad places.'
The great gods took their seats,
They set up festive drink, sat down to a banquet.
After they had made merry within it,
In Esagila, the splendid, had performed their rites,
The norms had been fixed (and) all their portents,
All the gods apportioned the stations of heaven and earth.
The fifty great gods took their seats.
The seven gods of destiny set up the three hundred in heaven.
Enlil raised the bow, his weapon, and laid (it) before them.
The gods, his fathers, saw the net he had made.
When they beheld the bow, how skilful its shape,
His fathers praised the work he had wrought.
Raising (it), Anu spoke up in the Assembly of the gods,
As he kissed the bow:

[The remainder of the epic is a long hymn of praise to Marduk
It culminates in a recitation of his fifty names, attributes reflecting
his power and mighty deeds.]

Notes

1 God of subterranean waters; the primeval sweet-water ocean.
2 An epithet of Tiamat; perhaps meaning 'mother.'
3 A water-deity; the primeval salt-water ocean.
4 I.e., the fresh waters of Apsu and the marine waters of Tiamat.
5 The waters of Apsu and Tiamat.
6 The first generation of gods.
7 Gods.
8 The sky-god.
9 One of the names of Ea, the earth and water-god.
10 Ea, the earth- and water-god.

11 That of Apsu and his vizier Mummu.
12 I.e., caused it to be in the waters of Apsu.
13 'The Deep.'
14 See note 13.
15 Cf. Ezekiel 1:6.
16 The weapon of the sun-god.
17 The gods who joined Tiamat in her war.
18 Here a collective name of the nether world gods.
19 Tiamat and Kingu.
20 The assembly hall of the gods.
21 A collective name of the heaven gods.
22 I.e., it has the authority of the sky-god Anu.
23 I.e., Marduk's destiny.
24 Red being the magic colour for warding off evil influence.
25 I.e., Kingu's course.
26 God of death.
27 By this action Marduk legalized his ownership of the Tablets of Fate.
28 The god of the wind, i.e., of the earth.
29 Out of his blood.
30 Meaning 'The king of the gods of heaven and earth.'
31 Ea.
32 For the New Year's Festival.
33 Name of the temple of Marduk in Babylon.
34 Meaning apparently that the height of Esagila corresponded to the depth of Apsu's waters.

Translation by E. A. Speiser, in *Ancient Near Eastern Texts* (Princeton, 1950), pp. 60-72, as reprinted in Isaac Mendelsohn (ed.), *Religions of the Ancient Near East*, Library of Religion, paperbook series (New York, 1955), pp. 19-46; notes by Mendelsohn

56. 'WHO CAN SAY WHENCE IT ALL CAME, AND HOW CREATION HAPPENED?'

('Rig Veda,' X, 129)

This creation hymn is at once a supreme expression of the poetry and philosophy of the Rig Veda and an eloquent murmur of doubt, which carries over into the Upanishads its sense of the depth, the mystery, and above all the unity of creation. In 'darkness concealed in darkness' (tamas in tamas), in those 'unillumined waters' which harbour no 'being' (sat) or 'non-being' (asat), there is generated, by cosmic heat (tapas) the primordial unitary force, That One (tad ekam). 'Desire' (kāma) now arose as the primal seed of 'mind' (manas), the firstborn of tad ekam, and the rishis, who 'see' that original moment when the gods were not, claim now to know the bond of sat in asat. 'But who knows truly,' concludes the poet, still in reverence before the mystery: perhaps That One 'whose eye controls this world'; but then perhaps he truly does not know.

Not only Upanshadic speculation, but also the evolutionary philosophy of the Sāmkhya system was deeply impressed by this hymn. It is important to consider this speculation of cosmic origins alongside other Rig Vedic creation accounts, such as X, 90 (see p. 226) and X, 112 (see p. 34) or I, 32.

1. Then[1] even nothingness was not, nor existence.[2]
    There was no air then, nor the heavens beyond it.
   What covered it? Where was it? In whose keeping?
   Was there then cosmic water, in depths unfathomed?

2. Then there were neither death nor immortality,
    nor was there then the torch of night and day.
   The One[3] breathed windlessly and self-sustaining.[4]
   There was that One then, and there was no other.

3. At first there was only darkness wrapped in darkness.
    All this was only unillumined water.[5]
   That One which came to be, enclosed in nothing,
   arose at last, born of the power of heat.[6]

4. In the beginning desire descended on it—
    that was the primal seed, born of the mind.
   The sages who have searched their hearts with wisdom
    know that which is, is kin[7] to that which is not.

5. And they have stretched their cord across the void,
    and know what was above, and what below.
   Seminal powers made fertile mighty forces.
    Below was strength, and over it was impulse.[8]

6. But, after all, who knows, and who can say
    whence it all came, and how creation happened?
   The gods themselves are later than creation,
    so who knows truly whence it has arisen?

7. Whence all creation had its origin,
    he, whether he fashioned it or whether he did not,
   he, who surveys it all from highest heaven,
    he knows—or maybe even he does not know.

The notes to this text are on p. 111.

Notes

1 In the beginning.
2 *Asat* nor *sat.*
3 *Tad ekam,* 'That One,' who 'breathes without air.'
4 *Svadhā,* energy, intrinsic power which makes self-generation possible.
5 Fluid (*salila*) and indistinguishable (*apraketa*)
6 *Tapas,* an archaic word which also defines those human austerities or techniques which, like this cosmic heat, generate power.
7 From 'bond' (*bandhu*).
8 This stanza is obscure. A. A. Macdonell suggests that the 'cord' (*rashmi*) implies the bond of the preceding stanza; thought measures out the distance between the non-existent and the existent and separates the male and female cosmogonic principles: impulse (*prayati*) above and energy (*svadhā*) below. (A *Vedic Reader for Students,* London: Oxford University, 1917, p. 210.)

Translation by A. L. Basham, *The Wonder That Was India* (London, 1954), pp. 247-8.

See also nos. 101, 292-4, 300

57. INDIAN COSMOGONY

('The Laws of Manu,' I, 5-16)

The Mānavadharmashāstra or Manusmriti, *known in the West as* The Laws of Manu *is the most important work regarding* dharma, *i.e., the principles, laws, and rules governing both the cosmos and human society. The dates assigned by scholars for the composition of the text vary from the second century* B.C. *to the second century* A.D. *The cosmogonic fragment reprinted below is known to be a late interpolation.*

5. This (universe) existed in the shape of Darkness,[1] unperceived, destitute of distinctive marks, unattainable by reasoning, unknowable, wholly immersed, as it were, in deep sleep.

6. Then the divine Self-existent[2] indiscernible, (but) making (all) this, the great elements and the rest, discernible, appeared with irresistible (creative) power, dispelling the darkness.

7. He who can be perceived by the internal organ[3] (alone), who is subtile, indiscernible, and eternal, who contains all created beings and is inconceivable, shone forth of his own (will).[4]

The notes on this text are on pp. 112-13.

8. He, desiring to produce beings of many kinds from his own body, first with a thought created[5] the waters, and placed [his] seed in them.

9. That (seed) became a golden egg,[6] in brilliancy equal to the sun; in that (egg) he himself was born as Brahmán, the progenitor of the whole world.

10. The waters were called *nārās*, (for) the waters are, indeed, the offspring of Nara; as they were his[7] first residence *(ayana)*, he thence is named Nārāyana.[8]

11. From that (first) cause, which is indiscernible, eternal, and both real and unreal,[9] was produced that male (Purusha),[10] who is famed in this world (under the appellation of) Brahmán.

12. The divine one resided in that egg during a whole year,[11] then he himself by his thought[12] (alone) divided it into two halves;

13. And out of those two halves he formed heaven and earth, between them the middle sphere, the eight points of the horizon, and the eternal abode of the waters.

14. From himself (ātmanas) he also drew forth the mind,[31] which is both real and unreal, likewise from the mind egoism,[14] which possesses the function of self-consciousness (and is) lordly:

15. Moreover, the great one,[15] the soul,[16] and all products affected by the three qualities,[17] and, in their order, the five organs which perceive the objects of sensation.[18]

16. But, joining minute particles even of those six,[19] which possess measureless power, with particles of himself he created all beings.

Notes

1 *Tamas*, a darkness both physical and mental. The Sāmkhya system finds considerable significance in this stanza: *tamas*, one of the three twisted strands *(gunas)* of cosmic substance, represents inertia.

2 *Svayambhū*, an epithet of Brahmán (masculine), who is the impersonal Absolute (Bráhman neuter) personified as manifest god.

3 *Atīndriya*, literally that spirit or mind 'beyond the senses.'

4 I.e., became self-manifest.

5 Or, released.

6 As 'the shape of Darkness' (vs. 1) and the environmental 'waters' recall the Rig Vedic creation hymn X, 120, so does this golden 'egg' *(anda)* and its seed *(bīja)* recall the *hiranyagarbha* of *Rig Veda*, X, 121.

7 Brahmán's.

8 An example of popular etymology, *nara* being primal man or eternal spirit.

9 Literally, having existence *(sat)* and non-existence *(asat)* as its nature.

10 See the Purushasūkta, *Rig Veda*, X, 90.

11 Early commentators disagreed, some saying that the 'year' was a 'year of Brahmán,' others maintaining that a human year is meant, as in the similar version of this selection, *Shatapatha-brāhmana*, XI, 1, 6, 1 *ff*.

12 Meditation (*dhyāna*).
13 *Manas*, mind or intelligence, as distinct from spirit (*ātman*).
14 *Ahamkāra*, literally 'the making of "I" (*aham*)'; the principle of individuation.
15 *Mahat*, the 'great'; in Sāmkhya also called *buddhi*, consciousness.
16 *Ātman*.
17 *Gunas*.
18 *Tanmātras*, subtle elements.
19 Again, the Indian commentators are at variance in their interpretations of these last three lines. Probably 'those six' are classes of *tattvas* (elements) mentioned in the preceding two verses, in the order: *manas, ahamkāra, mahat, ātman, tattvas* affected by the *gunas, tanmatras*. It is interesting to compare the Sāmkya evolutes of *prakriti*. Here twenty-five *tattvas*, a rearrangement of 'those six' above, evolve with greater systematization: (1) *purusha*; and from *prakriti*, (2) *mahat*, (3) *ahamkāra*, (4) *manas*, (5) five sense organs and five motor organs, (6) five subtle elements (*tanmātras*) and five gross elements (*mahābhūtas*).

Translation by G. Bühler, in *Sacred Books of the East*, XXV (Oxford, 1886), pp. 2-8

58. THE CREATION OF THE WORLD ACCORDING TO THE UPANISHADS

1. There was nothing whatsoever here in the beginning. By death indeed was this covered, or by hunger, for hunger is death. He created the mind, thinking 'let me have a self' (mind). Then he moved about, worshipping. From him, thus worshipping, water was produced. . . .

2. . . . That which was the froth of the water became solidified; that became the earth. On it he [i.e., death] rested. From him thus rested and heated (from the practice of austerity) his essence of brightness came forth (as) fire.

3. He divided himself threefold (fire is one-third), the sun one-third and the air one-third. He also is life [lit., breath] divided threefold, . . . (*Brihad-āranyaka Upanishad*, I, 2, 1-3.)

1. The Sun is *Brahman*—this is the teaching. An explanation thereof (is this). In the beginning this (world) was non-existent. It became existent. It grew. It turned into an egg. It lay for the period of a year. It burst open. Then came out of the eggshell, two parts, one of silver, the other of gold.

That which was of silver is this earth; that which was of gold is the sky. What was the outer membrane is the mountains; that which was the inner membrane is the mist with the clouds. What were the

veins were the rivers. What was the fluid within is the ocean.
(*Chāndogya Upanishad*, III, 19, 1-2.)

[*But further on, the sage Uddalaka presents another view: in the beginning was Being alone.*]

1. In the beginning, my dear, this was Being alone, one only without a second. Some people say 'in the beginning this was non-being alone, one only; without a second. From that non-being, being was produced.'

2. But how, indeed, my dear, could it be thus? said he [i.e., the sage Uddalaka], how could being be produced from non-being? On the contrary, my dear, in the beginning this was being alone, one only, without a second.

3. It thought, May I be many, may I grow forth. It sent forth fire. That fire thought, May I be many, may I grow forth. It sent forth water. . . .

4. That water thought, May I be many, may I grow forth. It sent forth food. . . . (*Chāndogya Upanishad*, VI, 2, 1-4.)

S. Radhakrishnan (editor and translator), *The Principal Upanishads* (New York: Harper & Row, 1953), pp. 151-2, 399, 447-9

59. HESIOD'S THEOGONY AND COSMOGONY

('Theogony,' 116-210)

The main themes of Hesiod's 'Theogony' are (1) the coming into being of Chaos (the Void), Earth, Eros, Sky and the first generation of gods (lines 116-53); (2) the castration of Sky by his son Cronus, instigated by his mother Earth (lines 154-210); (3) Zeus' escape from being swallowed by his father Cronus (lines 453-500); (4) the victorious battle of Zeus and the Olympian gods against the Titans (lines 617-735). Only the first two episodes are printed below. It is impossible to determine Hesiod's date, but he is later than Homer, probably eighth century B.C. The similarities to and differences from the Ancient Near East cosmogonies are discussed by Norman O. Brown in the introduction to his translation, 'Hesiod's Theogony,' pp. 36 ff.

First of all, the Void (*Chaos*) came into being, next broad-bosomed Earth, the solid and eternal home of all, and Eros [Desire], the most beautiful of the immortal gods, who in every man and every god softens the sinews and overpowers the prudent purpose of the mind. Out of Void came Darkness and black Night, and out of Night came Light and Day, her children conceived after union in love with Darkness. Earth first produced starry Sky, equal in size with herself, to cover her on all sides. Next she produced the tall mountains, the pleasant haunts of the gods, and also gave birth to the barren waters, sea with its raging surges—all this without the passion of love. Thereafter she lay with Sky and gave birth to Ocean with its deep current. Coeus and Crius and Hyperion and Iapetus; Thea and Rhea and Themia [Law] and Mnemosyne [Memory]; also golden-crowned Phoebe and lovely Tethys. After these came cunning Cronus, the youngest and boldest of her children; and he grew to hate the father who had begotten him.

Earth also gave birth to the violent Cyclopes—Thunderer, Lightner, and bold Flash—who made and gave to Zeus the thunder and the lightning bolt. They were like the gods in all respects except that a single eye stood in the middle of their foreheads, and their strength and power and skill were in their hands.

There were also born to Earth and Sky three more children, big, strong, and horrible, Cottus and Briareus and Gyes. This unruly brood had a hundred monstrous hands sprouting from their shoulders, and fifty heads on top of their shoulders growing from their sturdy bodies. They had monstrous strength to match their huge size.

Of all the children born of Earth and Sky these were the boldest, and their father hated them from the beginning. As each of them was about to be born, Sky would not let them reach the light of day; instead he hid them all away in the bowels of Mother Earth. Sky took pleasure in doing this evil thing. In spite of her enormous size, Earth felt the strain within her and groaned. Finally she thought of an evil and cunning stratagem. She instantly produced a new metal, grey steel, and made a huge sickle. Then she laid the matter before her children; the anguish in her heart made her speak boldly; 'My children, you have a savage father; if you will listen to me, we may be able to take vengeance for this evil outrage: he was the one who started using violence.'

This was what she said: but all the children were gripped by fear, and not one of them spoke a word. Then great Cronus, the cunning trickster, took courage and answered his good mother with these words: 'Mother, I am willing to undertake and carry through your plan. I have no respect for our infamous father, since he was the one who started using violence.'

This was what he said, and enormous Earth was very pleased. She hid him in ambush and put in his hands the sickle with jagged teeth, and instructed him fully in her plot. Huge Sky came drawing night behind him and desiring to make love; he lay on top of Earth stretched all over her. Then from his ambush his son reached out with his left hand and with his right took the huge sickle with its long jagged teeth and quickly sheared the organs from his own father and threw them away. The drops of blood that spurted from them were all taken in by Mother Earth, and in the course of the revolving years she gave birth to the powerful Erinyes [Spirits of Vengeance] and the huge Giants with shining armour and long spears. As for the organs themselves, for a long time they drifted round the sea just as they were when Cronus cut them off with the steel edge and threw them from the land into the waves of the ocean; then white foam issued from the divine flesh, and in the foam a girl began to grow. First she came near to holy Cythera, then reached Cyprus, the land surrounded by sea. There she stepped out, a goddess, tender and beautiful, and round her slender feet the green grass shot up. She is called Aphrodite by gods and men because she grew in the froth, and also Cytherea, because she came near to Cythera, and the Cyprian, because she was born in watery Cyprus. Eros [Desire] and beautiful Passion were her attendants both at her birth and at her first going to join the family of the gods. The rights and privileges assigned to her from the beginning and recognized by men and gods are these; to preside over the whispers and smiles and tricks which girls employ, and the sweet delight and tenderness of love.

Great Father Sky called his children the Titans, because of his feud with them: he said that they blindly had tightened the noose and had done a savage thing for which they would have to pay in time to come.

Translation by Norman O. Brown, in his *Hesiod's Theogony* (New York: Liberal Arts Press, 1953), pp. 56-9

The Creation of the World

60. ZOROASTRIAN DUALIST COSMOGONY: OHRMAZD AND AHRIMAN

('Greater Bundahishn,' I, 18-26)

The story of the two primal Spirits and the creation of the world is recounted in greatest detail in the first chapter of a ninth-century Pahlavi book known as the 'Bundahishn' or '(Book of) the Primal Creation.' The limitation of Time is Ohrmazd's first creative act, for he saw that if Ahriman were to be destroyed, he would have to be lured out of eternity, actualized in finite time, and forced into the open.

18. Ohrmazd, before the act of creation, was not Lord; after the act of creation he became Lord, eager for increase, wise, free from adversity, manifest, ever ordering aright, bounteous, all-perceiving. 19. [First he created the essence of the gods, fair (orderly) movement, that genius by which he made his own body better] for he had conceived of the act of creation; from this act of creation was his lordship.

20. And by his clear vision Ohrmazd saw that the Destructive Spirit would never cease from aggression and that his aggression could only be made fruitless by the act of creation, and that creation could not move on except through Time and that when Time was fashioned, the creation of Ahriman too would begin to move. 21. And that he might reduce the Aggressor to a state of powerlessness, having no alternative he fashioned forth Time. And the reason was this, that the Destructive Spirit could not be made powerless unless he were brought to battle. . . .

22. Then from Infinite Time he fashioned and made Time of the long Dominion: some call it finite Time. From Time of the long Dominion he brought forth permanence that the works of Ohrmazd might not pass away. From permanence discomfort was made manifest that comfort might not touch the demons. From discomfort the course of fate, the idea of changelessness, was made manifest, that those things which Ohrmazd created at the original creation might not change. From the idea of changelessness a perfect will (to create) material creation was made manifest, the concord of the righteous creation.

23. In his unrighteous creation Ahriman was without knowledge, without method. And the reason and interpretation thereof is this,

117

that when Ahriman joined battle with Ohrmazd the majestic wisdom, renown, perfection, and permanence of Ohrmazd and the powerlessness, self-will, imperfection and slowness in knowledge of the Destructive Spirit were made manifest when creation was created.

24. For Time of the long Dominion was the first creature that he fashioned forth; for it was infinite before the contamination of the totality of Ohrmazd. From the infinite it was fashioned finite; for from the original creation when creation was created until the consummation when the Destructive Spirit is made powerless there is a term of twelve thousand years which is finite. Then it mingles with and returns to the Infinite so that the creation of Ohrmazd shall for ever be with Ohrmazd in purity. 25. As it is said in the Religion, 'Time is mightier than both creations—the creation of Ohrmazd and that of the Destructive Spirit. Time understands all action and order (the law). Time understands more than those who understand. Time is better informed than the well-informed; for through Time must the decision be made. By Time are houses overturned—doom is through Time—and things graven shattered. From it no single mortal man escapes, not though he fly above, not though he dig a pit below and settle therein, not though he hide beneath a well of cold waters.'

26. From his own essence which is material light Ohrmazd fashioned forth the form of his creatures—a form of fire—bright, white, round and manifest afar. From the material (form) of that Spirit which dispels aggression in the two worlds—be it Power or be it Time—he fashioned forth the form of Vāy, the Good, for Vāy was needed: some call it Vāy of the long Dominion. With the aid of Vāy of the long Dominion he fashioned forth creation; for when he created creation, Vāy was the instrument he needed for the deed.

Translation and introductory comment by R. C. Zaehner, in his *Zurvan: A Zoroastrian Dilemma* (Oxford, 1955), pp. 314-16

See also nos. 37-9, 290, 303

B. A MYTH OF BEGINNING AND END

61. THE SCANDINAVIAN STORY OF CREATION AND A PROPHECY OF THE END OF THE WORLD

('Völuspá')

In the Elder, or Poetic, Edda the historian of religions finds no greater fascination than that of the Völuspá—the 'Sibyl's Prophecy.' In a few succinct verses this highly original poem of the gods sets forth a world view that sweeps powerfully from a vision of primordial chaos and creation through the turbulent lives of the gods to their ultimate doom in the ragnarök.

The poem is profoundly Scandinavian. A dark foreboding pursues each line as the poet unfolds the story of the world, told by a völva (a sibyl or seeress) whom the sovereign god Odin, maker of magic and lord of the dead, has called forth from the grave. The völva, abrupt and dramatic in her sombre vision, 'sees' first the abyss, Ginnungagap, in that age when sea and 'earth had not been, nor heaven above.' Chaos gives way to cosmos through the efforts of the gods, and soon giants, dwarfs and humans dwell on earth. The golden age of the young gods is terminated, however, when the first war—between the Æsir and the Vanir—takes its fateful course.

Like the Norns (the three goddesses who span past, present, and future), the sibyl 'sees' as well that which is to come, and to Odin she now describes the ragnorök, the 'fate of the gods.' The tribal battle has exploded into a great cosmic struggle between good and evil, light and darkness, harmony and chaos, life and death. Earth cannot bear this war and the völva's apocalyptic visions now portend its destruction by fire and flood. The world-tree Yggdrasill is shaken to the roots, the innocent god Baldr and then Odin himself are slain, 'the sun turns black, earth sinks in the sea,' and 'fire leaps high about heaven itself.'

Before the völva sinks again into earth, however, she concludes her vision with a scene of rebirth: 'Now do I see the earth anew/Rise all green from the waves again.' Baldr returns, the earth is fruitful, and a new golden hall of the gods appears.

Myths of Creation

The possibility of some influence from Christian symbolism, particularly in the final verses, has suggested a date of composition in the late tenth or early eleventh century, when Christianity began to penetrate the final northern frontiers. However, the Völuspá—terse, mystical, often obscure—has a unique perspective, and it survives for us as a last magnificent expression from an expiring heroic age.

1. Hearing I ask   from the holy races,
   From Heimdall's sons,   both high and low;
   Thou wilt, Valfather,   that well I relate
   Old tales I remember   of men long ago.

2. I remember yet   the giants of yore,
   Who gave me bread   in the days gone by;
   Nine worlds I knew,   the nine in the tree
   With mighty roots   beneath the mould.

3. Of old was the age   when Ymir lived;
   Sea nor cool waves   nor sand there were;
   Earth had not been,   nor heaven above,
   But a yawning gap,   and grass nowhere.

4. Then Bur's sons lifted   the level land,
   Midgard the mighty   there they made;
   The sun from the south   warmed the stones of earth,
   And green was the ground   with growing leeks.

5. The sun, the sister   of the moon, from the south
   Her right hand cast   over heaven's rim;
   No knowledge she had   where her home should be,
   The moon knew not   what might was his,
   The stars knew not   where their stations were.

6. Then sought the gods   their assembly-seats
   The holy ones,   and council held;
   Names then gave they   to noon and twilight,
   Morning they named   and the waning moon,
   Night and evening,   the years to number.

7. At Idavöll met   the mighty gods,
   Shrines and temples   they timbered high;
   Forges they set,   and they smithied ore,
   Tongs they wrought,   and tools they fashioned.

The notes on this text are on pp. 126-9.

8. In their dwellings at peace   they played at tables,
Of gold no lack   did the gods then know,
Till thither came up   giant-maids three,
Huge of might,   out of Jötunheim.

9. Then sought the gods   their assembly-seats
The holy ones,   and council held,
To find who should raise   the race of dwarfs
Out of Brimir's blood   and the legs of Blain. . . .

17. Then from the throng   did three come forth
From the home of the gods,   the mighty and gracious;
Two without fate   on the land they found,
Ask and Embla,   empty of might.

18. Soul they had not,   sense they had not,
Heat nor motion,   nor goodly hue;
Soul gave Odin,   sense gave Hönir,
Heat gave Lodur   and goodly hue.

19. An ash I know,   Yggdrasill its name,
With water white   is the great tree wet;
Thence come the dews   that fall in the dales,
Green by Urd's well   does it ever grow.

20. Thence come the maidens   mighty in wisdom,
Three from the dwelling   down 'neath the tree;
Urd is one named,   Verdandi the next,—
On the wood they scored,—   And Skuld the third.
Laws they made there,   and life allotted
To the sons of men,   and set their fates.

21. The war I remember,   the first in the world,
When the gods with spears   had smitten Gullveig.
And in the hall   of Har had burned her,—
Three times burned,   and three times born,
Oft and again,   yet ever she lives.

22. Heid they named her   who sought their home
The wide-seeing witch   in magic wise;
Minds she bewitched   that were moved by her magic,
To evil women   a joy she was.

23. On the host his spear   did Odin hurl
Then in the world   did war first come;

The wall that girdled   the gods was broken,
And the field by the warlike   Vanir was trodden.

24. Then sought the gods   their assembly-seats
     The holy ones,   and council held,
     Whether the gods   should tribute give,
     Or to all alike   should worship belong.

25. Then sought the gods   their assembly-seats,
     The holy ones,   and council held,
     To find who with venom   the air had filled,
     Or had given Od's bride   to the giants' brood.

26. In swelling rage   then rose up Thor,—
     Seldom he sits   when he such things hears,—
     And the oaths were broken,   the words and bonds,
     The mighty pledges   between them made.

27. I know of the horn   of Heimdall, hidden
     Under the high-reaching   holy tree;
     On it there pours   from Valfather's pledge
     A mighty stream: would you know yet more?

28. Alone I sat   when the Old One sought me,
     The terror of gods,   and gazed in mine eyes;
     'What hast thou to ask?   why comest thou hither?
     Odin, I know   where thine eye is hidden.'

29. I know where Odin's   eye is hidden,
     Deep in the wide-famed   well of Mimir;
     Mead from the pledge   of Odin each morn
     Does Mimir drink: would you know yet more?

30. Necklaces had I   and rings from Heerfather,
     Wise was my speech   and my magic wisdom;
     ....
     Widely I saw   over all the worlds.

31. On all sides saw I   Valkyries assemble
     Ready to ride   to the ranks of the gods;
     Skuld bore the shield,   and Skögul rode next,
     Gud, Hild, Gondul   and Geirskögul.
     Of Herjan's maidens   the list have ye heard,
     Valkyries ready   to ride o'er the earth.

32. I saw for Baldr, the bleeding god,
  The sons of Odin, his destiny set:
  Famous and fair in the lofty fields,
  Full grown in strength the mistletoe stood.

33. From the branch which
   seemed so slender and fair
  Came a harmful shaft that Höd should hurl;
  But the brother of Baldr was born ere long.
  And one night old fought Odin's son.

34. His hands he washed not, his hair he combed not,
  Till he bore to the bale-blaze Baldr's foe
  But in Fensalir did Frigg weep sore
  For Valhall's need: would you know yet more?

35. One did I see in the wet woods bound
  A lover of ill, and to Loki like;
  By his side does Sigyn sit, nor is glad
  To see her mate: would you know yet more?

36. From the east there pours through poisoned vales
  With swords and daggers the river Slid.
  ....
  ....

37. Northward a hall in Nidavellir
  Of gold there rose for Sindri's race;
  And in Okolnir another stood.
  Where the giant Brimir his beer-hall had.

38. A hall I saw, far from the sun.
  On Naströnd it stands and the doors face north;
  Venom drops through the smoke-vent down,
  For around the walls do serpents wind.

39. I saw there wading through rivers wild
  Treacherous men and murderers too,
  And workers of ill with the wives of men;
  There Nidhögg sucked the blood of the slain,
  And the wolf tore men; would you know yet more?

40. The giantess old in Ironwood sat,
  In the east, and bore the brood of Fenrir;
  Among these one in monster's guise
  Was soon to steal the sun from the sky.

41. There feeds he full   on the flesh of the dead,
    And the home of the gods   he reddens with gore;
    Dark grows the sun,   and in summer soon
    Come mighty storms: would you know yet more?

42. On a hill there sat,   and smote on his harp
    Eggther the joyous   the giants' warder;
    Above him the cock   in the bird-wood crowed,
    Fair and red   did Fjalar stand.

43. Then to the gods   crowed Gollinkambi,
    He wakes the heroes   in Odin's hall;
    And beneath the earth   does another crow,
    The rust-red bird   at the bars of Hel.

44. Now Garm howls loud   before Gnipahellir,
    The fetters will burst,   and the wolf run free;
    Much do I know,   and more can see
    Of the fate of the gods,   the mighty in fight.

45. Brothers shall fight   and fell each other,
    And sisters' sons   shall kinship stain;
    Hard is it on earth,   with mighty whoredom;
    Axe-time, sword-time,   shields are sundered,
    Wind-time, wolf-time   ere the world falls;
    Nor ever shall men   each other spare.

46. Fast move the sons   of Mim, and fate
    Is heard in the note   of the Gjallarhorn;
    Loud blows Heimdall,   the horn is aloft,
    In fear quake all   who on Hel-roads are.

47. Yggdrasill shakes,   and shiver on high
    The ancient limbs   and the giant is loose;
    To the head of Mim   does Odin give heed,
    But the kinsman of Surt   shall slay him soon.

48. How fare the gods?   how fare the elves?
    All Jötunheim groans,   the gods are at council;
    Loud roar the dwarfs   by the doors of stone,
    The masters of the rocks: would you know yet more?

49. Now Garm howls loud   before Gnipahellir,
    The fetters will burst,   and the wolf run free;
    Much do I know,   and more can see
    Of the fate of the gods,   the mighty in fight.

50. From the east comes Hrym   with shield held high;
In giant-wrath   does the serpent writhe;
O'er the waves he twists,   and the tawny eagle
Gnaws corpses screaming;   Naglfar is loose.

51. O'er the sea from the north   there sails a ship
With the people of Hel,   at the helm stands Loki;
After the wolf   do wild men follow,
And with them the brother   of Byleist goes.

52. Surt fares from the south   with the scourge of branches,
The sun of the battle-gods   shone from his sword;
The crags are sundered   the giant-women sink,
The dead throng Hel-way,   and heaven is cloven.

53. Now comes to Hlin   yet another hurt,
When Odin fares   to fight with the wolf,
And Beli's fair slayer   seeks out Surt,
For there must fall   the joy of Frigg.

54. Then comes Sigfather's   mighty son,
Vidar, to fight   with the foaming wolf;
In the giant's son   does he thrust his sword
Full to the heart: his father is avenged.

55. Hither there comes   the son of Heöthyn,
The bright snake gapes   to heaven above;
....
Against the serpent   goes Odin's son.

56. In anger smites   the warder of the earth—
Forth from their homes   must all men flee,—
Nine paces fares   the son of Fjörgyn.
And, slain by the serpent,   fearless he sinks.

57. The sun turns black,   earth sinks in the sea,
The hot stars down   from heaven are whirled;
Fierce grows the steam   and the life-feeding flame,
Till fire leaps high   about heaven itself.

58. Now Garm howls loud   before Gnipahellir,
The fetters will burst,   and the wolf run free;
Much do I know,   and more can see
Of the fate of the gods,   the mighty in fight.

59. Now do I see   *the earth anew*
    Rise all green   *from the waves again;*
    The cataracts fall,   *and the eagle flies,*
    And fish he catches   *beneath the cliffs.*

60. The gods in Idavoll   *meet together,*
    Of the terrible girdler   *of earth they talk.*
    And the mighty past   *they call to mind,*
    And the ancient runes   *of the Ruler of Gods.*

61. In wondrous beauty   *once again*
    Shall the golden tables   *stand mid the grass,*
    Which the gods had owned   *in the days of old,*
    ....

62. Then fields unsowed   *bear ripened fruit,*
    All ills grow better,   *and Baldr comes back;*
    Baldr and Höd dwell   *in Hropt's battle-hall,*
    And the mighty gods: *would you know yet more?*

63. Then Hönir wins   *the prophetic wand,*
    ....
    And the sons of the brothers   *of Tveggi abide*
    In Vindheim now: *would you know yet more?*

64. More fair than the sun,   *a hall I see,*
    Roofed with gold,   *on Gimle it stands;*
    There shall the righteous   *rulers dwell,*
    And happiness ever   *there shall they have.*

65. There comes on high.   *all power to hold,*
    A mighty lord,   *all lands he rules.*
    ....
    ....

66. From below the dragon   *dark comes forth,*
    Nidhögg flying   *from Nidafjöll;*
    The bodies of men   *on his wings he bears*
    The serpent bright: *but now I must sink.*

Notes (numbers refer to stanzas)

1 *Heimdall:* the watchman of the gods, son of nine giantesses, and ancestor of mankind. *Valfather:* Odin, 'Father of the Slain,' the sovereign god who receives the fallen warriors in his great palace, Valhall (*Valhöll,* 'Hall of the Slain').

A Myth of Beginning and End

2 The *völva* recalls here the cosmic tree Yggdrasill (the 'steed of Ygg [Odin]') which comprises the 'nine worlds.' We are reminded (as in stanzas 28-9) of how Odin gains occult wisdom (*seid*): he wins the secrets of the runes, nine magic songs, and the immortal drink (*mjöd*, 'mead') of poetry by hanging for nine nights on the tree and sacrificing himself to himself. The 'Rúnatals Tháttr' of the *Hávamál* (stanza 138) describes the scene:

> I know that I hung
> on the windswept tree
> for nine full nights,
> wounded with a spear
> and given to Odinn
> myself to myself; . . .

(Trans. E. O. G. Turville-Petre, *Myth and Religion of the North* [London: Weidenfeld & Nicolson, 1964], p. 42.)

3 *Ymir:* the giant from whose body the gods create a world. His function in this account of creation is unclear.

4 *Bur:* father of Odin and of Odin's brothers, Vili and Ve. (Bur's father, Buri, was created by the primeval cow, Audumla, according to Snorri's *Edda*.) *Midgard:* the world of men, the 'middle region' lifted from the waters by the gods.

7 *Idavöll:* the stronghold of the gods; see stanza 60, after *ragnarök*.

8 *Jötunheim:* the world of the giants.

9 *Brimir* and *Blain:* two giants, or possibly, names of the giant Ymir. Stanzas 10-16, an interpolated list of dwarf names, are here omitted.

17 The 'three' here are not the giant-maids of stanza 8, but the gods Odin, Hönir, and Lodur, who proceed to create primeval man and woman, Ask and Embla ('Ash' and 'Elm').

18 To these 'trees,' 'empty of might,' Odin gives *önd* (breath, life, spirit), Hönir gives sense, and Lodur gives heat.

19 Yggdrasill, the tree of fate, stretches from the lower world to heaven. At the centre of the world, it supports the universe, and beneath its roots lies Urdar-brunnr, the well of fate.

20 From the well come the three Norns, goddesses of fate: Urd, the Past; Verdandi, the Present; Skuld, the Future. The destinies of men are carved as magic signs (runes) on wood.

21 Here commences the war between the Æsir ('gods,' singular *ass*) and the special tribe of gods known as the Vanir. Apparently an assault on the principal goddess of the Vanir, Freyja (here called Gullveig and Heid), has precipitated strife between the gods. Gullveig has been speared and burned in the palace of Har (Odin), but survives as Heid by virtue of her dark magic (*seid*).

23 Odin declares war for the Æsir by ritually hurling his magic spear. The Vanir, equipped with magic of their own, breach the wall of Asgard, the Æsir's fortress.

24 A council of all the gods now determines the tribute which the Æsir should pay for the offence against Gullveig (Freyja).

25 *Od:* the husband of Freyja.

26 *Thor:* son of Odin and Jörd, the warrior god who wields his hammer Mjöllnir against the giants and demons. The cause of Thor's outburst may have been too well known to the hearers of the *Völuspá* to bear retelling. Snorri's *Edda*

recounts how a giant, employed by the Æsir to rebuild the walls of Asgard, demands as payment the sun, the moon, and the goddess Freyja as well. After trickery on the part of the Æsir, the giant threatens and is slain by Thor, and new occasion for enmity is found.

27 Heimdall's Gjallarhorn ('Ringing Horn'), the trumpet which he uses (stanza 46) to summon the gods to battle, lies under the cosmic tree Yggdrasill. There also is hidden one of Odin's eyes, pledged to Mimir, wisest of the Æsir, in exchange for wisdom.

28 *The Old One:* Odin.

29 The *völva* knows that Odin, whose most precious sense is sight, has sacrificed an eye to the well of Mimir, and that from the eye Mimir drinks the mead of immortality. 'Would you know yet more?' comes as a taunt to Odin, who has learned the past and now awaits the hearing of his fate.

30 *Heerfather:* Odin, 'Father of the Host.'

31 *Valkyries:* 'Choosers of the Slain,' who bear the fallen warriors to Odin at Valhall. The list of warrior-maidens may be an interpolation. *Herjan:* Odin, 'Leader of the Hosts.'

32 The seeress predicts the destiny of Baldr. Like the story of Freyja and the giant builder above, the episode of Baldr's death was well known to hearers of the *Völuspá* and required only a brief résumé. From all created things, with the sole exception of the young mistletoe, Frigg had secured an oath that none would hurt Baldr, her son. Loki, the trickster among the gods, brought mistletoe to a new sport of the Æsir—throwing harmless missiles at the seemingly indestructible Baldr—and by guiding the hand of Höd, the blind brother of Baldr, he contrived the death of the young god. Odin, in grief, begets Vali ('the brother of Baldr' in stanza 33) to avenge Baldr by slaying Höd.

34 *Fensalir:* the home of Frigg, who now weeps over these days of bloodshed.

35 The *völva* sees that Loki will not escape punishment for his part in the killing of Baldr. Sigyn sits by the side of her bound mate.

36 *Slid:* a river in the world of the giants.

37 *Nidavellir:* 'Dark Fields,' the home of the dwarfs. *Sindri:* the great worker in gold among the dwarfs. *Okolnir:* 'Never Cold,' possibly a volcano. *Brimir:* see stanza 9.

38 *Naströnd:* 'Corpse-shore,' the land of the dead, ruled by the goddess Hel.

39 Here in Naströnd the *völva* sees oath-breakers and murderers undergoing dreadful punishment: Nidhögg, the devouring serpent who lives under Yggdrasill, and a wolf, probably Fenrir, a son of Loki, are their tormenters.

40 Fenrir and the nameless giantess have the wolves Skoll and Hati as their offspring; Skoll steals the sun, Hati the moon.

42 *Eggther:* apparently the watchman of the giants, as is Heimdall for the gods. The cock Fjalar in the gallows tree awakes the giants for the great battle.

43 *Gollinkambi:* 'Gold-comb,' the cock who wakes the gods in Valhall. In the world of death a 'rust-red bird' is yet a third herald of *ragnarök*.

44 The *völva* sees that Fenrir (Garm) will break loose from his den, Gnipahellir, and run free. The stanza occurs again as a refrain.

46 *Mim:* Mimir.

47 *The giant:* Fenrir. This stanza recalls the episode where two of the Æsir, Mimir and Hönir, were sent to the Vanir as hostages in a treaty of peace. The Vanir decapitated Mimir and returned the head to Odin, who thereupon preserved it and consulted it for wisdom. *Surt:* the fire-giant who rules Muspell, a world in the south; his 'kinsman' is Fenrir.

50 *Hrym:* a leader of the giants who comes as the helmsman of the giants' ship, Naglfar, made from dead men's nails. The serpent Midgardsorm, another of Loki's offspring, churns the sea.

51 Having broken from their respective fetters (stanzas 35 and 44), Loki (the brother of Byleist) and Fenrir now are en route to battle.

52 *The scourge of branches:* fire.

53 *Hlin:* Frigg, Odin's wife. *Beli's slayer:* the god Freyr, one of the Vanir and brother to Freyja, who killed the giant Beli with his fist. Odin, the 'joy of Frigg,' is destined to fall before the wolf Fenrir.

54 *Sigfather:* Odin, 'Father of Victory.' Vidar, famed for his great shield and Thor-like strength, survives destruction and avenges his father by piercing Fenrir, 'the giant's son.'

55 *Hlödyn:* Jörd ('Earth'), the mother of Thor; Thor's father was Odin. Midgardsorm is the serpent.

56 Thor is 'warder of earth' and 'son of Fjörgyn (Jörd)'; momentarily victorious over the serpent, he himself falls slain 'nine paces' away.

60 *The girdler of earth:* Midgardsorm, the serpent in the chaos waters which encircle the world. Odin is 'Ruler of Gods' and master of the runes.

61 See stanza 8, where the gods play a game resembling chess or checkers.

62 Baldr and Höd, the brother who innocently slew him, now return in the new harmonious world. *Hropt:* Odin, whose 'battle-hall' is Valhall.

63 *Hönir:* see stanza 18. In this new age he has the gift of fortelling the future. *Tveggi:* Odin, 'The Twofold,' whose brothers are Vili and Ve. *Vindheim:* heaven, 'the home of the wind.'

64 *Gimle:* a hall roofed with gold where the worthy will dwell in the new age.

65 The stanza is obscure and the new ruler is unnamed.

66 *Nidhögg:* the dragon of stanza 39. *Nidarfjöll:* the 'Dark Crags.'

Translation by Henry Adams Bellows, *The Poetic Edda* (New York: American-Scandinavian Foundation, 1923), pp. 3-6, 8-26; notes by David Knipe; translation by Turville-Petre in note 2 added by M. Eliade

C. THE CREATION OF MAN

62. THE CREATION OF WOMAN FROM THE EARTH-MOTHER (MAORI)

To produce man it was therefore necessary for the god Tane, the Fertilizer, to fashion in human form a figure of earth upon the Earth Mother's body, and to vivify it. This event transpired in the following way. (The account, according to Best, is 'rendered as given by an old native'):

Tane proceeded to the *puke* (Mons *veneris*) of Papa [the Earth] and there fashioned in human form a figure in the earth. His next task was to endow that figure with life, with human life, life as known to human beings, and it is worthy of note that, in the account of this act, he is spoken of as Tane te waiora. It was the sun light fertilizing the Earth Mother. Implanted in the lifeless image were the *wairua* (spirit) and *manawa ora* (breath of life), obtained from Io, the Supreme Being. The breath of Tane was directed upon the image, and the warmth affected it. The figure absorbed life, a faint life sigh was heard, the life spirit manifested itself, and Hine-ahu-one, the Earth Formed Maid, sneezed, opened her eyes, and rose—a woman.

Such was the Origin of Woman, formed from the substance of the Earth Mother, but animated by the divine Spirit that emanated from the Supreme Being, Io the great, Io of the Hidden Face, Io the Parent, and Io the Parentless.

E. S. Craighill Handy, *Polynesian Religion*, Bernice P. Bishop Museum Bulletin 34 (Honolulu, 1927), p. 39; quoting Elsdon Best, 'Maori Personifications,' *Journal of the Polynesian Society*, XXXII (1923), pp. 110-11

63. ZUÑI GENESIS: THE CREATION AND EMERGENCE OF MAN

A myth from the Zuñi Indians of New Mexico

Before the beginning of the new-making, Awonawilona (the Maker and Container of All, the All-father Father), solely had being. There was nothing else whatsoever throughout the great space of the ages save everywhere black darkness in it, and everywhere void desolation.

In the beginning of the new-made, Awonawilona conceived within himself and thought outward in space, whereby mists of increase, steams potent of growth, were evolved and uplifted. Thus, by means of his innate knowledge, the All-container made himself in person and form of the Sun whom we hold to be our father and who thus came to exist and appear. With his appearance came the brightening of the spaces with light, and with the brightening of the spaces the great mist-clouds were thickened together and fell, whereby was evolved water in water; yea, and the world-holding sea.

With his substance of flesh outdrawn from the surface of his person, the Sun-father formed the seed-stuff of twain worlds, impregnating therewith the great waters, and lo! in the heat of his light these waters of the sea grew green and scums rose upon them, waxing wide and weighty until, behold! they became Awitelin Tsita, the 'Four-fold Containing Mother-earth,' and Apoyan Tä'chu, the 'All-covering Father-sky.'

The Genesis of Men and the Creatures:

From the lying together of these twain upon the great world-waters, so vitalizing, terrestrial life was conceived; whence began all beings of earth, men and the creatures, in the Four-fold womb of the World.

Thereupon the Earth-mother repulsed the Sky-father, growing big and sinking deep into the embrace of the waters below, thus separating from the Sky-father in the embrace of the waters above. As a woman forebodes evil for her first-born ere born, even so did the Earth-mother forebode, long withholding from birth her myriad progeny and meantime seeking counsel with the Sky-father. 'How,' said they to one another, 'shall our children, when brought forth, know one place from another, even by the white light of the Sun-father?'

Now like all the surpassing beings the Earth-mother and the Sky-father were 'hlimna (changeable), even as smoke in the wind; transmutable at thought, manifesting themselves in any form at will, like as dancers may by mask-making.

Thus, as a man and woman, spake they, one to the other. 'Behold!' said the Earth-mother as a great terraced bowl appeared at hand and within it water, 'this is as upon me the homes of my tiny children shall be. On the rim of each world-country they wander in, terraced mountains shall stand, making in one region many, whereby country shall be known from country, and within each, place from place. Behold, again !' said she as she spat on the water and rapidly smote and stirred it with her fingers. Foam formed, gathering about the terraced rim, mounting higher and higher. 'Yea,' said she, 'and from my bosom they shall draw nourishment, for in such as this shall they find the substance of life whence we were ourselves sustained, for see !' Then with her warm breath she blew across the terraces; white flecks of the foam broke away, and, floating over above the water, were shattered by the cold breath of the Sky-father attending, and forthwith shed downward abundantly fine mist and spray ! 'Even so, shall white clouds float up from the great waters at the borders of the world, and clustering about the mountain terraces of the horizons be borne aloft and abroad by the breaths of the surpassing of soul-beings, and of the children, and shall hardened and broken be by the cold, shedding downward, in rain spray, the water of life, even into the hollow places of my lap ! For therein chiefly shall nestle our children mankind and creature-kind, for warmth in thy coldness.'

Lo ! even the trees on high mountains near the clouds and the Sky-father crouch low towards the Earth-mother for warmth and protection ! Warm is the Earth-mother, cold the Sky-father, even as woman is the warm, man the cold being !

'Even so !' said the Sky-father; 'Yet not alone shalt thou helpful be unto our children, for behold !' and he spread his hand abroad with the palm downward and into all the wrinkles and crevices thereof he set the semblance of shining yellow corn grains; in the dark of the early world-dawn they gleamed like sparks of fire, and moved as his hand was moved over the bowl, shining up from and also moving in the depths of the water therein. 'See !' said he, pointing to the seven grains clasped by his thumb and four fingers, 'by such shall our children be guided; for behold, when the Sun-father is not nigh, and thy terraces are as the dark itself (being all hidden therein), then shall our children be guided by lights—like to these lights of all the six regions turning round the midmost one—as in and around the midmost place, where these our children shall abide, lie all the other regions of space ! Yea ! and even as these grains gleam up from the water, so shall seed-grains like to them, yet numberless, spring up from thy bosom when touched by my waters, to nourish our children'. Thus and in other ways many devised they for their offspring.

The Creation of Man

Anon in the nethermost of the four cave-wombs of the world, the seed of men and the creatures took form and increased; even as within eggs in warm places worms speedily appear, which growing, presently burst their shells and become as may happen, birds, tadpoles or serpents, so did men and all creatures grow manifoldly and multiply in many kinds. [But these are still imperfect beings: heaped and crowded together in the darkness, they crawl over one another like reptiles, grumbling, lamenting, spitting, and using indecent and insulting language. A few among them try to escape, however. One above all, distinguished from all the others as the most intelligent is the all-sacred master, Poshaiyankya, who somehow participates in the divine condition. He emerges all alone into the light after having traversed all the four telluric cave-wombs one after another. He arrives on the surface of the Earth, which has the appearance of a vast island, wet and unstable; and he makes his way towards the Sun-father to implore him to deliver mankind and the creatures there below. The Sun then repeats the process of the creation, but this time it is creation of another order. The Sun wishes to produce intelligent, free and powerful beings. He again impregnates the foam of the Earth-mother, and from this foam twins are born. The Sun endows them with every kind of magical power and orders them to be the ancestors and lords of men.] Well instructed of the Sun-father, they lifted the Sky-father with their great cloud-bow into the vault of the high zenith, that the earth might become warm and thus fitter for their children, men and the creatures. Then along the trail of the sun-seeking Poshaiyank'ya they sped backward swiftly on their floating fog-shield, westward to the Mountain of Generation. With the magic knives of the thunderbolt they spread open the uncleft depths of the mountain, and still on their cloud-shield—even as a spider in her web descendeth—so descend they, unerringly, into the dark of the under-world. There they abode with men and the creatures, attending them, coming to know them, and becoming known of them as masters and fathers, thus seeking the ways for leading them forth.

The Birth and Delivery of Men and the Creatures:

Now there were growing things in the depths, like grasses and crawling vines. So now the Beloved Twain breathed on the stems of these grasses (growing tall, as grass is wont to do toward the light, under the opening they had cleft and whereby they had descended), causing them to increase vastly and rapidly by grasping and walking round and round them, twisting them upward until lo! they reach forth even into the light. And where successively they grasped the stems ridges were formed and thumb-marks whence sprang branching leaf-stems. Therewith the two formed a great ladder whereon men and the creatures might ascend to the second cave-floor, and thus not be violently ejected in after-time by the throes of the Earth-mother, and thereby be made demoniac and deformed.

Up this ladder, into the second cave-world, men and the beings crowded, following closely the Two Little but Mighty Ones. Yet many fell back and, lost in the darkness, peopled the under-world, whence they were delivered in after-time amid terrible earth shakings, becoming the monsters and fearfully strange beings of olden time. Lo! in this second womb it was dark as is the night of a stormy season, but larger of space and higher than had been the first, because it was nearer the navel of the Earth-mother, hence named K'olin tebuli (the Umbilical-womb, or the Place of Gestation). Here again men and the beings increased, and the clamour of their complainings grew loud and beseeching. Again the Two, augmenting the growth of the great ladder, guided them upward, this time not all at once, but in successive bands to become in time the fathers of the six kinds of men (the yellow, the tawny grey, the red, the white, the mingled, and the black races), and with them the gods and creatures of them all. Yet this time also, as before, multitudes were lost or left behind. The third great cave-world, where unto men and the creatures had now ascended, being larger than the second and higher, was lighter, like a valley in starlight, and named Awisho tehuli—the Vaginal-womb, or the Place of Sex-generation or Gestation. For here the various peoples and beings began to multiply apart in kind one from another; and as the nations and tribes of men and the creatures thus waxed numerous as before, here, too, it became overfilled. As before, generations of nations now were led out successively (yet many lost, also as hitherto) into the next and last world-cave, Tepahaian tehuli, the Ultimate-uncoverable, or the Womb of Parturition.

Here it was light like the dawning, and men began to perceive and to learn variously according to their natures, wherefore the Twain taught them to seek first of all our Sun-father, who would, they said, reveal to them wisdom and knowledge of the ways of life—wherein also they were instructing them as we do little children. Yet like the other cave worlds, this too became, after long time, filled with progeny; and finally, at periods, the Two led forth the nations of men and the kinds of being, into this great upper world, which is called Tek'ohaian ulahnane, or the World of Disseminated Light and Knowledge or Seeing.

F. H. Cushing, *Outlines of Zuñi Creation Myths*, in *Thirteenth Annual Report*, Bureau of Ethnology (Washington, D.C., 1896), pp. 325-447; quotation from pp. 379-83

64. GOD AND THE FIVE WOMEN: A MYTH OF THE ORIGIN OF EARTH, FIRE, WATER AND WOMAN, FROM THE THOMPSON INDIANS OF THE NORTH PACIFIC COAST

Old One or Chief came down from the upper world on a cloud to the surface of the great lake or watery waste which was all that existed. The cloud rested on the lake. Old One pulled five hairs from his head and threw them down: they became five perfectly formed young women. He asked each in turn what she wished to be.

The first replied, 'A woman to bear children. I shall be bad and foolish, and seek after my own pleasure. My descendants will fight, steal, kill, and commit adultery.' The Chief answered that he was sorry, for because of her choice death and trouble would come into the world.

The second replied, 'A woman to bear children. I shall be good and virtuous. My descendants will be wise, peaceful, honest, truthful, and chaste.' The Chief commended her, and said that her way would triumph in the end.

The third chose to become Earth. From her, Old One said, everything would grow, and to her would return at death.

The fourth chose to be Fire, in grass, trees, and all wood, for the good of man. The fifth became Water, to 'cleanse and make wise' the people. 'I will assist all things on earth to maintain life.'

Then the Chief transformed them: first Earth, then Water, then Fire. He placed the two women (good and bad) upon the earth, and impregnated them. He told them they would be the parents of all the people. The evil would be more numerous at first, but the good would prevail eventually, he promised. Then the end will come: all the dead and living will be gathered together, Earth, Fire, and Water will resume their original forms, and all will be transformed and made new.

Condensed and paraphrased from James A. Teit, *Mythology of the Thompson Indians* (Publications of the Jessup North Pacific Expedition, vol. 8, pt. 2 [Leiden and New York: Brill and Stechert, 1912]), pp. 322-4

Myths of Creation

65. A THOMPSON INDIAN MYTH OF THE CREATION OF MAN

Before the world was formed, Stars, Moon, Sun, and Earth lived together (as people). Earth was a woman, and Sun was her husband. She was always finding fault with him, saying he was nasty, ugly, and too hot. At last the Sun grew weary of this scolding and left her. The Moon and the Stars went away with him. Earth-Woman was very sad.

The Old One appeared and transformed these people into their present forms. The Sun, Moon, and Stars he assigned to the sky, commanding them never to desert the earth again. Earth-Woman became the solid land: her hair became trees and grass, her flesh clay, her bones rocks, her blood springs of water. 'You will be as the mother of people, for from you their bodies will spring, and to you they will go back. People will live as in your bosom, and sleep on your lap. They will derive nourishment from you, and they will utilize all parts of your body.'

After this the Earth gave birth to people who were very similar in form to ourselves; but they knew nothing and required neither food nor drink. They had no appetites, desires, or thoughts. Then Old One travelled over the world and among the people, giving them appetites and desires. He caused all kinds of birds and fish to appear, to which he gave names and assigned functions. He taught women to make birch baskets, mats, and lodges, and how to dig roots, gather berries, and cure them. He taught men how to make fire, catch fish, trap and shoot game, etc. He instructed couples how to have intercourse and how to give birth to children.

When he had finished teaching the people, he bade them goodbye, saying, 'I now leave you; but if you . . . require my aid, I will come again to you. The Sun is your father, the Earth is your mother's body. You will be covered with her flesh as a blanket, under which your bones will rest in peace.'

Condensed and paraphrased from James A. Teit, *Mythology of the Thompson Indians* (Publications of the Jessup North Pacific Expedition, vol. 8, pt. 2 [Leiden and New York: Brill and Stechert, 1912]), pp. 321-2

66. A PAWNEE EMERGENCE MYTH: MOTHER CORN LEADS
THE FIRST PEOPLE TO THE SURFACE OF THE EARTH

From the ritual account given by the Pawnee Indian, Four Rings, to Dr. Melvin Gilmore.

Before the World was we were all within the Earth.
Mother Corn caused movement. She gave life.
Life being given we moved towards the surface:
We shall stand erect as men!
The being is become human! He is a person!
To personal form is added strength:
Form and intelligence united, we are ready to come forth—
But Mother Corn warns us that the Earth is still in flood.
Now Mother Corn proclaims that the flood is gone, and the Earth now green.
Mother Corn commands that the people ascend to the surface.
Mother Corn has gathered them together, they move half way to the surface;
Mother Corn leads them near to the surface of the Earth;
Mother Corn brings them to the surface. The first light appears!
Mother Corn leads them forth. They have emerged to the waist.
They step forth to the surface of the Earth.
Now all have come forth; and Mother Corn leads them from the East towards the West.
Mother Corn leads them to the place of their habitation. . . .
All is completed! All is perfect!

> H. B. Alexander, *The World's Rim* (Lincoln, Neb.: University of Nebraska Press, 1953), p. 89; quoting Dr. Gilmore

67. AN AFRICAN STORY OF THE CREATION OF MAN, FROM
THE SHILLUK, A NILOTIC PEOPLE

Turning now to Africa, we find the legend of the creation of mankind out of clay among the Shilluks of the White Nile, who ingeniously explain the different complexions of the various races by the different coloured clays out of which they were fashioned. They say that the creator Juok moulded all men of earth, and that while he was engaged in the work of creation he wandered about the world. In the land of the whites he found a pure white earth or sand, and out of it he shaped white men. Then he came to the land of Egypt and out of the mud of the Nile he made red or brown men. Lastly, he came to the land of the Shilluks, and finding there black earth he created black men out of it. The way in which he modelled men was this. He took a lump of earth and said to himself, 'I will make man, but he must be able to walk and run and go out into the fields, so I will give him two long legs, like the flamingo.' Having done so, he thought again, 'The man must be able to cultivate his millet, so I will give him two arms, one to hold the hoe, and the other to tear up the weeds.' So he gave him two arms. Then he thought again, 'The man must be able to see his millet, so I will give him two eyes.' He did so accordingly. Next he thought to himself, 'The man must be able to eat his millet, so I will give him a mouth.' And a mouth he gave him accordingly. After that he thought within himself, 'The man must be able to dance and speak and sing and shout, and for these purposes he must have a tongue.' And a tongue he gave him accordingly. Lastly, the deity said to himself, 'The man must be able to hear the noise of the dance and the speech of the great men, and for that he needs two ears.' So two ears he gave him, and sent him out into the world a perfect man.'

J. G. Frazer, *Folklore in the Old Testament*, I (London, 1919), pp. 22-3, translating and abridging W. Hofmayr, 'Die Religion der Schilluk,' *Anthropos*, VI (1906), pp. 128 *ff*.

D. MYTHS OF THE ORIGIN OF DEATH

J. G. Frazer distinguished four types of myths of the origin of Death: (1) the type of the Two Messengers; (2) the type of the Waxing and Waning Moon; (3) the type of the Serpent and his Cast Skin; (4) the type of the Banana-tree. Readers will find below examples of the last three types (nos. 68-70). The Aranda myth quoted below (no. 71) illustrates another motif: Death results from the arbitrary and cruel act of a mythical, theriomorphic Being.

The motif of the Two Messengers or 'the message that failed' is especially common in Africa. God sent the chameleon to the mythical ancestors with the message that they would be immortal, and he sent the lizard with the message that they would die. The chameleon sauntered along the way and the lizard arrived first. After she delivered her message, Death entered the world. Another African motif is that of 'Death in a bundle.' God allowed the first human beings to choose between two bundles, one of which contained Life, the other, Death. According to a third African motif, Death is the result of man's transgressing a divine commandment.

68. THE CAST SKIN: A MELANESIAN MYTH

At first men never died, but when they advanced in life they cast their skins like snakes and crabs, and came out with youth renewed. After a time a woman growing old went to a stream to change her skin. She threw off her old skin in the water, and observed that as it floated down it caught against a stick. Then she went home, where she had left her child. The child, however, refused to recognize her, crying that its mother was an old woman not like this young stranger; and to pacify the child she went after her cast integument and put it on. From that time mankind ceased to cast their skins and died.

R. H. Codrington, *The Melanesians* (Oxford, 1891), p. 265

139

69. THE STONE AND THE BANANA: AN INDONESIAN MYTH

Thus the natives of Poso, a district of Central Celebes, say that in the beginning the sky was very near the earth, and that the Creator, who lived in it, used to let down his gifts to men at the end of a rope. One day he thus lowered a stone; but our first father and mother would have none of it and they called out to their Maker, 'What have we to do with this stone? Give us something else.' The Creator complied and hauled away at the rope; the stone mounted up and up till it vanished from sight. Presently the rope was seen coming down from heaven again, and this time there was a banana at the end of it instead of a stone. Our first parents ran at the banana and took it. Then there came a voice from heaven saying: 'Because ye have chosen the banana, your life shall be like its life. When the banana-tree has offspring, the parent stem dies; so shall ye die and your children shall step into your place. Had ye chosen the stone, your life would have been like the life of the stone changeless and immortal.' The man and his wife mourned over their fatal choice, but it was too late; that is how through the eating of a banana death came into the world.

J. G. Frazer, *The Belief in Immortality*, I (London, 1913), pp. 74-5, quoting A. C. Kruijt

70. THE MOON AND RESURRECTION: AN AUSTRALIAN MYTH

In one of the Wotjobaluk legends it is said that at the time when all animals were men and women, some died, and the moon used to say, 'You up-again,' and they came to life again. There was at that time an old man who said, 'Let them remain dead.' Then none ever came to life again, except the moon, which still continued to do so.

A. W. Howitt, *The Native Tribes of South-East Australia* (London, 1904), p. 429

71. THE CRUEL BIRD: AN AUSTRALIAN (ARANDA TRIBE) MYTH

From a floor of rock they issued forth, south of Ilkanara, from a little rock-hole. The rock was first opened by a curfew woman, who thrust her nose through the hard stone. A second curfew woman followed, then a third, a fourth, a fifth, and so on. And then a curfew man appeared, followed by a second, a third, a fourth, a fifth, and so on to the last. Finally they had all emerged.

The men who had issued forth last all grew angry against the man who had appeared first perhaps because he had followed too closely upon the women. The first-born man lit a great blazing fire; and the others pointed a magic bone at him. The doomed man stretched himself out; he lay motionless for two nights. Then he died, and the rest buried him east of the floor of rock. Some of the women went to Tjolankuta, deep in grief; others went to Lkebalinja; others again sat down at the entrance of the gap where the Ilkaknara creek breaks through the range. They moved about in a women's dance, to the accompaniment of shouts by the men: 'bau! bau! bau! bau!'

But the dead man hollowed out the soil from underneath. Then his forehead emerged through the crust; next his temples reappeared; next his head became visible, up to his throat. His two shoulders, however, had become caught below.

Then the Urbura, the magpie, came from Urburakana. He rushed along in haste; he saw from a great distance away what was happening: 'See, he has begun to sprout up again only a moment ago; but his two shoulders have become caught tightly and are still pinning him down.' The dead man rose a little higher. The curfew women were approaching with dancing steps; they encircled him. The magpie rushed up, filled with deadly anger, to a mountain near-by, called Urburinka. Then he grasped a heavy mulga spear, thrust it deep into the neck of the dead man, stamped him back into the ground with his heel, trampling fiercely upon him: 'Remain rooted down firmly for all time; do not attempt to rise again; stay for ever in the grave!'

Then the curfews all turned into birds and flew to Running Waters; they all left, both men and women. Their wailing shrieks rang out without ceasing; their tears fell without ceasing; they were deeply stricken with grief.

The Urbura, too, soared up like a bird and returned to his own home, where he remained forever.

My informant added briefly that, but for the cruelty of the Urbura, the dead man would have grown up into life a second time; and if he had risen of his own accord, all men who died since that day, would have risen again after death in the same manner. But the Urbura had finally crushed the unfortunate curfew man, and stamped his head down a second time into the grave: 'And now all of us die and are annihilated for ever; and there is no resurrection for us.'

T. G. H. Strehlow, *Aranda Traditions* (Melbourne, 1947), pp. 44-5

72. MAUI AND HINE-NUI-TE-PO: A POLYNESIAN MYTH

Maui now felt it necessary to leave the village where Irawaru had lived, so he returned to his parents. When he had been with them for some time, his father said to him one day, 'Oh, my son, I have heard from your mother and others that you are very valiant, and that you have succeeded in all feats that you have undertaken in your own country, whether they were small or great. But now that you have arrived in your father's country, you will, perhaps, at last be overcome.'

Then Maui asked him, 'What do you mean? What things are there that I can be vanquished by?' His father answered him, 'By your great ancestress, by Hine-nui-te-po, who, if you look, you may see flashing, and, as it were, opening and shutting there, where the horizon meets the sky.' Maui replied, 'Lay aside such idle thoughts, and let us both fearlessly seek whether men are to die or live for ever.' His father said, 'My child, there has been an ill omen for us. When I was baptizing you, I omitted a portion of the fitting prayer, and that I know will be the cause of your perishing.'

Then Maui asked his father, 'What is my ancestress Hine-nui-te-po like?' He answered, 'What you see yonder shining so brightly red are her eyes. And her teeth are as sharp and hard as pieces of volcanic glass. Her body is like that of a man. And as for the pupils of her eyes, they are jasper. And her hair is like the tangles of long seaweed. And her mouth is like that of a barracouta.' Then his son answered him: 'Do you think her strength is as great as that of Tama-nui-te-Ra, who consumes man, and the earth, and the very waters, by the fierceness of his heat? Was not the world formerly saved alive by the speed with which he travelled? If he had then, in the days of his full strength and power, gone as slowly as he does now, not a remnant of mankind would have been left living upon the earth, nor, indeed, would anything else have survived. But I laid hold of Tama-nui-te-Ra, and now he goes slowly, for I smote him again and again, so that he is now feeble, and long in travelling his course, and he now gives but very little heat, having been weakened by the blows of my enchanted weapon. I then, too, split him open in many places, and from the wounds so made, many rays now issue forth and spread in all directions. So, also, I found the sea much larger than the earth, but by the power of the last born of your children, part of the earth was drawn up again, and dry land came forth.' And his father answered him, 'That is all very true, O, my last born, and the strength of my old age. Well, then, be bold, go and visit your great ancestress, who flashes so fiercely there, where the edge of the horizon meets the sky.'

Hardly was this conversation concluded with his father, when the young hero went forth to look for companions to accompany him upon this enterprise. There came to him for companions, the small robin, and the large robin, and the thrush, and the yellow-hammer, and every kind of little bird, and the water-wagtail. These all assembled together, and they all started with Maui in the evening, and arrived at the dwelling of Hine-nui-te-po, and found her fast asleep.

Then Maui addressed them all, 'My little friends, now if you see me creep into this old chieftainess, do not laugh at what you see. Nay, nay, do not, I pray you, but when I have got altogether inside her, and just as I am coming out of her mouth, then you may shout with laughter if you please.' His little friends, who were frightened at what they saw, replied, 'Oh, sir, you will certainly be killed.' He answered them, 'If you burst out laughing at me as soon as I get inside her, you will wake her up, and she will certainly kill me at once, but if you do not laugh until I am quite inside her, and am on the point of coming out of her mouth, I shall live, and Hine-nui-te-po will die.' His little friends answered, 'Go on then, brave sir, but pray take good care of yourself.'

Then the young hero started off. He twisted the strings of his weapon tight round his wrist, and went into the house. He stripped off his clothes, and the skin on his hips looked mottled and beautiful as that of a mackerel, from the tattoo marks, cut on it with the chisel of Uetonga [grandson of Ru, god of earthquakes; Uetonga taught tattooing to Mataora who taught it to man], and he entered the old chieftainess.

The little birds now screwed up their tiny cheeks, trying to suppress their laughter. At last the little Tiwakawaka could no longer keep it in, and laughed out loud, with its merry, cheerful note. This woke the old woman up. She opened her eyes, started up, and killed Maui.

Thus died this Maui we have spoken of. But before he died he had children, and sons were born to him. Some of his descendants yet live in Hawaiki, some in Aotearoa (or in these islands). The greater part of his descendants remained in Hawaiki, but a few of them came here to Aotearoa. According to the traditions of the Maori, this was the cause of the introduction of death into the world (Hine-nui-te-po was the goddess of death. If Maui had passed safely through her, then no more human beings would have died, but death itself would have been destroyed.) We express it by saying, 'The water-wagtail laughing at Maui-tiki-tiki-o Taranga made Hine-nui-te-po squeeze him to death.' And we have this proverb, 'Men make heirs, but death carries them off.'

Sir George Grey, *Polynesian Mythology* (London, 1855), pp. 56-8

E. MYTHS OF THE FLOOD

73. THE FLOOD NARRATIVE FROM THE GILGAMESH EPIC

Gilgamesh has made a long and difficult journey to learn how Utnapishtim acquired eternal life. In answer to his questions, Utnapishtim tells the following story. Once upon a time, the gods destroyed the ancient city of Shuruppak in a great flood. But Utnapishtim, forewarned by Ea, managed to survive by building a great ship. His immortality was a gift bestowed by the repentant gods in recognition of his ingenuity and his faithfulness in reinstituting the sacrifice.

Shurippak—a city which thou knowest,
(And) which on Euphrates' banks is set—
That city was ancient, (as were) the gods within it,
When their heart led the great gods to produce the flood.
There were Anu, their father,
Valiant Enlil, their counsellor,
Ninurta, their herald,
Ennuge, their irrigator.
Ninigiku-Ea was also present with them;
Their words he repeats to the reed-hut:[1]
'Reed-hut, reed-hut! Wall! Wall!
Reed-hut, hearken! Wall, reflect!
Man of Shuruppak,[2] son of Ubar-Tutu,
Tear down (this) house, build a ship!
Give up possessions, seek thou life.
Despise property and keep the soul alive.
Aboard the ship take thou the seed of all living things.
The ship that thou shalt build,
Her dimensions shall be to measure.
Equal shall be her width and her length.
Like the Apsu[3] thou shalt ceil her.'

The notes to this text are on p. 150.

I understood, and I said to Ea, my lord:
'Behold, my lord, what thou hast thus ordered,
I shall be honoured to carry out.
But what shall I answer the city, the people and elders?'
Ea opened his mouth to speak,
Saying to me, his servant:
'Thou shalt then thus speak unto them:
"I have learned that Enlil is hostile to me,
So that I cannot reside in your city,
Nor set my foot in Enlil's territory.
To the Deep I will therefore go down,
    To dwell with my lord Ea.
But upon you he will shower down abundance,
The choicest birds, the rarest fishes.
The land shall have its fill of harvest riches.
He who at dusk orders the husk-greens,
Will shower down upon you a rain of wheat." ' [4]
With the first glow of dawn,
The land was gathered about me.

   [too fragmentary for translation]

The little ones carried bitumen,
While the grown ones brought all else that was needful.
On the fifth day I laid her framework.
One (whole) acre was her floor space,
    Ten dozen cubits the height of each of her walls,
Ten dozen cubits each edge of the square deck.
I laid out the shape of her sides and joined her together.
I provided her with six decks,
Dividing her (thus) into seven parts.
Her floor plan I divided into nine parts.
I hammered water-plugs into her.
I saw to the punting-poles and laid in supplies.
Six 'sar' (measures) [5] of bitumen I poured into the furnace,
Three sar of asphalt I also poured inside.
Three sar of the basket-bearers transferred,
Aside from the one sar of oil which the calking consumed,
And the two sar of oil which the boatman stowed away.
Bullocks I slaughtered for the people,
And I killed sheep every day.
Must, red wine, oil, and white wine

I gave the workmen to drink, as though river water,
That they might feast as on New Year's Day. . . .
On the seventh day the ship was completed.
The launching was very difficult,
So that they had to shift the floor planks above and below,
Until two-thirds of the structure had gone into the water.
Whatever I had I laded upon her:
Whatever I had of silver I laded upon her;
Whatever I had of gold I laded upon her;
Whatever I had of all the living beings I laded upon her.
All my family and kin I made go aboard the ship.
The beasts of the field, the wild creatures of the field,
   All the craftsmen I made go aboard.
Shamash had set for me a stated time:
'When he who orders unease at night
   Will shower down a rain of blight,
Board thou the ship and batten up the gate!'
That stated time had arrived:
'He who orders unease at night showers down a rain of blight.'
I watched the appearance of the weather.
The weather was awesome to behold.
I boarded the ship and battened up the gate.
To batten up the (whole) ship, to Puzur-Amurri, the boatman,
I handed over the structure together with its contents.
With the first glow of dawn,
A black cloud rose up from the horizon.
Inside it Adad[6] thunders,
While Shallat and Hanish[7] go in front,
Moving as heralds over hill and plain.
Erragal[8] tears out the posts;[9]
Forth comes Ninurta and causes the dikes to follow.
The Anunnaki lift up the torches,
Setting the land ablaze with their glare.
Consternation over Adad reaches to the heavens,
Turning to blackness all that had been light.
The wide land was shattered like a pot!
For one day the south-storm blew,
Gathering speed as it blew, submerging the mountains,
Overtaking the people like a battle.
No one can see his fellow,
Nor can the people be recognized from heaven.

The gods were frightened by the deluge,
And, shrinking back, they ascended to the heaven of Anu.
The gods cowered like dogs
   Crouched against the outer wall.
Ishtar cried out like a woman in travail,
The sweet-voiced mistress of the gods moans aloud:
'The olden days are alas turned to clay,
Because I bespoke evil in the Assembly of the gods,
How could I bespeak evil in the Assembly of the gods,
Ordering battle for the destruction of my people,
When it is I myself who give birth to my people!
Like the spawn of the fishes they fill the sea!'
The Anunnaki gods weep with her,
The gods, all humbled, sit and weep,
Their lips drawn tight, . . . one and all.
Six days and six nights
Blows the flood wind, as the south-storm sweeps the land.
When the seventh day arrived,
   The flood (-carrying) south-storm subsided in the battle,
Which it had fought like an army.
The sea grew quiet, the tempest was still, the flood ceased.
I looked at the weather: stillness had set in,
And all of mankind had returned to clay.
The landscape was as level as a flat roof.
I opened a hatch, and light fell on my face.
Bowing low, I sat and wept,
Tears running down my face.
I looked about for coast lines in the expanse of the sea:
In each of fourteen (regions)
   There emerged a region (-mountain).
On Mount Nisir the ship came to a halt.
Mount Nisir held the ship fast,
   Allowing no motion.

....

[For six days the ship is held fast by Mount Nisir.]

When the seventh day arrived,
I sent forth and set free a dove.
The dove went forth, but came back;
There was no resting-place for it and she turned round.
Then I sent forth and set free a swallow.

The swallow went forth, but came back;
There was no resting-place for it and she turned round.
Then I sent forth and set free a raven.
The raven went forth and, seeing that the waters had diminished,
He eats, circles, caws, and turns not round.
Then I let out (all) to the four winds
    And offered a sacrifice.
I poured out a libation on the top of the mountain.
Seven and seven cult-vessels I set up,
Upon their plate-stands I heaped cane, cedarwood, and myrtle.
The gods smelled the savour,
The gods smelled the sweet savour,
The gods crowded like flies about the sacrificer.
As soon as the great goddess[10] arrived,
She lifted up the great jewels which Anu had fashioned to her liking:
'Ye gods here, as surely as this lapis
    Upon my neck I shall not forget,
I shall be mindful of these days, forgetting (them) never.
Let the gods come to the offering:
(But) let not Enlil come to the offering,
For he, unreasoning, brought on the deluge
And my people consigned to destruction.'
As soon as Enlil arrived,
And saw the ship, Enlil was wroth,
He was filled with wrath against the Igigi gods:[11]
'Has some living soul escaped?
    No man was to survive the destruction!'
Ninurta opened his mouth to speak,
    Saying to valiant Enlil:
'Who other than Ea can devise plans?
It is Ea alone who knows every matter.'
Ea opened his mouth to speak,
    Saying to valiant Enlil:
'Thou wisest of the gods, thou hero,
How couldst thou, unreasoning, bring on the deluge?
On the sinner impose his sin,
    On the transgressor impose his transgression!
(Yet) be lenient, lest he be cut off,
Be patient, lest he be dislodged!
Instead of thy bringing on the deluge,
    Would that a lion had risen up to diminish mankind!

Instead of thy brining on the deluge,
  Would that a wolf had risen up to diminish mankind!
Instead of thy bringing on the deluge,
  Would that a famine had risen up to lay low mankind!
Instead of thy bringing on the deluge,
  Would that pestilence had risen up to smite down mankind!
It was not I who disclosed the secret of the great gods.
I let Atrahasis[12] see a dream,
And he perceived the secret of the gods.
Now then take counsel in regard to him!'
Thereupon Enlil went aboard the ship.
Holding me by the hand, he took me aboard.
He took my wife aboard and made (her) kneel by my side.
Standing between us, he touched our foreheads to bless us:
'Hitherto Utnapishtim has been but human.
Henceforth Utnapishtim and his wife shall be like unto us gods.
Utnapishtim shall reside far away, at the mouth of the rivers!'
Thus they took me and made me reside far away,
  At the mouth of the rivers.

Notes

1 Probably the dwelling of Utnapishtim. The god Ea addresses him (through the barrier of the wall), telling him about the decision of the gods to bring on a flood and advising him to build a ship.
2 Utnapishtim.
3 The subterranean waters.
4 The purpose is to deceive the inhabitants of Shuruppak as to the real intent of the rain.
5 A 'sar' is about 8,000 gallons.
6 God of storm and rain.
7 Heralds of Adad.
8 I.e., Nergal, the god of the nether world.
9 Of the world dam.
10 Ishtar.
11 The heavenly gods.
12 'Exceeding wise,' an epithet of Utnapishtim.

Translation by E. A. Speiser, in *Ancient Near Eastern Texts* (Princeton, 1950), pp. 60-72, as reprinted in Isaac Mendelsohn (ed.), *Religions of the Ancient Near East*, Library of Religion paperbook series (New York, 1955), pp. 100-6; notes by Mendelsohn

See also no. 159

Myths of the Flood

74. A MYTH OF THE DELUGE FROM ANCIENT INDIA

('Shatapatha-Brāhmana,' I, 8, 1-6)

1. In the morning they brought to Manu water for washing, just as now also they (are wont to) bring (water) for washing the hands. When he was washing himself, a fish came into his hands.

2. It spake to him the word, 'Rear me, I will save thee!' 'Wherefrom wilt thou save me?' 'A flood will carry away all these creatures: from that I will save thee!' 'How am I to rear thee?'

3. It said, 'As long as we are small, there is great destruction for us: fish devours fish. Thou wilt first keep me in a jar. When I outgrow that, thou wilt dig a pit and keep me in it. When I outgrow that, thou wilt take me down to the sea, for then I shall be beyond destruction.'

4. It soon became a *ghasha* (a great fish); for that grows largest (of all fish). Thereupon it said, 'In such and such a year that flood will come. Thou shalt then attend to me (i.e. to my advice) by preparing a ship; and when the flood has risen thou shalt enter into the ship, and I will save thee from it.'

5. After he had reared it in this way, he took it down to the sea. And in the same year which the fish had indicated to him, he attended to (the advice of the fish) by preparing a ship; and when the flood had risen, he entered into the ship. The fish then swam up to him, and to its horn he tied the rope of the ship, and by that means he passed swiftly up to yonder northern mountain.

6. It then said, 'I have saved thee. Fasten the ship to a tree; but let not the water cut thee off whilst thou art on the mountain. As the water subsides, thou mayest gradually descend!' Accordingly he gradually descended and hence that (slope) of the northern mountain is called 'Manu's descent.' The flood then swept away all these creatures, and Manu alone remained here.

Translation by Julius Eggeling, *in Sacred Books of the East*, XII (Oxford, 1882), pp. 216-18

CHAPTER III

Man and the Sacred

A. SACRED WORLD, SACRED LIFE,
SACRED TIME

One of the outstanding characteristics of traditional societies is the opposition that they assume between their inhabited territory and the unknown and indeterminate space that surrounds it. The former is the World (more precisely, 'our world'), the cosmos; everything outside it is no longer a cosmos but a sort of 'other world,' a foreign, chaotic space, peopled by ghosts, demons, 'foreigners' (who are assimilated to demons and the souls of the dead). The world is a universe within which the sacred has already manifested itself. (Cf. M. Eliade, 'The Sacred and the Profane,' pp. 29 ff.)

The text reprinted below describes the religious conception of the Ngaju Dayak in southern Borneo; similar ideas are to be found among innumerable archaic and traditional societies.

75. THE SACRED WORLD: THE DAYAK OF BORNEO

The area inhabited by the sacred people is the sacred land. It was given to them by the godhead, which had shaped it out of the remains of the sun and the moon. It lies among the primeval waters, between Upperworld and Underworld, and rests on the back of the Watersnake. It is bounded by the raised tail and head of the deity of the Underworld. We also find in myths the idea that the world is enclosed in a circle formed by the Watersnake biting its own tail. The world is thus supported and enclosed by the godhead, a man lives under its protection, in divine peace and well-being. Man lives in the sacred, divine land of Mahatala and Jata. The mountains of the sacred land reach up to the Upperworld. The godhead descends on to them and on them he meets men and gives them his sacred gifts. Man lives in the sacred land in communion with the supreme deities. He climbs the sacred mountain and there practises asceticism (batapa), and Matahala draws close to him there and regards him. In the still of the night he lets himself drift on a small raft in the river, and the Watersnake emerges and sees him. The godhead is everywhere, and man can appear before it everywhere, for he is in the godhead's land and under its protection, and the godhead has created for him an approach to the Upperworld and the Underworld.

The world described here is the primeval village Batu Nindan Tarong, the origin of which is told in the creation myth, and which is pictured in the sacred designs. The head and tail of the Watersnake are usually represented in these drawings as the Tree of Life and this representation is meaningful in that the Watersnake and the Tree of Life are identical. The first human beings lived in this primeval village, and their three sons were born to them there, and when this time is spoken of or sung about the sacred legends and songs say: 'At that time, in the beginning, when our ancestors were still living in the mouth of the coiled Watersnake [which lay circled about the village], such-and-such happened,' and in this village the sacred ceremonies were first established.

With the exception of Maharaja Sangen, the three brothers did not stay in Batu Nindan Tarong. They left there and settled in the Upperworld and in our world. But the sacred people did not stay together in this world. The tribal organization collapsed, its members moved to other rivers and settled among strangers, and the idea of the sacred land diminished. Instead of a tribal area there is now the village, with its neighbouring villages upstream and downstream. The world and mankind *(kalunen)*, or man as part of this mankind, are synonymous and the same term *kalunen* is employed for both. The world is nothing but the sacred land, and the sacred land is inhabited only by the sacred people. The Ngaju calls his world (today, his village) by various names, e.g. *batu lewu*, home village, *lewu danumku*, my village and my native river. The name always used in myths and chants is *lewu injam tingang*, the village lent by the Watersnake, or it is also described as the village where the hornbill enjoyed the Watersnake. The real native village of mankind is not in this world: it is Batu Nindan Tarong, in the Upperworld. Man dwells only for a time in this world, which is 'lent' to him, and when the time has come and he is old, then he returns for ever to his original home. To die is not to become dead; it is called *buli*, to return home. This idea has nothing to do with any Christian influence; it is an ancient Dayak concept which is understandable in relation to the primeval sacred events and the mode of thought connected with them.

The Dayak loves the world into which he is born and where he grows up. His village is the largest and most beautiful place in the whole world, and he would change it for no other. If he leaves his village he takes with him sacred medicines which will guarantee his safe return, and if he himself never comes back his bones or his ashes are still brought back into the village and thereby he finds his last resting place in the sacred land. The description of the village and the world in myths and priestly chants has poetic force and beauty. There are old people, mostly women, who have never left their own village, not because they have never had a chance to, but because they simply never felt the need to do so. Why should one leave the village? Why roam far among strangers? Peace, safety, happiness, and the good life are to be found only in one's own village, only in one's own world where one is protected by the godhead, surrounded by the primevally maternal Watersnake, where one rests on its body and is enclosed by its head and tail.

The love for one's own world is expressed in the parting song of a dead person who leaves his village for ever to enter the village of the dead. He is fetched away by Tempon Telon and journeys to the Upperworld. His boat stops before the entrance. The dead person looks down once more on the world, and sings to his village and his river and to all those he loved ·

I can still not express my innermost thought properly,
Nor is it possible for me to speak what fills my heart.
I have thrown away the village lent by Hornbill, as one discards a
*   useless plate,*
I have pushed away the place where the hornbills live widely scattered
*   as one rejects an unusable dish,*
And I have myself become like a cast stone, never to return,
I am like a clod of earth thrown away, never again to come home.

This is not hopelessness, it is simply the farewell of the deceased, and with these words the boat travels on towards the true and eternal home to which the dead may return and where he will be joyfully received by the ancestors and by all who have travelled this road before him.

The world which is borne on the back of the Watersnake and enclosed by its body is the good, sacred land. The surroundings of the village, i.e. the area which is not bounded and fenced in by the Watersnake's body, is a strange, horrible, and fearsome land where one no longer feels at home, where one will not readily build a house, which one will not enter without taking grave precautions and providing oneself with protective medicines. Persons who have died bad deaths lie outside the village, and this is where criminals are buried, that is, those who are excluded from the sacred people by the community and even by the godhead itself. They do not rest in the midst of the sacred people and in the sacred land, nor are they enclosed in death by the Watersnake, and they are buried in unhallowed ground. God and man have no more to do with them, and they are separated for ever from them, they are thrust out into solitude and homelessness, banished to ominous surroundings. There they live in the company of those who have died bad deaths, i.e. who have lost their lives in an unnatural way, by accident or by a particularly dreaded illness (leprosy, small-pox), as punishment for some known or unknown offence. The godhead has caused them to die an 'unripe death' *(matei manta)*, has put a mark upon them and thrust them out for ever from the community of the living and from that of the ancestors. This community of unfortunate and homeless souls continues to live the existence of evil spirits in the bush and forests surrounding the village. As such, they attack people, make them ill, or take their lives. . . .

One's own world is the central point of all worlds, the focus of the whole divine cosmic order and harmony. This applies also to the village, which after the collapse of the tribal organization has taken over everything that we said above about the sacred land. The village also represents the social and cosmic totality; the village also possesses the dual division. The upper part of the village (i.e. the upstream, *ngaju*, part) is lived in by the superior group, and the lower part *(ngawa)* belongs to the lower group and to the slaves (if any). . . .

The sacred land is the land of the godhead. It was not only created and maintained by the godhead, it is the godhead itself and represents the totality of Upperworld and Underworld, of Mahatala and Jata. Man lives not only in the divine land, not only in the peace of the godhead, but actually in the godhead, for the sacred land is a part of the Tree of Life, it was created from the sun and the moon, which flank the tree, and which issued from the Gold Mountain and the Jewel Mountain, and thus from the total godhead.

Hans Schärer, *Ngaju Religion: The Conception of God among a South Borneo People*, translation by Rodney Needham (The Hague, 1963), pp. 59-62, 65, 66

76. THE SACRED WORLD AND THE SACRED LIFE
OF THE LENAPE

*The Delaware (or, as they call themselves, the Lenape) Indians in-
habited a vast region of eastern North America—particularly in
Ontario, Canada—and also Oklahoma. Their most important public
ritual, called the 'New Year Big House Ceremony,' took place in the
autumn after the harvest. A huge rectangular hut—symbolizing the
universe—was set up in a forest glade. The erection of the 'Big House'
represented a ritual recreation of the world and marked the beginning
of a new year. On the first evening of the ceremony the fire was
lighted and the assistants, wearing their best clothes, took their places
along the walls. The chief opened the ceremony with a prayer to the
Creator, such as the one printed here.*

'We are thankful that so many of us are alive to meet together here
once more, and that we are ready to hold our ceremonies in good faith.
Now we shall meet here twelve nights in succession to pray to
Gicelĕmû'kaong who has directed us to worship in this way. And
these twelve Misi'ng faces [carved on the posts of the house] are here
to watch and carry our prayers to Gicelĕmû'kaong in the highest
heaven. The reason why we dance at this time is to raise our prayers to
him.

'When we come into this house of ours we are glad, and thankful
that we are well, and for everything that makes us feel good which
the Creator has placed here for our use. We come here to pray Him
to have mercy on us for the year to come and to give us everything
to make us happy; may we have good crops, and no dangerous storms,
floods nor earthquakes. We all realize what He has put before us all
through life, and that He has given us a way to pray to Him and thank
Him. We are thankful to the East because everyone feels good in the
morning when they awake, and see the bright light coming from the
East and when the Sun goes down in the West we feel good and glad
we are well; then we are thankful to the West. And we are thankful to
the North, because when the cold winds come we are glad to have lived
to see the leaves fall again; and to the South, for when the South wind
blows and everything is coming up in the spring, we are glad to live
to see the grass growing and everything green again. We thank the
Thunders for they are the *mani'towuk* that bring the rain which the
Creator has given them power to rule over. And we thank our mother,

the Earth, whom we claim as mother because the Earth carries us and everything we need. When we eat and drink and look around, we know it is Gicelĕmû'kaong that makes us feel good that way. He gives us the purest thoughts that can be had. We should pray to Him every morning.

'Man has a spirit, and the body seems to be a coat for that spirit. That is why people should take care of their spirits, so as to reach Heaven and be admitted to the Creator's dwelling. We are given some length of time to live on earth, and then our spirits must go. When anyone's time comes to leave this earth, he should go to Gicelĕmû'kaong, feeling good on the way. We all ought to pray to Him to prepare ourselves for days to come so that we can be with Him after leaving the earth.

'We all must put our thoughts to this meeting, so that Gicelĕmû-'kaong will look upon us and grant what we ask. You all come here to pray; you have to reach Him all through life. Do not think of evil; strive always to think of the good which He has given us.

'When we reach that place, we shall not have to do anything or worry about anything, only live a happy life. We know there are many of our fathers who have left this earth and are now in this happy place in the Land of the Spirits. When we arrive we shall see our fathers, mothers, children, and sisters there. And when we have prepared ourselves so that we can go to where our parents and children are, we feel happy.

'Everything looks more beautiful there than here, everything looks new, and the waters and fruits and everything are lovely.

'No sun shines there, but a light much brighter than the sun, the Creator makes it brighter by his power. All people who die here, young or old, will be of the same age there; and those who are injured, crippled, or made blind will look as good as the rest of them. It is nothing but the flesh that is injured: the spirit is as good as ever. That is the reason that people are told to help always the cripples or the blind. Whatever you do for them will surely bring its rewards. Whatever you do for anybody will bring you credit hereafter. Whenever we think the thoughts that Gicelĕmû'kaong has given us, it will do us good.'

M. R. Harrington, *Religion and Ceremonies of the Lenape* (New York, 1921), pp. 87-92

77. THE COSMIC SYMBOLISM OF THE DELAWARE (LENAPE) CULTIC HOUSE

The Big House stands for the Universe; its floor, the earth; its four walls, the four quarters; its vault, the sky dome, atop which resides the Creator in his indefinable supremacy. To use Delaware expressions, the Big House being the universe, the centre post is the staff of the Great Spirit with its foot upon the earth, its pinnacle reaching to the hand of the Supreme Deity. The floor of the Big House is the flatness of the earth upon which sit the three grouped divisions of mankind, the human social groupings in their appropriate places; the eastern door is the point of sunrise where the day begins and at the same time the symbol of termination; the north and south walls assume the meaning of respective horizons; the roof of the temple is the visible sky vault. The ground beneath the Big House is the realm of the underworld while above the roof lie the extended planes or levels, twelve in number, stretched upward to the abode of the 'Great Spirit, even the Creator,' as Delaware form puts it. Here we might speak of the carved face images, . . . the representations on the centre pole being the visible symbols of the Supreme Power, those on the upright posts, three on the north wall and three on the south wall, the manitu of these respective zones; those on the eastern and western door posts, those of the east and west. . . . But the most engrossing allegory of all stands forth in the concept of the White Path, the symbol of the transit of life, which is met in the oval, hard-trodden dancing path outlined on the floor of the Big House, from the east door passing to the right down the north side past the second fire to the west door and doubling back on the south side of the edifice around the eastern fire to its beginning. This is the path of life down which man wends his way to the western door where all ends. Its correspondent exists, I assume, in the Milky Way, where the passage of the soul after death continues in the spirit realm. As the dancers in the Big House ceremony wend their stately passage following the course of the White Path they 'push something along,' meaning existence, with their rhythmic tread. Not only the passage of life, but the journey of the soul after death is symbolically figured in the ceremony.

Frank G. Speck, A *Study of the Delaware Indians Big House Ceremony*, Publications of the Pennsylvania Historical Commission, vol. 2 (Harrisburg, 1931), pp. 22-3

78. THE AUSTRALIAN CYCLE OF LIFE (ABORIGINE)

To the Aborigine, life is a cycle, though whether it is continuous or not, he does not always dare to say. Found by his parent in a spiritual experience, he is incarnated through his mother and so enters profane life. But a few years later, through the gate of initiation, he partially re-enters the sacred dream-time or sky-world which he has left for a season. After passing farther and farther into it, so far as the necessities of profane life allow, he dies, and through another gate, the transition rite of burial, he returns completely to his sacred spirit state in the sky, the spirit-home or totemic centre, perhaps to repeat the cycle later, perhaps to cease to be. In the case of a woman, the central part of the cycle does not exist—except in so far as she is the means of incarnation for sacred pre-existing spirits.

There are some interesting symbols of this return to spiritual existence. In north-western Australia, the individual's spirit came by way of a waterhole associated with the spirit of fertility or life; initiation gives him conscious knowledge of the source of his life, and after the final mourning ceremony his bones are put in a cave near by. In some of the desert areas, a hair-belt made from the deceased's hair, which contains something of his spirit, is finally returned to the cave or waterhold of the mythical serpent, from which the spirit issued for incarnation. In north-western Arnhem Land, the bones are finally placed in a totemic coffin and so identified with the totem and, therefore, with the source of life in man and nature. Finally, in parts of eastern Australia, the young fellow passes at his initiation to the sky-world which is symbolized on the initiation-ground by the marked trees, and when he dies, his burial-ground is likewise marked to symbolize the sky-world from which all life is believed to come and to which he now returns.

A. P. Elkin, *The Australian Aborigines* 3rd ed.
(Garden City, N.Y.: Doubleday and Co., 1964), pp. 336-7

See also no. 86

79. THE MEANING OF HUMAN EXISTENCE
(AUSTRALIAN ABORIGINE)

We often fail to realize how little meaning our way of life possesses for the Aborigines, even for those who are to all intents and purposes civilized. I can think of regions where they have been in touch with us for sixty years and where for six months of the year, the dry season of the north, they play a very valuable part in our country life, principally on the stations; during that time they dress in our way, shave and wash, appreciate our food and seem quite presentable. At the end of the time, they receive the small share of their pay which they are allowed to handle, buy a few objects (often at an exorbitant price) mostly of a kind which we regard as ridiculous for grown men, and then with their families go bush, casting off all their clothes and all else that belongs to our culture. They paint themselves, camp, hunt, perform corroborees and take part in secret ceremonies, and all this in spite sometimes of the fact that their social life has been most degraded and demoralized by association with whites during the past fifty years or so. We, of course, may think that their conduct in returning to this bush life every year is somewhat unintelligible and shows a lack of appreciation of the higher stage of living to which they adapt themselves for six months a year. But we must remember two things: in the first place, the only part of our life with which these seasonable native employees become familiar is its economic and material aspects, and they do not thereby gain the impression that our way of life is of more value to them than is their own; it has some interest for them, mainly because it enables them apparently to satisfy us and also to obtain a few material objects which they find either useful or fascinating. In the second place, our economic life is not their life—it is only an external means or a tool enabling them to do something which is obviously expedient, but it is not connected with their life of ritual and belief; on the other hand, the time in the bush with its paint and hunting and ceremonies is their life, and has meaning for them. What they do there is for themselves, and in the ritual they keep in touch with the heroes and ancestors of old, realize their common life, and derive hope for the future.

Such a fact as this helps us to understand why the young fellows are drawn towards initiation and the secret life in spite of the counter attractions and influences of missionary and other civilizing agents. It means, however, that they are drawn in two ways which seem to be incompatible. What then is the result? There are two alternatives: the missionary or civilizing agent may be succssful in putting an end to initiation and other secret rites, or in in getting such a grip over the rising generation that the old men make the initiation a mere form and not an entry into the full secret life of the tribe. But this implies a breakdown of tribal authority and a loss of the knowledge of, let alone the respect for these ideals, sentiments and sanctions which are essential to tribal cohesion; and in

Australia, such a condition is the accompaniment, and a cause, of tribal extinction. The other alternative is, for a period at least, the failure of the missionary or other civilizing agent. The old men and the glamour of the secret life win. The missionary may be quite unaware of this, for he is apt to rely on outward conformity to his demands and teaching, and if he is not conversant with the language and secrets of the tribe he cannot do otherwise. But slowly and surely, step by step, the young fellow advances along the secret path, and in heart is getting farther and farther away from the white man's doctrines and view of life. See him this morning outwardly playing his part on the station or in mission compound or church. But see him again this afternoon completely wrapped up in the performance of a secret rite and the exposition of a sacred myth by the elders—perhaps only a mile or so away from the mission or station, but an age away in mind. Yes, see him there and you will know where he finds meaning for life, sanction for conduct and hope for the future. And unless the tribal life breaks down, he will sooner or later spend a great deal of his time traversing the paths and localities sanctified by the wanderings and exploits of the great heroes of old, and performing the rites on which the life of the tribe and of nature depends.

What then is this secret life of the Aborigines? It is the life apart— a life of ritual and mythology, of sacred rites and objects. It is the life in which man really finds his place in society and in nature, and in which he is brought in touch with the invisible things of the world of the past, present and future. Every now and then we find the tribe, or groups from more than one tribe, going apart from the workaday world. A special camp is arranged where the women remain unless some of them are called upon to play a subsidiary part in the ceremony. Then the men go for a mile or so to a secret site or to sites where they spend hours, or maybe days and weeks and even months, singing and performing rites, and in some cases even eating or sleeping there. When they return later to the world of secular affairs they are refreshed in mind and spirit. They now face the vicissitudes of everyday life with a new courage and a strength gained from the common participation in the rites, with a fresh appreciation of their social and moral ideals and patterns of life, and an assurance that having performed the rites well and truly, all will be well with themselves and with that part of nature with which their lives are so intimately linked.

A. P. Elkin, *The Australian Aborigines* (3rd ed.; Garden City, N.Y.: Doubleday and Co., 1964), pp. 168-71

80. THE PHASES OF THE SACRED LIFE (THE NGAJU DAYAK OF SOUTH BORNEO)

Life is not a smoothly continuous process, but is broken into stages. There is life and death, becoming and passing away, and in this alternation man is continually returned to the primeval period, and he is thereby the object of divine creative activity whereby he can enter a new stage of life as a new man, until he has reached the highest stage of the true and perfect man, until indeed he has ascended by stages not only to the point of being godlike but of becoming divine. All ceremonies of transition, such as at birth, initiation, marriage and death, correspond very closely with each other in that on every occasion they repeat the drama of primeval creation. Man passes into death and returns to the total godhead and the Tree of Life, and then the godhead re-enacts the creation and man issues again from the Tree of Life as a new creature. . . .

Marriage. The marriage ceremony, which with all its rites lasts a fairly long time, is conducted by the elders, and they tell the couple from time to time what they have to do. The bride has to clasp the Tree of Life with her right hand and raised index finger. Then the bridegroom likewise encloses the finger of his bride and the Tree of Life with his right hand and raised index finger. . . .

What does the wedding really signify? From what we have already said it is clear that it has a deeper meaning, and is somehow connected with the conception of God and creation. It is not a simply social occasion; it is not primarily a matter of pairing together, but one of the most important religious affairs. To be married means to enter a new stage of sacred life. It means that something old is irrevocably past and something new comes about, it is death and life, passing away and coming into being. It is the same kind of event as birth, initiation, and death. The young couple die. The death is undergone through a representative, viz. the head, taken either in a raid or from a sacrificial slave, in which the spear, the stem of the Tree of Life, is stuck. According to old information from Schwaner, it used to be the case that the young pair were taken to the river, where the blood of a sacrificed slave has been mixed, and plunged into it. Immersion in the river means to die, but the dying was undergone by proxy in the person of the slave. Today the coconut is used as surrogate. . . . The couple are thus returned to mythical primeval time. They return to the Tree of Life. This return is indicated by the clasping of the Tree by the bridal pair. To clasp it means to be in the Tree of Life, to form a unity with it. In the ritual acts the godhead re-enacts the new creation, and through it the young couple leave the Tree and re-enter life, beginning their new existence in a new world, a new status, a new life. The wedding is the re-enactment of the creation, and the re-enactment of the creation of the first human couple from the Tree of Life. The bridal pair are the first human couple, and in their marital union, with its functions, duties, and rights, they are also the total godhead. . . . The ritually contracted marriage is fundamentally monogamous, as was that of the first ancestral pair. But what is a marriage according to the divine commandments? With marriage come bodily union, sexual intercourse, and the procreation of children. When these requirements are not met, the marriage does not resemble the Tree of Life from which children come, it is a withered tree and no marriage. And a marriage which is no marriage can be broken (in conformity with the relevant laws), or a second wife can be taken in addition to the first without this being thought an offence against *hadat*,[1] which it would be if the wife were rejected simply because she was old and the husband had fallen in love with a young girl, or if the man had more than two wives. In this respect, too, the conception of marriage is a very elevated one. The division of labour between man and woman, as well as reciprocal rights and duties, is regulated through the creation and the divine commandments, and these regulations are of a remarkably superior level. The Dayak woman is better protected by the law in many respects than is her European sister.

Birth. We shall refrain from describing here all religious observances and ceremonies which go before a birth, which surround it and succeed it. We shall ask ourselves only what birth means in relation to the conception of God. The period of pregnancy is a sacred time. The *pali*[2] are multiplied. They apply not only to the mother-to-be, but also to the future father, and these regulations show us the unbreakable and organic religious unity of man and wife. They are the total godhead and the Tree of Life, in their combination and in the coming of the new life as a ripe fruit from the Tree of Life. Every breach of this unity, every transgression of the *pali* which enclose this unity like a stout fence, causes the destruction of the Tree of Life and the ruin of its fruit. The child comes from the Tree of Life. . . . This unity and totality does not exist only during pregnancy, but during the birth also, and it lasts until the fortieth day after the delivery.

Initiation. The two rites just described belong to the rites of initiation, which bring about the transition from one stage in the sacred

The notes to this text are on p. 170.

life to another, but they by no means exhaust the list of such ceremonies. There is also the ritual bath of the infant, which takes place
either in a river or in the house, a few days or weeks after its birth.
The child is taken to the middle of the river in a sacred boat shaped
like the Watersnake, splendidly decorated with cloths and flags, and
there, at the entrance to the Underworld, it is immersed. The meaning
of the rite is clear. The total community returns in the godhead (the
boat) to the Underworld and commits the child to the godhead, who
bestows new life on the child so that it may go back to the world as a
new human being. Although this is primarily the affair of Jata,[3] the
deity of the Upperworld still has a part in this ritual bath. Before the
rite is begun, the priest invokes both of the supreme deities and begs
them to open the sources of the water of life and to let it flow in the
river, so that the child may be immersed in the water of life springing
from the Upperworld and the Underworld. The river-water is no use
in itself and the whole rite would be vain if it were not consecrated by
the consent, the presence, the water of life, and the deed, of the total
godhead. The sacred bath means here (and wherever and whenever it
is performed) a return to the godhead and a renewal of life in and
through the godhead.

Other initiation rites are the first step of the child on the ground,
the first touching of the fruit tree, and so on.

The real initiation ceremonies, which take place during and after
the end of puberty, are important. Formerly the youths spent the nights
during this period in the *balai* (meeting-house and guest house), not in
their own houses. There they were under the supervision of one of the
elders, who was responsible for instructing them in the rights and
duties of the adult men which they were to become. In this period they
were instructed in law, the secrets of headhunting and war, masculine
tasks, war-dances and games. At this time, too, their teeth were filed
(as were those of young girls also) and they circumcised themselves in
secret. We do not know enough about what these two activities mean.
The animistic and dynamistic interpretation can hardly be maintained,
and we ought probably to see them as partial self-sacrifice in connection
with the entire renovation of man, for the two activities do not stand
alone but form a whole together with all the others. A young man
becomes a full member of the society by passing through the initiation
rites, by taking part for the first time in human sacrifice and headhunting, and by the acquisition of costly possessions belonging to the
pusaka (sacred jars, gongs, weapons). . . .

Young girls approaching puberty were formerly shut up (*bakowo*), sometimes for two or three years, in a separately built room above or next to the room where the parents slept. This room (*kowo*) is identical with the *rahan* mentioned in myths and represented on the priests' maps, and stands for the primeval waters. All the rites connected with this period show us that the young girl is led to the Underworld. She stays there for a certain time, and when this is up she assumes the form of a watersnake. The ceremonies for the ending of the *kowo*-period are an occasion at which the whole community is represented; people gather from the surrounding villages and together ritually demolish the room, and then take the girl down to the river for a ritual bath. After this bath she comes back to earth from the Underworld, and as a new person begins her new life as a full member, socially and religiously, of the community. During the *kowo*-period the young girl used to be waited on by an old and respected female slave who instructed her in the rights, duties, and tasks of a woman. There are numerous *bakowo* myths in Dayak literature which tell us how after the destruction of the entire cosmos (usually through the fault of human beings), only a maiden remained alive, enclosed in a tall tree or in a rock. It was possible to communicate with her through a small hole, but she could not be seen. She was given the raw materials for skilled tasks such as weaving cloth or cane, and after a time beautifully executed objects were returned. During the *bakowo*-period the young girl may not be touched. This would cause not only her own death, viz. remaining for ever in the Underworld, but also the ruin of the entire cosmos, from which it could be saved only through the medium of human sacrifice. This event also is clearly told in the myths. Usually there is a young man burning with love for the imprisoned girl. He tries to free her from the tree or rock, and when this is unsuccessful he in despair cuts off the arm of his sweetheart. At this, the opening closes up and the girl disappears for ever. The *kowo*-period is sacred. The maiden lives with the godhead. She lives neither in this world nor in this present time, but in the primeval waters and in primeval time, and in her are accomplished the creative, beneficent activities of this time, which nothing may disturb or ruin, for any disturbance means an interference in the other world and will be punished by the angry, vengeful, divine judge with the destruction of the cosmos. As soon as the *kowo*-period is concluded the girl is again governed by worldly laws. . . .

Death. The most important and the concluding stage in the life of man is death. It does not mean passing away and the extinction of life, but returning home to the divine world and being taken up again into the social and divine unity of mythical primeval time. Death is a passage to a new existence, the transition to a new and true life. It is thus an event of the same kind as birth, initiation, and marriage, and it is not only the most important of all these stages of life but receives the fullest and the most detailed ceremonial expression: all the other stages reach their culmination and final conclusion in this.

The deceased person is removed from secular time and the laws of this world, and is placed back in mythical antiquity. This is shown by the rites performed at death, and by the preparation of the coffin. The coffin is made in the shape of a boat. But it is not only a boat, and it is not primarily intended for the journey of the dead person to the village of the dead, for his voyage on lake and river. This is not the explanation of the shape. The coffin is not only a boat but also the Hornbill or the Watersnake. The Hornbill coffin is for dead women, the Watersnake coffin for dead men. The sides of the coffin are decorated with a painted or carved liana which represents the Tree of Life and is named after it. The whole coffin is ornamented with coloured dots. They represent gold and jewels and are called after the Gold Mountain and Jewel Mountain of mythical antiquity. The coffin is provided with totemic emblems: cloth for a woman, blowpipe and sword for a man.

What is the meaning of this coffin? It is boat, Tree of Life, godhead, and primeval mountain. We might say that it is a material representation of the Creation Myth. The two coffins are identical with the two boats in which the first human couple drifted on the waters of life. They bear, too, the names of those boats (viz. *banama hintan* and *banama bulau*). Furthermore, they are identical with the Tree of Life (the liana), for they originated from it and are thus the Tree itself. They are also the godhead, for the total godhead is really the Tree of Life. Finally, they are also identical with the two primeval mountains, for out of their contact originated the head-dress of Mahatala from which came the Tree of Life. The coffin is thus the cosmic/divine totality of primeval times, and this totality is closely related, logically and theologically, to the creation myth. The dead return to the total godhead and the salvation of primeval time, and they are taken up into both of these.

The coffins, and many important rituals as well, show us clearly that the dead fall into two categories, one associated with the Upperworld and the other with the Underworld. This dichotomy, however, cannot be simply a sexual matter, as we have seen, but is connected with the divine and social dichotomy. We cannot therefore speak simply of a man's coffin and a woman's coffin, for both coffins must earlier have appertained to the two groups of which one was connected with the Upperworld and used the Hornbill coffin, while the other was connected with the Underworld and used the Watersnake coffin. . . .

In spite of this dichotomy, which also plays an important part in the action of conducting the dead during the mortuary ceremonies, it is the idea of unity that is far more stressed today. The deceased returns to the mythical primeval antiquity, to the divine totality, and to the primeval village Batu Nindan Tarong. In primeval time he finds himself again in the Tree of Life and in the godhead, and the godhead re-enacts a new creation in him. The deceased becomes again the first man floating in the boat, which itself is the godhead, on the primeval waters, until he is brought into the village of the dead, where he is united with his ancestors for ever. Man originated from the godhead. The godhead has guided him through the various stages of life until his death, until he returns to the godhead and is given new life and a new existence in the Upperworld from which he once departed and from which there will be no more separation.

Notes

1 Law, custom, right behaviour.   2 Taboo.
3 The deity of the Underworld or the primeval waters.

Hans Schärer, *Ngaju Religion: The Conception of God among a South Borneo People*, translation by Rodney Needham (The Hague, 1963), pp. 81-94

81. THE SACRED ERA (THE NGAJU DAYAK OF SOUTH BORNEO)

The sacred era of this world, created and given by the godhead, has a beginning and also an end. The beginning was the creation, the end will be brought about by the passage of time. Strictly speaking, this era lasts only one year. The beginning occurs with the appearance of the *patendo* (the constellation of Orion) and with the beginning of work in the fields. The course of the year is primarily determined by various tasks in the rice-fields which are begun about the second half of May. At this time the men, under the direction of the village headmen, look for places in the forest where they can make their fields. Each family makes its own field, and the clearing is marked out as their own possession. First the bushes and lianas are chopped down and the high trees are felled. From the middle of August to the middle of September the felled trees, which have dried out in the meantime, are burnt and the earth is fertilized with the ashes. The rice is planted from the middle of September to the middle of October. The harvest is reaped in February to March. During the sacred year life, work, and the division of labour between men and women are rigorously governed by divine regulations and carried out according to the will of the total godhead.

The hardest field tasks—felling trees, burning off, fencing, and building field huts—are carried out only by men. Sowing and havesting are shared by men and women. Guarding the fields against depredations by animals (monkeys, deer, wild pigs) and weeding are women's jobs. During this time the men go on trading expeditions or looking for forest products.

In the course of the sacred year working agreements must not be broken. The whole community forms a unity and the arbitrary or intentional breaking of this unity would result in harm not only to those taking part but also to the crops.

The sacred year (and with it the world-era) ends with the harvest. The two or three months between the harvest and the resumption of work in the fields are called *helat nyelo*, the time between the years. For a few weeks in this period the so-called harvest feast or new year's feast is held. But the ceremonies which are performed show that this feast has a far deeper significance. It is not only that another harvest has been brought in, or that another year is passed: there is much more to it than this, for a whole era in the existence of the world has elapsed, a period of creation is ended, and the people return not only from their fields to their village but they return also to the primeval time of myth and the beginning of everything. People return to the Tree of Life and the divine totality, and live and act in it. This is most clear in the lifting of all secular regulations and in the sub mission to the commandments of mythical antiquity and the total/ ambivalent godhead.

We should direct particular attention to this period of *helat nyelo*. It is, as we have said, the period in which all those in the fields return to the village. It is the time in which the representatives of the entire community gather, and in which the inhabitants of the different villages in any area (which are equivalent to the former total unity of the tribe) together hold feasts, perform rituals, compete in sporting events and go on fishing and hunting expeditions, for which they decorate their spears and equipment with ritual ornamentation (the spears with ribbons or woven bands, fishing equipment with cosmic colours). This custom displays the emphasis on totality in its cosmic/divine and social importance. This is a joyful and sublime period, in which the major sacrifices are offered, and after the expiry of the world-era (the old year) the creation is re-enacted and the entire cosmos renovated. It is the time in which Jata[1] emerges from the primeval waters and Mahatala[2] descends from the primeval mountain, when both are united, personally and in their totemic emblems, in the Tree of Life, from which the new creation originates. (The erection of a Tree of Life is one of the most important acts in the whole ceremony.) It is the time of passing away and becoming, of cosmic/divine and social totality. Life and laws are not undone but delivered, for the old passes away and the new comes into being. There is no question of disorder (even if it may appear so to us), but of another order. During this sacred period there is a return to cosmic/divine, social and sexual unity and wholeness. People live and act in the total/ambivalent godhead and in the Tree of Life. At this time they are the ambivalent godhead and the ambivalent Tree of Life and they remain thus until the re-enactment of the creation, until the renewal of the world, until the separation of the groups from the Tree of Life, and until the re-establishment of the entire secular, cosmic/divine, and social order. When the feast reaches its climax there is sexual exchange and intercourse between the participants. This total and mass sexual intercourse is not adulterous or contrary to hadat[3] and does not infringe or destroy the cosmic/divine order; it is the union of the Upperworld and Underworld, Matahala and Jata, in a personal and sexual whole and unity. It takes place in accordance with the commandments of the total/ambivalent godhead, and those who bring it about are in its accomplishment the total godhead itself. To describe it as disorder or unchastity, or to interpret it as a survival from a former promiscuity, is to see it with European eyes and from a European point of view. It takes place strictly according to the laws governing the period 'between the years,' and is only to be understood in relation to the conception of God and the myth of creation. In these lie its foundation and its religious meaning.

Notes

1 The deity of the Underworld or the primeval waters.
2 The deity of the Upperworld.   3 Law, custom, right behaviour.

Hans Schärer, *Ngaju Religion: The Conception of God among a South Borneo People*, translation by Rodney Needham (The Hague, 1963), pp. 94-7

82. HUNTING IS A HOLY OCCUPATION (NASKAPI INDIANS OF THE LABRADOR PENINSULA)

To the Montagnais-Naskapi hunters on the barest subsistence level—the animals of the forest, the tundra, and the waters of the interior and the coast, exist in a specific relation. They have become the objects of engrossing magico-religious activity, for to them hunting is a holy occupation. The animals pursue an existence corresponding to that of man as regards emotions and purpose in life. The difference between man and animals, they believe, lies chiefly in outward form. In the beginning of the world, before humans were formed, all animals existed grouped under 'tribes' of their kinds who could talk like men, and were even covered with the same protection. When addressing animals in a spiritual way in his songs, or using the drum, the conjuror uses an expresson which means freely, 'you and I wear the same covering and have the same mind and spiritual strength.' This statement was explained as meaning not that man had fur, not that animals wore garments, but their equality was spiritual and embraced or eclipsed the physical.

There has been no change in these native doctrines since they were first recorded in the seventeenth century in the words of the French priests. 'They believe that many kinds of animals have reasonable souls. They have superstitions against profaning certain bones of elk, beaver and other beasts or letting dogs gnaw them. They preserve them carefully or throw them into rivers. They pretend that the souls of these animals come to see how bodies are treated and go and tell the living beasts and those that are dead, so that if ill treated the beasts of the same kind will no longer allow themselves to be taken in this world or the next' (Father Le Clerq, 1691).

The belief of this same character among the central Algonkian is expressed succinctly by William Jones: 'It was thought that every living creature possessed a soul and that to get control of the soul made it possible to get control of the possessor of the soul. It was on such a theory that the Ojibwas hunted for game.'

The killing of animals, then, entails much responsibility in the spiritual sense. Since the animals' spirits at death are forgathered in their proper realms to be reincarnated later, the slaying of them places the hunter in the position, theoretically, of being their enemy. But he is not that in the ordinary sense of the term, because it is the ordained manner of procedure and one to which they are adjusted and inured. Requirements of conduct towards animals exist, however, which have to be known and carried out by the hunter. His success depends upon his knowledge, and, they argue, since no one can know everything and act to perfection, the subject of magico-religious science becomes, even from the native point of view, an inexhaustible one. Therefore, failure in the chase, the disappearance of the game from the hunter's districts, with ensuing famine, starvation, weakness, sickness, and death, are all attributed to the hunter's ignorance of some hidden principle of behaviour towards the animals or to his wilful disregard of them. The former is ignorance. The latter is sin. The two together constitute the educational sphere of the Montagnais-Naskapi, and the schooling is hard enough in reality although it may seem to the civilized imagination a mere travesty of mental training.

F. G. Speck, *Naskapi, The Savage Hunters of the Labrador Peninsula* (Norman, Okla: University of Oklahoma Press, 1935)

83. THE SACREDNESS OF AGRICULTURE: AHURA-MAZDA INSTRUCTS ZARATHUSTRA

('Vidēvdāt,' Fargard III)

'Unhappy is the land that has long lain unsown with the seed of the sower and wants a good husbandman, like a well-shapen maiden who has long gone childless and wants a good husband.

'He who would till the earth, O Spitama Zarathustra! with the left arm and the right, with the right arm and the left, unto him will she bring forth plenty of fruit: even as it were a lover sleeping with his bride on her bed; the bride will bring forth children, the earth will bring forth plenty of fruit.

'He who would till the earth, O Spitama Zarathustra! with the left arm and the right, with the right arm and the left, unto him thus says the Earth: "O thou man! who dost till me with the left arm and the right, with the right arm and the left, here shall I ever go on bearing, bringing forth all manner of food, bring corn first to thee."

'He who does not till the earth, O Spitama Zarathustra! with the left arm and the right, with the right arm and the left, unto him thus says the Earth: 'O thou man! who dost not till me with the left arm and the right, with the right arm and the left, ever shalt thou stand at the door of the stranger, among those who beg for bread; the refuse and the crumbs of the bread are brought unto thee, brought by those who have profusion of wealth." '

'Zarathustra asked :] O maker of the material world, thou Holy One ! What is the food that fills the Religion of Mazda?

Ahura Mazda answered : 'It is sowing corn again and again, O Spitama Zarathustra !

'He who sows corn, sows righteousness; he makes the Religion of Mazda walk, he suckles the Religion of Mazda; as well as he could do with a hundred men's feet, with a thousand women's breasts, with ten thousand sacrificial formulas.

'When barley was created; the Daevas started up, when it grew, then fainted the Daevas' hearts; when the knots came, the Daevas groaned; when the ear came, the Daevas flew away. In that house the Daevas stay, wherein wheat perishes. It is though red hot iron were turned about in their throats, when there is plenty of corn.'

Translation by James Darmester, *The Zend-Avesta*, part I, in *Sacred Books of the East*, IV (2nd ed.; Oxford, 1895), pp. 29-31

84. JAIN RESPECT FOR LIFE

('Acārānga-sūtra,' I, 1)

Earth is afflicted and wretched, it is hard to teach, it has no discrimination. Unenlightened men, who suffer from the effects of past deeds, cause great pain in a world full of pain already, for in earth souls are individually embodied. If, thinking to gain praise, honour, or respect . . . or to achieve a good rebirth . . , or to win salvation, or to escape pain, a man sins against earth or causes or permits others to do so, . . . he will not gain joy or wisdom. . . . Injury to the earth is like striking, cutting, maiming, or killing a blind man . . . Knowing this man should not sin against earth or cause or permit others to do so. He who understands the nature of sin against earth is called a true sage who understands karma. . . .

And there are many souls embodied in water. Truly water . . . is alive. . . . He who injures the lives in water does not understand the nature of sin or renounce it. . . . Knowing this, a man should not sin against water, or cause or permit others to do so. He who understands the nature of sin against water is called a true sage who understands karma. . . .

By wicked or careless acts one may destroy fire-beings, and moreover, harm other beings by means of fire. . . . For there are creatures living in earth, grass, leaves, wood, cowdung, or dustheaps, and jumping creatures which . . . fall into a fire if they come near it. If touched by fire, they shrivel up . . . lose their senses, and die. . . . He who understands the nature of sin in respect of fire is called a true sage who understands karma.

And just as it is the nature of a man to be born and grow old, so is it the nature of a plant to be born and grow old. . . . One is endowed with reason, and so is the other; one is sick, if injured, and so is the other; one grows larger and so does the other; one changes with time, and so does the other. . . . He who understands the nature of sin against plants is called a true sage who understands karma. . . .

All beings with two, three, four, or five senses, . . . in fact all creation, know individually pleasure and displeasure, pain, terror, and sorrow. All are full of fears which come from all directions. And yet there exist people who would cause greater pain to them. . . . Some kill animals for sacrifice, some for their skin, flesh, blood, . . . feathers, teeth, or tusks; . . . some kill them intentionally and some unintentionally; some kill because they have been previously injured by them, . . . and some because they expect to be injured. He who harms animals has not understood or renounced deeds of sin. . . . He who understands the nature of sin against animals is called a true sage who understands karma. . . .

A man who is averse from harming even the wind knows the sorrow of all things living. . . . He who knows what is bad for himself knows what is bad for others, and he who knows what is bad for others knows what is bad for himself. This reciprocity should always be borne in mind. Those whose minds are at peace and who are free from passions do not desire to live [at the expense of others]. . . . He who understands the nature of sin against wind is called a true sage who understands karma.

In short he who understands the nature of sin in respect of all the six types of living beings is called a true sage who understands karma.

Translation by A. L. Basham; from abridged version in Theodore de Bary, *Sources of Indian Tradition* (New York: Columbia University Press, 1958), pp. 62-3

B. ORIGIN AND DESTINY OF THE SOUL— AND THE POWERS OF MANA

85. SOULS, DREAMS, DEATH, ECSTASY

(E. B. Tylor's Theory of Animism)

To understand the popular conceptions of the human soul or spirit, it is instructive to notice the words which have been found suitable to express it. The ghost or phantasm seen by the dreamer or the visionary is in unsubstantial form, like a shadow or reflection, and thus the familiar term of the *shade* comes in to express the soul. Thus the Tasmanian word for the shadow is also that for the spirit, the Algonquins describe a man's soul as *otahchuk*, 'his shadow'; the Quiché language uses *natub* for 'shadow, soul'; the Arawak *ueja* means 'shadow, soul, image'; and Abipones made the one word *loákal* serve for shadow, soul, echo, image.' The Zulus not only use the word *tunzi* for 'shadow, spirit, ghost,' but they consider that at death the shadow of a man will in some way depart from the corpse, to become an ancestral spirit. The Basutos not only call the spirit remaining after death the *seriti* or 'shadow,' but they think that if a man walks on the river bank, a crocodile may seize his shadow in the water and draw him in; while in Old Calabar there is found the same identification of the spirit with the *ukpon* or 'shadow,' for a man to lose which is fatal. There are thus found among the lower races not only the types of those familiar classic terms, the *skia* and *umbra*, but also what seems the fundamental thought of the stories of shadowless men still current in the folklore of Europe, and familiar to modern readers in Chamisso's tale of Peter Schlemihl. Thus the dead in Purgatory knew that Dante was alive when they saw that, unlike theirs, his figure cast a shadow on the ground. Other attributes are taken into the notion of soul or spirit, with especial regard to its being the cause of life. Thus the Caribs, connecting the pulses with spiritual beings, and especially considering that in the heart dwells man's chief soul, destined to a future heavenly life, could reasonably use the one word *iouanni* for 'soul, life, heart.'

The Tongans supposed the soul to exist throughout the whole extension of the body, but particularly in the heart. . . .

The act of breathing, so characteristic of the higher animals during life, and coinciding so closely with life in its departure, has been repeatedly and naturally identified with the life or soul itself. . . . It is thus that West Australians used one word *waug* for 'breath, spirit, soul'; that in the Netela language of California, *piuts* means 'life, breath, soul'; that certain Greenlanders reckoned two souls to man, namely his shadow and his breath; that the Malays say the soul of the dying man escapes through his nostrils, and in Java use the same word *nawa* for 'breath, life, soul.' How the notions of life, heart, breath and phantom unite in the one conception of a soul or spirit, and at the same time how loose and vague such ideas are among barbaric races, is well brought into view in the answers to a religious inquest held in 1528 among the natives of Nicaragua. 'When they die, there comes out of their mouth something that resembles a person and is called *julio* [Aztec *yuli* = to live]. This being goes to the place where the man and woman are. It is like a person, but does not die, and the body remains here.'

. . . The conception of the soul as breath may be followed up through Semitic and Aryan etymology, and thus into the main streams of the philosophy of the world. Hebrew shows *nephesh*, 'breath,' passing into all the meanings of 'life, soul, mind, animal,' while *ruach* and *neshamah* make the like transition from 'breath' to 'spirit'; and to these the Arabic *nefs* and *ruh* correspond. The same is the history of Sanskrit *ātman* and *prāna*, of Greek *psychē* and *pneuma*, of Latin *animus, anima, spiritus*. So Slavonic *duch* has developed the meaning of 'breath' into that of soul or spirit; and the dialects of the Gypsies have this word *duk* with the meaning of 'breath, spirit, ghost,' whether these pariahs brought the word from India as part of their inheritance of Aryan speech, or whether they adopted it in their migration across Slavonic lands. German *geist* and English *ghost*, too, may possibly have the same original sense of breath. And if any should think such expressions due to mere metaphor, they may judge the strength of the implied connection between breath and spirit by cases of most unequivocal significance. Among the Seminoles of Florida, when a woman died in childbirth, the infant was held over her face to receive her parting spirit, and thus acquire strength and knowledge for its future use. These Indians could have well understood why at the death-bed of an ancient Roman, the nearest kinsman leant over to inhale the last breath of the departing (*et excipies hanc animam ore pio).*

Their state of mind is kept up to this day among Tyrolese peasants, who can still fancy a good man's soul to issue from his mouth at death like a little white cloud.

It will be shown that men, in their composite and confused notions of the soul, have brought into connection a list of manifestations of life and thought even more multifarious than this. But also, seeking to avoid such perplexity of combination, they have sometimes endeavoured to define and classify more closely, especially by the theory that man has a combination of several kinds of spirit, soul, or image, to which different functions belong. Already in the barbaric world such classification has been invented or adopted. Thus the Fijians distinguished between a man's 'dark spirit' or shadow, which goes to Hades, and his 'light spirit' or reflection in water or a mirror, which stays near where he dies. The Malagasy say that the *saina* or mind vanishes at death, the *aina* or life becomes mere air, but the *matoatoa* or ghost hovers round the tomb. In North America, the duality of the soul is a strongly marked Algonquin belief; one soul goes out and sees dreams while the other remains behind; at death one of the two abides with the body, and for this the survivors leave offerings of food, while the other departs to the land of the dead. A division into three souls is also known, and the Dakotas say that man has four souls, one remaining with the corpse, one staying in the village, one going in the air, and one to the land of spirits. The Karens distinguish between the 'la' or 'kelah,' the personal life-phantom, and the 'thah,' the responsible moral soul. . . .

The early animistic theory of vitality, regarding the function of life as caused by the soul, offers to the savage mind an explanation of several bodily and mental conditions, as being effects of a departure of the soul or some of its constituent spirits. This theory holds a wide and strong position in savage biology. The South Australians express it when they say of one insensible or unconscious, that he is 'wilyamarraba,' i.e., 'without soul.' Among the Algonquin Indians of North America, we hear of sickness being accounted for by the patient's 'shadow' being unsettled or detached from his body, and of the convalescent being reproached for exposing himself before his shadow was safely settled down in him; where we should say that a man was ill and recovered, they would consider that he died, but came again. Another account from among the same race explains the condition of men lying in lethargy or trance; their souls have travelled to the banks of the River of Death, but have been driven back and return to re-animate their bodies. Among the Fijians, 'when any one faints or dies, their spirit, it is said, may sometimes be brought back by calling after it; and occasionally the ludicrous scene is witnessed of a stout man lying at full length, and bawling out lustily for the return of his own soul.' . . . Thus, in various countries, the bringing back of lost souls becomes a regular part of the sorcerer's or priest's profession. The Salish Indians of Oregon regard the spirit as distinct from the vital principle, and capable of quitting the body for a short time without the patient being conscious of its absence; but to avoid fatal consequences it must be restored as soon as possible, and accordingly the medicine-man in solemn form replaces it down through the patient's head. . . . The Karens of Burma will run about pretending to catch a sick man's wandering soul, or as they say with the Greeks and Slavs, his 'butterfly' (leip-pya), and at last drop it down upon his head. The Karen doctrine of the 'la' is indeed a perfect and well-marked vitalistic system. This la, soul, ghost, or genius, may be separated from the body it belongs to and it is a matter of the deepest interest to the Karen to keep his la with him, by calling it, making offerings of food to it, and so forth. It is especially when the body is asleep, that the soul goes out and wanders; if it is detained beyond a certain time, disease ensues, and if permanently, then its owner dies. When the 'wee' or spirit-doctor is employed to call back the departed shade or life of a Karen, if he cannot recover it from the region of the dead, he will sometimes take the shade of a living man and transfer it to the dead, while its proper owner, whose soul has ventured out in a dream, sickens and dies. Or when a Karen becomes sick, languid and pining from his la having left him, his friends will perform a ceremony with a garment of the invalid's and a fowl which is cooked and offered with rice, invoking the spirit with formal prayers to come back to the patient. . . .

This same doctrine forms one side of the theory of dreams prevalent among the lower races. Certain of the Greenlanders, Cranz remarks, consider that the soul quits the body in the night and goes out hunting, dancing, and visiting; their dreams, which are frequent and lively, having brought them to this opinion. Among the Indians of North America, we hear of the dreamer's soul leaving his body and wandering in quest of things attractive to it. These things the waking man must endeavour to obtain, lest his soul be troubled, and quit the body altogether. The New Zealanders considered the dreaming soul to leave the body and return, even travelling to the region of the dead to hold converse with its friends. The Tagals of Luzon object to waking a sleeper, on account of the absence of his soul. The Karens, whose theory of the wandering soul has just been noticed, explain dreams to be what this la sees and experiences in its journeys when it has left the body asleep. They even account with much acuteness for the fact that we are apt to dream of people and places which we knew before; the leip-pya, they say, can only visit the regions where the body it belongs to has been already. . . .

The North American Indians allowed themselves the alternative of supposing a dream to be either a visit from the soul of the person or object dreamt of, or a sight seen by the rational soul, gone out for an excursion while the sensitive soul remains in the body. So the Zulu may be visited in a dream by the shade of an ancestor, the itongo, who comes to warn him of danger, or he may himself be taken by the itongo in a dream to visit his distant people, and see that they are in trouble; as for the man who is passing into the morbid conditions of the professional seer, phantoms are continually coming to talk to him in his sleep, till he becomes, as the expressive native phrase is, 'a house of dreams.' In the lower range of culture, it is perhaps most frequently taken for granted that a man's apparition in a dream is a visit from his disembodied spirit, where the dreamer, to use an expressive Ojibwa idiom, 'sees when asleep.' Such a thought comes out clearly in the Fijian opinion that a living man's spirit may leave the body, to trouble other people in their sleep or in a recent account of an old Indian woman of British Columbia sending for the medicine-man to drive away the dead people who came to her every night. A modern observer's description of the state of mind of the Negroes of West Africa in this respect is extremely characteristic and instructive. 'All their dreams are construed into visits from the spirits of their deceased friends. The cautions, hints, and warnings which come to them through this source are received with the most serious and deferential attention, and are always acted upon in their waking hours. The habit of relating their dreams, which is universal, greatly promotes the habit of dreaming itself, and hence their sleeping hours are characterized by almost as much intercourse with the dead as their waking are with the living. This is, no doubt, one of the reasons of their excessive superstitiousness. Their imaginations become so lively that they can scarcely distinguish between their dreams and their waking thoughts, between the real and the ideal, and they consequently utter falsehood without intending, and profess to see things which never existed.'

To the Greek of old, the dream-soul was what to the modern savage it still is. Sleep, loosing cares of mind, fell on Achilles as he lay by the sounding sea, and there stood over him the soul of Patroklos, like to him altogether in stature, and the beauteous eyes, and the voice, and the garments that wrapped his skin; he spake, and Achilles stretched out to grasp him with loving hands, but caught him not, and like a smoke the soul sped twittering below the earth. Along the ages that separate us from Homeric times, the apparition in dreams of men living or dead has been a subject of philosophic speculation and of superstitious fear. Both the phantom of the living and the ghost of the dead figure in Cicero's typical tale. Two Arcadians came to Megara together, one lodged at a friend's house, the other at an inn. In the night this latter appeared to his fellow-traveller, imploring his help, for the innkeeper was plotting his death; the sleeper sprang up in alarm, but thinking the vision of no consequence went to sleep again. Then a second time his companion appeared to him, to entreat that though he had failed to help, he would at least avenge, for the innkeeper had killed him and hidden his body in a dung-cart, wherefore he charged his fellow-traveller to be early next morning at the city-gate before the cart passed out. Struck with this second dream, the traveller went as bidden, and there found the cart; the body of the murdered man was in it, and the innkeeper was brought to justice. . . .

The evidence of visions corresponds with the evidence of dreams in their bearing on primitive theories of the soul, and the two classes of phenomena substantiate and supplement one another. . . . Human ghosts are among the principal of these phantasmal figures. There is no doubt that honest visionaries describe ghosts as they really appear to their perception, while even the impostors who pretend to see them conform to the description thus established; thus, in West Africa, a man's *kla* or soul, becoming at his death a *sisa* or ghost, can remain in the house with the corpse, but is only visible to the wong-man, the spirit-doctor. Sometimes the phantom has the characteristic quality of not being visible to all of an assembled company. Thus the natives of the Antilles believed that the dead appeared on the roads when one went alone, but not when many went together; thus among the Finns the ghosts of the dead were to be seen by the shamans, but not by men generally unless in dreams. Such is perhaps the meaning of the description of Samuel's ghost, visible to the witch of Endor, but not to Saul, for he has to ask her what it is she sees. . . .

That the apparitional human soul bears the likeness of its fleshly body, is the principle implicitly accepted by all who believe it really and objectively present in dreams and visions. My own view is that nothing but dreams and visions could have ever put into men's minds such an idea as that of souls being ethereal images of bodies. It is thus habitually taken for granted in animistic philosophy, savage or civilized, that souls set free from the earthly body are recognized by a likeness to it which they still retain, whether as ghostly wanderers on earth or inhabitants of the world beyond the grave. . . . This world-wide thought, coming into view here in a multitude of cases from all grades of culture, needs no collection of ordinary instances to illustrate it. But a quaint and special group of beliefs will serve to display the thoroughness with which the soul is thus conceived as an image of the body. As a consistent corollary to such an opinion, it is argued that the mutilation of the body will have a corresponding effect upon the soul, and very low savage races have philosophy enough to work out this idea. Thus it was recorded of the Indians of Brazil by one of the early European visitors, that they 'believe that the dead arrive in the other world wounded or hacked to pieces, in fact just as they left this.' Thus, too, the Australian who has slain his enemy will cut off the right thumb of the corpse, so that although the spirit will become a hostile ghost, it cannot throw with its mutilated hand the shadowy spear, and may be safely left to wander, malignant but harmless. . . .

In studying the nature of the soul as conceived among the lower races, and in tracing such conceptions onward among the higher, circumstantial details are available. It is as widely recognized among mankind that souls or ghosts have voices, as they have visible forms, and indeed the evidence for both of is of the same nature. Men who perceive evidently that souls do talk when they present themselves in dream or vision, naturally take for granted at once the objective reality of the ghostly voice, and of the the ghostly form from which it proceeds. This is involved in the series of narratives of spiritual communications with living men, from savagery onward to civilization, while the more modern doctrine of the the subjectivity of such phenomena recognizes the phenomena themselves, but offers a different explanation of them. One special conception, however, requires particular notice. This defines the spirit-voice as being a low murmur, chirp, or whistle, as it were the ghost of a voice. The Algonquin Indians of North America could hear the shadow-souls of the dead chirp like crickets. The divine spirits of the New Zealand dead, coming to converse with the living, utter their words in whistling tones, and such utterances by a squeaking noise are mentioned elsewhere in Polynesia. The Zulu diviner's familiar spirits are ancestral manes, who talk in a low whistling tone short of a full whistle, whence they have their name if 'imilozi' or whistlers. These ideas correspond with classic descriptions of the ghostly voice, as a 'twitter' or 'thin murmur.'. . .

The conception of dreams and visions as caused by present objective figures, and the identification of such phantom souls with the shadow and the breath, has led to the treatment of souls as substantial material beings. Thus it is a usual proceeding to make openings through solid materials to allow souls to pass. The Iroquois in old times used to leave an opening in the grave for the lingering soul to visit its body, and some of them still bore holes in the coffin for the same purpose. . . . The Chinese make a hole in the roof to let out the soul at death. And lastly, the custom of opening a window or door for the departing soul when it quits the body is to this day a very familiar superstition in France, Germany and England. Again, the souls of the dead are thought susceptible of being beaten, hurt and driven like any other living creatures. Thus the Queensland aborigines would beat the air in an annual mock fight, held to scare away the souls that death had let loose among the living since last year. Thus North American Indians, when they had tortured an enemy to death, ran about crying and beating with sticks to scare the ghost away. . . .

Explicit statements as to the substance of soul are to be found both among low and high races, in an instructive series of definitions. The Tongans imagined the human soul to be the finer or more aeriform part of the body, which leaves it suddenly at the moment of death; something comparable to the perfume and essence of a flower as related to the more solid vegetable fibre. The Greenland seers described the soul as they habitually perceived it in their visions; it is pale and soft, they said, and he who tries to seize it feels nothing, for it has no flesh nor bone sinew. The Caribs did not think the soul so immaterial as to be invisible, but said it was subtle and thin like a purified body. Turning to higher races, we may take the Siamese as an example of a people who conceive of souls as consisting of subtle matter escaping sight and touch, or as united to a swiftly moving aerial body. In the classic world, it is recorded as an opinion of Epicurus that 'they who say the soul is incorporeal talk folly, for it could neither do nor suffer anything were it such.' Among the Fathers, Irenaeus describes souls as incorporeal in comparison with mortal bodies, and Tertullian relates a vision or revelation of a certain Montanist prophetess, of the soul seen by her corporeally, thin and lucid, aerial in colour and human in form. . . .

Among rude races, the original conception of the human soul seems to have been that of etherality, or vaporous materiality, which has held so large a place in human thought ever since. In fact, the later metaphysical notion of immateriality could scarcely have conveyed any meaning to a savage. It is moreover to be noticed that, as to the whole nature and action of apparitional souls, the lower philosophy escapes various difficulties which down to modern times have perplexed metaphysicians and theologians of the civilized world. Considering the thin ethereal body of the soul to be itself sufficient and suitable for visability, movement, and speech, the primitive animist required no additional hypotheses to account for these manifestations. . . .

Departing from the body at the time of death, the soul or spirit is considered set free to linger near the tomb, to wander on earth or flit in the air, or to travel to the proper region of spirits—the world beyond the grave. . . . Men do not stop short at the persuasion that death releases the soul to a free and active existence, but they quite logically proceed to assist nature, by slaying men in order to liberate their souls for ghostly uses. Thus there arises one of the most widespread, distinct, and intelligible rites of animistic religion—that of funeral human sacrifice for the service of the dead. When a man of rank dies and his soul departs to its own place, wherever and whatever that place may be, it is a rational inference of early philosophy that the souls of attendants, slaves, and wives, put to death at his funeral, will make the same journey and continue their service in the next life, and the argument is frequently stretched further, to include the souls of new victims sacrificed in order that they may enter upon the same ghostly servitude. It will appear from the ethnography of this rite that it is not strongly marked in the very lowest levels of culture, but that, arising in the lower barbaric stage, it develops itself in the higher, and thenceforth continues or dwindles in survival.

Sir Edward Burnett Tylor, *Religion in Primitive Culture* (New York: Harper Torchbook, 1958), pp. 14-42 (originally published as *Primitive Culture*)

86. AN AUSTRALIAN CONCEPTION OF THE SOUL IN LIFE AND DEATH

(Murngin)

Each Murngin man and woman has two souls. One is looked upon as fundamental and real, and is felt to be the true soul, the soul from the heart, while the other is considered a trickster, of little value, and only in a vague way associated with the 'true man.' The first is the birimbir or warro, and the second is the mokoi or shadow soul. The warro is the totemic well spirit. It can be seen reflected in the water when one looks in it. It comes to one during good dreams. The warro, when a man dies, becomes 'all the same as a fish.' It lives with and in the totemic emblems. . . .

The trickster soul is called shadow soul before death and mokoi when it leaves the body and goes into the jungle and bush country. 'Our old people reckon that the shadow soul is all the same as a bad spirit. It's that thing that makes me bad. My shadow always comes with me. The shadows of other things and creatures [besides man] are not souls but only shadows.' The mokoi soul is supposed to live more or less all over the body. It is a kind of vague duplicate of it. Sometimes one is told that only the head of a man is made into a mokoi at his death and that mokoi has no body. In the pictures drawn of it and the representations made in the dances, the mokoi is always possessed of a body, but it is distorted and made to appear ugly and unpleasant.

The warro is constantly undergoing change of status. It originates in the totem well, comes to its human father in a dream under miraculous circumstances where it is directed to its mother's womb, lodges there, is born in a normal number of months, and then lives in the heart of the new human organism during the period of the organism's life of the flesh unless it is stolen by a black sorcerer. After death there is a period of some indecision between the land of the living and the land of the dead, but it finally returns to the totemic well whence it came. It is in the symbol of the soul and its relations to the sacred and profane elements in Murngin civilization that we find mirrored the structure and values of the society. The soul supplies the eternal element to the cultural life of an individual Murngin. It lifts man from the simple profane animal level and allows him to participate fully in the sacred eternal values of the civilization that was, is, and will be. It finally and eternally ties the man whose heart it occupies to his totem, the symbol of all clan unity in Murngin culture, since the soul at death is one of the prominent elements in the configuration of associated items found in the clan's totemic water, the water which is the essence of life. Here live the great totemic ancestors who existed in the time of the Wawilak creator sisters when the Wongar totems walked the earth, and whose sacred names are used by the profane living only when these living have been purified by the great rituals, when they are part of the sacred and eternal elements in the culture, when man and his totems participate as one in the totemic rituals. Here, too, in the well, lie the totemic ancestors who died at the beginning of time, and the more recently dead whose emotional bonds with the living are still strong. The more recent ancestors who have gone through the long purifying mortuary ritual which removed all the profane elements of the personality (whose mokoi spirit has gone into the bush with his other evil comrades) are, in their nature, of such sacredness that they can be absorbed into the body of the totem itself. And when the totemic essence of the totem animals is induced into the emblem, they also enter and participate in the spiritual life of the Murngin during the great rituals and then return to the sacred water hole. After the ritual, the emblem is buried beneath the mud of the totem well and allowed to rot, and the ancestor spirits and the totemic spirit return to the subterranean depths. Man goes through exactly the same cycle of existence as the totemic spirit. The totemic spirit enters into the sacred water hole, goes through the ordinary water at the top of the well into the subterranean depths, and finally into the totem water beneath, where the Wongar ancestors live, becoming a part of the sacred configuration. The soul exactly the same thing.

The soul, the totemic spirit, the Wongar or totemic ancestors, are all expressions of the fundamental sacred essence, the ultimate symbol of which is the totemic well, which is the repository of all the individual items which have been or will be incarnate in man or his religious objects.

W. Lloyd Warner, *A Black Civilization* (New York: Harper Torchbook, 1964), pp. 435-7

87. PRE-EXISTENCE AND INCARNATION AMONG NORTH AMERICAN INDIANS

It is in several places common for the breath of life to be conceived as proceeding from the Creator and returning to Him after death. Even without the connection with the breath being specified, the origin of the soul is ascribed to the Creator or the culture hero. The Bella Coola and Wind River Shoshoni thus consider that the Supreme Being is the giver of life and the life-soul. The Sauk Indian refers to his Creator as 'he that gave us life.' Also the kinsmen of the Sauk, the Fox, believe that the life-soul is a gift of the Great Spirit.

In the majority of cases our sources speak of the creation of the life-soul—or rather of life—but we also have data concerning the origin of the free-soul. The Supreme Being of the Bella Coola 'made a soul for each of those about to be born; one af the minor gods fashioned its face; and a goddess rocked it, and sent it below to be born.' The dream-soul of the Sinkaietk is conceived to have come from God—in contradistinction to the supernatural power, which is acquired from the animals. The Fox believe that just as the Supreme Being has given the life-soul, so the culture hero has given the free-soul. . . . The sky god Skan of the Oglala has given man the whole of his psychic equipment, including the life-soul and free-soul. The Wind River Shoshoni describe the free-soul as the gift of the supreme god. . . .

Where the direct statements fail us we with advantage have recourse to the remarks in the mythological tradition concerning the creation of the first human beings: the events of the primeval cosmic era are in many points repeated in the occurrences of later epochs, and the souls of the first man and modern man are of course conceived as having the same origin. Thus we are told in the Navajo myth concerning the first human beings: 'It was the wind that gave them life. It is the wind that comes out of our mouths now that gives us life.' . . .

If, however, a high divinity is conceived as the creator of the world, it is natural to expect that he will also be believed to have given man his soul(s) even if this is not directly stated. But we must remember the danger of reconstructing from logical premises a belief concerning whose existence nothing has been said. The origin of the soul is, it is true, often referred to the god who is also the creator of the earth. But even subordinate divinities may collaborate in the creative act to which the soul is due (the Navajo).

In a couple of cases, however, it seems justified—in certain circumstances—to deduce from the characteristics of the Supreme Being his significance for the origin of the soul. He is often referred to as the Breathmaker or Master of Life. The first of these terms, which has been used by some Muskhogean peoples (the Creek, Chickasaw, Seminole), of course speaks for itself. The second term, the Master of Life, which has for the most part been given to the Creator of the Algonquin Indians (and which in the literature is most frequently found as the designation for the supreme god of the Lenape Indians), presumably refers to the god's capacity as the giver and guardian of the soul. In some cases the supreme deity is called 'the Master of Life and Death.' This indicates, inter alia, that he is also the lord of the realm of the dead—a function which he fills even when he is only referred to as 'the Master of Life.' . . .

Thus, as a rule, the Indians of North America believe that man's spirit has its ultimate origin in the deity himself, either through creation or partial emanation. In a couple of cases, it is true, the father of the child has been stated to beget the soul as well as the physical embryo. But these exceptions are few, and are probably the products of a speculation that has tried to fill a gap in the existing knowledge of the soul or souls.

A soul that is commonly considered to derive from the gods is *ipso facto* not an ordinary profane creation. Whether it is conceived to be a gift of the deity or an emanation of his being, it belongs through its origin to the supernatural world. In its effect, on the other hand, it need not be supernatural in the same way as the mystical power.

The supernatural origin of the human soul finds particularly clear expression in the idea of pre-existence. Here we are not referring to the pre-existence that a reincarnated individual has had in a previous earthly life as man or animal: we are referring to the pre-incarnative existence, man's life before he is incarnated on earth. 'Man' stands here for the individual reality, which from the psychological viewpoint is the extra-physical soul, the free-soul, and which consequently represents man's ego in the pre-incarnative state. . . .

Where the belief in pre-existence in the form referred to here occurs (and it is reported from practically all parts of North America), the most widely varying places are conceived for the pre-incarnate existence. Among the Pueblo peoples of the Southwest the realm of the dead in the underworld is the place where the unborn dwell. One may naturally suspect that the new-born are consequently reincarnated deceased persons. But this is not always the case, for according to the agrarian Pueblo ideology the underworld is also the place for the renewal of life and is the original home of humanity. Also outside the Pueblo area we find the underworld regarded as man's constant place of generation. This is the case among, for instance, the Hidatsa, who possibly distinguished between this place and the realm of the dead. . . .

Where the prenatal original home does not coincide with the realm of the dead it is nevertheless localized to places that remind one of the abode of the dead. The Ingalik believe that 'there is a place filled with the spirits of little children, all impatient to be "called," i.e., born into this life.' In the depths of the forest there is according to Kwakiutl belief a mysterious house. 'Since one of the performances held in this house was that of giving birth, it was probably believed that from this house all generation of men, animals, and plants, took place.' The

Indians in the north-westernmost U.S.A. have a 'babyland' where the unborn children live and play before they come to the earth. The Chinook children lived 'a quite definite existence' before birth, in the sun, the daylight. The Montagnais tradition to the effect that children come from the clouds, on the other hand, is evidently only a pedagogical fiction. According to the Eastern Shawnee, unborn children live on the little stars of the Milky Way. But we also find the belief that they live together with the creator, 'Our Grandmother.'. . .

Narratives of medicine-men who before their human incarnation had been spirit-beings are known from many parts of North America. Le Mercier tells of a Huron medicine-man who declared that he had lived as an *oki* (spirit) under the earth together with a female spirit. Both, possessed by the desire to become human beings, had finally concealed themselves near a path and taken up their abode in a passing woman. She gave birth to them too early; the medicine-man lived, but his female partner, with whom he had fought in the womb, came to the world still-born.

The Central Algonquin and the adjacent Sioux believe that their medicine-men were thunder-beings in a previous life. Thus the Menomini think that 'some babies are actually manitous in human shape, as in the case of thunder boys, who are nothing less than these powerful god beings come to earth for a while; or girls who personify one of the sacred sisters of the eastern sky.' In such circumstances also the name of the person in question is pre-existent, and no other name must be substituted for it during his earthly existence. The reserved character and meditative behaviour of a child is a decisive criterion of its supernatural birth. . . .

Nowhere is the speculation concerning human pre-existence so subtle and sublime as in the notions of the pre-existence of medicine-men entertained by the Dakota tribes. Pond's splendid account of their ideas on this subject deserves to be quoted. He writes: 'The original essence of these men and women, for they appear under both sexes, first wakes into existence floating in ether. As the winged seed of the thistle or of the cottonwood floats on the air, so they are gently wafted by the 'four-winds'—'Taku-skan-skan'—through the regions of space, until, in due time, they find themselves in the abode of some one of the families of the superior gods by whom they are received into intimate fellowship. There the embryonic medicine-man remains till he becomes familiar with the characters, abilities, desires, caprices, and employment of the gods. He becomes essentially assimilated to them, imbibing their spirit and becoming acquainted with all the chants, feasts, fasts, dances and sacrificial rites which it is deemed necessary to impose on men.'. . . .

We find an echo of similar trains of thought in the belief of the Mohave shamans that 'they were present in spirit form at the beginning of the world, at the time when all power, shamanistic and other, was established and allotted.'. . . .

The future human being is often given the opportunity in his pre-existent life to choose the people he wishes to live among on earth and the woman of whom he wants to be born. An Iowa shaman 'inspected many tribes before he decided to be born an Iowa. He declined the Winnebago because they smelled fishy, and so he circled around until he discovered the Iowa. They suited him because they were clean, kept their camps swept up, and sent their women a long way off to menstruate. He came down and entered a dark lodge with a bearskin door, and after quite a stay he came out' (i.e. was born). The ethnocentric viewpoint also decides the future Dakota shaman's choice of parents: he does not want to be born of a white mother, partly because he wishes to have 'Dakota customs and dress,' and partly because his kinsmen the thunderers would kill him if he became white and thereby ignored their instructions. . . .

Concerning the soul's entry into the embryo and its role during the development of the embryo opinion is divided among North American Indians. . . .

The following collection of data shows how various are the conceptions of the soul's (or souls') incarnation.

Some Eskimo imagine that children, like eggs, live in the snow and creep into the womb. The Mackenzie Eskimo have many mutually incompatible notions concerning incarnation. One believes that the soul (*nappan*) comes with the water when the mother drinks, or from the ground when she urinates. Another believes that the child gets a soul at the same time as it is born. And a third believes that the soul comes at some time during the pregnancy, 'how or when she does not know.' The breath of a child to be enters a Tanaina woman like a cold puff of wind. The (free-) soul of a Tlingit Indian is not reincarnated until the body with which it is to be united has been born. The soul of the Hisla Indian is often the spirit of an uncle, which takes possession of his body even before the birth of the individual. The unitary soul among the Sanpoil appears already in the embryo. Among the Plains Cree the free-soul takes up its abode in the body at birth. The Naskapi Indian receives his 'Great Man' during the embryonic stage. According to the Shawnee, 'a soul goes to earth and jumps through the mother's vagina and into the body of the child through the fontanelle just before birth.' Jones writes that according to the belief of the Ojibway 'the manitou on the other side of the world' delivers their souls to people before their birth. The Fox imagine that the life-soul is with the human embryo during the embryonic development, while the free-soul remains outside the mother during this period, and does not enter the child's body until its birth. . . .

Evidence that the child is believed to have soul-activity during the embryonic stage is afforded in the Indian notion of the foetal consciousness: the child feels and thinks during the time it spends in the mother's body. Sometimes this consciousness is intensified to the point of precognition, prophetic clairvoyance.

A Bella Coola child that cries in the womb is believed to have an excellent intellect. A shaman from the Great Bear Lake district declared that before his birth he had seen a star, which revealed to him all the medicines that have power over man. The Chipewyan embryo warns its mother if she is approached by an evil spirit. The unborn Lummi Indian hears what his future relatives are saying and knows what they are thinking; if they have evil thought in their mind he leaves them before his birth. A sagacious Lenape declared that he had acquired supernatural knowledge even before his birth. . . . The Saulteaux relate that in former times the Indians had consciousness during the embryonic stage, and in this connection also certainty concerning the content of earthly life, a prophetic capacity that was one of the signs of magic power. Such things are now rare. A Saulteaux did, however, tell Hallowell the following: 'Four nights before I was born I knew that I would be born. My mind was as clear when I was born as it is now. I saw my father and my mother, and I knew who they were. I knew the things an Indian uses, their names and what they were good for. . . .' Such certainty is said to be founded on the fact that the person in question had earlier lived a life among human beings. The unborn Fox child understands what its mother is saying, and abandons her if she proves to be quarrelsome. The Winnebago medicine-man, who is sent down to a woman's womb from his pre-existence, retains his consciousness both at the conception and during the entire embryonic period. The Wahpeton shamans know everything about their future existence before their birth. . . .

The events after the incarnation, and especially at the actual moment of birth, have been dramatically described by a reincarnated Winnebago shaman: 'Then I was brought down to earth. I did not enter a woman's womb, but I was taken into a room. There I remained,

conscious at all times. One day I heard the noise of little children outside and some other sounds, so I thought I would go outside. Then it
seemed to me that I went through a door, but I was really being born
again from a woman's womb. As I walked out I was struck with the
sudden rush of cold air and I began to cry.'

Ake Hultkrantz, *Conceptions of the Soul among North*
American Indians (Stockholm, 1954), pp. 412-26

88. MAN'S SOUL IDENTIFIED BOTH WITH OSIRIS AND WITH NATURE

('*Coffin Texts,*' 330)

'*Coffin Texts,*' 330, contains the clearest identification of the soul with
nature that the ancients have left us.

Whether I live or die I am Osiris,
I enter in and reappear through you,
I decay in you, I grow in you,
I fall down in you, I fall upon my side.
The gods are living in me for I live and grow in the corn
    that sustains the Honoured Ones.
I cover the earth,
whether I live or die I am Barley.
I am not destroyed.
I have entered the Order,
I rely upon the Order,
I become Master of the Order,
I emerge in the Order,
I make my form distinct,
I am the Lord of the Chennet (Granary of Memphis?)
I have entered into the Order,
I have reached its limits. . . .

Translation by R. T. Rundle Clark in his *Myth and*
Symbol in Ancient Egypt (London, 1959), p. 142

Man and the Sacred

The Melanesian mind is entirely possessed by the belief in a super-natural power or influence, called almost universally *mana*. This is what works to effect everything which is beyond the ordinary power of men, outside the common processes of nature: it is present in the atmosphere of life, attaches itself to persons and things, and is manifested by results which can only be ascribed to its operation. When one has got it he can use it and direct it, but its force may break forth at some new point; the presence of it is ascertained by proof. A man comes by chance upon a stone which takes his fancy; its shape is singular, it is like something, it is certainly not a common stone, there must be *mana* in it. So he argues with himself, and he puts it to the proof; he lays it at the root of a tree to the fruit of which it has a certain resemblance, or he buries it in the ground when he plants his garden; an abundant crop on the tree or in the garden shows that he is right, the stone is *mana*, has that power in it. Having that power it is a vehicle to convey *mana* to other stones. In the same way certain forms of words, generally in the form of a song, have power for certain purposes; a charm of words is called a *mana*. But this power, though itself impersonal, is always connected with some person who directs it; all spirits have it, ghosts generally, some men. If a stone is found to have a supernatural power, it is because a spirit has associated itself with it; a dead man's bone has with it *mana*, because the ghost is with the bone; a man may have so close a connection with a spirit or ghost that he has *mana* in himself also, and can so direct it as to effect what he desires; a charm is powerful because the name of a spirit or ghost expressed in the form of words brings into it the power which the ghost or spirit exercises through it. Thus all conspicuous success is a proof that a man has *mana*; his influence depends on the impression made on the people's mind that he has it; he becomes a chief by virtue of it. Hence a man's power, though political or social in its character, is his *mana*; the word is naturally used in accordance with the native conception of the character of all power and influence as supernatural. If a man has been successful in fighting, it has not been his natural strength of arm, quickness of eye, or readiness of resource that has won success; he has certainly got the *mana* of a spirit or of some deceased warrior to empower him, conveyed in an amulet of a stone round his neck, or a tuft of leaves in his belt, in a tooth hung upon a finger of his bow hand, or in the form of words with which he brings supernatural assistance to his side. If a man's pigs multiply, and his gardens are productive, it is not because he is industrious and looks after his property, but because of the stones full of *mana* for pigs and yams that he possesses. Of course a yam naturally grows when planted, that is well known, but it will not be very large unless *mana* comes into play; a canoe will not be swift unless *mana* be brought to bear upon it, a net will not catch many fish, nor an arrow inflict a mortal wound.

R. H. Codrington, *The Melanesians* (Oxford, 1891), pp. 118-20

90. THE POLYNESIAN MANA

Mana has a meaning which has not a little in common with *tupu*,[1] but on a significant point they are radically different. Both denote unfolding activity and life; but whereas *tupu* is an expression of the nature of things and human beings as unfolded from within, *mana* expresses something participated, an active fellowship which according to its nature is never inextricably bound up with any single thing or any single human being. . . .

Mana thus is something which is found both in chief, tribe, and land, in other words, something common to a group; but there is a difference in their relation to this *mana* in that the chief owns the *mana* of the others. It is this very thing that makes his *mana* so much greater than that of the others, as it 'extends' into the land and the people.

This fellowship, *mana*, has something impersonal about it, in the way that it may be taken from the chief and taken over by another man. The impersonal, however, is only one aspect of *mana*, the one due to the fact that it contains the *mana* of the tribe as well as the land, and we may perhaps add, that of the chief as well. On the other hand there is something personal about *mana* in relation to tribe, chief or land, by the fact that they each have their share in it. This becomes evident if we consider the relation to *tupu* in more detail.

A man's *tupu* and his *mana* are intimately connected. We may say that his *tupu* attached his *mana* to it, or better that it extends into his *mana* so that they are in part identical. They both join in com-

The notes to this text are on p. 200.

promising a man's repute. The presents which the kinship group give a man at his wedding, are at once distributed by him among his wife's relatives, 'the *mana* is sufficient for the two, i.e., the married couple'; or in other words, the repute of the gifts is theirs. . . . Just as the conjunction of *tupu* and *mana* shows that these two belong together, but are not identical, so we may from a number of other conjunctions with *mana* learn what accompanies *mana* without being identical with it:

'It was Tane's *mana*, strength and insight which fixed Heaven above.'

'The *mana* and the strength of the divinity of the sacred place.'

'These heads (viz. those of the enemy) which were prepared as trophies, they were prepared in order to be a sign that the tribe had *mana* and the gift of victory.'

'His name (i.e. renown) and his *mana* were (both) very great.'

'It is hard to flee before the enemy . . . it is a sign that the *mana* and name (i.e. renown) of the tribe are destroyed by the blows of the weapons of the victorious tribe.'

'Therefore the fear of his name, the greatness of his *mana* and his nobility were greater than those of any other ancestor.'

'You possess the *mana*, you ought to say the words, i.e. you have the authority.'

Insight, the courage which bears victory in it *(mana)*, strength, name (i.e. renown), and the awe which the great name bears with it, authority, all this is connected with *mana* as something intimately bound up with it. These things are not *mana*, but they accompany *mana*, and we see how *mana* extends the inner vitality of *tupu* into strength, its courage into victorious courage, its honour into name (renown) and authority. . . .

Mana only refers to the urge towards realization; but this urge actually appears by the realization. 'If *Maui* had not been killed by this god (viz. Hinenuitepo), Maui's wish would have got *mana* and man would live for ever'; the realization of Maui's wish thus would have followed as a consequence of its *mana*. Similarly in the following passage: 'Only now did they repeat a *karakia* (incantation) to Rangi in order that the bung of the springs of the water should be taken out and the water come forth. Then their wish really got *mana* and the water rose.'

The dynamic element in *mana*, the unfolding, is brought out strongly when the word is used as a verb. The verbal character makes the aspect of *mana* as a communion or fellowship recede into the background, which is only justified if we do not forget that the dynamic element cannot be active except against this background. . . .

The *mana* common to the chief, the kinship group, and the land is owned by the chief; this causes his special position. It also means that his *tupu* extends over a wider field than that of other mortals. It may perhaps be translated into European languages by saying that his personality has a greater field of activity. We may say that he gets his field of activity with his *mana*, but the degree to which he can utilize it, will depend upon his personality. The chief who has a strong mind, strength, and courage, in short, a great *tupu*, can also be said to permeate the *mana* of the kinship group and the country with his being, his *mana*. It was said about Kupe, who was a chief from Hawaiki, that 'his *mana* penetrated into the population of the islands.'

This *mana*, which permeates the kinship group, is the basis of the chief's authority. It shows in practice by the fact that he can make others do what he wants. In a farewell letter to Governor Grey some Maoris wrote: 'It was your *mana* which put an end to the disturbances in this country.' The Maoris of course considered Grey as a kind of great chief and felt his *mana* in the authority by means of which he succeeded in making peace. . . .

This *mana* which extends into country and people thus in the great chief is permeated by his being. It is not a mysterious substance, but a fellowship on which he may leave his mark and which he may dominate by his personality. Therefore there is no paradox, either, in the statement that the greater the chief's *mana* is, the farther it extends itself, the more it is concentrated in his person. It can become so essential a part of him that the Maori briefly says, 'The chief is *mana*.' 'Farewell, thou, the *mana* of the country,' he will sing in the dirge on the deceased chief. . . .

Hence it is evident that the kinship group must honour (*manaaki*) its chief in order that his *mana* may endure. 'In him the chief-*mana* goes with being honoured,' it simply says. It is, however, inherent in the nature of fellowship that the chief must also yield something from his own life, and we see in a new light why he must understand how to honour his people. By this means he creates *mana* and by permeating the fellowship with his personality he attaches people to him. The greatest means to do so is by giving gifts. 'This is Rehua's *mana*,' says the Maori admiringly when seeing a chief being liberal, and as Rehua was of a divine nature it is understood that the chief provides a great *mana* for himself with his gifts.

From the intimate connection between *manaaki* and *mana* we also understand why it was impossible to decide whether a person honoured others most for his own sake or for the sake of the others. It is impossible because one honours for the sake of *mana*, the fellowship. . . .

Mana gives a plastic picture of the Maori's community because it denotes life in it. All free men have *mana*, i.e. they participate in the fellowship. Therefore everybody has a say in the matter according to his *mana*, i.e. his share in the fellowship. Therefore the chief is very far from being an absolute ruler, but the *mana* he contributes himself will always give him a corresponding influence. Add to this that he has a position as chief, which is expressed by the words that the *mana* of the kinship group is with him. This means that his personality is given the best possibility of asserting itself. The kinship group as a whole will not act without his being consulted. . . .

The important point that *mana* is the communal life does not otherwise seem to have been realized; but Best must at any rate have seen that it expresses life since he writes: 'When someone writes a treatise on the word *mana*, it will be seen that *mana* and *ora* (life) are almost synonymous terms, as applied to the old-time Maori.'

The secret of *mana* is that communal life, the 'fellowship,' permeates all the people to their innermost hearts; we may say that they live *mana*. A single strong personality may colour the whole fellowship. This does not take place by outward compulsion, but by the fact that the fellowship itself is stamped in such a way that they all obtain their 'being' or 'nature' according to the dominant element of *mana*. . . .

The chief's *mana* is not only the *mana* of the kinship group but that of the country as well. 'The great *mana* of this tract is in him alone,' it says somewhere about Te Rauparaha. So the *mana* of the country is as a matter of course part of that of the kinship groups as well, and as the latter stands in a similar determinative relationship to the country as the chief to the kinship group, the Maori may, of course, with equal right say that the *mana* of the country is with the kinship group without being guilty of any inconsistency.

The *mana* of the country was taken when they immigrated, and since then it has been the endeavour of every tribe and chief to cling to it. According to the sense of *mana* this simply takes place by living with the soil: 'This was a custom which originated from our ancestors, namely that we lived in some part of our country; later the tribe went to another part, lived there and cultivated the soil there, in order that our country's *mana* could be maintained by us, in order that our fires could always be burning on the extensive surface of our country so that the country was not taken by other tribes.'

The Maori must of course be able to maintain his right to the country with arms, but a passage like the one quoted shows that if possession of land is in practice identical with possessing its *mana*, then this is due to the fact that possession makes it possible to live with the country as one lives with the soil, inhabits it, cultivates it, and generally utilizes it. The factor mentioned last is not least in importance. The possession of the *mana* of the land must manifest itself in a true fellowship with the country, i.e. that one understands how to make the country yield. . . .

On the whole *mana* is so necessary to the Maori because he cannot very well affect his surroundings without involving it in a fellowship, i.e. without possessing its *mana*, or—in other words—without permeating its *mana* with his own being. He must possess the *mana* of the *kumara*[2] in order that it may thrive by his hand, and if its *mana* has been carried away, incorporated in a *mauri*,[3] he must fetch it back.

Mana, fellowship, is so necessary that the Maori must have *mana* even with an enemy whom he meets in open fight. In this connection it should also be mentioned that an enemy is called *hoa-riri*, or somewhat more rarely, *hoa-whawhai* and *hoa-ngangare*, the three words all with the literal sense of 'fighting-comrade,' as *hoa* means 'comrade, fellow,' whether referring to one's wife or to a travelling companion. Thus it is not nonsense to talk about fellowship, although this indeed is of quite a different character from that within the kinship group. The fellowship consists in the fact that the Maoris cannot meet and fight in a merely outward sense; they must necessarily stand in an inner relationship to their enemy. The outward manifestations of the fight are really only a question of who has the greatest *mana*, i.e. who can conquer the other from within and thus bring the antagonist's will and power to fight to its knees so that the weapons may reap the victory.

What is characteristic of the 'fellowship' of the fight in contrast to that of peace, is the fact that in the fight each party will try to dominate the 'fellowship' completely, which may be expressed as taking the enemy's *mana* or as dominating it with one's own *mana*. These are but two aspects of the same matter. As viewed from this angle there is but a difference of degree, but a very important difference, between the fellowship of peace and war. . . .

Against the background of these examples, which show how *mana* conquers and is conquered, we understand how it could be said about a *tangata haere*, a vagrant man, that he possesses *mana*. He could not like the chief possess his people's and his country's *mana*, but obviously this means that he was what we should term a powerful personality, who, wherever he went, forced people and things under his will, doing this—be it noted—from within by taking possession of their life, by creating a sphere which was his *mana*, but still a fellowship, as the point is that he included the others in it. The man in question actually became one of the great ancestors of one of the Waikato tribes, so that one of the tribes, the Ngatimahuta, was named after his son. . . .

Furthermore, we have now obtained a basis for completely understanding how *mana* is sometimes personal, sometimes impersonal. The personal aspect is in the fact that he who has the greatest *mana*, i.e. he who lives most intensely in the fellowship, by this also stamps the fellowship throughout by his personality. The impersonal aspect is at the other pole: that *mana* is a fellowship and therefore can be taken by somebody else if he is capable of doing so. Therefore the fellowship gets the character of an impersonal power which can be utilized by the person who understands how to do so.

Notes

1 Lit., 'to unfold one's nature'; honour.
2 Sweet potato.
3 Sacral objects.

J. Prytz Johansen, *The Maori and His Religion* (Copenhagen: Ejnar Munksgaard, 1954), pp. 85-99

C. TYPES OF SACRIFICE

91. NUER SACRIFICE

The Nuer are a cattle-herding people dwelling in the Nilotic Sudan. Their religious practices and beliefs have been studied with great care and understanding by E. E. Evans-Pritchard. The results of his twenty-five years of research have been published under the title 'Nuer Religion,' from which the following selection is taken.

Nuer sacrifice on a great many occasions: when a man is sick, when sin has been committed, when a wife is barren, sometimes on the birth of a first child, at the birth of twins, at initiation of sons, at marriages, at funerals and mortuary ceremonies, after homicides and at settlements of feuds, at periodic ceremonies in honour of one or other of their many spirits of a dead father, before war, when persons or property are struck by lightning, when threatened or overcome by plague or famine, sometimes before large-scale fishing enterprises, when a ghost is troublesome, etc.

When we examine this variety of occasions we see that Nuer sacrifices fall into two broad classes. Most sacrifices are made to prevent some danger hanging over people, for example on account of some sin, to appease an angry spirit, or at the birth of twins; or to curtail or to get rid of a misfortune which has already fallen, as in times of plague or in acute sickness. On all such occasions Spirit intervenes, or may intervene, for better or more often for worse, in the affairs of men, and its intervention is always dangerous. Any misfortune or grave danger is a sign of spiritual activity. Such sacrifices are made for a person or persons and not for social groups, and they involve ideas of propitiation, expiation, and related intentions. As they are the most common and the most specifically religious sacrifices I shall devote chief attention to them. There are other sacrifices which accompany various social activities, mostly of the *rites de passage* kind, such as initiation, marriage, and death. We cannot make an absolute distinction between the two sorts of sacrifice. A sacrifice of the *rites de passage* kind may contain elements of meaning characteristic of the other type. Sacrifices in marriage ceremonies—at betrothal, at the wedding, and at the consummation—are the best examples of the second type. A sacrifice to ward off the consequences of serious incest is a good example of the first type. A sacrifice to end mournings is an example of the blending of the two. It is a routine sacrifice in a *rites de passage* context, but it is also intended to get rid of the contamination of death and any evil there may be in men's hearts. For the purpose of discussing the meaning or meanings of sacrifice it is necessary to make the distinction, even if there is some overlapping. I shall speak of the one type as personal sacrifice and of the other as collective sacrifice. These terms draw attention to the formal distinction between sacrifices offered for persons and those offered on behalf of social groups, but we shall see that they differ also in intention, the first having primarily a piacular intention, and the second a confirmatory one; or, to use Hubert and Mauss's terms, the first are sacrifices of 'desacralization' (they make the sacred profane, they get rid of Spirit from man) and the second as sacrifices of 'sacralization' (they make the profane sacred, they bring Spirit to man).

The primary purpose of collective sacrifices, and also their main function, is to confirm, to establish, or to add strength to, a change in social status—boy to man, maiden to wife, living man to ghost—or a new relationship between social groups—the coming into being of a new age-set, the uniting of kin groups by ties of affinity, the ending of a blood-feud—by making God and the ghosts, who are directly concerned with the change taking place, witnesses of it. The ceremonies are incomplete and ineffective without sacrifice, but sacrifice may be only one incident in a complex of ceremonies, dances, and rites of various kinds, which have no religious significance in themselves. Its importance lies in the fact that it sacralizes the social event and the new relationship brought about by it. It solemnizes the change of status or relationship, giving it religious validation. On such occasions sacrifice has generally a conspicuously festal and eucharistic character. . . .

It is indicative of Nuer religious thought that these sacrifices·performed as part of social activities are concerned with relations within the social order and not with relations between men and their natural environment. We are often told in accounts of African peoples that their sacrifices are concerned with weather, rain, fertility of the soil, seed-time, fructification, harvest, and fishing and hunting. Generally no rite of any kind is performed by Nuer in connection with these processes, certainly no regular and obligatory rite; and if in certain circumstances one is performed, as before large-scale fishing, it is rarely a sacrifice, and if it is a sacrifice it is not regarded as either necessary or important. All this may be due to some extent to lack of interest in agriculture and hunting, but it is also because Nuer take nature for granted and are passive and resigned towards it. They do not think that they can influence it to their own advantage, being merely ignorant folk. What happens there is the will of God, and that has to be accepted. Hence Nuer are little interested in ritual for bringing rain and even consider it presumptuous to think of asking God for rain before sowing. This mentality is illustrated in one of their stories which relates how death came to a girl who asked that the setting of the sun might be delayed till she had finished her work. Nuer rather turn their eyes inwards, to the little closed social world in which they live, they and their cattle. Their sacrifices are concerned with moral and spiritual, not natural, crises.

We have now first to ask to whom sacrifices are made. This brings us again up against the problem of the one and the many. When a sin is expiated or pollution is wiped out by sacrifice it is made to God alone. Likewise in major calamities, such as plagues and murrains. Also when a person is struck by lightning, in connection with death, and in cases of sickness not attributed to a specific cause. We are here dealing with circumstances common to all men and with universals—with the moral law which is the same for all men, with effects of common interest and concern, and with dangers and misfortunes which fall on each and all alike. Sacrifices may, however, be made on some occasions to one or other spirit, for example, to a spirit of the air before battle or when it is thought to have brought about sickness in a man or if it is feared that it may do so; or to a totemic or other spirit of the below in circumstances already mentioned in earlier chapters. We are here dealing with something more particular and specific, the relation of certain persons to Spirit figured to them, and not to others, in one or other special form as a spirit. Nevertheless, as I have earlier explained, these spirits may be regarded as hypostases, representations, or refractions of God, and in the already defined sense in which this is so we can say that a sacrifice to any one of them is a sacrifice also to God. . . .

The sacrificial animal *par excellence* is an ox, and in important social ceremonies, such as weddings and those held for settlements of feuds, the victim must be an ox. Oxen are also sacrificed in times of general calamity, sometimes when people are dangerously ill, and occasionally to spirits. A barren cow may take the place of an ox. Bulls are only sacrificed in one of the rites closing a blood-feud, and occasionally, though only old beasts, in honour of a dead father. Except in these instances a male victim must be a neuter. If it is not, it is castrated before the rites begin. Fertile cows are only sacrificed at mortuary ceremonies, and then only for senior persons, as a tribute to their position in the community. It does not matter what is the colour of the victim, though in certain sacrifices there is a preference for beasts with certain markings. . . .

We have discussed to whom sacrifice is made and what is sacrificed. We have now to ask by whom it is made, and when and where. We have first to distinguish between the person (or social group) on whose behalf it is made, whom we may speak of as the sacrificer, though with some danger of misunderstanding, because he may not take an active part in the rite performed on his behalf, and those who act on his behalf, the actors in the drama. There may be a number of these. Several people may take part in the consecration and several men may deliver invocations. One man may present the victim, another consecrate and make the invocation over it, and yet another slay it. Nevertheless, there are always one or more prime actors, those who make the consecrations and invocations, which, rather than the actual killing, constitute for Nuer the main acts in the series of rites making up a sacrifice; and we may therefore speak of anyone, who, after consecrating the victim, makes an invocation over it as the officiant. There may be several of them. In certain sacrifices, particularly those of the collective kind, whoever else may invoke God, one or other particular functionary either must do so or it is thought highly desirable that he should do so. Normally any senior man, usually the head of the family of the sacrificer, can officiate at personal sacrifices. He would generally be one of the sacrificer's paternal kinsmen but it would not matter if he were not. The sacrifice is to God and not to ghosts, and it therefore does not matter who officiates. A youth would not officiate if there were an older man present, but this is a matter of social convention only: there is no ritual bar to his acting. Women do not sacrifice. They may assist in the act of consecration with ashes and they may pray, but they do not make invocations or slay victims. Neither the sacrificer nor the officiant has to be in a state of ceremonial purity. This is an idea entirely unknown to Nuer. . . . . .

Almost all sacrifices, whether personal or collective, have the same general features. A description of one is therefore, apart from details, a description of almost all. The victim is brought to the place of sacrifice and there are performed in succession the four acts which compose the sacrificial drama: presentation, consecration, invocation, and immolation. Other features may be added, such as libations and aspersions and, mostly in sacrifices to spirits, hymn-singing, but these are supernumerary acts. The essential rites of the sacrifice proper are the four I have mentioned. They form what might be called the canon of sacrifice. . . .

God takes the *yiegh*, the life. Man takes the *ring*, the flesh, what is left over after the sacrifice. The carcass is cut up and skinned as soon as the animal falls. In most sacrifices the meat is consumed by members of the family and kin of the person on whose behalf it was made. In marriage and most other collective sacrifices it is divided among relatives, both paternal and maternal, in traditional portions; and the age-mates of the owner of the beast and representatives of lineages collateral to his may also have rights to shares. If the principal officiant is not a member of the family or of the close kin but a master of ceremonies of the family or a priest or a prophet, he also receives his share. This part of the proceedings is of general interest and not merely for those directly concerned in the rites. If it is at all a public occasion people, whether they are concerned in the matter or not, gather round to watch the meat being cut up and handed to those to whom it is due, and there is often much shouting and argument as the distribution is goodhumouredly disputed and men tug at the carcass and snatch or beg pieces of meat. Even outsiders who get in the way and beg persistently enough are likely to receive pieces of it. According to the circumstances those who on such an occasion receive meat take it to their homes, maybe in different villages, for cooking and eating, or it is cooked by women of the homestead in which the sacrifice took place and eaten there by groups, according to sex, age, and kinship. The meat is cooked, served, and eaten as would be that of a wild beast slaughtered in hunting. It is boiled, though tid-bits may be roasted in the embers of a fire. I want to make it clear indeed that the cutting up of the victim, the preparation of its flesh, and the eating of it are not parts of the sacrifice. To regard the eating of the animal as part of the sacrificial rite would be like regarding a wedding feast as part of the marriage service in our own country. But if it does not form part of the rite and has no sacramental significance it forms part of the whole ceremony in the broader sense and has a social significance. We have always to remember that a sacrifice, even piacular sacrifice, furnishes a feast and that in the circumstances in which Nuer live and by convention this means that neighbours are likely in one way or another to share in it.

E. E. Evans-Pritchard, *Nuer Religion* (Oxford: Clarendon Press, 1956), pp. 197-215

See also no. 299

92. THE AINU BEAR SACRIFICE

The Ainu, now living in Hokkaido (northern Japan), Sakhalin, and the Kurile Islands, are the descendants of an archaic ethnic group probably originating from central or northern Siberia. The bear festival, 'Iyomante,' or 'Kamui Omante' (lit. 'to see off' or 'to send off' the 'kamui,' i.e., the 'god') is the most important of the Ainu rituals.

Ainu bear-hunters are very proud if they can secure a bear cub or two to bring up at home for the purpose of holding a great bear feast. Men have been known to risk their lives in order to secure one, and when they do catch a cub they bring it home with great glee, and, of course, get very drunk in honour of the occasion. Sometimes very young cubs may be seen living in the huts with the people, where they play with the children, and are cared for with great affection. In fact, some of them are treated even better than the children themselves, and I have known cases when the people have wept greatly when the cub has died. But as soon as they are grown big and strong enough to cause a little pain when they hug a person, or when their claws are too powerful to be pleasant, they are placed in a cage strongly made of pieces of timber. Here they generally remain until they arrive at the age of two or three years, at which time they are killed for the feast. . . .

When a young bear is about to be sacrificed, the day before this, to us, cruel and barbarous feast takes place, the owner sends round to all his people of the village, and invites them to come and take part in the festivities. . . . The last form of invitation I heard was as follows: —'I, so and so, am about to sacrifice the dear little divine thing who resides among the mountains. My friends and masters, come ye to the feast; we will then unite in the great pleasure of sending the god away. Come.'. . .

As the guests arrive at the place of sacrifice they enter the hut and sit around the fireplace, the men in front and the women behind. Millet dumplings are boiled and toasted, and a kind of white thick beer is brewed from millet. The women get what drink their husbands choose to give them, which, I have noticed, is very little indeed if the drink be the more expensive *sake* rather than millet beer. But this is not the real feast, but merely a sort of preliminary breaking of the fast.

When the guests have all come in, the men make numbers of *inao*,[1] and stick them into the hearth, and worship is performed. All the gods are worshipped and invited to partake of the feast with them. When this has been done, most of the *inao* are taken up reverently and carried to the *nusa*[2] place outside, and there stuck up. Next, two long and thickish poles are laid at their base. The men now come out of the hut, ornamented with their totem crowns, and solemnly approach the cage containing the bear. The women and children follow and sing, dance, and clap their hands. By-and-by all are ordered to the *nusa* place, and made to sit in a large circle, the old men in front. After this an Ainu is chosen who, having approached the bear, sits down before it and tells it that they are about to send it forth to its ancestors. He prays pardon for what they are about to do, hopes it will not be angry, tells it what an honour is about to be conferred upon it, and comforts it with the consolation that a large number of *inao* and plenty of wine, cakes, and other good cheer will be sent along with it. He also informs it that if it be a good and proper bear it will appear again to be treated in like manner. The last address I heard of ran thus: 'O thou divine one, thou wast sent into the world for us to hunt. O thou precious little divinity, we worship thee; pray hear our prayer. We have nourished thee and brought thee up with a deal of pains and trouble, all because we love thee so. Now, as thou hast grown big, we are about to send thee to thy father and mother. When thou comest to them please speak well of us, and tell them how kind we have been; please come to us again and we will sacrifice thee.'

After the prayer has been said another Ainu goes to the cub's cage and catches the victim's head in a rope having made a noose in it for that purpose. This noose is then passed round the neck and under the foreleg in such a manner as not to choke the animal when it struggles. Another noose is made in a second rope, and this is passed over the head in the same way, excepting that the end of it comes out on the opposite side of the bear. Thus, when the animal comes out of the cage it is led along by two men, one on each side. Sometimes, however, when the bear is a large one, a rope is put over the the hind quarters, and a man walks behind holding it tightly and ready to aid in case there should be any dangerous display of temper.

As soon as the poor beast is out or the cage the people who have formed the ring shout and clap their hands while it is being led into their midst, and upon its arrival they take blunt arrows, which they call *Hepere-ai*, i.e. 'cub arrows,' and shoot at it, thus trying to work it up into a passion. The shouting now becomes deafening, and the bear sometimes furious. But the wilder the bear becomes the more delighted do the people get. Should, however, the animal refuse to move, he is brushed down with a stick called *Takusa*, the tuft on the top of which is made of Arundinaria. When the excited and struggling brute shows signs of exhaustion a stake is driven into the ground in the centre of the ring of people, and to it the bear is tied. This stake is ornamented with *inao* shavings and leaves of Arundinaria, and is called *Tushop-ni*, i.e. 'tree having the rope.'

As soon as all is secure the blunt arrows are shot with renewed vigour, and the beast tears and rages till it is quite tired out. Then comes the most exciting time and true test of valour. All at once some brave young Ainu will rush forward and seize the brute by the ears and fur of the face, whilst another suddenly rushes out and seizes it by the hind quarters. These men both pull at the animal with all their might. This causes it to open its mouth. Another man then rushes forward with a round piece of wood about two feet long; this he thrusts into the bear's jaws. The poor beast in his rage bites hard at this, and holds it tight between its teeth. Next two men come forward, one on each side of the bear, and seize its fore-legs and pull them out as far as they can. Then two others will in a like manner catch hold of the two hind-legs. When all this has been done quite satisfactorily, the two long poles which were laid by the *nusa*, and which are called *Ok numba ni*, i.e. 'poles for strangling,' are brought forward. One is placed under its throat, and the other upon the nape of its neck.

A good shot with the bow, who has been previously determined on by the men, now comes up and shoots the arrow into the beast's heart, and so ends its misery. Care has to be taken to strike the brute that no blood is shed, for, for some reason or other, it is considered unfortunate to allow any of the blood to fall upon the earth. . . .

As soon then as the bear has been shot in the heart it is carried to the two poles, which have been previously placed upon the ground for this purpose, and its head placed upon one of them, while the other is put over its neck. Now all the people shout and rush forward, every one eager to assist in squeezing the animal till life is quite extinct. It is said that they must be careful not to allow the poor beast to utter any cries during its death struggles, for this is thought to be very unlucky; why I cannot learn. People become so very excited at the time the cub is throttled that they sometimes trample on one another in their eagerness to have a hand in the death. And so the poor brute is killed, and the first part of the act of sacrifice accomplished.

As soon as it is strangled to death the bear is skinned and its head cut off, the skin, however, being left attached to the head. This is taken to the east window and placed upon a mat called *inao-so*, and ornamented with *inao* shavings, earrings, beads, and other things; indeed, on one occasion I even saw one decorated with old sword hilts and a Japanese mirror. After having been placed here a piece of its own flesh is cut off and placed under the snout. This is called Not-pok-omap, i.e. 'that under the jaw.'

Then a piece of dried fish and a moustache lifter, neatly made up into a parcel, is put before it, also some millet dumplings, a cup of its own meat boiled, and some *sake*. The dried fish is called *Sat-chep shike*, i.e. 'the bundle of dried fish.' The cup containing the boiled meat is called *marapto itangi*, i.e. 'the cup of the feast.' This having been done, a man worships, saying, 'O cub, we give you these *inao* cakes, and dried fish; take them to your parents, and say, 'I have been brought up for a long time by an Ainu father and mother, and have been kept from all trouble and harm. As I am now grown big I am come to thee. I have also brought these *inao*, cakes, and dried fish. Please rejoice.' If you say this to them they will be very glad.'

Another prayer ran thus: 'My dear cub, pray listen to me. I have cared for you a long time, and now present thee with *inao*, cakes, wine and other precious things. Do thou ride upon the *inao*, and other good things herewith presented to thee, and go to thy father and mother. Go happily and make them rejoice. When you arrive call together multitudes of divine guests, and make a great feast. Do thou again come to this world that I, who reared thee, may meet with thee again, and once more bring thee up for sacrifice. I salute thee, my dear cub; depart in peace.'

After this worship has been performed millet dumplings are threaded on sticks, and placed beside the head. These are said to be for the feast in the new world, for it would never do to appear before one's ancestors without a small present sufficient to provide viands for a meal. They are called *Imoka-shike,* i.e. 'remnants of the feast.' The men now all readjust or don their crowns, for they have been either laid on one side or knocked off during the teasing and slaying of the cub. This done, they have a good dance altogether. . . . The dance over, they return to the hut, and make quantities of *inao,* which are carefully placed upon the bear's head. In the meantime some of the cub's flesh has been boiled. A cup of this is now taken, and set before the beast's snout, and he is said to be partaking of the *marapto itangi,* i.e. 'the cup of the feast.'

After a little time has elapsed the man who presides at the feast says, 'The little divinity has now finished eating; come, ye friends, let us worship.' He then takes the cup, salutes it, and divides the contents —a very small portion to each—among all the assembled guests, for it seems to be absolutely essential that each person, young and old alike, should take a little. Besides being called 'the cup of the feast,' this cup is also named *ipuni itangi,* i.e. 'the cup of offering.' This name refers to the fact of its having been offered to the divinity just sacrificed.

After this cup has been partaken of, more *inao* are made, while the rest of the beast is stewing in the pots. The entrails are then cut up fine, sprinkled with salt, and eaten raw. This, like the drinking of the blood, is said to be for the purpose of obtaining the prowess and other virtues of the bear. I must mention, also, that some of the men besmear themselves and their clothes with blood. This is said to be for the purpose of rendering themselves successful in hunting. This beastly habit is called *Yai-isho-ushi,* i.e. 'besmearing oneself with good sport,' or 'successful hunting.' . . .

As soon as the flesh has been sufficiently cooked it is shared out among the people present, and every number of the company partakes of some, however little it may be. It is thus that he obtains communion with his dear little divinity, as he calls the victim; and this appears to me to be the special way in which he shows his social and religious fellowship with his totem god and the people. Not to partake of this feast and not to make *inao* would be tantamount to confessing oneself outside the pale of Ainu fellowship. Every particle of the bear, bones excepted, formerly had to be eaten up, even to the entrails, though this rule is now relaxed. . . .

The head of the bear is at last detached from the skin and taken to the *nusa* heap, where it is placed among the other skulls. A tall pole is here set up having a fork in the top, the prongs of which are ornamented with *inao*. This pole is called *keomande-ni*, i.e. 'the pole for sending away.'

Notes

1 Wooden wands used for religious and ceremonial purposes.
2 A collection of *inao*.

> John Batchelor, *The Ainu and Their Folk-Lore* (London, 1901), pp. 483-95. Another, more elaborate, description of the ritual is in Joseph M. Kitagawa, 'Ainu Bear Festival,' in *History of Religions*, I (1961), pp. 95-151

93. HORSE SACRIFICE AND THE SHAMAN'S ASCENT TO THE SKY (ALTAIC)

Radlov's classic description of the Altaic ritual is based not only on his own observations but also on the texts of the songs and invocations recorded at the beginning of the nineteenth century by missionaries to the Altai and later edited by the priest V. L. Verbitsky. This sacrifice is celebrated from time to time by every family, and the ceremony continues for two or three consecutive evenings.

The first evening is devoted to preparation for the rite. The *kam* (shaman), having chosen a spot in a meadow, erects a new yurt there, setting inside it a young birch stripped of its lower branches and with nine steps *(tapty)* notched into its trunk. The higher foliage of the birch, with a flag at the top, protrudes through the upper opening of the yurt. A small palisade of birch sticks is erected around the yurt and a birch stick with a knot of horsehair is set at the entrance. Then a light-coloured horse is chosen, and after having made sure that the animal is pleasing to the divinity, the shaman entrusts it to one of the people present, called, for this reason, *bas-tut-kan-kisi*, that is, 'head-holder.' The shaman shakes a birch branch over the animal's back to force its soul to leave and prepare its flight to Bai Ülgän. He repeats the same gesture over the 'head-holder,' for his 'soul' is to accompany the horse's soul throughout its celestial journey and hence must be at the *kam's* disposition.

The shaman re-enters the yurt, throws branches on the fire, and fumigates his drum. He begins to invoke the spirits, bidding them enter his drum; he will need each one of them in the course of his ascent.

At each summons by name, the spirit replies, 'I am here, *kam!*' and the shaman moves his drum as if he were catching the spirit. After assembling his spirit helpers (which are all celestial spirits) the shaman comes out of the yurt. At a few steps' distance there is a scarecrow in the shape of a goose; he straddles it, rapidly waving his hands as if to fly, and sings:

> *Under the white sky,*
> *Over the white cloud;*
> *Under the blue sky,*
> *Over the blue cloud:*
> *Rise up to the sky, bird!*

To this invocation, the goose replies, cackling: 'Ungaigakgak ungai-gak, kaigaigakgak, kaigaigak.' It is, of course, the shaman himself who imitates the bird's cry. Sitting astride the goose, the *kam* pursues the soul of the horse (*pûra*)—which is supposed to have fled—and neighs like a charger.

With the help of those present, he drives the animal's soul into the palisade and laboriously mimes its capture; he whinnies, rears, and pretends that the noose that has been thrown to catch the animal is tightening around his own throat. Sometimes he lets his drum fall to show that the animal's soul has escaped. Finally it is recaptured, the shaman fumigates it with juniper and dismisses the goose. Then he blesses the horse and, with the help of several of the audience, kills it in a cruel way, breaking its backbone in such a manner that not a drop of its blood falls to the ground or touches the sacrificers. The skin and bones are exposed, hung from a long pole. After offerings are made to the ancestors and to tutelary spirits of the yurt, the flesh is prepared and eaten ceremonially, the shaman receiving the best pieces.

The second and most important part of the ceremony takes place on the following evening. It is now that the shaman exhibits his shamanic abilities during his ecstatic journey to the celestial abode of Bai Ülgän. The fire is burning in the yurt. The shaman offers horse meat to the Masters of the Drum, that is, the spirits that personify the shamanic powers of his family, and sings:

> *Take it, O Kaira Kan,*
>
> *Host of the drum with six bosses!*
> *Come tinkling here to me!*
>
> *If I cry: 'Cok!' bow thyself!*
> *If I cry: 'Mäl' take it to thee! . . .*

He makes a similar address to the Master of the Fire, symbolizing the sacred power of the owner of the yurt, organizer of the festival. Raising a cup, the shaman imitates with his lips the noise of a gathering of invisible guests busily drinking; then he cuts up pieces of the horse and distributes them among those present (who represent the spirits), who noisily eat them. He next fumigates the nine garments hung on a rope as an offering from the master of the house to Bai Ülgän, and sings:

> Gifts that no horse can carry,
>
> Alas, alas, alas!
>
> That no man can lift,
>
> Alas, alas, alas!
>
> Garments with triple collars,
>
> Thrice turning look upon them!
> Be they blankets for the courser,
>
> Alas, alas, alas!
>
> Prince Ulgan, thou joyous one!
>
> Alas, alas, alas!

Putting on his shamanic costume, the *kam* sits down on a bench, and while he fumigates his drum, begins to invoke a multitude of spirits, great and small, who answer, in turn: 'I am here, *kam!*' In this way he invokes: Yaik Kan, the Lord of the Sea, Kaira Kan, Paisyn Kan, then the family of Bai Ülgän (Mother Tasygan with nine daughters at her right and seven daughters at her left), and finally the Masters and Heroes of the Abakan and the Altai (Mordo Kan, Altai Kan, Oktu Kan, etc.) After this long invocation, he addresses the Märküt, the Birds of Heaven:

> Birds of Heaven, five Märküt,
> Ye with mighty copper talons,
> Copper is the moon's talon,
> And of ice the moon's beak;
> Broad thy wings, of mighty sweep,
> Like a fan thy long tail,
> Hides the moon thy left wing,
> And the sun thy right wing.
> Thou, the mother of the nine eagles,
> Who strayest not, flying through the Yaik,

Who weariest not about Edil,
Come to me, singing!
Come, playing, to my right eye,
Perch on my right shoulder! . . .

The shaman imitates the bird's cry to announce its presence: 'Kazak, kak, kak! I am here, *kam!*' And as he does so, he drops his shoulder, as if sinking under the weight of a huge bird.

The summons to the spirit continues, and the drum becomes heavy. Provided with these numerous and powerful protectors, the shaman several times circles the birch that stands inside the yurt,[1] and kneels before the door to pray the Porter Spirit for a guide. Receiving a favourable reply, he returns to the centre of the yurt, beating his drum, convulsing his body, and muttering unintelligible words. Then he purifies the whole gathering with his drum, beginning with the master of the house. It is a long and complex ceremony, at the end of which the shaman is in a state of exaltation. It is also the signal for the ascent proper, for soon afterward the *kam* suddenly takes his place on the first notch *(tapty)* in the birch, beating his drum violently and crying 'Cok! cok!' He also makes motions to indicate that he is mounting into the sky. In 'ecstasy' (?!) he circles the birch and the fire, imitating the sound of thunder, and then hurries to a bench covered with a horsehide. This represents the soul of the *pûra*, the sacrificed horse. The shaman mounts it and cries:

> *I have climbed a step,*
> *Aihai, aihai!*
> *I have reached a plane,*
> *Sagarbata!*
> *I have climbed to the* tapty's *head,*
> *Sagarbata!*
> *I have risen to the full moon,*
> *Sagarbata!*[2]

The shaman becomes increasingly excited and, continuing to beat his drum, orders the *bas-tut-kan-kisi* to hurry. For the soul of the 'head-holder' abandons his body at the same time as the soul of the sacrificed horse. The *bas-tut-kan-kisi* complains of the difficulty of the road, and the shaman encourages him. Then, mounting to the second *tapty*, he symbolically enters the second heaven, and cries:

The notes to this text are on p. 216.

I have broken through the second ground,
I have climbed the second level,
See, the ground lies in splinters.

And, again imitating thunder and lightning, he proclaims:

Sagarbata! Sagarbata!
Now I have climbed up two levels . . .

In the third heaven the *pûra* becomes extremely tired, and, to relieve it, the shaman summons the goose. The bird presents itself: 'Kagak! Kagak! I am here, *kam!*' The shaman mounts it and continues his celestial journey. He describes the ascent and imitates the cackling of the goose, which, in its turn, complains of the difficulties of the journey. In the third heaven there is a halt. The shaman now tells of his horse's weariness and his own. He also gives information concerning the coming weather, the epidemics and misfortunes that threaten, and the sacrifices that they collectively should offer. After the *bas-tut-kan-kisi* has had a good rest, the journey continues. The shaman climbs the notches in the birch one after the other, thus successively entering the other celestial regions. To enliven the performance, various episodes are introduced, some of them quite grotesque: the *kam* offers tobacco to Karakus, the Black Bird, in the shaman's service, and Karakus drives away the cuckoo; he waters the *pûra*, imitating the sound of a horse drinking; the sixth heaven is the scene of the last comic episode: a hare hunt. In the fifth heaven the shaman has a long conversation with the powerful Yayutsi (the 'Supreme Creator'), who reveals several secrets of the future to him; some of these the shaman communicates aloud, others are murmured. In the sixth heaven the shaman bows to the Moon, and to the Sun in the seventh. He passes through heaven after heaven to the ninth and, if he is really powerful, to the twelfth and higher; the ascent depends entirely on the shaman's abilities. When he has gone as high as his power permits, he stops and humbly addresses Bai Ülgän in the following terms:

Prince, to whom three ladders lead,
Bai Ülgän with the three flocks,
Blue slope that has appeared,
Blue sky that shows itself!
Blue cloud, drifting away,
Blue sky unattainable,
White sky unattainable,

Watering place a year away!
   Father Ülgän, thrice exalted,
Whom the moon's ax-edge spares,
Who uses the horse's hoof!
   Thou didst create all men, Ülgän,
All that makes a noise around us.
All cattle thou hast forsaken, Ülgän!
   Deliver us not to misfortune
Let us withstand the Evil One!
   Show us not Körmös [the evil spirit]
Give us not into his hand!
   Thou who the starry heaven
Hast turned a thousand, thousand times,
Condemn not my sins!

The shaman learns from Bai Ülgän if the sacrifice has been accepted and receives predictions concerning the weather and the coming harvest; he also learns what other sacrifice the divinity expects. This episode is the culminating point of the 'ecstasy': the shaman collapses, exhausted. The *bas-tut-kan-kisi* approaches and takes the drum and stick from his hands. The shaman remains motionless and dumb. After a time he rubs his eyes, appears to wake from a deep sleep, and greets those present as if after a long absence.

Notes

1 This birch symbolizes the World Tree, which stands at the Centre of the Universe, the Cosmic Axis that connects sky, earth, and underworld; the seven, nine, or twelve notches (*tapty*) represent the 'heavens,' the celestial planes. It should be noted that the shaman's ecstatic journey always takes place near the 'Centre of the World.'

2 All this is clearly an exaggeration due to intoxication at having broken through the first cosmic plane. For actually, the shaman has reached only the first heaven, he has not climbed to the highest *tapty*; he has not even risen to the full moon (which is in the sixth heaven).

M. Eliade, *Shamanism*, trans. Willard R. Trask (New York: Bollingen Series LXXVI, 1964), pp. 190-7; translating and summarizing Wilhelm Radlov, *Lose Blätter aus dem Tagebuche eines reisenden Linguisten*, two vols. in one (Leipzig, 1884), II, pp. 20-50

See also nos. 207, 205, 208

Types of Sacrifice

94. A MAZDEAN (ZOROASTRIAN) SACRIFICE TO THE SUN

('Khôrshêd Yasht,' 1-5)

1. We sacrifice unto the undying, shining, swift-horsed Sun.

When the light of the sun waxes warmer, when the brightness of the sun waxes warmer, then stand up the heavenly Yazatas, by hundreds and thousands; they gather together its Glory, they make its Glory, they make its Glory pass down, they pour its Glory unto the earth made by Ahura, for the increase of the world of holiness, for the increase of the creatures of holiness, for the increase of the undying, shining, swift-horsed Sun.

2. And when the sun rises up, then the earth, made by Ahura, becomes clean; the running waters become clean, the waters of the wells become clean, the waters of the sea become clean, the standing waters become clean; all the holy creatures, the creatures of the Good Spirit, become clean.

3. Should not the sun rise up, then the Daevas would destroy all the things that are in the seven Karshvares, nor would the heavenly Yazatas find any way of withstanding or repelling them in the material world.

4. He who offers up a sacrifice unto the undying, shining, swift-horsed Sun—to withstand darkness, to withstand the Daevas born of darkness, to withstand the robbers and bandits, to withstand the Yâtus and Pairikas, to withstand death that creeps in unseen—offers it up to Ahura Mazda, offers it up to the Amesha-Spentas, offers it up to his own soul. He rejoices all the heavenly and worldly Yazatas, who offers up a sacrifice unto the undying, shining, swift-horsed Sun.

5. I will sacrifice unto Mithra, the lord of wide pastures, who has a thousand ears, ten thousand eyes.

I will sacrifice unto the club of Mithra, the lord of wide pastures, well struck down upon the skulls of the Daevas.

I will sacrifice unto that friendship, the best of all friendships, that reigns between the moon and the sun.

Translation by James Darmesteter, The Zend-Avesta, part II in Sacred Books of the East, XXIII (Oxford, 1883), pp. 85-7

Man and the Sacred

95. A HOMERIC SACRIFICE FOR THE DEAD

(Homer, 'Odyssey,' XI, 18-50)

Odysseus speaks:
'Thither we came and beached our ship, and took out the sheep, and ourselves went beside the stream of Oceanus until we came to the place of which Circe had told us.

'Here Perimedes and Eurylochus held the victims, while I drew my sharp sword from beside my thigh, and dug a pit of a cubit's length this way and that, and around it poured a libation to all the dead, first with milk and honey, thereafter with sweet wine, and in the third place with water, and I sprinkled thereon white barley meal. And I earnestly entreated the powerless heads of the dead, vowing that when I came to Ithaca I would sacrifice in my halls a barren heifer, the best I had, and pile the altar with goodly gifts, and to Teiresias alone would sacrifice separately a ram, wholly black, the goodliest of my flocks. But when with vows and prayers I had made supplication to the tribes of the dead, I took the sheep and cut their throats over the pit, and the dark blood ran forth. Then there gathered from out of Erebus the spirits of those that are dead, brides, and unwedded youths, and toil-worn old men, and tender maidens with hearts yet new to sorrow, and many, too, that had been wounded with bronze-tipped spears, men slain in fight, wearing their blood-stained armour. These came thronging in crowds about the pit from every side, with a wondrous cry; and pale fear seized me. Then I called to my comrades and bade them flay and burn the sheep that lay there slain with the pitiless bronze, and to make prayers to the gods, to mighty Hades and dread Persephone. And I myself drew my sharp sword from beside my thigh and sat there, and would not suffer the powerless heads of the dead to draw near to the blood until I had enquired of Teiresias.'

Translation by A. T. Murray, in the Loeb Classical Library, vol. I (New York, 1919), pp. 387-9

Types of Sacrifice

96. A SACRIFICE TO RHEA, THE PHRYGIAN MOTHER-GODDESS

(Apollonius Rhodius, 'Argonautica,' I, 1078-1150)

After this, fierce tempests arose for twelve days and nights together and kept them there from sailing. But in the next night the rest of the chieftains, overcome by sleep, were resting during the latest period of the night, while Acastus and Mopsus the son of Ampycus kept guard over their deep slumbers. And above the golden head of Aeson's son there hovered a halcyon prophesying with shrill voice the ceasing of the stormy winds; and Mopsus heard and understood the cry of the bird of the shore, fraught with good omen. And some god made it turn aside, and flying aloft it settled upon the stern-ornament of the ship. And the seer touched Jason as he lay wrapped in soft sheepskins and woke him at once, and thus spake:

'Son of Aeson, thou must climb to this temple on rugged Dindymum and propitiate the mother (i.e., Rhea) of all the blessed gods on her fair throne, and the stormy blasts shall cease. For such was the voice I heard but now from the halcyon, bird of the sea, which, as it flew above thee in thy slumber, told me all. For by her power the winds and the sea and all the earth below and the snowy seat of Olympus are complete; and to her, when from the mountains she ascends the mighty heaven, Zeus himself, the son of Cronos, gives place. In like manner the rest of the immortal blessed ones reverence the dread goddess.'

Thus he spake, and his words were welcome to Jason's ear. And he arose from his bed with joy and woke all his comrades hurriedly and told them the prophecy of Mopsus the son of Ampycus. And quickly the younger men drove oxen from their stalls and began to lead them to the mountain's lofty summit. And they loosed the hawsers from the sacred rock and rowed to the Thracian harbour; and the heroes climbed the mountain, leaving a few of their comrades in the ship. And to them, the Macrian heights and all the coast of Thrace opposite appeared to view close at hand. And there appeared the misty mouth of Bosporus and the Mysian hills; and on the other side the stream of the river Aesepus and the city and Nepian plain of Adrasteia. Now there was a sturdy stump of vine that grew in the forest, a tree exceeding old; this they cut down, to be the sacred image of the mountain goddess; and Argos smoothed it skilfully, and they set it upon that rugged hill beneath a canopy of lofty oaks, which of all trees have their roots deepest. And near it they heaped an altar of small stones, and wreathed their brows with oak leaves and paid heed to sacrifice, invoking the mother of Dindymum, most venerable, dweller in Phrygia, and Titas and Cyllenus, who alone of many are called dispensers of doom and assessors of the Idaean mother—the Idaean Dactyls of Crete, whom once the nymph Anchiale, as she grasped with both hands the land of Oaxus, bare in the Dictaean cave. And with many prayers did Aeson's son beseech the goddess to turn aside the stormy blasts as he poured libations on the blazing sacrifice; and at the same time by command of Orpheus the youths trod a measure dancing in full armour, and clashed with their swords on their shields, so that the ill-omened cry might be lost in the air—the wail which the people were still sending up in grief for their king. Hence from that time forward the Phrygians propitiate Rhea with the wheel and the drum. And the gracious goddess, I ween, inclined her heart to pious sacrifices; and favourable signs appeared. The trees shed abundant fruit, and round their feet the earth of its own accord put forth flowers from the tender grass. And the beasts of the wild wood left their lairs and thickets and came up fawning on them with their tails. And she caused yet another marvel; for hitherto there was no flow of water on Dindymum, but then for them an unceasing stream gushed forth from the thirsty peak just as it was, and the dwellers around in after times called that stream, the spring of Jason. And then they made a feast in honour of the goddess on the Mount of Bears, singing the praises of Rhea most venerable; but at dawn the winds had ceased and they rowed away from the island.

Translation by R. C. Seaton, in the Loeb Classical Library (New York, 1912), pp. 77-81

97. EXPIATION OF AN UMBRIAN TOWN: AN ARCHAIC ROMAN SACRIFICE

The following has been translated from texts inscribed in Umbrian dialect on bronze tablets from Gubbio, ancient Iguvium. Iguvium is one hundred miles north of Rome. The ritual described was probably typical of early Italian religion generally.

(VI. A) This sacrifice must begin with observation of the birds, when the owl and the crow are favourable [prospering] and the woodpeckers, male and female, are on the right hand [legitimizing]. The one who goes to observe the birds must sit in a fenced enclosure and call upon the priest: 'Specify, that I observe favourable owls, favourable crows, a male woodpecker on the right hand, a female woodpecker on the right hand, birds on the right, voices of birds on the right, sent by the god.' The priest shall specify accordingly: 'Observe there favourable owls, favourable crows, a male woodpecker on the right hand, a female woodpecker on the right hand, birds on the right, voices of birds on the right, sent by the gods for me, for the community of Iguvium, at this particular time.' While he sits in his seat—the one who goes to listen to the voices of the birds—no noise [whispering] shall be made, and no one shall come between [to obstruct his view], until he has returned—i.e. the one who went to listen to the voices of the birds. If any noise is made or any person sits between [him and the birds], it shall be invalid. . . .

(16) When the voices of the birds are heard, the one sitting in the enclosure shall announce it, calling the priest by name, '[I announce] favourable owls, favourable crows, a male woodpecker on the right hand, a female woodpecker on the right hand, birds on the right, voices of birds on the right hand for thee, for the community of Iguvium, at this particular time.' For all these sacred acts, for the procession about the people, for the expiation of the city, he must carry the sacred staff. The sacrificial hearth at the Treblanian gate, which is to be laid for the expiation of the city, thou shalt so arrange that fire may be kindled from fire. So likewise at the two other gates, the Tesenacan and the Veiine.

Before the Treblanian gate, three oxen shall be sacrificed to Jupiter Grabovius. At the offering shall be said: 'To thee I offer prayers, O Jupiter Grabovius, for the Fisian city, for the town of Iguvium, for the names of the city, for the names of the town; be friendly, be gracious to the Fisian city, to the town of Iguvium, to the name of the city, to the name of the town, O holy one, to thee I pray with supplications, O Jupiter Grabovius, trusting in the sacred [sacrificial?] rite, I pray to thee with supplications, O Jupiter Grabovius. O Jupiter Grabovius, to thee [I offer] these fat oxen [as an expiation] for the Fisian city, for the town of Iguvium, for the names of the city, for the names of the town.

'O Jupiter Grabovius, by the effect of this [offering] . . . if in the Fisian city a fire breaks out [as a result of lightning], if in the town of Iguvium the due rites are neglected, [look upon it] as if it had been unintentional. O Jupiter Grabovius, if in thine offering [anything] is amiss, or neglected, or omitted, or [fraudulently] held back, or at fault, or if in thine offering there be any blemish, whether seen or unseen, O Jupiter Grabovius, let it be expiated by those fat oxen for an expiation, as is right. O Jupiter Grabovius, expiate the Fisian city, the town of Iguvium. O Jupiter Grabovius, expiate the name of the Fisian city, the town of Iguvium; the full citizens, the sacred rites, slaves, cattle, the fruits of the field, expiate. Be kind, be gracious with thy favour to the Fisian city, the town of Iguvium, the name of the city, the name of the town. O Jupiter Grabovius, preserve the Fisian city, preserve the town of Iguvium. O Jupiter Grabovius, preserve the Fisian city, preserve the town of Iguvium; full citizens, sacred rites, slaves, cattle, fruits of the field, preserve. Be kind, be gracious with thy favour to the Fisian city, to the town of Iguvium, the name of the city, the name of the town. O Jupiter Grabovius, with these fat oxen as an expiation for the Fisian city, for the town of Iguvium, for the names of the city, for the names of the town, O Jupiter Grabovius, I call upon thee.'

Translation by Frederick C. Grant, in his *Ancient Roman Religion*, Library of Religion paperbook series (New York, 1957), pp. 4-6, from Franz Bücheler, *Umbrica* (1883), VI A

98. AN OFFERING FOR JUPITER BEFORE THE SOWING

(Cato, 'On Agriculture,' 132)

Marcus Porcius Cato's work on agriculture, written about 160 B.C., is full of references to archaic and traditional rites, customs, and religious views.

The offering is to be made in this way: Offer to Jupiter Dapalis a cup of wine of whatever size you wish. Observe the day as a holiday (*feria*) for the oxen, their drivers, and those who make the offering. When you make the offering, say as follows: 'Jupiter Dapalis, since it is due and proper (*oportet*) that a cup of wine be offered thee, in my home among my family, for thy sacred feast; for that reason, be thou honoured by this feast that is offered thee.' Wash your hands, and then take the wine and say: 'Jupiter Dapalis, be thou honoured by this feast that is offered thee and be thou honoured by the wine that is placed before thee.' If you wish, make an offering to Vesta. The feast of Jupiter consists of roasted meat and an urn of wine. Present it to Jupiter religiously, in the proper form (*Jovi caste profanato sua contagione*). After the offering is made, plant millet, panic grass, garlic, and lentils.

Translation by Frederick C. Grant, in his *Ancient Roman Religion*, Library of Religion paperbook series (New York, 1957), p. 34

99. A ROMAN HARVEST SACRIFICE

(Cato, 'On Agriculture,' 134)

The offering of a pig preliminary to harvesting crops was perhaps originally intended to placate the 'Di Manes,' offended by the disturbance of the soil or by some accidental or unintentional wrong committed during the sowing, growth or maturing of the grain. Eventually it was understood to refer solely to the harvest.

Before the harvest the sacrifice of the *porca praecidanea* must be offered in this manner: Offer a sow as *porca praecidanea* to Ceres before you harvest spelt, wheat, barley, beans, and rape seed. Offer a prayer, with incense and wine, to Janus, Jupiter and Juno, before offering the sow. Offer a pile of cakes (*strues*) to Janus, saying, 'Father Janus, in offering these cakes to thee, I humbly pray that thou wilt be propitious and merciful to me and my children, my house and my household.' Then make an offering of cake (*fertum*) to Jupiter with these words: 'In offering thee this cake, O Jupiter, I humbly pray that thou, pleased with this offering, will be propitious and merciful to me and my children, my house and my household.' Then present the wine to Janus, saying: 'Father Janus, as I have prayed humbly in offering thee the cakes, so mayest thou in the same way be honoured by this wine now placed before thee.' Then pray to Jupiter thus: 'Jupiter, mayest thou be honoured in accepting this cake; mayest thou be honoured in accepting the wine placed before thee.' Then sacrifice the *porca praecidanea*. When the entrails have been removed, make an offering of cakes to Janus, and pray in the same way as you have prayed before. Offer a cake to Jupiter, praying just as before. In the same way offer wine to Janus and offer wine to Jupiter, in the same way as before in offering the pile of cakes, and in the consecration of the cake (fertum). Afterward offer the entrails and wine to Ceres.

Translation by Frederick C. Grant, in his *Ancient Roman Religion*, Library of Religion paperback series (New York, 1957), pp. 34-5

100. DEVOTIO: THE SACRIFICIAL DEATH OF DECIUS

(Livy, 'History of Rome,' VIII, 9, 1-11; 10, 3)

This legendary incident took place, presumably, during the Samnite wars, circa 340 B.C.

The Roman consuls, before they led their troops into the battle, offered sacrifices. It is said that the soothsayer [*haruspex*] pointed out to Decius that the head of the liver was on the friendly [right] side, that the victim was in other respects acceptable to the gods, and that the sacrifice of Manlius had been most favourable. 'It will do,' said Decius, 'if my colleague has received favourable omens.' In the formation above described they advanced into the field. Manlius commanded the right wing, Decius the left. At first the battle was fought with equal strength and ardour on both sides; but after a time the Roman *hastati* [spearmen] on the left, unable to resist the pressure of the Latins, fell back upon the *principes* [i.e., the heavy armed troops]. In this instant of alarm Decius the consul shouted with a loud voice to Marcus Valerius: 'We need help from the gods, Marcus Valerius! Come, state [or public] pontiff of the Roman people, dictate the words, so that I can devote myself for [i.e., save] the legions.' The pontiff bade him put on the purple-bordered toga and veil his head, with one hand thrust out from beneath the toga and touching his chin, and standing upon a spear that was laid beneath his feet to say as follows: 'Janus, Jupiter, Father Mars, Quirinus, Bellona, Lares, Divi Novensiles, Di Indigites, gods in whose power are both we and our enemies, and you also, Di Manes—I invoke and implore you, your favour I beg and beseech, that you may prosper the power and the victory of the Roman people of the Quirites, and visit upon the foes of the Roman people of the Quirites terror, fear, and death. As I have pronounced the words, even so on behalf of [*pro, in lieu of*] the republic of the Roman people of the Quirites, the army, the legions, and the auxiliaries of the Roman people of the Quirites, I hereby devote the legions and auxiliaries of the enemy, together with myself, to the Di Manes and to Earth [Tellus].'

Having uttered this prayer, he ordered the lictors to go to Titus Manlius at once and announce to his colleague that he had devoted himself for the good of the army. Then, girding himself with the Gabinian cincture and leaping, armed, upon his horse, he plunged into the thick of the enemy, a conspicuous sight to both armies and with something about him more august than human, as though he had been sent from heaven to expiate all the anger of the gods, and to avert destruction from his people and turn it upon their enemies. Thus the greatest terror and dread accompanied him, and, throwing the Latin front into disorder, it at once spread deeply into their whole army. This was most clearly evident from the fact that wherever he rode, men trembled as if struck by some baleful star; and when he fell beneath a hail of missiles, in that instant there could be no doubt of the consternation of the Latin cohorts, which everywhere deserted the field and took to flight. At the same time the Romans—their spirits now set free from religious fears—pressed on as if only then the signal had been given for the first time, and delivered a united blow. The light-armed men were running out between the first two ranks of foot soldiers and were adding their strength to that of the spearmen and the heavy armed troops, while the troops in the third rank, kneeling on their right knees, were waiting for the consul to signal them to rise [and advance]. . . .

For the rest, among all the citizens and allies the chief praise in that war belongs to the consuls, of whom one [Decius] had drawn upon himself above all the threats and dangers belonging to the gods above and the gods below, while the other had shown such courage and skill in battle that of those Romans and Latins who have handed down a report of the conflict all agree that whichever side was led by Titus Manlius would surely have won. The Latins fled to Minturnae. After the battle their camp was captured and many men—mostly Campanians—were seized and put to death there. The body of Decius could not be found that day, and night fell while the search continued. On the following day it was discovered in a great heap of enemy dead, covered with missiles, and was given burial by his colleagues in a manner befitting his death.

It seems appropriate at this point to add that the consul, dictator, or praetor who devotes the legions of the enemy need not also devote himself, but may instead devote any citizen he chooses from an enlisted Roman legion. If this man is killed, it is proof that all is well. If he does not die, then an image [*signum*] of him is buried seven feet or more beneath the ground and a sacrifice [*piaculum*, sin offering] is slain; and where the image is buried no Roman magistrate may lawfully ascend [i.e., upon the tumulus].

But if he chooses to devote himself, as Decius did, but does not die, he cannot rightly offer sacrifice either for himself or for the people, whether it is with a sacrificial victim or something else that he wishes to offer. The one who devotes himself may dedicate his arms to Vulcan or to any other god he chooses [as a rule, the enemies' weapons were dedicated to Vulcan]. The spear on which the consul had stood and prayed must not be allowed to fall into enemy hands. If this happens, expiation must be made to Mars, with swine, sheep and bull [*Marti suovetaurilibus piaculum fieri*]. These details, though the memory of both divine and human customs has now been wiped out by the preference shown to new and foreign ways rather than to the ancient and ancestral, I have thought it worth while to relate in the very words which were fashioned and handed down [from the days of old].

Translation by Frederick C. Grant, in his *Ancient Roman Religion*, Library of Religion paperback series (New York, 1957), pp. 23-5

101. THE COSMIC SACRIFICE

('Rig Veda,' x, 90)

Quite different from the impersonal creative force tad ekam *of Rig Veda,* X, 129 *(see p. 109), or the hymn of Prajāpati, Rig Veda,* X, 121 *(see p. 34) is the Purusha-sūkta. Purusha is at once supreme being, the cosmos, and (literally) 'man,' and as such he is sacrificed primordially as the very act of creation. As cosmic being, only one-quarter of Purusha is manifest; three-quarters of him are eternally unmanifest (like* Bráhman [neuter], *the absolute creative power).*

Self-immolated, his creative act becomes a prototype: all sacrifices henceforth are repetitions, reconstructing victim, altar, and even the consequences of that primeval sacrifice. In other words, the human microcosmic work, in correspondence with the macrocosmic original, recreates the world with each new sacrifice, producing as in illo tempore, not only all living creatures, celestial bodies, the three worlds, and the gods themselves, but also the substance of the three Vedas.

Of particular interest here (as it is the only Rig Vedic reference to the four social classes), the dismembered Purusha provides Brāhmans, Rājanyas (or Kshatriyas), Vaishyas and Shūdras from his own mouth, arms, thighs and feet, respectively. Thus does the Vedic creation hymn account for the origin of the non-Aryan serf (Shūdra), as well as the archaic tripartite distinction between the priest, concerned with the sacred utterance (bráhman), the warrior and his force (kshatra) of 'arms,' and the Vaishya, sprung from the loins of Purusha, who knows the secrets of animal and plant fertility and of wealth.

1. A thousand heads had Purusha, a thousand eyes, a thousand feet.
   He covered earth on every side, and spread ten fingers' breadth beyond.
2. This Purusha is all that yet hath been and all that is to be;
   The Lord of immortality which waxes greater still by food.[1]
3. So mighty is his greatness; yea, greater than this is Purusha.
   All creatures are one-fourth of him, three-fourths eternal life in heaven.
4. With three-fourths Purusha went up; one fourth of him again was here.
   Thence he strode out to every side over what eats not and what eats.
5. From him Virāj was born; again Purusha from Virāj was born.[2]
   As soon as he was born he spread eastward and westward[3] o'er the earth.
6. When gods prepared the sacrifice with Purusha as their offering,
   Its oil was spring, the holy gift was autumn; summer was the wood.
7. They balmed as victim on the grass[4] Purusha born in earliest time.
   With him the deities and all Sādhyas[5] and rishis sacrificed.
8. From that great general sacrifice the dripping fat was gathered up.
   He formed the creatures of the air, and animals both wild and tame.
9. From that great general sacrifice Rc- and Sāma-hymns were born;
   Therefrom the metres were produced, the Yajus had its birth from it.
10. From it were horses born, from it all creatures with two rows of teeth;
    From it were generated kine, from it the goats and sheep were born.

The notes to this text are on p. 228.

11. When they divided Purusha how many portions did they make?
    What do they call his mouth, his arms? What do they call his thighs and feet?

12. The Brāhman was his mouth, of both his arms was the Rājanya made.
    His thighs became the Vaishya, from his feet the Shūdra was produced.

13. The moon was gendered from his mind, and from his eye the sun had birth;
    Indra and Agni from his mouth were born, and Vāyu from his breath.

14. Forth from his navel came mid-air; the sky was fashioned from his head;
    Earth from his feet, and from his ear the regions. Thus they formed the worlds.

15. Seven fencing-logs[7] had he, thrice seven layers of fuel were prepared,
    When the gods, offering sacrifice, bound as their victim, Purusha.

16. Gods, sacrificing, sacrificed the victim; these were the earliest holy ordinances.
    The mighty ones attained the height of heaven, there where the Sādhyas, gods of old, are dwelling.

Notes

1 Although the Purusha is 'all that is,' sacrificial offerings yet provide him increase.

2 Virāj is obscure. As in other creation hymns (X, 129; X, 121), some primordial matter is presupposed. Here a cosmic 'man,' in lieu of the formless waters or undifferentiated sky-earth, is basal, but an intermediate stage of creation seems to be implied. 'From him' (the unmanifest quarter of Purusha) proceeds this secondary cosmic source, which in turn gives birth to (the manifest quarter of) Purusha. Aitareya-brāhmana I, 4 associates Virāj mystically with food, perhaps reflecting upon this passage and stanzas 2 and 4 above.

3 From one end of the earth (bhūmi) to the other.

4 Sacrificial grass.

5 Sādhyās, an ancient class of celestial beings; those who are worthy of propitiation.

6 The three Vedas: Rigveda, Sāmaveda and Yajurveda are here produced. This hymn is obviously then one of the latest to be included in the Rig Veda.

7 Borders of the sacrificial fire; usually three green sticks, but here a sacred number, seven.

Translation by Ralph T. H. Griffith, in his The Hymns of the Rigveda, IV (Benares, 1892), pp 289-93

See also no. 56

D. RITUALS, ORACLES, PRESCRIPTIONS, DEVOTION

102. RAIN-MAKING (AUSTRALIA)

It is universally believed by the tribes of the Karamundi nation, of the Darling River, that rain can be brought down by the following ceremony. A vein in the arm of one of the men is opened and the blood allowed to drop into a piece of hollow bark until there is a little pool. Into this is put a quantity of gypsum, ground fine, and stirred until it has the consistency of a thick paste. A number of hairs are pulled out of the man's beard and mixed up with this paste, which is then placed between two pieces of bark and put under the surface of the water in some river or lagoon, and kept there by means of pointed stakes driven into the ground. When the mixture is all dissolved away, the blackfellows say that a great cloud will come, bringing rain. From the time that this ceremony takes place until the rain comes, the men are tabooed from their wives, or the charm will be spoiled, and the old men say that if this prohibition were properly respected, rain would come every time that it is done. In a time of drought, when rain is badly wanted, the whole tribe meets and performs this ceremony.

A. W. Howitt, *The Native Tribes of South-East Australia* (London, 1904), pp. 396-7

See also nos. 198-201, 210

103. THE REVIVAL OF OSIRIS

('Pyramid Texts,' § 258 ff.)

One of the earliest hymns from the Osiris rituals, preserved in the pyramid of Wenis.

Hail to you, O Knowing One!
Geb has created you anew,

229

the Divine Company has brought you forth anew!
Horus is satisfied for his father,
Atum is satisfied for his offspring.
The gods of East and West are satisfied with this great event
which has come to pass through the action of the Divine Progeny.
Ah! Osiris! See! Behold!
Osiris! Hear! Attend!
Ah! Osiris! Lift yourself upon your side! Carry out what I ordain!
O Hater of Sleep! O Torpid One!
Rise up, you that were cast down in Nedit!
Take your bread with happiness in Pê!
Receive your sceptre in Heliopolis!
This is Horus [speaking], he has ordained action for his father,
he has shown himself master of the storm,
he has countered the blustering of Seth,
so that he (Seth) must bear you—
for it is he that must carry him who is [again] complete.

Translation by R. T. Rundle Clark, in his *Myth and
Symbol in Ancient Egypt* (London, 1959), p. 111

104. A SPELL FOR THE REVIVAL OF OSIRIS

('Coffin Texts,' 74)

Ah Helpless One!
Ah Helpless One Asleep!
Ah Helpless One in this place
    which you know not—yet I know it!
Behold, I have found you [lying] on your side—
    the great Listless One.
'Ah, Sister!' says Iris to Nephthys,
'This is our brother,
Come, let us lift up his head,
Come, let us [rejoin] his bones,
Come, let us reassemble his limbs,
Come, let us put an end to all his woe,
that, as far as we can help, he will weary no more.
May the moisture begin to mount for this spirit!
May the canals be filled through you!

May the names of the rivers be created through you!
Osiris, live!
Osiris, let the great Listless One arise!
I am Isis.'
        'I am Nephthys.
It shall be that Horus will avenge you,
It shall be that Thoth will protect you
—your two sons of the Great White Crown—
It shall be that you will act against him who acted against you,
It shall be that Geb will see,
It shall be that the Company will hear.
Then will your power be visible in the sky
And you will cause havoc among the [hostile] gods,
for Horus, your son, has seized the Great White Crown,
seizing it from him who acted against you.
Then will your father Atum call 'Come!'
Osiris, live!
Osiris, let the great Listless One arise!'

Translation by R. T. Rundle Clark, in his *Myth and Symbol in Ancient Egypt* (London, 1959), pp. 125-6

See also nos. 88, 167, 168

105. THE SACRED PIPE (DAKOTA INDIANS)

The sacred pipe plays a central ritual role among a great number of North American Indian tribes. The smoke is blown like incense to the celestial Beings, to the earth, and to the four cardinal points.

Two young men, in time of famine, were scouting for game upon the prairies. They encounter a beautiful woman, solitary. One of the young men, being lascivious in thought of her, is enveloped in a cloud, which, lifting, leaves only his bones. The other, reverent in heart, is instructed to hasten to the tribe and prepare them for the reception of the stranger. The Medicine Lodge is erected, and at sunrise on the following day to the awaiting tribesmen the mysterious maiden appears, bearing with her a sacred calumet. This she bestows, as something very precious, to the tribal custodians, at the same time charging the members of the tribe with their duties to one another. The version of Lone Man, a Teton, gives most fully the essential teaching. His narrative is recorded by Frances Densmore.

Braided sweet grass was dipped into a buffalo horn containing rain water and was offered to the Maiden. The chief said, 'Sister, we are now ready to hear the good message you have brought.' The pipe, which was in the hands of the Maiden, was lowered and placed on the rack. Then the Maiden sipped the water from the sweet grass.

Then, taking up the pipe again, she arose and said: 'My relatives, brothers and sisters: Wakantanka has looked down, and smiles upon us this day because we have met as belonging to one family. The best thing in a family is good feeling towards every member of the family. I am proud to become a member of your family—a sister to you all. The sun is your grandfather, and he is the same to me. Your tribe has the distinction of being always very faithful to promises, and of possessing great respect and reverence towards sacred things. It is known also that nothing but good feeling prevails in the tribe, and that whenever any member has been found guilty of committing any wrong, that member has been cast out and not allowed to mingle with the other members of the tribe. For all these good qualities in the tribe you have been chosen as worthy and deserving of all good gifts. I represent the Buffalo tribe, who have sent you this pipe. You are to receive this pipe in the name of all the common people (Indians). Take it, and use it according to my directions. The bowl of the pipe is red stone—a stone not very common and found only at a certain place. This pipe shall be used as a peacemaker. The time will come when you shall cease hostilities against other nations. Whenever peace is agreed upon between two tribes or parties this pipe shall be a binding instrument. By this pipe the medicine-men shall be called to administer help to the sick.'

Turning to the women, she said:

'My dear sisters, the women: You have a hard life to live in this world, yet without you this life would not be what it is. Wakantanka intends that you shall bear much sorrow—comfort others in time of sorrow. By your hands the family moves. You have been given the knowledge of making clothes and of feeding the family. Wakantanka is with you in your sorrows and joins you in your griefs. He has given you the great gift of kindness towards every living creature on earth. You he has chosen to have a feeling for the dead who are gone. He knows that you remember the dead longer than do the men. He knows that you love your children dearly.'

Then turning to the children:

'My little brothers and sisters. Your parents were once little children like you, but in the course of time they became men and women. All living creatures were once small, but if no one took care of them they would never grow up. Your parents love you and have made many sacrifices for your sake in order that Wakantanka may listen to them, and that nothing but good may come to you as you grow up. I have brought this pipe for them, and you shall reap some benefit from it. Learn to respect and reverence this pipe, and above all, lead pure lives. Wakantanka is your great grandfather.'

Turning to the men:

'Now my dear brothers: In giving you this pipe you are expected to use it for nothing but good purposes. The tribe as a whole shall depend upon it for their necessary needs. You realize that all your necessities of life come from the earth below, the sky above, and the four winds. Whenever you do anything wrong against these elements they will always take some revenge upon you. You should reverence them. Offer sacrifices through this pipe. When you are in need of buffalo meat, smoke this pipe and ask for what you need and it shall be granted you. On you it depends to be a strong help to the women in the raising of children. Share the women's sorrow. Wakantanka smiles on the man who has a kind feeling for a woman, because the woman is weak. Take this pipe, and offer it to Wakantanka daily. Be good and kind to the little children.'

Turning to the chief:

'My older brother: You have been chosen by these people to receive this pipe in the name of the whole Sioux tribe. Wakantanka is pleased and glad this day because you have done what is required and expected that every good leader should do. By this pipe the tribe shall live. It is your duty to see that this pipe is respected and reverenced. I am proud to be called a sister. May Wakantanka look down on us and take pity on us and provide us with what we need. Now we shall smoke the pipe.'

Then she took the buffalo chip which lay on the ground, lighted the pipe, and pointing to the sky with the stem of the pipe, she said, 'I offer this to Wakantanka for all the good that comes from above.' (Pointing to the earth:) 'I offer this to the earth, whence come all good gifts.' (Pointing to the cardinal points:) 'I offer this to the four winds, whence come all good things.' Then she took a puff of the pipe, passed it to the chief, and said, 'Now my dear brothers and sisters, I have done the work for which I was sent here and now I will go, but I do not wish any escort. I only ask that the way be cleared before me.'

Then, rising, she started, leaving the pipe with the chief, who ordered that the people be quiet until their sister was out of sight. She came out of the tent on the left side, walking very slowly; as soon as she was outside the entrance she turned into a white buffalo calf.

H. B. Alexander, *The World's Rim* (Lincoln, Neb.: University of Nebraska Press, 1953), pp. 155-7; quoting from and commenting on Frances Densmore, *Teton Sioux Music* (Bureau of American Ethnology, Bulletin 61, 1918), pp. 65-6

106. MEANING AND VALUE OF RITUALS: A CONFUCIAN APPRAISAL

('Hsün Tzu,' chapter 19, 'On Rites' [Li])

With Confucius and Mencius, Hsün Tzu was one of the outstanding philosophical figures of the Chou dynasty era. His exact dates are not known, but he flourished approximately 298-238 B.C.

Rites (li) rest on three bases: Heaven and earth, which are the source of all life; the ancestors, who are the source of the human race; sovereigns and teachers, who are the source of government. If there were no Heaven and earth, where would life come from? If there were no ancestors, where would the offspring come from? If there were no sovereigns and teachers, where would government come from? Should any of the three be missing, either there would be no men or men would be without peace. Hence rites are to serve Heaven on high and earth below, and to honour the ancestors and elevate the sovereigns and teachers. Herein lies the threefold basis of rites. . . .

In general, rites begin with primitive practices, attain cultured forms, and finally achieve beauty and felicity. When rites are at their best, men's emotions and sense of beauty are both fully expressed. When they are at the next level, either the emotion or the sense of beauty oversteps the others. When they are at still the next level, emotion reverts to the state of primitivity.

It is through rites that Heaven and earth are harmonious and sun and moon are bright, that the four seasons are ordered and the stars are on their courses, that rivers flow and that things prosper, that love and hatred are tempered and joy and anger are in keeping. They cause the lowly to be obedient and those on high to be illustrious. He who holds to the rites is never confused in the midst of multifarious change; he who deviates therefrom is lost. Rites—are they not the culmination of culture? . . .

Rites require us to treat both life and death with attentiveness. Life is the beginning of man, death is his end. When a man is well off both at the end and the beginning, the way of man is fulfilled. Hence the gentleman respects the beginning and is carefully attentive to the end. To pay equal attention to the end as well as to the beginning is the way of the gentleman and the beauty of rites and righteousness. . . .

Rites serve to shorten that which is too long and lengthen that which is too short, reduce that which is too much and augment that which is too little, express the beauty of love and reverence and cultivate the elegance of righteous conduct. Therefore, beautiful adornment and coarse sackcloth, music and weeping, rejoicing and sorrow, though pairs of opposites, are in the rites equally utilized and alternately brought into play. Beautiful adornment, music, and rejoicing are appropriate on occasions of felicity; coarse sackcloth, weeping, and sorrow are appropriate on occasions of ill-fortune. Rites make room for beautiful adornment but not to the point of being fascinating, for coarse sackcloth but not to the point of deprivation or self-injury, for music and rejoicing but not to the point of being lewd and indolent, for weeping and sorrow but not to the point of being depressing and injurious. Such is the middle path of rites. . . .

Funeral rites are those by which the living adorn the dead. The dead are accorded a send-off as though they were living. In this way the dead are served like the living, the absent like the present. Equal attention is thus paid to the end as well as to the beginning of life. . . .

Now the rites used on the occasion of birth are to embellish joy, those used on the occasion of death are to embellish sorrow, those used at sacrifice are to embellish reverence, those used on millitary occasions are to embellish dignity. In this respect the rites of all kings are alike, antiquity and the present age agree, and no one knows whence they came. . . .

Sacrifice is to express a person's feeling of remembrance and longing, for grief and affliction cannot be kept out of one's consciousness all the time. When men are enjoying the pleasure of good company, a loyal minister or a filial son may feel grief and affliction. Once such feelings arise, he is greatly excited and moved. If such feelings are not given proper expression, then his emotions and memories are disappointed and not satisfied, and the appropriate rite is lacking. Thereupon the ancient kings instituted rites, and henceforth the principle of expressing honour to the honoured and love to the beloved is fully realized. Hence I say: Sacrifice is to express a person's feeling of remembrance and longing. As to the fullness of the sense of loyalty and affection, the richness of ritual and beauty—these none but the sage can understand. Sacrifice is something that the sage clearly understands, the scholar-gentlemen contentedly perform, the officials consider a duty, and the common people regard as established custom. Among gentlemen it is considered the way of man; among the common people it is considered as having to do with the spirits.

Translation by Y. P. Mei, in Wm. Theodore de Bary (ed.), *Sources of Chinese Tradition* (New York: Columbia University Press, 1960), pp. 123-4

107. THE ENSHRINEMENT OF AMATERASU

('Nihongi,' I, 175-6)

The following entry in Nihongi (see p. 94), for the twenty-fifth year of the Emperor Suinin's reign (5 B.C. according to traditional dating but more probably around A.D. 260), describes the founding of the great shrine to Amaterasu at Ise. The moving of the Sun Goddess no doubt refers to the transporting of the mirror thought to be her embodiment.

Third month, 10th day. The Great Goddess Amaterasu was taken from [the princess] Toyo-suki-iri-hime, and entrusted to [the princess] Yamato-hime no Mikoto. Now Yamato-hime sought for a place where she might enshrine the Great Goddess. So she proceeded to Sasahata in Uda. Then turning back from thence, she entered the land of Omi, and went round eastwards to Mino, whence she arrived in the province of Ise.

Now the Great Goddess Amaterasu instructed Yamato-hime saying: 'The province of Ise, of the divine wind, is the land whither repair the waves from the eternal world, the successive waves. It is a secluded and pleasant land. In this land I wish to dwell.' In compliance, therefore, with the instruction of the Great Goddess, a shrine was erected to her in the province of Ise. Accordingly an Abstinence Palace[1] was built at Kawakami in Isuzu. This was called the palace of Iso. It was there that the Great Goddess Amaterasu first descended from Heaven.

Note

1 Abstinence Palace or Worship Palace.

Adapted from Aston's translation, by Wm. Theodore de Bary (ed.), *Sources of Japanese Tradition* (New York: Columbia University Press, 1958), pp. 34-5

108. A SHINTO HARVEST RITUAL

('Norito')

The Praying for Harvest, or Toshigohi no Matsuri, was celebrated on the 4th day of the 2nd month of each year, at the capital in the Zhingikuwan or Office for the Worship of the Shinto gods, and in the provinces by the chiefs of the local administration. At the Zhingikuwan there were assembled the ministers of state, the functionaries of that office, the priests and priestesses of 573 temples, containing 737 shrines, which were kept up at the expense of the Mikado's treasury, while the governors of the provinces superintended in the districts under their administration the performance of rites in honour of 2,395 other shrines.

The service began at twenty minutes to seven. The officials of the Zhingikuwan arranged the offering on the tables and below them, according to the rank of the shrines for which they were intended. The final preparations being now complete, the ministers of state, the virgin priestesses and the priests of the temples to which offerings were sent by the Mikado entered in succession, and took the places severally assigned to them. The horses which formed a part of the offerings were next brought in from the Mikado's stable, and all the congregation drew near, while the reader recited or read the *norito*. This reader was a member of the priestly family or tribe of Nakatomi, who traced their descent back to Amenokoyane, one of the principal advisers attached to the sun-goddess' grandchild when he first descended on earth.

The earliest account of the proceedings on these occasions is contained in a Record of the year 871. The harvest ritual translated by

Man and the Sacred

Satow contains 13 prayers and invocations. The text reproduced below is the third in that series.

He[1] says: 'I declare in the presence of the sovran gods of the HAR-VEST.[2] If the sovran gods will bestow in many-bundled ears and in luxuriant ears the late-ripening harvest which they will bestow, the late-ripening harvest which will be produced by the dripping of foam from the arms and by drawing the mud together between the opposing thighs,[3] then I will fulfil their praises by setting-up the first fruits in a thousand ears and many hundred ears,[4] raising-high the beer-jars, filling and ranging-in-rows the bellies of the beer-jars, I *will present them* [i.e. *the first-fruits*] in juice and in ear. As to things which grow in the great-field-plain—sweet herbs and bitter herbs: as to things which dwell in the blue-sea plain—things wide of fin and things narrow of fin, down to the weeds of the offing and weeds of the shore: and as to CLOTHES—with bright cloth, glittering cloth, soft cloth and coarse cloth will I fulfil praises. And having furnished a white horse, a white boar and a white cock,[5] and the various kinds of things in the presence of the sovran god of the HARVEST, I fulfil his praises by setting up the great OFFERINGS of the sovran GRANDCHILD's[6] augustness.'

Notes

1 'He' is the reader of the ritual, and the word rendered by 'says' signifies that the speaker is supposed to be speaking the words of the Mikado.
2 Who the gods of the Harvest were is unknown. According to the Ko-ji-ki, Susa-no-o begot the Great Harvest god, Ohotoshi no Kami, who begot the Harvest god, Mi-toshi no Kami, and several other names of deities, supposed to provide the human race with cereals, occur in various myths. The most famous of these are the goddess worshipped at the Outer Temple (Gekuu) at Watarahi in Ise, and the deity, Uka no mitama or Spirit of Food, to whom is dedicated the temple of Inari.
3 The process of preparing the half-liquid soil of the rice fields for the reception of the young plants is thus described.
4 Kahi, here rendered by 'ear,' is more exactly the seed of rice enclosed between the paleae.
5 The horse for the god to ride on, the cock to tell the time, and the boar (a domesticated animal,—not the wild boar) for the god's food.
6 I.e. Grandchild of Amaterasu, the Sun-Goddess. The epithet 'sovran grandchild' was first applied to the founder on earth of the Mikado's dynasty, but came in time to be applied to each and all of his successors on the throne.

Translation, introduction and notes by Ernest Satow, 'Ancient Japanese Rituals: no. 1—The Praying for Harvest,' Transactions of the Asiatic Society of Japan, vol. VII, part I (1879) pp. 97-132; quotation from pp. 113 ff.

109. THE AZTEC CEREMONIAL BATHING OF THE NEWBORN (FROM BERNARDINO DE SAHAGÚN)

The priest addresses the Goddess of the Flowing Waters:

'Merciful Lady Chalchiuhtlicue, thy servant here present is come into this world, sent by our father and mother, Ometecutli and Omeciuatl, who reside at the ninth heaven. We know not what gifts he bringeth; we know not what hath been assigned to him from before the beginning of the world, nor with what lot he cometh enveloped. We know not if this lot be good or bad, or to what end he will be followed by ill fortune. We know not what faults or defects he may inherit from his father or mother. Behold him between thy hands ! Wash him and deliver him from impurities as thou knowest should be, for he is confided to thy power. Cleanse him of the contamination he hath received from his parents; let the water take away the soil and the stain, and let him be freed from all taint. May it please thee, O Goddess, that his heart and his life be purified, that he may dwell in this world in peace and wisdom. May this water take away all ills, for which this babe is put into thy hands, thou who art mother and sister of the gods, and who alone art worthy to possess it and to give it, to wash from him the evils which he beareth from before the beginning of the world. Deign to do this that we ask, now that the child is in thy presence.'

H. B. Alexander, *The World's Rim* (Lincoln, Neb.: University of Nebraska Press, 1953), p. 177; translating Bernardino de Sahagún, *Historia de las Cosas de la Nueva España* (Mexico, 1946), bk. VI, chap. XXXII

110. THE EGYPTIAN 'NEGATIVE CONFESSION'

('Book of the Dead,' chapter 125)

When the deceased enters the hall of the goddesses of Truth, he says:

'Homage to thee, O great god, thou Lord of Truth. I have come to thee, my Lord, and I have brought myself hither that I may see thy beauties,' [i.e., experience thy gracious clemency]. 'I know thee, I know thy name. I know the names of the Two-and-Forty gods who live with thee in this Hall of Maāti, who keep ward over those who have done evil, who feed upon their blood on the day when the lives of men are reckoned up in the presence of Un-Nefer [i.e., Osiris]. In truth I have come to thee. I have brought Truth to thee. I have destroyed wickedness for thee.' [These words are followed by a statement of the offences which he had not committed, and he says:]

1. I have not sinned against men.
2. I have not oppressed (or wronged) [my] kinsfolk.
3. I have not committed evil in the place of truth.
4. I have not known worthless men.
5. I have not committed acts of abomination.
6. I have not done daily works of supererogation (?)
7. I have not caused my name to appear for honours.
8. I have not domineered over slaves.
9. I have not thought scorn of the god (or, God).
10. I have not defrauded the poor man of his goods.
11. I have not done the things which the gods abominate.
12. I have not caused harm to be done to the slave by his master.
13. I have caused no man to suffer.
14. I have allowed no man to go hungry.
15. I have made no man weep.
16. I have slain no man.
17. I have not given the order for any man to be slain.
18. I have not caused pain to the multitude.
19. I have not filched the offerings in the temples.
20. I have not purloined the cakes of the gods.
21. I have not stolen the offerings of the spirits.
22. I have had no dealing with the paederast.
23. I have not defiled myself in the pure places of the god of my city.
24. I have not cheated in measuring of grain.
25. I have not filched land or added thereto.
26. I have not encroached upon the fields of others.
27. I have not added to the weight of the balance.
28. I have not cheated with the pointer of the scales.
29. I have not taken away the milk from the mouths of the babes.
30. I have not driven away the beasts from their pastures.
31. I have not netted the geese of the preserves of the gods.
32. I have not caught fish with bait of their bodies.
33. I have not obstructed water when it should run.
34. I have not cut a cutting in a canal of running water.

35. I have not extinguished a flame when it ought to burn.
36. I have not abrogated the days of offering the chosen offerings.
37. I have not turned off cattle from the property of the gods.
38. I have not repulsed the god in his manifestations. I am pure. I am pure. I am pure. I am pure.

Translation by E. A. Wallis Budge, *Osiris, the Egyptian Religion of Resurrection*, vol I (1911), pp. 337-9; see also E. A. Wallis Budge, *The Book of the Dead*, vol. II (1901), pp. 365-371

111. AZTEC CONFESSION AND PENITENCE
(FROM BERNARDINO DE SAHAGÚN)

. . . the confessor speaks to the penitent saying: 'Oh brother, thou hast come to a place of great danger, and of much work and terror. . . . thou hast come to a place where snares and nets are tangled and piled one upon another, so that none can pass without falling into them. . . . these are thy sins, which are not only snares and nets and holes into which thou hast fallen, but also wild beasts, that kill and rend the body and the soul. . . . When thou wast created and sent here, thy father and mother Quetzalcoatl made thee like a precious stone . . . but by thine own will and choosing thou didst become soiled . . . and now thou hast confessed. . . . thou hast uncovered and made manifest all thy sins to our lord who shelters and purifies all sinners; and take not this as mockery, for in truth thou hast entered the fountain of mercy, which is like the clearest water with which our lord god, who shelters and protects us all, washes away the dirt from the soul. . . . now thou art born anew, now dost thou begin to live; and even now our lord god gives thee light and a new Sun; now also dost thou begin to flower, and to put forth shoots like a very clean precious stone issuing from thy mother's womb where thou art created. . . . It is fitting that thou do penance working a year in the house of god, and there shalt thou draw blood, and shalt thou pierce thy body with cactus thorns; and that thou make penance for the adulteries and other filth thou hast done, thou shalt pass osiers twice a day, one through thine ears and one through thy tongue; and not only as a penance for the carnal sins already mentioned, but for words and injuries with which thou hast affronted and hurt thy neighbours, with thy evil tongue. And for the ingratitude in which thou hast held the favours our lord hast done thee, and for thy inhumanity to thy neighbours in not making offering of the goods bestowed upon thee by god nor in giving to the poor the temporal goods our lord bestowed upon thee. It shall be thy duty to offer parchment and copal, and also to give alms to the needy who starve and who have neither to eat nor drink nor to be clad, though thou know how to deprive thyself of food to give them, and do thy best to clothe those who go naked and in rags; look that their flesh is as thine, and that they are men as thou art.'

> Laurette Séjourné, *Burning Water*, trans. Irene Nicholson (London, 1957), pp. 9-10; quoting from Bernardino de Sahagún, *Historia de las Cosas de la* Nueva España (Mexico, 1946), vol. II, p. 275

112. A CHINESE THEORY OF PORTENTS

(Tung Chung-shu, 'Ch'un-ch'iu fan-lu,' § 30)

Tung Chung-shu lived 179?-104? B.C. The title of this lengthy work from which the following selection is taken may be rendered in English as 'Deep Significance of the Spring and Autumn Annals.'

The creatures of Heaven and earth at times display unusual changes and these are called wonders. Lesser ones are called ominous portents. The portents always come first and are followed by wonders. Portents are Heaven's warnings, wonders are Heaven's threats. Heaven first sends warnings, and if men do not understand, then it sends wonders to awe them. This is what the *Book of Odes* means when it says: 'We tremble at the awe and the fearfulness of Heaven!' The genesis of all such portents and wonders is a direct result of errors in the state. When the first indications of error begin to appear in the state, Heaven sends forth ominous portents and calamities to warn men and announce the fact. If, in spite of these warnings and announcements, men still do not realize how they have gone wrong, then Heaven sends prodigies and wonders to terrify them. If, after these terrors, men still know no awe or fear, then calamity and misfortune will visit them. From this we may see that the will of Heaven is benevolent, for it has no desire to trap or betray mankind.

If we examine these wonders and portents carefully, we may discern the will of Heaven. The will of Heaven desires us to do certain things, and not to do others. As to those things which Heaven wishes and does not wish, if a man searches within himself, he will surely find warnings of them in his own heart, and if he looks about him at daily affairs, he will find verification of these warnings in the state. Thus we can discern the will of Heaven in these portents and wonders. We should not hate such signs, but stand in awe of them, considering that Heaven wishes to repair our faults and save us from our errors. Therefore it takes this way to warn us.

Translation by Burton Watson, in Wm. Theodore de Bary (ed.), *Sources of Chinese Tradition* (New York: Columbia University Press, 1960), p. 187

113. THE APPEARANCE OF A WHITE PHEASANT, A FAVOURABLE OMEN (ANCIENT JAPAN)

('Nihongi,' 11, 237-9)

The Emperor said: 'When a sage ruler appears in the world and rules the Empire, Heaven is responsive to him, and manifests favourable omens. In ancient times, during the reign of Ch'eng-wang of the Chou Dynasty, a ruler of the Western land (i.e., China), and again in the time of Ming Ti of the Han Dynasty, white pheasants were seen. In this Our Land of Japan, during the reign of the Emperor Homuda, a white crow made its nest in the Palace. In the time of the Emperor Ō-sazaki, a Dragon-horse appeared in the West. This shows that from ancient times until now, there have been many cases of auspicious omens appearing in response to virtuous rulers. What we call phoenixes, unicorns, white pheasants, white crows, and such like birds and beasts, even including herbs and trees, in short all things having the property of significant response, are favourable omens and auspicious signs produced by Heaven and Earth. Now that wise and enlightened sovereigns should obtain such auspicious omens is meet and proper. But why should We, who are so empty and shallow, have this good fortune? It is no doubt wholly due to Our Assistants, the Ministers, imperial Chieftains, Deity Chieftains, Court Chieftains and Local Chieftains, each of whom, with the utmost loyalty, conforms to the regulations that are made. For this reason, let us, from the Ministers down to the functionaries, with pure hearts reverence the Gods of Heaven and

Earth, and one and all accepting the glad omen, make the Empire to flourish.'

Again he commanded, saying:

'The provinces and districts in the four quarters having been placed in Our charge by Heaven, We exercise supreme rule over the Empire. Now in the province of Anato, ruled over by Our divine ancestors, this auspicious omen has appeared. For this reason We proclaim a general amnesty throughout the Empire, and begin a new year-period, to be called White Pheasant. Moreover We prohibit the flying of falcons within the limits of the province of Anato.'

> Adapted from Aston's translation, by Wm. Theodore de Bary (ed.), *Sources of Japanese Tradition* (New York: Columbia University Press, 1958), p. 80

114. THE ORACLE OF TROPHONIOS AT LEBADEIA

(Pausanias, 'Description of Greece,' IX, 39)

Trophonios, says Pausanias, is a figure similar to Asklepios, for in the grotto of Herkyna, in which are the sources of the river of that name (Herkyna is in fact the local river-nymph), 'there are standing statues, with serpents coiled round their sceptres. One might guess them to be Asklepios and Hygieia, but they may also be Trophonios and Herkyna, for even the serpents they reckon to be sacred to Trophonios no less than to Asklepios. . . . The most celebrated things in the grove are a temple and statue of Trophonios. The latter, which is the work of Praxiteles, also resembles Asklepios.' Pausanias then goes on:

As to the oracle, the procedure is as follows. When a man decides to go down to visit Trophonios, he is first of all lodged for a prescribed number of days in a building which is sacred to Agathos Daimon and Agathe Tyche [the Good Daimon and Good Fortune]. While living there he observes certain rules of purity, and in particular is allowed no warm baths; his bath is the river Herkyna. He gets plenty of meat from the sacrifices, for anyone who intends to make the descent sacrifices both to Trophonios himself and to the children of Trophonios, and also to Apollo and Kronos and Zeus surnamed Basileus [King] and Hera the Charioteer and Demeter whom they surname Europe and call the nurse of Trophonios. At each of the sacrifices a diviner is present who inspects the entrails of the victim, and having looked at them foretells to the man intending to descend whether Trophonios will receive him kindly and graciously. The entrails from the earlier sacrifices do not reveal the mind of Trophonios so clearly. But on the night on which a man is to go down, they sacrifice a ram into a trench, calling upon Agamedes. Though all the previous sacrifices may have been favourable, it goes for nothing if the entrails of this ram do not say the same thing; but if they too agree, then every man goes down with good hope. The method of descent is this. First of all, when night has fallen two boys of citizen families, aged about thirteen, bring him to the river Herkyna and there anoint him with olive oil and wash him. These boys are called Hermai, and it is they who wash the visitor to Trophonios and perform all needful services for him. After this he is brought by the priests, not straight to the oracle, but to springs of water which lie close to one another. Here he has to drink the water called Lethe, in order to achieve forgetfulness of all that he has hitherto thought of; and on top of it another water, the water of Mnemosyne, which gives him remembrance of what he sees when he has gone down. He next looks upon a statue which is said to be the work of Daidalos, and which the priests reveal to none save those who intend to go down to the abode of Trophonios, and when he has seen this statue and worshipped it and prayed, he approaches the oracle, wearing a linen chiton girdled with ribbons, and shod with the native boots of the country.

The oracle is situated above the grove on the mountain-side. It lies in the middle of a circular floor of white marble, about equal in circumference to the smallest size of threshing-floor and raised to a height of slightly under three feet. On the floor are set spikes with circular rails joining them, both spikes and railing being of bronze, and there are gates made through the railings. Inside the enclosure there is an opening in the earth, not a natural chasm but an accurate and skilful piece of building. In shape this chamber is like an oven. Its breadth across the middle is to all appearances about six feet, and even its depth one would not estimate to be more than twelve. It is made without any means of descent to the bottom, but whenever a man goes down to visit Trophonios they bring a light, narrow ladder for him. When he has gone down, he finds an opening between the bottom and the masonry, whose breadth appeared to be two spans, and its height a span. He lies down on the ground, and holding in his hand cakes kneaded with honey, he thrusts his feet into the opening and pushes forward himself, trying to get his knees inside the hole. The rest of his body is at once dragged in and follows his knees, just as a great and swift river would catch a man in its swirl and draw him under. From this stage on, once men are inside the *adyton*, they are not all instructed of the future in the same way; some have heard, others have seen as well. The way back is through the same opening, feet foremost.

They say that no one has died as the result of his descent, with the exception of one of the bodyguard of Demitrios, and as for him, he had not carried out any of the prescribed ritual at the sanctuary, nor did he go down to consult the god, but on the hope of getting gold and silver from the *adyton*. . . . When a man has come up from the abode of Trophonios, the priests take him over again and set him on a seat called the seat of Mnemosyne, which is not far from the *adyton*, and while he is seated there they ask him of all that he has seen and learned. Then when they have heard it they put him in charge of his friends, who lift him up and carry him to the house of Agathe Tyche and Agathos Daimon where he lodged before, for he is still in the grip of fear and unaware of himself or of those around him. But later on his wits will return to him unimpaired, and in particular he will recover the power of laughter. I do not write from hearsay, for I have consulted Trophonios myself, as well as seeing others who have done so.

Translation by W. K. C. Guthrie, in his *The Greeks and their Gods* (London, 1950), pp. 225-7. See also the commentary of J. G. Frazer, in *Pausanias's Description of Greece* (London, 1898), Bk. v, pp. 196-204

115. 'WE HAVE DRUNK SOMA, HAVE BECOME IMMORTAL . . .'

('Rig Veda,' VIII, 48, selections)

1. Of the sweet food I have partaken wisely,
   That stirs good thoughts, best banisher of trouble,
   On which to feast, all gods as well as mortals,
   Naming the sweet food 'honey,'[1] come together. . . .

3. We have drunk Soma, have become immortal,[2]
   Gone to the light have we, the gods discovered.
   What can hostility do against us?
   What, O Immortal,[3] mortal man's fell purpose?

The notes to this text are on pp. 247-8.

4. Joy to our heart be thou, when drunk, O Indu,[4]
   Like father to a son, most kind, O Soma;
   Thoughtful like friend to friend, O thou of wide fame,
   Prolong our years that we may live, O Soma.

5. These glorious freedom-giving drops by me imbibed
   Have knit my joints together as straps a chariot;
   From broken legs may Soma drops protect me,
   May they from every illness keep me far removed. . . .

8. Be gracious unto us for good, King Soma;
   We are thy devotees; of that be certain.
   When might and wrath display themselves, O Indu,
   Do not abandon us, as wished by foemen.

9. Protector of our body art thou, Soma,
   In every limb hast settled man-beholding:
   If we infringe thine ordinances be gracious
   As our good friend, O god, for higher welfare. . . .

11. Ailments have fled away, diseases vanished,
    The powers of darkness have become affrighted.
    With might hath Soma mounted up within us;
    The dawn we've reached, where men renew existence. . . .

13. Uniting with the Fathers hast thou, Soma,
    Thyself extended over earth and heaven.
    Thee, Indu, would we worship with oblation,
    And we ourselves become the lords of riches.

14. Ye gods, protectors, speak for us defending;
    Let neither sleep nor prattle overpower us.[5]
    May we beloved evermore of Soma
    With hero sons attended utter worship.

15. Soma, thou art our strengthener on all sides;
    Light-finder art thou; enter us, man-beholder.
    Do thou, O Indu, with thine aids accordant,
    Grant us protection both in front and rearward.

Notes

1 Madhu, the 'sweet' pressed juice known as *soma*. Cognates to *madhu* (Greek *méthy* [μέθυ]; Old Slavic *medu*; Icelandic *mjöd* [mjoär]; Anglo-Saxon *meodu*) suggest that a kind of honey mead of celestial origin, to which the religious values of intoxication and generative power were attributed, may have been part of an Indo-European cult; certain it is that *soma* (Avestan *haoma*) performed an essential role in the religion of the Indo-Iranians. The centrality of

the soma-sacrifice in the Vedic ritual brought the god Soma into a prominence in the hymns surpassed only by Indra and Agni who were themselves closely associated with the divine plant and its juice. All 114 hymns of the ninth book of the Rig Veda are addressed to the deity Soma.

2 At the climax of the Vājapeya, one of the seven forms of the soma-sacrifice the sacrificer ascends the sacrificial pole 'to heaven' and announces this accomplishment from the topmost step (cf. *Taittiriya-samhitā* 1.7.9).

3 *Amrita*, literally 'not dead'; like ambrosia (from ἀμβροτος), soma is the drink of the immortals.

4 The 'bright drop,' Soma.

5 Wakefulness and silence may refer to vows in the *dīkshā* (rite of initiation) to the soma-sacrifice. (A. A. Macdonell, *A Vedic Reader for Students* [London: Oxford University Press, 1917], p. 163).

Translation by H. D. Griswold, in his *The Religion of the Rigveda* (London, 1923), pp. 210-11

116. MYTH AND RITUAL: HOW TO BECOME A GANDHARVA

('Shatapatha Brāhmana,' XI, 5,)

This selection from one of the latest and best known of the Brāhmanas is a welcome expansion of a love story begun, but not concluded, in the most famous of the Rig Veda 'dialogue' (samvāda) hymns, X, 95. The tale recurs in the Mahābhārata and the Purānas, and was used by Kālidāsa for his drama Vikramorvashī.

The Gandharvas and the Apsarases—ancient classes of celestial beings who in the later Samhitās are often associated with waters and trees—are, like many forest creatures, sometimes friendly, sometimes hostile to men. King Purūravas falls happily in love with the nymph, Urvashī, until the Gandharvas separate the lovers by a ruse and the lonely king seeks the ritual means whereby he too may become a proper forest creature, a Gandharva.

The nymph Urvashī loved Purūravas the son of Idā.[1] When she married him she said: You must embrace me three times a day, but never lie with me against my will. Moreover I must never see you naked, for this is the proper way to behave to us women!'

She lived with him long, and she was with child by him, so long did she live with him. Then the Gandharvas said to one another: 'This Urvashī has been living too long among men! We must find a way to get her back!'

She kept a ewe with two lambs tied to her bed, and the Gandharvas

The notes to this text are on pp. 250-1.

carried off one of the lambs. 'They're taking away my baby,' she cried, 'as though there were no warrior and no man in the place!' Then they took away the second, and she cried out in the same way.

Then he thought to himself. 'How can the place where I am be without a warrior and a man?' And, naked as he was, he leapt up after them, for he thought it would take too long to put on a garment.

Then the Gandharvas produced a flash of lightning, and she saw him as clearly as if it were day—and she vanished. . . .

Bitterly weeping, he wandered all over Kurukshetra.[2] There is a lake of lotuses there, called Anyatahplakshā. He walked on its banks, and there were nymphs swimming in it in the form of swans.[3]

And she noticed him, and said: 'That's the man with whom I lived!' 'Let us show ourselves to him,' they said. 'Very well,' she replied, and they appeared to him [in their true forms].[4]

> Then he recognized her and entreated her:
>   'O my wife, with mind so cruel,
>   stay, let us talk together,
>   for if our secrets are untold
>   we shall have no joy in days to come!'

> Then she replied:
>   'What use is there in my talking to you!
>   I have passed like the first of dawns.
>   Purūravas, go home again!
>   I am like the wind, that cannot be caught.' . . .

> Mournfully Purūravas said:
>   'Today your lover will perish,
>   he will go to the furthest distance and never come back.
>   He will lie in the lap of disaster,[5]
>   and fierce wolves will devour him.' . . .

> She replied:
>   'Purūravas do not die! do not go away!
>   do not let the fierce wolves devour you!
>   Friendship is not to be found in women,
>   For they have hearts like half-tamed jackals!'[6]

> And then she said to him:
>   'When I dwelt in disguise in the land of mortals
>   and passed the nights of four autumns,[7]
>   I ate a little ghee[8] once a day,
>   and now I have had quite enough! . . .

But her heart pitied him, and she said, 'Come on the last evening of the year, then, when your son is born, you shall lie one night with me.'

He came on the last night of the year, and there stood a golden palace. They told him to enter, and brought her to him.

She said: 'Tomorrow the Gandharvas will grant you a boon and you must make your choice.' He said: 'You choose for me!' She answered: 'Say, "Let me become one of you!"'

In the morning the Gandharvas gave him a boon, and he asked: 'Let me become one of you.'

'There is no fire among men,' they said, 'which is so holy that a man may become one of us by sacrificing with it.' So they put fire in a pan, and said: 'By sacrificing with this you will become one of us.'

He took it and his son, and went homeward. On the way he left the fire in the forest and went to a village with the boy. When he came back the fire had vanished. In place of the fire was a pipal tree and in place of the pan a mimosa. So he went back to the Gandharvas.

They said: 'For a year you must cook enough rice for four [every day]. Each time [you cook] you must put on the fire three logs of the pipal anointed with ghee . . . and the fire which is produced [at the end of the year] will be the fire [which will make you one of us]. But that is rather difficult,' they added, 'so you should make an upper firestick of pipal wood and a lower one of mimosa wood, and the fire you get from them will be the fire [which will make you one of us]. But that too is rather difficult,' they added, 'so you must make both the upper and lower firestick[9] of pipal wood, and the fire you get from them will be the fire.'

So he made an upper and a lower firestick of pipal wood, and the fire he got from them was the fire [which would make him one of them]. He sacrificed with it and became a Gandharva.

Notes

1 And of Buddha, son of Soma. It is interesting to note that Purūravas belongs to the lunar race of kings, often mythically associated, like the Gandharvas themselves, with the heavenly soma. He is the ancestor of Puru, Bharata, Kuru, Pāndu and the other protagonists of the Mahābhārata.

2 The sacred 'field of the Kurus,' that great north Indian plain where the battle celebrated by the great epic was fought.

3 Some kind of aquatic bird (āti).

4 The following five stanzas are from *Rig Veda*, x, 95, 1, 2, 14-16, the 'dialogue' preserved by the priests who recite the *Rig Veda*. Our *Rig Veda* contains 18 stanzas; the *Satapatha-brānmana* was apparently aware of the first 15 of these.

5 Nirriti, Destruction, the wife of Adharma and mother of death. (Hopkins, E. W., *Epic Mythology* [Strassburg: Trübner, 1915], p. 41.)
6 *Sālāvrika*, of uncertain meaning. J. Eggeling translates as 'hyenas,' while A. Weber suggests 'werewolves' may be intended. (J. Eggeling [trans.], *Satapatha-brāhmana* [Oxford 1900; SBE XLIV], p. 71, *n.* 4.)
7 I.e., four years.
8 Clarified butter.
9 The churning-sticks used to produce fire.

Translation by A. L. Basham, in his *The Wonder That Was India* (London, 1954), pp. 405-7

117. PERFORM ACTION, FREE FROM ATTACHMENT TO ITS FRUITS ...

('Bhagavad Gītā,' III, 8-9, 19-24, 31, 35)

8. Perform thou action that is (religiously) required;
   For action is better than inaction.
   And even the maintenance of the body for thee
   Can not succeed without action.

9. Except action for the purpose of worship,
   This world is bound by actions;
   Action for that purpose, son of Kunti,
   Perform thou, free from attachment (to its fruits). . . .

19. Therefore unattached ever
    Perform action that must be done;
    For performing action without attachment
    Man attains the highest.

20. For only thru action, perfection
    Attained Janaka and others.
    Also for the mere control of the world
    Having regard, thou shouldst act.

21. Whatsoever the noblest does,
    Just that in every case other folk (do);
    What he makes his standard,
    That the world follows.

22. For Me, son of Prithā, there is nothing to be done
    In the three worlds whatsoever,
    Nothing unattained to be attained;
    And yet I still continue in action.

23. For if I did not continue
    At all in action unwearied,
    My path (would) follow
    Men altogether, son of Pritha.

24. These folk would perish
    If I did not perform action,
    And I should be an agent of confusion;
    I should destroy these creatures. . . .

31. Who this My doctrine constantly
    Follow, such men,
    Full of faith and not murmuring,
    They too are freed from (the effect of) actions. . . .

35. Better one's own duty, (tho) imperfect,
    Than another's duty well performed;
    Better death in (doing) one's own duty;
    Another's duty brings danger.

> Translation by Franklin Edgerton, *Bhagavad Gītā*, Vol.
> I, Harvard Oriental Series, Vol. 38 (Cambridge: Harvard University Press, 1944)

See also nos. 28, 264, 295-6

118. PERSONAL WORSHIP: PŪJĀ (HINDUISM)

The Purification and Dedication of the Body:
The dedication of the body of the worshipper to the deity is a necessary prelude to ceremonial worship. In this rite the worshipper purifies and consecrates each part of his person that he may become fit to appear before a god.

'No man should worship a deity so long as he himself has not become a deity. If the repetition of sacred utterances is performed without previous dedication of the parts of the body to the different deities, this repetition of *mantras* is demoniacal and without useful effect. To worship a deity, a man must become the Self of that deity through dedication, breath control, and concentration until his body becomes the deity's abode.' (*Gāndharva Tantra.*)

1. The first step is the purification of the worshipper and of the accessories of worship.

'The purification of the person of the worshipper consists in bathing.

The purification-of-the-subtle-elements (*bhuta shuddhi*) of the body is done through breath control and through the dedication of the six main parts of the body to the six deities to which they correspond. After this the other forms of dedication are performed.

2. 'The purification of the place of worship is done by cleaning it carefully, adorning it with an auspicious ornamentation made of powders of five colours, placing a seat and a canopy, using incense, lights, flowers, garlands, etc. All this must be done by the worshipper himself.

3. 'Purification of the ritual utterances, the *mantras*, is done by repeating the syllables which compose them in the regular order and then in the reverse order.

4. 'Purification of the accessories is done by sprinkling water consecrated with the basic *mantra* and the weapon-*mantra* (*astra-mantra*, i.e., the sound *phat*) and then displaying the cow-gesture (*dhenu-mudrā*).

5. 'Purification of the deity is done by placing the image on an altar invoking the presence of the deity through its secret *mantra* and the life-giving breathing-*mantra* (*prāna-mantra*), bathing the image three times while reciting the basic *mantra*, then adorning it with garments and jewels. After this an offering of incense and light should be made.' (*Kulārnava Tantra*.)

Removing Obstacles:
'The worshipper should bow with respect to the deities of the doors, first at the eastern door of the house of worship, then, successively at the southern door, the western door, and the northern door. After this he should bow to his chosen deity present in the form of its *yantra*.' (*Nigama-kalpalatā* 14.)

If the sanctuary has only one door, the worship of the deities of the three other directions should be done mentally. 'The sacrificial house should be entered with the right foot' (*Shivārcana Candrikā*); with the left foot if it is a left-hand sacrifice.

'The worshipper should remove obstacles of celestial origin by the godly look (looking with wide-open, unblinking eyes). Obstacles of the intermediary world are removed with the help of water consecrated with the *astra-mantra*. Terrestrial obstacles are avoided by doing three taps with the heel of the right foot.' (*Shāmbavī Tantra*.)

The Praise of the Deity:
'Just as gold is freed from its dross only by fire and acquires its

shining appearance from heat, so the mind of a living being, cleansed from the filth of his actions and his desires through his love for me, is transformed into my transcendent likeness. The mind is purified through the hearing and uttering of sacred hymns in my praise.' (*Bhāgavata Purāna* 11, 14, 25.)

The glorification of a deity is something different from meaningless praise. The *Brhad-devatā* (1, 6) says: 'The praise of something consists in the utterance of its name, the description of its shape, the proclaiming of its deeds, the mention of its family.'

'We cannot know a thing without knowing its merits, its qualities. All knowledge or science is based on a form of praise. A dictionary is but the praise of words. The works of science are filled with glorification. Everything which is an object of knowledge is as such a deity and is glorified in the Scripture that deals with it.' (Vijayānanda Tripāthī, 'Devatā tattva,' *Sanmārga*, III, 1942.)

Meditation:

'Meditation is of two kinds, gross and subtle. In the subtle form meditation is done on the "body of sound," that is, the *mantra*, of the deity. In the gross form meditation is on one image with hands and feet. . . . The suprasensory can seldom be reached by the mind; hence one should concentrate on the gross form.' (*Yāmala Tantra.*)

'The worshipper should engage in meditation, gradually concentrating his mind on all the parts of the body of his chosen deity, one after another, from the feet to the head. He can thus acquire such an intense state of concentration that during his undisturbed meditation the whole body of the chosen deity will appear to his mind's eye as an indivisible form. In this way the meditation on the deity in its formal aspect will gradually become profound and steady.' (Siva Candra Vidyārnava Bhattāchārya, *Principles of Tantra* [ed. Woodroffe], II (1916), 134, or p. 874 [1952 ed.], quoted with slight changes.)

Japa, the Repetition of Mantras:

'Japa, as the repetition of a mantra, has been compared to the action of a man shaking a sleeper to wake him up.' (Woodroffe, *The Garland of Letters*, p. 211, with slight changes.)

'Once the image of the chosen deity has been formed in the mind by concentration, the seed-mantra should be repeated, withdrawing the mind from all other thoughts. . . . Japa is of three kinds, audible, articulate but inaudible, and mental. . . . Japa concentration by this means is perfected, the consciousness of the worshipper is transferred

Rituals, Oracles, Prescriptions

to the deity represented by the utterance and he ceases to have an individuality distinct from that of the deity.' (Baradā Kantha Majumdar, *Principles of Tantra* [ed. Woodroffe], II [1916], 77-8, or pp. 648 f. [1952 ed.], quoted with slight changes.)

Translation by Alain Daniélou, in his *Hindu Polytheism* (New York: Bollingen Series LXXIII, 1964), pp. 377-9

119. PŪJĀ TO VISHNU AND OTHER GODS (HINDUISM)

(Agni-purāna, XXIII, 1-23)

Nārada said: I will now describe the mode of [offering] *pūjā*, by the performance of which *vipras* [sages] attain all objects of life. Washing his head, rinsing his mouth, and controlling his speech, one should sit well protected in a *svastika*, *padma*, or any other posture, with his face directed towards the east. He should then meditate in the middle of his navel on the mantra *yam*, smoke-coloured and identical with the terrific wind, and purify all the impurities of the body. Then meditating on the mantra *kshoum*, the ocean of light, situated in the lotus heart, he should, with flames going up, down, and in contrary directions, burn out all impurities. He should then meditate on the mantra *van*, of the shape of the moon, situated in the sky. And then the intelligent worshipper should sprinkle with nectarine drops his own body, extending from the lotus heart through the tubular organ *sushumnā*, passing through the generative organ and other tubes.

Having purified the *tattvas* [ingredients of worship], he should assign them. He should then purify his hand and the implements. First, he should assign, beginning with the thumb of the right hand, the fingers of the two hands to the principal limbs. Then with sixty-two mantras he should assign the twelve limbs to the body, namely heart, head, tuft of hair on the head, skin, two eyes, belly, back, arms, thighs, knee-joints, and feet. Then having offered *mudrā* and having recited his name one hundred and eight times, he should meditate on and adore Vishnu. Having placed a water-jar on his left and articles of worship on his right, he should wash them with the implements and then place flowers and scents. Having recited the adorable light of omnipresence and consciousness eight times, he should take up water in his palm with the mantra *phat* and then meditate on Hari [Vishnu-Krishna]. With his face directed towards the south-east, the direction presided over by Agni, he should pray for virtue, knowledge, dissociation from worldly objects and lordly powers; he should cast off his sins and physical impurities on the Yoga postures beginning with the east. In the *kūrma* (tortoise) posture, he should adore Ananta [Vishnu], Yama, the sun, and other luminous bodies. Having first meditated on them in his heart, invoked them, and adored them in the circle, he should again place offerings, water for washing the feet, water for rinsing the mouth, and *madhuparka* [a honey-and-milk offering]. Then by means of the knowledge of the art of worshipping the lotus-eyed deity [Vishnu], he should place water for bathing, cloth, sacred thread, ornaments, scents, flowers, incense, lamps, and edibles.

He should first adore the limbs at the gate in the east, and then Brahmā. He should then assign the discus and club to the southern quarter and the conch-shell and bow to the corner presided over by the moon. He should then assign arrows and the quiver to the left and right side of the deity. He should assign a leather fence and prosperity to the left and nourishment to the right. With mantras he should worship the garland of wild flowers, the mystic mark *Shrīvatsa* [Vishnu], and the *koustava* jem and all the deities of the quarters in the outside —all these paraphernalia and attendants of Vishnu. Either partially or wholly he should recite the mantras for adoring limbs, and adore them, circumambulate them, and then make offerings. He should meditate in his mind 'I am Brahmā, Hari' and he should utter the word 'come' in the ceremony of *āhvāna*[1] and 'forgive me' in the rite of *visarjana*.[2] Those who seek salvation should thus perform *pūjā* with the mantra of eight letters. I have described the worship of one form. Hear, and I will now describe that of nine *vyūhas* [parts of the body].

He should assign Vāsudeva, Bala, and others, first to his two thumbs and then severally to his head, forehead, mouth, heart, navel, buttocks, knees, and head, and afterwards worship them. He should then worship one *pītha* [the seat of a deity] and nine *vyūhas*. As before, he should worship in nine lotuses the nine forms and the nine parts of the body. In the midst thereof he should adore Vāsudeva.

Notes

1 'Invocation' of a deity; part of the rite in which the deity is installed in his image.
2 'Evacuation,' a concluding rite in which the image is thrown away.

Manmatha Nath Dutt, A *Prose English Translation of Agni Puranam*, vol. I (Calcutta, 1903), pp. 96-8; adapted by M. Eliade; notes by David Knipe

120. *THE MERITS OF BUILDING A TEMPLE (HINDUISM)*

('*Agni-purāna*,' XXXVIII, 1-50)

Agni said: I will now describe the fruits of making temples for the residence of Vāsudeva and other deities. He who attempts to erect temples for gods is freed from the sins of a thousand births. Those who think of building a temple in their minds are freed from the sins of a hundred births. Those who approve of a man's building a temple for Krishna go to the region of Acyuta [Vishnu] freed from sins. Having desired to build a temple for Hari, a man immediately takes a million of his generations, past and future, to the region of Vishnu. The departed manes of the person who builds a temple for Krishna live in the region of Vishnu, well adorned and freed from the sufferings of hell. The construction of a temple for a deity dissipates even the sin of Brahmanicide. By building a temple one reaps the fruit which he does not even gain by celebrating a sacrifice. By building a temple one acquires the fruits of bathing at all the sacred shrines. The construction of a temple, which gives heaven, by a religious or an irreligious man, yields the fruit reaped by persons slain in a battle undertaken on behalf of the celestials. By making one temple one goes to heaven; by making three one goes to the region of Brahmā; by making five one goes to the region of Shambhu; by making eight one goes to the region of Hari. By making sixteen one attains all objects of enjoyment and emancipation. A poor man, by building the smallest temple, reaps the same benefit which a rich man does by building the biggest temple for Vishnu. Having acquired wealth and built a temple with a small portion of it, a person acquires piety and gains favours from Hari. By making a temple with a lakh of rupees, or a thousand, or a hundred, or fifty, a man goes where the Garuda-emblemed deity resides. He who in his childhood even sportively makes a temple of Vāsudeva with sand, goes to his region. He who builds temples of Vishnu at sacred places, shrines, and hermitages, reaps three-fold fruits. Those who decorate the temple of Vishnu with scents, flowers, and sacred mud, go to the city of the Lord. Having erected a temple for Hari, a man, either fallen, about to fall, or half-fallen, reaps two-fold fruits. He who brings about the fall of a man is the protector of one fallen. By making a temple for Vishnu one attains to his region. As long as the collection of bricks of Hari's temple exists, the founder of his family lives gloriously in the region of Vishnu. He becomes pious and adorable both in this world and in the next.

He who builds a temple for Krishna, the son of Vāsudeva, is born as a man of good deeds and his family is purified. He who builds temples for Vishnu, Rudra, the sun-god, and other deities, acquires fame. What is the use to him of wealth which is hoarded by ignorant men? Useless is the acquisition of riches to one who does not have a temple built with hard earned money for Krishna, or whose wealth is not enjoyed by the Pitris, Brāhmanas, celestials, and friends. As death is certain for men, so is his destruction. The man who does not spend his money for his enjoyment or in charities and keeps it hoarded is stupid and is fettered even when alive. What is the merit of him who, obtaining riches either by an accident or manliness, does not spend it for a glorious work or for religion? [What is the merit of him] who, having given away his wealth to the leading twice-born, makes his gift circulated, or speaks of more than he gives away in charities? Therefore, a wise man should have temples built for Vishnu and other deities. Having entered the region of Hari, he acquires reverential faith in Narottama [Vishnu]. He pervades all the three worlds containing the mobile and the immobile, the past, future, and present, gross, subtle, and all inferior objects. From Brahmā to a pillar everything has originated from Vishnu. Having obtained entrance into the region of the Great Soul, Vishnu, the omnipresent god of gods, a man is not born again on earth.

By building temples for other gods, a man reaps the same fruit which he does by building one for Vishnu. By building temples for Shiva, Brahmā, the sun, Candī, and Lakshmī, one acquires religious merit. Greater merit is acquired by installing images. In the sacrifice attendant upon the setting up of an idol there is no end of fruits. One made of wood gives greater merit than one made of clay; one made of bricks yields more than a wooden one. One made of stone yields more than one made of bricks. Images made of gold and other metals yield the greatest religious merit. Sins accumulated in seven births are dissipated even at the very commencement. One building a temple goes to heaven; he never goes to hell. Having saved one hundred of his family, he takes them to the region of Vishnu. Yama said to his emissaries: 'Do not bring to hell persons who have built temples and adored idols. Bring those to my view who have not built temples. Range thus rightly and follow my commands.

'Persons can never disregard your commands, except those who are under the protection of the endless father of the universe. You should always pass over those persons who have their minds fixed on the

Lord. They are not to live here. You should avoid from a distance
those who adore Vishnu. Those who sing the glories of Govinda and
those who worship Janārdana [Vishnu or Krishna] with daily and
occasional rites should be shunned by you from a distance. Those who
attain to that station should not even be looked at by you. The persons
who adore Him with flowers, incense, raiment, and favourite ornaments should not be marked by you. They go to the region of Krishna.
Those who smear the body [of Vishnu] with unguents, who sprinkle
his body, should be left in the abode of Krishna. Even a son or any
other member born in the family of one who has built a temple of
Vishnu should not be touched by you. Hundreds of persons who have
built temples of Vishnu with wood or stone should not be looked at
by you with an evil mind.'

By building a golden temple one is freed from all sins. He who has
built a temple for Vishnu reaps the great fruit which one gains by
celebrating sacrifices every day. By building a temple for the Lord he
takes his family, a hundred generations past and a hundred to come,
to the region of Acyuta. Vishnu is identical with the seven worlds.
He who builds a temple for him saves the endless worlds and himself
attains immortality. As long as the bricks will last, the maker [of the
temple] will live for so many thousands of years in heaven. The
maker of the idol attains the region of Vishnu and he who consecrates
the installation of the same is immersed in Hari. The person who builds
a temple and an image, as well as he who consecrates them, come
before him.

This rite of *pratishthā* [installation] of Hari was related by Yama.
For creating temples and images of the deities, Hayashīrsha described
it to Brahmā.

Manmatha Nath Dutt, A *Prose English Translation of
Agni Puranam*, vol. I (Calcutta, 1903), pp. 142-6;
adapted by M. Eliade

121. ACTS AND REWARDS OF DEVOTION TO THE BUDDHA

('*Shikshāsamuccaya*,' 299-301 ['*Avalokana-sūtra*'])

Verily, for countless aeons he is not reborn blind or lame,
If, after he has decided to win enlightenment, he venerates a Stūpa
of the Teacher.
Firm in strength and vigour, a hero, firm in courage,

Speedily he wins fortune after he has circumambulated a Stūpa.

One who in this last age, this dreadful age, reveres a Stūpa, greater is his merit,

Than if for hundreds of thousands of Nayutas of Kotis of aeons he has honoured a similar number of Buddhas.

For the Buddha is pre-eminent, unequalled, most worthy of offerings, he who has travelled along the noblest pre-eminent way.

One who does worship to this Chief of Men, he has the best and unequalled reward.

Deceased here among men, he goes to the Heavens of the Thirty-Three,

And there he obtains a brilliant palace made of jewels.

If he here gives a pointed tower, he will there be waited upon by Apsaras.

If he places a garland on a Stūpa, he will be reborn among the Thirty-Three.

And there he gets a celestial lotus-pond, full of excellent water,

With a floor of golden sand, bestrewn with vaidurya and crystal.

And when he has enjoyed that celestial delight, and completed his life-span there,

The wise man, deceased from the Deva-world, becomes a man of wealth.

In hundreds of thousands of Nayutas of Kotis of births he will everywhere

Be honoured after he has placed a garland on a shrine.

When he has given but a strip of cloth to the Saviour of the world, to the Protector,

All his aims will prosper, both among Gods and among men.

He keeps out of the inferior and unlucky modes of life, and is not reborn in them.

When he has made a bower of garlands over the relics of the Saviour of the world,

He becomes a powerful king with a loyal retinue.

He is dear and cherished, honoured and praised,

By Gods and Nāgas, and the wise men in this world.

Wherever that hero is born, glorious with his merit's glory,

There his family is honoured, his country and his town.

Listen to me telling you of his advantages if he takes a speck of incense finer than a mustard seed,

And burns it at the shrines of the Lord: Serene in heart he forsakes all obstructions and all taints;

In whichever region he is, there he is full of merit, altogether full of health, firm in his intelligence, and alert;

He averts sorrow, and he goes his way dear and pleasant to many
    people.
If he should gain a kingdom, he honours the supreme Jina, a wise
    universal monarch of great might,
Golden his colour, adorned with marks, his body emits a pleasant odour
    in all worlds.
At birth already he receives the best of clothes, silken garments,
    heavenly, superb, well made.
He is blessed with a beautiful body when he has clothed the Saviour's
    shrines with robes.
It is because he has done worship with robes at the shrines of the
    unequalled Saviours,
That here in this world his body becomes unequalled, and armoured
    with the thirty-two marks.

Translation by Edward Conze, in Conze, *et al.*,
Buddhist Texts through the Ages (Oxford: Bruno
Cassirer (Publishers) Ltd., 1954)

122. MUHAMMAD PROCLAIMS THE PRESCRIPTIONS
OF ISLAM

(*'Koran,'* II, 166-75, 180-2, 186-93)

O believers, eat of the good things
wherewith We have provided you, and give thanks
to God, if it be Him that you serve.
These things only has He forbidden you;
carrion, blood, the flesh of swine,
what has been hallowed to other than God.
Yet whoso is constrained, not desiring,
nor transgressing, no sin shall be on him;
God is All-forgiving, All-compassionate.

Those who conceal what of the Book God has sent down
on them, and sell it for a little price—they shall eat
naught but the Fire in their bellies; God shall not
speak to them on the Day of Resurrection
neither purify them; there awaits them
        a painful chastisement.
Those are they that have bought error at
the price of guidance, and chastisement at

the price of pardon; how patiently they
shall endure the Fire!
That, because God has sent down the Book
with the Truth, and those that are
at variance regarding the Book
are in wide schism.

It is not piety, that you turn your faces
to the East and to the West.
True piety is this:
to believe in God, and the Last Day,
the angels, the Book, and the Prophets,
to give of one's substance, however cherished,
to kinsmen, and orphans,
the needy, the traveller, beggars,
and to ransom the slave,
to perform the prayer, to pay the alms,
And they who fulfil their covenant
when they have engaged in a covenant,
and endure with fortitude
misfortune, hardship and peril,
these are they who are true in their faith,
these are the truly godfearing.

O believers, prescribed for you is
retaliation, touching the slain;
freeman for freeman, slave for slave,
female for female. But if aught is pardoned
a man by his brother, let the pursuing
be honourable, and let the payment be
with kindliness. That is a lightening
granted you by your Lord, and a mercy;
and for him who commits aggression
after that—for his there awaits
a painful chastisement.
In retaliation there is life for you,
men possessed of minds; haply you
will be godfearing.

O believers, prescribed for you is
the Fast, even as it was prescribed for
those that were before you—haply you
will be godfearing—

*for days numbered; and if any of you
be sick, or if he be on a journey,
then a number of other days; and for those
who are able to fast, a redemption
by feeding a poor man. Yet better
it is for him who volunteers good,
and that you should fast is better for you,
    if you but know;
the month of Ramadan, wherein the Koran
was sent down to be a guidance
to the people, and as clear signs
of the Guidance and the Salvation.
So let those of you, who are present
at the month, fast it; and if any of you
be sick, or if he be on a journey,
then a number of other days; God desires
ease for you, and desires not hardship
for you; and that you fulfil the number, and
magnify God that He has guided you, and haply
    you will be thankful.*

*Permitted to you, upon the night of
the Fast, is to go in to your wives;
they are a vestment for you, and you are
a vestment for them. God knows that you have been
betraying yourselves, and has turned to you
and pardoned you. So now lie with them,
and seek what God has prescribed for you.
And eat and drink, until the white thread
shows clearly to you from the black thread
at the dawn; then complete the Fast
unto the night, and do not lie with them
while you cleave to the mosques. Those are
God's bounds; keep well within them. So God
makes clear His signs to men; haply they
    will be godfearing.*

*And fight in the way of God with those
who fight with you, but aggress not: God loves
    not the aggressors.
And slay them wherever you come upon them,
and expel them from where they expelled you;*

persecution is more grievous than slaying.
But fight them not by the Holy Mosque
until they should fight you there;
then, if they fight you, slay them—
such is the recompense of unbelievers—
but if they give over, surely God is
All-forgiving, All-compassionate.
Fight them, till there is no persecution
and the religion is God's; then if they
give over, there shall be no enmity
    save for evildoers.
The holy month for the holy month;
holy things demand retaliation.
Whoso commits aggression against you,
do you commit aggression against him
like as he has committed against you;
and fear you God, and know that God is
    with the godfearing.

And expend in the way of God;
and cast not yourselves by your own hands
into destruction, but be good-doers; God
    loves the good-doers.
Fulfil the Pilgrimage and the Visitation
unto God; but if you are prevented,
then such offering as may be feasible.
And shave not your heads, till the offering
reaches its place of sacrifice. If any
of you is sick, or injured in his head,
then redemption by fast, or freewill offering,
or ritual sacrifice. When you are secure,
then whosoever enjoys the Visitation
until the Pilgrimage, let his offering
be such as may be feasible; or if he
finds none, then a fast of three days
in the Pilgrimage, and of seven when
you return, that is ten completely;
that is for him whose family are not
present at the Holy Mosque. And fear
God, and know that God is terrible
    in retribution.

Translation by A. J. Arberry

123. 'THOSE WHO REPENT THEREAFTER, AND MAKE AMENDS . . .'

('Koran,' III, 78-84)

Say: 'We believe in God, and that which has been sent
down on us, and sent down on Abraham and Ishmael,
Isaac and Jacob, and the Tribes, and in that which was
given to Moses and Jesus, and the Prophets, of their
Lord; we make no division between any of them, and
   to Him we surrender.'
Whoso desires another religion than Islam, it shall
not be accepted of him; in the next world he shall
   be among the losers.
How shall God guide a people who have disbelieved
After they believed, and bore witness that the
Messenger is true, and the clear signs came to them?
God guides not the people of the evildoers.
Those—their recompense is that there shall rest
on them the curse of God and of the angels
and of men, altogether, therein dwelling forever;
the chastisement shall not be lightened
for them; no respite shall be given them.
But those who repent thereafter, and make amends—
God is All-forgiving, All-compassionate.

Translation by A. J. Arberry

124. PILGRIMAGE IN THE KORAN

('Koran,' XXII, 27-38)

And [make mention of] when We prepared as a habitation for Abraham the site of the House[1] [saying to him] : Do not associate anything with Me, but make pure My House for those who circumambulate, those who stand, those who bow and those who make prostration.

The notes to this text are on pp. 266-7.

And announce among the people the pilgrimage *(hajj)*. Let them come to thee on foot, on every kind of worn-out beast, coming in from every deep ravine, to witness things beneficial to them, and on days that have been specified to make mention of Allah's name over such beasts of the flocks as He has given them for provision. So eat ye of them and feed the misfortunate, the poor. Then let them finish with their uncleanness,[2] let them fulfill their vows, and let them circumambulate the ancient House. So! and if anyone makes much of [showing respect to] the things Allah has forbidden, that will be good for him with his Lord. Allowable for you are the cattle save what is recited to you,[3] so avoid the pollution of idols, and avoid any false speaking, being Hanifs to Allah, not such as associate [others] with Him. Should anyone associate [any other] with Allah it is like something that has fallen from heaven which the birds snatched away or the wind blew away to some distant place. So! and if anyone makes much of [showing respect to] Allah's rites,[4] that is [a sign] of purity of heart. Yours are the benefits from them (i.e., the cattle) until a set term, then their place is at the ancient house. For each communiy We have appointed some sacrificial rites *(mansak)* that they should mention the name of Allah over some of the beasts of the flocks which He has given them as provision. Your God is One God, so to Him surrender ye yourselves, and do thou [O Muhammad] give good tidings to those who humble themselves, whose hearts are moved with awe when Allah is mentioned, also to those who steadfastly endure what befalls them, and to those who observe prayer and from what We have given them as provision give freely (in charity). The sacrificial victims *(budn)* We have appointed for you as among Allah's rites in which there is good for you, so make mention over them of the name of Allah as they stand in line, and when they have fallen on their sides eat of them and feed both the contented and the clamourous. Thus have We subjected them (i.e., the cattle) to you. Mayhap ye will give thanks. Their flesh reaches not to Allah, nor does their blood, but piety on your part will reach Him.

Notes

1 I.e., the Ka'ba at Mecca, where it is the central shrine. *Bait*, 'house,' is the Arabic equivalent of the Hebrew *beth*, which we find in Beth-el, Beth-dagon, Beth-peor, Beth-shemesh, and such names in the Old Testament.

2 *Tafath* here means the state of neglect into which they have been forced to let their persons get because of the ritual restrictions of the sacral state as pilgrims. The rites being now over, they are to cut their nails, trim their beards, etc., in a kind of desacralization which allows them to resume normal life again.

3 I.e., the Qur'ānic passages concerning foods forbidden to a Muslim, such as

swine, the flesh of an animal that has died of itself, or of any animal offered in sacrifice to other than Allah. Such forbidden foods are listed in XVI, 115/116; 11, 173/168; v, 1-3/4.
4 *Sha'ā'ir* here probably means the rites and ceremonies at the holy sites other than the Ka'ba.

Translation and notes by Arthur Jeffery, *Islam: Muhammad and His Religion* (New York: Liberal Arts Press, 1958) pp. 200-1

E. PRAYERS AND HYMNS

125. A BUSHMAN DEMANDS THE HELP OF HIS GOD (SOUTH AFRICA)

Gauwa must help us that we kill an animal.
Gauwa, help us. We are dying of hunger.
Gauwa does not give us help.
He is cheating. He is bluffing.
Gauwa will bring something for us to kill next day
After he himself hunts and has eaten meat,
When he is full and is feeling well.

Lorna Marshall, '! Kung Bushman Religious Beliefs,' *Africa*, XXXII (1962), p. 247

126. A PRAYER TO IMANA, THE GREAT CREATOR OF THE RUANDA-URUNDI

Imana is the great Creator, the First Cause of all good. He does not enter into daily life at all, in a practical sense, and yet he is continually in the people's thoughts; all his acts are of his own volition, and he cannot be influenced by man. He is honoured but not feared, as he has no power to harm; there is no cult as there is for Ryangombe. . . .

There is little or no prayer made to Imana. All the worship goes to Ryangombe. There is, however, a cry for help, known as *Kwambaza*. A person in great distress can cry out to Imana for help wherever he is. As the cry is much the same in both countries [i.e., Ruanda and Urundi], I will give it without the vernacular, as the changes in language are too great to make either serve for both.

'O Imana of Urundi (Ruanda), if only you would help me! O Imana of pity, Imana of my father's house (or country), if only you would help me! O Imana of the country of the Hutu and the Tutsi, if only you would help me just this once! O Imana, if only you would give me a *rugo*[1] and children! I prostrate myself before you, Imana of Urundi (Ruanda). I cry to you: give me offspring, give me as you give to others! Imana, what shall I do, where shall I go? I am in distress, where is there room for me? O Merciful, O Imana of mercy, help this once!'

Note

1 The *rugo* is the fence surrounding the homestead and, by metonymy, the homestead itself.

Rosemary Guilleband, 'The Idea of God in Ruanda-Urundi,' in Edwin W. Smith (ed.), *African Ideas of God: A Symposium* (London, 1950), pp. 186, 192-3

127. A HYMN TO MWARI, THE GOD OF MASHONA (SOUTHERN RHODESIA)

Great Spirit!
Piler up of rocks into towering mountains!
When thou stampest on the stone,
The dust rises and fills the land.
Hardness of the precipice;
Waters of the pool that turn
Into misty rain when stirred.
Vessel overflowing with oil!
Father of Runji,
Who seweth the heavens like cloth:
Let him knit together that which is below.
Caller forth of the branching trees:
Thou bringest forth the shoots
That they stand erect.
Thou has filled the land with mankind,
The dust rises on high, oh Lord!
Wonderful One, thou livest
In the midst of the sheltering rocks,
Thou givest of rain to mankind:
We pray to thee,
Hear us, Lord!
Show mercy when we beseech thee, Lord.

Thou art on high with the spirits of the great.
Thou raisest the grass-covered hills
Above the earth, and createst the rivers,
Gracious One.

> Translation by F. W. T. Posselt, as quoted by Edwin
> W. Smith, 'The Idea of God among South African
> Tribes,' in Smith (ed.), *African Ideas of God: A Sym-
> posium* (London, 1950), p. 127

128. AN ARAPAHO PRAYER

*The Arapaho are an Algonquian tribe now settled in Oklahoma. With
this prayer pronounced by the priest, a woman is consecrated. She
impersonates the Mother of creation.*

My Father, have pity upon us! Remember that we are your children
since the time you created the heavens and the earth, with a man and
woman!

Our Grandfather, the Central-Moving Body, who gives light, watch
us in the painting of the belt which our Father directed, as it is before
us! Now speak to your servant who is to wear the belt! Look at her
with good gifts, and may she do this for the benefit of the new people
(children) so that this tribe shall have strength and power in the
future! . . .

We cannot cease praying to you, my Father, Man-Above, for we
desire to live on this earth, which we are now about to paint on this
occasion. We have given this belt to the sweet smoke for our purity
hereafter. May our thought reach to the sky where there is holiness.
Give us good water and an abundance of food!

> G. A. Dorsey, *The Arapaho Sun Dance*, Field Colum-
> bian Museum Anthropology Series, IV (1903), p. 74

129. 'GIVE THANKS TO MOTHER EARTH . . .'
(PAWNEE TRIBE, OKLAHOMA)

Behold! Our Mother Earth is lying here.
Behold! She giveth of her fruitfulness.

Truly, her power gives she us.
Give thanks to Mother Earth who lieth here.

Behold on Mother Earth the growing fields!
Behold the promise of her fruitfulness!
Truly, her power gives she us.
Give thanks to Mother Earth who lieth here.

Behold on Mother Earth the spreading trees!
Behold the promise of her fruitfulness!
Truly, her power gives she us.
Give thanks to Mother Earth who lieth here.

We see on Mother Earth the running streams;
We see the promise of her fruitfulness.
Truly, her power gives she us.
Our thanks to Mother Earth who lieth here!

> Alice C. Fletcher, *The Hako, a Pawnee Ceremony*, in
> Twenty-second Annual Report, part 2, Bureau of
> American Ethnology (Washington, D.C., 1904), p. 334

130. A TAHITIAN FAMILY PRAYER

This ancient prayer was repeated each night, in former times.

Save me! Save me! it is the night of the gods. Watch close to me, my God *(atua)*! Close to me, oh, my Lord *(fatu)*! Protect me from enchantments, sudden death, evil conduct, from slandering or being slandered, from intrigue, and from quarrels concerning the limits of land. Let peace reign about us, oh, my God! Protect me from the furious warrior, who spreads terror, whose hair bristles! May I and my spirit live and rest in peace this night, oh my God.

> E. S. Craighill Handy, *Polynesian Religion*, Bernice P.
> Bishop Museum Bulletin 34 (Honolulu, 1927), p. 201;
> translated from J. A. Moerenhout, *Voyages aux îles
> du Grand Ocean*, II (Paris, 1837), p. 83

131. A HAWAIIAN LAMENT

What is my great offence, O god!
I have eaten standing perhaps, or
   Without giving thanks,
Or these my people have eaten
   Wrongfully.
Yes, that is the offence, O Kane-of-the-water-of-life.
O spare; O let me live, thy devotee,
Look not with indifference upon me.
I call upon thee, O answer thou me,
O thou god of my body who art in heaven.
O Kane, let the lightning flash, let the thunder roar,
Let the earth shake.
I am saved; my god has looked upon me,
I am being washed. I have escaped the danger.

E. S. Craighill Handy, *Polynesian Religion*, Bernice P.
Bishop Museum Bulletin 34 (Honolulu, 1927), p. 242;
quoting Abraham Fornander

132. A SUMERO-AKKADIAN PRAYER TO EVERY GOD

This prayer is, in effect, a general prayer, asking any god for pardon
for any transgression. The writer, in his suffering, admits that he may
have broken some divine rule. But he does not know either what he
has done or what god he has offended. Furthermore, he claims that the
whole human race is ignorant of the divine will and thus is perpetually
committing sin. The gods, therefore, should have mercy and remove
his transgressions.

May the fury of my lord's heart be quieted toward me.
May the god who is not known be quieted toward me;
May the goddess who is not known be quieted toward me.
May the god whom I know or do not know be quieted toward me;
May the goddess whom I know or do not know be quieted toward me;
May the heart of my god be quieted toward me;
May the heart of my goddess be quieted toward me.
May my god and goddess be quieted toward me.

May the god who has become angry with me be quieted toward me;
May the goddess who has become angry with me be quieted toward me.

(lines 11-18 cannot be restored with certainty)

In ignorance I have eaten that forbidden by my god;
In ignorance I have set foot on that prohibited by my goddess.
O Lord, my transgressions are many; great are my sins.
O my god, (my) transgressions are many; great are (my) sins.
O my goddess, (my) transgressions are many; great are (my) sins.
O god whom I know or do not know, (my) transgressions are many; great are (my) sins;
O goddess whom I know or do not know, (my) transgressions are many; great are (my) sins;
The transgression which I have committed, indeed I do not know;
The sin which I have done, indeed I do not know.
The forbidden thing which I have eaten, indeed I do not know;
The prohibited (place) on which I have set foot, indeed I do not know;
The lord in the anger of his heart looked at me;
The god in the rage of his heart confronted me;
When the goddess was angry with me, she made me become ill.
The god whom I know or do not know has oppressed me;
The goddess whom I know or do not know has placed suffering upon me.
Although I am constantly looking for help, no one takes me by the hand;
When I weep they do not come to my side.
I utter laments, but no one hears me;
I am troubled; I am overwhelmed; I can not see.
O my god, merciful one, I address to thee the prayer, 'Ever incline to me';
I kiss the feet of my goddess; I crawl before thee.

(lines 41-9 are mostly broken and cannot be restored with certainty)

How long, O my goddess, whom I know or do not know, ere thy hostile heart will be quieted?
Man is dumb; he knows nothing;
Mankind, everyone that exists—what does he know?
Whether he is committing sin or doing good, he does not even know.
O my lord, do not cast thy servant down;
He is plunged into the waters of a swamp; take him by the hand.

The sin which I have done, turn into goodness;
The transgression which I have committed, let the wind carry away;
My many misdeeds strip off like a garment.
O my god, (my) transgressions are seven times seven; remove my
transgressions;
O my goddess, (my)transgressions are seven times seven; remove my
transgressions;
O god whom I know or do not know, (my) transgressions are seven
times seven; remove my transgressions;
O goddess whom I know or do not know, (my) transgressions are seven
times seven; remove my transgressions.
Remove my transgressions (and) I will sing thy praise.
May thy heart, like the heart of a real mother, be quieted toward me;
Like a real mother (and) a real father may it be quieted toward me.

Translation by Ferris J. Stephens, in *Ancient Near
Eastern Texts* (Princeton, 1950), pp. 391-2; reprinted in
Isaac Mendelsohn (ed.), *Religions of the Ancient Near
East*, Library of Religion paperbook series (New York,
1955), pp. 175-7

133. THE GREAT HYMN TO SHAMASH

Among the longest and most beautiful of the hymns that have come
down to us in cuneiform, this ranks as one of the best products of
Mesopotamian religious writing.

21. You climb to the mountains surveying the earth,
22. You suspend from the heavens the circle of the lands.
23. You care for all the peoples of the lands,
24. And everything that Ea, king of the counsellors, had created is
    entrusted to you.
25. Whatever has breath you shepherd without exception,
26. You are their keeper in upper and lower regions.
27. Regularly and without cease you traverse the heavens,
28. Every day you pass over the broad earth. . . .
33. Shepherd of that beneath, keeper of that above,
34. You, Shamash, direct, you are the light of everything.
35. You never fail to cross the wide expanse of sea,
36. The depth of which the Igigi know not.
37. Shamash, your glare reaches down to the abyss

38. So that monsters of the deep behold your light. . . .
45. Among all the Igigi there is none who toils but you,
46. None who is supreme like you in the whole pantheon of gods.
47. At your rising the gods of the land assemble;
48. Your fierce glare covers the land.
49. Of all the lands of varied speech,
50. You know their plans, you scan their way.
51. The whole of mankind bows to you,
52. Shamash, the universe longs for your light. . . .
88. A man who covets his neighbour's wife
89. Will [. . .] before his appointed day.
90. A nasty snare is prepared for him. [. . .]
91. Your weapon will strike at him, and there will be none to save him.
92. [His] father will not stand for his defence,
93. And at the judge's command his brothers will not plead.
94. He will be caught in a copper trap that he did not foresee.
95. You destroy the horns of a scheming villain,
96. A zealous [. . .], his foundations are undermined.
97. You give the unscrupulous judge experience of fetters,
98. Him who accepts a present and yet lets justice miscarry you make bear his punishment.
99. As for him who declines a present but nevertheless takes the part of the weak,
100. It is pleasing to Shamash, and he will prolong his life. . . .
124. The progeny of evil-doers will [fail.]
125. Those whose mouth says 'No'—their case is before you.
126. In a moment you discern what they say;
127. You hear and examine them; you determine the lawsuit of the wronged.
128. Every single person is entrusted to your hands;
129. You manage their omens; that which is perplexing you make plain.
130. You observe, Shamash, prayer, supplication, and benediction,
131. Obeisance, kneeling, ritual murmurs, and prostration.
132. The feeble man calls you from the hollow of his mouth,
133. The humble, the weak, the afflicted, the poor,
134. She whose son is captive constantly and unceasingly confronts you.
135. He whose family is remote, whose city is distant,
136. The shepherd [amid] the terror of the steppe confronts you,
137. The herdsman in warfare, the keeper of sheep among enemies.

138. Shamash, there confronts you the caravan, those journeying in fear,
139. The travelling merchant, the agent who is carrying capital.
140. Shamash, there confronts you the fisherman with his net,
141. The hunter, the bowman who drives the game,
142. With his bird net the fowler confronts you.
143. The prowling thief, the enemy of Shamash,
144. The marauder along the tracks of the steppe confronts you.
145. The roving dead, the vagrant soul,
146. They confront you, Shamash, and you hear all.
147. You do not obstruct those that confront you. . . .
148. For my sake, Shamash, do not curse them!
149. You grant revelations, Shamash, to the families of men,
150. Your harsh face and fierce light you give to them. . . .
154. The heavens are not enough as the vessel into which you gaze,
155. The sum of the lands is inadequate as a seer's bowl. . . .
159. You deliver people surrounded by mighty waves,
160. In return you receive their pure, clear libations. . . .
165. They in their reverence laud the mention of you,
166. And worship your majesty for ever. . . .
174. Which are the mountains not clothed with your beams?
175. Which are the regions not warmed by the brightness of your light?
176. Brightener of gloom, illuminator of darkness,
177. Dispeller of darkness, illuminator of the broad earth.

Translation by W. G. Lambert, in his *Babylonian Wisdom Literature* (Oxford, 1960), pp. 127 ff.

See also no. 20

134. 'LOOSE ME FROM SIN': A HYMN TO VARUNA

('Rig Veda,' II, 28)

1. This laud of the self-radiant wise Āditya[1] shall be supreme o'er all that is in greatness.
   I beg renown of Varuna the mighty, the god exceeding kind to him who worships.

The notes to this text are on p. 278.

2. Having extolled thee, Varuna, with thoughtful care may we have
   high fortune in thy service,
   Singing thy praises like the fires at coming, day after day, of
   mornings rich in cattle.

3. May we be in thy keeping, O thou leader, wide-ruling Varuna,
   lord of many heroes.
   O sons of Aditi,[2] for ever faithful, pardon us, gods, admit us to
   your friendship.

4. He made them flow, the Āditya, the sustainer: the rivers run by
   Varuna's commandment.[3]
   These feel no weariness, nor cease from flowing: swift have they
   flown like birds in air around us.

5. Loose me from sin as from a bond that binds me:[4] may we swell,
   Varuna, thy spring of Order.[5]
   Let not my thread, while I weave song, be severed, nor my work's
   sum before the time be shattered.

6. Far from me, Varuna, remove all danger: accept me graciously,
   thou holy sovereign.
   Cast off, like cords that hold a calf, my troubles: I am not even
   my eyelid's lord without thee.

7. Strike us not, Varuna, with those dread weapons which, Asura,
   at thy bidding wound the sinner.
   Let us not pass away from light to exile. Scatter that we may
   live, the men who hate us.

8. O mighty Varuna, now and hereafter, even as of old, will we
   speak forth our worship.
   For in thyself, infallible god, thy statutes ne'er to be moved are
   fixed as on a mountain.

9. Wipe out what debts I have myself contracted: let me not profit,
   king, by gain of others.
   Full many a morn remains to dawn upon us: in these, O Varuna,
   while we live direct us.

10. O king, whoever, be he friend or kinsman hath threatened me
    affrighted in my slumber—
    If any wolf or robber fain would harm us, therefrom, O Varuna,
    give thou us protection.

11. May I not live, O Varuna, to witness my wealthy, liberal, dear
    friend's destitution.
    King, may I never lack well-ordered riches. Loud may we speak,
    with heroes, in assembly.

Notes

1 The Ādityas, sovereign beings, are led by the god Varuna, who is universal ruler (*samrāj*), guardian of the cosmic law (*rita*), and *asura* par excellence. As maintainer of truth and the moral order Varuna must also be the punisher of sin, and with 'this laud supreme' the poet seeks not only to gain the material favours of Varuna, but also to escape his dreadful recompense for ill.
2 The mother of the Ādityas and a goddess also frequently invoked for release from sin.
3 Varuna as a celestial being merely orders the waters to flow; Indra, on the other hand (Rig Veda, II, 12, 3; see no.) must break resisting forces to release the cosmic waters.
4 Just as important as the fact that Varuna is the god who 'binds' sinners is the knowledge that he forgives and releases from the fetters (*pāsha*) those who are penitent.
5 *Rita*.

Translation by Ralph T. H. Griffith, in his *The Hymns of the Rigveda*, I (Benares, 1889), pp. 379-80

135. 'HOW MAY VARUNA AND I BE UNITED?'

('Rig Veda,' VII, 86)

1. The tribes of men have wisdom through his greatness who stayed even spacious heaven and earth asunder;[1]
   Who urged the high and mighty sky to motion, and stars of old, and spread the earth before him.
2. With my own heart I commune on the question how Varuna and I may be united.
   What gift of mine will he accept unangered? When may I calmly look and find him gracious?
3. Fain to know this my sin I question others: I seek the wise, O Varuna, and ask them.
   This one same answer even the sages gave me, Surely this Varuna is angry with thee.[2]
4. What, Varuna, hath been my chief transgression, that thou wouldst slay the friend who sings thy praises?
   Tell me, unconquerable Lord, and quickly sinless will I approach thee with my homage.

The notes to this text are on p. 279.

5. Loose us from sins committed by our fathers, from those wherein
   we have ourselves offended.
   O king, loose, like a thief who feeds the cattle,³ as from the cord a
   calf, set free Vasishtha.⁴

6. Not our own will betrayed us, but seduction, thoughtlessness,
   Varuna! wine, dice, or anger.
   The old is near to lead astray the younger: even slumber leadeth
   men to evil-doing.

7. Slavelike may I do service to the bounteous, serve, free from sin,
   the god inclined to anger.
   This gentle lord gives wisdom to the simple: the wiser god leads
   on the wise to riches.

8. O lord, O Varuna, may this laudation come close to thee and lie
   within thy spirit.
   May it be well with us in rest and labour. Preserve us evermore, ye
   gods, with blessings.

Notes

1 Heaven and earth, originally united, are 'propped apart' and established by
Varuna, the upholder of the cosmic order (*rita*).
2 Varuna 'binds' with fetters those who transgress, ritually or morally, his
universal law. The poet, perhaps suffering from illness, seeks to confess the sin
for which he is being punished, so that Varuna may forgive and 'release.' His
guilt is an uneasy burden while his sin goes unnamed, and the praiser of Varuna
seeks only to restore a right relationship with the god.
3 Or, 'like a cattle-stealing thief' (A. A. Macdonell, A *Vedic Reader for Students*
[London: Oxford University, 1917], p. 138.)
4 A well-known 'seer' (*rishi*).

Translation by Ralph T. H. Griffith, in his *The Hymns
of the Rigveda*, III (Benares, 1891), pp. 106-7

136. 'MAKE ME IMMORTAL . . .': A HYMN TO SOMA
PAVAMĀNA

('Rig Veda,' IX, 113, 7-11)

7. O Pavamāna,¹ place me in that deathless, undecaying world
   Wherein the light of heaven is set, and everlasting lustre shines.
   Flow, Indu,² flow for Indra's sake.

The notes to this text are on p. 280.

8. Make me immortal in that realm where dwells the king,[3] Vivas-
van's son,

    Where is the secret shrine of heaven, where are those waters,
young and fresh.

        Flow, Indu, flow for Indra's sake.

9. Make me immortal in that realm where they move even as they
list,

    In the third sphere of inmost heaven[4] where lucid worlds are full
of light.

        Flow, Indu, flow for Indra's sake.

10. Make me immortal in that realm of eager wish and strong desire,

    The region of the golden Sun, where food[5] and full delight are
found.

        Flow, Indu, flow for Indra's sake.

11. Make me immortal in that realm where happiness and transports,
where

    Joys and felicities combine, and longing wishes are fulfilled.

        Flow, Indu, flow for Indra's sake.

Notes

1 'Flowing clear,' an epithet of soma, the elixir of life, derived from the root
pū, 'to make clean, purify.' The juice is poured from the pressing through a
woolen filter and into jars or vats.

2 The 'bright drop,' soma, intoxicates the warrior Indra for his cosmic struggle
with the demon Vritra.

3 Yama, ruler of departed spirits, son of Vivasvān.

4 In the highest heaven, which Vishnu's third stride encompassed, dwell Yama
and the Fathers. Soma itself is found in all three worlds, just as in the ritual
soma, pressed thrice daily, is held in three tubs.

5 The translator has followed Sāyana here; the word is svadhā and is obscure.

Translation by Ralph T. H. Griffith, in his The Hymns
of the Rigveda, IV (Benares, 1892), pp. 105-6

137. HYMNS TO AGNI

('Rig Veda,' I, II, III, VII, selections)

1. I praise Agni, domestic priest, divine minister of sacrifice,
Invoker, greatest bestower of wealth.[1]

The notes to this text are on p. 282.

2. Worthy is Agni to be praised by living as by ancient seers:
   He shall bring hitherward the gods.[2]
7. To thee, dispeller of the night, O Agni, day by day with prayer,
   Bringing thee reverence, we come;
8. Ruler of sacrifices, guard of Law[3] eternal, radiant one,
   Increasing in thine own abode.
9. Be to us easy of approach, even as a father to his son:
   Agni, be with us for our weal. (I, 1, 1-2, 7-9.)

1. Thou, Agni, shining in thy glory through the days, art brought
   to life from out the waters, from the stone;
   From out the forest trees and herbs that grow on ground, thou,
   sovereign lord of men, art generated pure.[4]
2. Thine is the Herald's task and Cleanser's duly timed:
   Leader art thou, and Kindler for the pious man.
   Thou art Director, thou the ministering priest: thou
   art the Brahman, lord and master in our home.[5]
9. Agni, men seek thee as a father with their prayers, win thee,
   bright-formed, to brotherhood with holy act.
   Thou art a son to him who duly worships thee, and as a trusty
   friend thou guardest from attack.
14. By thee, O Agni, all the immortal guileless gods eat with thy
   mouth the oblation that is offered them.
   By thee do mortal men give sweetness to their drink.
   Pure art thou born, the embryo[6] of the plants of earth. (II, 1,
   1-2, 9, 14.)

2. That light of thine in heaven and earth,
   O Agni, in plants,
   O holy one, and in the waters,
   Wherewith thou hast spread wide
   the air's mid-region
   —bright that splendour, wavy, man-beholding. (III, 22, 2.)

4. I have begotten this new hymn for Agni, falcon of the sky:[7]
   will he not give us of his wealth?
8. Shine forth at night and morn: through thee with
   fires are we provided well.
   Thou, rich in heroes, art our friend.
10. Bright, purifier, meet for praise,
   immortal with refulgent glow,
   Agni drives Rākshasas[8] away.

Man and the Sacred

13. *Agni, preserve us from distress:*
consume our enemies, O God,
Eternal, with thy hottest flames.

14. *And, irresistible, be thou a mighty iron fort to us,*
with hundred walls for man's defence.

15. *Do thou preserve us, eve and morn, from sorrow,*
from the wicked man,
Infallible! by day and night. (VII, 15, 4, 8, 10, 13-15.)

Notes

1 Agni, addressed here in the first of 1028 hymns, is second only to Indra in Rig Vedic popularity. As 'Fire'—cosmic or ritual—his production, or rather his perpetual regeneration, becomes the subject of some 200 hymns. Typically, in this first brief stanza he is praised as domestic priest (*purohita*), performer (*ritvij*) of the sacrifice (*yajña*), the invoking and reciting priest (*hotar*), and bestower of wealth upon his worshippers.

2 Agni not only conveys the oblations to the gods, but brings the gods to the sacrifice as well.

3 *Rita.*

4 Agni is at home in the three worlds. In fact, his characteristics constantly fall into three-fold patterns. Here he is acknowledged as the vital heat in the waters, earth and plants of the terrestrial world. Similarly, he is child of the celestial waters, and as such is the separate deity Apām Nāpat; he is generated as a spark in the air from between two stones, as Indra generates him in lightning from the clouds (cf. *Rig Veda* II, 12, 3); and thirdly he is on earth the fire kindled in wood.

5 With more detail than in I, 1, 1, Agni's priestly roles are enumerated, illustrating not only the complexity of early Vedic ritual, but also the manner in which Agni is seen to pervade the entire sacrificial action. He is *hotar*, *potar* (the 'purifier'), *neshtar* (who 'leads' forward the wife of the sacrificer), *agnīdh* (the assistant to the *adhvaryu* who lights the fire by friction), *prashāstar* (the first assistant to the *hotar*), *adhvaryu* (who performs the manual aspects of sacrifice such as constructing the altar and preparing the *soma*), *brahman* (who in the later ritual is overseer of the sacrifice, but who is here perhaps an assistant), and, finally, Agni is the householder himself.

6 *Garbha.* Agni is the vital heat, the germ of life.

7 As mediator between the realms of men and of the gods, the characteristics of flight are often Agni's. As divine eagle or falcon (*shyena*) he is depicted in the Agnicayana (*Yajur Veda*), the ritual construction of a 10,800 brick fire-altar in the form of a flying bird. The iron fort with a hundred walls in stanza 14 below perhaps recalls the eagle's *soma*-theft in *Rig Veda*, IV, 26 and 27.

8 Terrestrial demons who attack and eat humans.

Translation by Ralph T. H. Griffith, in his *The Hymns of the Rigveda*, I-III (Benares, 1889-91); adapted by M. Eliade

See also nos. 25, 56, 101, 115

Prayers and Hymns

138. THE PRAYER OF SCIPIO AFRICANUS

(Livy, 'History of Rome,' XXIX, 27, 1-4)

As the great expedition was about to sail from Sicily to attack Carthage in 204 B.C., Scipio Africanus, on his flagship, offered the following prayer for a successful voyage.

'Ye gods and goddesses, who inhabit the seas and the lands, I supplicate and beseech you that whatever has been done under my command, or is being done, or will later be done, may turn out to my advantage and to the advantage of the people and the commons of Rome, the allies, and the Latins who by land or sea or on rivers follow me, [accepting] the leadership, the authority, and the auspices of the Roman people; that you will support them and aid them with your help; that you will grant that, preserved in safety and victorious over the enemy, arrayed in booty and laden with spoils, you will bring them back with me in triumph to our homes; that you will grant us the power to take revenge upon our enemies and foes; and that you will grant to me and the Roman people the power to enforce upon the Carthaginians what they have planned to do against our city, as an example of [divine] punishment.'

> Translation by Frederick C. Grant, in his *Ancient Roman Religion*, Library of Religion paperbook series (New York, 1957), p. 159

139. CLEANTHES' HYMN TO ZEUS

(Stobaeus, 'Eclogae,' I, I, 12)

Cleanthes of Assos (331-233 B.C.) was the disciple and successor of Zeno as head of the Stoic school. He was the real founder of Stoic theology.

> Most glorious of immortals, Zeus
> The many named, almighty evermore,
> Nature's great Sovereign, ruling all by law—
> Hail to thee! On thee 'tis meet and right

That mortals everyhere should call.
From thee was our begetting; ours alone
Of all that live and move upon the earth
The lot to bear God's likeness.
Thee will I ever chant, thy power praise!

For thee this whole vast cosmos, wheeling round
The earth, obeys, and where thou leadest
It follows, ruled willingly by thee.
In thy unconquerable hands thou holdest fast,
Ready prepared, that two-timed flaming blast,
The ever-living thunderbolt:
Nature's own stroke brings all things to their end.
By it thou guidest aright the sense instinct
Which spreads through all things, mingled even
With stars in heaven, the great and small—
Thou who art King supreme for evermore!

Naught upon earth is wrought in thy despite, O God.
Nor in the ethereal sphere aloft which ever winds
About its pole, nor in the sea—save only what
The wicked work, in their strange madness,
Yet even so, thou knowest to make the crooked straight.
Prune all excess, give order to the orderless;
For unto thee the unloved still is lovely—
And thus in one all things are harmonized,
The evil with the good, that so one Word
Should be in all things everlastingly.

One Word—which evermore the wicked flee!
Ill-fated, hungering to possess the good
They have no vision of God's universal law,
Nor will they hear; though if obedient in mind
They might obtain a noble life, true wealth.
Instead they rush unthinking after ill:
Some with a shameless zeal for fame,
Others pursuing gain, disorderly;
Still others folly, or pleasures of the flesh.
[But evils are their lot] and other times
Bring other harvests, all unsought—
For all their great desire, its opposite!

But, Zeus, thou giver of every gift,
Who dwellest within the dark clouds, wielding still

The flashing stroke of lightning, save, we pray,
Thy children from this boundless misery.
Scatter, O Father, the darkness from their souls,
Grant them to find true understanding—
On which relying thou justly rulest all—
While we, thus honoured, in turn will honour thee,
Hymning thy works forever, as is meet
For mortals while no greater right
Belongs even to the gods than evermore
Justly to praise the universal law!

Translation by Frederick C. Grant, in his *Hellenistic Religions* (New York, 1953), pp. 152-4

See also no. 304

140. MUHAMMAD PRESCRIBES THE DAILY PRAYERS OF THE MUSLIM

('Koran,' XVII, 80-3)

Perform the prayer
at the sinking of the sun to the darkening of the night
and the recital of dawn;
surely the recital of dawn is witnessed
And as for the night,
keep vigil a part of it, as a work of supererogation for thee;
it may be that thy Lord will
raise thee up to a laudable station.
And say: 'My Lord,
lead me in with a just ingoing, and lead me out with a
just outgoing; grant me
authority from Thee, to help me.'
And say:
'The truth has come, and falsehood has vanished away;
surely falsehood
is ever certain to vanish.'

Translation by A. J. Arberry

141. PRAYERS OF DERVISHES

I have naught but my destitution
     To plead for me with Thee.
And in my poverty I put forward that destitution as my plea.
I have no power save to knock at Thy door,
And if I be turned away, at what door shall I knock?
Or on whom shall I call, crying his name,
If Thy generosity is refused to Thy destitute one?
Far be it from Thy generosity to drive the disobedient one to despair!
Generosity is more freehanded than that.
In lowly wretchedness I have come to Thy door,
Knowing that degradation there finds help.
In full abandon I put my trust in Thee,
Stretching out my hands to Thee, a pleading beggar.

[Attributed to 'Abd al-Qādir al-Jīlānī as well as to Abuyad al-Tijāni]

O Lord, call down a blessing on Muhammad in the cooing of doves, in the hovering of birds, in the pasturing of cattle, in the excellence of the strong, in the might of the full-grown, in the sleeping of slumberers, . . . in the brightening of morning, in the murmur of the winds and in the tramp of cattle, in the girding on of swords and the brandishing of lances, and in the health of bodies and spirits.

[al-Salāt li-al-Busīrī]

Translation by Constance C. Padwick, in her *Muslim Devotions* (London, 1961), pp. 218, 257

F. PATTERNS OF INITIATION

142. AN AUSTRALIAN TRIBAL INITIATION

The terms 'tribal initiation,' 'puberty rites,' and 'initiation into an age group' designate the collective rituals whose function is to effect the transition from childhood or adolescence to adulthood, and which are obligatory for all members of a particular society. The puberty initiation represents above all the revelation of the sacred—and, for the primitive world, the sacred means not only everything that we now understand by religion, but also the whole body of the tribe's mythological and cultural traditions. Through initiation, the candidate passes beyond the natural mode—the mode of the child—and gains access to the cultural mode; that is, he is introduced to spiritual values. (Cf. M. Eliade, Birth and Rebirth [New York: Harper & Row, 1958].

Broadly speaking, the Australian initiation ceremony comprises the following phases: first, the preparation of the 'sacred ground,' where the men will remain in isolation during the festival; second, the separation of the novices from their mothers, and, in general, from all women; third, their segregation in the bush, or in a special isolated camp, where they will be instructed in the religious traditions of the tribe; fourth, certain operations performed on the novices, usually circumcision, the extraction of a tooth, or subincision, but sometimes scarring or pulling out the hair. Throughout the period of the initiation, the novices must behave in a special way, undergo a number of ordeals, and be subjected to various dietary taboos and prohibitions. Each element of this complex initiatory scenario has a religious meaning.

The separation of the novices from their mothers takes place more or less dramatically, in accordance with the customs of different tribes. The least dramatic method is found among the Kurnai, where the initiation ceremony is in any case quite simple. The mothers sit behind the novices; the men come forward in single file between the two groups and so separate them. The instructors raise the novices into the air several times, the novices stretching their arms as far as possible toward the sky. The meaning of this gesture is clear: the neophytes

287

are being consecrated to the Sky God. They are then led into the sacred enclosure where, lying on their backs with their arms crossed on their chests, they are covered with rugs. From then on they see and hear nothing. After a monotonous song, they fall asleep; later, the women withdraw. A Kurnai headman explained to A. W. Howitt—from whom we quote below—'If a woman were to see these things, or hear what we tell the boys, I would kill her.' When the neophytes wake, they are invested with a 'belt of manhood' and their instruction begins.

The central mystery of the Kurnai initiation is called 'Showing the Grandfather.'

'Showing the Grandfather.' This is the cryptic phrase used to describe the central mystery, which in reality means the exhibition to the novices of the *Tundun*, and the revelation to them of the ancestral beliefs. It is used, for instance, by the *Bullawangs* to their charges, as in telling them 'This afternoon we will take you, and show your grandfather to you.'

The Kurnai have two bull-roarers, a larger one called 'Tundun,' or 'the man,' and a smaller one called '*Rukat-Tundun*,' the woman, or wife of Tundun. The larger one is also called 'Grandfather,' *Wehntwin*, or *Mukbrogan*. In this the Kurnai differ from the Murring, who have only one bull-roarer, but they agree with several other Australian tribes. I think, but I cannot be sure, that where two bull-roarers are used, it indicates ceremonies in which the women take a certain part, whereas in tribes where there is only one, as the Murring, the women are totally excluded.

While the novices were thus under tutelage during the day following the sleeping ceremony, and while most of the men were out hunting, the Headmen and several others went away to prepare for the great ceremony of the grandfather. The spot chosen was, as I afterwards ascertained, over 2000 paces distant from the camp of the *Tutnurring*. While sitting there, talking to the *Bullawangs*, I several times heard the peculiar screech of the 'woman *Tundun*,' when the men who were making them tried one to see if it was satisfactory. When they were ready, about an hour before sunset, word was brought to the *Bullawangs*, who took their charges to the appointed place under the pretext 'Let us go for a walk. You must be tired with sitting there all day.'

On reaching the place, which was at the edge of an extensive and dense scrub of Ti-tree (*Melaleuca*), with a little open plain of some fifty acres in front, the novices were halted, and made to kneel down in a row, with their blankets drawn closely over their heads, so as to prevent their seeing anything. One of the *Bullawangs* knelt before each, and another stood behind. The principal Headman stood near, holding his throwing-stick in his hand. This being arranged satisfactorily, the ceremony commenced. The second Headman emerged from the scrub at about a hundred and fifty yards' distance, holding his bull-roarer, a 'man *Tundun*,' in his hand, which he commenced to whirl round, making a dull-sounding roar. The man immediately following him had a 'woman *Tundun*'; and in this way sixteen men came slowly forward, each one, as he came into the open, whirling his instrument and adding to the roaring and screeching din. By the time the last man had marched out into the clear ground, the leader had gained a point on the opposite side of the kneeling *Tutnurrings*, and the performers then halted in a semicircle, and produced a finale of discordant sounds. When this ceased, the Headman ordered the novices to stand up, and raise their faces towards the sky. Then, pointing upwards with his spear-thrower, the blanket was pulled off the head of each boy by his *Bullawang*, and the eyes of all the novices being directed to the uplifted throwing-stick, the Headman said, 'Look there! Look there! Look there!' successively pointing first to the sky, then lower, and finally to the *Tundun* men. Two old men now immediately ran from one novice to the other, saying in an earnest manner, 'You must never tell this. You must not tell your mother, nor your sister, nor any one who is not *Jeraeil*.' In the olden times spears were held pointed at the novices at this juncture, to emphasize the threats that were made, should they reveal the mysteries unlawfully. The old Headman then, in an impressive manner, revealed to the novices the ancestral beliefs, which I condense as follows:

Long ago there was a great Being, called *Mungan-ngaua*, who lived on the earth, and who taught the Kurnai of that time to make implements, nets, canoes, weapons—in fact, all the arts they know. He also gave them the personal names they bear, such as Tulaba. *Mungan-ngaua* had a son named *Tundun*, who was married, and who is the direct ancestor—(the *Wehntwin*, or father's father)—of the Kurnai. *Mungan-ngaua* instituted the *Jeraeil*, which was conducted by *Tundun*, who made the instruments which bear the names of himself and of his wife.

Some tribal traitor once impiously revealed the secrets of the *Jaraeil* to women, and thereby brought down the anger of *Mungan* upon the Kurnai. He sent fire (the Aurora Australis), which filled the whole space between earth and sky. Men went mad with fear, and speared one another, fathers killing their children, husbands their wives, and brothers each other. Then the sea rushed over the land, and nearly all mankind were drowned. Those who survived became the ancestors of the Kurnai. Some of them turned into animals, birds, reptiles, fishes; and *Tundun* and his wife became porpoises. Mungan left the earth, and ascended to the sky, where he still remains.

From that time, say the Kurnai, the knowledge of the Jeraeil and its mysteries has been handed down from father to son, together with the penalty for unlawfully revealing them, and for breaking the ordinance of *Mungan*—namely, destruction by his fire, or death at the hands of the men to whom his laws have been transmitted.

The novices, having been thus properly instructed, were told to take the *Tundun* in hand, and to sound it, which they did with evident reluctance and apprehension.

A. W. Howitt, *The Native Tribes of South-East Australia* (London, 1904), pp. 628-31

See also no. 1

143. DUKDUK, A MELANESIAN SECRET SOCIETY

There is a most curious and interesting institution, by which the old men of the tribe band themselves together, and, by working on the superstitions of the rest, secure for themselves a comfortable old age and unbounded influence. . . . The *Dukduk* is a spirit, which assumes a visible and presumably tangible form, and makes its appearance at certain fixed times. Its arrival is invariably fixed for the day the new moon becomes visible. It is announced a month beforehand by the old men, and is always said to belong to one of them. During that month great preparations of food are made, and should any young man have failed to provide an adequate supply on the occasion of its last appearance, he receives a pretty strong hint to the effect that the *Dukduk* is displeased with him, and there is no fear of his offending twice. When it is remembered that the old men, who alone have the power of summoning the *Dukduk* from his home at the bottom of the sea, are too weak to work, and to provide themselves with food or *dewarra* the reason for this hint seems to me pretty obvious. The day before the *Dukduk's* expected arrival the women usually disappear, or at all events remain in their houses. It is immediate death for a woman to look upon this unquiet spirit. Before daybreak everyone is assembled on the beach, most of the young men looking a good deal frightened. They have many unpleasant experiences to go through during the next fortnight, and the *Dukduk* is known to possess an extraordinary familiarity with all their shortcomings of the preceding month. At the first streak of dawn, singing and drum-beating is heard out at sea, and, as soon as there is enough light to see them, five or six canoes, lashed together with a platform built over them, are seen to be slowly advancing towards the beach. Two most extraordinary figures appear dancing on the platform, uttering shrill cries, like a small dog yelping. They seem to be about ten feet high, but so rapid are their movements that it is difficult to observe them carefully. However, the outward and visible form assumed by them is intended to represent a gigantic cassowary, with the most hideous and grotesque of human faces. The dress, which is made of the leaves of the *draconaena*, certainly looks much like the body of this bird, but the head is like nothing but the head of a *Dukduk*. It is a conical-shaped erection, about five feet high, made of very fine basket work, and gummed all over to give a surface on which the diabolical countenance is depicted. No arms or hands are visible, and the dress extends down to the knees. The old men, doubtless, are in the secret, but by the alarmed look on the faces of the others it is easy to see that they imagine that there is nothing human about these alarming visitors. As soon as the canoes touch the beach, the two *Dukduks* jump out, and at once the natives fall back, so as to avoid touching them. If a *Dukduk* is touched, even by accident, he very frequently tomahawks the unfortunate native on the spot. After landing, the *Dukduks* dance round each other, imitating the ungainly motion of the cassowary, and uttering their shrill cries. During the whole of their stay they make no sound but this. It would never do for them to speak, for in that case they might be recognized by their voices. Nothing more is to be done now till evening, and they occupy their time running up and down the beach, through the village, and into the bush, and seem to be very fond of turning up in the most unexpected manner, and frightening the natives half out of their wits. During the day a little house has been built in the bush, for the *Dukduks'* benefit. No one but the old men knows exactly where this house is, as it is carefully concealed. Here we may suppose the restless spirit unbends to a certain extent, and has his meals. Certainly no one would venture to disturb him. In the evening a vast pile of food is collected, and is borne off by the old men into the bush, every man making his contribution to the meal. The *Dukduk*, if satisfied, maintains a complete silence; but if he does not think the amount collected sufficient, he shows his disapprobation by yelping and leaping. When the food has been carried off, the young men have to go through a very unpleasant ordeal, which is supposed to prepare their minds for having the mysteries of the *Dukduk* explained to them at some very distant period. They stand in rows of six or seven, holding their arms high above their heads. When the *Dukduks* appear from their house in the bush, one of them has a bundle of stout canes, about six feet long, and the other a big club. The *Dukduk* with the canes selects one of them, and dances up to one of the young men, and deals him a most tremendous blow, which draws blood all round his body. There is, however, on the young man's part no flinching or sign of pain. After the blow with the cane he has to stoop down, on the 'tail,' which must be most unpleasant. Each of these young men has to go through this performance some twenty times in the course of the evening, and go limping home to bed. He will nevertheless be ready to place himself in the same position every night for the next fortnight. The time of a man's initiation may and often does last for about twenty years, and as the *Dukduk* usually appears at every town six times in every year, the novice has to submit to a considerable amount of flogging to purchase his freedom of the guild. Though I have never witnessed it, the *Dukduk* has the right, which he frequently exercises, of killing any man on the spot. He merely dances up to him, and brains him with a tomahawk or club. Not a man would dare dispute this right, nor would any one venture to touch the body afterwards. The *Dukduks* in such a case pick up the body, and carry it into the bush, where it is disposed of; how, one can only conjecture. Women, if caught suddenly, in the bush, are carried off, and never appear again, nor are any inquiries made after them. It is no doubt this power the *Dukduks* possess, of killing either man or woman with impunity, which makes them so feared. It is, above all things, necessary to preserve the mystery, and the way in which this is done is very clever. The man personating the *Dukduk* will retire to his house, take off his dress, and mingle with the rest of his tribe, so as not to be missed, and will put his share of food into the general contribution, thus making a present to himself. The last day on which the moon is visible, the *Dukduks* disappear, though no one sees them depart; their house in the bush is burned, and the dresses they have worn are destroyed. Great care is taken to destroy everything they have touched, the canes and clubs being burned every day by the old men.

H. Romilly, *The Western Pacific and New Guinea* (London, 1886), pp. 27-33

144. DĪKSHĀ, AN INDIAN INITIATORY RITUAL
(HINDUISM)

The *Dīkshā* must be performed by anyone who is preparing the *soma* sacrifice. The *Rig-Veda* seems to know nothing of the *dīkshā*, but it is documented in the *Atharva-Veda*. Here the *brahmacārin*—that is, the novice undergoing the initiatory puberty rite—is called the *dīkshita*, 'he who practices the *dīkshā*.' Herman Lommel has rightly emphasized the importance of this passage (*Atharva-Veda*, XI, 5, 6); the novice is homologized with one in the course of being reborn to make himself worthy to perform the *soma* sacrifice. For this sacrifice implies a preliminary sanctification of the sacrificer—and to obtain it he undergoes a return to the womb. The texts are perfectly clear. According to the *Aitareya Brāhmana* (1,3; 'Him to whom they give the *dīkshā*, the priests make into an embryo again. They sprinkle him with water; the water is man's sperm. . . . They conduct him to the special shed; the special shed is the womb of the *dīkshita*; thus they make him enter the womb that befits him. . . . They cover him with a garment; the garment is the caul. . . . Above that they put the black antelope skin; verily the placenta is above the caul. . . . He closes his hands; verily the embryo has its hands closed so long as it is within, the child is born with closed hands. . . . He casts off the black antelope skin to enter the final bath; therefore embryos come into the world with the placenta cast off. He keeps on his garment to enter it and therefore a child is born with a caul upon it.'

The parallel texts emphasize the embryological and obstetrical character of the rite with plentiful imagery. 'The *dīkshita* is an embryo, his garment is the caul,' and so on, says the *Taittirīya Samhitā* (I, 3, 2). The same work (VI, 2, 5, 5) also repeats the image of the *dikshita*-embryo, completed by that of the hut assimilated to the womb—an extremely ancient and widespread image; when the *dīkshita* comes out of the hut, he is like the embryo emerging from the womb. The *Maitrāyanī-Samhitā* (III, 6, 1) says that initiate leaves this world and 'is born into the world of the Gods'; the cabin is the womb for the *dikshita*, the antelope skin the placenta. The reason for this return to the womb is emphasized more than once. 'In truth man is unborn. It is through sacrifice that he is born' (III, 6, 7). And it is stressed that man's true birth is spiritual: 'The *dīkshita* is semen,' the *Maitrāyanī-Samhitā* adds (III, 6, 1)—that is, in order to reach the spiritual state that will enable him to be reborn among the Gods, the *dīkshita* must symbolically become what he has been from the beginning. He abolishes his biological existence, the years of his human life that have already passed, in order to return to a situation that is at once embryonic and primordial; he 'goes back' to the state of semen, that is, of pure virtuality.

M. Eliade, *Birth and Rebirth* (New York: Harper & Row, 1958), pp. 54-5

145. INITIATION OF A WARRIOR: GOING BERSERK

(Volsunga Saga, chapters 7-8)

In a passage that has become famous, the Ynglingasaga sets the comrades of Odin before us: 'They went without shields, and were mad as dogs or wolves, and bit on their shields, and were as strong as bears or bulls; men they slew, and neither fire nor steel would deal with them; and this is what is called the fury of the berserker.' This mythological picture has been rightly identified as a description of real men's societies—the famous *Männerbünde* of the ancient Germanic civilization. The berserkers were, literally, the 'warriors in shirts (*serkr*) of bear.' This is as much as to say that they were magically identified with the bear. In addition they could sometimes change themselves into wolves and bears. A man became a berserker as the result of an initiation that included specifically martial ordeals. So, for example, Tacitus tells us that among the Chatti the candidate cut neither his hair nor his beard until he had killed an enemy. Among the Taifali, the youth had to bring down a boar or a wolf; among the Heruli, he had to fight unarmed. Through these ordeals, the candidate took to himself a wild-animal mode of being; he became a dreaded warrior in the measure in which he behaved like a beast of prey. He metamorphosed himself into a superman because he succeeded in assimilating the magicoreligious force proper to the carnivora.

The *Volsunga Saga* has preserved the memory of certain ordeals typical of the initiations of berserkers. By treachery, King Siggeir obtains possession of his nine brothers-in-law, the Volsungs. Chained to a beam, they are all eaten by a she-wolf, except Sigmund, who is saved by a ruse of his sister Signy. Hidden in a hut in the depths of the forest, where Signy brings him food, he awaits the hour of revenge.

When her first two sons have reached the age of ten, Signy sends them to Sigmund to be tested. Sigmund finds that they are cowards, and by his advice Signy kills them. As the result of her incestuous relations with her brother, Signy has a third son, Sinfjotli. When he is nearly ten, his mother submits him to a first ordeal: she sews his shirt to his arms through the skin. Siggeir's sons, submitted to the same ordeal, had howled with pain, but Sinfjotli remains imperturbable. His mother then pulls off his shirt, tearing away the skin, and asks him if he feels anything. The boy answers that a Volsung is not troubled by such a trifle. His mother then sends him to Sigmund, who submits him to the same ordeal that Siggeir's two sons had failed to sustain: he orders him to make bread from a sack of flour in which there is a snake. When Sigmund comes home that night, he finds the bread baked and asks Sinfjotli if he did not find anything in the flour. The boy answers that he remembers having seen something, but he paid no attention to it and kneaded everything up together. After this proof of courage Sigmund takes the boy into the forest with him. One day they find two wolfskins hanging from the wall of a hut. The two sons of a king had been transformed into wolves and could only come out of the skins every tenth day. Sigmund and Sinfjotli put on the skins, but cannot get them off. They howl like wolves and understand the wolves' language. They then separate, agreeing that they will not call on each other for help unless they have to deal with more than seven men. One day Sinfjotli is summoned to help and kills all the men who had attacked Sigmund. Another time, Sinfjotli himself is attacked by eleven men, and kills them without summoning Sigmund to help him. Then Sigmund rushes at him and bites him in the throat, but not long afterward finds a way to cure the wound. Finally they return to their cabin to await the moment when they can put off their wolf-skins. When the time comes, they throw the skins into the fire. With this episode, Sinfjotli's initiation is completed, and he can avenge the slaying of the Volsungs.

The initiatory themes here are obvious: the test of courage, resistance to physical suffering, followed by magical transformation into a wolf. But the compiler of the *Volsunga Saga* was no longer aware of the original meaning of the transformation. Sigmund and Sinfjotli find the skins by chance and do not know how to take them off. Now transformation into a wolf—that is, the ritual donning of a wolfskin—constituted the essential moment of initiation into a men's secret society. By putting on the skin, the initiand assimilated the behaviour of a wolf; in other words, he became a wild-beast warrior, irresistible and invulnerable. 'Wolf' was the appellation of the members of the Indo-European military societies.

Summarized in M. Eliade, *Birth and Rebirth* (New York: Harper & Row, 1958), pp. 81-3; summarizing and commenting on *Volsunga Saga*, chaps. 7-8

146. CUCHULAINN'S INITIATION

('Tain Bo Cualnge')

According to the Old Irish *Tain Bo Cualnge*, Cuchulainn, nephew of Conchobar king of Ulster, one day overhead his master, the druid Cathba, saying: 'The little boy that takes arms this day shall be splendid and renowned for deeds of arms . . . but he shall be short-lived and fleeting.' Cuchulainn sprang up and, asking his uncle for arms and a chariot, set off for the castle of the three sons of Necht, the worst enemies of the kingdom of Ulster. Although these heroes were supposed to be invincible, the little boy conquered them and cut off their heads. But the exploit heated him to such a degree that a witch warned the king that if precautions were not taken, the boy would kill all the warriors in Ulster. The king decided to send a troop of naked women to meet Cuchulainn. And the text continues: 'Thereupon the young women all arose and marched out . . . and they discovered their nakedness and all their shame to him. The lad hid his face from them and turned his gaze on the chariot, that he might not see the nakedness or the shame of the women. Then the lad was lifted out of the chariot. He was placed in three vats of cold water to extinguish his wrath; and the first vat into which he was put burst its staves and its hoops like the cracking of nuts around him. The next vat into which he went boiled with bubbles as big as fists therein. The third vat into which he went, some men might endure it and others might not. Then the boys wrath (*ferg*) went down . . . and his festive garments were put on him.'

Translation by Joseph Dunn (*Tain Bo Cualnge* [London, 1914], pp. 60 *ff*.), as summarized in M. Eliade, *Birth and Rebirth* (New York: Harper & Row, 1958), pp. 84-5

147. DIONYSUS AND THE BACCHAE

(Euripides, 'The Bacchae,' 677-775)

According to the ancient authorities, the cult of Dionysus came to
Greece from Thrace or from Phrygia (the Phrygians were a Thracian
tribe). The cult was of a frenetic and ecstatic character, as this passage
from Euripides' Bacchae so strikingly illustrates. One of the herdsmen
describes to Pentheus, the king of Thebes, an attack of the maenads
(bacchae) upon the royal herd.

> About that hour
> when the sun lets loose its light to warm the earth
> our grazing herds of cows had just begun to climb
> the path along the mountain ridge. Suddenly
> I saw three companies of dancing women,
> one led by Autonoë the second captained
> by your mother Agave, while Ino led the third.
> There they lay in the deep sleep of exhaustion,
> some resting on boughs of fir, others sleeping
> where they fell, here and there among the oak leaves—
> but all modestly and soberly, not, as you think,
> drunk with wine nor wandering, led astray
> by the music of the flute, to hunt their Aphrodite
> through the woods.
>   But your mother heard the lowing
> of our horned herds, and springing to her feet,
> gave a great cry to waken them from sleep.
> And they too, rubbing the bloom of the sleep
> from their eyes, rose up lightly and straight—
> a lovely sight to see: all as one,
> the old women and the young and the unmarried girls.
> First they let the hair fall loose, down
> over their shoulders, and those whose straps had slipped
> fastened their skins of fawn with writhing snakes
> that licked their cheeks. Breasts swollen with milk,
> new mothers who had left their babies behind at home
> nestled gazelles and young wolves in their arms,
> suckling them. Then they crowned their hair with leaves,
> ivy and oak and flowering bryony. One woman

struck her thyrsus against a rock and a fountain
of cool water came bubbling up. Another drove
her fennel in the ground, and where it struck the earth,
at the touch of god, a spring of wine poured out.
Those who wanted milk scratched at the soil
with bare fingers and the white milk came welling up.
Pure honey spurted, streaming, from their wands.
If you had been there and seen these wonders for yourself,
you would have gone down on your knees and prayed
to the god you now deny.

  We cowherds and shepherds
gathered in small groups, wondering and arguing
among ourselves at these fantastic things,
the awful miracles those women did.
But then a city fellow with the knack of words
rose to his feet and said: 'All you who live
upon the pastures of the mountain, what do you say?
Shall we earn a little favour with King Pentheus
by hunting his mother Agave out of the revels?'
Falling in with his suggestion, we withdrew
and set ourselves in ambush, hidden by the leaves
among the undergrowth. Then at a signal
all the Bacchae whirled their wands for the revels
to begin. With one voice they cried aloud:
'O Iacchus! Son of Zeus!' 'O Bromius!' they cried
until the beasts and all the mountain seemed
wild with divinity. And when they ran,
everything ran with them.

  It happened, however,
that Agave ran near the ambush where I lay
concealed. Leaping up, I tried to seize her,
but she gave a cry: 'Hounds who run with me,
men are hunting us down! Follow, follow me!
Use your hands for weapons.'

  At this we fled
and barely missed being torn to pieces by the women.
Unarmed, they swooped down upon the herds of cattle
grazing there on the green of the meadow. And then
you could have seen a single woman with bare hands
tear a fat calf, still bellowing with fright,
in two, while others clawed the heifers to pieces.

Patterns of Initiation

There were ribs and cloven hooves scattered everywhere,
and scraps smeared with blood hung from the fig trees.
And bulls, their raging fury gathered in their horns,
lowered their heads to charge, then fell, stumbling
to the earth, pulled down by hordes of women
and stripped of flesh and skin more quickly, sire,
than you could blink royal eyes. Then,
carried up by their own speed, they flew like birds
across the spreading fields along Asopus' stream
where most of all the ground is good for harvesting.
Like invaders they swooped on Hysiae
and on Erythrae in the foothills of Cithaeron.
Everything in sight they pillaged and destroyed.
They snatched the children from their homes. And when
they piled their plunder on their backs, it stayed in place,
untied. Nothing, neither bronze nor iron,
fell to the dark earth. Flames flickered
in their curls and did not burn them. Then the villagers,
furious at what the women did, took to arms.
And there, sire, was something terrible to see.
For the men's spears were pointed and sharp, and yet
drew no blood, whereas the wands the women threw
inflicted wounds. And then the men ran,
routed by women! Some god, I say, was with them.
The Bacchae then returned where they had started,
by the springs the god had made, and washed their hands
while the snakes licked away the drops of blood
that dabbled their cheeks.

    Whoever this god may be,
sire, welcome him to Thebes. For he is great
in many other ways as well. It was he,
or so they say, who gave to mortal men
the gift of lovely wine by which our suffering
is stopped. And if there is no god of wine,
there is no love, no Aphrodite either,
nor other pleasure left to men.

Translation by William Arrowsmith, in Grene and
Lattimore (eds.), *The Complete Greek Tragedies*
(Chicago: University of Chicago Press, 1958), pp. 573-4

Man and the Sacred

148. THE ELEUSINIAN MYSTERIES

Happy is he among men upon earth who has seen these mysteries; but he who is uninitiate and who has no part in them never has lot of like good things once he is dead, down in the darkness and gloom.

> Hymn to Demeter, 480-2 (translation by Hugh G. Evelyn-White, Hesiod, the Homeric Hymns, and Homerica, Loeb Classical Library [New York, 1920], p. 323)

Thrice happy are those of mortals, who having seen those rites depart for Hades; for to them alone is it granted to have true life there; to the rest all there is evil.

> Sophocles, Frag. 719 (Dindorf) (translation by G. E. Mylonas, Eleusis and the Eleusinian Mysteries [Princeton: Princeton University Press, 1961], p. 284)

Happy is he who, having seen these rites, goes below the hollow earth; for he knows the end of life and he knows its god-sent beginning.

> Pindar, Frag. 102 (Oxford) (translation by Mylonas, op. cit., p. 285)

Beautiful indeed is the Mystery given us by the blessed gods: death is for mortals no longer an evil, but a blessing.

> Inscription found at Eleusis (translation by S. Angus, The Mystery Religions and Christianity [London, 1925], p. 140)

It was the common belief in Athens that whoever had been taught the Mysteries would, when he died, be deemed worthy of divine glory. Hence all were eager for initiation.

> Scholiast on Aristophanes (The Frogs, 158) (translation by S. Angus, op cit., p. 140)

Pausanias avoided explanations regarding the Mysteries and refrained from describing the buildings to be seen in the sacred precincts of Demeter both at Eleusis and Athens:

I purposed to pursue the subject, and describe all the objects that admit of description in the sanctuary at Athens called the Eleusinion, but I was prevented from so doing by a vision in a dream. I will, therefore, turn to what may be lawfully told to everybody.

Pausanias, I, 14, 3 (translation by Frazer)

My dream forbade me to describe what is within the wall of the sanctuary; and surely it is clear that the uninitiated may not lawfully hear of that from the sight of which they are debarred.

Pausanias, I, 38, 7 (translation by Frazer)

And the *synthema* (pass-word) of the Eleusinian mysteries is as follows: 'I fasted; I drank the *kykeon*; I took out of the chest; having done my task, I put again into the basket, and from the basket again into the chest.'

Clement of Alexandria, *Protreptikos*, II, 21. [*For the interpretations of this sacred formula, cf. George E. Mylonas, Eleusis and the Eleusinian Mysteries, pp. 294-305*]

The Phrygians, the Naassene says, assert that God is a fresh ear of cut-wheat, and following the Phrygians the Athenians, when they initiate in the Eleusinia exhibit in silence to the *epoptai* the mighty and marvellous and most complete epoptic mystery, an ear of cut-wheat.

Hippolytus, *Philosophoumena*, V, 8

[*According to Walter Otto, 'there can be no doubt of the miraculous nature of the event. The ear of wheat growing and maturing with a supernatural suddenness is just as much a part of the mysteries of Demeter as the vine growing in a few hours is part of the revels of Dionysus.' W. Otto, 'Meaning of the Eleusinian Mysteries,' p. 25, in The Mysteries (New York, 1955), pp. 14-31; see also Mylonas, op. cit. pp. 305-10.*]

Aristotle maintains that it is not necessary for the initiated to learn anything, but to receive impressions and to be put in a certain frame of mind by becoming worthy candidates.

Synesius, *De Dione*, 10. (Cf. Jeanne Groissant, *Aristotle et les Mystères*, Paris, 1932)

See also no. 35

149. DEATH AND INITIATION IN THE MYSTERIES

(Plutarch, 'On the Soul')

The soul [at the point of death] has the same experience as those who are being initiated into great mysteries. . . . At first one wanders and wearily hurries to and fro, and journeys with suspicion through the dark as one uninitiated: then come all the terrors before the final initiation, shuddering, trembling, sweating, amazement: then one is struck with a marvellous light, one is received into pure regions and meadows, with voices and dances and the majesty of holy sounds and shapes: among these he who has fulfilled initiation wanders free, and released and bearing his crown joins in the divine communion, and consorts with pure and holy men, beholding those who live here un-initiated, an uncleansed horde, trodden under foot of him and huddled together in mud and fog, abiding in their miseries through fear of death and mistrust of the blessings there.

> Plutarch, *On the Soul*, quoted in Stobaeus, IV, as translated by George E. Mylonas, in his *Eleusis and the Eleusinian Mysteries* (Princeton: Princeton University Press, 1961), pp. 246-65

150. INITIATION INTO THE MYSTERIES OF CYBELE: THE TAUROBOLIUM

(Prudentius, 'Peristephanon,' X, 1011-50)

The high priest who is to be consecrated is brought down under ground in a pit dug deep, marvellously adorned with a fillet, binding his festive temples with chaplets, his hair combed back under a golden crown, and wearing a silken toga caught up with Gabine girding.

Over this they make a wooden floor with wide spaces, woven of planks with an open mesh; they then divide or bore the area and repeatedly pierce the wood with a pointed tool that it may appear full of small holes.

Hither a huge bull, fierce and shaggy in appearance, is led, bound with flowery garlands about its flanks, and with its horns sheathed; Yea, the forehead of the victim sparkles with gold, and the flash of metal plates colours its hair.

Here, as is ordained, the beast is to be slain, and they pierce its breast with a sacred spear; the gaping wound emits a wave of hot blood, and the smoking river flows into the woven structure beneath it and surges wide.

Then by the many paths of the thousand openings in the lattice the falling shower rains down a foul dew, which the priest buried within catches, putting his shameful head under all the drops, defiled both in his clothing and in all his body.

Yea, he throws back his face, he puts his cheeks in the way of the blood, he puts under it his ears and lips, he interposes his nostrils, he washes his very eyes with the fluid, nor does he even spare his throat but moistens his tongue, until he actually drinks the dark gore.

Afterwards, the flamens draw the corpse, stiffening now that the blood has gone forth, off the lattice, and the pontiff, horrible in appearance, comes forth, and shows his wet head, his beard heavy with blood, his dripping fillets and sodden garments.

This man, defiled with such contagions and foul with the gore of the recent sacrifice, all hail and worship[1] at a distance, because profane blood[2] and a dead ox have washed him while concealed in a filthy cave.

Notes

1 *All hail and worship.* The consecrated priest, emerging from the blood bath with the gift of divine life (drawn from the sacred bull) himself becomes divine and is therefore worshipped. Those who received the *taurobolium* could be described as 'born again for eternity' (*renatus in aeternum*, C.I.L., vi, 510; many other inscriptions refer to the *taurobolium* and prove the rite to have been in use early in the second century A.D.).

2 *Profane blood.* It must be remembered that Prudentius was a Christian and that to him the blood was profane (*vilis*) and the whole rite not only repulsive but blasphemous.

> Translation and notes by C. K. Barrett, *The New Testament Background* (London, SPCK 1956), pp. 96-7

151. THE EPIPHANY OF THE MYSTERY GOD

Aristides records an experience in which 'there came from Isis a Light and other unutterable things conducing to salvation. In the same night appeared Serapis and Aesculapius himself, both marvellous in beauty and stature and in certain aspects resembling each other' (*Orat. Sac.*, III, p. 500). All ancient *epiphaneiae* were of the character of a dazzling

light. Porphyry knows that 'the eye of the body cannot bear' the brightness of divine apparitions (*De Mysteriis*, II, 8). The experience of Apuleius, 'I saw the sun shining at midnight,' and 'adoravi de proxumo,' refers to such an epiphany. In the Attis cult, 'Hail, Bridegroom, Hail, new Light' announced the epiphany. In the *Liturgy of Mithra* (Dieterich, p. 10) we read, 'Thou shalt see a youthful god, lovely in form, with red locks, wearing a white tunic and scarlet mantle, and holding a bright crown.'

S. Angus, *The Mystery Religions and Christianity*
(London, 1925), pp. 135-6

152. IDENTIFICATION WITH THE MYSTERY GOD

By mystic identification Lucius, after the sacrament of initiation, was 'arrayed like the sun and set up like an image of the god' before the spectators (Apuleius, *Metamorphoses*, XI, 24). The *mystes* of Attis became himself Attis. . . . A Greek papyrus has preserved a magical prayer based on Hermetic theology, in which occur the words: 'Enter thou into my spirit and my thoughts my whole life long, for thou art I and I am thou; thy name I guard as a charm in my heart.' In a similar prayer we read: 'I know thee Hermes, and thou knowest me: I am thou, and thou art I.'

S. Angus, *The Mystery Religions and Christianity*
(London, 1925), pp. 109-10

153. 'DEMORTALIZING' (APATHANATISMÓS)

'I a man . . . born of mortal womb . . . having been this day begotten again by thee, out of so many myriads rendered immortal in this hour by the good will of God in his abounding goodness' (the so called *Liturgy of Mithra*). 'This is the good end for those who have attained knowledge, namely, Deification,' we read in the Hermetic literature (*Poimandres*, I, 26), which recalls the famous statement of Clement of Alexandria that the true Gnostic 'practices being God.' In the thanksgiving prayer of the *Perfect Word* occurs the expression 'Saved by thee . . . we rejoice that even in our mortal bodies thou didst deify us by the Vision of Thyself' (Greek text in R. Reitzenstein, *Die Hellenistische Mysterienreligionen*, 2nd ed., p. 114).

S. Angus, *The Mystery Religions and Christianity* (London, 1925), pp. 110-11

154. PLATO ON INITIATION

('Phaedo,' 69 c)

The Neoplatonist Olympiodoros comments on this passage: 'He is adapting an Orphic verse.'

It looks as if those also who established rites of initiation for us were no fools, but that there is a hidden meaning in their teaching when it says that whoever arrives uninitiated in Hades will lie in mud, but the purified and initiated when he arrives there will dwell with gods. For there are in truth, as those who understand the mysteries say, 'Many who bear the wand, but few who become *Bakchoi.*' Now these latter are in my own opinion no others than those who have given their lives to true philosophy.

Translation and introductory note by Frederick C. Grant, in his *Hellenistic Religions* (New York, 1953), pp. 136-44

155. INITIATION IN THE MYSTERIES OF ISIS

(Apuleius, 'Metamorphoses,' XI, 1-26)

Apuleius of Madaura, in North Africa, lived in the second century A.D. He was a lawyer, a novelist, and an orator. His famous *Metamorphoses*, which used to be called *The Golden Ass*, is a thinly veiled apologetic and autobiographic work in eleven books, replete with charming tales (e.g., 'Cupid and Psyche' in IV, 28 MVI, 24). The hero, Lucius, being over-curious about magic, is accidentally turned into an ass. His restoration to human shape by the mercy of Isis and his initiation into her rites form the climax of the work and are regarded as being based on direct acquaintance with the Isis mysteries.

Man and the Sacred

Introduction

[Book XI opens with an auspicious note of mystery. Lucius is spending the night asleep on the warm sand of the seashore.]

(1) About the first watch of the night, I awoke in sudden terror; the full moon had risen and was shining with unusual splendour as it emerged from the waves. All about me lay the mysterious silence of the night. I knew that this was the hour when the goddess [Isis] exercised her greatest power and governed all things by her providence —not only animals, wild and tame, but even inanimate things were renewed by her divine illumination and might; even the heavenly bodies, the whole earth, and the vast sea waxed or waned in accordance with her will.

The Epiphany of Isis

[Lucius decides to make his appeal to Isis for release from his asinine disguise, and the goddess responds. His prayer in §2 recounts her titles as Queen of Heaven, Ceres, Proserpina, celestial Venus.]

(3) So I poured out my prayers and supplications, adding to them much pitiful wailing, and once more fell sound asleep on the same bed of sand. Scarcely had I closed my eyes when lo! from the midst of the deep there arose that face divine to which even the gods must do reverence. Then a little at a time, slowly, her whole shining body emerged from the sea and came into full view. I would like to tell you all the wonder of this vision, if the poverty of human speech does not prevent, or if the divine power dwelling within that form supplies a rich enough store of eloquence.

First, the tresses of her hair were long and thick, and streamed down softly, flowing and curling about her divine neck. On her head she wore as a crown many garlands of flowers, and in the middle of her forehead shone white and glowing a round disc like a mirror, or rather like the moon; on its right and left it was bound about with the furrowed coils of rising vipers, and above it were stalks of grain. Her tunic was of many colours, woven of the finest linen, now gleaming with snowy whiteness, now yellow like the crocus, now rosy-red like a flame. But what dazzled my eyes more than anything else was her cloak, for it was a deep black, glistening with sable sheen; it was cast about her, passing under her right arm and brought together on her left shoulder. Part of it hung down like a shield and drooped in many a fold, the whole reaching to the lower edge of her garment with tasseled fringe. (4) Here and there along its embroidered border, and also on its surface, were scattered sequins of sparkling stars, and in their midst the full moon of midmonth shone forth like a flame of fire. And all along the border of that gorgeous robe there was an unbroken garland of all kinds of flowers and fruits.

In her hands she held emblems of various kinds. In her right hand she carried a bronze rattle [the sistrum] made of a thin piece of metal curved like a belt, through which were passed a few small rods; this gave out a tinkling sound whenever she shook it three times with a quivering pulsation. In her left hand was a golden cup, from the top of whose slender handle rose an asp, towering with head erect and its throat distended on both sides. Her perfumed feet were shod with sandals woven of the palm of victory.

Such was the vision, and of such majesty. Then, breathing forth all the blessed fragrance of happy Arabia, she deigned to address me with voice divine; (5) 'Behold, Lucius, I have come, moved by thy prayers! I, nature's mother, mistress of all the elements, earliest off-spring of the ages, mightiest of the divine powers, Queen of the dead, chief of them that dwell in the heavens, in whose features are com-bined those of all the gods and goddesses. By my nod I rule the shining heights of heaven, the wholesome winds of the sea, and the mournful silences of the underworld. The whole world honours my sole deity [*numen unicum*] under various forms, with varied rites, and by many names . . . and the Egyptians mighty in ancient lore, honour-ing me with my peculiar rites, call me by my true name, *Isis the Queen*.

'I have come in pity for thy woes. I have come, propitious and ready to aid. Cease from thy weeping and lamentation, and lay aside thy grief. For thee, by my providence, the day of salvation is dawning! Therefore turn thy afflicted spirit, and give heed to what I command. The day, even the very day that follows this night, is dedicated to me by an everlasting dedication, for on this day, after I have laid to rest the storms of winter and stilled the tempestuous waves of the sea, my priests shall dedicate to the deep, which is now navigable once more, a new boat, and offer it in my honour as the first fruits of the year's seafaring. Thou must await this festival with untroubled heart and with no profane thoughts.'

[The goddess tells Lucius that he must mingle with the crowd at the Ploiaphesia and edge his way up to the priest, who will be wearing a garland of roses. Having been forewarned by the goddess in a vision, the priest will be prepared for what is to happen, namely, that Lucius (still the ass) will seize the priest's garland and eat it, whereupon he will be restored to human form. And so it takes place. Transformed once more into human shape, Lucius is exhorted by one of the priests, 'whose smiling face seemed more than mortal':]

(15) 'O Lucius, after enduring so many labours and escaping so many tempests of Fortune, you have now at length reached the port and haven of rest and mercy! Neither your noble lineage nor your high rank nor your great learning did anything for you; but because you turned to servile pleasures, by a little youthful folly you won the grim reward of your hapless curiosity. And yet while Fortune's blindness tormented you with various dangers, by her very malice she has brought you to this present state of religious blessedness. Let Fortune go elsewhere and rage with her wild fury, and find someone else to torment! For Fortune has no power over those who have devoted themselves to serve the majesty of our goddess. For all your afflictions —robbers, wild beasts, slavery, toilsome and futile journeys that ended where they began, and the daily fear of death—all these brought no advantage to wicked Fortune. Now you are safe, under the protection of that Fortune who is not blind but can see, who by her clear light enlightens the other gods. Therefore rejoice and put on a more cheerful countenance, appropriately matching your white robe, and follow with joyful steps the procession of this Saviour Goddess. Let all such as are not devout followers of the goddess see and acknowledge their error, [saying]; "See, here is Lucius, freed from his former miseries by the providence of the great goddess Isis, and rejoicing in triumph over his Fortune!" And in order that you may live even more safely and securely, hand in your name to this sacred militia [i.e., join the Isiac order]—for it is only a little while ago that you were asked to take the oath—and dedicate yourself to obey our religion and take upon yourself the voluntary yoke of ministry. For when you have begun to serve the goddess, then will you realize more fully the fruits of your liberty.'

The Initiation of Lucius

[And so the priest prophesied and made his appeal to Lucius, and Lucius consented and joined the procession, amid the jeers of the unbelievers. But his conversion, like that of many others, was a slow process, and only gradually did he come to identify himself with the Isiac priests; for, like many another, he believed the strict profession of religion was something too hard for him: 'The laws of chastity and abstinence are not easy to obey' (19). And yet he continued to frequent the services of worship (21), and eventually came to desire earnestly to be admitted to the mysteries of Isis. This took place on 'the night that is sacred to the goddess.']

(22) The priest finished speaking, and I did not mar my obedience by any impatience, but with a quiet and gentle and edifying silence I rendered attentive service at the daily observance of the sacred rites. Nor did the saving grace of the mighty goddess in any way deceive me or torture me with long delays, but in the dark of night, by commands that were not in the least dark, she clearly signified to me that the day so long desired had come, in which she would grant the fulfillment of my most earnest prayers. She also stated what amount I must provide for the supplications, and she appointed Mithras himself, her high priest, to administer the rites to me; for his destiny, she said, was closely bound up with mine by the divine conjunction of the stars.

These and other gracious admonitions of the supreme goddess refreshed my spirit, so that even before it was clear day I shook off sleep and hastened at once to the priest's lodging. I met him just as he was coming out of his bedchamber, and saluted him. I had decided to request with even more insistence that I should be initiated, now that it was due me. But he at once, as soon as he saw me, anticipated me, saying, 'Lucius, you happy, you greatly blessed man, whom the august deity deigns to favour with such good will! But why,' he asked, 'do you stand here idle, yourself delaying? The day you have so long asked by your unwearied prayers has come, when by the divine commands of the goddess of many names you are to be admitted by my hands into the most holy secrets of the mysteries.' Then, taking my right hand in his, the gentle old man led me to the very doors of the huge temple; and after celebrating with solemn ritual the opening of the gates and completing the morning sacrifice, he brought out from a hidden place in the temple certain books whose titles were written in undecipherable letters. Some of these [letters] were shaped like all kinds of animals and seemed to be brief ways of suggesting words; others had their extremities knotted or curved like wheels, or intertwined like the tendrils of a vine, which was enough to safeguard them from the curiosity of profane readers. At the same time he told me about the various preparations it was necessary to make in view of my initiation.

(23) I lost no time, but promptly and with a liberality even beyond what was required I either bought these things myself or had my friends buy them for me. And now, the time drawing near and requiring it, as he said, the priest conducted me with an escort of the

religiously-minded to the nearest baths; and when I entered the bath, where it is customary for the neophytes to bathe, he first prayed to the gods to be gracious to me and then sprinkled me with purest water and cleansed me. He then led me back to the temple, and since the day was now more than half over he placed me at the feet of the goddess herself; then, after confiding certain secret orders to me, those which were too holy to be spoken, he openly, before all who were present, bade me for ten successive days to abstain from all the pleasures of the table, to eat no meat and drink no wine. All these requirements I observed with scrupulous care. And at last came the day designated by the divine guarantee. The sun was sloping downward and bringing on the evening when lo! from everywhere came crowds of the initiates, flocking around me, and each of them, following the ancient rite, presented me with various gifts. Finally, all the uninitiated having withdrawn, they put on me a new linen robe, and the priest, seizing me by the hand, led me to the very inmost recesses of the holy place. . . .

. . . Hear then and believe, for what I tell you is true. I drew near to the confines of death, treading the very threshold of Proserpine. I was borne through all the elements and returned to earth again. At the dead of night, I saw the sun shining brightly. I approached the gods above and the gods below, and worshipped them face to face. See, I have told you things which, though you have heard them, you still must know nothing about. I will therefore relate only as much as may, without committing a sin, be imparted to the understanding of the uninitiate.

(24) As soon as it was morning and the solemn rites had been completed, I came forth clothed in the twelve gowns that are worn by the initiate, apparel that is really most holy, but about which no sacred ban forbids me to tell, since at that time there were many who saw me wearing it. For in the very midst of the holy shrine, before the image of the goddess, there was a wooden platform on which I was directed to stand, arrayed in a robe which, although it was only of linen, was so richly embroidered that I was a sight to behold. The precious cape hung from my shoulders down my back even to the ground, and it was adorned, wherever you looked, with the figures of animals in various colours. Here were Indian dragons, there griffins from the Hyperborean regions, winged like birds, but out of another world. This cape the initiates call the Olympian. In my right hand I carried a flaming torch, and my head was decorated with a crown made of white palm leaves, spread out to stand up like rays. After I had been

thus adorned like the sun and set up like an image of a god, the curtains were suddenly withdrawn, and the people crowded around to gaze at me. . . .

[There followed feast and parties, and on the third day a solemn fast-breaking ceremony. Unable at first to bear to leave the image of the goddess, finally Lucius addresses her one last time, sobbing:]

(25) 'O holy and eternal guardian of the human race, who dost always cherish mortals and bless them, thou carest for the woes of miserable men with a sweet mother's love. Neither day nor night, nor any moment of time, ever passes by without thy blessings, but always on land and sea thou watchest over men; thou drivest away from them the tempests of life and stretchest out over them thy saving right hand, wherewith thou dost unweave even the inextricable skein of the Fates; the tempests of Fortune thou dost assuage and restrainest the baleful motions of the stars. Thee the gods above adore, thee the gods below worship. It is thou that whirlest the sphere of heaven, that givest light to the sun, that governest the universe and trampled down Tartarus. To thee the stars respond, for thee the seasons return, in thee the gods rejoice, and the elements serve thee. At thy nod the winds blow, the clouds nourish [the earth], the seeds sprout, and the buds swell. Before thy majesty the birds tremble as they flit to and fro in the sky, and the beasts as they roam the mountains, the serpents hiding in the ground, and the monsters swimming in the deep. But my skill is too slight to tell thy praise, my wealth too slender to make thee due offerings of sacrifice. . . . Therefore the only thing one can do, if one is devout but otherwise a pauper, that I will strive to do. Thy face divine and thy most holy deity—these I will hide away deep within my heart; thine image I shall treasure forever!'

Having thus pleaded with the mighty deity, I embraced Mithras the priest, now my spiritual father, and hanging upon his neck with many a kiss I begged his forgiveness, since I could make no proper return for all the great benefits that he had conferred upon me. (26) Then, after many words of thanks, long drawn out, I finally set out for home by the shortest route. . . . A few days later, led on by the mighty goddess, I reached Rome on the eve of the Ides of December.

Translation and explanatory material by Frederick C Grant, in his *Hellenistic Religions* (New York, 1953), pp. 136-44

156. PERSONAL PIETY IN ROME (SECOND CENTURY A.D.)

(Apuleius, 'Apologia,' 55-6)

Apuleius is defending himself against the charge of practising magic, and especially of carrying magical objects wrapped in a handkerchief.

You ask, Aemilianus [the prosecutor], what I had in that handkerchief? Although I might deny that I had deposited any handkerchief whatsoever of mine in Pontianus' library—or even supposing I were to admit, at the most, that I did so deposit it—I can still deny that there was anything wrapped up in it. And if I should take this line, you have no evidence or argument by which to refute me; for there is no one who has ever touched it, and there is only one freedman, according to your own statement, who has ever seen it. Nevertheless, for all that, let me say that the cloth was jammed full. Imagine yourself now, if you please, to be on the verge of a great discovery—as when the comrades of Ulysses thought they had found a great treasure when they ran off with the bag full of all the winds! Would you like to have me tell you what it was I had wrapped up in that handkerchief and committed to the care of Pontianus' household gods? You shall have your wish.

I have been initiated into almost all of the Greek mysteries, and I have preserved with the greatest care certain of the emblems and tokens (*signa et monumenta*) of my initiations, which were presented to me by the priests. I am not talking now about anything strange or unheard-of. Even a single initiate (*mystes*) of the mysteries of Liber Pater who is present here knows what he keeps hidden away at home, safe from all profane touch, the object of his silent veneration. But I, as I have said, moved by religious zeal and a desire to know the truth, have devoted myself to many different mysteries (*sacra*), numerous rites, and various ceremonies relating to the gods. I am not making this up on the spur of the moment. Nearly three years ago, during the first days of my residence at Oea, in a public discourse which I delivered on the majesty of Aesculapius, I made the same statement and recounted the number of the mysteries with which I was familiar. That discourse was thronged, has been read far and wide, is in everyone's hands, and has won the approval of the pious inhabitants of Oea not so much through any eloquence of mine as because it speaks of Aesculapius. Will anyone who happens to remember it repeat the begin-

ning of that particular passage in my discourse?—Do you not hear,
Maximus [the presiding magistrate], how many voices are supplying
the words? Indeed, they are freely reciting it! Let me now order this
same passage to be read aloud, since you show by the gracious expression on your face that you will not be displeased to hear it. [The
passage is then read aloud.]

Can anyone who has the slightest recollection of religious rites be
surprised that a man who has been a partaker of so many divine
mysteries should preserve in his home certain mementos of these
sacred ceremonies, or that he should wrap them in a linen cloth,
which is the purest covering for holy things? For wool, produced by
the most lethargic of animals and stripped off the sheep's back, was
accordingly recognized by the followers of Orpheus and Pythagoras
as a profane vesture. But flax, the purest of all plants and among the
best of the fruits of the earth, is used by the most holy priests of
Egypt, not only for clothing and raiment but as a veil to hide sacred
things.

And yet I know that some persons, and chiefly this fellow Aemilli-
anus, think it a good joke to deride things divine. For I learn, from
certain men in Oea who know him, that up to the present he never
has prayed to any god or frequented any temple; if he happens to
pass by any shrine, he thinks it wrong to raise his hand to his lips as
an act of reverence. He has never given the first fruits of his crops
or vines or flocks to any of the rural gods who feed and clothe him;
there is no shrine at his villa, no holy place nor sacred grove. But
why should I speak of sacred groves or shrines? Those who have been
at his place say they never have seen there even one stone where an
offering of oil has been made or one bough where wreaths have been
hung (*ramum coronatum*). As a result, two nicknames have been given
him: He is called *Charon*, as I already have said, on account of his
truculence of tongue and manner, but he is also—and this is the
name he prefers—called *Mezentius*, because he despises the gods. For
this reason I can easily understand why he should regard my list of so
many initiations as something to jest about. It is even possible that,
because of his contumacy for things divine, it may never enter his
head that what I say is the truth, viz., that I guard most sacredly the
emblems and mementos of so many holy rites. But I—for what 'Mezentius' thinks of me I would not turn a hand; but to others I would
announce in the clearest voice: if any of you who happen to be
present have been partakers with me in these same solemn rites, give
the sign and you shall hear what it is that I am preserving. For no

consideration of personal safety will compel me to declare to the uninitiated (*ad profanos*) what things I have accepted to be kept in secret.

Translation by Frederick C. Grant, in his *Ancient Roman Religion*, Library of Religion paperbook series (New York, 1957), pp. 226-8

157. KŪKAI'S INITIATION IN THE ESOTERIC BUDDHISM

('Kōbō Daishi Zenshū,' 1, 98 ff.)

Kūkai (774-835) learned in China and introduced to Japan the Buddhism known as the True Words (Mantrayāna in Sanskrit, Shingon in Japanese). In Shingon Buddhism the mysteries are transmitted orally from master to disciple. This Esoteric Buddhism became the most important religion of Heian Japan.

The passage printed below is taken from the Memorial Presenting a List of Newly Imported Sūtras, which Kūkai wrote to the emperor upon his return from studying in China. Kūkai wrote reports on the results of his studies and cautiously relates his initiation.

During the sixth moon of 804, I, Kūkai, sailed for China aboard the Number One Ship, in the party of Lord Fujiwara ambassador to the T'ang court. We reached the coast of Fukien by the eighth moon, and four months later arrived at Ch'ang-an, the capital, where we were lodged at the official guest residence. The ambassadorial delegation started home for Japan on March 15, 805, but in obedience to an imperial edict, I alone remained behind in the Hsi-ming Temple where the abbot Yung-chung had formerly resided.

One day, in the course of my calls on eminent Buddhist teachers of the capital, I happened by chance to meet the abbot of the East Pagoda Hall of the Green Dragon Temple. This great priest, whose Buddhist name was Hui-kuo, was the chosen disciple of the Indian master Amoghavajra. His virtue aroused the reverence of his age; his teachings were lofty enough to guide emperors. Three sovereigns revered him as their master and were ordained by him. The four classes of believers looked up to him for instruction in the esoteric teachings.

I called on the abbot in the company of five or six monks from the Hsi-ming Temple. As soon as he saw me he smiled with pleasure, and he joyfully said, 'I knew that you would come! I have been waiting for such a long time. What pleasure it gives me to look on you today at last! My life is drawing to an end, and until you came there was no one to whom I could transmit the teachings. Go without delay to the ordination altar with incense and a flower.' I returned to the temple where I had been staying and got the things which were necessary for the ceremony. It was early in the sixth moon, then, that I entered the ordination chamber. I stood in front of the Womb Mandala [*Garbha mandala*] and cast my flower in the prescribed manner.[1] By chance it fell on the body of the Buddha Vairochana in the centre. The master exclaimed in delight, 'How amazing! How perfectly amazing!' He repeated this three or four times in joy and wonder. I was then given the fivefold baptism and received the instruction in the Three Mysteries that bring divine intercession. Next I was taught the Sanskrit formulas for the Womb Mandala, and learned the yoga contemplation on all the Honoured Ones.

Early in the seventh moon I entered the ordination chamber of the Diamond [*Vajra*] Mandala for a second baptism. When I cast my flower it fell on Vairochana again, and the abbot marvelled as he had before. I also received ordination as an āchārya early in the following month. On the day of my ordination I provided a feast for five hundred of the monks. The dignitaries of the Green Dragon Temple all attended the feast, and everyone enjoyed himself.

I later studied the Diamond Crown Yoga and the five divisions of the True Words teachings, and spent some time learning Sanskrit and the Sanskrit hymns. The abbot informed me that the Esoteric scriptures are so abstruse that their meaning cannot be conveyed except through art. For this reason he ordered the court artist Li Chen and about a dozen other painters to execute ten scrolls of the Womb and Diamond Mandalas, and assembled more than twenty scribes to make copies of the Diamond and other important esoteric scriptures. He also ordered the bronzesmith Chao Wu to cast fifteen ritual implements. These orders for the painting of religious images and the copying of the sūtras were issued at various times.

One day the abbot told me, 'Long ago, when I was still young, I met the great master Amoghavajra. From the first moment he saw me he treated me like a son, and on his visit to the court and his return

The note to this text is on pp. 316-17.

to the temple I was inseperable from him as his shadow. He confided to me. 'You will be the receptacle of the esoteric teachings. Do your best! Do your best!' I was then initiated into the teachings of both the Womb and Diamond, and into the secret mudrās as well. The rest of his disciples, monks and laity alike, studied just one of the mandalas or one Honoured One or one ritual, but not all of them as I did. How deeply I am indebted to him I shall never be able to express.

'Now my existence on earth approaches its term, and I cannot long remain. I urge you, therefore, to take the two mandalas and the hundred volumes of the Esoteric teachings, together with the ritual implements and these gifts which were left to me by my master. Return to your country and propagate the teachings there.

'When you first arrived I feared I did not have time enough left to teach you everything, but now my teaching is completed, and the work of copying the sūtras and making the images is also finished. Hasten back to your country, offer these things to the court, and spread the teachings throughout your country to increase the happiness of the people. Then the land will know peace and everyone will be content. In that way you will return thanks to Buddha and to your teacher. That is also the way to show your devotion to your country and to your family. My disciple I-ming will carry on the teachings here. Your task is to transmit them to the Eastern Land. Do your best! Do your best!' These were his final instructions to me, kindly and patient as always. On the night of the last full moon of the year he purified himself with a ritual bath and, lying on his right side and making the mudrā of Vairochana, he breathed his last.

That night, while I sat in meditation in the Hall, the abbot appeared to me in his usual form and said, 'You and I have long been pledged to propagate the esoteric teachings. If I am reborn in Japan, this time I will be your disciple.'

I have not gone into the details of all he said, but the general import of the Master's instructions I have given. [Dated 5th December 806].

Note

1 Mandala is a rather complex design, comprising a circular border and one or more concentric circles enclosing a square divided into four triangles; in the centre of each triangle, and in the centre of the mandala itself, are other circles containing images of divinities or their emblems. During the initiation, the *guru* blindfolds the disciple and puts a flower in his hand; the disciple throws it into the mandala, and the section into which it falls reveals the divinity who will be especially favourable to him. On the symbolism and the

rituals of mandal, cf. M. Eliade, *Yoga* (New York: Bollingen Series LVI, 1958), pp. 219 *ff*.; G. Tucci, *The Theory and Practice of the Mandala* (London, 1961).

Translation by Wm. Theodore de Bary, in De Bary (ed.), *Sources of Japanese Tradition* (New York: Columbia University Press, 1958), pp. 144-6. Introductory comment adapted from De Bary, pp. 137 *ff*. Note by M. Eliade.

See also nos. 193, 216, 217, 243-246

CHAPTER IV

Death, Afterlife, Eschatology

A. GODS, HEROES, AND DEATH

158. THE DESCENT OF ISHTAR TO THE NETHER WORLD

Ishtar, goddess of life and fertility, decides to visit her sister Ereshkigal, goddess of death and sterility. As Ishtar forces her way through the gates of the nether world, her robes and garments are stripped from her. Naked and helpless, she finally reaches Ereshkigal, who instantly has her put to death. Without Ishtar, there is no fertility on earth, and the gods soon realize their loss. Ea creates the beautiful eunuch Asushunamir, who tricks Ereshkigal into reviving Ishtar with the water of life and releasing her. The ending of the myth is obscure; perhaps Ishtar's lover, Tammuz, was released along with her. Like the Gilgamesh Epic the myth of the descent of Ishtar to the nether world has its Sumerian counterpart (see S. N. Kramer, 'Inanna's Descent to the Nether World,' ANET, pp. 52-7). Yet the Akkadian version differs substantially from its Sumerian prototype and is by no means a slavish translation of the former. The Sumerian version of the myth dates from the first half of the second millennium B.C.; the Semitic versions do not antedate the end of the second millennium B.C.

To the Land of no Return, the realm of Ereshkigal,
Ishtar, the daughter of Sin, set her mind.
Yea, the daughter of Sin set her mind
To the dark house, the abode of Irkalla,[1]
To the house which none leave who have entered it,
To the road from which there is no way back,
To the house wherein the dwellers are bereft of light,
Where dust is their fare and clay their food,
(Where) they see no light, residing in darkness,
(Where) they are clothed like birds, with wings for garments,
(And where) over door and bolt is spread dust.
When Ishtar reached the gate of the Land of no Return,

The notes to this text are on p. 325.

She said (these) words to the gatekeeper:
'O gatekeeper, open thy gate,
Open thy gate that I may enter!
If thou openest not the gate so that I cannot enter,
I will smash the door, I will shatter the bolt,
I will smash the doorpost, I will move the doors,
I will raise up the dead, eating the living,
So that the dead will outnumber the living.'
The gatekeeper opened his mouth to speak,
Saying to exalted Ishtar:
'Stop, my lady, do not throw it[2] down!
I will go to announce they name to Queen Ereshkigal.'
The gatekeeper entered, saying to Ereshkigal:
'Behold, thy sister Ishtar is waiting at the gate,
She who upholds the great festivals,
   Who stirs up the deep before Ea, the king.'
When Ereshkigal heard this,
Her face turned pale like a cut-down tamarisk,
While her lips turned dark like a bruised kunīnu-reed.
'What drove her heart to me? What impelled her spirit hither?
Lo, should I drink water with the Anunnaki?
Should I eat clay for bread, drink muddied water for beer?
Should I bemoan the men who left their wives behind?
Should I bemoan the maidens who were wrenched from the laps of
   their lovers?
(Or) should I bemoan the tender little one who was sent off before his
   time?[3]
Go, gatekeeper, open the gate for her,
Treat her in accordance with the ancient rules.'
Forth went the gatekeeper (to) open the door for her:
'Enter, my lady, that Cutha[4] may rejoice over thee,
That the palace of the Land of no Return may be glad at thy presence.'
When the first door he had made her enter,
   He stripped and took away the great crown on her head.
'Why O gatekeeper, didst thou take the great crown on my head?'
'Enter, my lady, thus are the rules of the Mistress of the Nether World.'

[*Ishtar passes through seven gates of the nether world. At each of
them the gatekeeper removes an ornament. At the second gate, he takes
the pendants on her ears; at the third, the chains round her neck; then
he removes, respectively, the ornaments on her breast, the girdle of*

birthstones on her hips, the clasps round her hands and feet, and the breechcloth on her body. Each time, she asks the same question; each time she receives the same answer.]

As soon as Ishtar had descended to the Land of no Return,
Ereshkigal saw her and was enraged at her presence.
Ishtar, unreasoning, flew at her.
Ereshkigal opened her mouth to speak,
Saying (these) words to Namtar, her vizier:
'Go, Namtar, lock her up in my palace!
Release against her, against Ishtar, the sixty miseries:
Misery of the eyes against her eyes,
Misery of the sides against her sides,
Misery of the feet against her feet,
Misery of the head against her head—
Against every part of her, against her whole body!'
After Lady Ishtar had descended to the Land of no Return,
The bull springs not upon the cow, the ass impregnates not the jenny,
In the street the man impregnates not the maiden.
The man lay in his (own) chamber, the maiden lay on her side.
....
The countenance of Papsukkal, the vizier of the great gods,
    Was fallen, his face was clouded.
He was clad in mourning, long hair he wore.
Forth went Papsukkal before Sin his father, weeping,
His tears flowing before Ea, the king:
'Ishtar has gone down to the nether world, she has not come up.
Since Ishtar has gone down to the Land of no Return,
The bull springs not upon the cow, the ass impregnates not the jenny,
In the street the man impregnates not the maiden.
The man lay down in his (own) chamber,
The maiden lay down on her side.'
Ea in his wise heart conceived an image,
And created Asushunamir, a eunuch:
'Up, Asushunamir, set thy face to the gate of the Land of no Return;
The seven gates of the Land of no Return shall be opened for thee.
Ereshkigal shall see thee and rejoice at thy presence.
When her heart is calmed, her mood is happy,
Let her utter the oath of the great gods.
(Then) lift up thy head, paying mind to the life-water bag:
'Pray, Lady, let them give me the life-water bag

That water therefrom I may drink.'[5]
As soon as Ereshkigal heard this,
She smote her thigh, bit her finger:
'Thou didst request of me a thing that should not be requested.
Come, Asushunamir, I will curse thee with a mighty curse!
The food of the city's plows[6] shall be thy food,
The sewers of the city shall be thy drink.
The shadow of the wall shall be thy station,
The threshold shall be thy habitation,
The besotted and the thirsty shall smite thy cheek!'
Ereshkigal opened her mouth to speak,
Saying (these) words to Namtar, her vizier:
'Ea, Namtar, knock at Egalgina,[7]
Adorn the thresholds with coral-stone,
Bring forth the Annunaki and seat (them) on thrones of gold,
Sprinkle Ishtar with the water of life and take her from my presence!'
Forth went Namtar, knocked at Egalgina,
Adorned the thresholds with coral-stone,
Brought forth the Anunnaki, seated (them) on thrones of gold,
Sprinkled Ishtar with the water of life and took her from her presence.
When through the first gate he had made her go out,
   He returned to her the breechcloth for her body.

[As Ishtar passes through each of the seven gates, her ornaments are
returned to her one by one.]

'If she does not give thee her ransom price, bring her back.[8]
As for Tammuz, the lover of her youth,
Wash him with pure water, anoint him with sweet oil;
Clothe him with a red garment, let him play on a flute of lapis.
Let courtesans turn his mood.'
When Belili[9] had . . . her jewelry,
And her lap was filled with 'eye-stones,'[10]
On hearing the sound of her brother, Belili struck the jewelry on . . .
So that the 'eye-stones' filled her chamber.
'My only brother, bring no harm to me!
On the day when Tammuz welcomes me,
   When with him the lapis flute (and) the carnelian ring welcome me,
When with him the wailing men and the wailing women welcome me,
May the dead rise and smell the incense.'

Notes

1 Another name of Ereshkigal, the queen of the nether world.
2 The door.
3 I.e. Ereshkigal would have cause for weeping if all these occupants of the nether world should be liberated by Ishtar.
4 A name of the nether world.
5 The scheme evidently succeeds, as Ereshkigal, distracted by the beauty of Asushunamir (meaning 'His Appearance is brilliant'), does not recover until it is too late.
6 This probably means 'dirt.'
7 'Palace of Justice.'
8 The concluding part of the myth and its allusions, particularly to Tammuz are obscure.
9 Apparently referring to Ishtar.
10 'Beads'?

> Translation by E. A. Speiser, *Ancient Near Eastern Texts* (Princeton, 1950), pp. 106-9; reprinted in Isaac Mendelsohn (ed.), *Religions of the Ancient Near East*, Library of Religion paperback series (New York, 1955), pp. 119-25; notes by Mendelsohn

159. GILGAMESH IN SEARCH OF IMMORTALITY

Although originally written in Akkadian, the Gilgamesh Epic was translated into several Near Eastern languages and became the most famous literary creation of the ancient Babylonians. Gilgamesh, king of Uruk, is two-thirds god and one-third man, and 'like a wild ox.' As the story begins, the nobles of Uruk are complaining to the gods that the mighty Gilgamesh in his restlessness and arrrogance is playing havoc with the city. His mother, the goddess Aruru, creates a companion for him—the wild man Enkidu, who runs with the animals on the steppe. Enkidu is first tamed and made human by a temple harlot. Then he is taken to Uruk, where he wrestles with Gilgamesh. The match is a draw and the two become inseparable companions.

One day, Gilgamesh, always looking for adventure, proposes that he and Enkidu travel to the distant cedar forest to kill Huwawa, its evil guardian. Enkidu protests that the journey is very dangerous and Huwawa very fierce, but Gilgamesh is determined and finally they set out. The undertaking is successful and the two are covered with glory.

But Enkidu has already had premonitions of disaster. On their return to Uruk, the goddess Ishtar sees the beauty of Gilgamesh and proposes

to him. He rejects her, reminding her of the fates of her previous lovers.
She is furious and has Anu send the sacred bull of heaven to attack
him. When Gilgamesh and Enkidu slay the bull, the gods become very
angry—this is too presumptuous. As punishment, Enkidu must die.

Enkidu's death is the occasion for the section which we have included
here, the climax and culmination of the Epic. For the first time Gilgamesh has had to face the fact of death, and it bewilders and terrifies
him. Hoping to learn the secret of immortality, he makes a long and
difficult journey in search of Utnapishtim, the one human being who
has acquired it. Utnapishtim tells his story—the famous story of the
flood. But Gilgamesh is, after all, human and very tired. He falls asleep.
Utnapishtim is about to send him away when his wife intervenes in
pity. Gilgamesh is told about a wonderful plant of immortality that
grows at the bottom of the sea. He obtains it; but as he stops to cool
himself in a quiet pool a snake carries off the plant. Gilgamesh, completely unsuccessful, returns to Uruk, and the text concludes as he
proudly shows his city to his ferryman.

For Enkidu, his friend, Gilgamesh
Weeps bitterly, as he ranges over the steppe:
'When I die, shall I not be like Enkidu?
Woe has entered my belly.
Facing death, I roam over the steppe.
To Utnapishtim,[1] Ubar-Tutu's son,
I have taken the road to proceed in all haste.
When arriving by night at mountain passes,
I saw lions and grew afraid.
I lifted my head to Sin[2] to pray.

[The remainder of the column is fragmentary or broken away. When
Gilgamesh next appears, he has arrived before a mountain.]

The name of the mountain is Mashu.
When he arrived at the mountain range of Mashu,
Which daily keeps watch over sunrise and sunset—
Whose peaks reach to the vault of heaven
(And) whose breasts reach to the nether world below—
Scorpion-men guard its gate,
Whose terror is awesome and whose glance was death.
Their shimmering halo sweeps the mountains
That at sunrise and sunset keep watch over the sun.

The notes to this text are on p. 334.

When Gilgamesh beheld them, with fear
And terror was darkened his face.
He took hold of his senses and bowed before them.
A scorpion-man calls to his wife:
'He who has come to us—his body is the flesh of the gods!'
His wife answers the scorpion-man:
'Two-thirds of him is god, one-third of him is human.'
The scorpion-man calls to the fellow,
Addressing (these) words to the offspring of the gods:
'Why hast thou come on this far journey?
Why hast thou arrived before me,
Traversing seas whose crossings are difficult?
The purpose of thy coming I would learn.'

[The remainder of the column is broken away. In the next part that
we have, Gilgamesh replies:]

'On account of Utnapishtim, my father, have I come,
Who joined the Assembly of the gods, in search of life.
About death and life I wish to ask him.'
The scorpion-man opened his mouth to speak,
Saying to Gilgamesh:
'Never was there, Gilgamesh, a mortal who could achieve that.
The mountain's trail no one has travelled.
For twelve leagues extends its inside.
Dense is the darkness and light there is none.

[The remainder is fragmentary or broken. Gilgamesh persists, and
eventually the scorpion-man opens the mountain to him.]

When Gilgamesh heard this,
To the word of the scorpion-man he gave heed.
Along the road of the sun he went.[3]
When one league he had attained,
Dense is the darkness and light there is none;
He can see nothing ahead or behind.

[Gilgamesh travels for eight leagues in total blackness. Beginning the
the ninth league, he feels the north wind fanning his face. He gradually
emerges from the cave.]

When eleven leagues he had attained, the dawn breaks.
And when he had attained twelve leagues, it had grown bright.
On seeing the grove of stones, he heads for . . .

The carnelian bears its fruit;
It is hung with vines good to look at.
The lapis bears foliage;
It, too, bears fruit lush to behold.

[The remainder of the tablet is mutilated or lost. There are two fairly
complete versions of the episodes in the following tablet—the Old
Babylonian and Assyrian recensions—as well as two, more fragmentary,
versions. We shall begin with the Old Babylonian version. The top
of the tablet is broken.]

Shamash was distraught, as he betook himself to him;
He says to Gilgamesh:
'Gilgamesh, whither rovest thou?
The life thou pursuest thou shalt not find.'
Gilgamesh says to him, to valiant Shamash:
'After marching (and) roving over the steppe,
Must I lay my head in the heart of the earth
That I may sleep through all the years?
Let mine eyes behold the sun
    That I may have my fill of the light!
Darkness withdraws when there is enough light.
May he who has died a death behold the radiance of the sun!'

[Again there is a break in the text. Gilgamesh is addressing Siduri,⁴
the ale-wife, who, according to the Assyrian text, 'dwells by the deep
sea.']

'He who with me underwent all hardships—
Enkidu, whom I loved dearly,
Who with me underwent all hardships—
Has now gone to the fate of mankind!
Day and night I have wept over him.
I would not give him up for burial—
In case my friend should rise at my plaint—
Seven days and seven nights,
Until a worm fell out of his nose.
Since his passing I have not found life,
I have roamed like a hunter in the midst of the steppe.
O ale-wife, now that I have seen thy face,
Let me not see the death which I ever dread.'
The ale-wife said to him, to Gilgamesh:
'Gilgamesh, whither rovest thou?

The life thou pursuest thou shalt not find.
When the gods created mankind,
Death for mankind they set aside,
Life in their own hands retaining.
Thou, Gilgamesh, let full be thy belly,
Make thou merry by day and by night.
Of each day make thou a feast of rejoicing,
Day and night dance thou and play!
Let thy garments be sparkling fresh,
Thy head be washed; bathe thou in water.
Pay heed to the little one that holds on to thy hand,
Let thy spouse delight in thy bosom!
For this is the task of mankind!'

[The remainder of the conversation is lost. The Assyrian text gives
a different version of Siduri's response.]

Gilgamesh also says to her, to the ale-wife:
'Now ale-wife, which is the way to Utnapishtim?
What are its markers? Give me, O give me, its markers!
If it be possible, the sea I will cross;
If it not be possible, over the steppe I will range!'
The ale-wife said to him, to Gilgamesh:
'Never, O Gilgamesh, has there been a crossing,
And none who came since the beginning of days could cross the sea.
Only valiant Shamash crosses the sea;
    Other than Shamash who can cross (it)?
Toilsome is the place of crossing
    Very toilsome the way thereto,
And deep are the Waters of Death that bar its approaches!
Where then, O Gilgamesh, wouldst thou cross the sea?
On reaching the Waters of Death, what wouldst thou do?
Gilgamesh, there is Urshanabi, boatman to Utnapishtim.
With him are the Stone Things.[5] In the woods he picks 'urnu'-snakes.[6]
Him let thy face behold.
If it be suitable, cross thou with him.
    If it be not suitable, draw thou back.'
When Gilgamesh heard this,
He raised the axe in his hand,
Drew the dirk from his belt, slipped into (the forest),
    And went down to them.[7]
Like an arrow he descended among them.

Death, Afterlife, Eschatology

[*The text is too fragmentary for translation. When it resumes, Gilgamesh is responding to Urshanabi's questions. He again tells of Enkidu's death and his own search and asks how he can find Utnapishtim. Urshanabi warns him that, by breaking the 'Stone Things,' he has hindered his own crossing. But he agrees to guide Gilgamesh, and sends him off to cut poles. They set sail and soon come to the waters of death, where Urshanabi instructs Gilgamesh: 'Press on, Gilgamesh, take a pole, / (But) let thy hand not touch the Waters of Death . . . !' Finally they reach Utnapishtim's island. Utnapishtim questions Gilgamesh, who repeats his long story again, concluding it as follows.*]

Gilgamesh also said to him, to Utnapishtim:
'That now I might come and behold Utnapishtim,
   Whom they call the Faraway,
I ranged and wandered over all the lands,
I traversed difficult mountains,
I crossed all the seas!
My face was not sated with sweet sleep,
I fretted myself with wakefulness;
I filled my joints with aches.
I had not reached the ale-wife's house
   When my clothing was used up.
I slew bear, hyena, lion, panther,
   Tiger, stag, (and) ibex—
The wild beasts and the creeping things of the steppe.
Their flesh I ate and their skins I wrapped about me.'

[*The remainder of the tablet is fragmentary and broken, except for the conclusion to Utnapishtim's response.*]

'Do we build houses for ever?
   Do we seal (contracts) for ever?
Do brothers divide shares for ever?
Does hatred persist for ever in the land?
Does the river for ever rise (and) bring on floods?
The dragon-fly leave (its) shell
That its face might (but) glance on the face of the sun?
Since the days of yore there has been no performance;
The resting and the dead, how alike they are!
Do they not compose a picture of death,
The commoner and the noble,
   Once they are near to their fate?
The Anunnaki, the great gods, foregather;

Mammetum. maker of fate, with them the fate decrees;
Death and life they determine.
(But) of death its days are not revealed.'
Gilgamesh said to him, to Utnapishtim the Faraway:
'As I look upon thee, Utnapishtim,
Thy features are not strange; even as I art thou.
My heart had regarded thee as resolved to do battle,
Yet thou liest indolent upon my back!
Tell me, how joinedst thou the Assembly of the gods,
  In thy quest of life?'
Utnapishtim said to him, to Gilgamesh:
'I will reveal to thee, Gilgamesh, a hidden matter
And a secret of the gods will I tell thee: . . .'

[Utnapishtim's revelation is the flood narrative printed on page 145.
He was made immortal, he says, through the intervention of the gods
after he managed to survive the great flood which destroyed Shurippak.]

'But now, who will for thy sake call the gods to Assembly
That the life which thou seekest thou mayest find?
Up, lie down to sleep
  For six days and seven nights.'
As he sits there on his haunches,
Sleep fans him like a mist.
Utnapishtim says to her, to his spouse:
'Behold this hero who seeks life!
Sleep fans him like a mist.'
His spouse says to him, to Utnapishtim the Faraway:
'Touch him that the man may awake,
That he may return safe on the way back whence he came,
That through the gate he left he may return to his land.'
Utnapishtim says to her, to his spouse:
'Since to deceive is human, he will seek to deceive thee.[8]
Up, bake for him wafers, put (them) at his head,
And mark on the walls the days he sleeps.'
She baked for him wafers, put (them) at his head,
And marked on the wall the days he slept.
His first wafer is dried out,
The second is leathery, the third is soggy;
  The crust of the fourth has turned white;
The fifth has a mouldy cast,
  The sixth (still) is fresh coloured;

And just as he touched the seventh, the man awoke.
Gilgamesh says to him, to Utnapishtim the Faraway:
'Scarcely had sleep surged over me,
When straightway thou dost touch and rouse me!'
Utnapishtim says to him, to Gilgamesh:
'Go, Gilgamesh, count thy wafers,
That the days thou hast slept may become known to thee:
Thy first wafer is dried out
The second is leathery, the third is soggy;
   The crust of the fourth has turned white;
The fifth has a mouldy cast,
   The sixth (still) is fresh coloured.
As for the seventh, at this instant thou hast awakened.'
Gilgamesh says to him, to Utnapishtim the Faraway:
'What then shall I do, Utnapishtim,
   Whither shall I go,
Now that the Bereaver has laid hold on my members?
In my bedchamber lurks death,
And wherever I set my foot, there is death!'
Utnapishtim says to him, to Urshanabi, the boatman:
'Urshanabi, may the landing-place not rejoice in thee,
   May the place of the crossing despise thee!
To him who wanders on its shore, deny thou its shore!
The man thou hast led (hither), whose body is covered with grime,
The grace of whose members skins have distorted,
Take him, Urshanabi, and bring him to the washing-place.
Let him wash off his grime in water clean as snow,
Let him cast off his skins; let the sea carry (them) away,
   That the fairness of his body may be seen.
Let him renew the band round his head,
Let him put on a cloak to clothe his nakedness,
That he may arrive in his city,
That he may achieve his journey.
Let not (his) cloak have a mouldy cast,
   Let it be wholly new.'
Urshanabi took him and brought him to the washing-place.
He washed off his grime in water clean as snow.
He cast off his skins, the sea carried (them) away,
That the fairness of his body might be seen.
He renewed the band round his head,
He put on a cloak to clothe his nakedness,

That he might arrive in his city,
That he might achieve his journey.
The cloak had not a mouldy cast, but was wholly new.
Gilgamesh and Urshanabi boarded the boat,
They launched the boat on the waves (and) they sailed away.
His spouse says to him, to Utnapishtim the Faraway:
'Gilgamesh has come hither, toiling and straining.
What wilt thou give him that he may return to his land?'
At that he, Gilgamesh, raised up (his) pole,
To bring the boat nigh to the shore.
Utnapishtim says to him, to Gilgamesh:
'Gilgamesh, thou hast come hither, toiling and straining.
What shall I give thee that thou mayest return to thy land?
I will disclose, O Gilgamesh, a hidden thing,
And . . . about a plant I will tell thee:
This plant, like the buckthorn is its . . .
Its thorns will prick thy hands just as does the rose.
If thy hands obtain the plant, thou wilt attain life.'
No sooner had Gilgamesh heard this,
    Than he opened the water-pipe,
He tied heavy stones to his feet.
They pulled him down into the deep and there he saw the plant.
He took the plant, though it pricked his hands.
He cut the heavy stones from his feet.
The sea cast him up upon its shore.
Gilgamesh says to him, to Urshanabi, the boatman:
'Urshanabi, this plant is a plant apart,
Whereby a man may regain his life's breath.
I will take it to ramparted Uruk,
    Will cause . . . to eat the plant . . . !
Its name shall be "Man Becomes Young in Old Age."
I myself shall eat (it)
    And thus return to the state of my youth.'
After twenty leagues they broke off a morsel,
After thirty (further) leagues they prepared for the night.
Gilgamesh saw a well whose water was cool.
He went down into it to bathe in the water.
A serpent snuffed the fragrance of the plant;
It came up from the water and carried off the plant.
Going back it shed its slough.
Thereupon Gilgamesh sits down and weeps,

His tears running down over his face.
He took the hand of Urshanabi, the boatman:
'For whom, Urshanabi, have my hands toiled?
For whom is being spent the blood of my heart?
I have not obtained a boon for myself.
For the earth-lion[9] have I effected a boon!
And now the tide will bear (it) twenty leagues away!
When I opened the water-pipe and spilled the gear,
I found that which had been placed as a sign for me:
  I shall withdraw,
And leave the boat on the shore!'
  After twenty leagues they broke off a morsel,
After thirty (further) leagues they prepared for the night.
  When they arrived in ramparted Uruk,
Gilgamesh says to him, to Urshanabi, the boatman:
'Go up, Urshanabi, walk on the ramparts of Uruk.
Inspect the base terrace, examine its brickwork,
  If its brickwork is not of burnt brick,
And if the Seven Wise Ones laid not its foundation.
One "sar"[10] is city, one sar orchards,
  One sar margin land; (further) the precinct of the Temple of Ishtar.
Three sar and the precinct comprise Uruk.'

Notes

1 The Babylonian hero of the Flood; in Sumerian his name is Ziusudra.
2 The moon-god.
3 Apparently from east to west.
4 The divine barmaid.
5 Apparently stone figures of unusual properties.
6 Meaning not clear. Perhaps some magic symbols possessing properties on a par with those of the Stone Things.
7 To the Stone Things.
8 By asserting that he had not slept at all.
9 An allusion to the serpent?
10 One sar is about 8,000 gallons.

Translation by E. A. Speiser, in *Ancient Near Eastern Texts* (Princeton, 1950), pp. 72-99, reprinted in Isaac Mendelsohn (ed.), *Religions of the Ancient Near East,* Library of Religion paperbook series (New York, 1955). pp. 47-115; notes by Mendelsohn

See also no. 73

B. DEATH AND THE INTERMEDIATE STATE

160. THE MOMENT OF DEATH AS DESCRIBED BY THE UPANISHADS

When this self gets to weakness, gets to confusedness, as it were, then the breaths gather round him. He takes to himself those particles of light and descends into the heart. When the person in the eye turns away, then he becomes non-knowing of forms.

⌐When his body grows weak and he becomes apparently unconscious, the dying man gathers his senses about him, completely withdraws their powers and descends into the heart. *Radhakrishnan.*]

He is becoming one, he does not see, they say; he is becoming one, he does not smell, they say; he is becoming one, he does not taste, they say; he is becoming one, he does not speak, they say; he is becoming one, he does not hear, they say; he is becoming one, he does not think, they say; he is becoming one, he does not touch, they say; he is becoming one, he does not know, they say. The point of his heart becomes lighted up and by that light the self departs either through the eye or through the head or through other apertures of the body. And when he thus departs, life departs after him. And when life thus departs, all the vital breaths depart after him. He becomes one with intelligence. What has intelligence departs with him. His knowledge and his work take hold of him as also his past experience. (*Brihad-āranyaka Upanishad*, IV, 4, 1-2.)

Verily, when a person departs from this world, he goes to the air. It opens out there for him like the hole of a chariot wheel. Through that he goes upwards. He goes to the sun. It opens out there for him like the hole of a *lambara*. Through that he goes upwards. He reaches the moon. It opens out there for him like the hole of a drum. Through that he goes upwards. He goes to the world free from grief, free from snow. There he dwells eternal years. (*ibid.*, V, 11, 1.)

S. Radhakrishnan (editor and translator), *The Principal Upanishads* (New York: Harper & Row, 1953), pp. 269-70, 296

161. THE BUDDHIST CONCEPTION OF THE INTERMEDIATE STATE

(*'Saddharma-smrityupasthāna Sūtra,'* from chapter XXXIV)

The Chinese translation of this material (from which the present English translation was made) dates from ca. A.D. 542.

When a human being dies and is going to be reincarnated as a human being . . . when the time of his death is approaching he sees these signs: he sees a great rocky mountain lowering above him like a shadow. He thinks to himself, 'The mountain might fall down on top of me,' and he makes a gesture with his hand as though to ward off this mountain. His brothers and kinsmen and neighbours see him do this; but to them it seems that he is simply pushing out his hand into space. Presently the mountain seems to be made of white cloth and he clambers up this cloth. Then it seems to be made of red cloth. Finally, as the time of his death approaches he sees a bright light, and being unaccustomed to it at the time of his death he is perplexed and confused. He sees all sorts of things such as are seen in dreams, because his mind is confused. He sees his (future) father and mother making love, and seeing them a thought crosses his mind, a perversity (*viparyāsa*) arises in him. If he is going to be reborn as a man he sees himself making love with his mother and being hindered by his father; or if he is going to be reborn as a woman, he sees himself making love with his father and being hindered by his mother. It is at that moment that the Intermediate Existence is destroyed and life and consciousness arise and causality begins once more to work. It is like the imprint made by a die; the die is then destroyed but the pattern has been imprinted.

Translation by Arthur Waley, in Conze *et al*, *Buddhist Texts through the Ages* (Oxford: Bruno Cassirer (Publishers) Ltd., 1954)

Death and the Intermediate State

Bardo Thödol, 'The Tibetan Book of the Dead,' is a guide for the dead and dying. The first part, called Chikhai Bardo, describes the moment of death. The second part, Chönyid Bardo, deals with the states which supervene immediately after death. The third part, Sidpa Bardo, concerns the onset of the birth instinct and of prenatal events.

When the expiration hath ceased, the vital-force will have sunk into the nerve-centre of Wisdom[1] and the Knower[2] will be experiencing the Clear Light of the natural condition.[3] Then the vital force, being thrown backwards and flying downwards through the right and left nerves,[4] the Intermediate State (*Bardo*) momentarily dawns.

The above [directions] should be applied before [the vital force hath] rushed into the left nerve [after first having traversed the navel nerve-centre].

The time [ordinarily necessary for this motion of the vital-force] is as long as the inspiration is still present, or about the time required for eating a meal.

Then the manner of application [of the instructions] is:

When the breathing is about to cease, it is best if the Transference hath been applied efficiently; if [the application] hath been inefficient, then [address the deceased] thus:

O nobly-born [so and so by name], the time hath now come for thee to seek the Path [in reality]. Thy breathing is about to cease. Thy *guru* hath set thee face to face before with the Clear Light; and now thou art about to experience in its Reality in the *Bardo* state, wherein all things are like the void and cloudless sky, and the naked, spotless intellect is like unto a transparent vacuum without circumference or centre. At this moment, know thou thyself; and abide in that state. I, too, at this time, am setting thee face to face.

Having read this, repeat it many times in the ear of the person dying, even before the expiration hath ceased, so as to impress it on the mind [of the dying one].

If the expiration is about to cease, turn the dying one over on the right side, which posture is called the 'Lying Posture of a Lion.' The

The notes to this text are on p. 341.

throbbing of the arteries [on the right and left side of the throat] is to be pressed.

If the person dying be disposed to sleep, or if the sleeping state advances, that should be arrested, and the arteries pressed gently but firmly. Thereby the vital-force will not be able to return from the median-nerve and will be sure to pass out through the Brahmanic aperture.[5] Now the real setting-face-to-face is to be applied.

At this moment, the first [glimpsing] of the Bardo of the Clear Light of Reality, which is the Infallible Mind of the Dharma-Kāya, is experienced by all sentient beings.

After the expiration hath completely ceased, press the nerves of sleep firmly; and, a lama, or a person higher or more learned than thyself, impress in these words, thus:

Reverend Sir, now that thou art experiencing the Fundamental Clear Light, try to abide in that state which now thou art experiencing.

And also in the case of any other person the reader shall set him face-to-face thus:

O nobly-born [so-and-so], listen. Now thou art experiencing the Radiance of the Clear Light of Pure Reality. Recognize it. O nobly-born, thy present intellect, in real nature void, not formed into anything as regards characteristics or colour, naturally void, is the very Reality, the All-Good.

Thine own intellect, which is now voidness, yet not to be regarded as of the voidness of nothingness, but as being the intellect itself, unobstructed, shining, thrilling, and blissful, is the very consciousness, the All-good Buddha.

Thine own consciousness, not formed into anything, in reality void, and the intellect, shining and blissful,—these two,—are inseparable. The union of them is the Dharma-Kāya state of Perfect Enlightenment.[6]

Thine own consciousness, shining, void, and inseparable from the Great Body of Radiance, hath no birth, nor death, and is the Immutable Light—Buddha Amitābha.

Knowing this is sufficient. Recognizing the voidness of thine own intellect to be Buddhahood, and looking upon it as beng thine own consciousness, is to keep thyself in the [state of the] divine mind of the Buddha.

Repeat this distinctly and clearly three or [even] seven times. That will recall to the mind [of the dying one] the former [i.e. when living] setting-face-to-face by the guru. Secondly, it will cause the naked consciousness to be recognized as the Clear Light; and, thirdly, recognizing one's own self [thus], one becometh permanently united with the Dharma-Kāya and liberation will be certain.

[*If when dying, one is familiar with this state, the wheel of rebirth is stopped and liberation is instantaneously achieved. But such spiritual efficiency is so very rare that the normal mental condition of the dying person is unequal to the supreme feat of holding on to the state in which the Clear Light shines. There follows a progressive descent into lower and lower states of the* Bardo *existence, and finally rebirth. Immediately after the first state of* Chikhai Bardo *comes the second stage, when the consciousness-principle leaves the body and says to itself: 'Am I dead, or am I not dead?' without being able to determine.*]

But even though the Primary Clear Light be not recognized, the Clear Light of the second *Bardo* being recognized, Liberation will be attained. If not liberated even by that, then that called the third *Bardo* or the *Chönyid Bardo* dawneth.

In this third stage of the *Bardo*, the karmic illusions come to shine. It is very important that this Great setting-face-to-face of the *Chönyid Bardo* be read: it hath much power and can do much good.

About this time [the deceased] can see that the share of food is being set aside, that the body is being stripped of its garments, that the place of the sleeping-rug is being swept;[7] can hear all the weeping and wailing of his friends and relatives, and, although he can see them and can hear them calling upon him, they cannot hear him calling upon them, so he goeth away displeased.

At that time, sounds, lights, and rays—all three—are experienced. These awe, frighten, and terrify, and cause much fatigue. At this moment, this setting-face-to-face with the *Bardo* [during the experiencing] of Reality is to be applied. Call the deceased by name, and correctly and distinctly explain to him, as follows:

O nobly-born, listen with full attention, without being distracted: There are six states of *Bardo*, namely: the natural state of *Bardo* while in the womb; the *Bardo* of the dream-state; the *Bardo* of ecstatic equilibrium, while in deep meditation; the *Bardo* of the moment of death; the *Bardo* [during the experiencing] of Reality; the *Bardo* of the inverse process of samsāric existence. These are the six.

O nobly-born, thou wilt experience three *Bardos*, the *Bardo* of the moment of death, the *Bardo* [during the experiencing] of Reality, and the *Bardo* while seeking rebirth. Of these three, up to yesterday, thou hadst experienced the *Bardo* of the moment of death. Although the Clear Light of Reality dawned upon thee, thou wert unable to hold on, and so thou hast to wander here. Now henceforth thou art going to experience the [other] two, the *Chönyid Bardo* and the *Sidpa Bardo*.[8]

Thou wilt pay undistracted attention to that with which I am about to set thee face to face, and hold on;

O nobly-born, that which is called death hath now come. Thou art departing from this world, but thou art not the only one; [death] cometh to all. Do not cling, in fondness and weakness, to this life. Even though thou clingest out of weakness, thou hast not the power to remain here. Thou wilt gain nothing more than wandering in this *Samsāra*.[9] Be not attached [to this world]; be not weak. Remember the Precious Trinity.[10]

O nobly-born, whatever fear and terror may come to thee in the *Chönyid Bardo*, forget not these words; and, bearing their meaning at heart, go forwards: in them lieth the vital secret of recognition:

Alas! when the Uncertain Experiencing of Reality is dawning upon me here,

With every thought of fear or terror or awe for all [apparitional appearances] set aside,

May I recognize whatever [visions] appear, as the reflections of mine own consciousness;

May I know them to be of the nature of apparitions in the Bardo:

When at this all-important moment [of opportunity] of achieving a great end.

May I not fear the bands of Peaceful and Wrathful [Deities], mine own thought-forms.

Repeat thou these [verses] clearly, and remembering their significance as thou repeatest them, go forwards, [O nobly-born]. Thereby, whatever visions of awe or terror appear, recognition is certain; and forget not this vital secret art lying therein.

O nobly-born, when thy body and mind were separating, thou must have experienced a glimpse of the Pure Truth, subtle, sparkling, bright dazzling, glorious, and radiantly awesome, in appearance like a mirage moving across a landscape in spring-time in one continuous stream of vibrations. Be not daunted thereby, nor terrified, nor awed. That is the radiance of thine own true nature. Recognize it.

From the midst of that radiance, the natural sound of Reality, reverberating like a thousand thunders simultaneously sounding, will come. That is the natural sound of thine own real self. Be not daunted thereby, nor terrified, nor awed.

Death and the Intermediate State

The body, which thou hast now is called the thought-body of propensities.[11] Since thou hast not a material body of flesh and blood, whatever may come,—sounds, lights, or rays,—are, all three, unable to harm thee: thou art incapable of dying. It is quite sufficient for thee to know that these apparitions are thine own thought-forms. Recognize this to be the *Bardo*.

O nobly-born, if thou dost not now recognize thine own thought-forms, whatever of meditation or of devotion thou mayest have performed while in the human world—if thou hast not met with this present teaching—the lights will daunt thee, the sounds will awe thee, and the rays will terrify thee. Shouldst thou not know this all-important key to the teachings,—not being able to recognize the sounds, lights, and rays,—thou wilt have to wander in the *Samsāra*.

Notes

1 The 'nerve-centres' are the 'psychic centres' (*cakra*). The 'nerve-centre of wisdom' is located in the heart-centre (*anāhata-cakra*).
2 'Knower,' i.e. the mind in its knowing functions.
3 The mind in its natural, or primal, state.
4 That is, the 'psychic nerves,' *pingāla-nādī* and *idā-nādī*.
5 *Brāhmarandhra*, the fissure on the top of the cranium identified with *sutura frontalis*.
6 From the union of the two states of mind, or consciousness, is born the state of Perfect Enlightenment, Buddhahood. The Dharma-Kāya ('Body of Truth') symbolizes the purest and the highest state of being, a state of supramundane consciousness.
7 The references are (1) to the share of food being set aside for the deceased during the funeral rites; (2) to his corpse being prepared for the shroud; (3) to his bed or sleeping-place.
8 The *Chönyid Bardo* is the intermediate state during the experiencing of Reality. The *Sidpa Bardo* represents the state wherein the deceased is seeking rebirth.
9 *Samsāra*, the universal becoming.
10 That is, the Buddha, the Dharma (=the Law, the Doctrine), the Samgha (the entire community of monks and hermits).
11 'Thought-body' or 'mind-body' born of the past worldly existence.

W. Y. Evans-Wentz (translator and editor), *The Tibetan Book of the Dead* (Oxford, 3rd ed.; 1957), pp. 90-2, 95-7, 101-4

C. FUNERARY RITUALS

163. 'AFFORD HIM EASY ACCESS, EARTH': A VEDIC FUNERARY HYMN

('Rig Veda,' X, 18)

1. Go hence, O Death,[1] pursue thy special pathway
   apart from that which gods are wont to travel.
   To thee I say it who hast eyes and hearest: touch
   not our offspring, injure not our heroes.
2. As ye have come effacing Mrityu's footstep,[2] to
   farther times prolonging your existence,
   May ye be rich in children and possessions, cleansed,
   purified, and meet for sacrificing.
3. Divided from the dead are these, the living: now
   is our calling on the gods successful
   We have come forth for dancing and for laughter,
   to farther times prolonging our existence.
4. Here I erect this rampart for the living; let none
   of these, none other reach this limit.
   May they survive a hundred lengthened autumns,
   and may they bury Death beneath this mountain.[3]
5. As the days follow days in close succession, as with
   the seasons duly come the seasons,
   As each successor fails not his foregoer, so form the
   lives of these, O great Ordainer[4]
6. Live your full lives and find old age delightful, all of
   you striving one behind the other.[5]
   May Tvashtar,[6] maker of fair things, be gracious,
   and lengthen out the days of your existence.
7. Let these unwidowed dames with noble husbands
   adorn themselves with fragrant balm and unguent.
   Decked with fair jewels, tearless, free from sorrow,
   first let the wives ascend unto the place.[7]

The notes to this text are on pp. 343-4.

8. Rise, come unto the world of life, O woman: come
    he is lifeless by whose side thou liest.
  Wifehood with this thy husband was thy portion,
    who took thy hand and wooed thee as a lover.[8]

9. From his dead hand I take the bow he carried, that
    it may be our power and might and glory.
  There art thou, there; and here with noble heroes
    may we o'ercome all hosts that fight against us.

10. Betake thee[9] to the lap of the earth the mother, of earth
    far-spreading, very kind and gracious.
  Young dame, wool-soft unto the guerdon-giver, may
    she preserve thee from Destruction's bosom.

11. Heave thyself, Earth, nor press thee downward
    heavily: afford him easy access, gently tending him.
  Earth, as a mother wraps her skirt about her child,
    so cover him.

12. Now let the heaving earth be free from motion: yea,
    let a thousand clods remain above him.
  Be they to him a home distilling fatness, here let
    them ever be his place of refuge.

13. I stay the earth from thee, while over thee I place
    this piece of earth. May I be free from injury.
  Here let the Fathers keep this pillar firm for thee,
    and there let Yama make thee an abiding place.[10]

14. Even as an arrow's feathers, they have laid me down
    at day's decline.
  My parting speech have I drawn back as 'twere a
    courser with the rein.

Notes

1 Mrityu, a personification of death, while Yama (see stanza 13 below) is the
god who rules the spirits of the departed.

2 I.e., 'losing' Death by erasing his tracks and frustrating his approach. The
stanza is addressed to those assembled for the funeral rites.

3 Having absolved the living from impurity (stanza 2), the *adhvaryu* priest
now raises a stone or earth mound, likened to a 'mountain,' to further bar
the path of Death and to limit his domain.

4 Dhātar, a divine being who is creator, arranger and maintainer of all things,
and who is particularly associated with matrimony and fertility.

5 Human lives should succeed one another, with their ideal 'hundred autumns'
each, in as orderly a fashion as the seasons.

6 The divine artisan, shaper of forms; a god celebrated for his generative
powers.

7 At this point the women now go up to the raised 'place' (*yoni*, a word which also means 'womb,' 'place of origin'), where the corpse lies with his widow beside him.

8 This stanza is addressed to the widow, either by the priest or by the husband's brother, as she is summoned to return to the realm of the living. (The levirate marriage is mentioned elsewhere in *Rig Veda*, x, e.g. 40.2).

9 The deceased.

10 After the committal of the body to the earth the priest has perhaps placed a beam or lid across the grave to 'stay the earth' and make the bodily resting place as secure as that which Yama provides for the spirit in the other world. This priestly act is cautious, nonetheless, as 'injury' may accrue from contact with the impurity of death. Stanza 14 is obviously a later addition.

Translation by Ralph T. H. Griffith, in his *The Hymns of the Rigveda*, IV (Benares, 1892), pp. 137-9; adapted by M. Eliade

164. THE AZTEC FUNERARY RITUAL (BERNARDINO DE SAHAGŪN)

When among the Aztecs a mortal died the 'straw death,' before the corpse the priest uttered these words: 'Our son, thou art finished with the sufferings and fatigues of this life. It hath pleased our Lord to take thee hence, for thou hast not eternal life in this world; our existence is as a ray of the sun. He hath given thee the grace of knowing us and of associating in our common life. Now the god Mictlantecutli and the goddess Mictecaciuatl [Lord and Lady of Hell] have made thee to share their abode. We shall all follow thee, for it is our destiny, and the abode is broad enough to receive the whole world. Thou wilt be heard of no longer among us. Behold, thou art gone to the domain of darkness, where there is neither light nor window. Neither shalt thou come hither again, nor needst thou concern thyself for thy return, for thine absence is eternal. Thou dost leave thy children poor and orphaned, not knowing what will be their end nor how they will support the fatigues of this life. As for us, we shall not delay to go to join thee there where thou wilt be.' Then upon the head of the body, like another baptism, the priest let fall a few drops of water and beside it placed a bowl of water: 'Lo, the water of which in this life thou hast made use; this for thy journey.' And like another Book of the Dead, in due order certain papers were laid upon the mummy-form corpse: 'Lo, with this thou shalt pass the two clashing mountains. . . . With this thou shalt pass the road where the serpent awaiteth thee. . . . With this thou shalt pass the lair of the green lizard. . . .

Lo, wherewith thou shalt cross the eight deserts. . . . And the eight hills. . . . And behold with what thou canst traverse the place of the winds that drive with obsidian knives.' Thus the perils of the Underworld Way were to be passed, and the soul to arrive before Mictlantecutli, whence after four years he should fare onward until, by the aid of his dog, sacrificed at his grave, he should pass over the Ninefold Stream, and thence, hound with master, enter into the eternal house of the dead, Chicomemictlan, the Ninth Hell.

H. B. Alexander, *The World's Rim* (Lincoln, Neb.: University of Nebraska Press, 1953), pp. 201-2; translating and summarizing Bernardino de Sahagún, *Historia de las Cosas de la Nueva España* bk. III, App. I

165. FUNERARY RITES OF THE TORADJA (CENTRAL CELEBES)

The Toradja had two funerals, which were separated by a considerable length of time. At the first of these the bodies were placed in temporary huts outside the village; at the second the bones were cleaned and given a definitive burial in caves.

Lamentations for the dead person began the moment he expired. They were always improvised, but stereotyped: it was said how much he was missed, he was asked why the mourners couldn't have gone in his place and his virtues were summed up. For many of the mourners, at least, it was a purely formal affair, unconnected with feelings of affection for the dead person. Many young girls, it would seem, participated merely to show off their voices. Men hardly took part in it and some were even quite annoyed by it.

The corpse was laid out soon after death, preferably by some one who fetched the bones for the second funeral *(tonggola)*, otherwise by an older member of the family. It was not washed, nor were its clothes usually removed, new and handsome ones being put on over the old ones or laid over the body. Cloths were bound about the knees, arms and around the head under the chin to make the body easier to carry and to keep the mouth from falling open. Now and then gold dust, a gold piece or beads (preferably white) were put into its mouth, supposedly as food for its *angga*.[1] In Pu'u-mboto they said on this

The notes to this text are on p. 352.

occasion : 'Just as white as the beads will be the grain of the rice which you will give us. Do not come to us, in the guise of pigs, mice or rice birds; give us the grain (*po'oe*).' Sometimes beads were placed on the eyes, a small mirror on the chest and pieces of money on the cheeks and forehead.

A bit of hair and the nails of the dead person were cut off and made up into a package along with the knife used for this purpose. They were either carried about or kept in the house (presumably by the closest relative, though from other remarks it would seem that the hair and nails of much loved or admired persons were in great demand) for a long time—by some as long as six generations. During the first funeral, from the time the body was removed from the house until the *moombe ue* had been performed, this package served as a substitute for the dead person, a bit of everything one ate or chewed being placed beside it. Hair and nails were said to be kept 'so that his *tanoana*[2] will be transferred to us.' Many said that they allayed their longing for the dead, and others, 'We keep hair and nails in order not to forget the dead, and the dead will then bless us.' They were also used as medicine for the crops, and it was said that, 'if we didn't cut off the nails of the dead they would pinch off the rice ears with them or dig up the roots of the plants.' A widow would keep the hair of her dead husband 'so that his *tanoana* would not part from hers,' but would throw it away when she remarried.

Once the corpse was dressed it was laid on a mat in the most appropriate part of the house and a sort of canopy *(batuwali)* was built over it. The *batuwali* (the word probably once meant 'room') consisted of four bamboo posts with cross bars, covered with a piece of cotton or sleeping mat to form the roof, and with curtains hung from the cross bars. Pinang blossoms were hung from the posts and beads by the head of the corpse. Beside the body was a basket with sirih-pinang and an egg, which served as its food. The *batuwali* was further decorated with various cotton goods, some of which later accompanied the corpse as presents.

While the body remained in the house it was fed. The food was placed beside it and removed after an hour and given to a slave to eat. At some point or other during the proceedings a buffalo and a few pigs were killed, the former being intended to serve as a means of transportation to the underworld for its master. The house was always full of people, especially at night. A circle which could not be broken was formed around the *batuwali* in order to protect the dead person from witches or the souls of the dead. The hearth fire and a torch had, moreover, to be kept burning. The people keeping watch could not sleep for a moment, as this would not only endanger the corpse but their own *tanoana* could easily be seized and taken to the underworld. Round dances *(kajori, raego)* and certain singing games were prohibited during these nights, though various others were especially performed on these occasions. Chief among the latter were the *djondjo awa* and the *lina*, which formed the greatest attractions for the young people. The first of these consisted in reciting improvised couplets which were alternated with a refrain beginning with the words *djondjo awa*. Kruyt thought these words probably came from *ndjo'u-ndjo'u wawa*, meaning 'go, go, accompany him' or 'take him away,' referring to the dead person. The *lina* was a song (plaintively sung, each line of which ended with the meaningless word *lina*, which Kruyt thought came from *linga*, 'to sing,' but which the Toradja equated with *ine*, 'mother.' The two games were alternated. They were said to be performed to distract and console the *angga* now that it had to leave the earth, and in them the *angga* was first taken on a trip to another region and then conducted to the underworld, or, in at least one case, to Buju mpotumangi, 'the mountain of weeping,' where it was handed over to other souls of the dead who had come to meet it. When leave was taken from the *angga* it was asked not to take the *tanoana* of the rice and other plants with it to the underworld, which would make the crops fail. Throughout the *djondjo awa* and *lina* a man and a young girl carried on a conversation of a piquant nature. . . .

The coffin was called either *bangka* or *jumu*. The second of these was a general term meaning 'covering'; the first meant 'boat,' and was still used in Pu'u-mboto in this sense. That the coffin was indeed thought of as a boat is borne out by the fact that if one dreamed of somebody rowing in a boat it was assumed that that person would soon die. The coffin was hollowed out of a tree trunk split lengthwise to form a cover, called *lakinja*, 'the man,' and a receptacle, called *tinanja*, 'the woman.' Aside from the handles at either end which were sometimes carved in the form of animal heads (Kruyt had seen those of pigs and goats) and which supposedly had no particular significance, the coffins were not decorated. . . .

Before the coffin was removed from the house a shaman performed the *mowurake mpo'onto tanoana*, 'shaman's ritual to hold back the *tanoana*,' over the closest relatives, supposedly to keep their souls from following the coffin. They squatted down near it and were covered by a costly old cloth *(bana)*. The shaman then touched all the heads under the cloth and finally the coffin with a *rare* consisting of a young arenga palm leaf and small bell and a basket in which was a branch of cordyline. This she repeated seven times and then touched the corpse with it seven times from the feet to the head while reciting a litany. . . .

Unfortunately Kruyt did not record the litanies recited on these occasions, so it is impossible to be sure of their significance, but it would seem that in all the cases the purpose was to prepare the people for a hazardous journey. The funeral ceremony was performed according to Kruyt to keep the *tanoana* of the surviving close relatives from following the dead person, but as we shall see, they too were supposed to be in the underworld while in mourning, so it is possible that the ceremony served to prepare them for this trip. As the dead person was similarly treated with the *rare* it may also have been done with the same intention. This, at any rate, was the explanation given by the Toradja for the *montende rare* performed over the corpse of a shaman.

When removing the coffin and on the way to its temporary shelter outside the village everything was done to prevent the soul of the dead from finding its way back to its home, except in the case of people who had left no relatives of the same generation behind. It was removed through the window, or if it was too small a wall was taken out for this purpose, and sometimes (generally in the case of infants) it was let out through the floor. . . .

The small hut which served as temporary resting place for the corpse *(tambea)* was a pile construction erected a short distance to the north, south or west of the village. It was never built to the east of it, as the village would then lie in the path of the *angga*, which went to the west. Account was also taken of the prevailing wind, to reduce to a minimum the smell of the rotting corpse in the village. It was solidly built, with no walls and a low roof. The roof was laid on differently than in houses for the living and the notched tree trunk which served as a ladder was placed so that the steps faced downwards, as the dead saw everything reversed. Long bamboo poles, each with a piece of white cotton attached, were erected about the hut. . . .

Upon arrival the coffin was placed in the hut with the feet pointing west. A hole was made in the bottom in which a long bamboo was inserted which reached to the ground and served to drain off the juices of decomposition. Then (in Lage at any rate and also Kruyt presumed, elsewhere) the shaman performed a ritual to lure back the *tanoana* of family members which might have gotten into the coffin so that they would not be taken by the *angga* to the underworld. The cover was then placed on the coffin, which was bound about with rattan, eight times for men and nine for women. Finally the cracks between the two parts were filled with fungus and covered with strips of bark cloth. A sleeping mat, a food basket, a cooking pot, the dead person's sirih pouch and sword and a few other articles and food were either hung from or laid on the roof of the hut.

Somewhat different customs were observed with respect to the corpse of a shaman. According to Kruyt these were to be explained by the fact that the soul *(angga)* of a shaman did not go to the underworld *(Torate)*, but to *Mungku mpe'anta-anta*, 'the mountain which serves as resting place,' in 'the land of the *wurake* spirits in the sky.' This was supposed to be where the roads from the upper and underworlds came together. Unfortunately, however, in the litany which Kruyt quoted in this connection her soul was spoken of as going to *Nanggi* or *Linduju*, both names for the underworld. Supposedly to demonstrate that her 'soul' went to heaven a small bamboo was placed in her mouth as a blow pipe through which she blew her 'breath' *(inosa)* to the sky. As we have seen, however, *inosa* is 'life force' and is closely akin to *tanoana*, thus quite different from *angga*. The ceremony by which, according to Kruyt, the shaman's soul was brought to heaven was called *montende rare*, 'to toss up the *rare*.' According to the Toradja it served 'to equip the dead person's *angga* (for its trip).' . . .

A hen or rooster, depending on whether or not the dead person was female or male respectively, was also tied to the hut or coffin. . . .

For the corpse of an important person a slave was designated as *tandojae*; at least that was the case in Onda'e, Lage and Lamusa according to the first edition of Kruyt and Adriani. He slept in the hut at night and kept a torch burning, and in the daytime he kept the flies away and wiped up the liquids from the corpse. His main duty was to prevent witches from 'eating up' the body. He could talk to no one and took his food where he could find it. . . .

After the coffin had been deposited in the hut leave was taken from the dead person. There was no set formula for this, though the sentiments expressed were apparently always pretty much the same. For example, 'O father (mother), we have put everything for you down here. Stay here. Your (dead) relatives are coming to keep you company, and among them is also so and so, who will tell you what you must do and not do. As for us, whom you have left, we too have some one whose orders we obey.' This is the end of our relationship. This far you have a claim on us as your children. We are making the steps of your house black. Do not come back to us.' 'Here you have your food. Give us rain so that our rice will succeed, and give us dry weather so that we can burn the wood on our fields. Do not let any rice birds loose on us, or mice or pigs.' Later on people returned from time to time, however, to bring food for the *angga (melo'a)*, as, for example, when people were called together to work in the fields *(mesale)*. Otherwise the dead would come to fetch it themselves.

Although official leave had been taken from the dead person his soul was still thought to return to visit the living, especially the first night after the disposal of the coffin, and for this reason the *batuwali* was left standing for eight nights (for a man) or nine nights (for a woman) after his death. If it was broken up earlier the sleeping mat was left for this length of time. Torch and hearth fire were kept burning and *wirih* and food were placed by its side. The shaman was helpful in preventing these visits, as she could see the *angga*. On this first night after the removal of the corpse she also descended to the underworld to fetch the *tanoana* of the relatives which might have followed the soul of the dead person there, and eight days after the removal (for a man; nine days after for a woman) she performed a ceremony with the aid of the *wurake* to rescue the *angga* from the juices of its decomposing corpse *(moombe ue)*. . . .

Aside from the general mourning there were special restrictions for a widow or widower. Until the body had been removed she (unless otherwise stated what follows applied equally to widows and widowers) remained by its head with a female companion of her family, who mourned for her, at its foot. A man likewise shared the mourning with a male member of the family (around the *Lake* a widow had eight companions and a widower nine). When the body was removed she was surrounded by rain mats and pieces of bark cloth, forming a small cubicle in which she remained as a rule for three days, sometimes less, 'in any case until the shaman had finished her work. . . .

In the case of the death of an important person, however, mourning was not ended until a head had been taken for him. Till then the mourners could put on no new clothes or take sirih from another's pouch, nor could coconuts be taken from the trees. If the village was at war then a head was taken from the enemy; otherwise a slave or somebody suspected of witchcraft or sorcery was bought from another village, brought home and cut to pieces. The person who had contributed most toward his purchase gave the first blow, holding onto the victim's hair, and he also took the head. The mourning could also be ended with a head taken by another tribe if necessary. The close relatives of the dead person were responsible for getting the head or sacrificial victim. A widower would not dare return until he had got one by some means or other, even if it took three years or longer. . . .

At the ceremonies ending the mourning the widow was told not to stay in the underworld, as she had been freed from the mourning restrictions by victory. The poles around the hut in which the coffin rested were cut down and a piece of the scalp of the victim was inserted in a notch in one of the handles of the coffin. Then the dead person was calmed by singing to him: 'Lie down again dead one, in the abode of the dead *(Nanggi)* is the resting place of your soul.' Then everybody returned to the village, where the clothes of the widow or widower were cut through and the mourning was declared to be ended. The leader of the troop of head-hunters cut a notch in the ridge pole on the east side of the house and inserted a piece of scalp in it, and then everybody repaired to the temple, where an old man addressed the dead person for whom the mourning had just been ended: 'Do not come to us in the form of mice or pigs, because we have mourned your death. From now on we will be happy: we will play the drums and sing; you see to it that our rice succeeds.' After a few strokes on the drum he continued: 'Any one who has anything to claim from others may demand payment from the debtor; he who wants to set out against the enemy or wants to marry let him go ahead, for the mourning period is over.'

After some time a second funeral was held for the bones of the dead. How soon this was done depended on various circumstances. In the first place a plentiful harvest was necessary because of the enormous amounts of food consumed, and for this reason was usually celebrated shortly after it. This had the further advantage that there was sufficient free time for it. It could not be celebrated every year in each village, however, because of the high cost, so either a village waited a few years until there were enough dead to make it worth while, or did it jointly with one or more villages. If there was no opportunity for holding a regular funeral, and certain signs, such as sickness or a plague of mice, made it urgent, then an emergency feast was organized which lasted only one day and to which no guests were invited. . . .

About eleven in the morning of the first day the bones were fetched by the bone collectors *(tonggola)*, roughly sorted out and made up into packages. When they returned to the village one of the oldest female *tonggola* treated everybody who felt the least bit sick with one of the skulls. After this the bones were brought to the feast grounds where the male *tonggola* slaughtered a tethered buffalo. . . .

The souls of the people whose bones had been assembled were brought from the underworld by the shamans. At the *mompemate* there was no prescribed number of them, but at the *motengke* there had to be five plus two male assistants. The litany described how the dead were waked, dressed themselves and were conducted through the underworld to the pinang tree which they climbed to reach the earth, where they came out in Mori (to the east of the Toradja), and finally were led to the temple or feast hut. There they were welcomed by their relatives and entertained by them and the rest of the participants with singing and dancing. In the songs the dead were brought up to date on the current affairs of the living. During this part of the ceremonies, which lasted a whole night from dusk to dawn, the men were permitted to ask a girl to be their partner. The man rested his elbow on the girl's shoulder and was allowed to touch her face and breast, in exchange for which he gave her a sarong or some other present. When she had had enough of it she would hang a white cotton or bark cloth sarong over his shoulder and the relationship would be ended. While they were together they were considered to be man and wife.

The next day the *angga* were conducted by the shamans to their final resting place.

Notes

1 Ghost; personality of a dead person.
2 The spiritual part of man.

R. E. Downs, *The Religion of the Bare'e Speaking Toradja of Central Celebes* (The Hague: Uitgeverij Excelsior, 1956), pp. 77-89; summarizing N. Adriani and A. C. Kruyt

D. EGYPTIAN CONCEPTIONS OF DEATH

166. THE DEAD PHARAOH ASCENDS TO HEAVEN

(From the 'Pyramid Texts')

The so-called Pyramid Texts are religious texts inscribed on the interior walls of the pyramids of certain pharaohs of the fifth and sixth dynasties (ca. 2425-2300 B.C.). The Pyramid Texts contain the oldest references to Egyptian cosmology and theology, but they are primarily concerned with the victorious passage of the dead pharaoh to his new, celestial abode.

Thy two wings are spread out like a falcon with thick plumage, like the hawk seen in the evening traversing the sky *(Pyr.* § 1048).

He flies who flies; this king Pepi flies away from you, ye mortals. He is not of the earth, he is of the sky. . . . This king Pepi flies as a cloud to the sky, like a masthead bird; this king Pepi kisses the sky like a falcon, this king Pepi reaches the sky like Horizon-god (Harakhte) *(Pyr.* § 890-1).

Thou ascendest to the sky as a falcon, thy feathers are (those of) geese *(Pyr.* § 913).

King Unis goes to the sky, king Unis goes to the sky! On the wind! On the wind! *(Pyr.* § 309).

Stairs to the sky are laid for him that he may ascend thereon to the sky *(Pyr.* § 365).

King Unis ascends upon the ladder which his father Re (the Sun-god) made for him *(Pyr.* § 390).

Atum has done that which he said he would do for this king Pepi II, binding for him the rope-ladder, joining together the (wooden) ladder for this king Pepi II; (thus) this king is far from the abomination of men *(Pyr.* § 2083).

'How beautiful to see, how satisfying to behold,' say the gods, 'when this god (meaning the king) ascends to the sky. His fearfulness is on his head, his terror is at his side, his magical charms are before him.' Geb has done for him as was done for himself (Geb). The gods and souls of Buto, the gods and souls of Hierakonpolis, the gods in the sky and the gods on earth come to him. They make supports for king Unis on their arms. Thou ascendest, O King Unis, to the sky. Ascend upon it in this its name 'Ladder' (*Pyr.* § 476-9).

[*Over and over again we find the assurance that the double doors of the sky are opened before the pharaoh.*]

Opened are the double doors of the horizon; unlocked are its bolts (*Pyr.* § 194; *n.b.* this is a constant refrain in the Pyramid Texts; cf. § 603, 604, 1408, etc).

[*The King's heralds hasten to announce his advent to the Sun god.*]

Thy messengers go, thy swift messengers run, thy heralds make haste. They announce to Re that thou hast come, (even) this king Pepi (§ 1539-40).

This king Pepi found the gods standing, wrapped in their garments, their white sandals on their feet. They cast off their white sandals to the earth, they throw off their garments. 'Our heart was not glad until thy coming,' say they (*Pyr.* § 1197).

[*More often the gods themselves proclaim the pharaoh's coming.*]

O Re-Atum! This king Unis comes to thee, an imperishable glorious-one, lord of the affairs of the place of the four pillars (the sky). Thy son comes to thee. This king Unis comes to thee (*Pyr. Ut.* 217).

[*The dead pharaoh boldly approaches the Sun god with the words:*]

I, O Re, am this one of whom thou didst say . . . 'My son!' My father are thou, O Re. . . . Behold king Pepi, O Re. This king Pepi is thy son. . . . This king Pepi shines in the east like Re, he goes in the west like Kheprer. This king Pepi lives on what whereon Horus (son of Re) lord of the sky lives, by command of Horus lord of the sky' (*Pyr.* § 886-8).

The king ascends to the sky among the gods dwelling in the sky. He stands on the great [dais], he hears (in judicial session) the (legal) affairs of men. Re finds thee upon the shores of the sky in this lake that is in Nut (the Sky-goddess). 'The arriver comes!' say the gods. He (Re) gives thee his arm on the stairway to the sky. 'He who knows his place comes,' say the gods. O Pure One, assume thy throne in the barque of Re and sail thou the sky. . . . Sail thou with the Imperishable Stars, sail thou with the Unwearied Stars. Receive thou the 'tribute' of the Evening Barque, become thou a spirit dwelling in Dewat. Live thou this pleasant life which the lord of the horizon lives (Pyr. § 1169-72).

Translation by J. H. Breasted, in his *Development of Religion and Thought in Ancient Egypt* (Chicago, 1912), pp. 109-15, 118-20, 122, 136

167. THE DEAD PHARAOH BECOMES OSIRIS

(From the 'Pyramid Texts')

A great number of Pyramid Texts *present the different phases of the ritual assimilation of the dead pharaoh with Osiris.*

As he (Osiris) lives, this king Unis lives; as he dies not, this king Unis dies not; as he perishes not, this king Unis perishes not (Pyr. Ut. 219).

[*The dead pharaoh receives the throne of Osiris, and becomes, like him, king of the dead.*]

Ho! king Neferkere (Pepi II)! How beautiful is this! How beautiful is this, which thy father Osiris has done for thee! He has given thee his throne, thou rulest those of the hidden places (the dead), thou leadest their august ones, all the glorious ones follow thee (Pyr. § 2022-3).

Translation by J. H. Breasted in his *Development of Religion and Thought in Ancient Egypt* (Chicago, 1912), pp. 145-6

168. OSIRIS—THE PROTOTYPE OF EVERY SOUL WHO HOPES TO CONQUER DEATH

('Coffin Texts,' I, 197)

The so-called Coffin Texts, *inscribed on the interior of coffins, belong to the Middle Kingdom (2250-1580 B.C.). They attest a marked* 'democratization' of the ancient funerary ritual of the pharaoh. Just as the pharaoh of earlier times had claimed to participate in the fate of Osiris, so each soul now hoped to achieve a ritual assimilation to the god.

Now are you a king's son, a prince,
as long as your soul exists, so long will your heart be with you.
Anubis is mindful of you in Busiris,
your soul rejoices in Abydos where your body is happy on the High Hill.
Your embalmer rejoices in every place.
Ah, truly, you are the chosen one!
you are made whole in this your dignity which is before me,
Anubis' heart is happy over the work of his hands
and the heart of the Lord of the Divine Hall is thrilled
when he beholds this good god,
Master of those that have been and Ruler over those that are to come.

Translation by R. T. Rundle Clark, in his *Myth and Symbol in Ancient Egypt* (London, 1960), p. 134

See also nos. 88, 109

169. SURVIVAL AS BA AND SURVIVAL IN THE TOMB ARE COMPLEMENTARY

Thou shalt come in and go out, thy heart rejoicing, in the favour of the Lord of the Gods, a good burial [being thine] after a venerable old age, when age has come, thou assuming thy place in the coffin, and joining earth on the high ground of the west.

Thou shalt change into a living Ba[1] and surely he will have power to obtain bread and water and air; and thou shalt take shape as a heron or swallow, as a falcon or a bittern, whichever thou pleasest.

Thou shalt cross in the ferryboat and shalt not turn back, thou shalt sail on the waters of the flood, and thy life shall start afresh. Thy Ba shall not depart from thy corpse and thy Ba shall become divine with the blessed dead. The perfect Ba's shall speak to thee, and thou shalt be an equal amongst them in receiving what is given on earth. Thou shalt have power over water, shalt inhale air, and

The note to this text is on p. 357.

shalt be surfeited with the desires of thy heart. Thine eyes shall be given to thee so as to see, and thine ears so as to hear, thy mouth speaking, and thy feet walking. Thy arms and thy shoulders shall move for thee, thy flesh shall be firm, thy muscles shall be easy and thou shalt exult in all thy limbs. Thou shalt examine thy body and find it whole and sound, no ill whatever adhering to thee. Thine own true heart shall be with thee, yea, thou shalt have thy former heart. Thou shalt go up to the sky, and shalt penetrate the Netherworld in all forms that thou likes.

Note

1 The dead man conceived as living an animated existence after death was called *Ba*. . . . The word *Ba* means 'animation, manifestation.'

> Translation by A. Gardiner, *The Attitude of the Ancient Egyptians to Death and the Dead* (Cambridge, Eng., 1935), pp. 29-30; as quoted in Henri Frankfort, *Ancient Egyptian Religion* (New York: Columbia University Press, 1948)

170. THE EGYPTIAN LAND OF SILENCE AND DARKNESS

In this song a woman laments the death of her husband.

How sad is the descent in the Land of Silence. The wakeful sleeps, he who did not slumber at night lies still forever. The scorners say: The dwelling-place of the inhabitants of the West is deep and dark. It has no door, no window, no light to illuminate it, no north wind to refresh the heart. The sun does not rise there, but they lie every day in darkness. . . . The guardian has been taken away to the Land of Infinity.

Those who are in the West are cut off, and their existence is misery; one is loathe to go to join them. One cannot recount one's experiences but one rests in one place of eternity in darkness.

> Translation by Henri Frankfort (after Kees), in Frankfort, *Ancient Egyptian Religion* (New York: Columbia University Press, 1948)

E. THE ROADS TO THE NETHER WORLD

171. THE INITIATES IN THE ORPHIC-PYTHAGOREAN BROTHERHOOD ARE TAUGHT THE ROAD TO THE LOWER WORLD

(The Funerary Gold Plates)

[Plate from Petelia, South Italy, fourth-third century B.C.]

Thou shalt find to the left of the House of Hades a spring,
And by the side thereof standing a white cypress.
To this spring approach not near.
But thou shalt find another, from the Lake of Memory
Cold water flowing forth, and there are guardians before it.
Say, 'I am a child of Earth and starry Heaven;
But my race is of Heaven (alone). This ye know yourselves.
But I am parched with thirst and I perish. Give me quickly
The cold water flowing forth from the Lake of Memory.'
And of themselves they will give thee to drink of the holy spring,
And thereafter among the other heroes thou shalt have lordship.

[Plate from Eleuthernai in Crete, second century B.C.]

I am parched with thirst and I perish—Nay, drink of me (or, But give
    me to drink of)
The ever-flowing spring on the right, where the cypress is.
Who art thou? . . .
Whence art thou?—I am the son of Earth and starry Heaven.

[Plate from Thurii, South Italy, fourth-third century B.C.]

But so soon as the spirit hath left the light of the sun,
Go to the right as far as one should go, being right wary in all things.
Hail, thou who hast suffered the suffering. This thou hadst never
    suffered before.
Thou art become god from man.
A kid thou art fallen into milk.

Hail, hail to thee journeying the right hand road
By holy meadows and groves of Persephone.

[Three more tablets from Thurii, of roughly the same date as the
previous one.]

I come from the pure, pure Queen of those below,
And Eukles and Eubuleus, and other Gods and Daemons:
For I also avow that I am of your blessed race.
And I have paid the penalty for deeds unrighteous,
Whether it be that Fate laid me low or the gods immortal
Or . . . with star-flung thunderbolt.
I have flown out of the sorrowful, weary circle.
I have passed with swift feet to the diadem desired.
I have sunk beneath the bosom of the Mistress, the Queen of the
    underworld.
And now I come a suppliant to holy Persephoneia,
That of her grace she send men to the seats of the Hallowed.
Happy and blessed one, thou shalt be god instead of mortal.
A kid I have fallen into milk.

> Translation by W. K. C. Guthrie, in his *Orpheus and
> Greek Religion* (London, 1935), pp. 172-3

See also nos. 148-55

172. THE IRANIAN AFTERLIFE: THE CROSSING OF THE CINVAT BRIDGE AND THE ROADS TO HEAVEN AND HELL

('Mēnōk i Khrat,' I, 71-122)

According to Zoroastrian belief, the soul of the departed hovers near
the body for three days. On the fourth day he faces a judgement on the
'Bridge of the Requiter' (Cinvat Bridge), where Rashn 'the righteous'
impartially weighs his good and evil deeds. If the good actions pre-
ponderate over the evil ones, the soul is permitted to ascend to Heaven;
if, on the contrary, there is a predominance of evil acts, it is dragged
off to Hell. But for the Zoroastrians, Hell is not eternal. At the Last
Judgement, at the end of time, the bodies are resurrected and reunited
with their souls. Then there is a final and universal purgation, from

which all men without exception emerge spotless, and enter into Paradise.

(71) Put not your trust in life, for at the last death must overtake you; (72) and dog and bird will rend your corpse and your bones will be tumbled on the earth. (73) For three days and nights the soul sits beside the pillow of the body. (74) And on the fourth day at dawn (the soul) accompanied by the blessed Srōsh, the good Vāy, and the mighty Vahrām, and opposed by Astvihāt (the demon of death), the evil Vāy, the demon Frēhzisht and the demon Vizisht, and pursued by the active ill-will of Wrath, the evil-doer who bears a bloody spear, (will reach) the lofty and awful Bridge of the Requiter to which every man whose soul is saved and every man whose soul is damned must come. Here does many an enemy lie in wait. (75) Here (the soul will suffer) from the ill-will of Wrath who wields a bloody spear and from Astvihāt who swallows all creation yet knows no sating, (76) and it will (benefit by) the mediation of Hihr, Srōsh, and Rashn, and will (needs submit) to the weighing (of his deeds) by the righteous Rashn who lets the scales of the spiritual gods incline to neither side, neither for the saved nor yet for the damned, nor yet for kings and princes: (77) not so much as a hair's breadth does he allow (the scales) to tip, and he is no respecter (of persons), (78) for he deals out impartial justice both to kings and princes and to the humblest of men.

(79) And when the soul of the saved passes over that bridge, the breadth of the bridge appears to be one parasang broad. (80) And the soul of the saved passes on accompanied by the blessed Srōsh. (81) And his own good deeds come to meet him in the form of a young girl, more beautiful and fair than any girl on earth. (82) And the soul of the saved says, 'Who art thou, for I have never seen a young girl on earth more beautiful or fair than thee.' (83) In answer the form of the young girl replies, 'I am no girl but thy own good deeds, O young man whose thoughts and words, deeds and religion were good: (84) for when on earth thou didst see one who offered sacrifice to the demons, then didst thou sit (apart) and offer sacrifice to the gods. (85) And when thou didst see a man do violence and rapine, afflict good men and treat them with contumely, and hoard up goods wrongfully obtained, then didst thou refrain from visiting creatures with violence and rapine of thine own; (86) (nay rather,) thou wast considerate to good men, didst entertain them and offer them hospitality, and give alms both to the man who came from near and to him who came from afar; (87) and thou didst amass thy wealth in righteousness. (88) And

when thou didst see one who passed a false judgement or took bribes or bore false witness, thou didst sit thee down and speak witness right and true. (89) I am thy good thoughts, good words, and good deeds which thou didst think and say and do. . . .'

(91) And when the soul departs from thence, then is a fragrant breeze wafted towards him,—(a breeze) more fragrant than any perfume. (92) Then does the soul of the saved ask Srōsh saying, 'What breeze is this, the like of which in fragrance I never smelt on earth?' (93) Then does the blessed Srōsh make answer to the soul of the saved, saying, 'This is a wind (wafted) from Heaven; hence is it so fragrant.'

(94) Then with his first step he bestrides (the heaven of) good thoughts, with his second (the heaven of) good words, and with his third (the heaven of) good deeds; and with his fourth step he reaches the Endless Light where is all bliss. (95) And all the gods and Amahraspands come to greet him and ask him how he has fared, saying, 'How was thy passage from those transient, fearful worlds where there is much evil to these worlds which do not pass away and in which there is no adversary, O young man whose thoughts and words, deeds and religion are good?'

(96) Then Ohrmazd, the Lord, speaks, saying, 'Do not ask him how he has fared, for he has been separated from his beloved body and has travelled on a fearsome road.' (97) And they served him with the sweetest of all foods even with the butter of early spring so that his soul may take its ease after the three nights terror of the Bridge inflicted on him by Astvihāt and the other demons, (98) and he is sat upon a throne everywhere bejewelled. . . . (100) And for ever and ever he dwells with the spiritual gods in all bliss for evermore.

(101) But when the man who is damned dies, for three days and nights does his soul hover near his head and weeps, saying, 'Whither shall I go and in whom shall I now take refuge?' (102) And during those three days and nights he sees with his eyes all the sins and wickedness that he committed on earth. (103) On the fourth day the demon Vizarsh comes and binds the soul of the damned in most shameful wise, and despite the opposition of the blessed Srōsh drags it off to the Bridge of the Requiter. (104) Then the righteous Rashn makes clear to the soul of the damned that it is damned (indeed).

(105) Then the demon Vizarsh seizes upon the soul of the damned, smites it and ill-treats it without pity, urged on by Wrath. (106) And the soul of the damned cries out with a loud voice, makes moan, and in supplication makes many a piteous plea; much does he struggle though his life-breath endures no more. (107) When all his struggling

and his lamentations have proved of no avail, no help is prof-
fered him by any of the gods nor yet by any of the demons, but
the demon Vizarsh drags him off against his will into nethermost
Hell.

(108) Then a young girl who yet has no semblance of a young
girl, comes to meet him. (109) And the soul of the damned says to
that ill-favoured wench, 'Who art thou? for I have never seen an
ill-favoured wench on earth more ill-favoured and hideous than thee.'
(110) And in reply that ill-favoured wench says to him, 'I am no
wench, but I am thy deeds,—hideous deeds,—evil thoughts, evil
words, evil deeds, and an evil religion. (111) For when on earth thou
didst see one who offered sacrifice to the gods, then didst thou sit (apart)
and offer sacrifice to the demons. (112) And when thou didst see one
who entertained good men and offered them hospitality, and gave alms
both to those who came from near and to those who came from afar,
then didst thou treat good men with contumely and show them dis-
honour, thou gavest them no alms and didst shut thy door (upon them).
(113) And when thou didst see one who passed a just judgement or
took no bribes or bore true witness or spoke up in righteousness,
then didst thou sit down and pass false judgement, bear false witness,
and speak unrighteously. . . .

(116) Then with his first step he goes to (the hell of) evil thoughts,
with his second to (the hell of) evil words, and with his third to (the
hell of) evil deeds. And with his fourth step he lurches into the
presence of the accursed Destructive Spirit and the other demons.
(117) And the demons mock at him and hold him up to scorn, saying,
'What grieved thee in Ohrmazd, the Lord, and the Amahraspands
and in fragrant and delightful Heaven, and what grudge or complaint
hadst thou of them that thou shouldst come to see Ahriman and
the demons and murky Hell? for we will torment thee nor shall
we have any mercy on thee, and for a long time shalt thou suffer
torment.'

(118) And the Destructive Spirit cries out to the demons, saying,
'Ask not concerning him, for he has been separated from his beloved
body, and has come through that most evil passage-way; (119) but
serve him (rather) with the filthiest and most foul food that Hell can
produce.'

(120) Then they bring him poison and venom, snakes and scorpions
and other noxious reptiles (that flourish) in Hell, and they serve him
with these to eat. (121) And until the Resurrection and the Final
Body he must remain in Hell, suffering much torment and many kinds

of chastisement. (122) And the food that he must for the most part eat there is all, as it were, putrid and like unto blood.

Mēnōk i Khrat, edited by Anklesaria. Translation by R. C. Zaehner, in his *The Teachings of the Magi* (London, 1956), pp. 133-8

173. A SIBERIAN (GOLDI) FUNERARY CEREMONY: THE SHAMAN GUIDES THE SOUL TO THE UNDERWORLD

The Goldi have two funerary ceremonies: the *nimgan*, which takes place seven days or even longer (two months) after the death, and the *kazatauri*, the great ceremony celebrated some time after the former and at the end of which the soul is conducted to the underworld. During the *nimgan* the shaman enters the dead person's house with his drum, searches for the soul, captures it, and makes it enter a sort of cushion (*fanya*). The banquet follows, participated in by all the relatives and friends of the dead person present in the *fanya*; the shaman offers the latter brandy. The *kazatauri* begins in the same way. The shaman dons his costume, takes his drum, and goes to search for the soul in the vicinity of the yurt. During all this time he dances and recounts the difficulties of the road to the underworld. Finally he captures the soul and brings it into the house, where he makes it enter the *fanya*. The banquet continues late into the night, and the food that is left over is thrown into the fire by the shaman. The women bring a bed into the yurt, the shaman puts the *fanya* in it, covers it with a blanket, and tells the dead person to sleep. He then lies down in the yurt and goes to sleep himself.

The following day he again dons his costume and wakes the deceased by drumming. Another banquet follows and at night (for the ceremony may continue for several days) he puts the *fanya* to bed again and covers it up. Finally one morning the shaman begins his song and, addressing the deceased, advises him to eat well but to drink sparingly, for the journey to the underworld is extremely difficult for the drunken person. At sunset preparations for the departure are made. The shaman sings, dances, and daubs his face with soot. He invokes his helping spirits and begs them to guide him and the dead man in the beyond. He leaves the yurt for a few minutes and climbs a notched tree that has been set up in readiness; from here he sees the road to the underworld. (He has, in fact, climbed the World Tree and is at the summit of the world.) At the same time he sees many other things: plentiful snow, successful hunting and fishing, and so on.

Returning to the yurt, he summons two powerful tutelary spirits to help him; *butchu*, a kind of one-legged monster with a human face and feathers, and *koori*, a long-necked bird. Without the help of these two spirits, the shaman could not come back from the underworld; he makes the most difficult part of the return journey sitting on the *koori*'s back.

After shamanizing until he is exhausted, he sits down, facing the west, on a board that represents a Siberian sled. The *fanya*, containing the dead person's soul, and a basket of food are set beside him. The shaman asks the spirits to harness the dogs to the sled and for a 'servant' to keep him company during the journey. A few moments later he 'sets off' for the land of the dead.

The songs he intones and the words he exchanges with the 'servant' make it possible to follow his route. At first the road is easy, but the difficulties increase as the land of the dead is approached. A great river bars the way, and only a good shaman can get his team and sled across to the other bank. Some time later, he sees signs of human activity; footprints, ashes, bits of wood—the village of the dead is not far away. Now, indeed, dogs are heard barking at no great distance, the smoke from the yurts is seen, the first reindeer appear. The shaman and the deceased have reached the underworld. At once the dead gather and ask the shaman to tell them his name and that of the newcomer. The shaman is careful not to give his real name; he searches through the crowd of spirits for the close relatives of the soul he is conducting, so that he may entrust it to them. Having done so, he hastens to return to earth and, arriving, gives a long account of all that he has seen in the land of the dead and the impressions of the dead man whom he escorted. He brings each of the audience greetings from their dead relatives and even distributes little gifts from them. At the close of the ceremony the shaman throws the *fanya* into the fire. The strict obligations of the living to the dead are now terminated.

M. Eliade, *Shamanism: Archaic Techniques of Ecstasy*, trans. Willard Trask (New York: Bollingen Series LXXVI), pp. 210-12, being a summary of Uno Harva, *Die religiösen Vorstellungen der altaischen Völker* (Helsinki, 1938), pp. 334-45

See also nos. 204, 205, 208, 209

Roads to the Nether World

174. THE WINNEBAGO INDIAN ROAD TO THE LAND OF THE DEAD

Before the spirit of the departed starts his journey to the nether world, he is carefully informed of the surprises and dangers of the voyage and is duly instructed how to overcome them.

I suppose you are not far away, that indeed you are right behind me. Here is the tobacco and here is the pipe which you must keep in front of you as you go along. Here also are the fire and the food which your relatives have prepared for your journey.

In the morning when the sun rises you are to start. You will not have gone very far before you come to a wide road. That is the road you must take. As you go along you will notice something on your road. Take your war club and strike it and throw it behind you. Then go on without looking back. As you go farther you will again come across some obstacle. Strike it and throw it behind you and do not look back. Farther on you will come across some animals, and these also you must strike and throw behind you. Then go on and do not look back. The objects you throw behind you will come to those relatives whom you have left behind you on earth. They will represent victory in war, riches, and animals for food.

When you have gone but a short distance from the last place where you threw the objects behind, you will come to a round lodge and there you will find an old woman. She is the one who is to give you further information. She will ask you, 'Grandson, what is your name?' This you must tell her. Then you must say, 'Grandmother, when I was about to start from the earth I was given the following objects with which I was to act as mediator between you and the human beings [i.e., the pipe, tobacco, and food].' Then you must put the stem of the pipe in the old woman's mouth and say, 'Grandmother, I have made all my relatives lonesome, my parents, my brothers, and all the others. I would therefore like to have them obtain victory in war, and honours. That was my desire as I left them downhearted upon the earth. I would that they could have all that life which I left behind me on earth. This is what they asked. This, likewise, they asked me, that they should not have to travel on this road for some time to come. They also asked to be blessed with those things that people are accustomed to have on earth. All this they wanted me to ask of you when I started from the earth. They told me to follow the four steps that would be

365

imprinted with blue marks, grandmother.' 'Well, grandson, you are young but you are wise. It is good. I will now boil some food for you.'

Thus she will speak to you and then put a kettle on the fire and boil some rice for you. If you eat it you will have a headache. Then she will say, 'Grandson, you have a headache, let me cup it for you.' Then she will break open your skull and take out your brains and you will forget all about your people on earth and where you came from. You will not worry about your relatives. You will become like a holy spirit. Your thoughts will not go as far as the earth, as there will be nothing carnal about you.

Now the rice that the old woman will boil will really be lice. For that reason you will be finished with everything evil. Then you will go on stepping in the four footsteps mentioned before and that were imprinted with blue earth. You are to take the four steps because the road will fork there. All your relatives who died before you will be there. As you journey on you will come to a fire running across the earth from one end to the other. There will be a bridge across it but it will be difficult to cross because it is continually swinging. However, you will be able to cross it safely, for you have all the guides about whom the warriors spoke to you. They will take you over and take care of you.

Well, we have told you a good road to take. If anyone tells a falsehood in speaking of the spirit-road, you will fall off the bridge and be burned. However you need not worry for you will pass over safely. As you proceed from that place the spirits will come to meet you and take you to the village where the chief lives. There you will give him the tobacco and ask for those objects of which we spoke to you, the same you asked of the old woman. There you will meet all the relatives that died before you. They will be living in a large lodge. This you must enter.

Paul Radin, *The Winnebago Tribe*, in Thirty-eighth Annual Report, Bureau of American Ethnology (Washington, D.C., 1923), pp. 143-4

175. THE ROAD TO THE SOUL'S WORLD, AS CONCEIVED BY THE THOMPSON RIVER TRIBES (BRITISH COLUMBIA)

The country of the souls is underneath us, toward the sunset; the trail leads through a dim twilight. Tracks of the people who last went over it. and of their dogs, are visible. The path winds along until it meets another road which is a short cut used by the shamans when trying to intercept a departed soul. The trail now becomes much straighter and smoother, and is painted red with ochre. After a while it winds to the westward, descends a long gentle slope, and terminates at a wide shallow stream of very clear water. This is spanned by a long slender log, on which the tracks of the souls may be seen. After crossing, the traveller finds himself again on the trail, which now ascends to a height heaped with an immense pile of clothes—the belongings which the souls have brought from the land of the living and which they must leave here. From this point the trail is level, and gradually grows lighter. Three guardians are stationed along this road, one on either side of the river and the third at the end of the path; it is their duty to send back those souls whose time is not yet come to enter the land of the dead. Some souls pass the first two of these, only to be turned back by the third, who is their chief and is an orator who sometimes sends messages to the living by the returning souls. All of these men are very old, grey-headed, wise, and venerable. At the end of the trail is a great lodge, mound-like in form, with doors at the eastern and the western sides, and with a double row of fires extending through it. When the deceased friends of a person expect his soul to arrive, they assemble here and talk about his death. As the deceased reaches the entrance, he hears people on the other side talking, laughing, singing, and beating drums. Some stand at the door to welcome him and call his name. On entering, a wide country of diversified aspect spreads out before him. There is a sweet smell of flowers and an abundance of grass, and all around are berry-bushes laden with ripe fruit. The air is pleasant and still, and it is always light and warm. More than half the people are dancing and singing to the accompaniment of drums. All are naked but do not seem to notice it. The people are delighted to see the new comer, take him up on their shoulders, run around with him, and make a great noise.

H. B. Alexander, *North American Mythology* (Boston, 1916), pp. 147-9; adapted from James Teit, *Traditions of the Thompson River Indians of British Columbia* (Boston and New York, 1898)

176. JOURNEY TO THE LAND OF THE GRANDFATHER: A GUARAYÚ BELIEF (EASTERN BOLIVIA)

Soon after burial the liberated soul of the deceased started on a long and dangerous journey to the land of the mythical ancestor, Tamoi, or Grandfather, who lived somewhere in the west. It had to choose first between two paths. One was wide and easy. The other was narrow and obstructed with weeds and tobacco plants, but it followed this if it was wide and courageous. Soon the soul came to a large river which it had to cross on the back of a ferocious alligator. The alligator ferried the soul over only if it knew how to accompany the alligator's chant by rhythmically stamping its bamboo tube. It then came to another river which it could pass only by jumping on a tree trunk that floated at great speed to and fro between the two banks. If the soul fell, palometa fish would tear it to pieces. Shortly after this it neared the abode of Izoi-tamoi, Grandfather of Worms, who looked enormous from a distance but became smaller and smaller as he was approached. If the deceased had been a bad man, however, the process was reversed; the Grandfather of Worms grew to gigantic proportions and cleaved the sinner in two. Next, the soul had to travel through a dark region where it lit its way by burning a bunch of straw which relatives had put in the grave. However, it had to carry its torch behind its back lest the light be put out by huge bats. When the soul arrived near a beautiful ceiba tree full of humming birds, it washed itself in a brook and shot a few of these birds, without hurting them, and plucked their feathers for Tamoi's headdress. Then the soul kicked the ceiba trunk to notify its relatives that it had reached that place. The next obstacle was the Itacaru, two rocks which clashed and recoiled on its path. The stones allowed the soul a short interval to pass through if it knew how to address them.

At a crossroad the soul was examined by a gallinazo bird, who made sure that, like all good Guarayú, it had perforated lips and ears. If it did not possess these mutilations, it was misled by the bird. Two further ordeals awaited the journeying soul; it had to endure being tickled by a monkey without laughing, and to walk past a magic tree without listening to the voices which issued from it and without even looking at it. The tree was endowed with complete knowledge of the soul's past life. To resist these temptations, the soul pounded its stamping tube on the ground. A further danger took the form of coloured grasses which blinded the soul and caused it to lose its way. Finally the soul arrived at a large avenue lined with blossoming trees full of harmonious birds and knew then that it had reached the land of the Grandfather. It announced its arrival by stamping the ground with its bamboo tube. The Grandfather welcomed the soul with friendly words and washed it with a magic water which restored its youth and good looks. From then

on, the soul lived happily, drinking chicha and carrying on the routine
activities of its former life.

Alfred Métraux, *The Native Tribes of Eastern Bolivia
and Western Matto Grosso*, Bureau of American
Ethnology, Bulletin 134 (Washington, D.C., 1942), pp.
105-6

177. A POLYNESIAN JOURNEY INTO THE NETHER WORLD

This story . . . was told to Mr. Shortland [Edward Shortland, on
whose account this summary is based] by a servant of his named Te
Wharewera. An aunt of this man died in a solitary hut near the banks
of Lake Rotorua. Being a lady of rank she was left in her hut, the
door and windows were made fast, and the dwelling was abandoned,
as her death had made it tapu. But a day of two after, Te Wharewera
with some others paddling in a canoe near the place at early morning
saw a figure on the shore beckoning to them. It was the aunt come to
life again, but weak and cold and famished. When sufficiently restored
by their timely help, she told her story. Leaving her body, her spirit
had taken the flight toward the North Cape, and arrived at the entrance
of Reigna. There, holding on by the stem of the creeping akeake-plant,
she descended the precipice, and found herself on the sandy beach of
a river. Looking around, she espied in the distance an enormous bird,
taller than a man, coming towards her with rapid strides. This terrible
object so frightened her, that her first thought was to try to return up
the steep cliff; but seeing an old man paddling a small canoe towards
her she ran to meet him, and so escaped the bird. When she had been
safely ferried across she asked the old Charon, mentioning the name
of her family, where the spirits of her kindred dwelt. Following the
path the old man pointed out, she was surprised to find it just such
a path as she had been used to on earth; the aspect of the country, the
trees, shrubs, and plants were all familiar to her. She reached the village
and among the crowd assembled there she found her father and many
near relations; they saluted her, and welcomed her with the wailing
chant which Maoris always address to people met after long absence.
But when her father had asked about his living relatives, and especially
about her own child, he told her she must go back to earth, for no one
was left to take care of his grandchild. By his orders she refused to
touch the food that the dead people offered her, and in spite of their

369

efforts to detain her, her father got her safely into the canoe, crossed with her, and parting gave her from under his cloak two enormous sweet potatoes to plant at home for his grandchild's especial eating. But as she began to climb the precipice again, two pursuing infant spirits pulled her back, and she only escaped by flinging the roots at them, which they stopped to eat, while she scaled the rock by help of the akeake-stem, till she reached the earth and flew back to where she had left her body. On returning to life she found herself in darkness, and what had passed seemed as a dream, till she perceived that she was deserted and the door fast, and concluded that she had really died and come to life again. When morning dawned, a faint light entered by the crevices of the shut-up house, and she saw on the floor near her a calabash partly full of red ochre mixed with water; this she eagerly drained to the dregs, and then feeling a little stronger, succeeded in opening the door and crawling down to the beach, where her friends soon after found her. Those who listened to her tale firmly believed the reality of her adventures, but it was much regretted that she had not brought back at least one of the huge sweet-potatoes, as evidence of her visit to the land of spirits.

Sir Edward Burnett Tylor, *Religion in Primitive Culture* (New York: Harper Torchbook, 1958), pp. 136-8; summarizing Edward Shortland, *Traditions and Superstitions of the New Zealanders* (London, 1854), pp. 150 ff. Tylor's book first published as *Primitive Culture*

F. GREEK AND ROMAN CONCEPTIONS OF DEATH AND IMMORTALITY

178. 'EVEN IN THE HOUSE OF HADES THERE IS LEFT SOMETHING...'

(Homer, 'Iliad,' XXIII, 61-81, 99-108)

The ghost of Patroklos appears to Achilleus.

And at that time sleep caught him and was drifted sweetly about him, washing
the sorrows out of his mind, for his shining limbs were grown weary
indeed, from running in chase of Hektor toward windy Ilion;
and there appeared to him the ghost of unhappy Patroklos
all in his likeness for stature, and the lovely eyes, and voice,
and wore such clothing as Patroklos had worn on his body.
The ghost came and stood over his head and spoke a word to him:
'You sleep, Achilleus; you have forgotten me; but you were not
careless of me when I lived, but only in death. Bury me
as quickly as may be, let me pass through the gates of Hades.
The souls, the images of dead men, hold me at a distance,
and will not let me cross the river and mingle among them,
but I wander as I am by Hades' house of the wide gates.
And I call upon you in sorrow, give me your hand; no longer
shall I come back from death, once you give me my rite of burning.
No longer shall you and I, alive, sit apart from our other
beloved companions to make our plans, since the bitter destiny
that was given me when I was born has opened its jaws to take me.
And you, Achilleus like the gods, have your own destiny;
to be killed under the wall of the prospering Trojans. . . .
So he spoke, and with his own arms reached for him, but could not
take him, but the spirit went underground, like vapour,
with a thin cry, and Achilleus started awake, staring,
and drove his hands together, and spoke, and his words were sorrowful:
'Oh, wonder! Even in the house of Hades there is left something,
a soul and an image, but there is no real heart of life in it.

For all night long the phantom of unhappy Patroklos
stood over me in lamentation and mourning, and the likeness
to him was wonderful, and it told me each thing I should do.'

Translation by Richmond Lattimore. Homer's *Iliad*
(Chicago: University of Chicago Press, 1951), pp. 136-7

179. THE MEAD OF ASPHODEL, WHERE THE SPIRITS DWELL . . .': THE HOMERIC OTHER WORLD

(Homer, 'Odyssey,' XXIV, 1-18)

Meanwhile Cyllenian Hermes called forth the spirits of the wooers.
He held in his hands his wand, a fair wand of gold, wherewith he lulls
to sleep the eyes of whom he will, while others again he wakens even
out of slumber; with this he roused and led the spirits, and they followed gibbering. And as in the innermost recess of a wondrous cave
bats flit about gibbering, when one has fallen from off the rock from
the chain in which they cling to one another, so these went with him
gibbering, and Hermes, the Helper, led them down the dank ways.
Past the streams of Oceanus they went, past the rock Leucus, past the
gates of the sun and the land of dreams, and quickly came to the
mead of the asphodel, where the spirits dwell, phantoms of men who
have done with toils. Here they found the spirit of Achilles, son of
Peleus, and those of Patroclus, of peerless Antilochus, and of Aias,
who in comeliness and form was the goodliest of all the Danaans after
the peerless son of Peleus.

Translation by A. T. Murray in the Loeb Classical
Library, vol. II (New York, 1919), p. 403

180. A ROMAN VIEW OF THE AFTER LIFE: THE DREAM OF SCIPIO

(Cicero, 'On the Republic,' VI, 14-26)

'The Dream of Scipio' is the conclusion of Cicero's treatise On the
Republic, probably written in 54 B.C. The dialogue is assumed to have
taken place during the Latin holidays in 129 B.C., in the garden of
Scipio Africanus the Younger. Scipio relates a dream in which he saw

his grandfather, Scipio Africanus the Elder. 'When I recognized him, I trembled with terror, but he said: "Courage, Scipio, do not be afraid, but remember carefully what I am to tell you."'

(14) By this time I was thoroughly terrified, not so much fearing death as the treachery of my own kind. Nevertheless, I [went on and] inquired of Africanus whether he himself was still alive, and also whether my father Paulus was, and also the others whom we think of as having ceased to be.

'Of course they are alive,' he replied. 'They have taken their flight from the bonds of the body as from a prison. Your so-called life [on earth] is really death. Do you not see your father Paulus coming to meet you?'

At the sight of my father I broke down and cried. But he embraced me and kissed me and told me not to weep. (15) As soon as I had controlled my grief and could speak, I began: 'Why, O best and saintliest of fathers, since here [only] is life worthy of the name, as I have just heard from Africanus, why must I live a dying life on earth? Why may I not hasten to join you here?'

'No indeed,' he replied. 'Unless that God whose temple is the whole visible universe releases you from the prison of the body, you cannot gain entrance here. For men were given life for the purpose of cultivating that globe, called Earth, which you see at the centre of this temple. Each has been given a soul, [a spark] from these eternal fires which you call stars and planets, which are globular and rotund and are animated by divine intelligence, and which with marvellous velocity revolve in their established orbits. Like all god-fearing men, therefore, Publius, you must leave the soul in the custody of the body, and must not quit the life on Earth unless you are summoned by the one who gave it to you; otherwise you will be seen to shirk the duty assigned by God to man.

(16) 'But Scipio, like your grandfather here, like myself, who was your father, cultivate justice and the sense of duty [*pietas*], which are of great importance in relation to parents and kindred but even more in relation to one's country. Such a life [spent in the service of one's country] is a highway to the skies, to the fellowship of those who have completed their earthly lives and have been released from the body and now dwell in that place which you see yonder' (it was the circle of dazzling brilliance which blazed among the stars), 'which you, using a term borrowed from the Greeks, call the Milky Way.'

Looking about from this high vantage point, everything appeared to me to be marvellous and beautiful. There were stars which we never see from the Earth, and the dimensions of all of them were greater than we have ever suspected. The smallest among them was the one which, being farthest from Heaven and nearest the Earth, shone with a borrowed light [the Moon]. The size of the stars. however, far exceeded that of the Earth. Indeed, the later seemed so small that I was humiliated with our empire, which is only a point where we touch the surface of the globe. . . .

(18) When I had recovered from my astonishment over this great panorama, and had come to myself, I asked: 'Tell me what is this loud, sweet harmony that fills my ears?'

He replied, 'This music is produced by the impulse and motion of these spheres themselves. The unequal intervals between them are arranged according to a strict proportion, and so the high notes blend agreeably with the low, and thus various sweet harmonies are produced. Such immense revolutions cannot, of course, be so swiftly carried out in silence, and it is only natural that one extreme should produce deep tones and the other high ones. Accordingly, this highest sphere of Heaven, which bears the stars, and whose revolution is swifter, produces a high shrill sound, whereas the lowest sphere, that of the Moon, rotates with the deepest sound. The Earth, of course, the ninth sphere, remains fixed and immovable in the centre of the universe. But the other eight spheres, two of which move with the same speed, produce seven different sounds—a number, by the way, which is the key to almost everything. Skilful men reproducing this celestial music on stringed instruments have thus opened the way for their own return to this heavenly region, as other men of outstanding genius have done by spending their lives on Earth in the study of things divine. . . .'

(26) 'Yes, you must use you best efforts,' he replied, 'and be sure that it is not you who are mortal, but only your body; nor is it you whom your outward form represents. Your spirit is your true self, not that bodily form that can be pointed out with the finger. Know yourself, therefore, to be a god—if indeed a god is a being that lives, feels, remembers, and foresees, that rules, governs, and moves the body over which it is set, just as the supreme God above us rules this world. And just as that eternal God moves the universe, which is partly mortal, so an eternal spirit moves the fragile body. . . .

Translation by Frederick C. Grant, in his *Ancient Roman Religion*, Library of Religion paperback series (New York, 1957), pp. 147-56

181. EMPEDOCLES ON THE TRANSMIGRATION OF THE SOUL

('Fragments' 115, 117, 118)

There is an oracle of Necessity, ancient decree of the gods, eternal and sealed with broad oaths: whenever one of those demi-gods, whose lot is long-lasting life, has sinfully defiled his dear limbs with bloodshed, or following strife has sworn a false oath, thrice ten thousand seasons does he wander far from the blessed, being born throughout that time in the forms of all manner of mortal things and changing one baleful path of life for another. The might of the air pursues him into the sea, the sea spews him forth on to the dry land, the earth casts him into the rays of the burning sun, and the sun into the eddies of air. One takes him from the other, but all alike abhor him. Of these I too am now one, a fugitive from the gods and a wanderer, who put my trust in raving strife. (*Frag.* 115)

I wept and wailed when I saw the unfamiliar place. (*Frag.* 118)

For already have I once been a boy and a girl, a fish and a bird and a dumb sea fish. (*Frag.* 117)

> Empedocles texts in G. S. Kirk and J. E. Raven, trans-
> lators, *The Presocratic Philosophers* (Cambridge, Eng.,
> 1957)

182. PLATO ON TRANSMIGRATION: THE MYTH OF ER

('Republic,' X, 614 b)

It is not, let me tell you, said I, the tale to Alcinous told that I shall unfold, but the tale of a warrior bold, Er, the son of Armenius, by race a Pamphylian. He once upon a time was slain in battle, and when the corpses were taken up on the tenth day already decayed, was found intact, and having been brought home, at the moment of his funeral, on the twelfth day as he lay upon the pyre, revived, and after coming to life related what, he said, he had seen in the world beyond. He said that when his soul went forth from his body he journeyed with a great company and that they came to a mysterious region where there were two openings side by side in the earth, and above and over against them in the heaven two others, and that judges were sitting between these, and that after every judgement they bade the righteous journey to the right and upward through the heaven with tokens attached to them in front of the judgement passed upon them, and the unjust to take the road to the left and downward, they too wearing behind signs of all that had befallen them, and that when he himself drew near they told him that he must be the messenger to mankind to tell them of that other world, and they charged him to give ear and to observe everything in the place. And so he said that here he saw, by each opening of heaven and earth, the souls departing after judgement had been passed upon them, while, by the other pair of openings, there came up from the one in the earth souls full of squalor and dust, and from the second there came down from heaven a second procession of souls clean and pure, and that those which arrived from time to time appeared to have come as it were from a long journey and gladly departed to the meadow and encamped there as at a festival, and acquaintances greeted one another, and those which came from the earth questioned the others about conditions up yonder, and those from heaven asked how it fared with those others. And they told their stories to one another, the one lamenting and wailing as they recalled how many and how dreadful things they had suffered and seen in their journey beneath the earth—it lasted a thousand years—while those from heaven related their delights and visions of a beauty beyond words. To tell it all, Glaucon, would take all our time, but the sum, he said, was this. For all the wrongs they had ever done to anyone and all whom they had severally wronged they had paid the penalty in turn tenfold each, and the measure of this was by periods of a hundred years each, so that on the assumption that this was the length of human life the punishment might be ten times the crime—as for example that if anyone had been the cause of many deaths or had betrayed cities and armies and reduced them to slavery, or had been participant in any other iniquity, they might receive in requital pains tenfold for each of these wrongs, and again if any had done deeds of kindness and had been just and holy men they might receive their due reward in the same measure. And other things not worthy of record he said of those who had just been born and lived but a short time, and he had still greater requitals to tell of piety and impiety towards the gods and parents and of self-slaughter.

Translation by Paul Shorey, in Hamilton and Cairns (eds.), *Plato: The Collected Dialogues* (New York: Bollingen Series LXXI, 1961), pp. 838-40

Greek Conceptions of Immortality

183. PLATO ON THE IMMORTALITY OF THE SOUL

('Meno,' 81 b)

MENO: What was it, and who were they?

SOCRATES: Those who tell it are priests and priestesses of the sort who make it their business to be able to account for the functions which they perform. Pindar speaks of it too, and many another of the poets who are divinely inspired. What they say is this—see whether you think they are speaking the truth. They say that the soul of man is immortal. At one time it comes to an end—that which is called death—and at another is born again, but is never finally exterminated. On these grounds a man must live all his days as righteously as possible. For those from whom

> Persephone receives requital for ancient doom,
> In the ninth year she restores again
> Their souls to the sun above.
> From whom rise noble kings
> And the swift in strength and greatest in wisdom,
> And for the rest of time
> They are called heroes and sanctified by men.[1]

Thus the soul, since it is immortal and has been born many times, and has seen all things both here and in the other world, has learned everything that is.

Note

1 Pindar, *Fragment* 133.

Translated by W. K. C. Guthrie, in Hamilton and Cairns (eds.), *Plato: The Collected Dialogues* (New York: Bollingen Series LXXI, 1961), p. 364

See also nos. 149, 159

G. ORPHEUS MYTHS

184. A POLYNESIAN ORPHEUS

A Maori hero, Hutu, went down to the underworld in search of the soul of the princess, Pare, who had committed suicide after being humiliated by him. This story is reminiscent of Orpheus' descent to Hades to bring back the soul of his wife, Eurydice.

Once, when the lance which he had thrown, led Hutu to Pare's door, the young noble-woman, whose heart had been won by the youth's skill and presence, revealed to him her admiration and love and invited him to enter her house. But he refused her and departed. Overwhelmed with shame, she 'ordered her attendants to arrange everything in the house and put it in order. When this was done she sat alone and wept, and rose and hung herself.' Hutu, remorseful, fearful of the people's anger, determined to save her soul in the world below. First he sat down and chanted the priestly incantations having to do with death and the abode of the dead; then he rose and proceeded on his journey. He met Hine-nui-te-po (Great-lady-of-the-night), who presides over the Land of Shades. Ill-humoured as usual, when Hutu asked the way, she pointed out the path taken by the spirits of dogs to the lower regions; but her favour was eventually won by the presentation of the seeker's precious greenstone hand club. Mollified by the gift, the goddess pointed out the true route, cooked some fern root for him and put it into a basket, at the same time admonishing him to eat sparingly of it, for it must suffice him throughout the journey. Should he eat the food of the lower world, it would mean that, instead of his being able to bring back the spirit of Pare to the world of light, his own soul would be condemned to remain forever in the lower regions. The goddess advised him further, 'When you fly from this world, bow your head as you descend to the dark world; but when you are near the world below a wind from beneath will blow on you, and will raise your head up again, and you will be in a right position to alight on your feet. . . .' Hutu arrived safely in the world below, and on inquiring the whereabouts of Pare, was told that she was 'in the village.' Although the girl knew that Hutu had come and was seeking her, her shame led her to conceal herself. In the hope of luring her from her house, he organized contests in top spinning and javelin throwing, games which he knew she loved to watch. But never did she appear. At last Hutu, sore at heart, said to the others, 'Bring a very long tree and let us cut the branches off it.' This done, ropes were plaited and tied to the top, and the crown of the tree was bent down to the earth by the people's tugging at the ropes. Hutu climbed into the top, and another man sat on his back. Then Hutu shouted, 'Let go.' And the tree flung the young adventurer and his companion high into the air. Delighted at this exhibition, all the people shouted with glee. This was too much for Pare and she came to watch the new game. Finally she said, 'Let me also swing, but let me sit on your shoulders.'

Exuberant, Hutu answered, 'Keep hold of my neck, O Pare!' The top of the tree being again drawn down, it was released on the signal and flew skyward with such a rush as to fling the ropes against the under side of the upper world where they became entangled in the grass at the entrance to the realm of the shades. Climbing up the ropes with Pare on his back, Hutu emerged into the world of light. He went straightway to the settlement where the dead body of Pare was lying, and the spirit of the young chieftess reentered her body and it became alive.

John White, *The Ancient History of the Maori* (Wellington, 1887-90), vol. II, pp. 164-7, as condensed by E. S. Craighill Handy, *Polynesian Religion*, Bernice P. Bishop Museum Bulletin 34 (Honolulu, 1927), pp. 81 ff. (Cf. M. Eliade, *Shamanism: Archaic Techniques of Ecstasy*, trans. Willard Trask [New York, 1964], p. 368)

185. A CALIFORNIAN ORPHEUS: A TACHI YOKUT MYTH

The Orpheus myth is also popular among North American Indian tribes, especially in the western and eastern parts of the continent.

A Tachi had a fine wife who died and was buried. Her husband went to her grave and dug a hole near it. There he stayed watching, not eating, using only tobacco. After two nights he saw that she came up, brushed the earth off herself, and started to go to the island of the dead. The man tried to seize her but could not hold her. She went southeast and he followed her. Whenever he tried to hold her she escaped. He kept trying to seize her, however, and delayed her. At daybreak she stopped. He stayed there, but could not see her. When it began to be dark the woman got up again and went on. She turned westward and crossed Tulare Lake (or its inlet). At daybreak the man again tried to seize her but could not hold her. She stayed in the place during the day. The man remained in the same place, but again he could not see her. There was a good trail there, and he could see the footprints of his dead friend and relatives. In the evening his wife got up again and went on. They came to a river which flows westward towards San Luis Obispo, the river of the Tulamni (the description fits the Santa Maria, but the Tulamni are in the Tulare drainage, on and about Buena Vista lake). There the man caught up with his wife and there they stayed all day. He still had nothing to eat. In the evening she went on again, now northward. Then somewhere to the west of the Tachi country he caught up with her once more and they spent the day there. In the evening the woman got up and they went on northward, across the San Joaquin river, to the north or east of it. Again he overtook his wife. Then she said: 'What are you going to do? I am nothing now. How can you get my body back? Do you think you shall be able to do it?' He said: 'I think so.' She said: 'I think not. I am going to a different kind of a place now.' From daybreak on that man stayed there. In the evening the woman started once more and went down along the river; but he overtook her again. She did not talk to him. Then they stayed all day, and at night went on again. Now they were close to the island of the dead. It was joined to the land by a rising and falling bridge called *ch'eleli*. Under this bridge a river ran swiftly. The dead passed over this. When they were on the bridge, a bird suddenly fluttered up beside them and frightened them. Many fell off into the river, where they turned into fish. Now the chief of the dead said: 'Somebody has come.' They told him: 'There are two. One of them is alive; he stinks.' The chief said: 'Do not let him cross.' When the woman came on the island, he asked her: 'You have a companion?' and she told him: 'Yes, my husband.' He asked her: 'Is he coming here?' She said, 'I do not know. He is alive.' They asked the man: 'Do you want to come to this country?' He said: 'Yes.' Then they told him: 'Wait, I will see the chief.' They told the chief: 'He says that he wants to come to this country. We think he does not tell the truth.' 'Well, let him come across.' Now they intended to frighten him off the bridge. They said: 'Come on. The chief says you can cross.' Then the bird (*kacha*) flew up and tried to scare him, but did not make him fall off the bridge into the water. So they brought him before the chief. The chief said: 'This is a bad country. You should

not have come. We have only your wife's soul *(ilit)*. She has left her
bones with her body. I do not think we can give her back to you.' In
the evening they danced. It was a round dance and they shouted. The
chief said to the man: 'Look at your wife in the middle of the crowd.
Tomorrow you will see no one.' Now the man stayed there three days.
Then the chief said to some of the people: 'Bring that woman. Her
husband wants to talk to her.' They brought the woman to him. He
asked her: 'Is this your husband?' She said: 'Yes.' He asked her: 'Do
you think you will go back to him?' She said: 'I do not think so. What
do you wish?' The chief said: 'I think not. You must stay here. You
cannot go back. You are worthless now.' Then he said to the man:
'Do you want to sleep with your wife?' He said: 'Yes, for a while.
I want to sleep with her and talk to her.' Then he was allowed to sleep
with her that night and they talked together. At daybreak the woman
was vanished and he was sleeping next to a fallen oak. The chief said
to him: 'Get up. It is late.' He opened his eyes and saw an oak instead
of his wife. The chief said: 'You see that we cannot make your wife as
she was. She is no good now. It is best that you go back. You have a
good country there.' But the man said: 'No, I will stay.' The chief
told him: 'No, do not. Come back here whenever you like, but go back
now.' Nevertheless he man stayed there six days. Then he said: 'I
am going back.' Then in the morning he started to go home. The chief
told him: 'When you arrive, hide yourself. Then after six days emerge
and make a dance.' Now the man returned. He told his parents: 'Make
me a small house. In six days I will come out and dance.' Now he
stayed there five days. Then his friends began to know that he had
come back. 'Our relative has come back,' they all said. Now the man
was in too much of a hurry. After five days he went out. In the evening
he began to dance and danced all night, telling what he saw. In the
morning when he had stopped dancing, he went to bathe. Then a
rattlesnake bit him. He died. So he went back to island. He is there
now. It is through him that the people know it is there. Every two
days the island becomes full. Then the chief gathers the people. 'You
must swim,' he says. The people stop dancing and bathe. Then the bird
frightens them, and some turn to fish, and some to ducks; only a few
come out of the water again as people. In this way room is made when
the island is too full. The name of the chief there is Kandjidji.

A. L. Kroeber, *Indian Myths of South Central California*, University of California Publications, *American
Archaeology and Ethnology*, vol. IV, no. 4 (1906-7), pp.
216-18

H. PARADISES

186. A MAHĀYĀNA PARADISE: THE PURE LAND

('Sukhāvatīvyūha,' chapters 15-18)

15. This world Sukhāvatī, Ānanda, which is the world system of the Lord Amitābha, is rich and prosperous, comfortable, fertile, delightful and crowded with many Gods and men. And in this world system, Ānanda, there are no hells, no animals, no ghosts, no Asuras and none of the inauspicious places of rebirth. And in this our world no jewels make their appearance like those which exist in the world system Sukhāvatī.

16. And that world system Sukhāvatī, Ānanda, emits many fragrant odours, it is rich in a great variety of flowers and fruits, adorned with jewel trees, which are frequented by flocks of various birds with sweet voices, which the Tathāgata's miraculous power has conjured up. And these jewel trees, Ānanda, have various colours, many colours, many hundreds of thousands of colours. They are variously composed of the seven precious things, in varying combinations, i.e. of gold, silver, beryl, crystal, coral, red pearls or emerald. Such jewel trees, and clusters of banana trees and rows of palm trees, all made of precious things, grow everywhere in this Buddha-field. On all sides it is surrounded with golden nets, and all round covered with lotus flowers made of all the precious things. Some of the lotus flowers are half a mile in circumference, others up to ten miles. And from each jewel lotus issue thirty-six hundred thousand kotis of rays. And at the end of each ray there issue thirty-six hundred thousand kotis of Buddhas, with golden-coloured bodies, who bear the thirty-two marks of the superman, and who, in all the ten directions, go into countless world systems, and there demonstrate Dharma.

17. And further, Ānanda, in this Buddha-field there are nowhere any mountains,—black mountains, jewel mountains, Sumerus, kings of mountains, circular mountains and great circular mountains. But the Buddha-field is everywhere even, delightful like the palm of the

hand, and in all its parts the ground contains a great variety of jewels and gems. . . .

18. And many kinds of rivers flow along in this world system Sukhāvatī. There are great rivers there, one mile broad, and up to fifty miles broad and twelve miles deep. And these rivers flow along calmly, their water is fragrant with manifold agreeable odours, in them are bunches of flowers to which various jewels adhere, and they resound with various sweet sounds. And the sound which issues from these great rivers is as pleasant as that of a musical instrument, which consists of hundreds of thousands of kotis of parts, and which, skilfully played, emits a heavenly music. It is deep, commanding, distinct, clear, pleasant to the ear, touching the heart, delightful, sweet, pleasant, and one never tires of hearing it, it always agrees with one and one likes to hear it, like the words 'Impermanent, peaceful, calm, and not-self.' Such is the sound that reaches the ears of those beings.

And, Ānanda, both the banks of those great rivers are lined with variously scented jewel trees, and from them bunches of flowers, leaves and branches of all kinds hang down. And if those beings wish to indulge in sports full of heavenly delights on those river-banks, then, after they have stepped into the water, the water in each case rises as high as they wish it to,—up to the ankles, or the knees, or the hips, or their sides, or their ears. And heavenly delights arise. Again, if beings wish the water to be cold, for them it becomes cold; if they wish it to be hot, for them it becomes hot; if they wish it to be hot and cold, for them it becomes hot and cold, to suit their pleasure. And those rivers flow along, full of water scented with the finest odours, and covered with beautiful flowers, resounding with the sounds of many birds, easy to ford, free from mud, and with golden sand at the bottom. And all the wishes those beings may think of, they all will be fulfilled, as long as they are rightful.

And as to the pleasant sound which issues from the water (of those rivers), that reaches all the parts of this Buddha-field. And everyone hears the pleasant sound he wishes to hear, i.e. he hears of the Buddha, the Dharma, the Samgha, of the (six) perfections, the (ten) stages, the powers, the grounds of self-confidence, of the special dharmas of a Buddha, of the analytical knowledge, of emptiness, the signless, and the wishless, of the uneffected, the unborn, of non-production, non-existence, non-cessation, of calm, quietude and peace, of the great friendliness, the great compassion, the great sympathetic joy, the great evenmindedness, of the patient acceptance of things which fail to be produced, and of the acquisition of the stage where one is consecrated (as a Tathāgata). And, hearing this, one gains the exalted zest and joyfulness, which is associated with detachment, dispassion, calm, cessation, Dharma, and brings about the state of mind which leads to the accomplishment of enlightenment. And nowhere in this world-system Sukhāvatī does one hear of anything unwholesome, nowhere of the hindrances, nowhere of the states of punishment, the states of woe and the bad destinies, nowhere of suffering. Even of feelings which are neither pleasant nor unpleasant one does not hear here, how much less of suffering! And that, Ānanda, is the reason why this world-system is called the 'Happy Land' (Sukhāvatī). But all this describes it only in brief, not in detail. One aeon might well reach its end while one proclaims the reasons for happiness in the world-system Sukhāvatī, and still one could not come to the end of (the enumeration of) the reasons for happiness.

Sukhāvatīvyūha, ch. 15-17, 18. Translation by Edward Conze, in Conze *et al.*, *Buddhist Texts through the Ages* (Oxford: Bruno Cassirer (Publishers) Ltd., 1954).

187. THE VISION OF ALLAH IN THE OTHER WORLD

Said Hammad b. Sulaiman: When the blessed have entered Paradise and have established themselves there in pleasure and delight, in a magnificent kingdom, a noble residence where they are in security and tranquility, they quite forget there what they were promised in this world of how they would [one day] see Allah and go to visit Him, so occupied are they with the blessings and the pleasures they are enjoying there. So while they are thus, behold, an angel from before Allah—mighty and majestic is He—looks down upon them from one of the mighty walls of Paradise, from an eminence so high that not a thing in Paradise is hidden from him. [It is a wall] made of glistening pearl whose light shines over against the Throne and shines to the highest point of heaven. This angel will call out at the top of his voice: 'O people of Paradise, greeting of peace to you,' yet with a voice so full of compassion that, though it is so loud, all ears incline to it and all faces turn toward it, all souls being moved by it, rejoicing at it, and responding eagerly to it. All of them hear the voice and take cognizance that this is a herald from before Allah—mighty and majestic is He. It will evoke no doubt in them, so they will respond:

'Labbaika! Labbaika!¹ O summoner from Allah, our Lord. We have heard and we respond.' Then he will say: 'Welcome to you, O ye saints of Allah! Welcome! most Welcome! Allah—mighty and majestic is He—sends you greeting of peace, saying that He is well pleased with you [and asking] are ye well pleased with Him.' They will reply: 'Praise be to Allah who has guided us to this, for we were not such as would have been guided had not Allah guided us (VII, 43/41). Praise be to Him, since He is well pleased with us and has made us well satisfied. To Him be praise and thanksgiving, since He has been bountiful to us and given us [all this].' Then (the angel) will say: 'O saints of Allah, Allah—glory be to Him—sends you greeting of peace and says: "Have I fulfilled the promises I made to you in the world, or have I come short of them in any way?" ' They will answer: 'Praise be to Allah, His are the gifts and the favours. He has indeed fulfilled His promises and bestowed on us bounty from Himself, this Paradise, in which we go about wherever we wish.' Then [the angel] will say to them: 'Allah—glory be to Him—gives you greeting of peace, and reminds you that in the world He promised you that in Paradise you would visit Him, approach Him, and look upon Him. Now He would fulfil what He promised you, so He gives you here and now permission to prepare yourselves to have your happiness made complete in His presence.'

When they hear that, everything they have been enjoying there and all they have so far attained in Paradise will seem to them a little thing compared with that exceeding great happiness. Indeed, all that Paradise contains will seem insignificant over against the fact that Allah is well pleased with them and [is allowing them] to visit Him and look upon Him. So they will get themselves ready for a visit to their Lord in their finest estate and their most beautiful attire. They will clothe themselves with the most precious robes and the most fragrant perfumes, and mount the finest of horses and the most nobly born steeds, the most precious that they have, and putting crowns upon their heads they will come forth, each man from his palace and his garden, till he reaches the farthest end of his property and moves out into the paths of Paradise, his *wildān*² preceding him and guiding him on the way to the visitation of the most illustrious King. Meanwhile they raise their voices in expressions of remembrance and encomium and hallelujahs (*tahlīl*), and whenever any man among them comes out into the paths of Paradise he meets his

The notes to this text are on p. 388.

brother [Muslim] who has come out for the same purpose that he has.

Thus they will journey along till they come to a broad open space at the borders of Paradise, where the ground is unencumbered, vacant, white, and camphored, its soil being of camphor mixed with musk and ambergris, and its stones of pearl and jacinth. There they will assemble, preceded by the angel who had summoned them and who has travelled on ahead of them till he has brought them to this Garden of Eden. Allah will have given a call to this Garden, [saying]; 'Adorn yourself, for I have called My saints to visit Me within you,' so the Garden will have adorned itself with the most exquisite and beautiful adornment, and its attendants and *wildān* will likewise have got themselves ready. So when the saints arrive at the gate of the Garden, the angel will precede them, having with him the people of Paradise, and all of them will cry; 'Greeting to you, O ye angels of our Lord.' Then there will be opened for them a gate between whose leaves is the distance between the East and the West here on earth. This gate is of green emerald and over it are curtains of light of such brightness as almost to destroy the sight. They will enter and pour out into a valley-bed there whose enormous size, both in length and breadth, is known only to Him who created it by His power and fashioned it in His wisdom. Its soil is of finest musk and saffron and ambergris, its stones of jacinths and jewels, its little pebbles and rubble are of gold, while on its banks are trees whose limbs hang down, whose branches are low, whose fruits are within easy reach, whose birds sing sweetly, whose colours shine brightly, whose flowers blossom in splendour, and from which comes a breeze [so delightful] as to reduce to insignificance all other delights, one needle's-eye full of which, were it sent to this world, would cure all the sick.

Beneath these trees are chairs and benches of light that gleam, chairs and benches of jacinth and of jewels, and the like of red gold, of green emerald, of musk and ambergris, set there for the prophets, the messengers, then for the saints and the pious, then for the martyrs and the just, then for the Blessed from among all the rest of the people. Over [these seats] are cloths of brocade and satin and green silk, very precious, the silk woven and hemmed with jacinths and with jewels, and [on them] also are cushions of red brocade. On these they will be given permission to seat themselves in accordance with the honourable rank each has. They will be met by cries of welcome and applause, with ascriptions of honour and merit. So each man of them will take his station according to the measure of honour he has with his Lord, and his position of nearness to Him and in His favour, while the angels and the *wildān* show them great respect in seating them. Then, when every man has taken his place and settled himself, according to his rank, orders will be given that they be served with the finest food. So they will eat it and enjoy it with such pleasure that they forget any food that they have eaten hitherto, and everything they have ever known before seems insignificant to them. [It will be served to them] on platters the like of which they have never seen before and on tables whose like they have never beheld. Then orders will be given that they be served the finest kinds of fruit such as they never before have seen, and they will eat of these fruits and enjoy thereof as much as they desire. Then orders will be given that they be served the finest varieties of drinks such as they never yet have drunk, [served to them] in vessels of pearl and jacinth which shine brilliantly, giving out lights the like of whose splendour and loveliness they have hitherto never beheld. So they will drink and enjoy it, and then orders will be given for them to be [perfumed] with perfumes such as they have never before enjoyed. Then orders will be given for them to be clothed with garments [of honour] the like of which they have not seen even in Paradise, and of such splendour and beauty as they have never before had for their delight.

This will be their state, so ask not about their happiness and their joy there, for all that they have had before now seems to them of no account. Then Allah—glory be to Him—will say: 'O My saints, O My servants, have I fulfilled to you what I promised you in the world? Have I amply fulfilled My promise?' They will answer: 'Yea, O our Lord, by Thy might, Thou hast fulfilled to us Thy promise and hast amply fulfilled what thou didst promise us.' Then He—glory be to Him—will say: 'Nay, by My might, there still remains for you one thing which you covet yet more and which has a still higher place in your estimation. What is there after you have come to Me but that you should look upon Me, that thereby your blessedness may be complete?' Then He—glory be to Him—will give command to the veils of light so they will be raised, and to the dread awfulness so that it is set aside. Then He—glory be to Him—will reveal Himself as them and they will look upon Him. Thus will they see Him without suffering any injury or any harm, and no joy can equal their joy in that, nor can any happiness or delight stand beside their happiness in that. So they will fall down before their Lord in prostration and deep humility, saying: 'Glory be to Thee, O our Lord. In Thy praise Thou art blessed and exalted, and blessed is Thy name.'

Notes

1 This exclamation, whose meaning is little understood, was the ancient cry which used to be raised by those approaching the sacred shrine at Mecca. It is still used by Muslim pilgrims at the present day. The technical word for making devotional use of this exclamation is *talbiya*.
2 Each of the Blessed in Paradise has a provision of male and female attendants of celestial origin. The *wildān* are the celestial youths who wait on them and the *hūrīs* are the celestial damsels.

Translation and notes by Arthur Jeffery, *Islam: Muhammad and His Religion* (New York: Liberal Arts Press, 1958) pp. 98-103; trans. from Ibn Makhlūf, *Kitāb al'Ulūm al-fākhira fī'n-nazr fī Umūr al-Ākhira* (Cairo, 1317 A.H.=A.D. 1899), II, 151-3

I. THE END OF THE WORLD

188. AHURA MAZDA TEACHES YIMA HOW TO SAVE ALL THAT IS BEST AND FAIREST IN THE WORLD

('Vidēvdāt,' Fargard II)

A terrible winter is approaching, a winter which is to destroy every living creature. Yima, the first man and first king, is advised to build a well-defended enclosure (vara) in which he is to keep the finest representatives of every kind of animal and plant. They live for a life of perfect happiness there.

(46) And Ahura Mazda spake unto Yima, saying:

'O fair Yima, son of Vīvanghat! Upon the material world the evil winters are about to fall, that shall bring the fierce, deadly frost; upon the material world the evil winters are about to fall, that shall make snowflakes fall thick, even in *aredvī* deep on the highest tops of the mountains.

(52) 'And the beasts that live in the wilderness, and those that live on the tops of the mountains, and those that live in the bosom of the dale shall take shelter in underground abodes.

(57) 'Before that winter, the country would bear plenty of grass for cattle, before the waters had flooded it. Now after the melting of the snow, O Yima, a place wherein the footprint of a sheep may be seen will be a wonder in the world.

(61) 'Therefore make thee a Vara (enclosure), long as a riding-ground on every side of the square, and thither bring the seeds of sheep and oxen, of men, of dogs, of birds, and of red blazing fires.

Therefore make thee a Vara, long as a riding-ground on every side of the square, to be an abode for men; a Vara, long as a riding-ground on every side of the square, for oxen and sheep.

(65) 'There thou shalt make waters flow in a bed a *hathra* long; there thou shalt settle birds, on the green that never fades, with food that never fails. There thou shalt establish dwelling-places consisting of a house with a balcony, a courtyard, and a gallery.

(70) 'Thither thou shalt bring the seeds of men and women, of the greatest, best, and finest on this earth; thither thou shalt bring the seeds of every kind of cattle, of the greatest, best, and finest on this earth.

(74) 'Thither thou shalt bring the seeds of every kind of tree, of the highest of size and sweetest of odour on this earth; thither thou shalt bring the seeds of every kind of fruit, the best of savour and sweetest of odour. All those seeds shalt thou bring, two of every kind, to be kept inexhaustible there, so long as those men shall stay in the Vara.

(80) 'There shall be no humpbacked, none bulged forward there; no impotent, no lunatic; no one malicious, no liar; no one spiteful, none jealous; no one with decayed tooth, no leprous to be pent up, nor any of the brands wherewith Angra Mainyu stamps the bodies of mortals.

(87) 'In the largest part of the place thou shalt make nine streets, six in the middle part, three in the smallest. To the streets of the largest part thou shalt bring a thousand seeds of men and women; to the streets of the middle part, six hundred; to the streets of the smallest part, three hundred. That Vara thou shalt seal up with thy golden seal, and thou shalt make a door, and a window self-shining within.'

(93) Then Yima said within himself: 'How shall I manage to make that Vara which Ahura Mazda has commanded me to make?'

And Ahura Mazda said unto Yima: 'O fair Yima, son of Vīvanghat! Crush the earth with a stamp of thy heel, and then knead it with thy hands, as the potter does when kneading the potter's clay.'

Translation by James Darmesteter, *The Zend-Avesta*, part I, in *Sacred Books of the East*, IV (2nd ed.; Oxford 1895), pp. 15-18

189. THE BUDDHA FORETELLS THE GRADUAL DECLINE OF RELIGION

(*'Anāgatavamsa'*)

Praise to that Lord, Arahant, perfect Buddha.
Thus have I heard: At one time the Lord was staying near Kapilavatthu in the Banyan monastery on the bank of the river Rohani.

The End of the World

Then the venerable Sariputta questioned the Lord about the future Conqueror:

> 'The Hero that shall follow you,
> The Buddha—of what sort will he be?
> I want to hear of him in full.
> Let the Visioned One describe him.'

> When he had heard the Elder's speech
> The Lord spoke thus:
> 'I will tell you, Sariputta,
> Listen to my speech.

> 'In this auspicious aeon
> Three leaders have there been:
> Kakusandha, Konāgamana
> And the leader Kassapa too.

> 'I am now the perfect Buddha;
> And there will be Metteyya [i.e., Maitreya] too
> Before this same auspicious aeon
> Runs to the end of its years.

> 'The perfect Buddha, Metteyya
> By name, supreme of men.'

(Then follows a history of the previous existence of Metteyya . . . and then the description of the gradual decline of the religion:)

'How will it occur? After my decease there will first be five disappearances. What five? The disappearance of attainment (in the Dispensation), the disappearance of proper conduct, the disappearance of learning, the disappearance of the outward form, the disappearance of the relics. There will be these five disappearances.

'Here attainment means that for a thousand years only after the Lord's complete Nirvāna will monks be able to practise analytical insights. As time goes on and on these disciples of mine are non-returners and once-returners and stream-winners. There will be no disappearance of attainment for these. But with the extinction of the last stream-winner's life, attainment will have disappeared.

'This, Sariputta, is the disappearance of attainment.

'The disappearance of proper conduct means that, being unable to practise jhana, insight, the Ways and the fruits, they will guard no more the four entire purities of moral habit. As time goes on and on they will only guard the four offences entailing defeat. While there are even a hundred or a thousand monks who guard and bear in mind the four offences entailing defeat, there will be no disappearance of proper conduct. With the breaking of moral habit by the last monk or on the extinction of his life, proper conduct will have disappeared.

'This, Sariputta, is the disappearance of proper conduct.

'The disappearance of learning means that as long as there stand firm the texts with the commentaries pertaining to the word of the Buddha in the three Pitakas, for so long there will be no disappearance of learning. As time goes on and on there will be base-born kings, not Dhamma-men; their ministers and so on will not be Dhamma-men, and consequently the inhabitants of the kingdom and so on will not be Dhamma-men. Because they are not Dhamma-men it will not rain properly. Therefore the crops will not flourish well, and in consequence the donors of requisites to the community of monks will not be able to give them the requisites. Not receiving the requisites the monks will not receive pupils. As time goes on and on learning will decay. In this decay the Great Patthanā itself will decay first. In this decay also (there will be) Yamaka, Kathāvatthu, Puggalapaññati, Dhātukathā, Vibhanga and Dhammasangani. When the Abhidhamma Pitaka decays the Suttanta Pitaka will decay. When the Suttantas decay the Anguttara will decay first. When it decays the Samyutta Nikāya, the Majjhima Nikāya, the Dīgha Nikāya and the Khuddaka-Nikāya will decay. They will simply remember the Jātaka together wit the Vinaya-Pitaka. But only the conscientious (monks) will remember the Vinaya-Pitaka. As time goes on and on, being unable to remember even the Jātaka, the Vessantara-jātaka will decay first. When that decays the Āpannaka-jātaka will decay. When the Jātakas decay they will remember only the Vinaya-Pitaka. As time goes on and on the Vinaya-Pitaka will decay. While a four-line stanza still continues to exist among men, there will not be a disappearance of learning. When a king who has faith has had a purse containing a thousand (coins) placed in a golden casket on an elephant's back, and has had the drum (of proclamation) sounded in the city up to the second or third time, to the effect that: "Whoever knows a stanza uttered by the Buddhas, let him take these thousand coins together with the royal elephant"—but yet finding no one knowing a four-line stanza, the purse containing the thousand (coins) must be taken back into the palace again—then will be the disappearance of learning.

'This, Sariputta, is the disappearance of learning.

'As time goes on and on each of the last monks, carrying his robe, bowl, and tooth-pick like Jain recluses, having taken a bottle-gourd and turned it into a bowl for almsfood, will wander about with it in his forearms or hands or hanging from a piece of string. As time goes on and on, thinking: "What's the good of this yellow robe?" and cutting off a small piece of one and sticking it on his nose or ear or in his hair, he will wander about supporting wife and children by agriculture, trade and the like. Then he will give a gift to the Southern community for those (of bad moral habit). I say that he will then acquire an incalculable fruit of the gift. As time goes on and on, thinking: "What's the good of this to us?", having thrown away the piece of yellow robe, he will harry beasts and birds in the forest. At this time the outward form will have disappeared.

'This, Sariputta, is called the disappearance of the outward form.

'Then when the Dispensation of the Perfect Buddha is 5,000 years old, the relics, not receiving reverence and honour, will go to places where they can receive them. As time goes on and on there will not be reverence and honour for them in every place. At the time when the Dispensation is falling into (oblivion), all the relics, coming from every place: from the abode of serpents and the deva-world and the Brahma-world, having gathered together in the space round the great Bo-tree, having made a Buddha-image, and having performed a "miracle" like the Twin-miracle, will teach Dhamma. No human being will be found at that place. All the devas of the ten-thousand world system, gathered together, will hear Dhamma and many thousands of them will attain to Dhamma. And these will cry aloud, saying: "Behold, devatas, a week from today our One of the Ten Powers will attain complete Nirvāna." They will weep, saying: "Henceforth there will be darkness for us." Then the relics, producing the condition of heat, will burn up that image leaving no remainder.

'This, Sariputta, is called the disappearance of the relics.'

Translation and explanatory material by Edward Conze, in Conze *et al.*, *Buddhist Texts through the Ages* (Oxford: Bruno Cassirer (Publishers) Ltd., 1954).

190. IRANIAN ESCHATOLOGY: THE RAISING OF THE DEAD AND THE FINAL BODY

(Greater Bundahishn)

(1) It is said in the Religion that just as Mashyē and Mashyānē, after they had grown out of the earth, consumed water first, then plants,

then milk, and then meat, so do men when they are [are about to] die, abstain first from the eating of meat and milk and then from bread; but right up to the moment of death they drink water.

(2) So too in the millennium of Oshētarmāh (the last millennium before the coming of Sōshyans) the power of Āz (gluttony) is so diminished that men are satisfied by eating one meal every three days and nights. After that they abstain from eating meat, and eat (only) plants and the milk of domestic animals. After that they abstain from drinking milk also; then they abstain from eating plants too, and drink only water. Ten years before the coming of Sōshyans they reach a state in which they eat nothing, yet do not die.

(3) Then Sōshyans will raise up the dead, as (the Religion) says, 'Zoroaster asked Ohrmazd, "From whence can the body which the wind has carried off and the water swept away, be put together again; and how will the raising of the dead come to pass?" And Ohrmazd made answer (and said): "When [I established] the sky without pillar on an invisible (*mēnōk*) support, its ends flung wide apart, bright with the substance of shining metal, and when I created the earth which supports the whole material creation though itself has no material support, and when I set the Sun, Moon, and stars—forms of light— on their courses in the atmosphere, and when I created grain on earth and scattered it abroad so that it grows up again and yields a greater crop, and when I created various and variegated colours in the plants, and when I gave fire to the plants and other things and it did not burn (them), and when I created the embryo in its mother's womb and gave it nourishment, giving to it its several organs, . . . when I created each one of these things, each was more difficult than the raising of the dead. For in the raising of the dead I have the assistance of the likes of these. When they were still [uncreated], I had [no such assistance].

(4) ' "Behold! If I created what had not been, why should it be impossible for me to recreate what once was? For at that time I shall demand from the Spirit of the Earth the bones, from the water the blood, from the plants the hair, from the wind the spirit (*jān*) even as they received them at the primal creation." '

(5) First will be raised the bones of Gayōmart, then the bones of Mashyē and Mashyānē: then will the bones of (all) other men be raised up. For fifty-seven years will Sōshyans raise the dead and all men will be resurrected, both those who were saved and those who were damned. And each man will arise in the place where his spirit left him or where first he fell to the ground. . . .

(7) Then will men recognize each other, that is, soul will recognize soul and body (thinking), 'This is my father,' or 'This is my brother,' or 'This is my wife,' or 'This is whatever close relative it may be.' Then the assembly of Isat-vāstar will convene when men stand upon the earth in that assembly; and every man will see his good and evil deeds, and the saved will be as clearly distinguished from the damned as is a white sheep from a black.

(8) And in that assembly the damned man who had on earth a friend who was saved, will upbraid the man who was saved, saying, 'Why didst thou not apprise me on earth of the good deeds that thou thyself wast doing?' And if in truth the man who was saved did not so apprise him, then must he needs be put to shame in that assembly.

(9) Then will they separate the saved from the damned, and carry off the saved to Paradise (garōdhmān) and hurl the damned back into Hell; and for three days and nights these denizens of Hell will endure punishment in Hell, in their bodies and in their souls (jān) while the saved experience joy in their bodies during their three days and nights in Paradise.

(10) For it is said that on that day when damned is separated from saved, and saved from damned, tears will flow down from (the eyes of) all men, right down to their feet. When son is separated from the company of father, brother from brother, friend from friend, then will every man bewail the deeds he did, the saved weeping for the damned, and the damned weeping for themselves. It may be the father who is saved and the son who is damned, or it may be one brother who is saved and the other who is damned. . . .

(13) And Gōchihr, the serpent in the heavenly sphere, will fall from the summit of the Moon to the earth, and the earth will suffer pain like unto the pain a sheep feels when a wolf rends out its wool.

(14) Then will the Fire-god and the god Airyaman melt the metals that are in the mountains and hills, and they will flow over the earth like rivers. And they will make all men to pass through that molten metal and (thereby) make them clean. And it will seem to him who was saved as if he were walking through warm milk, but to the man who was damned it will seem exactly like walking through molten metal.

(15) Then will all men come together in the greatest joy, father and son, brothers and all friends. And one man will ask another, 'How has thy soul fared in all these many years? Wast thou saved, or wast thou damned?' Next the soul will see its body, will question it and be answered by it.

(16) All men will become of one voice and give praise with a loud

voice to Ohrmazd and the Amahraspands. At this time Ohrmazd will
have brought his creation to its consummation, and there will be no
(further) work he need do.

(17) While the resurrection of the dead proceeds, Sōshyans and his
helpers will perform the sacrifice of the raising of the dead, and in that
sacrifice the bull Hadhayans will be slain, and from the fat of the
bull they will prepare the white Hōm (Haoma), (the drink of) immortality, and give it to all men. And all men will become immortal for
ever and ever. . . .

(19) To each man his wife and children will be restored, and they
will have intercourse with their wives even as they do on earth today,
but no children will be born to them. . . .

(22) Then Ohrmazd will seize hold of the Destructive Spirit, Vahu-
man (the Good Mind) will seize Akōman (the Evil Mind), Artvahisht
Indar, Shahrēvar Sāvul, Spandarmat Tarōmat (Arrogance) who is
Nānghaith, Hurdāt and Amurdāt will seize Tairich and Zairich, True
Speech False Speech, and the blessed Srōsh will seize upon Eshm
(Wrath) of the bloody banner.

(23) Then (only) two Lies will remain, Ahriman and Āz (Con-
cupiscence). Ohrmazd will come (down) to earth, himself the 'Zōt'-priest
with the blessed Srōsh as his 'Raspik'-priest, and he will hold the sacred
girdle in his hand. By that Gāthic ritual Ahriman and Āz, their
weapons smashed, will be made powerless; and by the same passage
through the sky by which they rushed in, they will hurtle into the
darkness and gloom.

(24) And the serpent Gōchihr will be burnt up in the molten metal;
and the molten metal will flow out into Hell. And (all) the stench and
corruption that was in Hell will be burnt up by this molten metal and
made clean. And [the hole in (?)] Hell by which the Destructive Spirit
rushed in, will be sealed up by that molten metal, and the earth that
was in Hell will be brought up to the broad expanse of (this) material
world.

(25) Then will the final Resurrection take place in the two worlds;
and in accordance with its own desire the material world will become
immortal for ever and ever.

(26) This too is said, that this earth will become flat, with neither
hills nor dales. There will be neither mountains nor ridges nor pits,
neither high ground nor low.

Translation by R. C. Zaehner, in his *The Teachings of
the Magi* (London, 1956), pp. 145-50; from *Bundahishn*
(edited by Anklesaria), pp. 220-8

The End of the World

191. MUHAMMAD SPEAKS OF THE DAY OF DOOM

('Koran,' LVI, 1-55; LXIX, 14-39)

In the Name of God, the Merciful, the Compassionate

> When the Terror descends
> (and none denies its descending)
> abasing, exalting,
> when the earth shall be rocked
> and the mountains crumbled
> and become a dust scattered,
> and you shall be three bands—

Companions of the Right (O Companions of the Right!)
Companions of the Left (O Companions of the Left!)
> and the Outstrippers: the Outstrippers
> those are they brought nigh the Throne,
> in the Gardens of Delight
> (a throng of the ancients
> and how few of the later folk)
> upon close-wrought couches
> reclining upon them, set face to face,
> immortal youths going round about them
> with goblets, and ewers, and a cup from a spring
> (no brows throbbing, no intoxication)
> and such fruits as they shall choose,
> and such flesh of fowl as they desire,
> and wide-eyed houris
> as the likeness of hidden pearls,
> a recompense for that they laboured.
Therein they shall hear no idle talk, no cause of sin,
> only the saying 'Peace, Peace!'

The Companions of the Right (O Companions of the Right!)
> mid thornless lote-trees and serried acacias,
> and spreading shade and outpoured waters,
> and fruits abounding
> unfailing, unforbidden,
> and upraised couches.

Perfectly We formed them, perfect,
and We made them spotless virgins,
    chastely amorous, like of age
for the Companions of the Right.
    A throng of the ancients
and a throng of the later folk.

The Companions of the Left (O Companions of the Left!)
    mid burning winds and boiling waters
    and the shadow of a smoking blaze
      neither cool, neither goodly;
    and before that they lived at ease,
      and persisted in the Great Sin,
        ever saying,
    'What, when we are dead and become
dust and bones, shall we indeed
    be raised up?
What, and our fathers, the ancients?'

Say: 'The ancients, and the later folk
shall be gathered to the appointed time
    of a known day.
Then you erring ones, you that cried lies,
you shall eat of a tree called Zakkoum,
and you shall fill therewith your bellies
and drink on top of that boiling water
lapping it down like thirsty camels.
This shall be their hospitality on the
    Day of Doom. (LVI, 1-55.)

So, when the Trumpet is blown with a single blast
and the earth and the mountains are lifted up and
    crushed with a single blow,
then, on that day, the Terror shall come to pass,
and heaven shall be split, for upon that day it
    shall be very frail,
and the angels shall stand upon its borders, and
upon that day eight shall carry above them the
    Throne of thy Lord.
On that day you shall be exposed, not one secret
    of yours concealed.

The End of the World

Then as for him who is given his book in his right hand,
he shall say, 'Here, take and read my book! Certainly
I thought that I should encounter my reckoning.' So he
      shall be in a pleasing life
      in a lofty Garden,
      its clusters nigh to gather.
'Eat and drink with wholesome appetite for that you did
      long ago, in the days gone by.'
But as for him who is given his book in his left hand,
he shall say, 'Would that I had not been given my book
and not known my reckoning! Would it had been the end!
      My wealth has not availed me,
      my authority is gone from me.'
Take him, and fetter him, and then roast him in Hell,
then in a chain of seventy cubits' length insert him!
Behold, he never believed in God the All-mighty, and
he never urged the feeding of the needy; therefore he
today has not here one loyal friend, neither any food
saving foul pus, that none excepting the sinners eat.

                               (LXIX, 41-39.)

Translation by A. J. Arberry

J. MESSIANIC PROPHECIES AND MILLENARIAN MOVEMENTS

192. THE PROPHECY CONCERNING MAITREYA, THE FUTURE BUDDHA

('Maitreyavyākarana')

Maitreya will appear in the future, some thirty thousand years hence. At present Maitreya is believed to reside in the Tushita heaven, awaiting his last rebirth when the time is ripe. His name is derived from mitra, 'friend,' friendliness being a basic Buddhist virtue, akin to Christian love.

Sariputra, the great general of the doctrine, most wise and resplendent, from compassion for the world asked the Lord: 'Some time ago you have spoken to us of the future Buddha, who will lead the world at a future period, and who will bear the name of Maitreya. I would now wish to hear more about his powers and miraculous gifts. Tell me, O best of men, about them !'

The Lord replied: 'At that time, the ocean will lose much of its water, and there will be much less of it than now. In consequence a world-ruler will have no difficulties in passing across it. India, this island of Jambu, will be quite flat everywhere, it will measure ten thousand leagues, and all men will have the privilege of living on it. It will have innumerable inhabitants, who will commit no crimes or evil deeds, but will take pleasure in doing good. The soil will then be free from thorns, even, and covered with a fresh green growth of grass; when one jumps on it, it gives way, and becomes soft like the leaves of the cotton tree. It has a delicious scent, and tasty rice grows on it, without any work. Rich silken, and other, fabrics of various colours shoot forth from the trees. The trees will bear leaves, flowers, and fruits simultaneously; they are as high as the voice can reach and they last for eight myriads of years. Human beings are then without any blemishes, moral offences are unknown among them, and they are full of zest and joy. Their bodies are very large and their skin has a fine hue. Their strength is quite extraordinary. Three kinds of illness only are known—people must relieve their bowels, they must eat, they must get old. Only when five hundred years old do the women marry.

'The city of Ketumatī will at that time be the capital. In it will reside the world-ruler, Shankha by name, who will rule over the earth up to the confines of the ocean; and he will make the Dharma prevail. He will be a great hero, raised to his station by the force of hundreds of meritorious deeds. His spiritual adviser will be a Brahmin, Subrahmana by name, a very learned man, well versed in the four Vedas, and steeped in all the lore of the Brahmins. And that Brahman will have a wife, called Brahmavatī, beautiful, attractive, handsome, and renowned.

'Maitreya, the best of men, will then leave the Tushita heavens, and go for his last rebirth into the womb of that woman. For ten whole months she will carry about his radiant body. Then she will go to a grove full of beautiful flowers, and there, neither seated nor lying down, but standing up, holding on to the branch of a tree, she will give birth to Maitreya. He, supreme among men, will emerge from her right side, as the sun shines forth when it has prevailed over a bank of clouds. No more polluted by the impurities of the womb than a lotus by drops of water, he will fill this entire Triple world with his splendour. As soon as he is born he will walk seven steps forward, and where he puts down his feet a jewel or a lotus will spring up. He will raise his eyes to the ten directions, and will speak these words: "This is my last birth. There will be no rebirth after this one. Never will I come back here, but, all pure, I shall win Nirvāna!"

'And when his father sees that his son has the thirty-two marks of a superman, and considers their implications in the light of the holy mantras, he will be filled with joy, for he will know that, as the mantras show, two ways are open to his son: he will either be a universal monarch, or a supreme Buddha. But as Maitreya grows up, the Dharma will increasingly take possession of him, and he will reflect that all that lives is bound to suffer. He will have a heavenly voice which reaches far; his skin will have a golden hue, a great splendour will radiate from his body, his chest will be broad, his limbs well developed, and his eyes will be like lotus petals. His body is eighty cubits high, and twenty cubits broad. He will have a retinue of 84,000 persons, whom he will instruct in the mantras. With this retinue he will one day go forth into the homeless life. A Dragon tree will then be the tree under which he will win enlightenment; its branches rise up to fifty leagues, and its foliage spreads far and wide over six Kos. Underneath it Maitreya, the best of men, will attain enlightenment—

there can be no doubt on that. And he will win his enlightenment the very same day that he has gone forth into the homeless life.

'And then, a supreme sage, he will with a perfect voice preach the true Dharma, which is auspicious and removes all ill, i.e. the fact of ill, the origination of ill, the transcending of ill, and the holy eightfold path which brings security and leads to Nirvāna. He will explain the four Truths, because he has seen that generation, in faith, ready for them, and those who have listened to his Dharma will thereupon make progress in the religion. They will be assembled in a park full of beautiful flowers, and his assembly will extend over a hundred leagues. Under Maitreya's guidance, hundreds of thousands of living beings shall enter upon a religious life.

'And thereupon Maitreya, the compassionate teacher, surveys those who have gathered around him, and speaks to them as follows: "Shākyamuni has seen all of you, he, the best of sages, the saviour, the world's true protector, the repository of the true Dharma. It was he who has set you on the path to deliverance, but before you could finally win it you have had to wait for my teaching. It is because you have worshipped Shākyamuni with parasols, banners, flags, perfumes, garlands, and unguents that you have arrived here to hear my teaching. It is because you have offered to the shrines of Shākyamuni unguents of sandalwood, or powdered saffron, that you have arrived here to hear my teaching. It is because you have always gone for refuge to the Buddha, the Dharma, and the Samgha, that you have arrived here to hear my teaching. It is because, in Shākyamuni's dispensation, you have undertaken to observe the moral precepts, and have actually done so, that you have arrived here to hear my teaching. It is because you have given gifts to the monks—robes, drink, food, and many kinds of medicines—that you have arrived here to hear my teaching. It is because you have always observed the sabbath days that you have arrived here to hear my teaching.". . .

'For 60,000 years Maitreya, the best of men, will preach the true Dharma, which is compassionate towards all living beings. And when he has disciplined in his true Dharma hundreds and hundreds of millions of living beings, then that leader will at last enter Nirvāna. And after the great sage has entered Nirvāna, his true Dharma still endures for another ten thousand years.

'Raise therefore your thoughts in faith to Shākyamuni, the Conqueror! For then you shall see Maitreya, the perfect Buddha, the best of men! Whose soul could be so dark that it would not be lit up with a serene faith when he hears these wonderful things, so potent of future good! Those therefore who long for spiritual greatness, let them show respect to the true Dharma, let them be mindful of the religion of the Buddhas!'

Translation by Edward Conze, in his *Buddhist Scriptures* (Penguin Books, 1959), pp. 238-42

193. NICHIREN SEES JAPAN AS THE CENTRE OF BUDDHISM'S REGENERATION

Nichiren (1222-82) was a Japanese religious teacher who established a Buddhist sect.

When, at a certain future time, the union of the state law and the Buddhist Truth shall be established, and the harmony between the two completed, both sovereign and subjects will faithfully adhere to the Great Mysteries. Then the golden age, such as were the ages under the reign of the sage kings of old, will be realized in these days of degeneration and corruption, in the time of the Latter Law. Then the establishment of the Holy See will be completed, by imperial grant and the edict of the Dictator, at a spot comparable in its excellence with the Paradise of Vulture Peak. We have only to wait for the coming of the time. Then the moral law *(kaihō)* will be achieved in the actual life of mankind. The Holy See will be the seat where all men of the three countries [India, China and Japan] and the whole Jambudvīpa [world] will be initiated into the mysteries of confession and expiation; and even the great deities, Brahmā and Indra, will come down into the sanctuary and participate in the initiation.

Masaharu Anesaki, *Nichiren, the Buddhist Prophet* (Cambridge, Mass., 1916), p. 110; as quoted in Wm. Theodore de Bary (ed.), *Sources of Japanese Tradition* (New York: Columbia University Press, 1958), p. 230

194. A SIOUX NATIVISTIC MOVEMENT: THE GHOST-DANCE RELIGION

The great underlying principle of the Ghost dance doctrine is that the time will come when the whole Indian race, living and dead, will be reunited upon a regenerated earth, to live a life of aboriginal happiness, forever free from death, disease, and misery. On this foundation each tribe has built a structure from its own mythology, and each apostle and believer has filled in the details according to his own mental capacity or ideas of happiness, with such additions as come to him from the trance. Some changes, also, have undoubtedly resulted from the transmission of the doctrine through the imperfect medium of the sign language. . . .

All this is to be brought about by overruling spiritual power that needs no assistance from human creatures; and though certain medicine-men were disposed to anticipate the Indian millennium by preaching resistance to the further encroachments of the whites, such teachings form no part of the true doctrine, and it was only where chronic dissatisfaction was aggravated by recent grievances, as among the Sioux, that the movement assumed a hostile expression. On the contrary, all believers were exhorted to make themselves worthy of the predicted happiness by discarding all things warlike and practising honesty, peace, and good will, not only among themselves, but also toward the whites, so long as they were together. Some apostles have even thought that all race distinctions are to be obliterated, and that the whites are to participate with the Indians in the coming felicity; but it seems unquestionable that this is equally contrary to the doctrine as originally preached.

Different dates have been assigned at various times for the fulfillment of the prophecy. Whatever the year, it has generally been held, for very natural reasons, that the regeneration of the earth and the renewal of all life would occur in the early spring. In some cases July, and particularly the 4th of July, was the expected time. This, it may be noted, was about the season when the great annual ceremony of the sun dances formerly took place among the prairie tribes. The messiah himself has set several dates from time to time, as one prediction after another failed to materialize, and in his message to the Cheyenne and Arapaho, in August, 1891, he leaves the whole matter an open question. The date universally recognized among all the tribes immediately prior to the Sioux outbreak was the spring of 1891. As springtime came and passed, and summer grew and waned, and autumn faded again into winter without the realization of their hopes and longings, the doctrine gradually assumed its present form—that some time in the unknown future the Indian will be united with his friends who have gone before, to be forever supremely happy, and that this happiness may be anticipated in dreams, if not actually hastened in reality, by earnest and frequent attendance on the sacred dance. . . .

As I had always shown a sympathy for their ideas and feelings, and had now accomplished a long journey to the messiah himself at the cost of considerable difficulty and hardship, the Indians were at last fully satisfied that I was really desirous of learning the truth concerning their new religion. A few days after my visit to Left Hand, several of the delegates who had been sent out in the preceding August came down to see me, headed by Black Short Nose, a Cheyenne. After preliminary greetings, he stated that the Cheyenne and Arapaho were now convinced that I would tell the truth about their religion, and as they loved their religion and were anxious to have the whites know that it was all good and contained nothing bad or hostile they would now give me the message which the messiah himself had given to them, that I might take it back to show to Washington. He then took from a beaded pouch and gave to me a letter, which proved to be the message or statement of the doctrine delivered by Wovoka to the Cheyenne and Arapaho delegates, of whom Black Short Nose was one, on the occasion of their last visit to Nevada, in August, 1891, and written down on the spot, in broken English, by one of the Arapaho delegates, Caspar Edson, a young man who had acquired some English education by several years' attendance at the government Indian school at Carlisle, Pennsylvania. On the reverse page of the paper was a duplicate in somewhat better English, written out by a daughter of Black Short Nose, a school girl, as dictated by her father on his return. These letters contained the message to be delivered to the two tribes, and as is expressly stated in the text were not intended to be seen by a white man. The daughter of Black Short Nose had attempted to erase this clause before her father brought the letter down to me, but the lines were still plainly visible. It is the genuine official statement of the Ghost-dance doctrine as given by the messiah himself to his disciples. . . .

The Messiah Letter (free rendering)

When you get home you must make a dance to continue five days. Dance four successive nights, and the last night keep up the dance until the morning of the fifth day, when all must bathe in the river and then disperse to their homes. You must all do in the same way.

I, Jack Wilson, love you all, and my heart is full of gladness for the gifts you have brought me. When you get home I shall give you a good cloud [rain?] which will make you feel good. I give you a good spirit and give you all good paint. I want you to come again in three months, some from each tribe there [the Indian Territory].

There will be a good deal of snow this year and some rain. In the fall there will be such a rain as I have never given you before.

Grandfather [a universal title or reverence among Indians and here meaning the messiah] says, when your friends die you must not cry. You must not hurt anybody or do harm to anyone. You must not fight. Do right always. It will give you satisfaction in life. This young man has a good father and mother. [Possibly this refers to Casper Edson, the young Arapaho who wrote down this message of Wovoka for the delegation].

Do not tell the white people about this. Jesus is now upon the earth. He appears like a cloud. The dead are alive all again. I do not know when they will be here; maybe this fall or in the spring. When the time comes there will be no more sickness and everyone will be young again.

Do not refuse to work for the whites and do not make any trouble with them until you leave them. When the earth shakes [at the coming of the new world] do not be afraid. It will not hurt you.

I want you to dance every six weeks. Make a feast at the dance and have food that everybody may eat. Then bathe in the water. That is all. You will receive good words again from me some time. Do not tell lies.

The mythology of the doctrine is only briefly indicated, but the principal articles are given. The dead are all risen and the spirit hosts are advancing and have already arrived at the boundaries of this earth, led forward by the regenerator in shape of cloud-like indistinctness. The spirit captain of the dead is always represented under this shadowy semblance. The great change will be ushered in by a trembling of the earth, at which the faithful are exhorted to feel no alarm. The hope held out is the same that has inspired the Christian for nineteen centuries—a happy immortality in perpetual youth. As to fixing a date, the messiah is as cautious as his predecessor in prophecy, who declares that 'no man knoweth the time, not even the angels of God.' His weather predictions also are about as definite as the inspired utterances of the Delphian oracle. . . .

We may now consider details of the doctrine as held by different tribes, beginning with the Paiute, among whom it originated. The best account of the Paiute belief is contained in a report to the War Department by Captain J. M. Lee, who was sent out in the autumn of 1890 to investigate the temper and fighting strength of the Paiute and other Indians in the vicinity of Fort Bidwell in northeastern California. We give the statement obtained by him from Captain Dick, a Paiute, as delivered one day in a conversational way and apparently without reserve, after nearly all the Indians had left the room:

'Long time, twenty years ago, Indian medicine-man in Mason's valley at Walker lake talk same way, same as you hear now. In one year, maybe, after he begin talk he die. Three years ago another medicine-man begin same talk. Heap talk all time. Indians hear about it everywhere. Indians come from long way off to hear him. They come from the east; they make signs. Two years ago me go to Winnemucca and Pyramid lake, me see Indian Sam, a head man, and Johnson Sides. Sam he tell me he just been to see Indian medicine-man to hear him talk. Sam say medicine-man talk this way:

'"All Indians must dance, everywhere, keep on dancing. Pretty soon in next spring Big Man [Great Spirit] come. He bring back all game of every kind. The game be thick everywhere. All dead Indians come back and live again. They all be strong just like young man, be young again. Old blind Indian see again and get young and have fine time. When Old Man [God] comes this way, then all the Indians go to mountains, high up away from whites. Whites can't hurt Indians then. Then while Indians way up high, big flood comes like water and all white people die, get drowned. After that water go way and then nobody but Indians everywhere and game all kinds thick. Then medicine-man tell Indians to send word to all Indians to keep up dancing and the good time will come. Indians who don't dance, who don't believe in this word, will grow little, just about a foot high, and stay that way. Some of them will be turned into wood and be burned in fire." That's the way Sam tell me the medicine-man talk.'

Lieutenant N. P. Phister, who gathered a part of the material embodied in Captain Lee's report, confirms this general statement and gives a few additional particulars. The flood is to consist of mingled mud and water, and when the faithful go up into the mountains, the sceptics will be left behind and will be turned to stone. The prophet claims to receive these revelations directly from God and the spirits of the dead Indians during his trances. He asserts also that he is invulnerable, and that if soldiers should attempt to kill him they would fall down as if they had no bones and die, while he would still live, even though cut into little pieces.

One of the first and most prominent of those who brought the doctrine to the prairie tribes was Porcupine, a Cheyenne, who crossed the mountains with several companions in the fall of 1889, visited Wovoka, and attended the dance near Walker Lake, Nevada. In his report of his experiences, made some months later to a military officer, he states that Wovoka claimed to be Christ himself, who had come back again, many centuries after his first rejection, in pity to teach his children. He quoted the prophet as saying:

'I found my children were bad, so I went back to heaven and left them. I told them that in so many hundred years I would come back to see my children. At the end of this time I was sent back to try to teach them. My father told me the earth was getting old and worn out and the people getting bad, and that I was to renew everything as it used to be and make it better.

'He also told us that all our dead were to be resurrected; that they were all to come back to earth, and that, as the earth was too small for them and us, he would do away with heaven and make the earth itself large enough to contain us all; that we must tell all the people we met about these things. He spoke to us about fighting; and said that was bad and we must keep from it; that the earth was to be all good hereafter, and we must all be friends with one another. He said that in the fall of the year the youth of all good people would be renewed, so that nobody would be more than forty years old, and that if they behaved themselves well after this the youth of everyone would be renewed in the spring. He said if we were all good he would send people among us who could heal all our wounds and sickness by mere touch and that we would live forever. He told us not to quarrel or fight or strike each other, or shoot one another; that the whites and Indians were to be all one people. He said if any man disobeyed what he ordered his tribe would be wiped from the face of the earth; that we must believe everything he said, and we must not doubt him or say he lied; that if we did, he would know it; that he would know our thoughts and actions in no matter what part of the world we might be.'

Here we have the statement that both races are to live together as one. We have also the doctrine of healing by touch. Whether or not this is an essential part of the system is questionable, but it is certain that the faithful believe that great physical good comes to them, to their children, and to the sick from the imposition of hands by the priests of the dance, apart from the ability thus conferred to see the things of the spiritual world.

Another idea here presented, namely, that the earth becomes old and decrepit, and requires that its youth be renewed at the end of certain great cycles, is common to a number of tribes, and has an important place in the oldest religions of the world. As an Arapaho who spoke English expressed it, 'This earth too old, grass too old, trees too old, our lives too old. Then all be new again.' Captain H. L. Scott also found among the southern plains tribes the same belief that the rivers, the mountains, and the earth itself are worn out and must be renewed, together with an indefinite idea that both races alike must die at the same time, to be resurrected in new but separate worlds. . . .

The manner of the final change and the destruction of the whites has been variously interpreted as the doctrine was carried from its original centre. East of the mountains it is commonly held that a deep sleep will come on the believers, during which the great catastrophe will be accomplished, and the faithful will awake to immortality on a new earth. The Shoshoni of Wyoming say this sleep will continue four nights and days, and that on the morning of the fifth day all will open their eyes in a new world where both races will dwell together forever. The Cheyenne, Arapaho, Kiowa, and others, of Oklahoma, say that the new earth, with all the resurrected dead from the beginning, and with the buffalo, the elk, and other game upon it, will come from the west and slide over the surface of the present earth, as the right hand might slide over the left. As it approaches, the Indians will be carried upward and alight on it by the aid of the sacred dance feather which they wear in their hair and which will act as wings to bear them up. They will then become unconscious for four days, and on waking out of their trance will find themselves with their former friends in the midst of all the old time surroundings. By Sitting Bull, the Arapaho apostle, it is thought that this new earth as it advances will be preceded by a wall of fire which will drive the whites across the water to their original and proper country, while the Indians will be enabled by means of the sacred feathers to surmount the flames and reach the promised land. When the expulsion of the whites has been accomplished, the fire will be extinguished by a rain continuing twelve days. By a few it is believed that a hurricane with thunder and lightning will come to destroy the whites alone. This last idea is said to be held also by the Walapai of Arizona, who extend its provisions to include the unbelieving Indians as well. The doctrine held by the Caddo, Wichita, and Delaware, of Oklahoma, is practically the same as is held by the Arapaho and Cheyenne from whom they obtained it. All these tribes believe that the destruction or removal of the whites is to be accomplished entirely by supernatural means, and they severely blame the Sioux for having provoked a physical conflict by their impatience instead of waiting for their God to deliver them in his own good time.

Among all the tribes which have accepted the new faith it is held that frequent devout attendance on the dance conduces to ward off disease and restore the sick to health, this applying not only to the actual participants, but also to their children and friends. The idea of obtaining temporal blessings as the reward of a faithful performance of religious duties is too natural and universal to require comment. The purification by the sweat-bath, which forms an important preliminary to the dance among the Sioux, while devotional in its purpose, is probably also sanitary in its effect.

Among the powerful and warlike Sioux of the Dakotas, already restless under both old and recent grievances, and more lately brought to the edge of starvation by a reduction of rations, the doctrine speedily assumed a hostile meaning and developed some peculiar features, for which reason it deserves particular notice as concerns this tribe. The earliest rumours of the new messiah came to the Sioux from the more western tribes in the winter of 1888-89, but the first definite account was brought by a delegation which crossed the mountains to visit the messiah in the fall of 1889, returning in the spring of 1890. On the report of these delegates the dance was at once inaugurated and spread so rapidly that in a few months the new religion had been accepted by the majority of the tribe.

Perhaps the best statement of the Sioux version is given by the veteran agent, James McLaughlin, of Standing Rock Agency. In an official letter of October 17, 1890, he writes that the Sioux, under the influence of Sitting Bull, were greatly excited over the near approach of a predicted Indian millennium or 'return of the ghosts,' when the white man would be annihilated and the Indian again supreme, and which the medicine-men had promised was to occur as soon as the grass was green in the spring. They were told that the Great Spirit had sent upon them the dominant race to punish them for their sins, and that their sins were now expiated and the time of deliverance was at hand. Their decimated ranks were to be reinforced by all the Indians who had ever died, and these spirits were already on their way to reinhabit the earth, which had originally belonged to the Indians, and were driving before them, as they advanced, immense herds of buffalo and fine ponies. The Great Spirit, who had so long deserted his red children, was now once more with them and against the whites, and the white man's gunpowder would no longer have power to drive a bullet through the skin of an Indian. The whites themselves would soon be overwhelmed and smothered under a deep landslide, held down by sod and timber, and the few who might escape would become small fishes in the rivers. In order to bring about this happy result, the Indians must believe and organize the Ghost dance.

James Mooney, *The Ghost-Dance Religion and the Sioux Outbreak of 1890*, Fourteenth Annual Report, part 2, Bureau of American Ethnology (Washington, D.C., 1896), pp. 641-1110; quotation from pp. 777-87

195. THE GHOST-DANCE RELIGION (SIOUX): THE CEREMONY

The dance commonly begins about the middle of the afternoon or later, after sundown. When it begins in the afternoon, there is always an intermission of an hour or two for supper. The announcement is made by the criers, old men who assume this office apparently by tacit understanding, who go about the camp shouting in a loud voice to the people to prepare for the dance. The preliminary painting and dressing is usually a work of about two hours. When all is ready, the leaders walk out to the dance place, and facing inward, join hands so as to form a small circle. Then, without moving from their places they sing the opening song, according to previous agreement, in a soft undertone. Having sung it through once more they raise their voices to their full strength and repeat it, this time slowly circling around in the dance. The step is different from that of most other Indian dances, but very simple, the dancers moving from right to left, following the course of the sun, advancing the left foot and following it with the right, hardly lifting the feet from the ground. For this reason it is called by the Shoshoni the 'dragging dance.' All the songs are adapted to the simple measure of the dance step. As the song rises and swells the people come singly and in groups from the several tipis, and one after another joins the circle until any number from fifty to five hundred men, women, and children are in the dance. When the circle is small, each song is repeated through a number of circuits. If large, it is repeated only through one circuit, measured by the return of the leaders to the starting point. Each song is started in the same manner, first in an undertone while the singers stand still in their places, and then with full voice as they begin to circle around. At intervals between the songs, more especially after the trances have begun, the dancers unclasp hands and sit down to smoke or talk for a few minutes. At such times the leaders sometimes deliver short addresses or sermons, or relate the recent trance experience of the dancer. In holding each other's hands the dancers usually intertwine the fingers instead of grasping the the hand as with us. Only an Indian could keep the blanket in place as they do under such circumstances. Old people hobbling along with sticks, and little children hardly past the toddling period sometimes form a part of the circle, the more vigorous dancers accommodating the movement to their weakness. Frequently a woman will be seen to join the circle with an infant upon her back and dance with the others, but should she show the least sign of approaching excitement watchful friends lead her away that no harm may come to the child. Dogs are driven off from the neighbourhood of the circle lest they should run against any of those who have fallen into a trance and thus awaken them. The dancers themselves are careful not to disturb the trance subjects while their souls are in the spirit world. Full Indian dress is worn, with buckskin, paint, and feathers, but among the Sioux the women discarded the belts ornamented with discs of German silver, because the metal had come from the white man. Among the southern tribes, on the contrary, hats are sometimes worn in the dance, although this was not considered in strict accordance with the doctrine.

No drum, rattle, or other musical instrument is used in the dance, excepting sometimes by an individual dancer in imitation of a trance vision. In this respect particularly the Ghost dance differs from every other Indian dance. Neither are any fires built within the circle, so far as known, with any tribe excepting the Walapai. The northern Cheyenne, however, built four fires in a peculiar fashion outside of the circle, as already described. With most tribes the dance was performed around a tree or pole planted in the centre and variously decorated. In the southern plains, however, only the Kiowa seem ever to have followed this method, they sometimes dancing around a cedar tree. On breaking the circle at the end of the dance the performers shook their blankets or shawls in the air, with the idea of driving away all evil influences. On later instructions from the messiah all then went down to bathe in the stream, the men in one place and the women in another, before going to their tipis. The idea of washing away evil things, spiritual as well as earthly, by bathing in running water is too natural and universal to need comment. . . .

The most important feature of the Ghost dance, and the secret of the trances, is hypnotism. . . . Immediately on coming among the Arapaho and Cheyenne in 1890, I heard numerous stories of wonderful things that occurred in the Ghost dance—how people died, went to heaven and came back again, and how they talked with dead friends and brought back messages from the other world. Quite a number who had thus 'died' were mentioned and their adventures in the spirit land were related with great particularity of detail, but as most of the testimony came from white men, none of whom had seen the dance for themselves, I preserved the scientific attitude of scepticism. So far as could be ascertained, none of the intelligent people of the agency had thought the subject sufficiently worthy of serious consideration to learn whether the reports were true or false. On talking with the Indians I found them unanimous in their statements as to the visions, until I began to think there might be something in it.

The first clue to the explanation came from the statement of his own experience in the trance, given by Paul Boynton, a particularly bright Carlisle student, who acted as my interpreter. His brother had died some time before, and as Paul was anxious to see and talk with him, which the new doctrine taught was possible, he attended the next Ghost dance, and putting his hands upon the head of Sitting Bull, according to the regular formula, asked him to help him see his dead brother. Paul is of an inquiring disposition, and, besides his natural longing to meet his brother again, was actuated, as he himself said, by a desire to try 'every Indian trick.' He then told how Sitting Bull had hypnotized him with the eagle feather and the motion of his hands, until he fell unconscious and did really see his brother, but awoke just as he was about to speak to him, probably because one of the dancers had accidentally brushed against him as he lay on the ground. He embodied his experience in a song which was afterward sung in the dance. From his account it seemed almost certain that the secret was hypnotism.

James Mooney, *The Ghost-Dance Religion and the Sioux Outbreak of 1890*, Fourteenth Annual Report, part 2, Bureau of American Ethnology (Washington, D.C., 1896), pp. 920-3

196. JOHN FRUM: A MILLENARIAN MOVEMENT IN TANNA, NEW HEBRIDES

Millenarian tendencies had been noted just before the turn of the century, when there had been rumours that Jesus would descend and lead the Christians to Heaven while Tanna and the pagans were consumed by fire. But the first important signs of native unrest did not become apparent until much later. In early 1940, there were signs of disturbance, exacerbated no doubt by a fall in copra prices. Meetings were held from which Whites were excluded, as were women. These meetings were to receive the message of one John Frum (spelt sometimes Jonfrum), described as a 'mysterious little man with bleached hair, high-pitched voice and clad in a coat with shining buttons.' He used 'ingenious stage-management . . . appearing at night, in the faint light of a fire, before men under the influence of kava.' John Frum issued pacific moral injunctions against idleness, encouraged communal gardening and co-operation, and advocated dancing and kava-drinking. He had no anti-White message at first and prophesied on traditional lines.

The prophet was regarded as the representative or earthly manifestation of Karaperamun, god of the island's highest mountain, Mount Tukosmeru. Karaperamun now appeared as John Frum, who was to be hidden from the Whites and from women.

John Frum prophesied the occurrence of a cataclysm in which Tanna would become flat, the volcanic mountains would fall and fill the river-beds to form fertile plains, and Tanna would be joined to the neighbouring islands of Eromanga and Aneityum to form a new island. Then John Frum would reveal himself, bringing in a reign of bliss, the natives would get back their youth, and there would be no sickness; there would be no need to care for gardens, trees or pigs. The Whites would go; John Frum would set up schools to replace mission schools, and would pay chiefs and teachers.

Only one difficulty prevented the immediate attainment of this happy state—the presence of the Whites, who had to be expelled first. The use of European money was also to cease. A corollary was the restoration of many ancient customs prohibited by the missionaries; kava-drinking above all, and also dancing, polygyny, etc. Immigrants from other islands were to be sent home.

This was not simply a programme of 'regression.' Only some of the ancient customs were to be revived, and they were customs banned by the missions. And the future envisaged was not the restoration of primitive tribalism and hand-agriculture, but a new life with 'all the material riches of the Europeans' accruing to the natives. John Frum would provide all the money needed.

Natives now started a veritable orgy of spending in European stores in order to get rid of the Europeans' money, which was to be replaced by John Frum's with a coconut stamped on it. Some even hurled their long-hoarded savings into the sea, believing that 'when there would be no money left on the island the White traders would have to depart, as no possible outlet would be found for their activity.' Lavish feasts were also held to use up food. There was thus no puritan or medieval-European 'asceticism' in these general joyful expectations of plenty. Rather, solidarity between rich and poor alike was expressed in this orgy of consumption, since, existing wealth was meaningless in the light of the prodigious riches to come. Friday, the day on which the millenium was expected, became a holy day, whilst on Saturday dances and kava-drinking took place. 'A certain licence accompanied the festivals,' Guiart remarks. We may be sure that this represents some socially-recognized breaking of existing conventions.

The movement was organized through messengers known as 'ropes of John Frum.' The enthusiasts broke away from the existing Christian villages which the missions had set up under Christian chiefs, and broke up into small family units living in 'primitive shelters,' or else joined pagan groups in the interior. This development, though formally the opposite of Santoese domestic communism, symbolizes the same basic social fact: a break with the mission-controlled villages and the old pattern of group life.

The first John Frum wave in April 1940 occasioned little alarm, but the revival of the movement in May 1941 created considerable perturbation. Large amounts of money were suddenly brought in by natives. Even gold sovereigns, which had not been seen since 1912 when they were paid to the chiefs who accepted the authority of the Government, appeared; this perhaps symbolized renunciation of the agreement. Some natives came in with over £100 in cash; cows and pigs were killed, kava drunk, and there was all-night dancing at the Green Point villages on the west coast where the movement had its centre. The Presbyterian missions, on Sunday the eleventh of May, found their services unattended. One of the most influencial chiefs had given the order to abandon the mission and their schools. Dominican services were equally neglected.

After a lapse of a week, Nicol [the British Agent] visited Green Point, only to find it empty except for a few women and children. He summoned twenty police reinforcements from Vila and, with the aid of one of the chiefs, arrested the John Frum leaders. A menacing crowd followed him shouting 'Hold firm for John Frum !'

In the trial, it transpired that John Frum was a native named Manehivi in his mid-thirtes. He was illiterate (though he pretended to read), and refused to say where he had obtained his gold-buttoned coat. Manehivi was sentenced to three years' internment, and five years' exile from Tanna; nine others received a year's imprisonment, Nicol had Manehivi tied to a tree and exposed as an imposter for a day, and made five chiefs sign a statement asserting that they renounced John Frum, and fined him £100.

The movement still flourished in spite of repression. December 1941 was the significant date of the next major outbreak. News of Pearl Harbour had percolated through even to the natives of Tanna, though the defeat was credited to the Germans, who were going to win. Because of growing anti-British feeling, Nicol had twenty men arrested and sent to Vila, and recommended the establishment of a permanent police force.

Meanwhile the John Frum leaders in Vila were active. Manehivi was not the real John Frum, people said; the latter was still at large. Missionaries intercepted messages written from Vila by a second John Frum, a Tama police-boy, Joe Nalpin, and addressed to a west coast chief and two other men. They contained a new theme: John Frum was King of America, or would send his son to America to seek the King, or his son was coming from America, or his sons were to seek John Frum in America. Mount Tukosmeru would be 'covered by invisible planes belonging to John Frum.' Nalpin actually helped to direct the new phase from gaol, where he was serving a nine months' sentence.

In January, Australian Cataline flyingboats on patrol were the probable origin of the rumour that three sons of John Frum—Isaac, Jacob and Lastuan (Last-One?)—had landed by plane on the other side of the island from Green Point. 'Junketings' were going on night and day, as it was believed that John Frum's advent was imminent. The appearance of the first Americans and of numerous planes added fuel to the flames. . . .

As the Americans moved in to meet the Japanese threat, the news of their arrival swept the islands. A man was arrested for saying that Mount Tukomeru was 'full of soldiers'; it would open on the Day, and the soldiers would fight for John Frum. But the most astounding piece of information was the news that many of these U.S. troops were *black!* It was prophesied that large numbers of black Americans were coming to rule over the natives. Their dollars would become the new money; they would release the prisoners, and pay wages.

Consequently, the Americans met with a splendid response when they set out to hire native labour. The movement now revived on Tanna, and kava-drinking and dancing were the order of the day, especially on the east coast; the missions were still boycotted. More arrests were made, and the prisoners sent to Vila, where many were allowed to work for the U.S. Air Force. . . .

In October, Nicol returned. His arrival precipitated a new John Frum demonstration which was broken up by the police. Natives armed with guns and clubs resisted arrest and reinforcements were summoned. A new leader in the north of the island, Neloaig (Nelawihang), proclaimed himself John Frum, King of America and of Tanna. He organized an armed force which conscripted labour for the construction of an aerodrome which the Americans had told him to build for American Liberator planes bringing goods from John Frum's father. Those who refused to work would be bombed by planes. This pressed labour was resisted by a few natives who were wounded. The District Agent, under the pretence of demanding a ship to evacuate him from the island, radioed for help. He arrested Neloaig when the latter visited him at his office.

The arrest of Neloaig produced demands for his release. The supporters of John Frum, undaunted, went on feverishly building the airstrip, and a band of Neloaig's followers even attempted to liberate their leader from gaol. The police reinforcements, with two U.S. officers, were quickly despatched to the John Frum airstrip. There they found 200 men at work, surrounded by others with guns. After the latter was disarmed, an American officer spoke to the natives, trying to persuade them of their folly. This was backed up by a demonstration of the power of a tommy-gun turned on a John Frum poster pinned to a nearby tree. Many fled in panic; the police then burned down a John Frum hut and took forty-six prisoners. Neloaig received two years, ten others one year, and the rest three months. Later Neloaig escaped from gaol and hid in the bush on Efate for three years before he gave himself up. In April 1948 he was committed to a lunatic asylum. His wife was detained at Vila, but the people of north Tanna still paid homage to her.

Though illiterate, Neloaig had pretended to read and had started his own schools. When the missionaries at Lenakel tried to restart classes in 1943, only fifty children out of a total population of 2,500 attended. Dances and kava-drinking still flourished, and villages were allowed to fall into untidiness. John Frumism still flourished. Pagans, too, provided recruits; pagan leaders had long attempted to play off Government against mission, Neloaig's father among them.

Peter Worsley, *The Trumpet Shall Sound: A Study of 'Cargo' Cults in Melanesia* (London: MacGibbon & Kee, 1957), pp. 153-9

197. A MESSIANIC NAKED CULT IN SANTO, NEW HEBRIDES

Some time about 1944 or 1945 a curious wave of feeling which we shall call the Naked Cult in imitation of the Santo bushmen themselves, passed over the bush communities of central Santo (i.e., Espiritu Santo). They refer to the followers of the Cult as the *malamala* (naked) folk. . . .

Our trek of 1948 has put a very different complexion on the whole movement. We found that the further we penetrated inland in a westerly direction the more we discovered the people to be affected. We passed through quite a number of villages where the people were openly practising the Cult, and had greatly modified their traditional heathen ways. We even met a measure of hostility—which is signficant in trying to analyse the character of the driving force behind the movement.

It is not easy to judge of the approximate numbers of active followers, but I should estimate it at not less than 500. This represents a proportion of about one-third of the heathen population of those parts of Santo which are affected. Although we called at villages with more than 100 of these followers in them (all told) we did not really penetrate far enough into the western highlands to get to the hearts of the movement. What follows here is, however, the testimony of native chiefs who were intimidated into brief participation in the Cult, or who managed to resist its emissaries when they visited their villages. . . .

Last year all that I could get, in reply to enquiries, was the fact that a man called Tieka (English—Jack) was the moving influence behind the Cult. When I asked where he lived I was vaguely told 'on top'; which is pidgin for 'further inland.' This year I got more information about him. He lives on the Bierai river on the eastern slopes of Tava Masana and has two villages about six miles apart, called Naku and Lori. He is a young man, whom I judge, from inquiry, to be between thirty-five and forty. He has not, so far as my informants knew, ever worked for whites but some of his people have done so, in the past. He is married to two wives (but one informant says only one).

The war was already well towards its close when he started the Cult by sending about thirty of his men—from villages near to his own —on a crusade through the villages of inland Santo. Their message everywhere they went was the same:

1. Take off your loin-cloths. Women take off their leaf coverings. Take off your bead necklaces and armlets. All these things make you dirty.

2. Destroy all your property which you have taken from the white man—calico, money, implements; in addition destroy all your own bush crafts such as basket-making and mat-making. It is best to be free from these.

3. Burn down all your present houses and build on the following new plan:

(i) Two big community houses to be erected in each village—one for the men to sleep in at night; and another for the women to sleep in at night. No cohabitation of families at night.

(ii) Build a large kitchen with each community house. No cooking is to be done in the community houses.

4. All food is to be cooked in the *morning*. No night cooking.

5. Do not work for the white man.

6. Destroy all animals in your villages: dogs, cats, pigs, etc.

7. It also appears that they were promised that soon 'America' would come; they would receive everything good; they would never die; they would live for ever.

8. A common language, called 'Maman,' was adopted among all Cult followers even though the villages represent widely separated language groups.

9. Many old taboos have been scrapped; the prohibition on marriage within the totem-group; the segregation period after childbirth; the necessity for buying brides; the burial custom has been changed so that now the corpse is exposed on a wooden platform in the bush (as on parts of Malekula) instead of being buried in the floor of the deceased person's house (as is the tradition in central Santo).

Not every village fell for this. The basic thing was the taking-off of the loin-cloth. In three different villages we were given an interesting account of what actually ensued when the intimidation partly arrived. They were strong enough to overawe the average bush community of twenty to forty souls, and the fact that they repeated their visits showed some determination to force their viewpoint.

J. Graham Miller, 'Naked Cult in Central West Santo,' *The Journal of the Polynesian Society*, vol. 57, (1948), pp. 330-41; quotation from pp. 330-2

Specialists of the Sacred: From Medicine Men to Mystics and Founders of Religions

A. SHAMANS AND MEDICINE MEN

Shamanism is a religious phenomenon characteristic of Siberian and Ural-Altaic peoples. The word 'shaman' is of Tungus origin (saman) and it has passed, by way of Russian, into European scientific terminology. But shamanism, although its most complete expression is found in the Arctic and central Asian regions, must not be considered as limited to those countries. It is encountered, for example, in southeast Asia, Oceania, and among many North American aboriginal tribes. A distinction is to be made, however, between the religions dominated by a shamanistic ideology and by shamanistic techniques (as is the case with Siberian and Indonesian religions) and those in which shamanism constitutes rather a secondary phenomenon.

The shaman is medicine man, priest, and psychopompos; that is to say, he cures sickness, he directs the communal sacrifices, and he escorts the souls of the dead to the other world. He is able to do all this by virtue of his techniques of ecstasy, i.e., by his power to leave his body at will. In Siberia and in northeast Asia a person becomes a shaman by hereditary transmission of the shamanistic profession or by spontaneous vocation or 'election.' More rarely a person can become a shaman by his own decision or upon request of the clan, but the self-made shamans are regarded as weaker than those who inherit the profession or who are 'elected' by the supernatural beings. In North America, on the other hand, the voluntary 'quest' for the powers constitutes the principal method. No matter how the selection takes place, a shaman is recognized as such only following a series of initiatory trials after receiving instruction from qualified masters.

In North and Central Asia as a rule the trials take place during an indefinite period of time during which the future shaman is sick and stays in his tent or wanders in the wilderness, behaving in such an eccentric way that it could be mistaken for madness. Several authors went so far as to explain Arctic and Siberian shamanism as the ritualized expression of a psychomental disease, especially of Arctic hysteria. But the 'chosen' one becomes a shaman only if he can interpret his pathological crisis as a religious experience and succeeds in curing himself. The serious crises that sometimes accompany the 'election' of the future shaman are to be regarded as initiatory trials. Every initiation involves the symbolic death and resurrection of the neophyte. In the dreams and hallucinations of the future shaman may be found the classical pattern of the initiation: he is tortured by demons, his body is cut in pieces, he descends to the nether world or ascends to heaven and is finally resuscitated. That is to say, he acquires a new mode of being, which allows him to have relations with the supernatural worlds. The shaman is now enabled to 'see' the spirits, and he himself behaves like a spirit; he is able to leave his body and to travel in ecstasy in all cosmic regions. However, the ecstatic experience alone is not sufficient to make a shaman. The neophyte must be instructed by masters in the religious traditions of the tribe, and he is taught to recognize the various diseases and to cure them.

Among certain Siberian peoples the consecration of the shaman is a public event. Among the Buriats, for example, the neophyte climbs a birch, a symbol of the world tree, and in doing this he is thought to ascend to heaven. The ascension to heaven is one of the specific characteristics of Siberian and central Asian shamanism. At the occasion of the horse sacrifice, the Altaic shaman ascends to heaven in ecstasy in order to offer to the celestial god the soul of the sacrificed horse. He realizes this ascension by climbing the birch trunk, which has nine notches, each symbolizing a specific heaven.

The most important function of the shaman is healing. Since sickness is thought of as a loss of the soul, the shaman has to find out first whether the soul of the sick man has strayed far from the village or has been stolen by demons and is imprisoned in the other world. In the former case the healing is not too difficult: the shaman captures the soul and reintegrates it in the body of the sick person. In the latter case he has to descend to the nether world, and this is a complicated and dangerous enterprise. Equally stirring is the voyage of the shaman to the other world to escort the soul of the deceased to its new abode; the shaman narrates to those present all the vicissitudes of the voyage as it takes place.

198. THE MAKING OF A MEDICINE MAN: WIRADJURI TRIBE (SOUTHEAST AUSTRALIA)

My father is Yibai-dthulin. When I was a small boy he took me into the bush to train me to be a Wulla-mullung. He placed two large quartz crystals against my breast, and they vanished into me. I do not know how they went, but I felt them going through me like warmth. This was to make me clever and able to bring things up. He also gave me some things like quartz crystals in water. They looked like ice and the water tasted sweet. After that I used to see things that my mother could not see. When out with her I would say, 'What is out there like men walking?' She used to say, 'Child, there is nothing.' These were the *jir* (ghosts) which I began to see.

When I was about ten years old, I was taken to the Burbung[1] and saw what the old men could bring out of themselves; and when my tooth was out the old men chased me with the *wallungs*[2] in their mouths, shouting, '*Ngai, Ngai*,' and moving their hands towards me. I went into the bush for a time, and while there my old father came out to me. He said, 'Come here to me'; and he then showed me a piece of quartz crystal in his hand, and when I looked at it he went down into the ground and I saw him come up all covered with red dust. It made me very frightened. He then said, 'Come to me,' and I went to him, and he said, 'Try and bring up a Wallung.' I did try, and brought one up. He then said, 'Come with me to this place.' I saw him standing by a hole in the ground, leading to a grave. I went inside and saw a dead man, who rubbed me all over to make me clever, and who gave me some Wallung. When we came out, my father pointed to a Gunr (tiger-snake) saying 'That is your *budjan*;[3] it is mine also.' There was a string tied to the tail of the snake, and extending to us. It was one of those strings which the doctors bring up out of themselves, rolled up together.

He took hold of it, saying, 'Let us follow him.' The tiger-snake went through several tree trunks, and let us through. Then we came to a great Currajong tree, and went through it, and after that to a tree with a great swelling round its roots. It is in such places that Dara-mulun lives. Here the Gunr went down into the ground, and we followed him, and came up inside the tree, which was hollow. There I saw a lot of little Daramuluns, the sons of Baiame. After we came out again the snake took us into a great hole in the ground in which were a number of snakes, which rubbed themselves against me, but did not hurt me, being my *Budjan*. They did this to make me a clever man, and to make me a *Wulla-mullung*. My father then said to me, 'We will go up to Baiame's camp.' He got astride of a *Mauir* (thread) and put me on another, and we held by each other's arms. At the end of the thread was Wombu, the bird of Baiame. We went through the clouds, and on the other side was the sky. We went through the place where the Doctors go through, and it kept opening and shutting very quickly. My father said that, if it touched a Doctor when he was going through, it would hurt his spirit, and when he returned home he would sicken and die. On the other side we saw Baiame sitting in his camp. He was a very great old man with a long beard. He sat with his legs under him and from his shoulders extended two great quartz crystals to the sky above him. There were also numbers of the boys of Baiame and of his people, who are birds and beasts.

Notes

1 The initiation ceremonies.
2 Quartz crystals.
3 *Budjan* is a secret personal totem.

A. W. Howitt, *The Native Tribes of South-East Australia* (London, 1904), pp. 406-8

199. A MEDICINE MAN'S INITIATION: KURNAI TRIBE (SOUTHEAST AUSTRALIA)

The Medicine Man speaks:

'When I was a big boy about getting whiskers I was at Alberton camped with my people. Bunjil-gworan was there and other old men. I had some dreams about my father, and I dreamed three times about the same thing. The first and the second time, he came with his brother and a lot of other old men, and dressed me up with lyre-bird's feathers round my head. The second time they were all rubbed over with Naial (red ochre), and had Bridda-briddas on. The third time they tied a cord made of whale's sinews round my neck and waist, and swung me by it and carried me through the air over the sea at Corner Inlet, and set me down at Yiruk [Wilson's Promontory]. It was at the front of a big rock like the front of a house. I noticed that there was something like an opening to the rock. My father tied something over my eyes and led me inside. I knew this because I heard the rocks make a sound as of knocking behind me. Then he uncovered my eyes, and I found that I was in a place as bright as day, and all the old men were round about. My father showed me a lot of shining bright things, like glass, on the walls, and told me to take some. I took one and held it tight in my hand. When we went out again my father taught me how to make these things go into my legs, and how I could pull them out again. He also taught me how to throw them at people. After that, he and the other old men carried me back to the camp and put me on the top of a big tree. He said, "Shout out loud and tell them that you are come back." I did this, and I heard the people in the camp waking up, and the women beginning to beat their rugs for me to come down, because now I was a Mulla-mullung. Then I woke up and found that I was lying along the limb of a tree. The old men came out with firesticks, and when they reached the tree, I was down, and standing by it with the thing my father had given me in my hand. It was like glass, and we call it Kiin. I told the old men all about it, and they said that I was a doctor. From that time I could pull things out of people, and I could throw the Kiin like light in the evening at people, saying to it Blappan (go!). I have caught several in that way. After some years I took to drinking, and then I lost my Kiin and all my power, and have never been able to do anything since. I used to keep it in a bag made of the skin of a ring-tail opossum, in a hole of a tree. One night I dreamed that I was sleeping in the camp, and my wife threw some kruk [menstrual blood] at me, and after that my Kiin went out of my bag. I do not know where. I have slept under the tree where I left it, thinking that my power might come back, but I have never found the Kiin, and I never dream any more about it.'

A. W. Howitt, The Native Tribes of South-East Australia (London, 1904), pp. 408-10

200. THE INITIATION OF A BINBINGA MEDICINE MAN (CENTRAL AUSTRALIA)

The Binbinga hold that medicine men are consecrated by the spirits Mundadji and Munkaningi (father and son). The magician Kurkutji told how, entering a cave one day, he came upon the old Mundadji, who caught him by the neck and killed him.

Mundadji cut him [Kurkutji] open, right down the middle line, took out all of his insides and exchanged them for those of himself, which he placed in the body of Kurkutji. At the same time he put a number of sacred stones in his body. After it was all over the younger spirit, Munkaninji, came up and restored him to life, told him that he was now a medicine man, and showed him how to extract bones and other forms of evil magic out of men. Then he took him away up into the sky and brought him down to earth close to his own camp, where he heard the natives mourning for him, thinking that he was dead. For a long time he remained in a more or less dazed condition, but gradually he recovered and the natives knew that he had been made into a medicine man. When he operates the spirit Munkaninji is supposed to be near at hand watching him, unseen of course by ordinary people. When taking a bone out, an operation usually conducted under the cover of darkness, Kurkutji first of all sucks very hard at the stomach of the patient and removes a certain amount of blood. Then he makes passes over the body, punches, pounds and sucks, until at last the bone comes out and is then immediately, before it can be seen by the onlookers, thrown in the direction of the spot at which Munkaninji is sitting down quietly watching. Kurkutji then tells the natives that he must go and ask Munkaninji if he will be so kind as to allow him, Kurkutji, to show the bone to them, and permission having been granted, he goes to the spot at which he has, presumably, previously deposited one, and returns with it.

B. Spencer and F. J. Gillen, *The Northern Tribes of Central Australia* (London, 1904), pp. 487-8

201. THE INITIATION OF AN AUSTRALIAN MEDICINE MAN: UNMATJERA TRIBE (CENTRAL AUSTRALIA)

Just as in the case of northern Asiatic or American shamanism, in Australia too one becomes a shaman in three ways: by inheriting the profession, by call or election, or by personal quest. But whatever way he has taken, a candidate is not recognized as a medicine man until he has been accepted by a certain number of medicine men or been taught by some of them, and, above all, after a more or less laborious initiation. In the majority of instances, the initiation consists in an ecstatic experience, during which the candidate undergoes certain operations performed by mythical Beings, and undertakes ascents to Heaven or descents to the subterranean World. (Cf. M. Eliade, Shamanism: Archaic Techniques of Ecstasy [New York: Bollingen Series LXXVI, *1964], pp. 45 ff.)*

428

Shamans and Medicine Men

Following are the words of Ilpailurkna, a famous magician of the Unmatjera tribe, as reported by Spencer and Gillen.

When he was made into a medicine man, a very old doctor came one day and threw some of his *atnongara* stones[1] at him with a spear-thrower. Some hit him on the chest, others went right through his head, from ear to ear, killing him. The old man then cut out all his insides, intestines, liver, heart, lungs—everything in fact, and left him lying all night long on the ground. In the morning the old man came and looked at him and placed some atnongara stones inside his body and in his arms and legs, and covered his face with leaves. Then he sang over him until his body was all swollen up. When this was so he provided him with a complete set of new inside parts, placed a lot more *atnongara* stones in him, and patted him on the head, which caused him to jump up alive. The old medicine man then made him drink water and eat meat containing *atnongara* stones. When he awoke he had no idea as to where he was, and said, 'Tju, tju, tju'—'I think I am lost.' But when he looked round he saw the old medicine man standing beside him, and the old man said, 'No, you are not lost; I killed you a long time ago.' Ipailurkna had completely forgotten who he was and all about his past life. After a time the old man led him back to his camp and showed it to him, and told him that the woman there was his lubra, for he had forgotten all about her. His coming back this way and his strange behaviour at once showed the other natives that he had been made into a medicine man.

Note

1 These *atnongara* stones are small crystalline structures which every medicine man is supposed to be able to produce at will from his body, through which it is believed that they are distributed. In fact it is the possession of these stones which gives his virtue to the medicine man.

B. Spencer and J. Gillen, *The Northern Tribes of Central Australia* (London, 1904), pp. 480-1

202. HOW LEBID BECAME A SHAMAN (KWAKIUTL INDIAN)

'Lebid had been sick for a long time,' said the one who told the tale. 'For three winters he had been sick abed and he was just bones. It was real mid-winter and it was very cold. . . .

Specialists of the Sacred

[*After Lebid had died, his body was wrapped in blankets and laid at the far end of the village site. It was too cold to bury him.*]

Night came. When all the Gwasila lay down, a wolf began to howl behind Gwekelis. It was not long that one wolf was howling, when many wolves began to howl. They gathered at the place where Lebid was wrapped up on the rock. Then the Gwasila guessed that the wolves were going to eat him. Probably the wolves were sitting around the dead one, for they were all howling together. The Gwasila did not sleep for they were afraid. When it was near daylight the wolves were still howling, many. Then all the Gwasila heard Lebid singing his sacred song among the howling wolves and they knew that Lebid had now become a shaman. When day came in the morning the many howling wolves went back into the woods, and Lebid went also into the woods, singing his sacred song. He kept together with the wolves. Now the sisters of Lebid and his late wife, Maxmaklodalaogwa were running about in vain, looking at the place where he had been wrapped up on the rocks. They saw the tracks of Lebid who had been walking among the wolves. Now the Gwasila were asked by the shamans of the Nakwaxdax that they should all go and wash, with the women and children in the morning and in the evening, so that they should all purify themselves. Then they did so. Now he had been away for two days, then he was heard singing his sacred song inland from the village of Gwekelis. . . . When day came in the morning the Gwasila went to get fire wood. Lebid's wife and daughters and sisters cleared Lebid's house so as to make it clean. . . . All the Gwasila were purified. When it got dark in the evening he came singing his sacred song. They could hardly hear him in the woods. Now at once the Gwasila started a fire in the middle of the house. All the men and the women who were not menstruating and the children went in. Now the shaman of Nakwaxdax told all those who went into the house to carry batons. When they were all holding the batons the shaman of the Nakwaxdax, whose name was Making-alive (Qwequlagila) told the Gwasila to beat fast time together. They all beat time together. For a long time they were beating time. Then they stopped beating time and the sound of Lebid came nearer as he was singing his sacred song behind the village. Three times the Gwasila beat fast time. Then the sound of the sacred song came to the front of the house. Again they beat fast time; the fourth time Lebid came into the door, really naked, only hemlock was wound around his head and hemlock was wound around his neck. He was really lean. The Gwasila beat fast time. He went around the fire in the middle of the house still singing his sacred song. These are the words of his sacred song:

1. I was taken away far inland to the edge of the world by the magical power of heaven, the treasure, ha, wo, ho.
2. Only then was I cured by it, when it was really thrown into me, the past life bringer of Naualakume, the treasure, ha, wo, ho.
3. I come to cure with this means of healing of Naualakume, the treasure. Therefore I shall be a life bringer, ha, wo, ho.
4. I come with the water of life given into my hand by Naualakume, the means of bringing to life, the treasures, ha, wo, ho.

Then Lebid sang his other sacred song:

1. He turns to the right side, poor one, this supernatural one, so as to obtain the supernatural one, ha, wo, ho.
2. Let the supernatural one be the life bringer, the supernatural one, ha, wo, ho.
3. That the poor one may come to life with the lifebringer of Naualakume, ha, wo, ho.
4. The poor one comes, this supernatural one, to give protection with the means of giving protection of Naualakume, ha, wo, ho.

After he had danced, all those went out of the house who were not shamans. Then the real shamans of the Gwasila sat down in the house. Lebid sat down on a new mat in the rear of the house. All had their faces blackened, the old shamans, and all had on their heads the shamans' head rings of red cedar bark. All had around their necks shamans' neck rings of red cedar bark. Then they all lay on their backs and there was no talking. Only Lebid, the new shaman who had come back to life was sitting on his new mat. . . . They were waiting for all the men and women who were not shamans to go to sleep. When they thought they were all asleep they sent four real shamans to go and look into the doors of all the houses of the Gwasila to see whether they were not barred. Then they found that all the doors of the houses were barred. They came into the meeting house of the shamans and they barred the door of the house. Then they sat down. They were sitting quite a while in silence, then arose one of the shamans, whose name was Bringing-Life-out-of-the-Woods (Qulamol-telsila). He spoke and said, 'Indeed, friends, indeed, this is the way it is done, for we came here to this house, that Lebid, who is newly added to us, our friend, may tell us how it was brought right down to this shaman. Now he will tell us why he came to life again. He will keep nothing hidden from his friends.' Thus he said and sat down.

Then Lebid spoke and said, 'Indeed, friends, you fellow-shamans, thus you must do to a new shaman. Now I will tell you, friends. I was very sick, and a man came into the place where I was lying in another house and invited me to follow him. Immediately I arose and followed him. Then I saw that my body was still lying here groaning. We had not gone far into the woods before we arrived at a house and we entered the house. I was asked by the other man to go and sit down in the rear of the house. When I had seated myself, then spoke the man who was sitting on the right hand side of the doorway of the house. He said, "Go on, speak, Naualakume, he who is the great shaman, of what we shall do to him who has come and is sitting among us," said he. Then a man came who had tied around his head a thick ring of red cedar bark and a thin neck ring of cedar bark. He spoke and said, "Our friend will not stay away, for I wish him to go back to his tribe so that he may become a great shaman and that he may cure the sick in his tribe. And he shall have my name for his name. Now he shall have the name Naualakume. And I shall take out the breath from his body so that I may keep it," said he as he went out of the door of the house. It was not long before he came back. He spoke and said, "Now his body is dead on the ground, for I am holding his breath, which is the owner of the soul of our friend. Now I shall give him my shamanistic power," said he and he vomited a quartz crystal. Then all the men beat fast time on the boards. He sang his sacred song as he threw the quartz crystal into the lower part of my sternum, and now I had become a shaman after this as it was getting daylight. Then Naualakume said, "Again we shall beat time for our friend tonight," said he. Then all the wolves who were now men, went to sleep. In the evening they all went into the house, for Lebid was still sitting there. And when the men were all in, Naualakume came singing his sacred song outside the house. Then he came in. There was a wolf carved out of yew wood on the back of his rattle. He went around the fire in the middle of the house. After he had gone around four times he sat down near me and pressed (on top) with his right hand on the top of my head, and he put down his rattle and pressed with his left hand the top of my head; then he sang his sacred song. Then he pressed down with both his hands on both sides of my head, down to the lower end of my trunk.' And so he brought his hands together, put his hands flat together, and raised his hands throwing up the sickness of Lebid. After he had done this four times he finished. . . . Then all the men put on their wolf masks and when they were

all dressed, they all went out of the door of the house, and also Lebid.
As soon as all had come out, all the wolves howled. Lebid walked
among them, and also Naualakume kept the breath of the body of
Lebid, for only his soul had been taken by the wolves. Now they went
to where the body of Lepid was wrapped on the rocks. As soon as
they had arrived there, Naualakume asked the other wolves to take
off the mat that had been spread over the body and the wrapping of
two pairs of blankets. As soon as all had been taken off, Naualakume
went there. He called Lebid to sit by his side. He took his breath and
drew it into his mouth. Then he blew it into the mouth of Lebid's
body. He asked the many wolves that they all should lick the body
of the dead one. 'Now my soul was sitting on the ground and was just
watching the wolves as they were licking the body. They had not
been licking it long when it began to breathe. Then Naualakume
pressed both his hands on the head of the soul of Lebid and he pressed
down with both his hands on his head. Then the soul began to get
small and it was of the size of a large fly. He took it and put it on
top of the head of Lebid and blew it in. Immediately Lebid arose and
sang his sacred song. Now he was singing among the wolves who
were howling and they went back into the woods and went home to
their house. Lebid also followed them. Again the wolves beat time at
night. And now they really taught Lebid who had now the name
Naualakume how to treat the sick. He said that he could not throw
(sickness); and other Gwasila say that he could throw (sickness), he
who had now the name Naualakume. Then said the great shaman of
the wolves [i.e. Lebid] that he would always make him dream "about
what I should do when curing really sick ones, as he was giving instructions to me." Now I came into this house where we are sitting now.'

Franz Boas, *The Religion of the Kwakiutl Indians*, vol.
II (New York: Columbia University Press, 1930), pp.
46-50

203. THE 'ENLIGHTENMENT' OF THE ESKIMO
SHAMANS (IGLULIK)

*During the shaman's initiation, the master helps the disciple to obtain
'lighting' or 'enlightenment,' angákok, also called quamanek.*

The *angákoq* consists 'of a mysterious light which the shaman suddenly feels in his body, inside his head, within the brain, an inexplicable searchlight, a luminous fire, which enables him to see in the dark, both literally and metaphorically speaking, for he can now, even with closed eyes, see through darkness and perceive things and coming events which are hidden from others: thus they look into the future and into the secrets of others.'

The candidate obtains this mystical light after long hours of waiting, sitting on a bench in his hut and invoking the spirits. When he experiences it for the first time 'it is as if the house in which he is suddenly rises; he sees far ahead of him, through mountains, exactly as if the earth were one great plain, and his eyes could reach to the end of the earth. Nothing is hidden from him any longer; not only can he see things far, far away, but he can also discover souls, stolen souls, which are either kept concealed in far, strange lands or have been taken up or down to the Land of the Dead.'

> M. Eliade, *Shamanism: Archaic Techniques of Ecstasy*
> (New York: Bollingen Series LXXVI, 1964), pp. 60-1,
> based on and quoted from Knud Rasmussen, *Intel-
> lectual Culture of the Iglulik Eskimos* (Copenhagen,
> 1930), pp. 112-13

204. AN INITIATORY DREAM OF A SAMOYED SHAMAN

A. A. Popov gives the following account concerning a shaman of the Avam Samoyed. Sick with smallpox, the future shaman remained unconscious for three days and so nearly dead that on the third day he was almost buried. His initiation took place during the time. He remembered having been carried into the middle of a sea. There he heard his Sickness (that is, smallpox) speak, saying to him: 'From the Lords of the Water you will receive the gift of shamanizing. Your name as a shaman will be *Huottarie* (Diver).' Then the Sickness troubled the water of the sea. The candidate came out and climbed a mountain. There he met a naked woman and began to suckle at her breast. The woman, who was probably the Lady of the Water, said to him: 'You are my child; that is why I let you suckle at my breast. You will meet many hardships and be greatly wearied.' The husband of the Lady of the Water, the Lord of the Underworld, then gave him two guides, an ermine and a mouse, to lead him to the underworld. When they came to a high place, the guides showed him seven tents with torn roofs. He entered the first and there found the inhabitants of the underworld and the men of the Great Sickness (syphilis). These men tore out his heart and threw it into a pot. In other tents he met the Lord of Madness and the Lords of all the nervous disorders, as well as the evil shamans. Thus he learned the various diseases that torment mankind.

Still preceded by his guides, the candidate then came to the Land of the Shamanesses, who strengthened his throat and his voice. He was then carried to the shores of the Nine Seas. In the middle of one of them was an island, and in the middle of the island a young birch tree rose to the sky. It was the Tree of the Lord of the Earth. Beside it grew nine herbs, the ancestors of all the plants on earth. The tree was surrounded by seas, and in each of these swam a species of bird with its young. There were several kinds of ducks, a swan, and a sparrow-hawk. The candidate visited all these seas; some of them were salt, others so hot he could not go near the shore. After visiting the seas, the candidate raised his head and, in the top of the tree, saw men of various nations: Tavgi Samoyed, Russians, Dolgan, Yakut, and Tungus. He heard voices: 'It has been decided that you shall have a drum (that is, the body of a drum) from the branches of this tree.' He began to fly with the birds of the seas. As he left the shore, the Lord of the Tree called to him: 'My branch has just fallen; take it and make a drum of it that will serve you all your life.' The branch had three forks, and the Lord of the Tree bade him make three drums from it, to be kept by three women, each drum being for a special ceremony— the first for shamanizing women in childbirth, the second for curing the sick, the third for finding men lost in the snow.

The Lord of the Tree also gave branches to all the men who were in the top of the tree. But, appearing from the tree up to the chest in human form, he added: 'One branch only I give not to the Shamans, for I keep it for the rest of mankind. They can make dwellings from it and so use it for their needs. I am the Tree that gives life to all men.' Clasping the branch, the candidate was ready to resume his flight when again he heard a human voice, this time revealing to him the medicinal virtues of the seven plants and giving him certain instructions concerning the art of shamanizing. But, the voice added, he must marry three women (which, in fact, he later did by marrying three orphan girls whom he had cured of smallpox).

And after that he came to an endless sea and there he found trees and seven stones. The stones spoke to him one after the other. The first had teeth like bears' teeth and a basket-shaped cavity, and it revealed to him that it was the earth's holding stone; it pressed on the fields with its weight, so that they should not be carried away by the wind. The second served to melt iron. He remained with these stones for seven days and so learned how they could be of use to men.

Then his two guides, the ermine and the mouse, led him to a high, rounded mountain. He saw an opening before him and entered a bright cave, covered with mirrors, in the middle of which there was something like a fire. He saw two women, naked but covered with hair, like reindeer. Then he saw that there was no fire burning but that the light came from above, through an opening. One of the women told him that she was pregnant and would give birth to two reindeer; one would be the sacrificial animal of the Dolgan and Evenki, the other that of the Tavgi. She also gave him a hair, which was to be useful to him when he shamanized for reindeer. The other woman also gave birth to two reindeer, symbols of the animals that would aid man in all his works and also supply his food. The cave had two openings, toward the north and toward the south; through each of them the young women sent a reindeer to serve the forest people (Dolgan and Evenki). The second woman, too, gave him a hair. When he shamanizes, he mentally turns toward the cave.

Then the candidate came to a desert and saw a distant mountain. After three days' travel he reached it, entered an opening, and came upon a naked man working a bellows. On the fire was a cauldron 'as big as half the earth.' The naked man saw him and caught him with a huge pair of tongs. The novice had time to think, 'I am dead!' The man cut off his head, chopped his body into bits, and put everything in the cauldron. There he boiled his body for three years. There were also three anvils, and the naked man forged the candidate's head on the third, which was the one on which the best shamans were forged. Then he threw the head into one of three pots that stood there, the one in which the water was the coldest. He now revealed to the candidate that, when he was called to cure someone, if the water in the ritual pot was very hot, it would be useless to shamanize, for the man was already lost; if the water was warm, he was sick but would recover; cold water denoted a healthy man.

The blacksmith then fished the candidate's bones out of a river, in which they were floating, put them together, and covered them with flesh again. He counted them and told him that he had three too many; he was therefore to procure three shaman's costumes. He forged his head and taught him how to read the letters that are inside it. He changed his eyes; and that is why, when he shamanizes, he does not see with his bodily eyes but with these mystical eyes. He pierced his ears, making him able to understand the language of plants. Then the candidate found himself on the summit of a mountain, and finally he woke in the yurt, among the family. Now he can sing and shamanize indefinitely, without ever growing tired.

M. Eliade, *Shamanism: Archaic Techniques of Ecstasy* (New York: Bollingen Series, LXXVI, 1964), pp. 38-42; translating and summarizing A. A. Popov, *Tavgytsy. Materialy po etnografii avamskikh i vedeyevskikh tavgytsev* (Moscow and Leningrad, 1936, pp. 84 ff.

205. MYSTICAL MARRIAGE OF A SIBERIAN (GOLDI) SHAMAN

The Goldi clearly distinguish between the tutelary spirit (ayami), *which chooses the shaman, and the helping spirits* (syvén), *which are subordinate to it and are granted to the shaman by the* ayami *itself. According to Sternberg the Goldi explain the relations between the shaman and his* ayami *by a complex sexual emotion. Here is the report of a Goldi shaman.*

Once I was asleep on my sick-bed, when a spirit approached me. It was a very beautiful woman. Her figure was very slight, she was no more than half an arshin (71 cm.) tall. Her face and attire were quite as those of one of our Gold women. Her hair fell down to her shoulders in short black tresses. Other shamans say they have had the vision of a woman with one half of her face black, and the other half red. She said: 'I am the "ayami" of your ancestors, the Shamans. I taught them shamaning. Now I am going to teach you. The old shamans have died off, and there is no one to heal people. You are to become a shaman.'

Next she said: 'I love you, I have no husband now, you will be my husband and I shall be a wife unto you. I shall give you assistant spirits. You are to heal with their aid, and I shall teach and help you myself. Food will come to us from the people.'

I felt dismayed and tried to resist. Then she said, 'If you will not obey me, so much the worse for you. I shall kill you.'

She has been coming to me ever since, and I sleep with her as with my own wife, but we have no children. She lives quite by herself without any relatives in a hut, on a mountain, but she often changes her abode. . . . Sometimes she comes under the aspect of an old woman, and sometimes under that of a wolf, so she is terrible to look at. Sometimes she comes as a winged tiger. I mount it and she takes me to show me different countries. I have seen mountains, where only old men and women live, and villages, where you see nothing but young people, men and women: they look like Golds and speak Goldish, sometimes those people are turned into tigers.

Now my ayami does not come to me as frequently as before. Formerly, when teaching me, she used to come every night. She has given me three assistants—the 'jarga' (the panther), the 'doonto' (the bear) and the 'amba' (the tiger). They come to me in my dreams, and appear whenever I summon them while shamaning. If one of them refuses to come, the 'ayami' makes them obey, but, they say, there are some who do not obey even the 'ayami.' When I am shamaning, the 'ayami' and the assistant spirits are possessing me; whether big or small, they penetrate me, as smoke or vapour would. When the 'ayami' is within me, it is she who speaks through my mouth, and she does everything herself. When I am eating the 'sukdu' (the offerings) and drinking pig's blood (the blood of pigs is drunk by shamans alone, lay people are forbidden to touch it), it is not I who eat and drink, it is my 'ayami' alone.

M. Eliade, *Shamanism, op. cit.*, pp. 72-3, quoting Leo Sternberg, 'Divine Election in Primitive Religion' (1924), pp. 476 *ff*. Cf. *Shamanism*, pp. 421 *ff*., for autobiographies of South-Indian Savara shamans and shamanesses, whose marriages to spirits are in striking parallel to the documents collected by Sternberg

206. A POWERFUL SHAMAN (APACHE)

'My white brother,' an Apache shaman told Reagan, 'you probably will not believe it, but I am all powerful. I will never die. If you shoot me, the bullet will not enter my flesh, or if it enters it will not hurt me. . . . If you stick a knife in my throat, thrusting it upwards, it will come out through my skull at the top of my head. . . . I am all powerful. If I wish to kill any one, all I need to do is to thrust out my hand and touch him and he dies. My power is like that of a god.'

Albert B. Reagan, *Notes on the Indians of the Fort Apache Region*, American Museum of Natural History, Anthropological Papers, XXXV, part V (1930), p. 391

207. SOUL-LOSS AND MAGICAL CURE (APINAYÉ OF EASTERN BRAZIL)

When Meōka's little daughter had the dysentery at the age of six months, Ka'ta'm (according to the story he told me [Nimiendaju]) effected the cure as follows:

'I was walking toward the brook with Iré [Ka'ta'm's wife] to bathe. Passing the plantation, I heard a little child crying. "Do you hear something?" I asked Iré. "No," she said, "I do not hear anything." But I myself heard it distinctly and thought, "Who could this be?" Letting my wife wait, I walked toward the sound. There I saw the shadow of Meōka's daughter sitting in the plantation, right in the middle of the shadows of the white watermelons, which had already been harvested and eaten, and of which only the stalks remained. For that is the very time when the shadows of all cultivated fruits dance in the plantation. They had taken the little one to the farm and allowed her to taste of the watermelon, and the shadows of the fruits had retained the child's.

'I went to her mother and told her not to cry, for her little child would recover. I advised her to wait for several days, then the shadow would spontaneously return. The grandmother thought the girl's body was already too feeble and would not be able to hold out. Then I went thither and fetched back the shadow.'

I [Nimiendaju] witnessed this last-mentioned procedure. Ka'ta'm had himself painted in the afternoon and went down to the plantation by himself. The mother sat down in front of the door, with her sick child on her lap, surrounded by a number of women. After a while Ka'ta'm slowly returned from the farm. He was carrying the child's invisible shadow-soul precisely as though its body were in his arms. When the women caught sight of him, they burst out crying aloud, imagining how the little patient's shadow had spent days all alone, surrounded only by the shadows of the fruits, without fire and shelter. Ka'ta'm put the shadow on the child's head and stroked it down her body.

Some time before this accident Ka'ta'm had similarly cured his own child, whose shadow had been captured by the fruits' shadows; and several days later he discovered the shadow of another sick child at the bathing-hole in the creek and brought it back. Its mother had taken the child along to bathe, and while so engaged it had lost its shadow in the water. Ka'ta'm heard and learned the pitiful song of the lost soul, and sang it in the evening for the women, who at first wept, then took up the tune.

Curt Nimiendaju, *The Apinayé* (Washington, D.C., 1937), pp. 144-5

208. A YUKAGIR SHAMANISTIC SÉANCE (NORTHEASTERN SIBERIA)

The shaman sits down on the ground and, after drumming for a long time, invokes his tutelary spirits, imitating the voices of animals. 'My fore-father, my ancestors, stand near by me. In order to help me, stand near me, my girl spirits. . . .' He begins drumming again and, rising with the help of his assistant, goes to the door and breathes deeply, in order to swallow the souls of his ancestors and other spirits that he has summoned. 'The soul of the patient, it seems, has travelled along the road to the Kingdom of Shadows,' the spirits of the ancestors announce through the shaman's voice. The patient's relatives encourage him: 'Be strong, strength do not spare!' The shaman drops his drum and lies face down on the reindeer skin; he remains motionless, the sign that he has left his body and is journeying in the beyond. He has descended into the Kingdom of Shadows 'through the drum as through a lake.' For a long time he does not stir and all those present patiently wait for him to wake. His return is indicated by a few motions. Two girls massage his legs, and, now completely restored to himself, he replaces the soul in the patient's body. He then goes to the door and dismisses his helping spirits.

At the end of such a séance the shaman gave Jochelson the particulars of his ecstatic journey. Accompanied by his helping spirits, he had followed the road that leads to the Kingdom of Shadows. He came to a little house and found a dog that began to bark. An old woman, who guarded the road, came out of the house and asked him if he had come for ever or for a short time. The shaman did not answer her; instead, he addressed his spirits: 'Do not listen to the old woman's words, walk on without stopping.' Soon they came to a stream. There was a boat, and on the other bank the shaman saw tents and men. Still accompanied by his spirits, he entered the boat and crossed the stream. He met the souls of the patient's dead relatives, and entering their tent, found the patient's soul there too. As the relatives refused to give it to him, he had to take it by force. To carry it safely back to the earth, he inhaled the patient's soul and stuffed his ears to prevent it from escaping.

M. Eliade, *Shamanism*, op. cit., pp. 247-8; summarizing Waldemar Jochelson, *The Yukaghir and the Yukaghirize Tungus* (Leiden and New York, 1924-6) pp. 196-9

209. AN ESKIMO SHAMAN DESCENDS TO THE BOTTOM OF THE OCEAN

Descent to the abode of Takánakapsâluk, the Mother of the Sea Beasts, is undertaken at an individual's request, sometimes because of illness, sometimes because of bad luck in hunting; only in the latter case is the shaman paid. But it sometimes happens that no game at all is to be found and the village is threatened with famine; then all the villagers gather in the house where the seance is held, and the shaman's ecstatic journey is made in the name of the whole community. Those present must unfasten their belts and laces, and remain silent, their eyes closed. For a time the shaman breathes deeply, in silence, before summoning his helping spirits. When they come the shaman begins to murmur, 'The way is made ready for me; the way opens before me!' and the audience answer in chorus: 'Let it be so.' And now the earth opens, and the shaman struggles for a long time with unknown forces before he finally cries: 'Now the way is open.' And the audience exclaim in chorus: 'Let the way be open before him; let there be way for him.' Now, first under the bed, then farther away, under the passage, is heard the cry, 'Halala-he-he-he, Halala-he-he-he'; this is the sign that the shaman has set off. The cry grows more and more distant until it is no longer heard.

During this time the audience sing in chorus, their eyes closed, and sometimes the shaman's clothes—which he had taken off before the séance—come to life and start flying about the house, over the heads of the audience. The signs and deep breathing of people long dead are also heard; they are dead shamans come to help their colleague on his dangerous journey. And their signs and their breathing seem to come from very far under water, as if they were sea beasts.

Reaching the bottom of the ocean, the shaman finds himself facing three great stones in constant motion barring his road; he must pass between them at the risk of being crushed. (This is another image of the 'strait gate' that forbids access to the plane of higher being to anyone but an 'initiate,' that is, one who can act like a 'spirit.') Successfully passing this obstacle, the shaman follows a path and comes to a sort of bay; on a hill stands Takánakapsâluk's house, made of stone and with a narrow entrance. The shaman hears sea beasts blowing and panting, but does not see them. A dog with bared teeth defends the entrance; the dog is dangerous to anyone who is afraid of it, but the shaman passes over it, and it understands that he is a very powerful magician. (All these obstacles oppose the ordinary shaman, but the really powerful shamans reach the bottom of the sea and the presence of Takánakapsâluk directly, by diving beneath their tent or snow hut, as if slipping through a tube.)

If the goddess is angry with men, a great wall rises before her house. And the shaman has to knock it down with his shoulder. Others say that Takánakapsâluk's house has no roof, so that the goddess can better see men's acts from her place by the fire. All kinds of marine animals are gathered in a pool to the right of the fire, and their cries and breathings are heard. The goddess's hair hangs down over her face and she is dirty and slovenly; this is the effect of men's sins, which have almost made her ill. The shaman must approach her, take her by the shoulder, and comb her hair (for the goddess has no fingers with which to comb herself). Before he can do this, there is another obstacle to be overcome; Takánakapsâluk's father, taking him for a dead man on the way to the land of shades, tries to seize him, but the shaman cries, 'I am flesh and blood!' and succeeds in passing.

As he combs Takánakapsâluk's hair, the shaman tells her that men have no more seal. And the goddess answers in the spirit language: 'The secret miscarriages of the women and breaches of taboo in eating boiled meat bar the way for the animals.' The shaman now has to summon all his powers to appease her anger; finally she opens the pool and sets the animals free. The audience hears their movements at the bottom of the sea, and soon afterward the shaman's gasping breathing, as if he were emerging from the surface of the water. A long silence follows. Finally the shaman speaks: 'I have something to say.' All answer. 'Let us hear, let us hear.' And the shaman, in the spirit language, demands the confession of sins. One after another, all confess their miscarriages or their breaches of taboos and repent.

M. Eliade, *Shamanism*, op. cit., pp. 294-6; summarizing Knud Rasmussen, *Intellectual Culture of the Iglulik Eskimos* (Copenhagen, 1930), pp. 124 ff.

210. BLACK MAGIC: AN AUSTRALIAN SORCERER
(ARNHEM LAND)

One of the most noted killers in the southeastern Murngin country was Laindjura, who had destroyed many victims by black magic. As an individual he was not very different from the ordinary man in the tribe, although possibly a bit more alert. He was a good hunter as well as an excellent wood carver, and had several wives and a number of children. There was nothing sinister, peculiar, or psychopathic about him; he was perfectly normal in all of his behaviour. Among his own people the attitudes were no different toward him than toward any other man in the clan. It was extremely difficult, however, to obtain Laindjura's confidence to the point where he would talk about his activities as a sorcerer. Although he and I were on very friendly terms, it was not until my second field trip into the area that he gave me long accounts of his various killings.

It is impossible definitely to evaluate how far Laindjura and other killers believed the case histories which they gave me. There was no doubt in my own thinking that Laindjura believed a great part of them. Since he was constantly credited and blamed by friends and enemies for certain deaths, he may at first have taken an attitude 'as if' he had done these things and ultimately have come to believe that he had actually performed the operations he claimed he had. A black sorcerer who is credited with many killings has a rather difficult time among the people surrounding his own group, and under most circumstances it is more difficult and unpleasant to be so classed than as an ordinary man; hence a man would not practise such complete duplicity as these stories might indicate unless the setting were extraordinary from our point of view.

The Killing of Bom-li-tjir-i-li's wife—'All of us were camping at Marunga Island. We were looking for oysters. This woman I was about to kill was hunting for lilies that day, for the other women had gone another way to search for oysters. I carried a hatchet with me and watched her. The woman gathered her lily bulbs, then left the swamp, went back on to the sandy land and lay down in the shade. She covered herself with paper bark to keep warm because she had been in the lily pond and felt cold. Only her head came out from the bark. She could not see.

'I sneaked up and hit her between the eyes with the head of a tomahawk. She kicked and tried to raise up but she couldn't. Her eyes turned up like she was dead. I picked her up under the arms and dragged her to a mangrove jungle and laid her down. She was a young girl.

'I split a mangrove stick from off a tree and sharpened it. I took some djel-kurk (orchid bulb) first and got it ready. I did not have my spear-thrower with me, so I took the handle off my tomahawk and jabbed about the skin on her Mount of Venus which was attached to her vagina and pushed it back. I pushed the skin up to her navel.

'Her large intestine protruded as though it were red calico. I covered my arm with orchid juice. I covered the killing stick with it too. I put the stick in the palm of my hand so that I could push the point upward with my thumb. When she inhaled, I pushed my arm in a little. When she exhaled I stopped. Little by little I got my hand inside her. Finally I touched her heart. I pushed the killing stick with my thumb up over the palm, which pressed the stick against my fingers, into her heart. She had a very large heart and I had to push harder than usual.

'I pulled the stick out. I stood back of her and held her up with her breasts in my hands. She was in a squatting position.

'Her heart's blood ran out into the paper-bark basket I had left to catch it in. It ran slower and slower and then stopped. I laid her down and took the blood away. I hid it. I came back and broke a nest of green ants off a tree. I laid it near her. I put the live ants on her skin. I did not squeeze them, for I was in a hurry because I was afraid her relatives would come looking for her. The skin, when bitten by the ants, moved by itself downward from her navel and covered her bones over her Mount of Venus.

'I then took some dry mud from an old lily pond. I put my sweat on the mud and warmed it over the fire. I put it against her to heal the wound so that no trace would be left of what I had done. I was careful none of her pubic hair would be left inside her vagina so that it would be felt by her husband or seen by the women. I kept up the mud applications until the vagina looked as it did before. I put blood and sweat in the mud and warmed it and put it inside the uterus. I did this again, using the mud, sweat, and blood. I did this six or eight times. The inside now was like it was before.

'I turned her over. Her large intestine stuck out several feet. I shook some green ants on it. It went in some little way. I shook some more on, and a little receded. I shook some more, and all of it went in. Everything was all right now. There was no trace of the wound.

'I took the tomahawk handle which had her heart's blood on it

I whirled it around her head. Her head moved slowly. I whirled it again. She moved some more. The spirit that belonged to that dead woman went into my heart then. I felt it go in. I whirled the stick again and she gasped for breath. I jumped over her and straightened her toes and fingers. She blew some breath out of her mouth, and was all right.

'It was noontime. I said to her, "You go eat some lilies." The woman got up and walked away. She went round another way. I said to that woman "You will live two days. One day you will be happy, the next day you will be sick." The woman went to the place where I had found her. She went to sleep. I took her blood and went away. The other women came from where they had been gathering oysters. They were laughing and talking. They awakened the girl. She picked up her lily bulbs and went to the camp with the women.

'The next day she walked around and played, laughed, talked and made fun and gathered a lot of oysters and lilies. She came back to camp that night. She brought the things she had gathered into camp. She laid down and died that night.'

W. Lloyd Warner, A Black Civilization (New York, 1958), pp. 188-90

B. HOLY PERSONAGES

211. AN AFRICAN DIVINE KING (NYASALAND)

Mbande is a hill on the plain of north Nyasaland with a commanding view of the surrounding country and well suited to defence. The west side is precipitous and below the scarp edge there used to be a marsh; to the north the hill is protected by a wide reach of the Lukulu river. It is a sacred place and for many generations was the home of the 'divine king,' the Kyungu. Like the Lwembe he was the living representative of a hero, and was selected by a group of hereditary nobles from one of two related lineages, the office alternating (if suitable candidates were available) between the two. They sought a big man, one who had begotten children and whose sons were already married, not a young man for, the nobles said, 'young men always want war, and destroy the country.' He must be a man of wisdom (*gwa mahala*) and generous in feeding his people.

The Kyungu's life was governed by taboos even more rigorous than those surrounding the Lwembe. He must not fall ill, or suffer a wound, or even scratch himself and bleed a little, for his ill health, or his blood falling on the earth would bring sickness to the whole country. 'Men feared when Kyungu's blood fell on the ground, they said, "It is his life." ' 'If he had a headache his wives (if they loved him) told him not to mention it, they hid his illness; but if the nobles entered and found him ill they dug the grave and put him in it, saying, "He is the ruler (*ntemi*), it's taboo for him to be ill." Then he thought: "Perhaps it is so" (with a gesture of resignation).'

Great precautions were taken to preserve his health. He lived in a separate house with his powerful medicines. His food was prepared by boys below the age of puberty lest a menstruating woman, or a youth who had laid with a woman, should touch it and so bring sickness upon him; and his numerous wives were immured in the royal enclosure—a great stockade—and jealously guarded, for any infidelity on their part was thought to make their husband ill, and with him the whole country.

When the Kyungu did fall ill he was smothered by the nobles who

446

lived around him at Mbande, and buried in great secrecy, with a score
or more of living persons—slaves—in the grave beneath him, and one
or two wives and the sons of commoners above. And in the midst of
all this slaughter the nobles brought a sheep to look into the grave
that the dead Kyungu might be gentle (*mololo*) like the sheep!

The living Kyungu was thought to create food and rain, and his
breath and the growing parts of his body—his hair and nails and the
constantly replaced mucus of his nose—were believed to be magically
connected with the fertility of the Ngonde plain. When he was killed
his nostrils were stopped so that he was buried 'with the breath in his
body'; while portions of his hair and nails and of his nasal mucus were
taken from him beforehand and buried by the nobles of Ngonde in the
black mud near the river. This was 'to defend the country against
hunger,' to close up the land, to keep it rich and heavy and fertile as
it was when he himself lived in it.'

His death was kept secret—a relatively easy matter since he lived
in seclusion—and one of the nobles (Ngosi) impersonated him wearing his clothes. After a month or two when the nobles had decided
whom to choose as the new Kyungu, the luckless man was summoned
to Mbande: 'Your father calls you.' Then he came with his companions and entered the house to make obeisance; they seized him and
put the sacred cloth on him and set him on the stool 'Kisumbi,' saying,
'Thou Kyungu, thou art he,' and he became the Kyungu. Then they
struck the drum, Mwenekelwa, and everyone knew that the Kyungu
had died and another had been installed. Men feared greatly to be
seized as the Kyungu, just as they feared to be seized as the Lwembe,
because the life of a divine king was short. Ngonde historians quote
a number of cases of sons of the Kyungu who fled to escape being
set on the stool; once they had sat on it they dared not flee lest they
die. . . .

In time of drought the nobles of Ngonde would go to a diviner to
inquire who it was who was angry; they would mention all the names
of the sacred groves of the Kyungus in turn and he would tell them
that it was so and so. They would inform the living Kyungu and he
would give them a bull or a sheep, together with some beer—they
would take one of the pots of beer from his own house, brought by
his people as tribute. And he would give them some flour and cloths
also. Then they would go with them into the grove and build a
miniature hut. Next they would kill the beast and hang some of the
meat up on a tree—the rest they would eat later outside the grove.
Then they would tear up the cloths and fasten some of the pieces on

to the hut in the grove—an action they would explain as 'giving him cloths.' And finally, they would pour out some of the beer and the flour. Nearly always, in time of drought, they would thus build a hut and make an offering in the grove of the Kyungu whom the diviner had mentioned.

But occasionally, if one of the chiefs had recently insulted the Kyungu, they concluded that it was the living Kyungu himself who was angry. They would go to a diviner and mention all the names of the dead Kyungus, but he would refuse to accept any of them: 'No . . . no.' And at length he would tell them that it was the living Kyungu who was angry because so-and-so had insulted him. Then there would be no sacrifice at the grove at all, but the nobles of Ngonde would go to the one who had insulted the Kyungu and charge him with it, asking him what he meant by thus killing them all, would not the whole land starve? And so the wrongdoer would take a cow to the Kyungu who, thereupon, would address the nobles of Ngonde, saying: 'If it was my anger which brought the drought then it will rain (for I am no longer angry). But if the rain does not come then it cannot have been my anger, it must have been someone [of the dead Kyungus] whom you forgot to ask about it.' 'And if, after that, the rain came soon, then it was not likely that anyone would insult the Kyungu again.'. . .

Thus to insult Kyungu was not only treasonable, it was blasphemous, and the whole plain was believed to be cursed with drought or disease in reply. An 'insult' might mean any neglect of the obligations of the chiefs and nobles and commoners of the plain to their lord. . . .

The majesty (*ubusisya*) of the Kyungu was cultivated in a variety of ways. He smeared himself with ointment made from lion fat, and his bed was built up with elephant tusks and lion pelts. He was enthroned on the sacred iron stool called Kisumbi, he had a spear, Kamisa, and Mulima, a porous piece of iron 'like a mouth organ' used to make rain, all handed down from the first Kyungu. His zebra tails, set with medicines in horn handles, were waved in war and during prayer to the shades, and he also had the famous drum on which the blood of a child was poured.

But the majority of their subjects only worshipped from afar in fear and trembling. At Mbande no ordinary commoner was ever conducted into the sacred enclosure, but only the territorial nobles and the elder chiefs, and they only occasionally; while when the Kyungu travelled through his country all men save the very oldest fled from his approach. Even in speech fearful circumlocutions were used to refer to his journeying—'The country is on the move'—'the great hill is moving'—'the mystery is coming.' It was taboo both for the old men who stayed to see him, and for those who entered the sacred enclosure, ever to greet him in the usual way. Falling down and clapping the hands was the only greeting for the Kyungu.

From the wives of the Kyungu also men fled in terror, fearing lest they be compromised and thrown over the cliff of Mbande, and this both added to the atmosphere of terror which surrounded him and was an expression of it.

Monica Wilson, *Communal Rituals of the Nyakyusa* (London: Oxford University Press, 1959), pp. 40-6

212. THE DEATH OF ORPHEUS

Orpheus, the son of Oiagros, and of Kalliope, one of the Muses, was king of the Macedonians and of the country of the Odrysai. He was skilled in music and particularly in the lyre; and, since the Thracians and Macedonians are a music-loving race, he won great favour with the people thereby. The manner of his death was this: he was torn in pieces by the women of Thrace and Macedonia because he would not allow them to take part in his religious rites, or it may be on other pretexts too; for they do say that after the misfortune that he had with his own wife he became the foe of the whole sex. Now on appointed days a throng of armed Thracians and Macedonians used to gather at Leibethra, and come together in a certain building which was large and well adapted for the performance of initiatory rites; and when they entered to take part in the rites, they laid down their arms before the door. The women watched for this, and, filled with anger at the slight put upon them, seized the arms, slew those who attempted to overpower them, and rending Orpheus limb from limb, cast the scattered remains into the sea. No requital was exacted from the women, and a plague afflicted the land. Seeking relief from their troubles, the inhabitants received an oracle, saying that if they should find the head of Orpheus and bury it, then they should have rest. After much difficulty they found it through a fisherman at the mouth of the river Meles. It was still singing, and in no way harmed by the sea, nor had it suffered any of the other dreadful changes which the fates of man bring upon dead bodies. Even after so long time it was fresh, and blooming with the blood of life. So they took it and buried it under a great mound, and fenced off a precinct around it, which at first was a hero-shrine but later grew to be a temple. That is, it is honoured with sacrifices and all the other tributes which are paid to gods. No woman may ever set foot within it.

Konon, *Fab.* 45, printed in Kern, *Testt.* 39 and 115. Translated by W. K. C. Guthrie, in Guthrie, *Orpheus and the Greek Religion* (London: Methuen, 1935), pp. 61-2

See also nos. 147, 148-54

213. EMPEDOCLES GOES AMONG MEN AS AN IMMORTAL

Friends who dwell throughout the great town of golden Acragas, up by the citadel, men mindful of good deeds, unversed in wickedness, havens of respect for strangers, all hail. I go about among you all an immortal god, mortal no more, honoured as is my due and crowned with garlands and verdant wreaths. Whenever I enter the prosperous townships with these my followers, men and women both, I am revered; they follow me in countless numbers, asking where lies the path to gain, some seeking prophecies, while others, for many a day stabbed by grievous pains, beg to hear the word that heals all manner of illness. (*Frag.* 112.)

But at the end they come among men on earth as prophets, bards, doctors and princes; and thence they arise as gods mighty in honour, sharing with the other immortals their hearth and their table, without part in human sorrows or weariness. (*Frags.* 146, 147.)

Translation by G. S. Kirk and J. E. Raven, *The Presocratic Philosophers* (Cambridge, Eng.: Cambridge University Press, 1957), p. 354

214. THE FLAMEN DIALIS AND HIS WIFE

(Aulus Gellius, 'Attic Nights,' X, 15)

A great many ceremonies are imposed upon the Flamen Dialis [the priest of Jupiter], and also many restraints [*castus multiplices*, taboos], about which we read in the books *On The Public Priesthoods* and also in Book I of Fabius Pictor's work. Among them I recall the following: it is forbidden [*religio est*] the Flamen Dialis to ride a horse; it is likewise forbidden him to view the 'classes arrayed' outside the pomerium [the sacred boundary of Rome], i.e., armed and in battle order; hence only rarely is the Flamen Dialis made a consul, since [the conduct of] wars is entrusted to the consuls; it is likewise unlawful [*fas numquam est*] for him ever to take an oath by Jupiter [*jurare dialem*]; it is likewise unlawful for him to wear a ring, unless it is cut through and empty [i.e., without a jewel?]. It is also unlawful to carry out fire from the *flaminia*, i.e., the Flamen Dialis' dwelling, except for a sacral purpose; if a prisoner in chains enters the house he must be released and the chains must be carried up through the *impluvium* [the opening in the roof above the *atrium* or living room] onto the roof tiles and dropped down from there into the street. He must have no knot in his head gear or in his girdle or in any other part of his attire. If anyone is being led away to be flogged and falls at his feet as a suppliant, it is unlawful [*piaculum est*] to flog him that day. The hair of the [Flamen] Dialis is not to be cut, except by a free man. It is customary [*mos est*] for the Flamen neither to touch nor even to name a female goat, or raw (?) meat, ivy, or beans.

He must not walk under a trellis for vines. The feet of the bed on which he lies must have a thin coating of clay, and he must not be away from this bed for three successive nights, nor is it lawful for anyone else to sleep in this bed. At the foot of his bed there must be a box containing a little pile of sacrificial cakes. The nail trimmings and hair of the Dialis must be buried in the ground beneath a healthy tree. Every day is a holy day [*feriatus est*] for the Dialis. He must not go outdoors [*sub divo*] without a head-covering—this is now allowed indoors, but only recently by decree of the pontiffs, as Masurius Sabinus has stated; it is also said that some of the other ceremonies have been remitted and cancelled.

It is not lawful for him to touch bread made of fermented meal [i.e., with yeast]. His underwear ['inner tunic'] he does not take off except in covered places, lest he appear nude under the open sky, which is the same as under the eye of Jove. No one else outranks him in the seating at a banquet except the *Rex sacrificulus*. If he loses his his wife, he must resign his office. His marriage cannot be dissolved [*dirimi ius non est*] except by death. He never enters a burying ground, he never touches a corpse. He is, however, permitted [*non est religio*] to attend a funeral.

Almost the same ceremonial rules belong to the Flaminica Dialis [i.e., his wife]. They say that she observes certain other and different ones, for example, that she wears a dyed gown, and that she has a twig from a fruitful tree tucked in her veil [which was worn over her head at a sacrifice], and that it is forbidden [*religiosum est*] for her to ascend more than three rungs of a ladder (except what the Greeks call 'ladders' [steps?]) and even that when she goes to the Argei [when twenty-four puppets were thrown into the Tiber] she must neither comb her head nor arrange her hair.

Translation by Frederick G. Grant, in his *Ancient Roman Religion*, Library of Religion paperbook series (New York, 1957), pp. 30-2

215. AUGUSTUS—'FATHER OF HIS OWN FATHERLAND' (HALICARNASSUS)

Following is an inscription found at Halicarnassus, dating from some time after 2 B.C.

Since the eternal and deathless nature of the universe has perfected its immense benefits to mankind in granting us as a supreme benefit, for our happiness and welfare, Caesar Augustus, Father of his own Fatherland, divine Rome, Zeus Paternal, and Saviour of the whole human race, in whom Providence has not only fulfilled but even surpassed the prayers of all men: land and sea are at peace, cities flourish under the reign of law, in mutual harmony and prosperity; each is at the very acme of fortune and abounding in wealth; all mankind is filled with glad hopes for the future, and with contentment over the present; [it is fitting to honour the god] with public games and with statues, with sacrifices and with hymns.

Translation by Frederick C. Grant, *Ancient Roman Religion*, op. cit., pp. 174-5

216. NICHIREN PROCLAIMS HIMSELF THE 'BODHISATTVA OF SUPERB ACTION

Nichiren (1222-82) was a Japanese religious teacher.

I, Nichiren, a man born in the ages of the Latter Law, have nearly achieved the task of pioneership in propagating the Perfect Truth, the task assigned to the Bodhisattva of Superb Action (Vishishtachāritra). The eternal Buddhahood of Shākyamuni, as he revealed himself in the chapter on Life-duration, in accordance with his primeval entity; the Buddha Prabhūtaratna, who appeared in the Heavenly Shrine, in the chapter on its appearance, and who represents Buddhahood in the manifestation of its efficacy; the Saints [bodhisattvas] who sprang out of the earth, as made known in the chapter on the Issuing out of Earth —in revealing all these three, I have done the work of the pioneer [among those who perpetuate the Truth]; too high an honour, indeed, for me, a common mortal ! . . .

I, Nichiren, am the one who takes the lead of the Saints-out-of-Earth. Then may I not be one of them? If I, Nichiren, am one of them, why may not all my disciples and followers be their kinsmen? The Scripture says 'If one preaches to anybody the Lotus of Truth, even just one clause of it, he is, know ye, the messenger of the Tathāgata, the one commissioned by the Tathāgata, and the one who does the work of the Tathāgata.' How, then, can I be anybody else than this one? . . .

By all means, awaken faith by seizing this opportunity ! Live your life through as the one who embodies the Truth, and go on without hesitation as a kinsman of Nichiren ! If you are one in faith with Nichiren, you are one of the Saints-out-of-Earth; if you are destined to be such, how can you doubt that you are the disciple of the Lord Shākyamuni from all eternity? There is assurance of this in a word of Buddha, which says: 'I have always, from eternity, been instructing and quickening all these beings.' No attention should be paid to the difference between men and women among those who would propagate the Lotus of the Perfect Truth in the days of the Latter Law. To utter the Sacred Title is, indeed, the privilege of the Saints-out-of-Earth. . . .

When the Buddha Prabhūtaratna sat in the Heavenly Shrine side by side with the Tathāgata Shākyamuni, the two Buddhas lifted up the banner of the Lotus of the Perfect Truth, and declared themselves to be the Commanders [in the coming fight against vice and illusion]. How can this be a deception? Indeed, they have thereby agreed to raise us mortal beings to the rank of Buddha. I, Nichiren, was not present there in the congregation, and yet there is no reason to doubt the statements of the Scripture. Or, is it possible that I was there? Common mortal that I am, I am not well aware of the past, yet in the present I am unmistakably the one who is realizing the Lotus of Truth. Then in the future I am surely destined to participate in the communion of the Holy Place. Inferring the past from the present and the future, I should think that I must have been present at the Communion in the Sky. [The present assures the future destiny, and the future destiny is inconceivable without its cause in the past.] The present, future, and past cannot be isolated from one another. . . .

In this document, the truths most precious to me are written down. Read, and read again; read into the letters and fix them into your mind! Thus put faith in the Supreme Being, represented in a way unique in the whole world! Ever more strongly I advise you to be firm in faith, and to be under the protection of the threefold Buddhahood. March strenuously on in the ways of practice and learning! Without practice and learning the Buddhist religion is nullified. Train yourself, and also instruct others! Be convinced that practice and learning are fruits of faith! So long as, and so far as, there is power in you, preach, if it be only a phrase or a word [of the Scripture]! *Namu Myōhō-renge-kyō! Namu Myōhō-renge-kyō!* [Adoration to the Lotus of Perfect Truth.]

Masaharu Anesaki, *Nichiren, the Buddhist Prophet* (Cambridge, Mass., 1916), pp. 83-5; as quoted in Wm. Theodore de Bary (ed.), *Sources of Japanese Tradition* (New York: Columbia University Press, 1958), pp. 228-9

217. NICHIREN'S TRANSFIGURATION WHILE LIVING IN RETIREMENT

This spot among the mountains is secluded from the worldly life, and there is no human habitation in the neighbourhood—east, west, north, or south. I am now living in such a lonely hermitage; but in my bosom, in Nichiren's fleshly body, is secretly deposited the great mystery which the Lord Shākyamuni revealed on Vulture Peak, and has entrusted to me. Therefore I know that my breast is the place where all Buddhas are immersed in contemplation; that they turn the Wheel of Truth upon my tongue; that my throat is giving birth to them; and that they are attaining the Supreme Enlightenment in my mouth. This place is the abode of such a man, who is mysteriously realizing the Lotus of Truth in his life; surely such a place is no less dignified than the Paradise of Vulture Peak. As the Truth is noble, so is the man who embodies it; as the man is noble, so is the place where he resides. We read in the chapter on the 'Mysterious Power of the Tathāgata' as follows:

'Be it a forest, or at the foot of a tree, or in a monastery . . . on that spot erect a stūpa dedicated to the Tathāgata. For such a spot is to be regarded as the place where all Tathāgatas have arrived at the Supreme Perfect Enlightenment; on that spot all Tathāgatas have turned the Wheel of Truth, on that spot all Tathāgatas have entered the Great Decease.' Lo, whoever comes to this place will be purged of all sins and depravities which he has accumulated from eternity, and all his evil deeds will at once be transformed into merits and virtues.

Masaharu Anesaki, *Nichiren, the Buddhist Prophet* (Cambridge, Mass., 1916), p. 129, as quoted in Wm. Theodore de Bary (ed.), *Sources of Japanese Tradition* (New York: Columbia University Press, 1958), p. 231

See also nos. 157, 193, 246

C. FORMS OF ASCETICISM

218. THE INDIAN ASCETIC

('The Laws of Manu,' VI, 33-65)

33. But having thus passed the third part of (a man's natural term of) life in the forest, he may live as an ascetic during the fourth part of his existence, after abandoning all attachments to worldly objects.[1]

34. He who after passing from order to order, after offering sacrifices and subduing his senses, becomes, tired with (giving) alms and offerings of food, an ascetic, gains bliss after death.

35. When he has paid the three debts, let him apply his mind to (the attainment of) final liberation; he who seeks it without having paid (his debts) sinks downwards.

36. Having studied the Vedas in accordance with the rule, having begat sons according to the sacred law, and having offered sacrifices according to his ability, he may direct his mind to (the attainment of) final liberation. . . .

41. Departing from his house fully provided with the means of purification (Pavitra),[2] let him wander about absolutely silent, and caring nothing for enjoyments that may be offered (to him).

42. Let him always wander alone, without any companion, in order to attain (final liberation), fully understanding that the solitary (man, who) neither forsakes nor is forsaken, gains his end.

43. He shall neither possess a fire, nor a dwelling, he may go to a village for his food, (he shall be) indifferent to everything, firm of purpose, mediating (and) concentrating his mind on Brahman. . . .

45. Let him not desire to die, let him not desire to live; let him wait for (his appointed) time, as a servant (waits) for the payment of his wages.

46. Let him put down his foot purified by his sight,[3] let him drink water purified by (straining with) a cloth, let him utter speech purified by truth, let him keep his heart pure.

The notes to this text are on p. 457.

47. Let him patiently bear hard words, let him not insult anybody, and let him not become anybody's enemy for the sake of this (perishable) body.

48. Against an angry man let him not in return show anger, let him bless when he is cursed, and let him not utter speech, devoid of truth, scattered at the seven gates.[4]

49. Delighting in what refers to the Soul,[5] sitting (in the postures prescribed by the Yoga), independent (of external help), entirely abstaining from sensual enjoyments, with himself for his only companion, he shall live in this world, desiring the bliss (of final liberation). . . .

60. By the restraint of his senses, by the destruction of love[6] and hatred, and by the abstention from injuring the creatures,[7] he becomes fit for immortality.

61. Let him reflect on the transmigrations of men, caused by their sinful deeds, on their falling into hell, and on the torments in the world of Yama,

62. On the separation from their dear ones, on their union with hated men, on their being overpowered by age and being tormented with diseases,

63. On the departure of the individual soul from this body and its new birth in (another) womb, and on its wanderings through ten thousand millions of existences,

64. On the infliction of pain on embodied (spirits), which is caused by demerit, and the gain of eternal bliss, which is caused by the attainment of their highest aim, (gained through) spiritual merit.

65. By deep meditations, let him recognize the subtile nature of the supreme Soul,[8] and its presence in all organisms, both the highest and the lowest.

Notes

1 Reference here is to the ideal four stages (āshramas) of the Brahman's life: student (brahmacārin), householder (grihastha), hermit or forest-dweller (vānaprastha), and finally, ascetic or mendicant (yati, bhikshu, parivrājaka, samnyāsin).

2 Construed as either his capacities after having completed three states of life, or his 'equipment' such as staff and water-pot.

3 Lest he injure any small animal, or step on something impure.

4 The seven bodily orifices?

5 Ātman.

6 Or, affection, passion (rāga).

7 Ahimsā, non-injury.

8 Brahman.

Translation by G. Bühler in *Sacred Books of the East*, XXV (Oxford, 1886), pp. 204-10

Specialists of the Sacred

219. GOTAMA BUDDHA TALKS OF HIS ASCETIC
PRACTICES

('Majjhima-nikāya,' XII *['Māha-sīhanāda-sutta'])*

Gotama Buddha is speaking to Sāriputta, one of his favourite disciples.

Aye, Sāriputta, I have lived the fourfold higher life;—I have been an
ascetic of ascetics; loathly have I been, foremost in loathliness, scrupulous have I been, foremost in scrupulosity; solitary have I been, foremost in solitude.

(i) To such a pitch of asceticism have I gone that naked was I,
flouting life's decencies, licking my hands after meals, never heeding
when folk called to me to come or to stop, never accepting food brought
to me before my rounds or cooked expressly for me, never accepting
an invitation, never receiving food direct from pot or pan or within
the threshold or among the faggots or pestles, never from (one only of)
two people messing together, never from a pregnant woman or a nurs-
ing mother or a woman *in coitu*, never from gleanings (in time of
famine) nor from where a dog is ready at hand or where (hungry) flies
congregate, never touching flesh or spirits or strong drink or brews of
grain. I have visited only one house a day and there taken only one
morsel; or I have visited but two or (up to not more than) seven
houses a day and taken at each only two or (up to not more than)
seven morsels; I have lived on a single saucer of food a day, or on two,
or (up to) seven saucers; I have had but one meal a day, or one every
two days, or (so on, up to) every seven days, or only once a fortnight,
on a rigid scale of rationing. My sole diet has been herbs gathered
green, or the grain of wild millets and paddy, or snippets of hide, or
water-plants, or the red powder round rice-grains within the husk, or
the discarded scum of rice on the boil, or the flour of oil-seeds, or grass,
or cow-dung. I have lived on wild roots and fruit, or on windfalls only.
My raiment has been of hemp or of hempen mixture, of cerements,
of rags from the dust-heap, of bark, of the black antelope's pelt either
whole or split down the middle, of grass, of strips of bark or wood, of
hair of men or animals woven into a blanket or of owl's wings. In fulfil-
ment of my vows, I have plucked out the hair of my head and the hair
of my beard, have never quitted the upright for the sitting posture,
have squatted and never risen up, moving only a-squat, have couched
on thorns, have gone down to the water punctually thrice before night-

fall to wash (away the evil within). After this wise, in divers fashions, have I lived to torment and to torture my body—to such a length in asceticism have I gone.

(ii) To such a length have I gone in loathliness that on my body I have accumulated the dirt and filth of years till it dropped off of itself—even as the rank growths of years fall away from the stump of a tinduka-tree. But never once came the thought to me to clean it off with my own hands or to get others to clean it off for me;—to such a length in loathliness have I gone.

(iii) To such a length in scrupulosity have I gone that my footsteps out and in were always attended by a mindfulness so vigilant as to awake compassion within me over even a drop of water lest I might harm tiny creatures in crevices;—to such a length have I gone in scrupulosity.

(iv) To such a length have I gone as a solitary that when my abode was in the depths of the forest, the mere glimpse of a cowherd or neatherd or grasscutter, or of a man gathering firewood or edible roots in the forest, was enough to make me dart from wood to wood, from thicket to thicket, from dale to dale, and from hill to hill,—in order that they might not see me or I them. As a deer at the sight of man darts away over hill and dale, even so did I dart away at the mere glimpse of cowherd, neatherd, or what not, in order that they might not see me or I them;—to such a length have I gone as a solitary.

When the cowherds had driven their herds forth from the byres, up I came on all fours to find a subsistence on the droppings of the young milch-cows. So long as my own dung and urine held out, on that I have subsisted. So foul a filth-eater was I.

I took up my abode in the awesome depths of the forest, depths so awesome that it was reputed that none but the passion-less could venture in without his hair standing on end. When the cold season brought chill wintry nights, then it was that, in the dark half of the months when snow was falling, I dwelt by night in the open air and in the dank thicket by day. But when there came the last broiling month of summer before the rains, I made my dwelling under the baking sun by day and in the stifling thicket by night. Then there flashed on me these verses, never till then uttered by any:

> Now scorched, now froze, in forest dread, alone,
> naked and fireless, set upon his quest,
> the hermit battles purity to win.

In a charnel ground I lay me down with charred bones for pillow.

When the cowherds' boys came along, they spat and staled upon me, pelted me with dirt and stuck bits of wood into my ears. Yet I declare that never did I let an evil mood against them arise within me.—So poised in equanimity was I.

[80] Some recluses and brahmins there are who say and hold that purity cometh by way of food, and accordingly proclaim that they live exclusively on jujube-fruits, which, in one form or other, constitute their sole meat and drink. Now I can claim to have lived on a single jujube-fruit a day. If this leads you to think that this fruit was larger in those days, you would err; for, it was precisely the same size then that it is today. When I was living on a single fruit a day, my body grew emaciated in the extreme; because I ate so little, my members, great and small, grew like the knotted joints of withered creepers; like a buffalo's hoof were my shrunken buttocks; like the twists in a rope were my spinal vertebrae; like the crazy rafters of a tumble-down roof, that start askew and aslant, were my gaunt ribs; like the starry gleams on water deep down and afar in the depths of a well, shone my gleaming eyes deep down and afar in the depths of their sockets; and as the rind of a cut gourd shrinks and shrivels in the heat, so shrank and shrivelled the scalp of my head,—and all because I ate so little. If I sought to feel my belly, it was my backbone which I found in my grasp; if I sought to feel my backbone, I found myself grasping my belly, so closely did my belly cleave to my backbone;—and all because I ate so little. If for ease of body I chafed my limbs, the hairs of my body fell away under my hand, rotted at their roots;—and all because I ate so little.

Other recluses and brahmins there are who, saying and holding that purity cometh by way of food, proclaim that they live exclusively on beans—or sesamum—or rice—as their sole meat and drink.

[81] Now I can claim to have lived on a single bean a day—on a single sesamum seed a day—or a single grain of rice a day; and [the result was still the same]. Never did this practice or these courses or these dire austerities bring me to the ennobling gifts of super-human knowledge and insight. And why?—Because none of them lead to that noble understanding which, when won, leads on to Deliverance and guides him who lives up to it onward to the utter extinction of all ill.

Translation by Lord Chalmers, *Further Dialogues of the Buddha*, I (London, 1926), pp. 53-7

220. GOTAMA BUDDHA PRACTISED THE MOST SEVERE ASCETICISM AND BECAME A MASTER IN YOGA

('Majjhima-nikāya,' XXXVI *['Mahā-saccaka-sutta']*)

Thought I then to myself:—Come, let me, with teeth clenched and with tongue pressed against my palate, by sheer force of mind restrain, coerce, and dominate my heart. And this I did, till the sweat streamed from my armpits. Just as a strong man, taking a weaker man by the head or shoulders, restrains and coerces and dominates him, even so did I, with teeth clenched and with tongue pressed against my palate, by sheer force of mind restrain, coerce, and dominate my heart, till the sweat streamed from my armpits. Resolute grew my perseverance which never quailed; there was established in me a mindfulness which knew no distraction,—though my body was sore distressed and afflicted, because I was harassed by these struggles as I painfully struggled on.— Yet even such unpleasant feelings as then arose did not take possession of my mind.

Thought I to myself:—Come, let me pursue the Ecstasy that comes from not breathing. So I stopped breathing, in or out, through mouth and nose; and then great was the noise of the air as it passed through my ear-holes, like the blast from a smith's bellows. Resolute grew my perseverance . . . did not take possession of my mind.

Thought I to myself:—Come, let me pursue further the Ecstasy that comes from not breathing. So I stopped breathing, in or out, through mouth and nose and ears; and then violent winds wracked my head, as though a strong man were boring into my skull with the point of a sword. Resolute grew my perseverance . . . did not take possession of my mind.

Thought I to myself:—Come, let me pursue still further the Ecstasy that comes from not breathing. So I kept on stopping all breathing, in or out, through mouth and nose and ears; and then violent pains attacked my head, as though a strong man had twisted a leather thong round my head. Resolute grew my perseverance . . . did not take possession of my mind.

Thought I to myself:—Come, let me go on pursuing the Ecstasy that comes from not breathing. So I kept on stopping breathing, in or out, through mouth and nose and ears; and then violent winds pierced my inwards through and through,—as though an expert butcher or his man were hacking my inwards with sharp cleavers. Resolute grew my perseverance . . . did not take possession of my mind.

Thought I to myself: --Come, let me still go on pursuing the Ecstasy that comes from not breathing. So I kept on stopping all breathing, in or out, through mouth and nose and ears; and then there was a violent burning within me,—as though two strong men, taking a weaker man by both arms, were to roast and burn him up in a fiery furnace. Resolute grew my perseverance . . . did not take possession of my mind.

At the sight of me, some gods said I was dead; others said I was not dead but dying; while others again said that I was an Arahat and that Arahats lived like that !

Thought I to myself:—Come, let me proceed to cut off food altogether. Hereupon, gods came to me begging me not so to do, or else they would feed me through the pores with heavenly essences which would keep me alive. If, thought I to myself, while I profess to be dispensing with all food whatsoever, these gods should feed me all the time through the pores with heavenly essences which keep me alive, that would be imposture on my part. So I rejected their offers, peremptorily.

Thought I to myself:—Come, let me restrict myself to little tiny morsels of food at a time, namely the liquor in which beans or vetches, peas or pulse, have been boiled. I rationed myself accordingly, and my body grew emaciated in the extreme. My members, great and small, grew like the knotted joints of withered creepers . . . (etc., as in Sutta XII) . . . rotted at their roots; and all because I ate so little.

Thought I to myself:—Of all the spasms of acute and severe pain that have been undergone through the ages past—or will be undergone through the ages to come—or are now being undergone—by recluses or brahmins, mine are pre-eminent; nor is there aught worse beyond. Yet, with all these severe austerities, I fail to transcend ordinary human limits and to rise to the heights of noblest understanding and vision. Could there be another path to Enlightenment?

A memory came to me of how once, seated in the cool shade of a rose-apple tree on the lands of my father the Shākyan, I, divested of pleasures of sense and of wrong states of mind, entered upon, and abode in, the First Ecstasy, with all its zest and satisfaction,—a state bred of inward aloofness but not divorced from observation and reflection. Could this be the path to Enlightenment? In prompt response to this memory, my consciousness told me that here lay the true path to Enlightenment.

Thought I to myself:—Am I afraid of a bliss which eschews pleasures of sense and wrong states of mind?—And my heart told me I was not afraid.

Forms of Asceticism

Thought I to myself: It is no easy matter to attain that bliss with a body so emaciated. Come, let me take some solid food, rice and junket; and this I ate accordingly.

With me at the time there were the Five Almsmen, looking for me to announce to them what truth I attained; but when I took the rice and junket, they left me in disgust, saying that luxuriousness had claimed me and that, abandoning the struggle, I had reverted to luxuriousness.

Having thus eaten solid food and regained strength, I entered on, and abode in, the First Ecstasy. –Yet, such pleasant feelings as then arose in me did not take possession of my mind; nor did they as I successively entered on, and abode in, the Second, Third, and Fourth Ecstasies.

Translation by Lord Chalmers, *Further Dialogues of the Buddha,* I (London, 1926), pp. 174-7

See also nos. 225-30, 282-9

221. JAIN DOCTRINES AND PRACTICES OF NONVIOLENCE (AHIMSĀ): THE EXAMPLE OF MAHĀVĪRA

('Akārānga-sūtra, I, 8, i.3—iv.8)

Vardhamāna Mahāvīra ('The Great Hero') was a contemporary of the Buddha. He is said to have left his home at the age of thirty and wandered for twelve years in search of salvation. At the age of forty-two he obtained enlightenment and became a 'conqueror' (jina, term from which the Jain took their name). Mahāvīra founded an order of naked monks and taught his doctrine of salvation for some thirty years. He died in 468 B.C., at the age of seventy-two, in a village near Patna.

I. 3. For a year and a month he did not leave off his robe. Since that time the Venerable One, giving up his robe, was a naked, world-relinquishing, houseless (sage).

4. Then he meditated (walking) with his eye fixed on a square space before him of the length of a man. Many people assembled, shocked at the sight; they struck him and cried.

5. Knowing (and renouncing) the female sex in mixed gathering places, he meditated, finding his way himself: I do not lead a worldly life.

6. Giving up the company of all householders whomsoever, he meditated. Asked, he gave no answer; he went and did not transgress the right path.

7. For some it is not easy (to do what he did), not to answer those who salute; he was beaten with sticks, and struck by sinful people. . . .

10. For more than a couple of years he led a religious life without using cold water; he realize.l singleness, guarded his body, had got intuition, and was calm.

11. Thoroughly knowing the earth-bodies and water-bodies and fire-bodies and wind-bodies, the lichens, seeds, and sprouts,

12. He comprehended that they are, if narrowly inspected, imbued with life, and avoided to injure them; he, the Great Hero.

13. The immovable (beings) are changed to movable ones, and the movable beings to immovable ones; beings which are born in all states become individually sinners by their actions.

14. The Venerable One understands thus: he who is under the conditions (of existenece), that fool suffers pain. Thoroughly knowing (karman), the Venerable One avoids sin.

15. The sage, perceiving the double (karman), proclaims the incomparable activity, he, knowing one; knowing the current of worldliness, the current of sinfulness, and the impulse.

16. Practising the sinless abstinence from killing, he did no acts, neither himself nor with the assistance of others; he to whom women were known as the causes of all sinful acts, he saw (the true sate of the world). . . .

III. 7. Ceasing to use the stick (i.e. cruelty) against living beings, abandoning the care of the body, the houseless (Mahāvīra), the Venerable One, endures the thorns of the villages (i.e. the abusive language of the peasants), (being) perfectly enlightened.

8. As an elephant at the head of the battle, so was Mahāvīra there victorious. Sometimes he did not reach a village there in Ladha.

9. When he who is free from desires approached the village, the inhabitants met him on the outside, and attacked him, saying, 'Get away from here.'

10. He was struck with a stick, the fist, a lance, hit with a fruit, a clod, a potsherd. Beating him again and again, many cried.

11. When he once (sat) without moving his body, they cut his flesh, tore his hair under pains, or covered him with dust.

12. Throwing him up, they let him fall, or disturbed him in his religious postures; abandoning the care of his body, the Venerable One humbled himself and bore pain, free from desire.

13. As a hero at the head of the battle is surrounded on all sides, so was there Mahāvīra. Bearing all hardships, the Venerable One, undisturbed, proceeded (on the road to Nirvāna). . . .

IV. 1. The Venerable One was able to abstain from indulgence of the flesh, though never attacked by diseases. Whether wounded or not wounded, he desired not medical treatment.

2. Purgatives and emetics, anointing of the body and bathing, shampooing and cleaning of the teeth do not behove him, after he learned (that the body is something unclean).

3. Being averse from the impressions of the senses, the Brāhmana wandered about, speaking but little. Sometimes in the cold season the Venerable One was meditating in the shade.

4. In summer he exposes himself to the heat, he sits squatting in the sun; he lives on rough (food); rice, pounded jujube, and beans.

5. Using these three, the Venerable One sustained himself eight months. Sometimes the Venerable One did not drink for half a month or even for a month.

6. Or he did not drink for more than two months, or even six months, day and night, without desire (for drink). Sometimes he ate stale food.

7. Sometimes he ate only the sixth meal, or the eighth, the tenth, the twelfth; without desires, persevering in meditation.

8. Having wisdom, Mahāvīra committed no sin himself, nor did he induce other to do so, nor did he consent to the sins of others.

Translation from Prākrit by Herman Jacobi, *Jaina Sūtra*, part I, in *Sacred Books of the East*, (Oxford, 1884), pp. 85-7

222. MILAREPA EXTOLS HIS 'FIVE COMFORTS'

Milarepa (Mi-la-ras-pa, 1040-1123), magician, yogi and poet, disciple of Mar-pa of Lho-brag (1012-97), is perhaps the most famous figure in the religious history of Tibet. His complete poetical works, Mila Gnubum, 'The Hundred Thousand Songs of Milarepa,' have been recently translated into English by Garma C. C. Chang (New York: University Books, 1962). The following selection is from Mila Khabum, the 'Biography of Milarepa,' written by a mysterious yogi, 'The mad yogi from gTsan' in the latter part of the twelfth or in the beginning of the thirteenth century.

One night, a person, believing that I possessed some wealth, came and, groping about, stealthily pried into every corner of my cave. Upon my observing this, I laughed outright, and said, 'Try if thou canst find anything by night where I have failed by daylight.' The person himself could not help laughing, too; and then he went away.

About a year after that, some hunters of Tsa, having failed to secure any game, happened to come strolling by the cave. As I was sitting in Samādhi, wearing the above triple-knotted apology for clothing, they prodded me with the ends of their bows, being curious to know whether I was a man or a *bhūta*. Seeing the state of my body and clothes, they were more inclined to believe me a *bhūta*. While they were discussing this amongst themselves, I opened my mouth and spoke, saying, 'Ye may be quite sure that I am a man.' They recognized me from seeing my teeth, and asked me whether I was Thöpaga. On my answering in the affirmative, they asked me for a loan of some food, promising to repay it handsomely. They said, 'We heard that thou hadst come once to thy home many years ago. Hast thou been here all the while?' I replied, 'Yes; but I cannot offer you any food which ye would be able to eat.' They said that whatever did for me would do for them. Then I told them to make fire and boil nettles. They did so, but as they expected something to season the soup with, such as meat, bone, marrow, or fat, I said, 'If I had that, I should then have food with palatable qualities; but I have not had that for years. Apply the nettles in place of the seasoning.' Then they asked for flour or grain to thicken the soup with. I told them if I had that, I should then have food with sustaining properties; but that I had done without that for some years, and told them to apply nettle tips instead. At last they asked for some salt, to which I again said that salt would have imparted taste to my food; but I had done without that also for years, and recommended the addition of more nettle tips in place of salt. They said, 'Living upon such food, and wearing such garments as thou hast on now, it is no wonder that thy body hath been reduced to this miserable plight. Thine appearance becometh not a man. Why, even if thou should serve as a servant, thou wouldst have a bellyful of food and warm clothing. Thou art the most pitiable and miserable person in the whole world.' I said, 'O my friends, do not say that. I am one of the most fortunate and best amongst all who have obtained the human life. I have met with Marpa the Translator, of Lhobrak, and obtained from him the Truth which conferreth Buddhahood in one lifetime; and now, having entirely given up all worldly thoughts, I am passing my life in strict asceticism and devotion in these solitudes, far away from human habitations. I am obtaining that which will avail me in Eternity. By denying myself the trivial pleasures to be derived from food, clothing, and fame, I am subduing the Enemy [Ignorance] in this very lifetime. Amongst the World's entire human population I am one of the most courageous, with the highest aspirations. . . .

I then sang to them a song about my Five Comforts:
'Lord! Gracious Marpa! I bow down at Thy Feet!
Enable me to give up worldly aims.
'Here is the Dragkar-Taso's Middle Cave,
On this the topmost summit of the Middle Cave,
I, the Yogi Tibetan called Repa,
Relinquishing all thoughts of what to eat or wear, and this life's aims,
Have settled down to win the perfect Buddhahood.

'Comfortable is the hard mattress beneath me,
Comfortable is the Nepalese cotton-padded quilt above me,
Comfortable is the single meditation-band which holdeth up my knee,
Comfortable is the body, to a diet temperate inured,
Comfortable is the Lucid Mind which discerneth present clingings and
    the Final Goal;
Nought is there uncomfortable; everything is comfortable.

'If all of ye can do so, try to imitate me;
But if inspired ye be not with the aim of the ascetic life,
And to the error of the Ego Doctrine will hold fast,
I pray that ye spare me your misplaced pity;
For I a Yogi am, upon the Path of the Acquirement of Eternal Bliss.

'The Sun's last rays are passing o'er the mountain tops;
Return ye to your own abodes.
And as for me, who soon must die, uncertain of the hour of death,
With self-set task of winning perfect Buddhahood,
No time have I to waste on useless talk;
Therefore shall I into the State Quiescent of Samādhi enter now.'

Translation by W. Y. Evans-Wentz and Lama Kazi Dawa-Samdup, in Evans-Wentz, *Tibet's Great Yogi Milarepa* (Oxford, 1928), pp. 199-202

Specialists of the Sacred

*Al-Hasan al-Basrī flourished in the eighth century A.D. (died A.D. 728=
110 A.H.).*

Beware of this world *(dunyā)* with all wariness; for it is like to a snake,
smooth to the touch, but its venom is deadly. . . . The more it pleases
thee, the more thou be wary of it, for the man of this world, whenever
he feels secure in any pleasure thereof, the world drives him over
into some unpleasantness, and whenever he attains any part of it and
squats him down in it, the world turns him upside down. And again
beware of this world, for its hopes are lies, its expectations false; its
easefulness is all harshness, muddied its limpidity. . . . Even had the
Almighty not pronounced upon the world at all or coined for it any
similitude . . . yet would the world itself have awakened the slum-
berer and roused the heedless; how much more then, seeing that God
has Himself sent us a warning against it! . . . For this world has
neither worth nor weight with God, so slight it is. . . . It was offered
to our Prophet, with all its keys and treasures . . . but he refused
to accept it, and nothing prevented him from accepting it—for there
is naught that can lessen him in God's sight—but he disdained to
love what his creator hated, and to exalt what his Sovereign had
debased. As for Muhammad, he bound a stone upon his belly when he
was hungry; and as for Moses . . . it is said of him in the stories
that God revealed to him, 'Moses, when thou seest poverty approaching,
say, 'Welcome to the badge of the righteous!' And when thou seest
wealth approaching, say, 'Lo! a sin whose punishment has been put on
aforetime.' If thou shouldst wish, thou mightest name as a third the
Lord of the Spirit and the Word [Jesus], for in his affair there is a
marvel; he used to say, 'My daily bread is hunger, my badge is fear,
my raiment is wool, my mount is my foot, my lantern at night is
the moon, and my fire by day is the sun, and my fruit and fragrant
herbs are such things as the earth brings forth for the wild beasts and
the cattle. All the night I have nothing, yet there is none richer than I!'

Translation by A. J. Arberry, in his *Sufism* (London,
1950), pp. 33-5; as abridged by John Alden Williams,
Islam (New York, 1961), pp. 139-40

D. PROPHETS AND FOUNDERS OF RELIGIONS

224. ZARATHUSTRA IS BEING REPULSED BY EVERYBODY

('Yasna' 46)

At the beginning of the Yasna 46 Zarathustra is being repulsed by everybody. He knows the reason for his lack of success: his poverty 'in men and in cattle.' Therefore he turns to the wise Lord—Ahura Mazda—as a friend to a friend (stanza 2). In his prayers he calls for the reform of existence which is to be accomplished one day through the action of the saviour. He, Zarathustra, was chosen by the Lord to announce this good news (stanza 3). The following stanzas—4, and 7 to 11—depict the hosility which those who promote the Righteousness have to face from the wicked. In stanzas 12 to 17 the scene is changed; here Zarathustra enumerates his protectors. Whoever works at the renewal of the world on his, Zarathustra's, behalf, will obtain prosperity in the future life (stanzas 18-19).

1. To what land shall I flee? Where bend my steps?
   I am thrust out from family and tribe;
   I have no favour from the village to which I would belong,
   Nor from the wicked rulers of the country:
   How then, O Lord, shall I obtain thy favour?

2. I know, O Wise One, why I am powerless:
   My cattle are few, and I have few men.
   To thee I address my lament: attend unto it, O Lord,
   And grant me the support which friend would give to friend.
   As Righteousness teach the possession of the Good Mind.

3. When, O Wise One, shall the wills of the future saviours come
   forth,
   The dawns of the days when, through powerful judgment,
   The word shall uphold Righteousness?
   To whom will I help come through the Good Mind?
   To me, for I am chosen for the revelation by thee, O Lord.

4. The wicked one, ill-famed and of repellent deeds,
   Prevents the furtherers of Righteousness from fostering the cattle
   In the district and in the country.
   Whoever robs him of Dominion or of life, O Wise One,
   Shall walk foremost in the ways of the doctrine. . . .

7. Who, O Wise One, shall be sent as a protector to such as I am,
   If the evil one seeks to do me harm?
   Who but thy fire and thy mind, O Lord,
   Whose acts shall bring Righteousness to maturity?
   Do thou proclaim this mystery to my conscience!

8. Whoever seeks to injure my living possessions,
   May danger not come to me through his deeds!
   May all his actions turn against him with hostility, O Wise One,
   And take him from the good life, not the bad life!

   (A listener):
9. Who is he, the zealous man who first
   Taught me to honour thee as the most powerful,
   As the righteous Lord, holy in his action?
   (Zarathustra:)
   What he said to thee, to thee as Righteousness,
   What he said to Righteousness, the creator of the cattle,
   They ask it of me through thy Good Mind.

10. Whoever, man or woman, O wise Lord,
    Shall give me what thou knowest is the best of this existence,
    —To wit: reward for Righteousness and the Dominion (?) with
       (?) the Good Mind—
    And all those whom I shall induce to worship such as you,
    With all those will I cross the Bridge of the Separator!

11. The sacrificers and the sorcerer princes
    Have subdued mankind to the yoke of their Dominion,
    To destroy existence through evil deeds;
    They shall be tortured by their own soul and their own conscience,
    When they come to the Bridge of the Separator,
    For ever to be inmates of the house of Evil. . . .

13. Whoever among mortals pleases Spitama Zarathustra (? by his
        readiness?),
    He is worthy to be heard.
    To him shall the Wise One give existence,
    And as Good Mind he shall further his living possessions,

(?) For his Righteousness (?) we shall consider him your faithful
 friend,
(To you and to Righteousness?). . . .

18. Whoever is true to me, to him I promise, through the Good Mind,
    That which I myself do most desire;
    But oppression to him who seeks to oppress us.
    O Wise One, I strive to satisfy your wish through Righteousness.
    Thus the decision of my will and of my mind.

19. He who for me, who for Zarathustra,
    According to Righteousness will bring to pass
    That which is most renewing by the will (of the Lord),
    To him as a reward, when he attains the future life,
    Shall come two pregnant cows with the ox and all that he desires
      through the Mind.
    This thou hast revealed to me, O Wise One, thou who knowest
      best!

> Translation and introductory commentary by Jacques
> Duchesne-Guillemin, in his *The Hymns of Zarathustra*
> (London, 1952), pp 75-83

225. PRINCE SIDDĀRTHA ENCOUNTERS OLD AGE, SICKNESS AND DEATH

('Dīgha-nikāya,' XIV ['Mahāpadāna suttanta'])

Now the young lord Gotama, when many days had passed by, bade
his charioteer make ready the state carriages, saying: 'Get ready the
carriages, good charioteer, and let us go through the park to inspect
the pleasaunce.' 'Yes, my lord,' replied the charioteer, and harnessed
the state carriages and sent word to Gotama: 'The carriages are ready,
my lord; do now what you deem fit.' Then Gotama mounted a state
carriage and drove out in state into the park.

Now the young lord saw, as he was driving to the park, an aged
man as bent as a roof gable, decrepit, leaning on a staff, tottering as
he walked, afflicted and long past his prime. And seeing him Gotama
said: 'That man, good charioteer, what has he done, that his hair
is not like that of other men, nor his body?'

'He is what is called an aged man, my lord.'

'But why is he called aged?'

'He is called aged, my lord, because he has not much longer to live.'

'But then, good charioteer, am I too subject to old age, one who has not got past old age?'

'You, my lord, and we too, we all are of a kind to grow old; we have not got past old age.'

'Why then, good charioteer, enough of the park for today. Drive me back hence to my rooms.'

'Yea, my lord,' answered the charioteer, and drove him back. And he, going to his rooms, sat brooding sorrowful and depressed, thinking, 'Shame then verily be upon this thing called birth, since to one born old age shows itself like that!'

Thereupon the rāja sent for the charioteer and asked him: 'Well, good charioteer, did the boy take pleasure in the park? Was he pleased with it?'

'No, my lord, he was not.'

'What then did he see on his drive?'

(And the charioteer told the rāja all.)

Then the rāja thought thus: We must not have Gotama declining to rule. We must not have him going forth from the house into the homeless state. We must not let what the brāhman soothsayers spoke of come true.

So, that these things might not come to pass, he let the youth be still more surrounded by sensuous pleasures. And thus Gotama continued to live amidst the pleasures of sense.

Now after many days had passed by, the young lord again bade his charioteer make ready and drove forth as once before. . . .

And Gotama saw, as he was driving to the park, a sick man, suffering and very ill, fallen and weltering in his own water, by some being lifted up, by others being dressed. Seeing this, Gotama asked: 'That man, good charioteer, what has he done that his eyes are not like others' eyes, nor his voice like the voice of other men?'

'He is what is called ill, my lord.'

'But what is meant by ill?'

'It means, my lord, that he will hardly recover from his illness.'

'But I am too, then, good charioteer, subject to fall ill; have I not got out of reach of illness?'

'You, my lord, and we too, we are all subject to fall ill; we have not got beyond the reach of illness.'

'Why then, good charioteer, enough of the park for today. Drive me back hence to my rooms. 'Yea, my lord,' answered the charioteer, and drove him back. And he, going to his rooms, sat brooding sorrowful and depressed, thinking: Shame then verily be upon this thing called birth, since to one born decay shows itself like that, disease shows itself like that.

Thereupon the rāja sent for the charioteer and asked him: 'Well, good charioteer, did the young lord take pleasure in the park and was he pleased with it?'

'No, my lord, he was not.'

'What did he see then on his drive?'

(And the charioteer told the rāja all.)

Then the rāja thought thus: We must not have Gotama declining to rule; we must not have him going forth from the house to the homeless state; we must not let what the brāhman soothsayers spoke of come true.

So, that these things might not come to pass, he let the young man be still more abundantly surrounded by sensuous pleasures. And thus Gotama continued to live amidst the pleasures of sense.

Now once again, after many days . . . the young lord Gotama . . . drove forth.

And he saw, as he was driving to the park, a great concourse of people clad in garments of different colours constructing a funeral pyre. And seeing this he asked his charioteer: 'Why now are all those people come together in garments of different colours, and making that pile?'

'It is because someone, my lord, has ended his days.'

'Then drive the carriage close to him who has ended his days.'

'Yea, my lord,' answered the charioteer, and did so. And Gotama saw the corpse of him who had ended his days and asked: 'What, good charioteer, is ending one's days?'

'It means, my lord, that neither mother, nor father, nor other kinsfolk will now see him, nor will he see them.'

'But am I too then subject to death, have I not got beyond reach of death? Will neither the rāja, nor the ranee, nor any other of my kin see me more, or shall I again see them?'

'You, my lord, and we too, we are all subject to death; we have not passed beyond the reach of death. Neither the rāja, nor the ranee, nor any other of your kin will see you any more, nor will you see them.'

'Why then, good charioteer, enough of the park for today. Drive me back hence to my rooms.'

'Yea, my lord,' replied the charioteer, and drove him back.

And he, going to his rooms, sat brooding sorrowful and depressed, thinking: Shame verily be upon this thing called birth, since to one born the decay of life, since disease, since death shows itself like that!

Thereupon the rāja questioned the charioteer as before and as before let Gotama be still more surrounded by sensuous enjoyment. And thus he continued to live amidst the pleasures of sense.

Now once again, after many days . . . the lord Gotama . . . drove forth.

And he saw, as he was driving to the park, a shaven-headed man, a recluse, wearing the yellow robe. And seeing him he asked the charioteer, 'That man, good charioteer, what has he done that his head is unlike other men's heads and his clothes too are unlike those of others?'

'That is what they call a recluse, because, my lord, he is one who has gone forth.'

'What is that, "to have gone forth"?'

'To have gone forth, my lord, means being thorough in the religious life, thorough in the peaceful life, thorough in good action, thorough in meritorious conduct, thorough in harmlessness, thorough in kindness to all creatures.'

'Excellent indeed, friend charioteer, is what they call a recluse, since so thorough in his conduct in all those respects, wherefore drive me up to that forthgone man.'

'Yea, my lord,' replied the charioteer and drove up to the recluse. Then Gotama addressed him, saying, 'You master, what have you done that your head is not as other men's heads, nor your clothes as those of other men?'

'I, my lord, am one whose has gone forth.'

'What, master, does that mean?'

'It means, my lord, being thorough in the religious life, thorough in the peaceful life, thorough in good actions, thorough in meritorious conduct, thorough in harmlessness, thorough in kindness to all creatures.'

'Excellently indeed, master, are you said to have gone forth since so thorough is your conduct in all those respects.' Then the lord Gotama bade his charioteer, saying: 'Come then, good charioteer, do you take the carriage and drive it back hence to my rooms. But I will even here cut off my hair, and don the yellow robe, and go forth from the house into the homeless state.'

'Yea, my lord,' replied the charioteer, and drove back. But the prince Gotama, there and then cutting off his hair and donning the yellow robe, went forth from the house into the homeless state.

Now at Kapilavatthu, the rāja's seat, a great number of persons, some eighty-four thousand souls, heard of what prince Gotama had done and thought: Surely this is no ordinary religious rule, this is no common going forth, in that prince Gotama himself has had his head shaved and has donned the yellow robe and has gone forth from the house into the homeless state. If prince Gotama has done this, why then should not we also? And they all had their heads shaved and donned the yellow robes, and in imitation of the Bodhisat they went forth from the house into the homeless state. So the Bodhisat went up on his rounds through the villages, towns and cities accompanied by that multitude.

Now there arose in the mind of Gotama the Bodhisat, when he was meditating in seclusion, this thought: That indeed is not suitable for me that I should live beset. 'Twere better were I to dwell alone, far from the crowd.

So after a time he dwelt alone, away from the crowd. Those eighty-four thousand recluses went one way, and the Bodhisat went another way.

Now there arose in the mind of Gotama the Bodhisat, when he had gone to his place and was meditating in seclusion, this thought: Verily, this world has fallen upon trouble—one is born, and grows old, and dies, and falls from one state, and springs up in another. And from the suffering, moreover, no one knows of any way of escape, even from decay and death. O, when shall a way of escape from this suffering be made known—from decay and from death?'

> From Clarence H. Hamilton, *Buddhism* (New York, 1952), pp. 6-11, quoting translation by E. H. Brewster, in his *Life of Gotama the Buddha*, pp. 15-19. See also Rhys Davids, *Dialogues of the Buddha*, part 2 (Oxford, 1910), pp. 18 ff., which follows Brewster translation closely

226. GOTAMA'S FIRST MASTERS: KĀLĀMA AND RĀMAPUTTA

('Majjhima-nikāya,' XXVI ['Ariya-pariyesana-sutta'])

Yes, I myself too, in the days before my full enlightenment, when I was but a Bodhisatta, and not yet fully enlightened,—I too, being subject in myself to rebirth, decay and the rest of it, pursued what was no less subject thereto. But the thought came to me:—Why do I pursue what, like myself, is subject to rebirth and the rest? Why, being myself subject thereto, should I not, with my eyes open to the perils which these things entail, pursue instead the consummate peace of Nirvāna,—which knows neither rebirth nor decay, neither disease nor death, neither sorrow nor impurity?

There came a time when I, being young, with a wealth of coal-black hair untouched by grey and in all the beauty of my early prime—despite the wishes of my parents, who wept and lamented—cut off my hair and beard, donned the yellow robes and went forth from home to homelessness on Pilgrimage. A pilgrim now, in search of the right, and in quest of the excellent road to peace beyond compare, I came to Ālāra Kālāma and said:—It is my wish, reverend Kālāma, to lead the higher life in this your Doctrine and Rule. Stay with us, venerable sir, was his answer; my Doctrine is such that ere long an intelligent man can for himself discern, realize, enter on, and abide in, the full scope of his master's teaching. Before long, indeed very soon, I had his Doctrine by heart. So far as regards mere lip-recital and oral repetition, I could say off the (founder's) original message and the elders' exposition of it, and could profess, with others, that I knew and saw it to the full. Then it struck me that it was no Doctrine merely accepted by him on trust that Ālāra Kālāma, preached, but one which he professed to have entered on and to abide in after having discerned and realized it for himself; and assuredly he had real knowledge and vision thereof. So I went to him and asked him up to what point he had for himself discerned and realized the Doctrine he had entered on and now abode in.

Up to the plane of Naught, answered he.

Hereupon, I reflected that Ālāra Kālāma was not alone in possessing faith, perseverance, mindfulness, rapt concentration, and intellectual insight; for, all these were mine too. Why, I asked myself, should not I strive to realize the Doctrine which he claims to have entered on and to abide in after discerning and realizing it for himself? Before long, indeed very soon, I had discerned and realized his Doctrine for myself and had entered on it and abode therein. Then I went to him and asked him whether this was the point up to which he had discerned and realized for himself the Doctrine which he professed. He said yes; and I said that I had reached the same point for myself. It is a great thing, said he, a very great thing for us, that in you, reverend sir, we find such a fellow in the higher life. That same Doctrine which I for myself have discerned, realized, entered on, and profess,—that have you for yourself discerned, realized, entered on and abide in; and that same Doctrine which you have for yourself discerned, realized, entered on and profess,—that have I for myself discerned, realized, entered on, and profess. The Doctrine which I know, you too know; and the Doctrine which you know, I too know. As I am, so are you; and as you are, so am I. Pray, sir, let us be joint wardens of this company! In such wise did Ālāra Kālāma, being my master, set me, his pupil, on precisely the same footing as himself and show me great worship. But, as I bethought me that his Doctrine merely led to attaining the plane of Naught and not to Renunciation, passionlessness, cessation, peace, discernment, enlightenment and Nirvāna,—I was not taken with his Doctrine but turned away from it to go my way.

Still in search of the right, and in quest of the excellent road to peace beyond compare, I came to Uddaka Rāmaputta and said;—It is my wish, reverend sir, to lead the higher life in this your Doctrine and Rule. Stay with us . . . vision thereof. So I went to Uddaka Rāmaputta and asked him up to what point he had for himself discerned and realized the Doctrine he had entered on and now abode in.

Up to the plane of neither perception or non-perception, answered he.

Hereupon, I reflected that Uddaka Rāmaputta was not alone in possessing faith . . . show me great worship. But, as I bethought me that his Doctrine merely led to attaining the plane of neither perception nor non-perception, and not to Renunciation, passionlessness, cessation, peace, discernment, enlightenment and Nirvāna,—I was not taken with his Doctrine but turned away from it to go my way.

Still in search of the right, and in quest of the excellent road to peace beyond compare, I came, in the course of an alms-pilgrimage through Magadha, to the Camp township at Uruvelā and there took up my abode. Said I to myself on surveying the place:—Truly a delightful spot, with its goodly groves and clear flowing river with ghāts and amenities, hard by a village for sustenance. What more for his striving can a young man need whose heart is set on striving? So there I sat me down, needing nothing further for my striving.

Subject in myself to rebirth—decay—disease—death—sorrow—and impurity, and seeing peril in what is subject thereto, I sought after the consummate peace of Nirvāna, which knows neither sorrow nor decay, neither disease nor death, neither sorrow nor impurity;—this I pursued, and this I won; and there arose within me the conviction, the insight, that now my Deliverance was assured, that this was my last birth, nor should I ever be reborn again.

Translation by Lord Chalmers, *Further Dialogues of the Buddha*, I (London, 1926), pp. 115-18

227. AFTER THE ILLUMINATION THE BUDDHA PROCLAIMS:
'I AM THE HOLY ONE IN THIS WORLD, I AM THE HIGHEST
TEACHER . . .'

('Mahāvagga,' I, 7-9)

Now Upaka, a man belonging to the Ājīvaka sect (i.e. the sect of
naked ascetics), saw the Blessed One travelling on the road, between
Gayā and the Bodhi tree; and when he saw him, he said to the Blessed
One: 'Your countenance, friend, is serene; your complexion is pure and
bright. In whose name, friend, have you retired from the world? Who
is your teacher? Whose doctrine do you profess?'

When Upaka the Ājīvaka had spoken thus, the Blessed One addressed
him in the following stanzas: 'I have overcome all foes; I am all-wise;
I am free from stains in every way; I have left everything; and have
obtained emancipation by the destruction of desire. Having myself
gained knowledge, whom should I call my master? I have no teacher;
no one is equal to me; in the world of men and of gods no being is like
me. I am the holy One in this world, I am the highest teacher, I
alone am the Absolute Sambuddha; I have gained coolness (by the
extinction of all passion) and have obtained Nirvāna. To found the
Kingdom of Truth I go to the city of the Kāsis (Benares); I will beat
the drum of the Immortal in the darkness of this world.'

(Upaka replied): 'You profess then, friend, to be the holy, absolute
Jina.[1]

(Buddha said): 'Like me are all Jinas who have reached extinction
of the Āsavas;[2] I have overcome all states of sinfulness; therefore,
Upaka, am I the Jina.'

When he had spoken thus, Upaka, the Ājīvaka replied: 'It may
be so, friend': shook his head, took another road, and went away.

Notes

1 Jina, or the victorious One, is one of the many appellations common to the
founders of Buddhism and Jainism.
2 Āsava,—sensuality, individuality, delusion, and ignorance.

Translation and notes by T. W. Rhys Davids and
Hermann Oldenberg, Vinaya Texts, part I, in Sacred
Books of the East, XIII, (Oxford, 1881), pp. 90-1

228. GOTAMA BUDDHA PONDERS: 'MUST I NOW PREACH
WHAT I SO HARDLY WON?'

('Majjhima-nikāya,' XXVI *['Āriya-pariyesana-sutta']*)

I have attained, thought I, to this Doctrine profound, recondite, hard
to comprhend, serene, excellent, beyond dialectic, abstruse, and only
to be perceived by the learned. But mankind delights, takes delight,
and is happy in what it clings on to, so that for it, being thus minded
it is hard to understand causal relations and the chain of causation,—
hard to understand the stilling of all plastic forces, or the renunciation
of all worldly ties, the extirpation of craving, passionlessness, peace
and Nirvāna. Were I to preach the Doctrine, and were others not to
understand it, that would be labour and annoyance to me! Yes, and
on the instant there flashed across my mind these verses, which no
man had heard before:—

> *Must I now preach what I so hardly won?*
> *Men sunk in sin and lusts would find it hard*
> *to plumb this Doctrine,—up stream all the way,*
> *abstruse, profound, most subtle, hard to grasp.*
> *Dear lusts will blind them that they shall not see,*
> *—in densest mists of ignorance befogged.*

As thus I pondered, my heart inclined to rest quiet and not to preach
my Doctrine. But, Brahmā Sahāmpati's mind came to know what
thoughts were passing within my mind, and he thought to himself:—
The world is undone, quite undone, inasmuch as the heart of the
Truth-finder inclines to rest quiet and not to preach his Doctrine!
Hereupon, as swiftly as a strong man might stretch out his arm or
might draw back his outstretched arm, Brahmā Sahāmpati vanished
from the Brahmā-world and appeared before me. Towards me he came
with his right shoulder bared, and with his clasped hands stretched
out to me in reverence, saying:—May it please the Lord, may it
please the Blessed One, to preach his doctrine! Beings there are whose
vision is but little dimmed, who are perishing because they do not
hear the Doctrine;—these will understand it!

Translation by Lord Chalmers, *Further Dialogues of
the Buddha,* I (London, 1926), pp. 118-19

Specialists of the Sacred

229. GOTAMA BUDDHA REMEMBERS HIS EARLIER
EXISTENCES

('Majjhima-nikāya,' iv ['Bhaya-bherava-sutta])

With heart thus steadfast, thus clarified and purified, clean and cleansed of things impure, tempered and apt to serve, stablished and immutable,—it was thus that I applied my heart to the knowledge which recalled my earlier existences. I called to mind my divers existences in the past,—a single birth, then two . . . [and so on to] . . . a hundred thousand births, many an aeon of disintegration of the world, many an aeon of its redintegration, and again many an aeon both of its disintegration and of its redintegration. In this or that former existence, I remembered, such and such was my name, my sept, my class, my diet, my joys and sorrows, and my term of life. When I passed thence, I came by such and such subsequent existence, wherein such and such was my name and so forth. Thence I passed to my life here. Thus did I call to mind my divers existences of the past in all their details and features.—This, brahmin, was the first knowledge attained by me, in the first watch of that night,—ignorance dispelled and knowledge won, darkness dispelled and illumination won, as befitted my strenuous and ardent life, purged of self.

That same steadfast heart I now applied to knowledge of the passage hence, and re-appearance elsewhere, of other beings. With the Eye Celestial, which is pure and far surpasses the human eye, I saw things in the act of passing hence and of re-appearing elsewhere,—being high and low, fair or foul to view, in bliss or woe; I saw them all faring according to their past. Here were beings given over to evil in act, word and thought, who decried the Noble and had a wrong outlook and became what results from such wrong outlook;—these, at the body's dissolution after death, made their appearance in states of suffering, misery and tribulation and in purgatory. Here again were beings given to good in act, word and thought, who did not decry the Noble, who had the right outlook and became what results from right outlook;—these, at the body's dissolution after death, made their appearance in states of bliss in heaven. All this did I see with the Eye Celestial; and this, brahmin, was the second knowledge attained by me, in the second watch of that night,—ignorance dispelled and knowledge won, darkness dispelled and illumination won, as befitted my strenuous and ardent life, purged of self.

That same steadfast heart I next applied to knowledge of the eradication of Cankers. I comprehended, aright and to the full, Ill, the origin of Ill, the cessation of Ill, and the course that leads to the cessation of Ill. I comprehend, aright and to the full, what the Cankers were, with their origin, cessation, and the course that leads to their cessation. When I knew this and when I saw this, then my heart was delivered from the Canker of sensuous pleasure, from the Canker of continuing existence, and from the Canker of ignorance; and to me thus delivered came the knowledge of my Deliverance in the conviction—Rebirth is no more; I have lived the highest life; my task is done; and now for me there is no more of what I have been. This, Brahmin, was the third knowledge attained by me, in the third watch of that night,—ignorance dispelled and knowledge won, darkness dispelled and illumination won, as befitted my strenuous and ardent life, purged of self.

> Translation by Lord Chalmers, *Further Dialogues of the Buddha*, I (London, 1926), pp. 15-17

230. THE BUDDHA ENTERS NIRVĀNA

(Ashvagosha, 'Buddhacarita,' XXVI, 83-6, 88-106)

Thereupon the Buddha turned to his Disciples, and said to them: 'Everything comes to an end, though it may last for an aeon. The hour of parting is bound to come in the end. Now I have done what I could do, both for myself and for others. To stay here would from now on be without any purpose. I have disciplined, in heaven and on earth, all those whom I could discipline, and I have set them in the stream. Hereafter this my Dharma, O monks, shall abide for generations and generations among living beings. Therefore, recognize the true nature of the living world, and do not be anxious; for separation cannot possibly be avoided. Recognize that all that lives is subject to this law; and strive from today onwards that it shall be thus no more! When the light of gnosis has dispelled the darkness of ignorance, when all existence has been seen as without substance, peace ensues when life draws to an end, which seems to cure a long sickness at last. Everything, whether stationary or moveable, is bound to perish in the end. Be ye therefore mindful and vigilant! The time for my entry into Nirvāna has now arrived. These are my last words!'

Thereupon, supreme in his mastery of the trances, He at that moment entered into the first trance, emerged from it and went on to the second, and so in due order he entered all of them without omitting one. And then, when he had ascended through all the nine stages of meditational attainment, the great Seer reversed the process, and returned again to the first trance. Again he emerged from that, and once more he ascended step by step to the fourth trance. When he emerged from the practice of that, he came face to face with everlasting Peace.

And when the Sage entered Nirvāna, the earth quivered like a ship struck by a squall, and firebrands fell from the sky. The heavens were lit up by a preternatural fire, which burned without fuel, without smoke, without being fanned by the wind. Fearsome thunderbolts crashed down on the earth, and violent winds raged in the sky. The moon's light waned, and, in spite of a cloudless sky, an uncanny darkness spread everywhere. The rivers, as if overcome with grief, were filled with boiling water. Beautiful flowers grew out of season on the Sal trees above the Buddha's couch, and the trees bent down over him and showered his golden body with their flowers. Like as many gods the five-headed Nāgas stood motionless in the sky, their eyes reddened with grief, their hoods closed and their bodies kept in restraint, and with deep devotion they gazed upon the body of the Sage. But, well-established in the practice of the supreme Dharma, the gathering of the gods round king Vaishravana was not grieved and shed no tears, so great was their attachment to the Dharma. The Gods of the Pure Abode, though they had great reverence for the Great Seer, remained composed, and their minds were unaffected; for they hold the things of this world in the utmost contempt. The Kings of the Gandharvas and Nāgas, as well as the Yakshas and the Devas who rejoice in the true Dharma—they all stood in the sky, mourning and absorbed in the utmost grief. But Mara's hosts felt that they had obtained their heart's desire. Overjoyed they uttered loud laughs, danced about, hissed like snakes, and triumphantly made a frightful din by beating drums, gongs and tom-toms. And the world, when the Prince of Seers had passed beyond, became like a mountain whose peak has been shattered by a thunderbolt; it became like the sky without the moon, like a pond whose lotuses the frost has withered, or like learning rendered ineffective by lack of wealth.

Translation by Edward Conze, in Conze (ed.), *Buddhist Scriptures* (Penguin Books, 1959), pp. 62-4

231. MUHAMMAD'S CALL (AT-TABARĪ)

Ahmad b. 'Uthman, who is known as Abu'l-jawza', has related to me on the authority of Wahb b. Jarir, who heard his father say that he had heard from an-Nu'man b. Rashid, on the authority of az-Zuhri from 'Urwa, from 'A'isha, who said: The way revelation (wahy) first began to come to the Apostle of Allah—on whom be Allah's blessing and peace—was by means of true dreams which would come like the morning dawn. Then he came to love solitude, so he used to go off to a cave in Hira[1] where he would practise tahannuth[2] certain nights before returning to his family. Then he would come back to his family and take provisions for the like number [of nights] until unexpectedly the truth came to him.

He (i.e., Gabriel) came to him saying: 'O Muhammad, thou art Allah's Apostle (rasūl[3]).' Said the Apostle of Allah—upon whom be Allah's blessing and peace: 'Thereat I fell to my knees where I had been standing, and then with trembling limbs dragged myself along till I came in to Khadija,[4] saying: "Wrap ye me up! Wrap ye me up!"[5] till the terror passed from me. Then [on another occasion] he came to me again and said: "O Muhammad, thou art Allah's Apostle," [which so disturbed me] that I was about to cast myself down from some high mountain cliff. But he appeared before me as I was about to do this, and said: "O Muhammad, I am Gabriel, and thou art Allah's Apostle." Then he said to me: "Recite!"; but I answered: "What should I recite?"; whereat he seized me and grievously treated me three times, till he wore me out. Then he said: "Recite, in the name of thy Lord who has created" (Sūra XCVI, 1). So I recited it and then went to Khadija, to whom I said: "I am worried about myself." Then I told her the whole story. She said: "Rejoice, for by Allah, Allah will never put thee to shame. By Allah, thou art mindful of thy kinsfolk, speakest truthfully, renderest what is given thee in trust, bearest burdens, art ever hospitable to the guest, and dost always uphold the right against any wrong." Then she took me to Waraqua b. Naufal b. Asad [to whom] she said: "Give ear to what the son of thy brother [has to report]." So he questioned me, and I told him [the whole] story. Said he: "This is the nāmūs[6] which was sent down upon Moses the son of Amram. Would that I might be a stalwart youth [again to take part] in it. Would that I might still be alive when your people turn you out." "And will they turn me out?" I

The notes to this text are on p. 484.

asked. "Yes," said he, "never yet has a man come with that with which you come but has been turned away. Should I be there when your day comes I will lend you mighty assistance." '

Notes

1 A mountain in the environs of Mecca.
2 This is probably intended to represent the Hebrew word *tihinnōth* 'prayers.'
3 *Rasūl* is literally 'messenger,' but like the New Testament *apostolos*, as a messenger of God it technically means an Apostle.
4 His first wife, an elderly and wealthy Meccan widow who had married him some years earlier.
5 See Sūra LXXIII, 1.
6 This is from the Syriac transliteration of the Greek word *nomos*, 'law,' which is used in the Septuagint and the New Testament for the Mosaic law, i.e., the Torah.

Translation and notes by Arthur Jeffery, *Islam. Muhammad and His Religion* (New York: Liberal Arts Press, 1958), pp. 15-17; from at-Tabarī, *Ta'rīkh ar-rusul wa'l-mulūk* (Leiden, 1881), I, 1147-52

232. MUHAMMAD IS THE MESSENGER OF GOD

('Koran,' XLVIII, 30-3)

Muhammad is the Messenger of God,
and those who are with him are hard
against the unbelievers, merciful
one to another. Thou seest them
bowing, prostrating, seeking bounty
from God and good pleasure. Their
mark is on their faces, the trace of
prostration. That is their likeness
in the Torah, and their likeness
in the Gospel: as a seed that puts
forth its shoot, and strengthens it,
and it grows stout and rises straight
upon its stalk, pleasing the sowers,
that through them He may enrage
the unbelievers. God has promised
those of them who believe and do deeds
of righteousness forgiveness and
a mighty wage.

Translation by A. J. Arberry
484

233. MUHAMMAD PROCLAIMS THE KORAN, 'THE BOOK WHEREIN IS NO DOUBT . . .'

('Koran,' II, 1-23)

That is the book, wherein is no doubt,
   a guidance to the godfearing
who believe in the Unseen, and perform the prayer,
and expend of that We have provided them;
who believe in what has been sent down to thee
   and what has been sent down before thee,
   and have faith in the Hereafter;
those are upon guidance from their Lord,
   those are the ones who prosper.

As for the unbelievers, alike it is to them
whether thou hast warned them or hast not warned them,
   they do not believe.
God has set a seal on their hearts and on their hearing,
   and on their eyes is a covering,
and there awaits them a mighty chastisement.

   And some men there are who say,
'We believe in God and the Last Day';
   but they are not believers.
They would trick God and the believers,
   and only themselves they deceive,
     and they are not aware.
   In their hearts is a sickness,
   and God has increased their sickness,
and there awaits them a painful chastisement
   for that they have cried lies.
When it is said to them, 'Do not corruption in the land,'
they say, 'We are only ones that put things right.'
   Truly, they are the workers of corruption
     but they are not aware.
When it is said to them, 'Believe as the people believe,'
they say, 'Shall we believe, as fools believe?'
   Truly, they are the foolish ones,
     but they do not know.
When they meet those who believe, they say, 'We believe';

but when they go privily to their Satans, they say,
  'We are with you; we were only mocking.'
  God shall mock them, and shall lead them on
  blindly wandering in their insolence.
  Those are they that have bought error
    at the price of guidance,
  and their commerce has not profited them,
    and they are not right-guided.
The likeness of them is as the likeness of a man
who kindled a fire, and when it lit all about him
God took away their light, and left them in darkness
        unseeing,
    deaf, dumb, blind—
  so they shall not return;
or as a cloudburst out of heaven
in which is darkness, and thunder, and lightning—
  they put their fingers in their ears
  against the thunderclaps, fearful of death;
    and God encompasses the unbelievers;
the lightning wellnigh snatches away their sight;
whensoever it gives them light, they walk in it,
and when the darkness is over them, they halt;
  had God willed, He would have taken away
    their hearing and their sight.
Truly, God is powerful over everything.

O you men, serve your Lord Who created you,
and those that were before you; haply so
  you will be godfearing;
who assigned to you the earth for a couch,
and heaven for an edifice, and sent down
out of heaven water, wherewith He brought forth
fruits for your provision; so set not up
  compeers to God wittingly.
And if you are in doubt concerning that We have
sent down on Our servant, then bring a sura
like it, and call your witnesses, apart from
  God, if you are truthful.
And if you do not—and you will not—then
fear the Fire, whose fuel is men and stones,
  prepared for unbelievers.

Give thou good tidings to those who believe
and do deeds of righteousness, that for them
await gardens underneath which rivers flow;
whensoever they are provided with fruits therefrom
they shall say, 'This is that wherewithal
we were provided before'; that they shall be
given in perfect semblance; and there
for them shall be spouses purified; therein
  they shall dwell forever.

Translation by A. J. Arberry

234. ALLAH TELLS MUHAMMAD THE STORY OF ABRAHAM

('Koran,' XIX, 42-52)

And mention in the Book Abraham;
surely he was a true man, a Prophet.
When he said to his father, 'Father,
why worshippest thou that which neither
hears nor sees, nor avails thee anything?
Father, there has come to me knowledge
such as came not to thee; so follow me,
And I will guide thee on a level path.
Father, serve not Satan; surely Satan
is a rebel against the All-merciful.
Father, I fear that some chastisement
from the All-merciful will smite thee,
so that thou becomest a friend to Satan.'
Said he, 'What, art thou shrinking
from my gods, Abraham? Surely, if thou
givest not over, I shall stone thee;
so forsake me now for some while.'
He said, 'Peace be upon thee!
I will ask my Lord to forgive thee;
surely He is ever gracious to me.
Now I will go apart from you
and that you call upon, apart from

God; I will call upon my Lord,
and haply I shall not be, in calling
upon my Lord, unprosperous.'
So, when he went apart from them
and that they were serving, apart
from God, We gave him Isaac and
Jacob, and each We made a Prophet
and We gave them of Our mercy,
and We appointed unto them
a tongue of truthfulness, sublime.

Translation by A. J. Arberry

235. ALLAH REVEALS TO MUHAMMAD HOW HE SAVED THE CHILDREN OF ISRAEL

('Koran,' XVII, 104-9)

And We gave Moses nine signs,
clear signs. Ask the Children of Israel
when he came to them, and Pharaoh
said to him, 'Moses, I think thou art bewitched.'
He said, 'Indeed thou knowest that none
sent these down, except the Lord
of the heavens and earth, as clear
proofs; and, Pharaoh, I think thou art accursed.'
He desired to startle them from the land;
and We drowned him and those with him, all together.
And We said to the Children of Israel
after him, 'Dwell in the land; and
when the promise of the world to come
comes to pass, we shall bring you a rabble.'

With the truth We have sent it down,
and with the truth it has come down;
and We have sent thee not, except
good tidings to bear, and warning;
and a Koran We have divided,
for thee to recite it to mankind

at intervals, and We have sent it down successively.
Say: 'Believe in it, or believe not';
those who were given the knowledge before it
when it is recited to them, fall down
upon their faces prostrating, and say,
'Glory be to our Lord! Our Lord's promise is performed.'

Translation by A. J. Arberry

236. ALLAH SENT THE TORAH, THE PROPHETS, AND
JESUS, SON OF MARY

('Koran,' V, 50-3)

And We sent, following
in their footsteps, Jesus
son of Mary, confirming
the Torah before him;
and We gave to him
the Gospel, wherein
is guidance and light,
and confirming the Torah
before it, as a guidance
and an admonition
unto the godfearing.
So let the People of the Gospel judge
according to what God has sent down
therein. Whosoever judges not
according to what God has sent down—
they are the ungodly.

And We have sent down to thee the Book
with the truth, confirming the Book
that was before it, and assuring it.
So judge between them according to what
God has sent down, and do not follow
their caprices, to forsake the truth
that has come to thee. To every one
of you We have appointed a right way
and an open road.

Translation by A. J. Arberry

237. MUHAMMAD SPEAKS BY REVELATION

('Koran,' XLII, 50-4)

It belongs not to any mortal that
God should speak to him, except
by revelation, or from behind a veil,
or that He should send a messenger
and He reveal whatsoever He will
by His leave; surely He is
     All-high, All-wise.
Even so We have revealed to thee a
Spirit of Our bidding. Thou knewest
not what the Book was, nor belief;
but We made it a light, whereby We
guide whom We will of Our servants. And thou,
surely thou shalt guide unto a straight path—
the path of God, to whom belongs whatsoever is in
the heavens and whatsoever is in the earth. Surely
     unto God all things come home.

Translation by A. J. Arberry

See also nos. 43, 252, 268, 269

E. SPIRITUAL TECHNIQUES AND MYSTICAL EXPERIENCES

238. A NEOPLATONIST PHILOSOPHER ON THE ARTS AND EFFECTS OF ECSTASY

(Iamblichus, 'On the Mysteries,' III, 4-6)

Iamblichus was born in Syria and lived from ca. 250 to 325 A.D. His book On the Mysteries *is in the form of a reply by a certain Abammon to a letter by Porphyry addressed 'To Anebo' and is a defence of ritualistic magic or theurgy. Iamblichus' presentation of Neoplatonism fell far below the high teaching of Plotinus and incorporated much popular superstition.*

(4) Among the signs by which those who are truly possessed by the gods may be known, the greatest is the fact that many [of those who experience ecstasy] are not burned, though fire is applied to them, since the deity breathing within them does not permit the fire to touch them; many, though burned, are unaware of it, since at that moment they are not dwelling in the body [literally, not living an animal life]. Many have daggers thrust through their bodies without feeling it; others have their backs cut [open] with hatchets, or cut their arms with knives, without taking any notice. The activities in which they are engaged are not of a human kind, and since they are borne by God they can reach places which are inaccessible to men; they pass through fire unharmed; they tread upon fire and cross over streams, like the priestess in Castabala [who walked barefoot on snow and hot coals]. This proves that in their enthusiasm [i.e., their state of inspiration] they are not aware of what they are doing and are not living a human or bodily existence as far as sensation and volition are concerned, but live instead another and diviner kind, which fills them and takes complete possession of them.

(5) There are many different kinds of divine possession, and there are different ways of awakening the divine spirit; consequently there are many different indications of this state. For one thing, there are

different gods from whom we receive the spirit [i.e., are inspired], and this results in a variety of forms in which the inspiration manifests itself; further, the kinds of influence exerted are different, and so there are various ways in which the divine seizure takes place. For either the god takes possession of us, or else we are entirely absorbed in him, or else [thirdly] we co-operate with him. At times we partake of the lowest power of God, at others of the middle [power], at still others of the highest [i.e., first]. Sometimes it is a mere participation, again it is a communion [fellowship or sharing], or again it becomes a union of these [two] kinds. Now the soul enjoys complete separation; again it is still involved in the body, or [else] the whole nature is laid hold of [and controlled].

Hence the signs of possession are manifold: either movement of the body and its parts, or complete relaxation; [either] singing choirs, round dances, and harmonious voices, or the opposite of these. [The] bodies have been seen to rise up, grow, or move freely in the air, and the opposite has also been observed. They have been heard to utter [different] voices of equal strength, or with great diversity and inequality, in tones that alternated with silence; and again in other cases harmonious crescendo or diminuendo of tone, and in still other cases other kinds of utterance.

(6) But the greatest thing [about this experience] is that the one who thus draws down a deity beholds the greatness and the nature of the invading spirit; and he is secretly guided and directed by him. So too he who receives a god sees also a fire before he takes it into himself. Now and then the god manifests himself to all who are present, either as he comes or as he goes. From this it is made known, to those who have the knowledge, wherein his truth and his power chiefly consist and his place [in the divine hierarchy], and what qualifies him by his nature to make known the truth; and also what power he is able to grant or to maintain. Those, however, who without this beatifying view invoke the spirits are merely reaching out and touching things in the dark, and do not know what they are doing, save for certain minor signs in the body of the possessed person and other indubitable, visible symptoms; but the full understanding of divine possession is denied them, being hid in the invisible.

Translation and introduction by Frederick C. Grant, in his *Hellenistic Religions* (New York, 1953), pp. 173-5

TECHNIQUES OF YOGA

239. CONCENTRATION 'ON A SINGLE POINT'

The point of departure of Yoga meditation is concentration on a single object; whether this is a physical object (the space between the eyebrows, the tip of the nose, something luminous, etc.), or a thought (a metaphysical truth), or God (Ishvara) makes no difference. This determined and continuous concentration, called *ekāgratā* ('on a single point'), is obtained by integrating the psychomental flux (*sarvārthatā*, 'variously directed, discontinuous, diffused attention'). This is precisely the definition of yogic technique: *yogah cittavritti-nirodhyah*, i.e., the yoga is the suppression of psychomental states (*Yoga-sūtras*, I, 2).

The immediate result of *ekāgratā*, concentration on a single point, is prompt and lucid censorship of all the distractions and automatisms that dominate—or, properly speaking, compose—profane consciousness. Completely at the mercy of associations (themselves produced by sensations and the *vāsanās*), man passes his days allowing himself to be swept hither and thither by an infinity of disparate moments that are, as it were, external to himself. The senses or the subconscious continually introduce into consciousness objects that dominate and change it, according to their form and intensity. Associations disperse consciousness, passions do it violence, the 'thirst for life' betrays it by projecting it *outward*. Even in his intellectual efforts, man is passive, for the fate of secular thoughts (controlled not by *ekāgratā* but only by fluctuating moments of concentration, *kshiptavikshiptas*) is to be thought by objects. Under the appearance of thought, there is really an indefinite and disordered flickering, fed by sensations words, and memory. The first duty of the yogin is to think—that is, not to let *himself* think. This is why Yoga practice begins with *ekāgratā*, which dams the mental stream and thus constitutes a 'psychic mass,' a solid and unified continuum.

The practice of *ekāgratā* tends to control the two generators of mental fluidity: sense activity (*indriya*) and the activity of the subconscious (*samskāra*). Control is the ability to intervene, at will and directly, in the functioning of these two sources of mental 'whirlwinds' (*cittavritti*). A yogin can obtain discontinuity of consciousness at will;

in other words, he can, at any time and any place, bring about concentration of his attention on a 'single point' and become insensible to any other sensory or mnemonic stimulus. Through *ekāgratā* one gains a genuine will—that is, the power freely to regulate an important sector of biomental activity. It goes without saying that *ekāgratā* can be obtained only through the practice of numerous exercises and techniques, in which physiology plays a role of primary importance. One cannot obtain *ekāgratā* if, for example, the body is in a tiring or even uncomfortable posture, or if the respiration is disorganized, unrhythmical. This is why, according to Patañjali, yogic technique implies several categories of physiological practices and spiritual exercises (called *angas*, 'members'), which one must have learned if one seeks to obtain *ekāgratā* and, ultimately, the highest concentration, *samādhi*. These 'members' of Yoga can be regarded both as forming a group of techniques and as being stages of the mental ascetic itinerary whose end is final liberation. They are: (1) restraints (*yama*), (2) disciplines (*niyama*); (3) bodily attitudes and postures (*āsana*); (4) rhythm of respiration (*prānāyāma*); (5) emancipation of sensory activity from the domination of exterior objects (*pratyāhāra*); (6) concentration (*dhāranā*); (7) yogic meditation (*dhyāna*); (8) *samādhi* (*Yoga-sūtras*, II, 29).

Each class (*anga*) of practices and disciplines has a definite purpose. Patañjali hierarchizes these 'members of Yoga' in such a way that the yogin cannot omit any of them, except in certain cases. The first two groups, *yama* and *niyama*, obviously constitute the necessary preliminaries for any type of asceticism, hence there is nothing specifically yogic in them. The restraints (*yama*) purify from certain sins that all systems of morality disapprove but that social life tolerates. Now, the moral law can no longer be infringed here—as it is in secular life—without immediate danger to the seeker for deliverance. In Yoga, every sin produces its consequences immediately. The five restraints are *ahimsā*, 'not to kill,' *satya*, 'not to lie,' *asteya*, 'not to steal,' *brahmacarya*, 'sexual abstinence,' *aparigraha*, 'not to be avaricious.'

Together with these restraints, the yogin must practise the *niyamas* —that is, a series of bodily and psychic 'disciplines.' 'Cleanliness, serenity "samtosha," asceticism "tapas," the study of Yoga metaphysics, and the effort to make God "Īshvara," the motive of all one's actions constitute the disciplines.' (*Y.S.*, II, 32.)

M. Eliade, *Yoga: Immortality and Freedom*, trans. Willard R. Trask (New York: Bollingen Series LVI, 1958), pp. 47-50

240. YOGIC POSTURES (ĀSANA) AND RESPIRATORY DISCIPLINE (PRĀNĀYĀMA)

It is only with the third 'member of Yoga' (*yogānga*) that yogic technique, properly speaking, begins. This third 'member' is *āsana*, a word designating the well-known yogic posture that the *Yoga-sūtras* (II, 46) define as *sthirasukham*, 'stable and agreeable.' *Āsana* is described in numerous Hatha Yoga treatises; Patañjali defines it only in outline, for *āsana* is learned from a *guru* and not from descriptions. The important thing is that *āsana* gives the body a stable rigidity, at the same time reducing physical effort to a minimum. Thus, one avoids the irritating feeling of fatigue, of enervation in certain parts of the body, one regulates the physical processes, and so allows the attention to devote itself solely to the fluid part of consciousness. At first an *āsana* is uncomfortable and even unbearable. But after some practice, the effort of maintaining the body in the same position becomes inconsiderable. Now (and this is of the highest importance), effort must disappear, the position of meditation must become natural; only then does it further concentration. 'Posture becomes perfect when the effort to attain it disappears, so that there are no more movements in the body. In the same way, its perfection is achieved when the mind is transformed into infinity—that is, when it makes the idea of its infinity its own content' (Vyāsa, ad Y.S. II, 47.) And Vācaspatimishra, commenting on Vyāsa's interpretation, writes: 'He who practises *āsana* must employ an effort that consists in suppressing the natural efforts of the body. Otherwise this kind of ascetic posture cannot be realized.' As for 'the mind transformed into infinity,' this means a complete suspension of attention to the presence of one's own body.

Āsana is one of the characteristic techniques of Indian asceticism. It is found in the Upanishads and even in Vedic literature, but allusions to it are more numerous in the *Mahābhārata* and in the Purānas. Naturally, it is in the literature of Hatha Yoga that the *āsanas* play an increasingly important part; the *Gheranda Samhitā* describes thirty-two varieties of them. Here, for example, is how one assumes one of the easiest and most common of the meditational positions, the *padmāsana*: 'Place the right foot on the left thigh and similarly the left one on the right thigh, also cross the hands behind the back and firmly catch the great toes of the feet so crossed (the right hand on the right great toe and the left hand on the left). Place the chin on the chest and fix the gaze on the tip of the nose.' (II, 8.) Lists and descriptions of *āsanas* are to be found in most of the tantric and Hatha-yogic treatises. The purpose of these meditational positions is always the same; 'absolute cessation of trouble from the pairs of opposites' (*Yoga-sūtras*, II, 48.) In this way one realizes a certain 'neutrality' of the senses; consciousness is no longer troubled by the 'presence of the body.' One realizes that first stage towards isolation of consciousness; the bridges that permit communication with sensory activity begin to be raised.

On the plane of the 'body,' *āsana* is an *ekāgratā*, a concentration on a single point; the body is 'tense,' concentrated in a single position. Just as *ekāgratā* puts an end to the fluctuation and dispersion of the states of consciousness, so *āsana* puts an end to the mobility and dis-posability of the body, by reducing the infinity of possible positions to a single archetypal, iconographic posture. Refusal to move (*āsana*), to let oneself be carried along on the rushing stream of states of conscious-ness (*ekāgratā*) will be continued by a long series of refusals of every kind.

The most important—and, certainly, the most specifically yogic—of these various refusals is the disciplining of respiration (*prānāyāma*)—in other words, the 'refusal' to breathe like the majority of mankind, that is, nonrhythmically. Patañjali defines this refusal as follows: '*Prānāyāma* is the arrest [*viccheda*] of the movements of inhalation and exhalation and it is obtained after *āsana* has been realized. (*Y.S.*, II, 49.) Patañjali speaks of the 'arrest,' the suspension, of respiration; however, *prānāyāma* begins with making the respiratory rhythm as slow as possible; and this is its first objective. There are a number of texts that treat of this Indian ascetic technique, but most of them do no more than repeat the traditional formulas. Although *prānāyāma* is a specifically yogic exercise, and one of great importance, Patañjali devotes only three *sūtras* to it. He is primarily concerned with the theoretical bases of ascetic practices; technical details are found in the commentaries by Vyāsa, Bhoja, and Vācaspatimishra, but especially in the Hatha-yogic treatises.

A remark of Bhoja's reveals the deeper meaning of *prānāyāma*: 'All the functions of the organs being preceded by that of respiration—there being always a connection between respiration and conscious-ness in their respective functions—respiration, when all the functions of the organs are suspended, realizes concentration of consciousness on a single object' (ad *Y.S.* I, 34.). The statement that a connection always exists between respiration and mental states seems to us highly important. It contains far more than mere observation of the bare fact, for example, the respiration of a man in anger is agitated, while that of one who is concentrating (even if only provisionally and without any yogic purpose) becomes rhythmical and automatically slows down, etc. The relation connecting the rhythm of respiration with the states of consciousness mentioned by Bhoja, which has undoubtedly been observed and experienced by yogins from the earliest times—this relation has served them as an instrument for 'unifying' consciousness. The 'unification' here under consideration must be understood in the sense that, by making his respiration rhythmical and progressively slower, the yogin can 'penetrate'—that is, he can experience, in perfect lucidity—certain states of consciousness that are inaccessible in a waking condition, particularly the states of consciousness that are peculiar to sleep. For there is no doubt that the respiratory system of a man asleep is slower than that of a man awake. By reaching this rhythm of sleep through the practice of *prāṇāyāma*, the yogin, without renouncing his lucidity, penetrates the states of consciousness that accompany sleep.

The Indian ascetics recognize four modalites of consciousness (beside the enstatic 'state'): diurnal consciousness, consciousness in sleep with dreams, consciousness in sleep without dreams, and 'cataleptic consciousness.' By means of *prāṇāyāma*—that is, by increasingly prolonging inhalation and exhalation (the goal of this practice being to allow as long an interval as possible to pass between the two moments of respiration)—the yogin can, then, penetrate all the modalities of consciousness. For the noninitiate, there is discontinuity between these several modalities; thus he passes from the state of waking to the state of sleep unconsciously. The yogin must preserve continuity of consciousness—that is, he must penetrate each of these states with determination and lucidity.

But experience of the four modalities of consciousness (to which a particular respiratory rhythm naturally corresponds), together with *unification* of consciousness (resulting from the yogin's getting rid of the discontinuity between these four modalities), can only be realized after long practice. The immediate goal of *prāṇāyāma* is more modest. Through it one first of all acquires a 'continuous consciousness,' which alone can make yogic meditation possible. The respiration of the ordinary man is generally arhythmic; it varies in accordance with external circumstances or with mental tension. This irregularity produces a dangerous psychic fluidity, with consequent instability and diffusion of attention. One can become attentive by making an effort to do so. But, for Yoga, effort is an exteriorization. Respiration must be made rhythmical, if not in such a way that it can be 'forgotten' entirely, at least in such a way that it no longer troubles us by discontinuity. Hence, through *prāṇāyāma*, one attempts to do away with the effort of respiration, rhythmic breathing must become something so automatic that the yogin can forget it.

Rhythmic respiration is obtained by harmonizing the three 'moments'; inhalation *(pūraka)*, exhalation *(recaka)*, and retention of the inhaled air *(kumbhaka)*. These three moments must each fill an equal space of time. Through practice the yogin becomes able to prolong them considerably, for the goal of *prāṇāyāma* is, as Patañjali says, to suspend respiration as long as possible; one arrives at this by progressively retarding the rhythm.

M. Eliade, *Yoga, op. cit.*, pp. 53-8

241. YOGIC CONCENTRATION AND MEDITATION

Āsana, prāṇāyāma and *ekāgratā* succeed—if only for the short time the respective exercise continues—in abolishing the human condition. Motionless. breathing rhythmically, eyes and attention fixed on a single point, the yogin experiences a passing beyond the secular modality of existence. He begins to become autonomous in respect to the cosmos: external tensions no longer trouble him (having passed beyond 'the opposites,' he is equally insensible to heat and cold, to light and darkness, etc.); sensory activity no longer carries him outward, toward the objects of the senses; the psychomental stream is no longer either invaded or directed by distractions, automatisms, and memory: it is 'concentrated,' 'unified.' This retreat outside the cosmos is accompanied by a sinking into the self, progress in which is directly proportional to progress in the retreat. The yogin returns to himself, takes, so to speak, possession of himself, surrounds himself with increasingly stronger 'defences' to protect him against invasion from without—in a word, he becomes invulnerable. . . .

Making respiration rhythmical and, as far as possible, suspending it greatly promote concentration *(dhāraṇā)*. For, Patañjali tells us (Y.S., II, 52, 53), through *prāṇāyāma* the veil of darkness is rent and the intellect becomes capable *(yogyata)* of concentration *(dhāraṇā)*. The yogin can test the quality of his concentration by *pratyāhāra* (a term usually translated 'withdrawal of the senses' or 'abstraction,' which we prefer to translate 'ability to free sense activity from the domination of external objects'). According to the *Yoga-sūtras* (II, 54), *pratyāhāra* could be understood as the faculty through which the intellect (*citta*) possesses sensations as if the contact were real.

This withdrawal of sensory activity from the domination of exterior objects (*pratyāhāra*) is the final stage of psychophysiological *ascesis*. Thenceforth the yogin will no longer be 'distracted' or 'troubled' by the senses, by sensory activity, by memory, etc. All activity is suspended. The *citta*—being the psychic mass that orders and illuminates sensations coming from without—can serve as a mirror for objects, without the senses interposing between it and its object. The non-initiate is incapable of gaining this freedom, because his mind, instead of being stable is constantly violated by the activity of the senses, by the subconscious, and by the 'thirst for life.' By realizing *cittavritti nirodhyah* (i.e., the suppression of psychomental states), the *citta* abides in itself *(svarūpamātre)*. But this 'autonomy' of the intellect does not result in the suppression of phenomena. Even though detached from phenomena, the yogin continues to contemplate them. Instead of knowing through forms (*rūpa*) and mental states (*cittavritti*), as formerly, the yogin now contemplates the essence *(tattva)* of all objects directly.

Autonomy with respect to stimuli from the outer world and to the dynamism of the subconscious—an autonomy that he realizes through *pratyāhāra*—allows the yogin to practise a threefold technique, which the texts call *samyama*. The term designates the last stages of yogic meditation, the last three 'members of Yoga' *(yoganga)*. These are concentration (*dhāranā*), meditation properly speaking (*dhyāna*), and stasis *(samādhi)*.

Concentration (*dhāranā*, from the root *dhrī*, 'to hold fast') is in fact an *ekāgratā*, a 'fixing on a single point,' but its content is strictly notional. In other words, *dhāranā*—and this is what distinguishes it from *ekāgratā*, whose sole purpose is to arrest the psychomental flux and 'fix it on a single point'—realizes such a 'fixation' for the purpose of *comprehension*. Patañjali's definition of it is: 'fixation of thought on a single point' (*deshabandhashcittasya dhāranā*; Y.S. III, 1); Vyāsa adds that the concentration is usually on 'the centre [*cakra*] of the navel, on the lotus of the heart, on the light within the head, on the tip of the nose, on the tip of the tongue, or on any external place or object.' Vācaspatimishra further adds that one cannot obtain *dhāranā* without the aid of an object on which to fix one's thought.

In his *Yogasāra-samgraha*, Vijñānabhikshu quotes a passage from the

Ishvara Gītā according to which a *dhāranā* takes the time of twelve *prānāyāmas*. 'The time necessary for concentration of the mind on an object [*dhāranā*] is equal to the time taken by twelve *prānāyāmas*' (i.e., by twelve controlled, equal, and retarded respirations). By prolonging this concentration on an object twelve times, one obtains 'yogic meditation,' *dhyāna*. Patañjali defines *dhyāna* as 'a current of unified thought' (Y.S., III, 2), and Vyāsa adds the following gloss to the definition: 'Continuum of mental effort to assimilate other objects.' Vijñānabhikshu explains this process as follows: when, after achieving *dhāranā* on some point, one's mind has succeeded for a sufficient time in holding itself before itself under the form of the object of meditation, without any interruption caused by the intrusion of any other function, one attains *dhyāna*.

M. Eliade, *Yoga, op. cit.,* pp. 66-72

242. SAMĀDHI

The passage from 'concentration' to 'meditation' does not require the application of any new technique. Similarly, no supplementary yogic exercise is needed to realize *samādhi*, once the yogin has succeeded in 'concentrating' and 'meditating.' *Samādhi*, yogic 'enstasis,' is the final result of the crown of all the ascetic's spiritual efforts and exercises. The meanings of the term *samādhi* are union, totality; absorption in, complete concentration of mind; conjunction. The usual translation is 'concentration,' but this embarks the risk of confusion with *dhāranā*. Hence we have preferred to translate it 'entasis,' 'stasis,' and conjunction.

. . . Patañjali and his commentators distinguish several kinds or stages of supreme concentration. When *samādhi* is obtained with the help of an object or idea (that is, by fixing one's thought on a point in space or on an idea), the stasis is called *samprajñāta samādhi* ('enstasis with support,' or 'differentiated enstasis'). When, on the other hand, *samādhi* is obtained apart from any 'relation' (whether external or mental)—that is, when one obtains a 'conjunction' into which no 'otherness' enters, but which is simply a full comprehension of being— one has realized *asamprajñāta samādhi* ('undifferentiated stasis'). Vijñānabhikshu adds that *samprajñāta samādhi* is a means of liberation in so far as it makes possible the comprehension of truth and ends every kind of suffering. But *asamprajñāta samādhi* destroys the 'impressions [*samskāra*] of all antecedent mental functions' and even succeeds in arresting the karmic forces already set in motion by the yogin's past activity. During 'differentiated stasis,' Vijñābhikshu continues, all the mental functions are 'arrested' ('inhibited'), except that which 'meditates on the object'; whereas in *asamprajñāta samādhi* all 'consciousness' vanishes, the entire series of mental functions are blocked. 'During this stasis, there is no other trace of the mind [*citta*] save the impressions [*samskāra*] left behind (by its past functioning). If these impressions were not present, there would be no possibility of returning to consciousness.'

We are, then, confronted with two sharply differentiated classes of 'states.' The first class is acquired through the yogic technique of concentration (*dhāranā*) and meditation (*dhyāna*); the second class comprises only a single 'state'—that is, unprovoked enstasis, 'raptus.' No doubt, even this *asamprajñāta samādhi* is always owing to prolonged efforts on the yogin's part. It is not a gift or a state of grace. One can hardly reach it before having sufficiently experienced the kinds of *samādhi* included in the first class. It is the crown of the innumerable 'concentrations' and 'meditations' that have preceded it. But it comes without being summoned, without being provoked, without special preparation for it. That is why it can be called a 'raptus.'

Obviously, 'differentiated enstasis,' *samprajñāta samādhi*, comprises several stages. This is because it is perfectible and does not realize an absolute and irreducible 'state.' Four stages or kinds are generally distinguished: 'argumentative' *(savitarka)*, 'nonargumentative' *(nirvitarka)*, 'reflective' *(savicāra)*, 'super-reflective' *(nirvicāra)*. Patañjali also employs another set of terms: *vitarka, vicāra, ānanda, asmitā.* (*Y.S.*, 1, 17). But, as Vijñānabhikshu, who reproduces this list, remarks, 'the four terms are purely technical, they are applied conventionally to different forms of realization.' These four forms or stages of *samprajñāta samādhi*, he continues, represent an ascent; in certain cases the grace of God (Īshvara) permits direct attainment of the higher states, and in such cases the yogin need not go back and realize the preliminary states. But when this divine grace does not intervene, he must realize the four states gradually, always adhering to the same object of meditation (for example, Vishnu). These four grades or stages are also known as *samāpattis*, 'coalescences.' (*Y.S.*, 1, 41.)

All these four stages of *samprajñāta samādhi* are called *bīja samādhi* ('*samādhi* with seed') or *sālambana samādhi* ('with support'); for Vijñānabhikshu tells us, they are in relation with a 'substratum' (support) and produce tendencies that are like 'seeds' for the future functions of consciousness. *Asamprajñāta samādhi*, on the contrary, is *nirbīja*, 'without seed,' without support. By realizing the four stages of *samprajñāta*, one obtains the 'faculty of absolute knowledge' (*Y.S.*, I, 48). This is already an opening towards *samādhi* 'without seed,' for absolute knowledge discovers the ontological completeness in which *being* and *knowing* are no longer separated. Fixed in *samādhi*, consciousness *(citta)* can now have direct revelation of the Self *(purusha)*. Through the fact that this contemplation (which is actually a 'participation') is realized, the pain of existence is abolished.

Vyāsa (ad *Y.S.*, III, 55) summarizes the passage from *samprajñāta* to *asamprajñāta samādhi* as follows: through the illumination (*prajñā*, 'wisdom') spontaneously obtained when he reaches the stage of *dharma-megha-samādhi*, the yogin realizes 'absolute isolation' *(kaivalya)*—that is, liberation of *purusha* from the dominance of *prakriti*. For his part, Vācaspatimishra says that the 'fruit' of *samprajñāta samādhi* is *asamprajñāta samādhi*, and the 'fruit' of the latter is *kaivalya*, liberation. It would be wrong to regard this mode of being of the Spirit as a simple 'trance' in which consciousness was emptied of all content. Nondifferentiated enstasis is not absolute emptiness.' The 'state' and the 'knowledge' simultaneously expressed by this term refer to a total absence of objects in consciousness, not to a consciousness absolutely empty. For, on the contrary, at such a moment consciousness is saturated with a direct and total intuition of being. As Mādhava says, 'nirodha [final arrest of all psychomental experience] must not be imagined as a nonexistence, but rather as the support of a particular condition of the Spirit.' It is the enstasis of total emptiness, without sensory content or intellectual structure, an unconditioned state that is no longer 'experience' (for there is no further relation between consciousness and the world) but 'revelation.' Intellect *(buddhi)*, having accomplished its mission, withdraws, detaching itself from the Self *(purusha)* and returning into *prakṛti*. The Self remains free, autonomous: it contemplates itself. 'Human' consciousness is suppressed; that is, it no longer functions, its constituent elements being reabsorbed into the primordial substance. The yogin attains deliverance; like a dead man, he has no more relation with life; he is 'dead in life.' He is the *jīvan-mukta*, the 'liberated in life.' He no longer lives in time and under the domination of time, but in an eternal present, in the *nunc stans* by which Boethius defined eternity.

M. Eliade, *Yoga*, op. cit., pp. 77, 79-81, 83-4, 93-4

JAPANESE BUDDHISM

243. KŪYA, 'THE SAINT OF THE STREETS': A PIONEER OF THE PURE LAND BUDDHISM

The rise of Pure Land Buddhism was not merely an outgrowth of the new feudal society, translating into religious terms the profound social changes which then took place. Already in the late Heian period we find individual monks who sensed the need for bringing Buddhist faith within the reach of the ordinary man, and thus anticipated the mass religious movements of medieval times. Kūya (903-72), a monk on Mt. Hiei, was one of these. The meditation on the Buddha Amida, which had long been accepted as an aid to the religious life, he promoted as a pedestrian devotion. Dancing through the city streets with a tinkling bell hanging from around his neck, Kūya called out the name of Amida and sang simple ditties of his own composition, such as:

> He never fails
> To reach the Lotus Land of Bliss
> Who calls,
> If only once,
> The name of Amida.

> A far, far distant land
> Is Paradise,
> I've heard them say;
> But those who want to go
> Can reach there in a day.

In the market places all kinds of people joined him in his dance and sang out the invocation to Amida, 'Namu Amida Butsu.' When a great epidemic struck the capital, he proposed that these same people join him in building an image of Amida in a public square, saying that common folk could equal the achievement of their rulers, who had built the Great Buddha of Nara, if they cared to try. In country districts he built bridges and dug wells for the people where these were needed, and to show that no one was to be excluded from the blessings of

Paradise, he travelled into regions inhabited by the Ainu and for the
first time brought to many of them the evangel of Buddhism.

Wm. Theodore de Bary (ed.), *Sources of Japanese
Tradition* (New York: Columbia University Press,
1958), pp. 193-4

244. HŌNEN AND THE INVOCATION OF AMIDA, THE BUDDHA OF BOUNDLESS LIGHT

*Hōnen (1133-1212) believed that the invocation of Amida's name,
Namu Amida Butsu, was the only sure hope of salvation. This invocation became known as the Nembutsu, a term which originally signified meditation on the name of Amida, but later meant simply the
fervent repetition of his name.*

*The wife of the ex-Regent, Kanezane Tsukinowa, already converted
to Hōnen's faith, asked him some questions regarding the practice
of Nembutsu. Hōnen replied as follows:*

I have the honour of addressing you regarding your inquiry about
the *Nembutsu*. I am delighted to know that you are invoking the
sacred name. Indeed the practice of the *Nembutsu* is the best of all
for bringing us to Ōjō,[1] because it is the discipline prescribed in Amida's
Original Vow. The discipline required in the Shingon, and the meditation of the Tendai, are indeed excellent, but they are not in the Vow.
This *Nembutsu* is the very thing that Shākya himself entrusted[2] to
his disciple, Ānanda. As to all other forms of religious practice belonging to either the meditative or non-meditative classes, however excellent
they may be in themselves, the great Master did not specially entrust
them to Ānanda to be handed down to posterity. Moreover, the *Nembutsu* has the endorsation of all the Buddhas of the six quarters; and,
while the disciples of the exoteric and esoteric schools, whether in
relation to the phenomenal or noumenal worlds, are indeed most
excellent, the Buddhas do not give them their final approval. And so,
although there are many kinds of religious exercise, the *Nembutsu*
far excels them all in its way of Attaining Ōjō. Now there are some
people who are unacquainted with the way of birth into the Pure
Land, who say, that because the *Nembutsu* is so easy, it is all right

The notes to this text are on p. 505.

for those who are incapable of keeping up the practices required in the Shingon, and the meditation of the Tendai sects, but such a cavil is absurd. What I mean is, that I throw aside those practices not included in Amida's Vow, nor prescribed by Shākyamuni, nor having the endorsement of the Buddhas of all quarters of the universe, and now only throw myself upon the Original Vow of Amida, according to the authoritative teaching of Shākyamuni, and in harmony with what the many Buddhas of the six quarters have definitely approved. I give up my own foolish plans of salvation, and devote myself exclusively to the practice of that mightily effective discipline of the Nembutsu, with earnest prayer for birth into the Pure Land. This is the reason why the abbot of the Eshin-in Temple in his work Essentials of Salvation (Ōjōyōshū) makes the Nembutsu the most fundamental of all. And so you should now cease from all other religious practices, apply yourself to the Nembutsu alone, and in this it is all-important to do it with undivided attention. Zendō,[3] who himself attained to that perfect insight (samādhi) which apprehends the truth, clearly expounds the full meaning of this in his Commentary on the Meditation Sūtra, and in the Two-volumed Sūtra the Buddha (Shākya) says, 'Give yourself with undivided mind to the repetition of the name of the Buddha who is in Himself endless life.' And by 'undivided mind' he means to present a contrast to a mind which is broken up into two or three sections, each pursuing its own separate object, and to exhort to the laying aside of everything but this one thing only. In the prayers which you offer for your loved ones, you will find that the Nembutsu is the one most conducive to happiness. In the Essentials of Salvation, it says that the Nembutsu is superior to all other works. Also Dengyō Daishi, when telling how to put an end to the misfortunes which result from the seven evils, exhorts to the practice of the Nembutsu. Is there indeed anything anywhere that is superior to it for bringing happiness in the present or the future life? You ought by all means to give yourself up to it alone.'

Notes

1 Rebirth in the Pure Land.
2 This refers to the passage in the Meditation Sūtra which says: 'Buddha said to Ānanda, "Preserve well these words. I mean to preserve well the name of the Buddha of Endless Life." '
3 Chinese Patriarch of Pure Land Sect.

Translation and notes by Rev. Harper Havelock Coates and Rev. Ryugaku Ishizuka, Hōnen, the Buddhist Saint, III (Kyoto, 1925), pp. 371-3

245. SHINRAN: 'THE NEMBUTSU ALONE IS TRUE'

('Tannishō,' selections)

Shinran (1173-1262), who claimed to be Hōnen's true disciple, is regarded as the founder of the most important of all 'Pure Land' sects. Shinran's utter reliance on the power of Amida is emphasized by his reinterpretation of the Nembutsu. A single, sincere invocation is enough, said Shinran, and any additional recitation of the Name should merely be an expression of thanksgiving to Amida.

The collection of Shinran's sayings is said to have been made by his disciple Yuiembō, who was concerned over heresies and schisms developing among Shinran's followers and wished to compile a definitive statement of his master's beliefs.

Your aim in coming here, travelling at the risk of your lives through more than ten provinces, was simply to learn the way of rebirth in the Pure Land. Yet you would be mistaken if you thought I knew of some way to obtain rebirth other than by saying the *Nembutsu*, or if you thought I had some special knowledge of religious texts not open to others. Should this be your belief, it is better for you to go to Nara or Mt. Hiei, for there you will find many scholars learned in Buddhism and from them you can get detailed instruction in the essential means of obtaining rebirth in the Pure Land. As far as I, Shinran, am concerned, it is only because the worthy Hōnen taught me so that I believe salvation comes from Amida by saying the *Nembutsu*. Whether the *Nembutsu* brings rebirth in the Pure Land or leads one to Hell, I myself have no way of knowing. But even if I had been misled by Hōnen and went to Hell for saying the *Nembutsu*, I would have no regrets. If I were capable of attaining Buddhahood on my own through the practice of some other discipline, and yet went down to Hell for saying the *Nembutsu*, then I might regret having been misled. But since I am incapable of practising such disciplines, there can be no doubt that I would be doomed to Hell anyway.

If the Original Vow of Amida is true, the teaching of Shākyamuni cannot be false. If the teaching of the Buddha is true, Zendō's commentary on the *Meditation Sūtra* cannot be wrong. And if Zendō is right, what Hōnen says cannot be wrong. So if Hōnen is right, what I, Shinran, have to say may not be empty talk.

Such, in short, is my humble faith. Beyond this I can only say that, whether you are to accept this faith in the *Nembutsu* or reject it, the choice is for each of you to make. . . .

'If even a good man can be reborn in the Pure Land, how much more so a wicked man.'

People generally think, however, that if even a wicked man can be reborn in the Pure Land, how much more so a good man! This latter view may at first sight seem reasonable, but it is not in accord with the purpose of the Original Vow, with faith in the Power of Another. The reason for this is that he who, relying on his own power, undertakes to perform meritorious deeds, has no intention of relying on the Power of Another and is not the object of the Original Vow of Amida. Should he, however, abandon his reliance on his own power and put his trust in the Power of Another, he can be born in the True Land of Recompense. We who are caught in the net of our own passions cannot free ourselves from bondage to birth and death, no matter what kind of austerities or good deeds we try to perform. Seeing this and pitying our condition, Amida made his Vow with the intention of bringing wicked men to Buddhahood. Therefore the wicked man who depends on the Power of Another is the prime object of salvation. This is the reason why Shinran said, 'If even a good man can be reborn in the Pure Land, how much more so a wicked man!' . . .

It is regrettable that among the followers of the *Nembutsu* there are some who quarrel, saying 'These are my disciples, those are not.' There is no one whom I, Shinran, can call my own disciple. The reason is that, if a man by his own efforts persuaded others to say the *Nembutsu*, he might call them his disciples, but it is most presumptuous to call those 'my disciples' who say the *Nembutsu* because they have been moved by the grace of Amida. If it is his karma to follow a teacher, a man will follow him; if it is his karma to forsake a teacher, a man will forsake him. It is quite wrong to say that the man who leaves one teacher to join another will not be saved by saying the *Nembutsu*. To claim as one's own and attempt to take back that faith which is truly the gift of Amida—such a view is wholly mistaken. In the normal course of things a person will spontaneously recognize both what he owes to the grace of Amida and what he owes to his teacher [without the teacher having to assert any claims]. . . .

The Master was wont to say, 'When I ponder over the Vow which Amida made after meditating for five kalpas, it seems as if the Vow were made for my salvation alone. How grateful I am to Amida, who thought to provide for the salvation of one so helplessly lost in sin!'

When I now reflect upon this saying of the Master, I find that it is fully in accordance with the golden words of Zendō. 'We must realize that each of us is an ordinary mortal, immersed in sin and crime, subject to birth and death, ceaselessly migrating from all eternity and ever sinking deeper into Hell, without any means of delivering ourselves from it.'

It was on this account that Shinran most graciously used himself as an example, in order to make us realize how lost every single one of us is and how we fail to appreciate our personal indebtedness to the grace of Amida. In truth, none of us mentions the great love of Amida, but we continually talk about what is good and what is bad. Shinran said, however, 'Of good and evil I am totally ignorant. If I understood good as Buddha understands it, then I could say I knew what was good. If I understood evil as Buddha understands it, then I could say I knew what was bad. But I am an ordinary mortal, full of passion and desire, living in this transient world like the dweller in a house on fire. Every judgment of mine, whatever I say, is nonsense and gibberish. The *Nembutsu* alone is true.'

> Translation in Wm. Theodore de Bary (ed.), *Sources of Japanese Tradition* (New York: Columbia University Press, 1958), pp. 216-18. Introductory note based on De Bary

246. NICHIREN AND THE 'ADORATION TO THE LOTUS OF THE PERFECT TRUTH'

Nichiren (1222-82) held that the Lotus Sūtra represents the final and supreme teaching of the Buddha Shākyamuni, revealing the one and only way of salvation. While the prevailing schools of Japanese Buddhism emphasize one form of Buddha at the expense of the others, the Lotus Sūtra alone upholds the truth of the triune Buddha (i.e., Dharmakāya, Sambhogakāya, and Nirmānakāya). For Nichiren, only in this trinity is the salvation of all assured. So it is the name of the Lotus Sūtra, not the name of Amida Buddha, which should be on the lips of every Buddhist.

If you desire to attain Buddhahood immediately, lay down the banner of pride, cast away the club of resentment, and trust yourselves to the unique Truth. Fame and profit are nothing more than vanity of this life; pride and obstinacy are simply fetters to the coming life. . . .

When you fall into an abyss and some one has lowered a rope to pull you out, should you hesitate to grasp the rope because you doubt the power of the helper? Has not Buddha declared, 'I alone am the protector and saviour'? There is the power! Is it not taught that faith is the only entrance [to salvation]? There is the rope! One who hesitates to seize it, and will not utter the Sacred Truth, will never be able to climb the precipice of Bodhi (Enlightenment). . . . Our hearts ache and our sleeves are wet [with tears], until we see face to face the tender figure of the One, who says to us, 'I am thy Father.' At this thought our hearts beat, even as when we behold the brilliant clouds in the evening sky or the pale moonlight of the fast-falling night. . . . Should any season be passed without thinking of the compassionate promise, 'Constantly I am thinking of you'? Should any month or day be spent without revering the teaching that there is none who cannot attain Buddhahood? . . . Devote yourself wholeheartedly to the 'Adoration to the Lotus of the Perfect Truth,' and utter it yourself as well as admonish others to do the same. Such is your task in this human life.

Masaharu Anesaki, *Nichiren, the Buddhist Prophet* (Cambridge, Mass., 1916), pp. 46-7; as quoted in Wm. Theodore de Bary (ed.), *Sources of Japanese Tradition* (New York: Columbia University Press, 1958), pp. 222-23

See also nos. 193, 216, 217

ZEN BUDDHISM

To bring salvation within the reach of ordinary men—this was the common aim of the Buddhist sects which spread abroad in medieval Japan. Yet to achieve this same end, and to guide men through the uncertainties, turmoil and suffering of that difficult age, these new movements sometimes employed quite different means. The Pure Land and Nichiren sects stressed the need for complete faith in something beyond oneself: the saving power of Amida or of the *Lotus Sūtra*. To find rest and security, they said, man had to turn himself and this world to the Other World. By contrast Zen Buddhism, which first rose to prominence in these same times, firmly opposed the idea that

Buddhahood is something to be sought outside oneself or in another world. Every man has a Buddha-nature, and to realize it he need only look within. Self-understanding and self-reliance are the keynote of Zen.

The means by which this inner realization may be achieved is indicated by the term Zen, meaning 'meditation' or 'concentration.' To speak of it as a 'means,' however, is appropriate only with reference to the specific procedure involved in the practice of meditation: sitting erect, cross-legged and motionless, with the mind concentrated so as to achieve, first, tranquility, and then active insight. But in the light of this insight the method and realization are seen to be one; no 'means' is employed, no 'end' is attained.

Wm. Theodore de Bary (ed.), *Sources of Japanese Tradition* (New York: Columbia University Press, 1958), p. 232

247. REALIZING THE SOLUTION (GENJŌ KŌAN)

[Against the notion that enlightenment is a single, momentary experience.]

To study the way of the Buddha is to study your own self. To study your own self is to forget yourself. To forget yourself is to have the objective world prevail in you. To have the objective world prevail in you, is to let go of your 'own' body and mind as well as the body and mind of 'others.' The enlightenment thus attained may seem to come to an end, but though it appears to have stopped this momentary enlightenment should be prolonged and prolonged.

[Against the notion that the objective world is merely a projection of one's own mind.]

When you go out on a boat and look around, you feel as if the shore were moving. But if you fix your eyes on the rim of the boat, you become aware that the boat is moving. It is exactly the same when you try to know the objective world while still in a state of confusion in regard to your own body and mind; you are under the misapprehension that your own mind, your own nature, is something real and enduring [while the external world is transitory]. Only when you sit straight and look into yourself, does it become clear that [you yourself are changing and] the objective world has a reality apart from you.

[The fullness of enlightenment.]

Our attainment of enlightenment is something like the reflection of the moon in water. The moon does not get wet, nor is the water cleft apart. Though the light of the moon is vast and immense, it finds a home in water only a foot long and an inch wide. The whole moon and the whole sky find room enough in a single dewdrop, a single drop of water. And just as the moon does not cleave the water apart, so enlightenment does not tear man apart. Just as a dewdrop or drop of water offers no resistance to the moon in heaven, so man offers no obstacle to the full penetration of enlightenment. Height is always the measure of depth. [The higher the object, the deeper will seem its reflection in the water.]

> From Hashida, *Shōbō genzō shakui*, I, 142-64, selections translated in De Bary (ed.), *Sources of Japanese Tradition*, op. cit., pp. 251-2

248. SITTING AND THE KŌAN

In the pursuit of the Way [Buddhism] the prime essential is sitting (*zazen*). . . . By reflecting upon various 'public-cases' (*kōan*) and dialogues of the patriarchs, one may perhaps get the sense of them but it will only result in one's being led astray from the way of the Buddha, our founder. Just to pass the time in sitting straight, without any thought of acquisition, without any sense of achieving enlightenment —this is the way of the Founder. It is true that our predecessors recommended both the *kōan* and sitting, but it was the sitting that they particularly insisted upon. There have been some who attained enlightenment through the test of the *kōan*, but the true cause of their enlightenment was the merit and effectiveness of sitting. Truly the merit lies in the sitting.

> From the *Shōbō genzō zuimonki*, pp. 98-9, translated in De Bary (ed.), *Sources of Japanese Tradition*, op. cit., p. 253

249. THE IMPORTANCE OF SITTING

When I stayed at the Zen lodge in T'ien-t'ung [China], the venerable Ching used to stay up sitting until the small hours of the morning and then after only a little rest would rise early to start sitting again. In the meditation hall we went on sitting with the other elders, without letting up for even a single night. Meanwhile many of the monks went off to sleep. The elder would go around among them and hit the sleepers with his fist or a slipper, yelling at them to wake up. If their sleepiness persisted, he would go out to the hallway and ring the bell to summon the monks to a room apart, where he would lecture to them by the light of a candle.

'What use is there in your assembling together in the hall only to go to sleep? Is this all that you left the world and joined holy orders for? Even among laymen, whether they be emperors, princes, or officials, are there any who live a life of ease? The ruler must fulfill the duties of the sovereign, his ministers must serve with loyalty and devotion, and commoners must work to reclaim land and till the soil —no one lives a life of ease. To escape from such burdens and idly while away the time in a monastery—what does this accomplish? Great is the problem of life and death; fleeting indeed is our transitory existence. Upon these truths both the scriptural and meditation schools agree. What sort of illness awaits us tonight, what sort of death tomorrow? While we have life, not to practise Buddha's Law, but to spend the time in sleep is the height of foolishness. Because of such foolishness Buddhism today is in a state of decline. When it was at its zenith monks devoted themselves to the practice of sitting in meditation (*zazen*), but nowadays sitting is not generally insisted upon and consequently Buddhism is losing ground.' . . .

Upon another occasion his attendants said to him, 'The monks are getting overtired or falling ill, and some are thinking of leaving the monastery, all because they are required to sit too long in meditation. Shouldn't the length of the sitting period be shortened?' The master became highly indignant. 'That would be quite wrong. A monk who is not really devoted to the religious life may very well fall asleep in a half hour or an hour. But one truly devoted to it who has resolved to persevere in his religious discipline will eventually come to enjoy the practice of sitting, no matter how long it lasts. When I was young I used to visit the heads of various monasteries, and one of them explained to me, "Formerly I used to hit sleeping monks so hard that my fist just about broke. Now I am old and weak, so I can't hit them hard enough. Therefore it is difficult to produce good monks. In many monasteries today the superiors do not emphasize sitting strongly enough, and so Buddhism is declining. The more you hit them the better," he advised me.'

From the *Shōbō genzō zuimonki*, pp. 50-2, translated by Wm. Theodore de Bary, in De Bary (ed.), *Sources of Japanese Tradition, op. cit.*, pp. 253-4

250. CONTEMPT FOR THE SCRIPTURES

There are Zen masters of a certain type who join in a chorus to deny that the sūtras contain the true teaching of the Buddha. 'Only in the personal transmission from one patriarch to another is the essential truth conveyed; only in the transmission of the patriarchs can the exquisite and profound secrets of Buddha be found.' Such statements represent the height of folly, they are the words of madmen. In the genuine tradition of the patriarchs there is nothing secret or special, not even a single word or phrase, at variance with the Buddhist sūtras. Both the sūtras and the transmission of the patriarchs alike represent the genuine tradition deriving from Shākyamuni Buddha. The only difference between them is that the patriarchs' transmission is a direct one from person to person. Who dares, then, to ignore the Buddha's sūtras? Who can refuse to study them, who can refuse to recite them? Wisely it has been said of old, 'It is you who get lost in the sūtras, not the sūtras that lead you astray.' Among our worthy predecessors there were many who studied the Scriptures. Therefore these loose-tongued individuals should be told, 'To discard the sūtras of the Buddha, as you say, is to reject the mind of the Buddha, to reject the body of the Buddha. To reject the mind and body of the Buddha is to reject the children [followers] of the Buddha. To reject children of the Buddha is to reject the teaching of the Buddha. And if the teaching of the Buddha itself is to be rejected, why should not the teaching of the patriarchs be rejected? And when you have abandoned the teaching of the Buddha and the patriarchs, what will be left except a lot of bald-headed monks? Then you will certainly deserve to be chastised by the rod. Not only would you deserve to be enslaved by the rulers of the world, but to be cast into Hell for punishment.'

From Etō, *Shūso to shite no Dōgen Zenji*, p. 246, translated by Wm. Theodore de Bary, in De Bary (ed.), *Sources of Japanese Tradition, op, cit.,* pp. 255-6

ISLAM

251. MUHAMMAD'S ASCENSION

Each year throughout the Muslim world, on the night of the 27th day of the month Rajah, is celebrated the festical called *Lailat al-Mi'raj*, i.e., the Night of the Prophet's Ascension. The Qur'anic basis for this is Sura XVII, 1 : 'Glory be to Him Who took His servant by night from the sacred temple [at Mecca] to the more remote temple, whose precincts We have blessed, to show him some of Our signs.' On this night mosques are lit up and special services of celebration held at which it is customary to read certain little chapbooks which give more or less elaborate accounts of the famous Night Journey. The brief account of the *Mi'raj* given here is that found in the well-known compendium of Traditions, al-Baghawi's *Masabih as-Sunna* (Khairiyya edition: Cairo, A.H. 1318=A.D. 1900) II, 169-72.

[It is related] from Quatada, quoting from Anas b. Malik—with whom may Allah be pleased—from Malik b. Sa'sa'a, who said that the Prophet of Allah—on whom be Allah's blessing and peace— related to them [the story of] the night on which he was taken on his heavenly journey, saying: While I was in al-Hatim[1]—or maybe he said, While I was in al-Hijr—lying at rest, one came to me,[2] split all between here and here—i.e., from the hollow of his throat to his pubic hair—and drew out my heart. Then there was brought a golden basin filled with faith in which he washed my heart and my bowels and then they were returned [to their place]. According to another line of transmission [the Prophet] said: Then he washed my stomach with water of Zazam,[3] and filled it with faith and wisdom. Then a white riding beast was brought, somewhat smaller than a mule yet

The notes to this text are on p. 517.

bigger than an ass, whose every bound carried him as far as his eye could reach. Him I mounted and Gabriel set off with me till we came to the lowest heaven, which he asked should be opened. 'Who is this?' he was asked. 'Gabriel,' he replied. 'And who is that with you?' 'Muhammad,' said he. 'And has he had revelation sent him?' 'Assuredly,' said he. 'Then welcome to him. How blessed a coming.' Thereat [the gate] was opened, and when I had cleared it, lo! there was Adam. [Gabriel] said: 'This is your father Adam, greet him.' So I gave him greeting, which he returned, saying: 'Welcome to you, O righteous son, righteous prophet.' Then Gabriel mounted up with me till we came to the second heaven, which he asked should be opened. 'Who is this?' he was asked. 'Gabriel,' he replied. 'And who is that with you?' 'Muhammad,' said he. 'And has he had revelation sent him?' 'Assuredly,' said he. 'Then welcome to him. How blessed a coming.' Thereat [the gate] was opened, and when I had cleared it, lo! there was John [the Baptist] and Jesus, who were cousins on their mothers' side. Said [Gabriel]: 'These are John and Jesus, give them greeting.' So I greeted them and they returned it saying: 'Welcome to the righteous brother, the righteous prophet.' Then he ascended with me to the third heaven, which he asked should be opened. 'Who is this?' he was asked. 'Gabriel,' he replied. 'And who is that with you?' 'Muhammad,' said he. 'And has he had revelation sent him?' 'Assuredly,' said he. 'Then welcome to him. How blessed a coming.' Thereat [the gate] was opened, and when I had cleared it, lo! there was Joseph. [Gabriel] said: 'This is Joseph, greet him.' So I gave him greeting, which he returned, saying, 'Welcome to the righteous brother, the righteous prophet.' Then he ascended with me till we came to the fourth heaven, which he asked should be opened. 'Who is this?' he was asked. 'Gabriel,' he replied. 'And who is that with you?' 'Muhammad,' said he. 'And has he had revelation sent him?' 'Assuredly,' said he. 'Then welcome to him. How blessed a coming.' Thereat [the gate] was opened, and when I had cleared it, lo! there was Idris (Enoch). Said [Gabriel]: 'This is Idris, give him greeting.' So I greeted him, and he returned it, saying: 'Welcome to the righteous brother, the righteous prophet.' Then he ascended with me to the fifth heaven, which he asked should be opened. 'Who is this?' he was asked. 'Gabriel,' he replied. 'And who is that with you?' 'Muhammad,' said he. 'And has he had revelation sent him?' 'Assuredly,' said he. 'Then welcome to him. How blessed a coming.' When I had cleared [the gate], lo! there was Aaron. Said [Gabriel]: 'This is Aaron, give him greeting.' So I greeted him, and he returned it, saying: 'Welcome to the righteous brother, the righteous prophet.' Then he ascended with me to the sixth heaven, which he asked should be opened. 'Who is this?' he was asked. 'Gabriel,' he replied. 'And who is that with you?' 'Muhammad,' said he. 'And has he had revelation sent him?' 'Assuredly,' said he. 'Then welcome to him. How blessed a coming.' When I had cleared [the gate] lo! there was Moses. Said [Gabriel]: 'This is Moses, give him greeting.' So I greeted him, and he returned it saying: 'Welcome to the righteous brother, the righteous prophet.' When I passed on he wept, and one asked him why he wept. 'I weep,' said he, because of a youth who has been sent [as an Apostle] after me, more of whose community will enter Paradise than my community.' Then [Gabriel] ascended with me till we reached the seventh heaven, which he asked should be opened. 'Who is this?' he was asked. 'Gabriel,' he replied. 'And who is that with you?' 'Muhammad,' said he. 'And has he had revelation sent him?' 'Assuredly,' said he. 'Then welcome to him. How blessed a coming.' When I had cleared [the gate], lo! there was Abraham. Said [Gabriel]: 'This is your father Abraham, so greet him.' I gave him greeting, which he returned, saying: 'Welcome to the righteous son, the righteous prophet.'

Then I ascended to the Sidrat al-Muntaha, whose fruits were the size of Hajar[4] waterpots and its leaves like elephants' ears. Said [Gabriel]: 'This is the Sidrat al-Muntaha.'[5] There I beheld four streams, two within and two without, so I asked: 'What are these, O Gabriel?' 'The two within,' he answered, are the two rivers of Paradise, but the two without are the Nile and the Euphrates.' Then I was taken up to the Frequented Fane, where a vessel of wine, a vessel of milk, and a vessel of honey were brought to me. I took the milk, whereat he said: 'This is the *fitra*[6] of you and your community.' Then there was laid on me the religious duty of performing fifty prayer services daily, and I departed. As I passed by Moses he asked: 'With what have you been commanded?' 'With fifty prayer services each day,' I replied. 'But your community,' said he, 'will never be able to perform fifty prayer services a day. By Allah, I have had experience with people before you, and I had to strive hard with the Children of Israel. Return to your Lord and ask Him to lighten it for your community.' So I went back and He remitted ten. Then I returned to Moses, but he said the like [of what he had said before], so I went back and He remitted ten more. When, however, I got back to Moses he said the like again, so I returned and He remitted another ten. When I returned to Moses he again said the like, so I went back and was commanded ten prayer services each day and night. When I got back to Moses he said as he had said before, so I went back and was bidden perform five prayer services daily. When I got back to Moses, he said: 'And with what are you commanded now?' 'I am bidden,' I replied, 'perform five prayer services day and night.' 'Your community,' said he, 'will never be able to perform five prayer services daily. I have had experience with people before you, and have had to strive hard with the Children of Israel. Go back to your Lord and ask Him to lighten it for your community.' 'I have been asking of my Lord,' I replied, 'till I am ashamed, I am content and I submit.' Then as I passed on a Crier cried: 'I have settled my ordinance, and have made things easy for My servants.'

Notes

1 The Hatim is a semi-circular, low, and thick wall to the northwest of the Ka'ba at Mecca. The Hijr is the space between this wall and the Ka'ba itself.
2 Lit. 'a comer came,' a common way of expressing the coming of some supernatural visitor. From what follows we may assume that it was the archangel Gabriel.
3 This is the sacred well in the precincts of the shrine of Mecca from which the pilgrims drink as an act of piety and thereby partake of its blessedness.
4 Hajar is the district of Arabia which includes Bahrain over on the Persian Gulf. The *Sidrat al-Muntaha*, i.e., 'lote tree of the boundary,' is said to be a celestial tree which marks the boundary beyond which creatures may not ascend. It is mentioned in Sura LIII, 14.
5 This is the celestial Ka'ba, the navel of the celestial world, situated directly above the earthly Ka'ba.
6 A *fifra* is a natural, inborn disposition. The meaning here is that the Muslim community will be a 'middler' community, like milk, which has neither the intoxicating qualities of wine nor the cloying sweetness of honey.

Translation, introductory comment, and notes by Arthur Jeffery, *Islam. Muhammad and His Religion* (New York: Liberal Arts Press, 1958) pp. 35-9

252. MUHAMMAD'S MEETING WITH HIS LORD

A favourite episode in the account of Muhammad's Ascension is that which tells of the Prophet being taken into the presence of Allah. As Enoch walked with God, as Abraham was the friend of God, as Moses spoke with God face to face on Mt. Sinai, as Jesus had a son's relationship with his Father, so this story is intended to show how Muhammad had an equally intimate acquaintance with his Lord. There are many versions of the story. That given here is from *as-Suyūti's al-La'ālī al-masnū'sa* (Cairo. 1317 A.H.=A.D. 1899), I, 39.

Now when I was brought on my Night Journey to the [place of the] Throne and drew near to it, a green *rafraf*[1] was let down to me, a thing too beautiful for me to describe to you, whereat Gabriel advanced and seated me on it. Then he had to withdraw from me, placing his hands over his eyes, fearing lest his sight be destroyed by the scintillating light of the Throne, and he began to weep aloud, uttering *tasbih*, *tahmid* and *tathniya* to Allah. By Allah's leave, as a sign of His mercy towards me and the perfection of His favour to me, that *rafraf* floated me into the [presence of the] Lord of the Throne, a thing too stupendous for the tongue to tell of or the imagination to picture. My sight was so dazzled by it that I feared blindness. Therefore I shut my eyes, which was by Allah's good favour. When I thus veiled my sight Allah shifted my sight [from my eyes] to my heart, so with my heart I began to look at what I had been looking at with my eyes. It was a light so bright in its scintillation that I despair of ever describing to you what I saw of His majesty. Then I besought my Lord to complete His favour to me by granting me the boon of having a steadfast vision of Him with my heart. This my Lord did, giving me that favour, so I gazed at Him with my heart till it was steady and I had a steady vision of Him.

There He was, when the veil had been lifted from Him, seated on His Throne, in His dignity, His might, His glory, His exaltedness, but beyond that it is not permitted me to describe Him to you. Glory be to Him! How majestic is He. How bountiful are His works! How exalted is His position! How brilliant is His light! Then He lowered somewhat for me His dignity and drew me near to Him, which is as He has said in His book, informing you of how He would deal with me and honour me: 'One possessed of strength. He stood erect when He was at the highest point of the horizon. Then He drew near and descended, so that He was two bows' lengths off, or even nearer' (LIII, 6-9). This means that when He inclined to me He drew me as near to Him as the distance between the two ends of a bow, nay, rather, nearer than the distance between the crotch of the bow and its curved ends. 'Then He revealed to His servant what He revealed' (v. 10), i.e., what matters He had decided to enjoin upon me. 'His heart did not falsify what it saw' (v. 11), i.e., my vision of him with my heart. 'Indeed he was seeing one of the greatest signs of his Lord.' (v. 18).

Now when He—glory be to Him—lowered His dignity for me He placed one of His hands between my shoulders and I felt the coldness of his finger tips for a while on my heart, whereat I experienced such a sweetness, so pleasant a perfume, so delightful a coolness, such a sense of honour in [being granted this] vision of Him, that all my terrors melted away and my fears departed from me, so my heart became tranquil. Then was I filled with joy, my eyes were refreshed, and such delight and happiness took hold of me that I began to bend and sway to right and left like one overtaken by slumber. Indeed, it seemed to me as though everyone in heaven and earth had died, for I heard no voices of angels, nor during the vision of my Lord did I see any dark bodies. My Lord left me there such time as He willed, then brought me back to my senses, and it was as though I had been asleep and had awakened. My mind returned to me and I was tranquil, realizing where I was and how I was enjoying surpassing favour and being shown manifest preference.

Then my Lord, glorified and praised be He, spoke to me, saying: 'O Muhammad, do you know about what the Highest Council is disputing?' I answered: 'O Lord, Thou knowest best about that, as about all things, for Thou art the One who knows the unseen' (cf. v. 109/108). 'They are disputing,' He said, 'about the degrees (darajat) and the excellences (hasanat). Do you know, O Muhammad, what the degrees and the excellences are?' 'Thou, O Lord,' I answered, 'knowest better and art more wise.' Then He said: 'The degrees are concerned with performing one's ablutions at times when that is disagreeable, walking on foot to religious assemblies, watching expectantly for the next hour of prayer when one time of prayer is over. As for the excellences, they consist of feeding the hungry, spreading peace, and performing the Tahajjud prayer at night when other folk are sleeping.' Never have I heard anything sweeter or more pleasant than the melodious sound of His voice.

Such was the sweetness of His melodious voice that it gave me confidence, and so I spoke to Him of my need. I said: 'O Lord, Thou didst take Abraham as a friend, Thou didst speak with Moses face to face, Thou didst raise Enoch to a high place, Thou didst give Solomon a kingdom such as none after him might attain, and didst give to David the Psalter. What then is there for me, O Lord?' He replied: 'O Muhammad, I take you as a friend just as I took Abraham as a friend. I am speaking to you just as I spoke face to face with Moses. I am giving you the Fatiha (Sūra 1) and the closing verses of al-Baqara (11, 284-6), both of which are from the treasuries of My Throne and which I have given to no prophet before you. I am sending you as a prophet to the white folk of the earth and the black folk and the red folk, to jinn and to men thereon, though never before you have I sent a prophet to the whole of them. I am appointing the earth, its dry land and its sea, for you and for your community as a place for purification and for worship. I am giving your community the right to booty which I have given as provision to no community before them. I shall aid you with such terrors as will make your enemies flee before you while you are still a month's journey away. I shall send down to you the Master of all Books and the guardian of them, a Qur'an which We Ourselves have parcelled out (XVII, 106/107). I shall exalt your name for you (XCIV, 4), even to the extent of conjoining it with My name, so that none of the regulations of My religion will ever be mentioned without you being mentioned along with Me.'

Then after this He communicated to me matters which I am not permitted to tell you, and when He had made His covenant with me and had left me there such time as He willed, He took His seat again upon His Throne. Glory be to Him in His majesty, his dignity, His might. Then I looked, and behold, something passed between us and a veil of light was drawn in front of Him, blazing ardently to a distance that none knows save Allah, and so intense that were it to be rent at any point it would burn up all Allah's creation. Then the green *rafraf* on which I was desecended with me, gently rising and falling with me in 'Illiyun[2] . . . till it brought me back to Gabriel, who took me from it. Then the *rafraf* mounted up till it disappeared from my sight.

Notes

1 The lexicons give as one meaning of *rafraf* 'a narrow piece of silk brocade.' It was an ancient idea that a human must be accompanied during ascent to celestial places. Gabriel had accompanied Muhammad so far, but now he can go no further, so a kind of magic carpet is sent down to bring the Prophet the rest of the way into the Divine Presence.

2 'Illiyun is said to be the highest of all celestial regions. It is mentioned in *Sūra* LXXXIII, 18-21.

Translation, introductory comment, and notes by Arthur Jeffery, *Islam. Muhammad and His Religion* (New York: Liberal Arts Press, 1958) pp. 42-6

See also nos. 43, 237, 268, 269

253. A SUFI MYSTIC SPEAKS TO HIS GOD

The following is from the writing of Dhu 'l-Nūn, the Egyptian, who died A.D. *861 (246* A.H.*).*

O God, I never hearken to the voices of the beasts or the rustle of the trees, the splashing of waters or the song of birds, the whistling of the wind or the rumble of thunder, but I sense in them a testimony to Thy Unity (*wahdānīya*), and a proof of Thy Incomparableness; that Thou art the All-prevailing, the All-knowing, the All-wise, the All-just, the All-true, and that in Thee is neither overthrow nor ignorance nor folly nor injusice nor lying. O God, I acknowledge Thee in the proof of Thy handiwork and the evidence of Thy acts; grant me, O God, to seek Thy Satisfaction with my satisfaction, and the Delight of a Father in His child, remembering Thee in my love for Thee, with serene tranquility and firm resolve.

[In his poetry Dhu 'l-Nūn uses the passionate language of the devoted lover, as Rābi'a of Basra had done before him, and so helped to fix a tradition that is thereafter so prominent a characteristic of Sufi literature:]

> *I die, and yet not dies in me*
> *The ardour of my love for Thee,*
> *Nor hath Thy Love, my only goal,*
> *Assuaged the fever of my soul.*

> *To Thee alone my spirit cries;*
> *In Thee my whole ambition lies,*
> *And still Thy Wealth is far above*
> *The poverty of my small love.*

> *I turn to Thee in my request,*
> *And seek in Thee my final rest;*
> *To Thee my loud lament is brought,*
> *Thou dwellest in my secret thought.*

> *However long my sickness be,*
> *This wearisome infirmity,*
> *Never to men will I declare*
> *The burden Thou hast made me bear.*

To Thee alone is manifest
The heavy labour of my breast,
Else never kin nor neighbours know
The brimming measure of my woe.

A fever burns below my heart
And ravages my every part;
It hath destroyed my strength and stay,
And smouldered all my soul away.

Guidest Thou not upon the road
The rider wearied by his load,
Delivering from the steeps of death
The traveller as he wandereth?

Didst Thou not light a Beacon too
For them that found the Guidance true
But carried not within their hand
The faintest glimmer of its brand?

O then to me Thy Favour give
That, so attended, I may live
And overwhelm with ease from Thee
The rigour of my poverty.

> Translation and parenthetical note by A. J. Arberry,
> in his *Sufism, An Account of the Mystics of Islam*
> (London, 1950), pp. 52-4.)

245. ABŪ YAZĪD'S MYSTICAL ASCENSION

Abū Yazīd (Bāyazīd) of Bistam, the Persian (d. 261/875), was the
first to take the Prophet's Ascension (miʻrāj) as a theme for expressing
his own mystical experience, thereby setting a fashion which others
later followed.

I saw that my spirit was borne to the heavens. It looked at nothing and
gave no heed, though Paradise and Hell were displayed to it, for it was
freed of phenomena and veils. Then I became a bird, whose body was of
Oneness and whose wings were of Everlastingness, and I continued to
fly in the air of the Absolute, until I passed into the sphere of Purification, and gazed upon the field of Eternity and beheld there the tree

of Oneness. When I looked I myself was all those. I cried: 'O Lord, with my egoism I cannot attain Thee, and I cannot escape from my selfhood. What am I to do?' God spake: 'O Abū Yazīd, thou must win release from thy thou-ness by following my Beloved (sc. Muḥammad). Smear thine eyes with the dust of his feet and follow him continually.'

> Translation and introductory note by A. J. Arberry,
> *Sufism, op. cit.,* pp. 54-5

255. AL-JUNAID ON UNION AND SEPARATION

Al-Junaid of Baghdad (d. 298/910), called in later times 'the Shaikh of the Order,' was the most original and penetrating intellect among the Sufis of his time. He elaborated a consistent system of Islam's theosophy.

> Now I have known, O Lord,
> What lies within my heart;
> In secret, from the world apart,
> My tongue hath talked with my Adored.

> So in a manner we
> United are, and One;
> Yet otherwise disunion
> Is our estate eternally.

> Though from my gaze profound
> Deep awe hath hid Thy Face,
> In wondrous and ecstatic Grace
> I feel Thee touch my inmost ground.

> Translation and introductory note by A. J. Arberry,
> *Sufism, op. cit.,* p. 59

256. AL-HALLĀJ SPEAKS OF GOD: 'I AM HE WHOM I LOVE . . .'

Husayn ibn Mausūr al-Hallāj (d. 309/922) chose Jesus as his model and claimed: 'I am the Truth' (Ana al-Haqq) (cf. John 14:6). Since al-Haqq, the Truth, is one of the names of God, he was accused of claiming divinity and finally was publicly scourged and crucified.

Betwixt me and Thee there lingers an 'it is I' that torments me.
Ah, of Thy grace, take this 'I' from between us!

I am He whom I love, and He whom I love is I,
We are two spirits dwelling in one body.
If thou seest me, thou seest Him,
And if thou seest Him, thou seest us both.

Ibrāhim ibn Fātik, his servant, said: 'When al-Hallāj was brought to be crucified and saw the cross and the nails . . . he prayed a prayer of two inclinations, and I was standing near him. He recited in the first the Opening of the Qur'an and the verse 'And we shall try you with something of fear and of hunger' (Sūra 21:35). In the second he recited the Opening and the verse beginning 'Every soul shall taste of death' (Sūra 29:57). When he was finished he said some words I do not remember, but of what I remember was: '. . . Oh my God, who art revealed in every place and who art not in any place, I beseech Thee by the truth of Thy Divine word which declared that I am, and by the truth of my weak human word which declares that Thou art, sustain me in gratitude for this Thy grace, that Thou didst hide from others what Thou didst reveal to me of the glory of Thy countenance, and didst forbid to them what thou didst permit to me: the sight of things hidden by Thy mystery.

'And these Thy servants, who are gathered together to slay me in zeal for Thy religion, seeking Thy favour, forgive them. For if Thou hadst revealed to them that which Thou hast revealed to me, they would not have done that which they have done; hadst Thou withheld from me what Thou hast withheld from them, I should never have been tried with this tribulation. To Thee be praise in all Thou doest; to Thee be praise in whatsoever Thou willest.'

Then he was silent. The Herdsman stepped up and dealt him a smashing blow which broke his nose, and the blood ran onto his white robe. The mystic al-Shiblī, who was in the crowd, cried aloud and rent his garment, and Abū Husayn al-Wasitī fell fainting, and so did other famous Sufis who were there, so that a riot nearly broke out. Then the executioners did their work.

Translation and introduction by John Alden Williams, *Islam* (New York, 1961), pp. 148-9, from L. Massignon and Kraus (eds.), *Akhbār al-Hallāj* (Paris, 1936), pp. 7-8. The poem quoted at the beginning was translated by R. A. Nicholson, *The Legacy of Islam* (London, 1939), p. 218

257. THE 'REVELATION' OF AL-NIFFARI

The following is from Kitāb al-Mawāqif by Muhammad b. Abd al-Jabbār al-Niffari (fl. 350/961).

The writer pictures himself as standing before God (mauqif—a term perhaps originally borrowed from the descriptions of the Last Day) in a spiritual state, and hears God speaking to him.

He stayed me in Death; and I saw the acts, every one of them, to be evil. And I saw Fear holding sway over Hope; and I saw Riches turned to fire and cleaving to the fire; and I saw Poverty an adversary adducing proofs; and I saw every thing, that it had no power over any other thing; and I saw this world to be a delusion, and I saw the heavens to be a deception. And I cried out, 'O Knowledge!' and it answered me not. Then I cried out, 'O Gnosis!'; and it answered me not. And I saw every thing, that it had deserted me, and I saw every created thing, that it had fled from me; and I remained alone. And the act came to me, and I saw in it secret imagination, and the secret part was that which persisted; and naught availed me, save the Mercy of my Lord. And he said to me, 'Where is thy knowledge?' And I saw the Fire. And he said to me, 'Where is thy act?' and I saw the Fire. And he said to me, 'Where is thy gnosis?' And I saw the Fire. And He unveiled for me His Gnoses of Uniqueness, and the Fire died down. And He said to me, 'I am thy Friend.' And I was stablished. And He said to me, 'I am thy Gnosis.' And I spoke. And He said to me, 'I am thy Seeker.' And I went forth.

Translation and comment on it by A. J. Arberry, *Sufism, op. cit.,* pp. 64-5

258. AL-GHAZĀLĪ'S CONVERSION TO SUFISM

Abū Hāmid Muhammad b. Muhammad al-Ghazālī (451/1059-505/1111) was a leading orthodox theologian and lawyer; yet he was dissatisfied with the intellectual and legalistic approach to religion and felt a yearning for a more personal experience of God. He tells about his conversion to Sufism in an autobiographical work.

Then I turned my attention to the Way of the Sufis. I knew that it could not be traversed to the end without both doctrine and practice, and that the gist of the doctrine lies in overcoming the appetites of the flesh and getting rid of its evil dispositions and vile qualities, so that the heart may be cleared of all but God; and the means of clearing it is *dhikr Allah*, i.e., commemoration of God and concentration of every thought upon Him. Now, the doctrine was easier to me than the practice, so I began by learning their doctrine from the books and sayings of their Shaykhs, until I acquired as much of their Way as it is possible to acquire by learning and hearing, and saw plainly that what is most peculiar to them cannot be learned, but can only be reached by immediate experience and ecstasy and inward transformation. I became convinced that I had now acquired all the knowledge of Sufism that could possibly be obtained by means of study; as for the rest, there was no way of coming to it except by leading the mystical life. I looked on myself as I then was. Worldly interests encompassed me on every side. Even my work as a teacher—the best thing I was engaged in—seemed unimportant and useless in view of the life hereafter. When I considered the intention of my teaching, I perceived that instead of doing it for God's sake alone I had no motive but the desire for glory and reputation. I realized that I stood on the edge of a precipice and would fall into Hell-fire unless I set about to mend my ways. . . . Conscious of my helplessness and having surrendered my will entirely, I took refuge with God as a man in sore trouble who has no resource left. God answered my prayer and made it easy to turn my back on reputation and wealth and wife and children and friends.

> Translation by A. J. Arberry, *Sufism, op. cit.*, p. 80.
> Introduction adapted from Arberry

259. RŪMĪ DOES NOT RECOGNIZE HIMSELF

Jalāl al-Dīn Rūmī (d. 1273) came under the influence of the Sufi Shams al-Dīn Tabrizi, who was killed by an angry mob. In acknowledgment of the influence of his master, Rūmī called his collection of poems (Diwān) The Diwān of Shams-i-Tabrīz.

What is to be done, O Moslems? for I do not recognize myself.
I am neither Christian nor Jew nor Gabr nor Moslem.
I am not of the East, nor of the West, nor of the land, nor of the sea;

Spiritual Techniques

I am not of Nature's mint, nor of the circling heavens.

I am not of earth, nor of water, nor of air, nor of fire;

I am not of the empyrean, nor of the dust, nor of existence, nor of
entity.

I am not of the Kingdom of 'Iraquain, nor of the country of Khorāsān,

I am not of this world, nor of the next, nor of Paradise, nor of hell.

My place is the Placeless, my trace is the Traceless;

'Tis neither body nor soul, for I belong to the soul of the Beloved.

I have put duality away, I have seen that the two worlds are one;

One I seek, One I know, One I see, One I call.

He is the first, He is the last, He is the outward, He is the inward.

I know none other except 'Yā Hū' [O He!] and 'Yā man Hū.'

I am intoxicated with Love's cup; the two worlds have passed out of
my ken.

I have no business save in carouse and revelry.

If once in my life I spent a moment without thee,

From that time and from that hour I repent of my life.

If once in this world I win a moment with thee,

I will trample on both worlds, I will dance in triumph forever.

Oh Shamsi Tabrīz, I am drunken in this world,

That except of drunkenness and revelry I have no tale to tell.

Translation by R. A. Nicholson, *Dīvānī Shamsi Tabrīz*
(Cambridge, 1898), p. 125. Introduction adapted from
Nicholson

CHAPTER VI

Speculations on Man and God

A. DIFFERENT UNDERSTANDINGS
OF THE HUMAN CONDITION

The name of the author of 'A Dispute over Suicide' has not survived. The text is written in hieratic on a papyrus in the Berlin Museum: no other copies are known. The handwriting dates the papyrus to the Middle Kingdom (ca. 2000-1740 B.C.). It seems probable that the work was composed a few hundred years previously in the First Intermediate Period (ca. 2280-2000 B.C.), like the Instruction for King Meri-ka-re, when the troubled times caused men to reassess religious and ethical beliefs.

The 'Dispute' is in the form of a dialogue between an unnamed man, who is weary of his life, and his soul. The man speaks in the first person and tries to convince his soul of the desirability of suicide and death. The course of the argument is difficult to follow and the text is very obscure in places, especially the first half where there are parables and metaphors, the point of which often escapes the modern reader. It seems not improbable that the man consistently argues in favour of suicide while his soul attempts throughout to dissuade him, but such is the difficulty of the text that sometimes the attitude of the soul is not clear and scholars hold varying views on the tenor of some of its speeches.

My soul opened its mouth to me that it might answer what I had said. If thou recallest burial, it is a sad matter. It is the bringing of tears, making a man sad. It is dragging a man from his house and casting him on the hillside. Thou shalt never go up that thou mayest see the sun. Those who built in granite[1] and who hewed chambers in fine pyramid(s) with good work, when the builders became gods their offering stelae[2] were destroyed like (those of) the weary ones that died on the dyke, through lack of a survivor, the water having taken its toll, and the sun likewise to whom the fishes of the river banks talk. Listen to me.

The notes to this text are on p. 534.

Behold it is good for men to listen. Follow pleasure and forget care. . . .
I opened my mouth to my soul that I might answer what it had said.

> Behold my name stinks
>> Behold more than the stench of fish
>> On a summer's day when the sky is hot. . . .
> Behold my name stinks
>> Behold more than a woman
>> About whom a lie has been told to a man.
> Behold my name stinks
>> Behold more than a sturdy lad
>> About whom it is said 'He belongs to his rival.'[3]

> To whom shall I speak today?
>> Brothers are evil,
>> The companions of yesterday do not love.
> To whom shall I speak today?
>> Hearts are rapacious,
>> Every man seizes the goods of his neighbour . . .
> To whom shall I speak today?
>> Men are contented with evil,
>> Goodness is neglected everywhere.
> To whom shall I speak today?
>> One who should make a man enraged by his evil behaviour
>> Makes everyone laugh, though his iniquity is grievous. . . .
> To whom shall I speak today?
>> The wrongdoer is an intimate,
>> The brother with whom one should act is become an enemy.
> To whom shall I speak today?
>> Yesterday is not remembered,
>> No one now helps him that hath done (good).
> To whom shall I speak today?
>> Faces are averted,
>> Every man has (his) face downcast towards his brethren.
> To whom shall I speak today?
>> Hearts are rapacious,
>> No man has a heart upon which one can rely.
> To whom shall I speak today?
>> There are no righteous men.
>> The land is left over to workers of iniquity. . . .
> To whom shall I speak today?
>> I am laden with misery

> Through lack of an intimate.
> To whom shall I speak today?
>> The sin that roams the land,
>> It has no end.
> Death is in my sight today
>> (Like) the recovery of a sick man,
>> Like going abroad after detention.
> Death is in my sight today
>> Like the smell of myrrh,
>> Like sitting under an awning on a windy day
> Death is in my sight today
>> Like the scent of lotus flowers,
>> Like sitting on the bank of drunkenness.
> Death is in my sight today
>> Like a well trodden way,
>> As when a man returns home from an expedition.
> Death is in my sight today
>> Like the clearing of the sky,
>> Like a man attracted thereby to what he knows not.
> Death is in my sight today
>> Like the longing of a man to see home,
>> When he has spent many years held in capitvity.
> Surely he who is yonder[4] shall
>> Be a living god,
>> Punishing the sin of him who commits it.
> Surely he who is yonder shall
>> Stand in the barque of the sun,
>> Causing the choicest things to be given therefrom to the
>> temples.
> Surely he who is yonder shall
>> Be a man of knowledge,
>> Who cannot be prevented from petitioning Re when he
>> speaks.

What my soul said to me. Put care aside, my comrade and brother. Make an offering on the brazier and cling to life, according as I (?) have said.[5] Desire me here and reject the West, but desire to reach the West when thy body goes into the earth, that I may alight after thou hast grown weary.[6] Then let us make an abode together.

IT IS FINISHED FROM ITS BEGINNING TO ITS END, AS IT WAS FOUND IN WRITING.

Notes

1 *Those who built in granite* refers to the kings and nobles of the Old Kingdom who built the great pyramids and who erected fine tombs for themselves in order that their mortal remains should be preserved for ever. Preservation of the physical body was essential for life after death. The sense of the passage is that these kings and nobles are now no better off than poor men who died in the open, without shelter and without relatives to perform the mortuary rites for them. Soon after the great ones *became gods* (i.e., died), their pyramids and tombs were plundered and their offering stelae were destroyed, thus reducing them to the level of the paupers.

2 *offering stelae* were necessary for the mortuary cult. It was believed that the deceased needed food and drink after death. Stelae were erected on the outside of the tomb, at which such offerings were made. The wealthy endowed mortuary priests to make the offerings daily while the less fortunate relied on relatives and friends.

3 *his rival*, i.e., the lad's father's rival for his mother's affections. The imputation levelled against the lad is that he is a bastard.

4 *he who is yonder* is a euphemism for 'the dead.'

5 *as I (?) have said.* The original has 'as you have said.' The pronoun of the second person is emended to that of the first person.

6 *grown weary* is a euphemism for 'died'; cp. earlier in the text *like (those of) the weary ones that died on the dyke.*

> Translation, introduction, and notes by T. W. Thacker, in D. Winton Thomas (ed.), *Documents from Old Testament Times* (London: Thomas Nelson, 1958)

261. THE EGYPTIAN SONG OF THE HARPIST: 'NONE RETURNETH AGAIN THAT IS GONE THITHER'

> *How prosperous is this good prince!*[1]
> *It is a goodly destiny, that the bodies diminish,*
> *Passing away while others remain,*
> *Since the time of the ancestors,*
> *The gods who were aforetime,*
> *Who rest in their pyramids,*
> *Nobles and the glorious departed likewise,*
> *Entombed in their pyramids.*
> *Those who built their (tomb)-temples,*
> *Their place is no more.*
> *Behold what is done therein.*
> *I have heard the words of Imhotep and Hardedef,*[2]
> *(Words) greatly celebrated as their utterances.*

The notes to this text are on p. 535.

Different Understandings

Behold the places thereof;
Their walls are dismantled,
Their places are no more,
As if they had never been.

None cometh from thence
That he may tell (us) how they fare;
That he may tell (us) of their fortunes,
That he may content our heart,
Until we (too) depart
To the place whither they have gone.

Encourage thy heart to forget it,
Making it pleasant for thee to follow thy desire,
While thou livest.
Put myrrh upon thy head,
And garments on thee of fine linen,
Imbued with marvellous luxuries,
The genuine things of the gods.

Increase yet more thy delights,
And let (not) thy heart languish.
Follow thy desire and thy good,
Fashion thine affairs on earth
After the mandates of thine (own) heart.
(Till) that day of lamentation cometh to thee,
Then the silent-hearted hears not their lamentation,
Nor he that is in the tomb attends the mourning.

Celebrate the glad day,
Be not weary therein.
Lo, no man taketh his goods with him.
Yea, none returneth again that is gone thither.

Notes

1 Meaning the dead king in whose tomb the song was written.
2 Imhotep was grand vizier, chief architect, and famous wise man under king Zoser of the Third Dynasty (thirtieth century B.C.). Hardedef was a royal prince, son of Khufu of Gizeh, and hence connected with the greatest pyramid. He lived about a century after Imhotep. Both of them had thus become proverbial wise men a thousand years after they passed away.

Translation and notes by J. H. Breasted, in his
*Development of Religion and Thought in Ancient
Egypt*, 1912, pp. 182-3. Cf. translation by John A.
Wilson, in ANET, p. 467

262. EGYPTIAN DISILLUSION AND DESPAIR: THE ADMONITIONS OF *IPU*

The Admonitions *date originally from the twenty-second century* B.C.

It used to be said that he was every man's shepherd, that there was no evil in his heart, that however insignificant his flock he would spend the whole day caring for them. . . . Ah! Had he understood the character of men in the first generation he would have launched his curse and raised his arm against them. He would have destroyed their heirs, although they were his own seed. But he wished that birth should continue . . . it could not come to an end as long as these gods (the righteous kings of the past) were there. Progeny still comes forth from the wombs of the women of Egypt but one does not find it [playing?] in the road. It is rapine and violence against the weak that these gods (the recent kings) have wrought. There has been no true pilot in their time. Where is he? Does he sleep perchance? Behold, one sees no sign of his almighty power!

> A. H. Gardiner, *The Admonitions of an Egyptian Sage* (Leipzig, 1909), as printed in R. T. Rundle Clark, *Myth and Symbol in Ancient Egypt* (New York, 1960), pp. 68-9

See also nos. 18-20, 166-70, 272, 273

263. A JAIN PARABLE: THE MAN IN THE WELL

(Haribhadra, 'Samarādityakathā,' II, 55-88)

A certain man, much oppressed by the woes of poverty,
Left his own home, and set out for another country.
He passed through the land, with its villages, cities, and harbours,
And after a few days he lost his way.

And he came to a forest, thick with trees . . . and full of wild beasts.
There, while he was stumbling over the rugged paths, . . . a prey to thirst and hunger, he saw a mad elephant, fiercely trumpeting, charg-

ing him with upraised trunk. At the same time there appeared before him a most evil demoness, holding a sharp sword, dreadful in face and form, and laughing with loud and shrill laughter. Seeing them he trembled in all his limbs with deathly fear, and looked in all directions. There, to the east of him, he saw a great banyan tree. . . .

And he ran quickly, and reached the mighty tree.
But his spirits fell, for it was so high that even the birds could not
    fly over it,
And he could not climb its high unscalable trunk. . . .
All his limbs trembled with terrible fear,
Until, looking round, he saw nearby an old well covered with grass.
Afraid of death, craving to live if only a moment longer,
He flung himself into the well at the foot of the banyan tree.
A clump of reeds grew from its deep wall, and to this he clung,
While below him he saw terrible snakes, enraged at the sound of
    his falling;
And at the very bottom, known from the hiss of its breath, was a
    black and mighty python
With mouth agape, its body thick as the trunk of a heavenly elephant,
    with terrible red eyes.
He thought, 'My life will only last as long as these reeds hold fast,'
And he raised his head; and there, on the clump of reeds, he saw two
    large mice,
One white, one black, their sharp teeth ever gnawing at the roots of
    the reed-clump.
Then up came the wild elephant, and, enraged the more at not catching
    him,
Charged time and again at the trunk of the banyan tree.
At the shock of his charge a honeycomb on a large branch
Which hung over the old well, shook loose and fell.
The man's whole body was stung by a swarm of angry bees,
But, just by chance, a drop of honey fell on his head,
Rolled down his brow, and somehow reached his lips,
And gave him a moment's sweetness. He longed for other drops,
And he thought nothing of the python, the snakes, the elephant, the
    mice, the well, or the bees,
In his excited craving for yet more drops of honey.
This parable is powerful to clear the minds of those on the way to
    freedom.
Now hear its sure interpretation.

The man is the soul, his wandering in the forest the four types of
existence.

The wild elephant is death, the demoness old age.

The banyan tree is salvation, where there is no fear of death, the
elephant,

But which no sensual man can climb.

The well is human life, the snakes are passions,

Which so overcome a man that he does not know what he should do.

The tuft of reed is man's allotted span, during which the soul exists
embodied;

The mice which steadily gnaw it are the dark and bright fortnights.

The stinging bees are manifold diseases,

Which torment a man until he has not a moment's joy.

The awful python is hell, seizing the man bemused by sensual pleasure,

Fallen in which the soul suffers pains by the thousand.

The drops of honey are trivial pleasures, terrible at the last.

How can a wise man want them, in the midst of such peril and hardship?

Translation by A. L. Basham, in Wm. Theodore de
Bary (ed.), *Sources of Indian Tradition* (New York:
Columbia University Press, 1958), pp. 56-8

264. THE INDESTRUCTIBLE, ETERNAL SELF: KRISHNA'S TEACHING TO ARJUNA

('Bhagavad Gītā,' II, 16-26, 47)

16. Of what is not, no coming to be occurs;
    No coming not to be occurs of what is;
    But the dividing-line of both is seen,
    Of these two, by those who see the truth.

17. But know that that is indestructible,
    By which this all is pervaded;
    Destruction of this imperishable one
    No one can cause.

18. These bodies come to an end,
    It is declared, of the eternal embodied (soul),
    Which is indestructible and unfathomable.
    Therefore fight, son of Bharata!

Different Understandings

19. Who believes him a slayer,
    And who thinks him slain,
    Both these understand not:
    He slays not, is not slain.

20. He is not born, nor does he ever die;
    Nor, having come to be, will he ever more come not to be.
    Unborn, eternal, everlasting, this ancient one
    Is not slain when the body is slain.

21. He knows as indestructible and eternal
    This unborn, imperishable one,
    That man, son of Prithā, how
    Can he slay or cause to slay—whom?

22. As leaving aside worn-out garments
    A man takes other, new ones,
    So leaving aside worn-out bodies
    To other, new ones goes the embodied (soul).

23. Swords cut him not,
    Fire burns him not,
    Water wets him not,
    Wind dries him not.

24. Not to be cut is he, not to be burnt is he,
    Not to be wet nor yet dried;
    Eternal, omnipresent, fixed,
    Immovable, everlasting is he.

25. Unmanifest he, unthinkable he,
    Unchangeable he is declared to be;
    Therefore knowing him thus
    Thou shouldst not mourn him.

26. Moreover, even if constantly born
    Or constantly dying thou considered him,
    Even so, great-armed one, thou
    Shouldst not mourn him. . . .

47. On action alone be thy interest,
    Never on its fruits;
    Let not the fruits of action be thy motive,
    Nor be thy attachment to inaction.

Translation by Franklin Edgerton, *The Bhagavad Gītā* (Vol. I, Harvard Oriental Series, Vol. 38 (Cambridge: Harvard University Press, 1944)

265. GREEK PESSIMISM

What life is there, what pleasure without golden Aphrodite? May I die, as soon as I have no part in her ways. Stealthy wooing, lovers' gifts and lovers' unions—these alone are flowers of youth worth plucking for man or woman. Once let old age come on, making a man evil and ugly at once, and heavy cares gnaw at the heart continually. No joy has he in seeing the sun's light, unhonoured by the young and despised by womankind. Thus bitter is old age, as the god hath willed.

Like are we to the leaves that flowery springtime bears, when swiftly they wax strong beneath the rays of the sun. Like them we enjoy for a span the flowers of youth, knowing from the gods neither good nor evil. But the black fates stand by, and one holds in her hand the goal of bitter old age, the other that of death. Brief is the fruit of youth, no longer than the daily spread of the sunshine over the earth; but when once that springtime of life is past, then verily to die is better than life, for many are the ills that invade the heart.

Mimnermos of Kolophon, seventh century B.C.

Honourable it is and glorious for a man to fight with foes for his country, his children and his wedded wife. As for death, it will come whenever the Fates with their spindle decide. . . . For in no way is it decreed that a man may escape death, though he have the Immortals themselves for forebears. He may retire and shun the fray and the javelin's blow, but in his house the Fate of death finds him out. Then is he less loved and less regretted by the people, but the warrior if aught befall him is mourned by low and high, and in life is the equal of the demi-gods.

Kallinos, seventh century B.C.

My son, the end of all things is in the hand of Zeus the heavy thunderer. There is no wit in man. Creatures of a day, we live like cattle, knowing nothing of how the god will bring each one to his end. Hope and self-persuasion are the nourishment of us all as we seek the unattainable. [One man, he continues, is caught up by old age before he reaches his goal, others have wasting diseases, are taken off by war or shipwreck or commit suicide; and so it goes on.] Thus evil is with everything. Yea ten thousand dooms, woes and grief beyond speaking are the lot of mankind.

Semonides, seventh century B.C.

Men? Small is their strength, fruitless their cares, brief their life, toil upon toil. Death unescapable hangs over all alike, dealing impartially with good and bad.

All wisdom is with God. In mortal life nothing is free from woe.

Simonides of Keos, seventh century B.C.

Translation by W. K. C. Guthrie, in his *The Greeks and Their Gods* (London, 1950), pp. 129-31

266. A PAGAN PHILOSOPHER ON THE USE OF IMAGES

(Maximus of Tyre, 'Oration,' VIII, 10)

Maximus of Tyre (ca. A.D. 125-185) was a Sophist and eclectic philosopher who travelled widely and lectured both at Athens and at Rome.

For the God who is the Father and Creator of all that is, older than the sun, older than the sky, greater than time and eternity and the whole continual flow of nature, is not to be named by any lawgiver, is not to be uttered by any voice, is not to be seen by any eye. But we, being unable to grasp his essence, make use of sounds and names and pictures, of beaten gold and ivory and silver, of plants and rivers, of mountain peaks and torrents, yearning for the knowledge of him, and in our weakness naming all that is beautiful in this world after his nature. The same thing happens to those who love others; to them the sweetest sight will be the actual figures of their children, but sweet also will be their memory—they will be happy at [the sight of] a lyre, a little spear, or a chair, perhaps, or a running ground, or anything whatever that wakens the memory of the beloved. Why should I go any further in examining and passing judgment about images? Let all men know what is divine; let them know, that is all. If Greeks are stirred to the remembrance of God by the art of Phidias, or the Egyptians by paying worship to animals, or others by a river, or others by fire, I will not quarrel with their differences. Only let them know, let them love, let them remember.

Translation by Frederick C. Grant, in his *Hellenistic Religions* (New York, 1953), p. 168

Speculations on Man and God

(Cicero, 'The Nature of the Gods,' III, *79-95)*

This work of Cicero's was one of the most important writings in the history of ancient religious thought and in the philosophy of religion. It marked a summation and turning point in the perennial discussion, for Cicero recognized the difficulties which educated men faced in his time, viz., the decline of confidence in the traditional gods and in divine providence (i.e., the divine rule of the world) while at the same time having a half-conscious longing for a rational and defensible belief in divine purpose.

The Nature of the Gods was written in the summer of 45 B.C. The arrangement of the dialogue is simple. Cotta and his friends have gathered at his villa during the Latin Festival in the summer of the year 76 B.C. They are Gaius Velleius, the leading Roman expert in Epicureanism, Balbus, the renowned Stoic, and Cotta, the host, an acute and eminent exponent of the New Academy. Cicero is present. In book I, Velleius sets forth the main principles of Epicurean teachings on the existence and nature of gods (§§ 18-56). The remainder of book I is the reply made by Cotta the Academic, who completely demolishes Epicurean theology and shows that philosophy to be wholly destructive of religion (§§ 57-124).

Book II sets forth in detail the positive teachings of the Stoic theology as expounded by Balbus under four main headings: (1) the existence of the gods, proved by many arguments (§§ 4-44); (2) their nature (§§ 45-72); and their providential government of the world (§§ 73-153); and (3) their providential care for man (§§ 154-168). Book III contains Cotta's criticism, from the Academic point of view, of Balbus' exposition of Stoicism.

'However, we need say nothing more on a point that is already perfectly clear. Telamon dismisses the whole subject, viz., that the gods pay no attention to man, in a single line [of Ennius' play]:

> If they cared [for us], the good would prosper
> and the evil suffer:
> But this does not happen.
> (Frag. 330)

Indeed, the gods should have made all men good, if they were really

542

concerned over the welfare of the human race; (80) or at the very least they should certainly have taken care of the good. But why, then, were the two Scipios, the bravest and best of men, defeated in Spain by the Carthaginians? Why did Maximus have to bury his son, a consul? Why was Hannibal permitted to kill Marcellus? Why was Paulus overwhelmed at Cannae? Why was Regulus handed over to be tortured by the Carthaginians? Why was not Africanus protected by his own walls? [He was murdered in bed by an unknown assassin.] But these instances and many others belong to the past; let us look at more recent ones. Why is my uncle, Publius Rutilius, a man of unsullied character and of the greatest learning, now in exile? Why was my colleague Drusus murdered in his own house? Why was that model of temperance and prudence, Quintus Scaevola, the Pontifex Maximus, assassinated in the very presence of the statue of Vesta? And before that, why were so many of the foremost citizens put to death by Cinna? Why was the most treacherous man of all, Gaius Marius, given the power to order the death of that noblest of men, Quintus Catulus? (81) The day would be too short if I set out to make a list of the good men who have been overwhelmed by adversity, or, equally, the wicked who have prospered. Why did Marius die comfortably at home, an old man, and a consul for the seventh time? Why did that utterly cruel man Cinna rule for so long? "But," you say, "he was punished." It would have been far better had he been prevented from murdering all those eminent men, rather than himself eventually punished. . . . Further, we are told that Anaxarchus, the follower of Democritus, was slaughtered by the tyrant of Cyprus, and that Zeno of Elea was tortured to death. Why should I mention Socrates, of whose death I can never read, in Plato [in the *Phaedo*], without weeping? Do you not see, then, that the judgment of the gods, supposing they pay any attention to human affairs, has obliterated all distinctions? [i.e., between good and evil, or between the upright and the wicked. Cf. § 84 *ad fin.*]

(83) 'Diogenes the Cynic used to say that Harpalus, a bandit in those days who was looked upon as a happy man, was the standing witness against the gods, since he lived and prospered for so long. Dionysius, whom I have just mentioned, after plundering the temple of Proserpine at Locri, was sailing back to Syracuse, and as he held his course with a strong following wind, smiled and said, "Do you see, my friends, what a fine voyage the immortal gods provide those who commit sacrilege?" He was a very clever fellow, and he caught hold of the truth so thoroughly and so clearly that he persevered in this view.

When his fleet touched the coast of the Peloponnese and he arrived at the temple of Olympian Zeus, he stripped off the immensely heavy gold mantle of the god which the tyrant Celo had devoted to Jove out of the spoils taken from the Carthaginians; and he actually joked about it, saying that a golden mantle was much too heavy for summer and too cold for winter and tossing him a woollen mantle, which was good for any time of year.

'He also ordered the removal of the gold beard of Aesculapius at Epidaurus, saying it was not proper for the son to wear a beard when his father [Apollo] in all his temples appeared without one. (84) He even ordered the silver tables removed from the shrines, since in accordance with ancient Greek custom they were inscribed, "The property of the good gods"; for he said he wished to benefit by their goodness. . . .

(86) ' "But," it may be urged, "the gods pay no attention to little matters (cf. 11, 167), and are not concerned with the tiny farms and poor vines of individual persons, so that any small damage done by blight or hail can scarcely have come to Jupiter's attention. In kingdoms the rulers do not look after every last detail of affairs." This is your argument. As if it were Publius Rutilius' estate at Formiae about which I was complaining [§ 80], and not his total loss of safety! But this is a way mortals have: their external commodities ["the good things of life"], vineyards, grain, fields, olive groves, abundant harvests of fruit and grain—in short, all the comforts and prosperity which enrich their life—these, they say, are derived from the gods; but no one ever looked upon virtue as the gift of a god! (87) And no doubt with good reason, since our virtue entitles us to receive praise from others, and in virtue we have a right to take pride, which we could not do if it came as a gift from God, and not from ourselves. On the other hand, when we gain new honours, or are blessed with some increase in our property, or when we receive any other of the good things that come by fortune or luckily escape any of the evils, we then return thanks to the gods, and do not assume that any praise is due to ourselves. But who ever thanked the gods that he was a good man? No, but we thank them that we are rich, honoured, safe and sound. . . .

(89) ' "But good men sometimes end their lives happily." Yes, and so we seize their examples and without the least show of reason attribute their success to the gods. Diagoras, who was called the Atheist, once visited Samothrace, where one of his friends showed him several pictures of people who had survived very dangerous storms. "You assume," he said, "that the gods pay no attention to human affairs. Do you

not recognize from these painted tablets how many persons through their vows to the gods have escaped the violence of tempests and reached ports in safety?" "Sure enough," replied Diagoras, "but there are no pictures of those who were shipwrecked and lost at sea." On another voyage he himself ran into a storm, and the sailors, alarmed and terrified, told him they justly deserved their misfortune for admitting him on board their ship. But he pointed out to them several other ships labouring through the storm and asked if they thought these ships also had a Diagoras on board. And so with regard to good or bad fortune, it makes not the slightest difference what you are or how you have lived.

(90) ' "The gods, like kings, do not pay attention to everything," it is said [cf. § 86]. But what is the parallel here? If kings knowingly overlook anything [for which they are responsible], they are very guilty; but a god cannot be plead ignorance as an excuse. Yet what an extraordinary defence you make for his case when you say that even if a wicked man escapes his punishment by dying, the penalty is inflicted on his children, his children's children, and all his posterity. What a marvellous example of divine justice! Would any city tolerate the proposal of a law like that, which sentenced a son or a grandson for the crime committed by a father or a grandfather? . . .

(93) ' "Providence," you say, "does not concern itself with individual men" (cf. II, 164). No wonder!—since it does not care for cities. Not even for cities? No, nor for whole nations of peoples. If, therefore, it even despises whole nations, what wonder is there if it scorns the whole human race? But how can you assert that the gods do not concern themselves with all the petty circumstances of life, and at the same time hold that specific, individual dreams are distributed to men by the immortal gods! I take up this question with you because your school believes in the truth of dreams. And do you also maintain that men ought to obligate themselves with vows? But vows are taken by individuals; hence it appears that the divine mind listens even to private matters, and can you not see, accordingly, that it is not so heavily engrossed [with public affairs] as you supposed? Assume that it is busily engaged in moving the heavens and looking after the earth and controlling the seas: why does it permit so many gods to be idle and do nothing? Why is not the management of human affairs handed over to some of those idle deities, which you, Balbus, described as innumerable?

'This is about what I have to say concerning the nature of the gods; not with a desire to destroy [the idea], but merely to let you see how obscure a subject it is, and how difficult to explain' [cf. I, 1].

(94) When he had said this, Cotta ceased speaking. But Lucilius replied, 'You have been very severe in your attack upon divine providence, that doctrine established by the Stoics with the greatest piety and wisdom! But as it is growing late, please set another day for our answer to your views. For it is my duty to challenge you in defence of our altars and hearths, the temples and shrines of the gods, nay, even the walls of the City, which you pontiffs declare to be sacred—for you surround the City with religion [ceremonies] even more carefully than you do with walls. This is something which, as long as I am able to breathe, I think it utterly wrong for me to abandon.'

(95) To which Cotta replied, 'I really wish that you would refute me, Balbus! What I have set forth was intended not to decide this debate, but to discuss it; and I am sure that you can easily defeat me.'

'No doubt of that,' said Velleius, 'when he even believes that our dreams are sent from Jupiter, which, unsubstantial as they are, still have more weight than a Stoic discourse on the nature of the gods!'

Translation by Frederick C. Grant, in his *Ancient Roman Religion*, Library of Religion paperbook series (New York, 1957), pp. 140 *ff.*; introduction adapted from Grant

268. ALLAH IS NEARER TO MAN THAN THE JUGULAR VEIN

('Koran,' L, 1-15)

Nay, but they marvel that a warner has come to
them from among them; and the unbelievers say,
    'This is a marvellous thing!
What, when we are dead and become dust? That
    is a far returning!'
We know what the earth diminishes of them;
    with Us is a book recording.
    Nay, but they cried lies to the truth
    when it came to them, and so they are
    in a case confused.
What, have they not beheld heaven above them,
how We have built it, and decked it out fair,
    and it has no cracks?

And the earth—We stretched it forth, and cast on it
    firm mountains,
and We caused to grow therein of every joyous kind
    for an insight
and a reminder to every penitent servant.
    And We sent down out of heaven
        water blessed,
    and caused to grow thereby gardens
        and grain of harvest
and tall palm-trees with spathes compact,
    a provision for the servants,
and thereby We revived a land that was dead.
    Even so is the coming forth.

Cried lies before them the people of Noah
    and the men of Er-Rass, and Thamood, and
    Ad and Pharaoh, the brothers of Lot, the
    men of the Thicket, the people of Tubba',
    Every one cried lies to the Messengers,
    and My threat came true.
What, were We wearied by the first creation?
No indeed; but they are in uncertainty
    as to the new creation.

We indeed created man; and We know
what his soul whispers within him,
and We are nearer to him than the
    jugular vein.

        Translation by A. J. Arberry

269. GOD 'KNOWS THE THOUGHTS WITHIN THE BREASTS'

('Koran,' XXXIX, 5-10)

Surely God guides not him who is a liar,
    unthankful.
Had God desired to take to Him a son,
He would have chosen whatever He willed of that
He has created. Glory be to Him! He is God,
    the One, the Omnipotent.

He created the heavens and the earth in truth,
  wrapping night about the day, and
  wrapping the day about the night;
and He has subjected the sun and the moon, each of them running
  to a stated term.

Is not He the All-mighty, the All-forgiving?
  He created you of a single soul, then
  from it He appointed its mate;
and He sent down to you of the cattle eight couples.
  He creates you in your mothers' wombs
  creation after creation
  in threefold shadows.
  That then is God, your Lord;
  to Him belongs the Kingdom;
  there is no god but He;
  so how are you turned about?
If you are unthankful, God is independent of you,
yet He approves not unthankfulness in His servants;
but if you are thankful, He will approve it in you.
And no soul laden bears the load of another. Then
to your Lord shall you return, and He will tell you
  what you have been doing.
  He knows the thoughts within the breasts.

Translation by A. J. Arberry

See also nos. 73, 237, 252

270. 'WHERE IS THE LAND IN WHICH ONE DOES NOT DIE?' (NAHUATL)

The Nahuatl were an ancient people in Mexico.

The more I weep, the more I am afflicted,
the more my heart may not desire it,
have I not, when all is said, to go to the Land of the Mystery?

Here on earth our hearts say:
'Oh my friends, would that we were immortal,
oh friends, where is the land in which one does not die?

Shall it be that I go? Does my mother live there? Does my
    father live there?

In the Land of the Mystery . . . my heart shudders:
if only I had not to die, had not to perish. . . .
I suffer and feel pain.

Thou hast left thy fame already well-founded,
O Prince Tlacahuepantzin.
The fact is that here we are but slaves.
Men are simply standing
before him through whom everything lives.
Birth comes, life comes upon earth.
For a short while it is lent us,
the glory of that by which everything lives.
Birth comes, life comes upon earth.

We come only to sleep,
We come only to dream:
It is not true, not true we come to live on the earth:

Spring grass are we become:
It comes, gloriously trailing, it puts out buds, our heart,
the flower of our bodies opens a few petals, then withers!

> Nahuatl poem quoted by Laurette Séjourné, *Burning
> Water*, trans. Irene Nicholson (London, 1957), pp.
> 63-4

271. A MEXICAN LAMENT (NAHUATL)

1. Weeping, I, the singer, weave my song of flowers of sadness; I call
to memory the youths, the shards, the fragments, gone to the land
of the dead; once noble and powerful here on earth, the youths were
dried up like feathers, were split into fragments like an emerald, before
the face and in the sight of those who saw them on earth, and with
the knowledge of the Cause of All.

2. Alas! Alas! I sing in grief as I recall the children. Would that I
could turn back again; would that I could grasp their hands once more;
would that I could call them forth from the land of the dead; would
that we could bring them again on earth, that they might rejoice and
delight the Giver of Life; is it possible that we His servants should reject

him or should be ungrateful? Thus I weep in my heart as I, the singer, review my memories, recalling things sad and grievous.

3. Would only that I knew they could hear me, there in the land of the dead, were I to sing some worthy song. Would that I could gladden them, that I could console the suffering and the torment of the children. How can it be learned? Whence can I draw the inspiration? They are not where I may follow them; neither can I reach them with my calling as one here on earth.

Daniel G. Brinton, *Ancient Nahuatl Poetry* (Philadelphia, 1890), p. 73; as quoted in Charles Samuel Braden, *The Scriptures of Mankind* (New York, 1952), pp. 30-1

B. HUMILITY, WISDOM, TOLERANCE

EGYPTIAN TEACHING

272. AN EGYPTIAN RELIGIOUS THINKER:
THE INSTRUCTION FOR KING MERI-KA-RE

The extract which follows is taken from a work composed by an Egyptian king for the benefit of his son Meri-ka-re, who succeeded him on the throne. They lived in the period of confusion and anarchy known as the First Intermediate Period, which followed the downfall of the Old Kingdom (ca. 2280 B.C.) and which preceded the rise of the Middle Kingdom (ca. 2000 B.C.). The Instruction for King Meri-ka-re was thus composed in times of violence and intrigue, and it is in this setting that it must be interpreted and understood. . . .

In the Leningrad Papyrus (the only one in which this portion of the text is fully preserved), the first sentence of each of the two paragraphs is written in red. Capitals are used here to reproduce these headings.

DO JUSTICE SO LONG AS THOU ABIDEST ON EARTH. Calm the weeper and oppress not the widow. Do not oust a man from the property of his father. Do not harm officials in respect of their posts.[1] Beware of punishing wrongfully. Do not kill: it shall not profit thee. Punish with caution[2] by beating—so shall this country[3] be peaceful—except (for) the rebel when his plans have been discovered, for God knows the treacherous of heart and God requiteth his sins in blood. It is the mild man who . . . a lifetime. Do not slay a man whose good qualities thou knowest, one with whom thou didst chant the writings[4] and read in the inventory. . . . God, bold of thy step in difficult places. The soul cometh to the place it knoweth: it cannot stray from the paths of yesterday and no magic can oppose it. It cometh to those that give it water.

THE JUDGES[5] WHO JUDGE THE DEFICIENT, thou knowest that

The notes to this text are on p. 552.

they are not lenient on that day of judging the miserable, in the hour of performing (their) duty. It is hard when the accuser is possessed of knowledge.[6] Put not thy trust in length of years:[7] they regard a lifetime as an hour. A man surviveth after death and his deeds are placed beside him in heaps. Eternal is the existence yonder. He who makes light of it is a fool. As for him who reaches it without doing wrong, he shall exist yonder like a god, striding forth like the Lords of Eternity.

Notes

1 *posts*. The Egyptian word is of uncertain meaning and the translation is a guess.

2 *caution*. The meaning of the Egyptian word is uncertain.

3 *this country* is a common expression for Egypt, exactly as 'this country' is used by Englishmen in speaking of England.

4 *with whom thou didst chant the writings*. This expression seems to mean 'with whom you were at school.'

5 The *Judges* are a tribunal of gods who judge the dead and decide their fate on the basis of their behaviour whilst on earth.

6 *It is hard when the accuser is possessed of knowledge*, i.e., when the accuser is armed with facts detrimental to the dead person appearing before the divine judges it goes ill with him.

7 *Put not thy trust in length of years*. However long it may be since a sin was committed, the accuser and the judges will remember.

Translation, introduction, and notes by T. W. Thacker, in D. Winton Thomas (ed..), *Documents from Old Testament Times* (London: Thomas Nelson, 1958)

273. THE TEACHING OF AMENEMOPE

The literary remains of the ancient Egyptians reveal that didactic treatises containing wise maxims and proverbial truths were very greatly to their taste. It had long been suspected that for some, at least, of the Hebrew proverbs, models had been provided by this Wisdom Literature, but it was not until the publication of the 'Teaching of Amenemope' that definite evidence to support this conjecture was forthcoming. A number of passages in the Egyptian text were then seen to be so remarkable in resemblance to passages in the book of Proverbs that, even if it could not be proved that the Hebrew borrowed directly from the Egyptian, or *vice-versa*, nevertheless there could be little doubt that both were essentially related. It has been suggested that an international, pan-oriental, common stock of proverbial literature existed in the ancient Near East. Certainly the resemblances between Amenemope's work and the book of Proverbs indicate that the proverbial literature of O.T. times knew no national boundaries.

The papyrus roll containing the 'Teaching of Amenemope' was secured for the British Museum in 1888. . . . The date of the British Museum text is open to question. Suggested dates range from ca. 1000 B.C. to *ca.* 600 B.C. . . . Possibly the original work was written at the end of the Eighteenth or the beginning of the Nineteenth Dynasty (*ca.* 1300 B.C.), when contact between Egypt and Syria was particularly close.

Second Chapter

> Guard thyself against robbing the wretched
> And against being puissant over the man of broken arm.
> Stretch not forth thy hand to repel an old man,
> Nor anticipate the aged.
> 5. Let not thyself be sent on a wicked mission,
> Nor love him who hath performed it.
> Cry not out against him whom thou hast injured,
> Nor answer him back to justify thyself.
> He who hath done evil, the river-bank abandons him,
> 10. And his flooded land carries him away.
> The north wind cometh down that it may end his hour;
> It is united to the tempest;
> The thunder is loud, and the crocodiles are evil.
> O hot-head, what is thy condition?
> 15. He is crying out, his voice to heaven.
> O Moon, arraign his crime!
> Steer that we may ferry the wicked man across,
> For we shall not act like him—
> Lift him up, give him thy hand;
> 20. Leave him (in) the hands of the god;
> Fill his belly with bread that thou hast,
> So that he may be sated and may cast down his eye.

Notes

Lines 1 f. Cp. Prov. xxii, 22. *The man of broken arm,* i.e., helpless; cp. a similar use in Hebrew in reference to the weakness of Pharaoh (Ezek. xxx, 21 f., 24) and of Moab (Jer. xlviii, 25).
Line 4. *anticipate,* i.e., not allowing the aged to speak.

Line 9. *the river-bank abandons him.* Perhaps the meaning is that it crumbles away under his feet because it has been weakened by the inundation.

Line 16. *O Moon.* The moon was the symbol of Thoth, the Ibis-headed god who presided at the Judgment of the Dead when a man's heart was weighed against the feather of Truth. The scene is often depicted in copies of the Book of the Dead.

Lines 17-22. This remarkable passage is in striking contrast to the *lex talionis* of ancient times.

Line 18. Cp. Prov. xxiv, 29.

Line 20. Cp. Deut. xxxiii, 27.

Lines 21 f. Cp. Prov. xxv, 21. *cast down his eye,* i.e., to be ashamed.

Sixth Chapter

> Remove not the landmark at the boundaries of the arable land.
> Nor disturb the position of the measuring-cord;
> Covet not a cubit of land,
> Nor throw down the boundaries of a widow. . . .
> 5. Beware of throwing down the boundaries of the fields,
> Lest a terror carry thee off. . . .
> Better is poverty in the land of the god
> Than riches in a storehouse;
> Better is bread, when the heart is happy,
> 10. Than riches with vexation.

Notes

Lines 1-4. Cp. Prov. xxiii, 10 (also xxii, 28).

Lines 5 f. Cp. Prov. xxiii, 11.

Lines 7-10. Cp. Prov. xv, 16 f., xviii, 1.

Seventh Chapter

> Cast not thy heart after riches;
> There is no ignoring Shay and Renent.
> Place not thy heart upon externals;
> Every man belongeth to his hour.
> 5. Labour not to seek for increase;
> Thy needs are safe for thee.
> If riches are brought to thee by robbery,
> They will not spend the night with thee;
> At daybreak they are not in thy house:
> 10. Their places may be seen, but they are not.
> The ground has opened its mouth—'Let him enter that it may swallow,'
> They sink into the underworld.

They have made for themselves a great breach suitable to their
size
And are sunken down in the storehouse.

15. They have made themselves wings like geese
And are flown away to heaven.
Rejoice not thyself (over) riches (gained) by robbery.
Nor groan because of poverty.

Notes

Line 2. *Shay* and *Renent* were deities of fortune. Perhaps 'Fate and Fortune' is
the best translation.
Line 4. *his hour.* This is possibly a reference to a man's horoscope.
Lines 5-16. Cp. the remarkable parallel in Prov. xxiii, 4 f.
Line 11. 'Let him enter . . . swallow' is a descriptive epithet of the devouring
mouth of the earth.
Line 15. *geese.* In the book of Proverbs it is the soaring eagle which is the
simile of the flight of wealth (xxiii, 5).

Thirteenth Chapter

Injure not a man, [with] pen upon papyrus—
O abomination of the god!
Bear not witness with lying words,
Nor seek another's reverse with thy tongue.

5. Make not a reckoning with him who hath nothing,
Nor falsify thy pen.
If thou hast found a large debt against a poor man,
Make it into three parts,
Forgive two, and let one remain,

10. In order that thou shalt find thereby the ways of life.
Thou wilt lie down—the night hasteneth away—(lo!) thou art
in the morning;
Thou has found it like good news.
Better is praise for one who loves men
Than riches in a storehouse;

15. Better is bread, when the heart is happy,
Than riches with contention.

Notes

Line 6. Cp. Jer. viii, 8.
Lines 7-10. It has been suggested that the difficult parable of the Unjust Steward,
recorded in St. Luke's Gospel, but absent from the other Gospels, may be a
reminiscence of these lines (Luke xvi, 1 ff.).
Lines 13 f. Cp. Prov. xvi, 8. Lines 13 f. Cp. Prov. xvii, 1.

Thirtieth Chapter

See for thyself these thirty chapters:
They give pleasure; they instruct;
They are the foremost of all books;
They instruct the ignorant.
5. If they are read out in the presence of the ignorant,
Then he will be cleansed by reason of them.
Fill thyself with them; put them in thy heart,
And be a man who can explain them,
Interpreting them as a teacher.
10. As for the scribe who is experienced in his office,
He shall find himself worthy to be a courtier.

Colophon

It has come to its end
In the writing of Senu, son of the God's Father Pa-miu

Notes

Line 1. Cp. Prov. xxii, 20.
Lines 10 f. Cp. Prov. xxii, 29.
Lines 12 f. The colophon records the successful completion of the copying of the text and gives the name of the copyist. Egyptian books were normally concluded in this way. *the God's Father* was a title given to a class of elder temple priests.

> Translation, introduction, and notes by J. M. Plumley, in D. Winton Thomas (ed.), *Documents from Old Testament Times* (London : Thomas Nelson, 1958)

GREEK THOUGHT

274. 'I AM A MORTAL, A MAN'

(Aeschylus, 'Agamemnon,' 914-30)

Clytaemnestra's handmaidens spread a bright carpet between the chariot and the door, and Agamemnon speaks.

Daughter of Leda, you who kept my house for me,
there is one way your welcome matched my absence well.

You strained it to great length. Yet properly to praise
me thus belongs by right to other lips, not yours.
And all this—do not try in women's ways to make
me delicate, nor, as if I were some Asiatic
bow down to earth and with wide mouth cry out to me,
nor cross my path with jealousy by strewing the ground
with robes. Such state becomes the gods, and none beside.
I am a mortal, a man; I cannot trample upon
these tinted splendours without fear thrown in my path.
I tell you, as a man, not god, to reverence me.
Discordant is the murmur at such treading down
of lovely things; while God's most lordly gift to man
is decency of mind. Call that man only blest
who has in sweet tranquillity brought his life to close.
If you could only act as such, my hope is good.

Translation by Richmond Lattimore. Published by University of Chicago Press, 1959

JAIN BELIEF

275. THE JAIN CONCEPTION OF KARMAN

('Sūtrakritānga,' I, 2, 1)

The Jain believe that the essentials of their doctrine were revealed in the most ancient times (as a matter of fact, in mythical time) by a series of prophets or founders of religion, called Tīrthamkara. Rishabha, the supposed inspirer of the following text, was the first Tīrthamkara.

(Rishabha said to his sons):
Acquire perfect knowledge of the Law! Why do you not study it? It is difficult to obtain instruction in it after this life. The days (that are gone by) will never return, nor is it easy a second time to obtain human birth.

See, young and old men, even children in the mother's womb die. As a hawk catches a quail, so (life) will end when its time is spent.

(A man) may suffer for the sake of his parents; he will not easily obtain happiness after this life. A pious man should consider these causes of danger and cease to act.

For in this world living beings suffer individually for their deeds; for the deed they have done themselves, they obtain (punishment), and will not get over it before they have felt it.

Even gods, Gandharvas, Rākshasas, and Asuras; animals who live on earth, and snakes; kings, common people, merchants, and Brāhmanas; they all must leave their rank and suffer.

Notwithstanding their pleasures and relations, all men must suffer in due time the fruit of their works; as a cocoa-nut detaching itself from its stalk (falls down), so (life) will end when its time is spent.

Even a very learned or virtuous man, or a Brāhmana or an ascetic, will be severely punished for his deed when he is given to actions of deceit.

See, those (heretics) who search for the knowledge of truth, but who do not cross the Samsāra, talk only about the highest good (without reaching it).

How will you understand what is near you and what is beyond? In the meanwhile you suffer for your deeds.

He who walks about naked and lean, he who eats only once after a month, if he is filled with deceit, will be born an endless number of times.

Man, cease from sins! For the life of men will come to an end. Men who are drowned (in lust, as it were), and addicted to pleasure will, for want of control, be deluded.

Exert and control yourself! For it is not easy to walk on ways where there are minutely small animals. Follow the commandments which the Arhats have well proclaimed.

Heroes (of faith) who desist (from sins) and exert themselves aright, who subdue wrath, fear, etc., will never kill living beings; they desist from sins and are entirely happy.

It is not myself alone who suffers, all creatures in the world suffer; this a wise man should consider, and he should patiently bear (such calamities) as befall him, without giving way to his passions.

As a wall covered with a plastering (of dried cowdung) is by a shock made thin, so (a monk) should make his body lean by fasting, etc. He should abstain from slaughter of living beings. This is the Law proclaimed by the Sage.

As a bird covered with dust removes the grey powder by shaking itself, so a worthy and austere Brāhmana, who does penance, annihilates his Karman.

Young and old people claim a houseless Shrāmana as their own, though he begs according to the Law, observes the rules of conduct, and performs austerities. People will ever cry themselves hoarse, but will not captivate him.

Whatever they will do to move his pity, however they will cry about their son, they will not captivate a worthy and virtuous monk or make him return to domestic life.

Though they tempt him with pleasures, and though they should bind him and carry him home, if he does not care for a (worldly) life, they will not captivate him or make him return to domestic life.

His father and mother, his children and wife who claim him, will admonish him; 'See, you are our supporter; care not for the next world in order to support us.'

Some people are (foolishly) attached to others, and are thereby deluded; the unrighteous make them adopt unrighteousness, and they exult in their wickedness.

Therefore a worthy and wise man should be careful, ceasing from sin and being entirely happy. The virtuous heroes of faith (have chosen) the great road, the right and certain path to perfection.

He who has entered the road leading to the destruction (of Karman), who controls his mind, speech, and body, who has given up his possessions and relations and all undertakings, should walk about subduing his senses.

> Translation from prakrit by Herman Jacobi. *Jaina Sūtras*, Part II, in *Sacred Books of the East*, XLV (Oxford, 1895), pp. 249 53

A BUDDHIST EMPEROR AND PHILOSOPHER: ASHOKA

The Edicts of Ashoka.

Ashoka (*ca.* 274-232 B.C.) was an emperor and conqueror who was afflicted by repentance after the short and sanguinary Kalinga war. He revealed himself a philosopher in the consequences he draws from his repentance—a political philosopher who expressed himself in proclamations and laws, bounding his country with Rock Edicts to publish his ideals and aims to his neighbours and to his subjects along the frontiers, erecting Pillar Edicts in the important places of his empire to express his moral and social objectives, and dedicating in the Cave Edicts places for religious observance; and a moral philosopher who found a substitute for conquests by arms in conquest by Dharma, by righteousness and morality. He was a religious leader who turned from external observances to internal meditations, from temporal possessions to eternal truths. But above all he was a teacher and. in particular, a teacher of understanding and tolerance.

Ashoka sums up his teaching in a single word, 'Dharma.' His Edicts make it clear that he conceived his mission to consist in defining, publishing and propagating Dharma; and the strength and originality of his teaching are underlined by the meaning he gave to that ambiguous term. 'Dharma' means the insights and percepts of religion and piety; it also means the principles and prescriptions of ethics and morality. With remarkable clarity, Ashoka recognized the interplay of the various dimensions of the moral life: it reflects a man's duties as determined by his station in life; it reflects a basic order in the universe and a truth discerned in that order; it is a bond uniting people in their associations in families, communities, religions, and nations; it is a fundamental insight, differently expressed in different cultures and religions, which serves as a basis for mutual understanding and peace; it is a guide to action and to self-realization and happiness; it is achieved by action, advanced by instruction, and protected by sanctions, and in turn it provides a basis for policy, education, and justice; it is discovered by self-scrutiny, meditation, and conversion, and it entails renunciation of whatever is inconsistent with it.

Ashoka attributes his own interest in Dharma to repentance for the violence and cruelty of the Kalinga war. The change of heart brought about by his reflections on war inspired him to the promulgation of his Edicts by providing an insight for moral reform. His interest throughout is practical in its orientation. He devoted himself to study of Dharma, to action according to Dharma, and to inculcation of Dharma, but the three are inseparable—the study of Dharma translates Dharma into concrete action; action according to Dharma provides examples to guide inculcation; inculcation of Dharma, although it depends on instruction, supervision, administration, and institutions, is achieved finally only by meditation and study.

The Edicts of Asoka, edited and translated by N. A. Vicam and Richard McKeon (Chicago: University of Chicago Press, 1959), pp. ix-xii

276. KING ASHOKA DISCRIMINATES BETWEEN
MEANINGLESS CEREMONIES AND THE
'CEREMONIES OF DHARMA'

('Rock Edict' IX)

King Priyadarshī, the Beloved of the Gods, says : People perform various ceremonies. Among the occasions on which ceremonies are performed are sicknesses, marriages of sons or daughters, children's births, and departures on journeys. Women in particular have recourse to many diverse, trivial, and meaningless ceremonies.

It is right that ceremonies be performed. But this kind bears little fruit. The ceremony of Dharma (*Dharma-mangala*), on the contrary, is very fruitful. It consists in proper treatment of slaves and servants, reverence to teachers, restraint of violence towards living creatures, and liberality to priests and ascetics. These and like actions are called the ceremonies of Dharma.

Therefore, a father, son, brother, master, friend, acquaintance, or even a neighbour ought to say about such actions, 'They are good; they should be performed until their purpose is achieved. I shall observe them.'

Other ceremonies are of doubtful value. They may achieve their purpose, or they may not. Moreover, the purposes for which they are performed are limited to this world.

The ceremony of Dharma, on the other hand, is not limited to time. Even if it does not achieve its object in this world, it produced unlimited merit in the next world. But if it produces its object in this world, it achieves both effects; the purpose desired in this world and unlimited merit in the next.

It has also been said that liberality is commendable. But there is no greater liberality than the gift of Dharma or the benefit of Dharma. Therefore, a friend, well-wisher, relative, or companion should urge one when the occasion arises, saying, 'You should do this; this is commendable. By doing this you may attain heaven.' And what is more worth doing than attaining heaven?

Translation by N. A. Nikam and Richard McKeon,
The Edicts of Asoka, op. cit., pp. 46-7

561

277. ASHOKA'S CHANGE OF HEART AND THE IDEAL OF CONQUEST BY DHARMA

('Rock Edict' XIII)

The Kalinga country was conquered by King Priyadarshī, Beloved of the Gods, in the eighth year of his reign. One hundred and fifty thousand persons were carried away captive, one hundred thousand were slain, and many times that number died.

Immediately after the Kalingas had been conquered, King Priyadarshī became intensely devoted to the study of Dharma, to the love of Dharma, and to the inculcation of Dharma.

The Beloved of the Gods, conqueror of the Kalingas, is moved to remorse now. For he has felt profound sorrow and regret because the conquest of a people previously unconquered involves slaughter, death, and deportation.

But there is a more important reason for the King's remorse. The Brāhmanas and Shramanas [the priestly and ascetic orders] as well as the followers of other religions and the householders—who all practised obedience to superiors, parents, and teachers, and proper courtesy and firm devotion to friends, acquaintances, companions, relatives, slaves, and servants—all suffer from the injury, slaughter and deportation inflicted on their loved ones. Even those who escaped calamity themselves are deeply afflicted by the misfortunes suffered by those friends, acquaintances, companions, and relatives for whom they feel an undiminished affection. Thus all men share in the misfortune, and this weighs on King Priyadarshī's mind.

[Moreover, there is no country except that of the Yōnas (that is, the Greeks) where Brahmin and Buddhist ascetics do not exist] and there is no place where men are not attached to one faith or another.

Therefore, even if the number of people who were killed or who died or who were carried away in the Kalinga war had been only one one-hundredth or one one-thousandth of what it actually was, this would still have weighed on the King's mind.

King Priyadarshī now thinks that even a person who wrongs him must be forgiven for wrongs that can be forgiven.

King Priyadarshī seeks to induce even the forest peoples who have come under his dominion [that is, primitive peoples in the remote sections of the conquered territory] to adopt this way of life and this ideal. He reminds them, however, that he exercises the power to punish, despite his repentance, in order to induce them to desist from their crimes and escape execution.

For King Priyadarshī desires security, self-control, impartiality, and cheerfulness for all living creatures.

King Priyadarshī considers moral conquest [that is, conquest by Dharma, *Dharma-vijaya*] the most important conquest. He has achieved this moral conquest repeatedly both here and among the peoples living beyond the borders of his kingdom, even as far away as six hundred *yojanas* [about three thousand miles], where the Yōna [Greek] king Antiyoka rules, and even beyond Antiyoka in the realms of the four kings named Turamaya, Antikini, Maka, and Alikasudara[1] and to the south among the Cholas and Pandyas [in the southern tip of the Indian peninsula] as far as Ceylon.

Here in the King's dominion also, among the Yōnas [inhabitants of a northwest frontier province, probably Greeks] and the Kambōjas [neighbours of the Yōnas], among the Nābhakas and Nābhapanktis [who probably lived along the Himalayan frontier], among the Bhojas and Paitryanikas, among the Andhras and Paulindas [all peoples of the Indian peninsula], everywhere people heed his instructions in Dharma.

Even in countries which King Priyadarshī's envoys have not reached, people have heard about Dharma and about his Majesty's ordinances and instructions in Dharma, and they themselves conform to Dharma and will continue to do so.

Wherever conquest is achieved by Dharma, it produces satisfaction. Satisfaction is firmly established by conquest by Dharma [since it generates no opposition of conquered and conqueror]. Even satisfaction, however, is of little importance. King Priyadarshī attaches value ultimately only to consequences of action in the other world.

This edict on Dharma has been inscribed so that my sons and great-grandsons who may come after me should not think new conquests worth achieving. If they do conquer, let them take pleasure in moderation and mild punishments. Let them consider moral conquest the only true conquest.

That is good, here and hereafter. Let their pleasure be pleasure in morality [Dharma-rati]. For this alone is good, here and hereafter.

Note

1 The five kings referred to have been identified as follows: Antiyoka—Antiochus II Theos of Syria (261-246 B.C.); Turamaya—Ptolemy II Philadelphos of Egypt (285-247 B.C.); Antikini—Antigonos Gonatas of Macedonia (278-239

B.C.); Maka—Magas of Cyrene (300-258 B.C.); and Alikasudra—Alexander of
Epirus (272?-258 B.C.). The passage is of extreme importance not only for dating
the events of Ashoka's reign but also for judging the extent of communications
in his times. It indicates, moreover, the date 258 B.C., as the latest date at which
all five could be referred to simultaneously and therefore fixes the approximate
date of the edict.

Translation and note by N. A. Nikam and Richard
McKeon, *The Edicts of Asoka, op. cit.*, pp. 27-30

278. KING ASHOKA AGAINST RELIGIOUS INTOLERANCE

('Rock Edict' XII)

King Priyadarshī honours men of all faith, members of religious orders
and laymen alike, with gifts and various marks of esteem. Yet he does
not value either gifts or honours as much as growth in the qualities
essential to religion in men of all faiths.

This growth may take many forms, but its root is in guarding one's
speech to avoid extolling one's own faith and disparaging the faith of
others improperly or, when the occasion is appropriate, immoderately.

The faiths of others all deserve to be honoured for one reason or
another. By honouring them, one exalts one's own faith and at the
same time performs a service to the faith of others. By acting otherwise, one injures one's own faith and also does disservice to that of
others. For if a man extols his own faith and disparages another because
of devotion to his own and because he wants to glorify it, he seriously
injures his own faith.

Therefore concord alone is commendable, for through concord men
may learn and respect the conception of Dharma accepted by others.

King Priyadarshī desires men of all faiths to know each other's doctrines and to acquire sound doctrines. Those who are attached to their
particular faiths should be told that King Priyadarshī does not value
gifts or honours as much as growth in the qualities essential to religion
in men of all faiths.

Many officials are assigned to tasks bearing on this purpose—the
officers in charge of spreading Dharma, the superintendents of women
in the royal households, the inspectors of cattle and pasture lands, and
other officials.

The objective of these measures is the promotion of each man's particular faith and the glorification of Dharma.

Translation by N. A. Nikam and Richard McKeon,
The Edicts of Asoka, op. cit., pp. 51-2

279. ASHOKA AGAINST AGGRESSION AND
TENSION BETWEEN STATES

('Kalinga Edict' 11)

King Priyadarshī says:

I command that the following instructions be communicated to my official at Samāpā:

Whenever something right comes to my attention, I want it put into practice and I want effective means devised to achieve it. My principal means to do this is to transmit my instructions to you.

All men are my children. Just as I seek the welfare and happiness of my own children in this world and the next, I seek the same things for all men.

Unconquered peoples along the borders of my dominions may wonder what my disposition is towards them. My only wish with respect to them is that they should not fear me, but trust me; that they should expect only happiness from me, not misery; that they should understand further that I will forgive them for offences which can be forgiven; that they should be induced by my example to practise Dharma; and that they should attain happiness in this world and the next.

I transmit these instructions to you in order to discharge my debt [to them] by instructing you and making known to you my will and my unshakable resolution and commitment. You must perform your duties in this way and establish their confidence in the King, assuring them that he is like a father to them, that he loves them as he loves himself, and that they are like his own children.

Having instructed you and informed you of my will and my unshakable resolution and commitment, I will appoint officials to carry out this programme in all the provinces. You are able to inspire the border peoples with confidence in me and to advance their welfare and happiness in this world and the next. By doing so, you will also attain heaven and help me discharge my debts to the people.

This edict has been inscribed here so that my officials will work at all times to inspire the peoples of neighbouring countries with confidence in me and to induce them to practise Dharma.

This edict must be proclaimed every four months [at the beginning of the three seasons—hot, rainy and cold] on Tisya days [i.e., when the moon is in the constellation containing Tisya, Sirius]; it may also be proclaimed in the intervals between those days; and on appropriate occasions it may be read to individuals.

By doing this, you will be carrying out my commands.

Translation by N. A. Nikam and Richard McKeon, *The Edicts of Asoka, op. cit.,* pp. 53-4

CONFUCIUS

280. THE GOLDEN AGE: THE CONFUCIAN AGE OF GRAND UNITY

(Li-chi', 9)

Once Confucious was taking part in the winter sacrifice. After the ceremony was over, he went for a stroll along the top of the city gate and sighed mournfully. He sighed for the state of Lu.

His disciple Yet Yen [Tzu lu], who was by his side, asked: 'Why should the gentleman sigh?'

Confucius replied: 'The practice of the Great Way, the illustrious men of the Three Dynasties—these I shall never know in person. And yet they inspire my ambition! When the Great Way was practised, the world was shared by all alike. The worthy and the able were promoted to office and men practised good faith and lived in affection. Therefore they did not regard as parents only their own parents, or as sons only their own sons. The aged found a fitting close to their lives, the robust their proper employment; the young were provided with an upbringing and the widow and widower, the orphaned and the sick, with proper care. Men had their tasks and women their hearths. They hated to see goods lying about in waste, yet they did not hoard them for themselves; they disliked the thought that their energies were not fully used, yet they used them not for private ends. Therefore all evil plotting was prevented and thieves and rebels did not arise, so that people could leave their outer gates unbolted. This was the age of Grand Unity.

'Now the Great Way has become hid and the world is the possession of private families. Each regards as parents only his own parents, as sons only his sons; goods and labour are employed for selfish ends. Hereditary offices and titles are granted by ritual law while walls and moats must provide security. Ritual and righteousness are used to regulate the relationship between ruler and subject, to insure affection between father and son, peace between brothers, and harmony between husband and wife, to set up social institutions, organize the farms and villages, honour the brave and wise, and bring merit to the individual. Therefore intrigue and plotting come about and men take up arms. Emperor Yu, kings T'ang, Wen, Wu, and Ch'eng and the Duke of Chou achieved eminence for this reason: that all six rulers were constantly attentive to ritual, made manifest their righteousness and acted in complete faith. They exposed error, made humanity their law and humility their practice, showing the people wherein they should constantly abide. If there were any who did not abide by these principles, they were dismised from their positions and regarded by the multitude as dangerous. This is the period of Lesser Prosperity.'

Translation by Wm. Theodore de Bary and others, in de Bary, *et al.* (eds.), *Sources of Chinese Tradition* (New York: Columbia University Press, 1960), pp. 191-2

281. THE TEACHINGS OF CONFUCIUS

('Analects,' selections)

'Confucius,' the Latinized form of K'ung Fu-tzu or 'Master K'ung,' is the title commonly used in referring to him in Chinese. Confucius was born in 551 B.C. in what is now Shantung Province. His father died when he was very young, leaving him to struggle alone with the problem of securing an education and making his way in the world. Confucius believed that his place was in the world of politics, and with almost pathetic persistence he sought throughout the states of China a ruler who would be willing to employ him and his ideas in the government. But on the whole his political career was a failure, and more and more he turned his attention to the teaching of young men. He was said to have had some three thousand students. He died in 479 B.C.

Confucius said: 'At fifteen, I set my heart on learning. At thirty, I was firmly established. At forty, I had no more doubts. At fifty, I knew the will of Heaven. At sixty, I was ready to listen to it. At seventy, I could follow my heart's desire without transgressing what was right.' (II, 4.)

When Confucius was in Ch'i, he heard the Shao music and for three months he forgot the taste of meat, saying: 'I never thought music could be so beautiful.' (VII, 13.)

Confucius said: 'When walking in a party of three, I always have teachers, I can select the good qualities of the one for imitation, and the bad ones of the other and correct them in myself.' (VII, 21.)

Confucius said: 'I am a transmitter and not a creator. I believe in and have a passion for the ancients. I venture to compare myself with our old P'eng (China's Methuselah).' (VII, 1.)

Confucius said: 'Sometimes I have gone a whole day without food and a whole night without sleep, giving myself to thought. It was no use. It is better to learn.' (XV, 30.)

There were four things that Confucius was determined to eradicate: a biased mind, arbitrary judgments, obstinacy, and egotism. (IX, 4.)

Confucius said: 'Those who know the truth are not up to those who love it; those who love the truth are not up to those who delight in it.' (VI, 18.)

Confucius said: 'Having heard the Way (Tao) in the morning, one may die content in the evening.' (IV, 8.)

Humanity (jen)

Fan Ch'ih asked about humanity. Confucius said: 'Love men.' (XII, 22.)

Tzu Chang asked Confucius about humanity. Confucius said: 'To be able to practise five virtues anywhere in the world constitutes humanity.' Tzu Chang begged to know what these were. Confucius said: 'Courtesy, magnaminity, good faith, diligence, and kindness. He who is courteous is not humiliated, he who is magnanimous wins the multitude, he who is of good faith is trusted by the people, he who is diligent attains his objective, and he who is kind can get service from the people.' (XVII, 6.)

Confucius said: 'Without humanity a man cannot long endure adversity, nor can he long enjoy prosperity. The humane rest in humanity; the wise find it beneficial' (IV, 2.)

Confucius said: 'Only the humane man can love men and can hate men.' (IV, 3.)

Filial Piety

Tzu Yu asked about filial piety. Confucius said: 'Nowadays a filial son is just a man who keeps his parents in food. But even dogs or horses are given food. If there is no feeling of reverence, wherein lies the difference?' (II, 7.)

Tzu Hsia asked about filial piety. Confucius said: 'The manner is the really difficult thing. When anything has to be done the young people undertake it; when there is wine and food the elders are served —is this all there is to filial piety?' (II, 8.)

Religious Sentiment

Tzu Lu asked about the worship of ghosts and spirits. Confucius said: 'We don't know yet how to serve men, how can we know about serving the spirits?' 'What about death, was the next question. Confucius said: 'We don't know yet about life, how can we know about death?' (XI, 11.)

Fan Ch'ih asked about wisdom. Confucius said: 'Devote yourself to the proper demands of the people, respect the ghosts and spirits but keep them at a distance—this may be called wisdom.' (VI, 20.)

Translation by Wm. Theodore de Bary and others, in de Bary, et al. (eds.), Sources of Chinese Tradition (New York: Columbia University Press, 1960), pp. 24-5, 28-31

C. BUDDHA EXPLAINS THE MIDDLE PATH

282. THE PARABLE OF THE ARROW: GOTAMA BUDDHA
REFUSES TO DISCUSS METAPHYSICAL PROBLEMS

('Majjhima-nikāya,' I, 426 ff. [LXII *'Cūla-mālunkyā-sutta'*])

Thus I have heard: The Lord was once dwelling near Sāvatthī, at
Jetavana in the park of Anāthapindika. Now the elder Mālunkyāputta
had retired from the world, and as he meditated the thought arose:
'These theories have been left unexplained by the Lord, set aside, and
rejected, whether the world is eternal or not eternal, whether the
world is finite or not, whether the soul (life) is the same as the body,
or whether the soul is one thing and the body another, whether a
Buddha (Tathāgata) exists after death or does not exist after death,
and whether a Buddha both exists and does not exist after death, and
whether a Buddha is non-existent and not non-existent after death—
these things the Lord does not explain to me, and that he does not
explain them to me does not please me, it does not suit me. I will
approach the Lord, and ask about this matter. . . . If the Lord does
not explain to me, I will give up the training, and return to a worldly
life.'

[When Mālunkyāputta had approached and put his questions the
Lord replied:] 'Now did I, Mālunkyāputta, ever say to you, 'Come
Mālunkyāputta, lead a religious life with me, and I will explain to you
whether the world is eternal or not eternal [and so on with the other
questions]?'' 'You did not, reverend sir.' 'Anyone, Mālunkyāputta,
who should say 'I will not lead a religious life with the Lord, until
the Lord explains to me whether the world is eternal or not eternal
[etc.] . . .' that person would die, Mālunkyāputta, without its
being explained. It is as if a man had been wounded by an arrow
thickly smeared with poison, and his friends, companions, relatives, and
kinsmen were to get a surgeon to heal him, and he were to say, "I
will not have this arrow pulled out, until I know by what man I was
wounded, whether he is of the warrior caste, or a brahmin, or the
agricultural, or the lowest caste." Or if he were to say, "I will not have

this arrow pulled out until I know of what name or family the man is
. . . or whether he is tall, or short, or of middle height . . . or
whether he is black, or dark, or yellowish . . . or whether he comes
from such and such a village, or town, or city. . . . or until I know
whether the bow with which I was wounded was a chāpa or a kondanda,
or until I know whether the bow-string was of swallow-wort, or
bamboo-fibre, or sinew. or hemp, or of milk-sap tree, or until I know
whether the shaft was from a wild or cultivated plant . . . or whether
it was feathered from a vulture's wing or a heron's or a hawk's, or a pea-
cock's, or a sithilahanu-bird's . . . or whether it was wrapped round
with the sinew of an ox, or of a buffalo, or of a ruru-deer, or of a
monkey . . . or until I know whether it was an ordinary arrow, or
a razor arrow, or a vekanda, or an iron arrow, or a calf-tooth arrow,
or one of a karavīra leaf." That man would die, Mālunkyāputta,
without knowing all this.

'It is not on the view that the world is eternal, Mālunkyāputta
that a religious life depends; it is not on the view that the world is not
eternal that a religious life depends. Whether the view is held that
the world is eternal, or that the world is not eternal, there is still
re-birth, there is old age, there is death, and grief, lamentation, suffering, sorrow, and despair, the destruction of which even in this life I
announce. It is not on the view that the world is finite. . . . It is not
on the view that a Tathāgata exists after death. . . . Therefore, Mālunkyāputta, consider as unexplained what I have not explained, and consider as explained what I have explained. And what, Mālunkyāputta,
have I not explained? Whether the world is eternal I have not explained, whether the world is not eternal . . . whether a Tathāgata is
both non-existent and not non-existent after death I have not explained. And why Mālunkyāputta, have I not explained this? Because
this, Mālunkyāputta, is not useful, it is not concerned with the principle of a religious life, does not conduce to aversion, absence or passion,
cessation, tranquillity, supernatural faculty, perfect knowledge, Nirvāna, and therefore I have not explained it.

'And what, Mālunkyāputta, have I explained? Suffering have I
explained, the cause of suffering, the destruction of suffering, and the
path that leads to the destruction of suffering have I explained. For
this, Mālunkyāputta, is useful, this is concerned with the principle of
a religious life; this conduces to aversion, absence of passion, cessation,
tranquillity, supernatural faculty, perfect knowledge, Nirvāna and
therefore have I explained it. Therefore, Mālunkyāputta, consider as
unexplained what I have not explained, and consider as explained

what I have explained.' Thus spoke the Lord and with joy the elder Mālunkyāputta applauded the words of the Lord.

Translation by E. J. Thomas, *Buddhist Scriptures* (London, 1913), pp. 64-7. Cf. Lord Chalmers, *Further Dialogues of the Buddha*, vol. I (London, 1926, pp. 304 ff.

283. THE MIDDLE PATH WHICH LEADS TO WISDOM AND CONDUCES TO NIRVĀNA

('*Mahāvagga*,' I, 6, 17-30)

17. And the Blessed One thus addressed the five Bhikkhus: There are two extremes, O Bhikkhus, which he who has given up the world, ought to avoid. What are these two extremes? A life given to pleasures, devoted to pleasures and lusts: this is degrading, sensual, vulgar, ignoble, and profitless; and a life given to mortifications: this is painful, ignoble and profitless. By avoiding these two extremes, O Bhikkhus, the Tathāgata has gained the knowledge of the Middle Path which leads to insight, which leads to wisdom, which conduces to calm, to knowledge, to the Sambodhi, to Nirvāna.

18. Which, O Bhikkhus, is this Middle Path the knowledge of which the Tathāgata has gained, which leads to insight, which leads to wisdom, which conduces to calm, to knowledge, to the Sambodhi, to Nirvāna? It is the holy eightfold Path, namely, Right Belief, Right Aspiration, Right Speech, Right Conduct, Right Means of Livelihood, Right Endeavour, Right Memory, Right Meditation. This, O Bhikkhus, is the Middle Path the knowledge of which the Tathāgata has gained, which leads to insight, which leads to wisdom, which conduces to calm, to knowledge, to the Sambodhi, to Nirvāna.

19. This, O Bhikkhus, is the Noble Truth of Suffering: Birth is suffering: decay is suffering; illness is suffering; death is suffering. Presence of objects we hate, is suffering; Separation from objects we love, is suffering; not to obtain what we desire, is suffering. Briefly, the fivefold clinging to existence is suffering.

20. This, O Bhikkhus, is the Noble Truth of the Cause of suffering: Thirst, that leads to re-birth, accompanied by pleasure and lust, finding its delight here and there. (This thirst is threefold), namely, thirst for pleasure, thirst for existence, thirst for prosperity.

The Middle Path

21. This, O Bhikkhus, is the Noble Truth of the Cessation of suffering: (it ceases with) the complete cessation of this thirst—a cessation which consists in the absence of every passion —with the abandoning of this thirst, with the doing away with it, with the deliverance from it with the destruction of desire.

22. This, O Bhikkhus, is the Noble Truth of the Path which leads to the cessation of suffering: that holy eightfold Path, that is to say, Right Belief, Right Aspiration, Right Speech, Right Conduct, Right Means of Livelihood, Right Endeavour, Right Memory, Right Meditation. . . .

29. Thus the Blessed One Spoke. The five Bhikkhus were delighted, and they rejoiced at the words of the Blessed One. And when this exposition was propounded, the venerable Kondanna obtained the pure and spotless Eye of the Truth (that is to say, the following knowledge): 'Whatsover is subject to the condition of origination, is subject also to the condition of cessation.

30. And as the Blessed One had founded the Kingdom of Truth (by propounding the four Noble Truths), the earth-inhabiting *devas* shouted: Truly the Blessed One has founded at Benares, in the deer park Isipatana, the highest kingdom of Truth, which may be opposed neither by a Samana nor by a Brāhmana, neither by a deva, nor by Māra, nor by Brahma, nor by any being in the world.

Translation by T. W. Rhys Davids and Hermann Oldenberg, *Vinaya Texts*, part I, in *Sacred Books of the East*, XIII (Oxford, 1881), pp. 94-7

284. PROFITABLE AND UNPROFITABLE DOCTRINES

('Samyutta-nikāya,' V, 437)

At one time the Lord dwelt at Kosambi in the sisu-grove. Then the Lord took a few sisu leaves in his hand and addressed the monks: 'What do you think, monks, which are the more, the few sisu leaves I have taken in my hand, or those that are in the sisu-grove?' 'Small in number, Lord, and few are the leaves that the Lord has taken in his hand: those are far more that are in the sisu-grove.' 'Even so, monks, that is much more which I have realized and have not declared to you; and but little have I declared.

'And why, monks, have I not declared it? Because it is not profitable,

573

does not belong to the beginning of the religious life, and does not tend to revulsion, absence of passion, cessation, calm, higher knowledge, enlightenment, Nirvāna. Therefore have I not declared it.

'And what, monks, have I declared? This is pain, I have declared; this is the cause of pain, I have declared; this is the cessation of pain, I have declared; this is the Way leading to the cessation of pain, I have declared. And why, monks, have I declared it? Because it is profitable, it belongs to the beginning of the religious life, and tends to revulsion, absence of passion, cessation, calm, higher knowledge, enlightenment, Nirvāna. Therefore have I declared it.

'Therefore, monks, to this you must be devoted: this is pain, this is the cause of pain, this is the cessation of pain, this is the Way, leading to the cessation of pain.'

Translation by Edward J. Thomas, *Early Buddhist Scriptures* (London, 1935), pp. 117-18

285. THE BUDDHA EXPLAINS THE NOBLE EIGHTFOLD WAY

('*Samyutta-nikāya,*' v, 8)

'The Noble Eightfold Way, monks, I will expound and analyse to you. Listen to it, reflect on it well, I will speak.' 'Even so, Lord,' the monks replied to the Lord.

The Lord said, 'What, monks, is the Noble Eightfold Way? It is namely right view, right intention, right speech, right action, right livelihood, right effort, right mindfulness, right concentration.

'And what, monks, is the right view? The knowledge of pain, knowledge of the cause of pain, knowledge of the cessation of pain, and knowledge of the way that leads to the cessation of pain: that monks is called right view.

'And what is right intention? The intention to renounce, the intention not to hurt, the intention not to injure: that, monks, is called right intention.

'And what is right speech? Refraining from falsehood, from malicious speech, from harsh speech, from frivolous speech: that, monks, is called right speech.

'And what is right action? Refraining from taking life, from taking what is not given, from sexual intercourse: that, monks, is called right action.

'And what is right livelihood? Here a noble disciple abandoning a false mode of livelihood gets his living by right livelihood: that, monks, is called right livelihood.

'And what is right effort? Here a monk with the nonproducing of bad and evil thoughts that have not yet arisen exercises will, puts forth effort, begins to make exertion, applies and exerts his mind; with the dispelling of bad and evil thoughts that had arisen he exercises will, puts forth effort, begins to make exertion, applies and exerts his mind; with the producing of good thoughts that had not arisen he exercises will, puts forth effort, begins to make exertion, applies and exerts his mind; with the fixing, freeing from confusion, increasing, enlarging, developing and filling up of good thoughts that had arisen he exercises will, puts forth effort, begins to make exertion, applies and exerts his mind: that, monks, is called right effort.

'And what is right mindfulness? Here (1) on the body: a monk abides contemplating the body, ardent, thoughtful, and mindful, dispelling his longing and dejection towards the world; (2) on feelings: he abides contemplating the feelings, ardent, thoughtful, and mindful, dispelling his longing and dejection towards the world; (3) on the mind: he abides contemplating the mind, ardent, thoughtful, and mindful, dispelling his longing and dejection towards the world; (4) on thoughts: he abides contemplating thoughts, ardent, thoughtful, and mindful, dispelling his longing and dejection towards the world. That, monks is called right mindfulness.

'And what is right concentration? Here (1) a monk free from passions and evil thoughts attains and abides in the first trance of joy and pleasure, which is accompanied by reasoning and investigation and arises from seclusion. (2) With the ceasing of reasoning and investigation, in a state of internal serenity, with his mind fixed on one point, he attains and abides in the second trance of joy and pleasure arising from concentration, and free from reasoning and investigation. (3) With equanimity and indifference towards joy he abides mindful and self-possessed, and with his body experiences pleasure that the noble ones call "Dwelling with equanimity, mindful and happy," and attains and abides in the third trance. (4) Dispelling pleasure and pain, and even before the disappearance of elation and depression, he attains and abides in the fourth trance, which is without pleasure and pain, and with the purity of mindfulness and equanimity: that, monks, is called right concentration.'

Translation by E. J. Thomas, *Early Buddhist Scriptures*
(London, 1935), pp. 94-6

286. THE PARABLE OF THE FIRE:
A TATHĀGATA IS LIKE A BURNED-OUT FIRE

('Majjhima-nikāya,' I, 485 ff. [LXXII 'Aggi-vacchagotta-sutta'])

'Vaccha, the view that the world is eternal is a jungle, a wilderness, a theatrical show, a perversion, a fetter, and is coupled with suffering, destruction, despair, and pain, and does not tend to aversion, absence of passion, cessation, tranquillity, supernatural faculty, perfect knowledge, Nirvāna. . . . Considering it disadvantageous, Vaccha, I have accordingly none of these views.' 'But has Gotama any view?' 'The Tathāgata, Vaccha, is free from views, for this is what the Tathāgata holds: form, the cause of form, the destruction of form, sensation, the cause of sensation, perception, the aggregates of qualities, consciousness, how they arise and perish. Therefore with the destruction of, and indifference towards, and the ceasing and abandonment of all imaginings, all agitations, all false views of the self or of anything belonging to a self, the Tathāgata is liberated, thus I say.'

'But where is the monk reborn, sir Gotama, whose mind is thus liberated?' 'It does not fit the case, Vaccha, to say he is reborn.' 'Then, sir Gotama, he is not reborn.' 'It does not fit the case, Vaccha, to say he is not reborn.' 'Then, sir Gotama, he is both reborn and not reborn.' 'It does not fit the case, Vaccha, to say he is neither reborn nor not reborn. . . .' 'In this matter, sir Gotama, I feel in a state of ignorance and confusion, and the small amount of faith that I had in Gotama through a former conversation has now disappeared.' 'Enough of your ignorance and confusion, Vaccha, for deep is this doctrine, difficult to be seen and comprehended, good, excellent, beyond the sphere of reasoning, subtle, intelligible only to the wise. It is difficult to be understood by you, who hold other views, another faith, other inclinations, another discipline, and have another teacher. Therefore, Vaccha, I will ask you this, and do you explain it as you may please. Do you think, Vaccha, that if a fire were burning before you, you would know that a fire was burning before you?' 'If a fire was burning before me, sir Gotama, I should know that a fire was burning before me.' 'And if some one asked you on what the fire burning before you depends, how would you explain it? . . .' 'I should say that this fire which is burning before me depends on its clinging to grass and sticks.' 'If the fire before you were to go out, would you know that the fire before you had gone out?' 'If the fire before me were to go out, I should know that the fire had gone out.' 'And if some one were to ask you, "Vaccha, in what direction has the fire gone which has gone out, to the east, west, north or south," if you were thus asked, how would you explain it?' 'It does not fit the case, sir Gotama, to say so, for the fire burned through depending on its clinging to grass and sticks, and through its consuming this, and not getting any other, it is without food, and comes to be what is called extinct.' 'And just so, Vaccha, that form by which one would assert the existence of a Tathāgata has ceased, it is uprooted, it is pulled up like a taliput-palm, made non-existent, and not liable to arise again in the future. The Tathāgata, who is released from what is called form, is deep, immeasurable, hard to fathom, and like a great ocean. It does not fit the case to say he is born again, to say he is not born again, to say he is both born again and not born again, or to say he is neither born again nor not born again.

Translation by E. J. Thomas, *Buddhist Scriptures* (London, 1913), pp. 71-3. Cf. Lord Chalmers, *Further Dialogues of the Buddha*, vol. I (London, 1926), pp. 342 *ff.*

287. THE PARABLE OF THE OIL LAMP: THE EXTINCTION OF CRAVING

('Samyutta-nikāya,' II, 86)

He dwelt at Sāvatthi. 'In one, monks, who abides reflecting on the enjoyment of things that fetter, craving increases. With craving as a cause there is grasping. With grasping as a cause there is becoming (the desire to be). With the desire to be as a cause there is rebirth. With rebirth as a cause old age and death, grief, lamentation, pain, dejection, and despair arise. Even so is the cause of this whole mass of pain.

'Just as, monks, on account of oil and on account of a wick an oil lamp would burn, and a man from time to time were to pour oil thereon and trim the wick, even so, monks, an oil lamp with that nutriment, that fuel, would burn for a long time.

'Even so, monks, in one who abides reflecting on the enjoyment of things that fetter, craving increases. . . . 'Even so is the cause of this whole mass of pain.

'In one, monks, who reflects on the wretchedness of things that fetter, craving ceases. With the cessation of craving grasping ceases. . . . Even so is the cessation of this whole mass of pain.

'Just as monks, on account of oil and on account of a wick an oil lamp would burn, and a man from time to time were not to pour oil thereon and not to trim the wick, even so, monks, an oil lamp with the exhaustion of the original fuel and being without nutriment through being unfed with any more would become extinct.

'Even so, monks, in one who abides reflecting on the wretchedness of things that fetter, craving ceases. With the ceasing of craving grasping ceases. With the ceasing of grasping the desire to be ceases. With the ceasing of the desire to be rebirth ceases. With the ceasing of rebirth old age and death, grief, lamentation, pain, dejection, and despair cease. Even so is the cessation of this whole mass of pain.'

Translation by E. J. Thomas, Early Buddhist Scriptures
(London, 1935), pp. 122-3

288. THE BUDDHA'S ADVICE TO SARIPUTRA

('Sutta Nipāta,' 964-975)

The monk alert, rapt farer on the edge,
Should have no fear of these five fears:
Gadflies and stinging bees and things that creep,
Attacks of men and of four-footed beasts.

Nor should he be afraid of others' views,
When the great perils of them he hath seen;
So should the expert seeker overcome
All other troubles that may here befall.

When stricken by disease or hunger's pangs,
Cold and excessive heat should he endure;
When stricken sore by them, that homeless man
Must stir up energy and strive with strength.

Let him not steal nor let him tell a lie,
Let him show amity to weak and strong;
And when he knows disquiet of the mind,
Let him expel that as dark as Mara's gloom.

Nor must he fall a prey to wrath and pride,
But digging up their roots, let him stay poised;
And, as he wrestles, let him overcome
All that is dear to him, all that repels.

With joy in what is lovely, wisdom-led,
Let him then put to flight these troubles here,

Conquer dislike for his lone lodging place,
Conquer the four that cause him discontent:

With food and clothing timely gotten, he
Must therein measure know for his content;
He, faring thus, restrained and curbed, would speak
In village no harsh words, tho' vexed indeed.

Then let him loiter not, but eyes downcast,
Be ever bent on musing, much awake;
Then let him strive for poise, intent-of-self
Cut doubt and hankering and fretful ways.

Alert, let him rejoice, when urged by words,
Break fallowness in fellow-wayfarers,
Utter in season due the expert word,
Not ponder on the views and talk of folk.

Alert, then let him train to discipline
Those things which are the five dusts in the world;
To conquer lust for forms and sounds and tastes,
To conquer lust for scents and things of touch.

When he hath disciplined desire for these,
Alert, with mind released in full, that monk
As studies he the thing aright, in time
Alone, uplifted, may the darkness rend.

Thus spake the master.

Translation by Edward Conze in Conze (ed.) *Buddhist Scriptures* (Baltimore, 1959), pp. 77-9

289. THE BUDDHA'S 'WAY OF VIRTUE'

('Dhammapada,' selections)

The Dhammapada although accepted at the Council of Ashoka in 240 B.C. as a collection of the sayings of Gotama, was not put into writing until some generations had passed. It probably contains accretions of later date.

47. He who is busy culling pleasure, as one plucks flowers, Death seizes and hurries off, as a great flood bears away a sleeping village.

48. The Destroyer treads him underfoot as he is culling worldly pleasures, still unsated with lusts of the flesh.

50. Be not concerned with other men's evil words or deeds or neglect of good: look rather to thine own sins and negligence [lit. 'sins of commission and omission': things done and undone.]

51. As some bright flower—fair to look at, but lacking fragrance—so are fair words which bear no fruit in action.

52. As some bright flower, fragrant as it is fair, so are fair words whose fruit is seen in action.

63. The fool who knows his folly is so far wise; but the fool who reckons himself wise is called a fool indeed.

76. Look upon him who shows you your faults as a revealer of treasure: seek his company who checks and chides you, the sage who is wise in reproof: it fares well and not ill with him who seeks such company.

78. Avoid bad friends, avoid the company of the evil: seek after noble friends and men of lofty character.

83. Freely go the righteous; the holy ones do not whine and pine for lusts: unmoved by success or failure, the wise show no change of mood.

85. Few amongst men are they who reach the farther shore: the rest, a great multitude, stand only on the bank.

92. Some there are who have no treasure here, temperate ones whose goal is the freedom which comes of realizing that life is empty and impermanent: their steps are hard to track as the flight of birds through the sky.

93. He whose taints are purged away, who is indifferent to food, whose goal is the freedom which comes of realizing life's emptiness and transiency, is hard to track as the flight of birds in the sky.

94. Even the gods emulate him whose senses are quiet as horses well-tamed by the charioteer, who has renounced self-will, and put away all taints.

100. Better than a thousand empty words is one pregnant word, which brings the hearer peace.

101. Better than a thousand idle songs is a single song, which brings the hearer peace.

102. Better it is to chant one verse of the law, that brings the hearer peace, than to chant a hundred empty songs.

103. If one were to conquer a thousand thousand in the battle—he who conquers self is the greatest warrior.

104, 105. Self-conquest is better than other victories; neither god nor demi-god, neither Māra nor Brahmā, can undo the victory of such a one, who is self-controlled and always calm.

106. If month by month throughout a hundred years, one were to offer sacrifices costing thousands, and if for a moment another were to reverence the self-controlled—this is the better worship.

107. If one for a hundred years tended the sacred fire in the glade, and another for a moment reverenced the self-controlled, this is the better worship.

110. Better than a hundred years of impure and intemperate existence is a single day of moral, contemplative life.

111. Better is one day of wise and contemplative life than a thousand years of folly and intemperance.

141. Not nakedness, nor matted hair, not dirt, nor fastings, not sleeping in sanctuaries, nor ashes, nor ascetic posture—none of these things purifies a man who is not free from doubt.

145. Engineers control the water, fletchers fashion their shafts, carpenters shape the wood: it is themselves that the pious fashion and control.

146. Where is the joy, what the pleasure, whilst all is in flames? Benighted, would ye not seek a torch?

147. Look at this painted image, wounded and swollen, sickly and full of lust, in which there is no permanence;

148. This wasted form is a nest of disease and very frail: it is full of putrid matter and perishes. Death is the end of life.

149. What delight is there for him who sees these grey bones scattered like gourds in autumn?

150. Here is a citadel of bones plastered with flesh and blood, and manned by old age and death, self-will and enmity.

151. Even as the king's bright chariot grows old, so the body of man also comes to old age. But the law of the holy never ages; the holy teach it to the holy.

165. Thou art brought low by the evil thou hast done thyself: by the evil thou hast left undone art thou purified. Purity and impurity are things of man's inmost self; no man can purify another.

169. Follow after virtue, not after vice. The virtuous live happy in this world and the next.

170. The King of Death sees not him who regards the world as a bubble, a mirage. . . .

174. Blinded are the men of this world; few there are who have eyes to see; few are the birds which escape the fowler's net; few are they who go to heaven. . . .

178. Good is kingship of the earth; good is birth in heaven; good is universal empire; better still is the fruit of conversion. . . .

197. O Joy! We live in bliss; amongst men of hate, hating none. Let us indeed dwell among them without hatred.

198. O Joy! In bliss we dwell; healthy amidst the ailing. Let us indeed dwell amongst them in perfect health.

199. Yea in very bliss we dwell: free from care amidst the care-worn. Let us indeed dwell amongst them without care.

200. In bliss we dwell possessing nothing: let us dwell feeding upon joy like the shining ones in their splendour.

201. The victor breeds enmity; the conquered sleeps in sorrow. Regardless of either victory or defeat the calm man dwells in peace.

202. There is no fire like lust; no luck so bad as hate. There is no sorrow like existence: no bliss greater than Nirvāna [rest].

211. Take a liking for nothing; loss of the prize is evil. There are no bonds for him who has neither likes nor dislikes.

212. From attachment comes grief, from attachment comes fear. He who is pure from attachment knows neither grief nor fear.

213. From affection comes grief and fear. He who is without affection knows neither grief nor fear.

214. From pleasure comes grief and fear. He who is freed from pleasure knows neither grief nor fear.

215. From lust come grief and fear. He who is freed from lust knows neither grief nor fear.

216. From desire comes grief and fear. He who is free of desire knows neither grief nor fear. . . .

223. By calmness let a man overcome wrath; let him overcome evil by good; the miser let him subdue by liberality, and the liar by truth.

224. Speak the truth, be not angry, give of thy poverty to the suppliant: by these three virtues a man attains to the company of the gods.

237. Thy life is ended; thou art come into the Presence of Death: there is no resting-place by the way, and thou hast no provision for the journey.

238. Make for thyself a refuge; come, strive and play the sage! Burn off thy taints, and thou shalt know birth and old age no more.

252. To see another's fault is easy: to see one's own is hard. Men winnow the faults of others like chaff: their own they hide as a crafty gambler hides a losing throw.

264. Not by his shaven crown is one made a 'religious' who is intemperate and dishonourable. How can he be a 'religious' who is full of lust and greed?

286. 'Here I will pass the wet season; here the winter and summer,' thinks the fool, unmindful of what may befall.

287. Then comes Death and sweeps him away infatuated with children and cattle, and entangled with this world's goods, as a flood carries off a sleeping village.

288. There is no safety in sons, or in father, or in kinsfolk when Death overshadows thee: amongst thine own kith and kin is no refuge;

289. Knowing this clearly, the wise and righteous man straightway clears the road that leads to Nirvāna.

385. Him I call the Brahmin whom desire assails not from within nor from without, in whom is no fear, he is indeed free.

386. Him I call Brahmin who is meditative, clean of heart, solitary, who has done his duty and got rid of taints, who has reached the goal of effort. . . .

393. Not by matted locks, nor by lineage, nor by caste is one a Brahmin; he is the Brahmin in whom are truth and righteousness and purity. . . .

396. Not him do I call Brahmin who is merely born of a Brahmin mother; men may give him salutation as a Brahmin, though he be not detached from the world: but him I call a Brahmin who has attachment to nothing.

397. Him I call a Brahmin who has cut the bonds, who does not thirst for pleasures, who has left behind the hindrances.

398. Whoso has cut the cable, and the rope and the chain with all its links, and has pushed aside the bolt, this wise one I call a Brahmin. . . .

400. He is the Brahmin who does not give way to anger, who is careful of religious duties, who is upright, pure, and controlled, who has reached his last birth.

406. Not opposing those who oppose, calm amidst the fighters, not grasping amidst men who grasp, he is the Brahmin.

Translation by W. D. C. Wagiswara and K. J. Saunders, *The Buddha's 'Way of Virtue'* (London: John Murray, 1912)

See also nos. 220, 225-30

D. THE ULTIMATE REALITY:
QUESTIONS AND ANSWERS

290. ZARATHUSTRA ASKS THE LORD . . .

('Gāthā-Yasna' 44)

This *Gāthā-Yasna* 44 might be called the *Questions to the Lord*, for each of its stanzas, except the last, is introduced by this formula: 'This I ask thee, O Lord, answer me truly . . .'

Stanzas 3 to 7 are concerned with the origin of the world and its organization, and stanzas 8 to 19 with its future. The last four of these in particular are devoted to the mission of Zarathustra and to the expectation of the Saviour. Such is the body of the hymn, preceded by two introductory stanzas and ended by a final stanza.

1. This I ask thee, O Lord, answer me truly:
   May a wise one like thee reveal it to a friend such as I am,
   In virtue of my veneration,—such as is due to a being like you—
   And as Righteousness may he lend us his friendly support,
   Coming unto us through the Good Mind!

2. This I ask thee, O Lord, answer me truly:
   When the best existence begins,
   Shall they have their fill of the rewards who have desired them?
   For this man, the holy one through Righteousness,
   Holds in his spirit the force which heals existence,
   Beneficent unto all, as a sworn friend, O Wise One.

3. This I ask thee, O Lord, answer me truly:
   Who was the first father of Righteousness at the birth?
   Who appointed their path to sun and stars?
   Who but thou is it through whom the moon waxes and wanes?
   This I would know, O Wise One, and other things too!

4. This I ask thee, O Lord, answer me truly:
   Who set the Earth in its place below, and the sky of the clouds,
      that it shall not fall?

Who the waters and the plants?
Who yoked the two steeds to wind and clouds?
Who, O Wise One, is the creator of the Good Mind?

5. This I ask thee, O Lord, answer me truly:
What artificer made light and darkness?
What artificer sleep and waking?
Who made morning, noon, and night,
To remind the wise man of his task?

11. This I ask thee, O Lord, answer me truly:
Shall Devotion extend to those to whom thy religion shall be
    proclaimed?
From the beginning was I chosen for this by thee:
All others I shall look upon with hostile spirit.

12. This I ask thee, O Lord, answer me truly:
Who among those to whom I speak is righteous and who is
    wicked?
Which of the two? Am I evil myself,
Or is he the evil one who would wickedly keep me far from thy
    salvation?
How should I not think him the wicked one?

13. This I ask thee, O Lord, answer me truly:
(How?) shall we rid ourselves of evil
By throwing it back on these who, full of disobedience,
Care naught for following Righteousness
And do not trouble to take counsel with the Good Mind?

14. This I ask thee, O Lord, answer me truly:
(How?) shall I deliver evil into the hands of Righteousness,
That it may put it down according to the rules of thy doctrine,
That it may cause a mighty schism among the wicked
And bring them blindness and hostilities, O Wise One.

16. This I ask thee, O Lord, answer me truly:
Who will be victorious and protect the living by thy doctrine?
May visible signs be given to me:
Make known the judge that shall heal existence!
And may it be given to obey him, through the Good Mind,
To all those in whom thou seekest it, O Wise One!

17. This I ask thee, O Lord, answer me truly:
    Shall I attain my goal with you, O Wise One?
    May I become one with you and may my word have power,
    That Integrity and Immortality according to thy order
    May join themselves with the follower of Righteousness.

18. This I ask thee, O Lord, answer me truly:
    Shall I receive for my wage, through Righteousness,
    Two mares with a stallion and a camel,
    Which were promised to me, O Wise One,
    Together with thy gift of Integrity and Immortality?

19. This I ask thee, O Lord, answer me truly:
    He that does not give his hire to the one who earned it,
    He that does not give it according to his word,
    What shall be his present punishment,
    —knowing that which shall come to him at the end?

20. Have the false gods ever been good masters?
    This I ask of those who see, in their cult,
    How the sacrificer and the usig deliver the ox to fury,
    And how the sorcerer prince makes him to moan in his soul,
    And who do not sprinkle the water of the cattle on the pastures
    To make it prosper through Righteousness.

> Translation and commentary by Jacques Duchesne-
> Guillemin, in his The Hymns of Zarathustra (London,
> 1952), pp. 63-73

See also nos. 37, 60, 303

291. NACIKETAS' THIRD WISH

('Katha Upanishad,' I, 1, selections)

A poor and pious Brāhman, Vājasravasa, performs a sacrifice and gives
as presents to the priests a few old and feeble cows. His son, Naciketas,
feeling disturbed by the unreality of his father's observance of the sacrifice, proposes that he himself may be offered as offering (daksinā) to
a priest. When he persisted in his request, his father in rage said, 'Unto
Yama, (death) I give thee.' Naciketas goes to the abode of Yama and

finding him absent, waits there for three days and nights unfed. Yama, on his return, offers three gifts in recompense for the delay and discomfort caused to Naciketas. For the first, Naciketas said, 'Let me return alive to my father.' For the second, 'Tell me how my good works may not be exhausted'; and for the third, 'Tell me the way to conquer re-death.'

20. There is this doubt in regard to a man who has departed, some (holding) that he is and some that he is not. I would be instructed by thee in this knowledge. Of the boons this is the third boon.

21. (Yama said): Even the gods of old had doubt on this point. It is not, indeed, easy to understand; (so) subtle is this truth. Choose another boon, O Naciketas. Do not press me. Release me from this. . . .

23. (Yama said): Choose sons and grandsons that shall live a hundred years, cattle in plenty, elephants, gold and horses. Choose vast expanses of land and life for thyself as many years as thou wilt.

24. If thou deemest (any) boon like unto this, choose (that) as also wealth and long life. O Naciketas, prosper then on this vast earth. I will make thee the enjoyer of thy desires. . . .

26. (Naciketas said): Transient (are these) and they wear out, O Yama, the vigour of all the senses of men. All life (a full life), moreover, is brief. Thine be the chariots, thine the dance and song.

27. Man is not to be contented with wealth. Shall we enjoy wealth when we have seen thee? Shall we live as long as thou art in power? That alone is (still) the boon chosen by me.

28. Having approached the undecaying immortality, what decaying mortal on this earth below who (now) knows (and meditates on) the pleasures of beauty and love, will delight in an over-long life?

29. Tell us that about which they doubt, O Death, what there is in the great passing-on. This boon which penetrates the mystery, no other than that does Naciketas choose.

S. Radhakrishnan (editor and translator), *The Principal Upanishads* (New York: Harper & Row, 1953), pp. 603 ff.

292. 'EXPLAIN TO ME THE BRAHMAN . . .'

('Brihad-āranyaka Upanishad,' III, 4, 1-2)

1. Then Ushasta Cākrāyana asked him: 'Yājñavalkya,' said he, 'explain to me the Brahman that is immediately present and directly perceived, who is the self in all things?' 'This is your self. That is within all things.' 'Which is within all things, Yājñavalkya?' 'He who breathes in with your breathing in is the self of yours which is in all things. He who breathes out with your breathing out is the self of yours which is in all things. He who breathes about with your breathing about is the self of yours which is in all things. He who breathes up with your breathing up is the self of yours which is in all things. He is your self which is in all things.'

2. Ushasta Cākrāyana said: 'This has been explained by you as one might say 'This is cow,' 'This is a horse.' Explain to me the *Brahman* that is immediately present and directly perceived, that is the self in all things.' 'This is your self that is within all things.' 'Which is within all things, Yājñavalkya?' 'You cannot see the seer of seeing, you cannot hear the hearer of hearing, you cannot think the thinker of thinking, you cannot understand the understander of understanding. He is your self which is in all things. Everything else is of evil.' Thereupon Ushasta Cākrāyana kept silent.

S. Radhakrishnan (editor and translator), *The Principal Upanishads, op. cit.,* pp. 219-20

293. 'HOW MANY GODS ARE THERE, YĀJÑAVALKYA?' . . . 'ONE'

('Brihad-āranyaka Upanishad,' III, 9, 1)

1. Then Vidagdha Sakalya asked him: 'How many gods are there Yājñavalkya?' He answered, in accord with the following *nivid* (invocation of the gods). 'As many as are mentioned in the *nivid* of the hymn of praise to the Vishve-devas, namely, three hundred and three, and three thousand and three.' 'Yes,' he said, 'but how many gods are there, Yājñavalkya?' 'Thirty-three.' 'Yes,' he said, 'but how many gods are there, Yājñavalkya?' 'Six.' 'Yes,' said he, 'but how many gods are

there, Yājñavalkya?' 'Three.' 'Yes,' said he, 'but how many gods are
there, Yājñavalkya?' 'Two.' 'Yes,' said he, 'but how many gods
are there, Yājñavalkya?' 'One and a half.' 'Yes,' said he, 'but how many
gods are there, Yājñavalkya?' 'One.' . . .

S. Radhakrishnan (editor and translator), *The Principal
Upanishads, op. cit.,* pp. 234-5

294. 'THIS IS THE SELF OF MINE . . . THIS IS BRAHMAN'

('Upanishads,' selections)

1. Verily, this whole world is *Brahman*, from which he comes forth,
without which he will be dissolved, and in which he breathes. Tranquil,
one should meditate on it.

2. He who consists of mind, whose body is life, whose form is light,
whose conception is truth, whose soul is space, containing all works,
containing all desires, containing all odours, containing all tastes,
encompassing this whole world, being without speech and without
concern.

3. This is my self within the heart, smaller than a grain of rice,
than a barley corn, than a mustard seed, than a grain of millet or than
the kernel of a grain of a millet. This is myself within the heart, greater
than the earth, greater than the atmosphere, greater than the sky,
greater than these worlds.

4. Containing all works, containing all desires, containing all odours,
containing all tastes, encompassing this whole world, without speech,
without concern, this is the self of mine within the heart; this is
Brahman. Into him, I shall enter, on departing hence. Verily, he who
believes this, will have no more doubts. *(Chāndogya Upanishad,* III,
14, 1-4.)

. . . But the self *(ātman)* is not this, not this. He is incomprehensible
for he is never comprehended. He is indestructible for he cannot be
destroyed. He is unattached for he does not attach himself. . . .
(Brihad-āranyaka Upanishad, IV, 2, 4.)

This self *(ātman)* is (like) honey for all beings and all beings are (like)
honey for this self. This shining, immortal person who is in this self
and the shining, immortal person who is in this (individual) self, he is

just this Self, this is immortal, this is *Brahman*, this is all. *(Brihad-
āranyaka Upanishad, II, 5, 14.)*

Manifest, well-fixed, moving, verily, in the secret place (of the heart)
such is the great support. In it is centred all this which moves, breathes
and winks. Know that as being, as non-being, as the supreme object to
be desired, as the highest beyond the reach of man's understanding.
(Mundaka Upanishad, II, 2, 1.)

> S. Radhakrishnan (editor and translator), *The Princi-
> pal Upanishads, op. cit.*

See also nos. 56, 101, 300

295. WHENEVER ORDER (DHARMA) LANGUISHES,
KRISHNA MANIFESTS HIMSELF

('Bhagavad Gītā, IV, 1-9, 14)

The Blessed One said:

1. This discipline to Vivasvant
   I proclaimed; 'tis eternal;
   Vivasvant told it to Manu,
   Manu spake it to Ikshvāku.

2. Thus received in line of succession,
   The royal seers knew it.
   In a long course of time in this world this
   Discipline became lost, scorcher of the foe.

3. This very same by Me to thee today,
   This ancient discipline, is proclaimed.
   Thou art My devotee and friend, that is why;
   For this is a supreme secret.

   Arjuna said:

4. Later Thy birth,
   Earlier the birth of Vivasvant:
   How may I understand this,
   That Thou didst proclaim it in the beginning, as Thou sayest?

   The Blessed One said:

5. For Me have passed many
   Births, and for thee, Arjuna;

These I know all;
Thou knowest not, scorcher of the foe.

6. Tho unborn, tho My self is eternal.
   Tho Lord of Beings,
   Resorting to My own material nature
   I come into being by My own mysterious power.

7. For whenever of the right
   A languishing appears, son of Bharata,
   A rising up of unright,
   Then I send Myself forth.

8. For protection of the good,
   And for destruction of evil-doers,
   To make a firm footing for the right,
   I come into being in age after age.

9. My wondrous birth and actions
   Whoso knows thus as they truly are,
   On leaving the body, to rebirth
   He goes not; to Me he goes, Arjuna! . . .

14. Actions do not stain Me,
    (Because) I have no yearning for the fruit of actions.
    Who comprehends Me thus
    Is not bound by actions.

> Translation by Franklin Edgerton. *The Bhagavad Gītā*,
> vol I Harvard Oriental Series, Vol. 38 (Cambridge:
> Harvard University Press, 1944)

296. THE TEACHINGS OF THE BHAGAVAD GĪTĀ: 'WHATEVER THOU DOEST, DO AS AN OFFERING TO ME'

('Bhagavad Gītā, IX, VI, VIII, *selections)*

4. By Me is pervaded all this
   Universe, by Me in the form of the unmanifest.
   All beings rest in Me,
   And I do not rest in them.

5. And (yet) beings do not rest in Me:
   Behold My divine mystery (or magic)!
   Supporter of being, and not resting in beings,
   Is My Self, that causes beings to be.

6. As constantly abides in the ether
     The great wind, that penetrates everywhere,
   So all beings
     Abide in Me; make sure of that.

7. All beings, son of Kuntī,
     Pass into My material nature
   At the end of a world-eon; them again
     I send forth at the beginning of a (new) world-eon.

8. Taking as base My own material nature
     I send forth again and again
   This whole host of beings,
     Which is powerless, by the power of (My) material nature.

9. And Me these actions do not
     Bind Dhanamjaya,—
   Sitting in as one sitting out (participating as one indifferent),
     Unattached to these actions.

10. With Me as overseer, material nature
     Brings forth (the world of) moving and unmoving (beings);
   By this motive force, son of Kuntī,
     The world goes around.

11. Fools despise Me
     That have assumed human form,
   Not knowing the higher state
     Of Me, which is the great lord of beings. . . .

16. I am the ritual act, I am the act of worship,
     I am the offering to the dead, I am the medicinal herb,
   I am the sacred formula, I alone am the sacrificial butter,
     I am the fire of offering, I am the poured oblation.

17. I am the father of this world,
     The mother, the establisher, the grandsire,
   The object of knowledge, the purifier, the sacred syllable om,
     The verse of praise, the chant, and the sacrificial formula.

18. The goal, supporter, lord, witness,
     The dwelling-place, refuge, friend,
   The origin, dissolution, and maintenance,
     The treasure-house, the imperishable seed.

19. I give heat; the rain I
    Hold back and send forth;
    Both immortality and death,
    Both the existent and the non-existent am I, Arjuna. . . .

23. Even those who are devotees of other gods,
    And worship them permeated with faith,
    It is only Me, son of Kuntī, that even they
    Worship, (tho) not in the enjoined fashion.

24. For I of all acts of worship
    Am both the recipient and the lord;
    But they do not recognize Me
    In the true way; therefore they fall (from the 'heaven' they
    win).

25. Votaries of the gods go to the gods,
    Votaries of the (departed) fathers go to the fathers,
    Worshippers of goblins go to the goblins,
    Worshippers of Me also go to Me.

26. A leaf, a flower, a fruit, or water,
    Who presents to Me with devotion,
    That offering of devotion I
    Accept from the devout-souled (giver).

27. Whatever thou doest, whatever thou eatest,
    Whatever thou offerest in oblation or givest,
    Whatever austerity thou performest, son of Kuntī,
    That do as an offering to Me. . . .

30. Even if a very evil doer
    Reveres Me with single devotion,
    He must be regarded as righteous in spite of all;
    For he has the right resolution.

31. Quickly his soul becomes righteous,
    And he goes to eternal peace.
    Son of Kuntī, make sure of this:
    No devotee of Mine is lost.

32. For if they take refuge in Me, son of Prithā,
    Even those who may be of base origin,
    Women, men of the artisan caste, and serfs too,
    Even they go to the highest goal. (IX, 4-11, 16-19, 23-7, 30-2.)

30. Who sees Me in all,
     And sees all in Me,
   For him I am not lost,
     And he is not lost for Me.

31. Me as abiding in all beings whoso
     Reveres, adopting (the belief in) one-ness,
   Tho abiding in any possible condition,
     That disciplined man abides in Me. (VI, 30-1.)

5. And at the hour of death, on Me alone
    Meditating, leaving the body
   Whoso dies, to My estate he
    Goes; there is no doubt of that.

6. Whatsoever state (of being) meditating upon
    He leaves the body at death,
   To just that he goes, son of Kuntī,
    Always, being made to be in the condition of that.

7. Therefore at all times
    Think on Me, and fight;
   With thought-organ and consciousness fixed on Me
    Thou shalt go just to Me without a doubt. (VIII, 5-7.)

> Translation by Franklin Edgerton, *The Bhagavad Gītā*
> vol. I, Harvard Oriental Series, vol. 38 (Cambridge:
> Harvard University Press, 1944)

See also nos. 28, 117, 264

297. TAO, THE ULTIMATE REALITY

('Tao Tê Ching,' selections)

Tao is the way that those must walk who would 'achieve without doing.' But tao is not only a means, a doctrine, a principle. It is the ultimate reality in which all attributes are united, 'it is heavy as a stone, light as a feather'; it is the unity underlying unity. 'It is that by losing of which men die; by getting of which men live. Whatever is done without it, fails; whatever is done by means of it, succeeds. It has neither root nor stalk, leaf nor flower. Yet upon it depends the generation and growth of the ten thousand things, each after its kind' (Kuan Tzu, 49).

The Ultimate Reality

We do not know, and it is unlikely that we shall ever know, who wrote the Tao Tê Ching. But for two thousand years the name of Lao Tan or 'Master Lao' (Lao Tzu) has been connected with this book.

Chapter IV

The Way is like an empty vessel
That yet may be drawn from
Without ever needing to be filled.
It is bottomless; the very progenitor of all things in the world.
In it all sharpness is blunted,
All tangles untied,
All glare tempered,
All dust[1] smoothed.
It is like a deep pool that never dries.
Was it too the child of something else? We cannot tell,
But as a substanceless image[2] it existed before the Ancestor.[3]

Notes

1 Dust is the Taoist symbol for the noise and the fuss of everyday life.
2 A *hsiang*, an image such as the mental images that float before us when we think.
3 The Ancestor in question is almost certainly the Yellow Ancestor who separated Earth from Heaven and so destroyed the Primal Unity, for which he is frequently censured in Chuang Tzu.

Chapter VI

The Valley Spirit never dies.
It is named the Mysterious Female.
And the Doorway of the Mysterious Female
Is the base from which Heaven and Earth sprang.
It is there within us all the while;
Draw upon it as you will, it never runs dry.

Chapter VII

Heaven is eternal, the Earth everlasting.
How come they to be so? It is because they do not foster their
   own lives;
That is why they live so long.
Therefore the Sage

595

Puts himself in the background; but is always to the fore.
Remains outside; but is always there.
Is it not just because he does not strive for any personal end
That all his personal ends are fulfilled?

Chapter XI

We put thirty spokes together and call it a wheel;
But it is on the space where there is nothing that the
  usefulness of the wheel depends.
We turn clay to make a vessel;
But it is on the space where there is nothing that the
  usefulness of the vessel depends.
We pierce doors and windows to make a house;
And it is on these spaces where there is nothing that the
  usefulness of the house depends.
Therefore just as we take advantage of what is, we should
  recognize the usefulness of what is not.

Chapter XXII

'To remain whole, be twisted!
To become straight, let yourself be bent.
To become full, be hollow.
Be tattered, that you may be renewed.
Those that have little, may get more,
Those that have much, are but perplexed.
Therefore the Sage
Clasps the Primal Unity,
Testing by it everything under heaven.
He does not show himself; therefore he is seen everywhere.
He does not define himself, therefore he is distinct.
He does not boast of what he will do, therefore he succeeds.
He is not proud of his work, and therefore it endures.
He does not contend,
And for that very reason no one under heaven can contend with him.

So then we see that the ancient saying 'To remain whole, be twisted!'
was no idle word; for true wholeness can only be achieved by return.[1]

Note

1 To the way.

The Ultimate Reality

Chapter XXV

There was something formless yet complete,
That existed before heaven and earth;
Without sound, without substance,
Dependent on nothing, unchanging,
All pervading, unfailing.
One may think of it as the mother of all things under heaven.
Its true name[1] we do not know;
'Way' is the by-name that we give it.
Were I forced to say to what class of things it belongs I should call
    it Great (ta).
Now ta also means passing on,
And passing on means going Far Away,
And going far away means returning.[2]
Thus just as Tao[3] has 'this greatness' and as earth has it
and as heaven has it, so may the ruler also have it. Thus
'within the realm there are four portions of greatness,' and
one belongs to the king. The ways of men are conditioned by
those of earth. The ways of earth, by those of heaven. The
ways of heaven by those of Tao, and the ways of Tao by the Self-so.[4]

Notes

1 I.e., we do not know to what class of things it belongs.
2 Returning to 'what was there at the Beginning.'
3 Henceforward I shall use the Chinese word Tao instead of the Way; to do
so avoids many inconveniences.
4 The 'unconditioned'; the 'what-is-so-of-itself.'

Chapter XXVII

Perfect activity leaves no track behind it;
Perfect speech is like a jade-worker whose tool leaves no mark
The perfect reckoner needs no counting-slips;
The perfect door has neither bolt nor bar,
Yet cannot be opened.
The perfect knot needs neither rope nor twine,
Yet cannot be untied.
Therefore the Sage
Is all the time in the most perfect way helping men,
He certainly does not turn his back on men;
Is all the time in the most perfect way helping creatures,
He certainly does not turn his back on creatures. . . .

Speculations on Man and God

Chapter XXXIV

Great Tao is like a boat that drifts;
It can go this way; it can go that.
The ten thousand creatures owe their existence to it and it does
not disown them;
Yet having produced them, it does not take possession of them.
Tao, though it covers the ten thousand things like a garment,
Makes no claim to be master over them,
And asks for nothing from them.
Therefore it may be called the Lowly.
The ten thousand creatures obey it,
Though they know not that they have a master;
Therefore it is called the Great.
So too the Sage just because he never at any time makes a show
of greatness in fact achieves greatness.

Chapter XLII

Tao gave birth to the One; the One gave birth successively to two things, three things, up to ten thousand.[1] These ten thousand creatures cannot turn their backs to the shade without having the sun on their bellies,[2] and it is on this blending of the breaths[3] that their harmony[4] depends. To be orphaned, needy, ill-provided is what men most hate, yet princes and dukes style themselves so. Truly, 'things are often increased by seeking to diminish them and diminished by seeking to increase them.' The maxims that others use in their teaching I too will use in mine. Show me a man of violence that came to a good end, and I will take him for my teacher.

Commentary

To be a prince is a 'sunny' as opposed to a 'shady' thing. But a prince does not feel properly 'harmonized' unless he also has 'the shade at his back,' which he obtains by humbling himself.

A proverb says: 'The man of violence never yet came to a good end; nor did he that delights in victory fail to meet his match.' Another proverb says: 'The best doctor cannot save one whose life-span has run out; nor can the man of violence strive with Heaven.' It is possible that Ch'iang-liang, 'man of violence,' is in reality the name of a mythological figure, a sort of Titan who warred unsuccessfully against Heaven. Chi'iang means 'violent'; but liang means 'rafter,' and though

The notes to this text are on p. 599.

the two together are said to mean 'man of violence,' no proof is adduced; and I suspect that this Titan was called 'Rafter' because his image was carved on the ends of rafters. This theory is borne out by a passage in *Chuang Tzu* (VI, 9) which speaks of a strong man called Chü-liang, 'holder of the rafters' who like Samson 'lost his strength.' In order to conform to a quotation by Huai-nan Tzu, many modern editors have tampered with the text at the beginning of the chapter.

Notes

1 I.e., everything.
2 Which symbolizes the fact that they are themselves a mixture of light and dark, hard and soft, water and fire, etc.
3 The warm 'breath' of the sun and the cold 'breath' of the shade. Hence 'breath' comes to mean a 'state of the atmosphere' in a wider sense.
4 Or 'balance,' as we should say.

Chapter LII

That which was the beginning of all things under heaven
We may speak of as the 'mother' of all things.
He who apprehends the mother[1]
Thereby knows the sons.[2]
And he who has known the sons
Will hold all the tighter to the mother,
And to the end of his days suffer no harm:
'Block the passages, shut the doors,
And till the end your strength shall not fail.
Open up the passages, increase your doings,
And till your last day no help shall come to you.'
As good sight means seeing what is very small
So strength means holding on to what is weak.[3]
He who having used the outer-light[4] can return to the
*   inner-light*
Is thereby preserved from all harm.
This is called resorting to the always-so.

Notes

1 Tao, the One, the Whole.
2 The Many, the universe.
3 I.e., Tao.
4 This corresponds to 'knowing the sons.' *Ming* ('inner-light') is self-knowledge.

Speculations on Man and God

Chapter LVI

Those who know do not speak;
Those who speak do not know.
Block the passages,
Shut the doors,
Let all sharpness be blunted,
All tangles untied,
All glare tempered.
All dust smoothed.
This is called the mysterious levelling.
He who has achieved it cannot either be drawn into friendship
  or repelled,
Cannot be benefited, cannot be harmed,
Cannot either be raised or humbled,
And for that very reason is highest of all creatures under
  heaven.

Chapter LVII

'Kingdoms can only be governed if rules are kept;
Battles can only be won if rules are broken.'[1]
But the adherence of all under heaven can only be won by letting-
  alone.
How do I know that it is so?
By this.[2]
The more prohibitions there are, the more ritual avoidances,
The poorer the people will be.
The more 'sharp weapons'[3] *there are,*
The more benighted will the whole land grow.
The more cunning craftsmen there are,
The more pernicious contrivances[4] *will be invented.*
The more laws are promulgated,
The more thieves and bandits there will be.
Therefore a sage has said:
So long as I 'do nothing' the people will of themselves be trans-
  formed.
So long as I love quietude, the people will of themselves go
  straight.

The notes to this text are on p. 601.

So long as I act only by inactivity the people will of themselves
become prosperous.

So long as I have no wants the people will of themselves return to
the 'state of the Uncarved Block.'

Notes

1 A military maxim, to the pattern of which the author proceeds to fit his
Taoist formula. Cf. Lionel Giles, *Sun Tzu*, pp. 34, 35. *Ch'i* means unexpected
manoeuvres. *Cheng* 'rules kept' is not here used in its technical military sense
of 'open attack.'

2 Through what I have found inside myself, 'in the belly'; through the light of
my inner vision.

3 I.e., clever people.

4 Cf. the story in *Chuang Tzu* (XII 11) about the man in whom the idea of a
simple labour-saving contrivance inspired feelings similar to those aroused in
Wordsworth by the sight of a railway train.

Chapter LXXXI

True words are not fine-sounding;

Fine-sounding words are not true.

The good man does not prove by argument;

And he who proves by argument is not good.

True wisdom is different from much learning;

Much learning means little wisdom.

The Sage has no need to hoard;

When his own last scrap has been used up on behalf of others,

Lo, he has more than before!

When his own last scrap has been used up in giving to others,

Lo, his stock is even greater than before!

For Heaven's way is to sharpen without cutting,

And the Sage's way is to act without striving.

> Translation, commentary, and notes by Arthur
> Waley, in his *The Way and Its Power: A Study of
> the Tao Tê Ching* (Grove Press, New York)

298. CHUANG TZU DISCOURSES ON TAO

The second great figure of the early Taoist school is the philosopher
Chuang Tzu or Chuang Chou, whose dates are tentatively given as
369 to 286 B.C., making him a contemporary of Mencius. Although he

was a minor official at one time, he seems to have lived most of his life as a recluse and almost nothing is known about him. The book which bears his name, actually probably a combination of his own essays and those of his disciples and imitators, is one of the most witty and imaginative works of all Chinese literature. Like the Lao Tzu it does not depend for its effect upon methodical argumentation, but upon the use of parable and allegory, paradox and fanciful imagery. A favourite device of the work is to make an actual historical figure like Confucius serve as an illustration of Taoist ideas, thus involving the great men of Chinese history in all sorts of whimsical and purely imaginative anecdotes.

Chuang Tzu shares with the Lao Tzu its central conception of the Tao as the principle underlying and governing all existence. He is, however, less concerned with the Tao as a guide in life than as that which possesses a supreme value in itself, transcending all mundane uses. . . . Chuang Tzu is almost indifferent to human society. He seeks neither to reform things nor to keep them as they are, but only to rise above them. The philosophy of Chuang Tzu is essentially a plea for the freedom of the individual. But it is a kind of spiritual freedom, liberating the individual more from the confines of his own mind than from external restraints. What he must be freed from are his own prejudices, his own partial view of things, his tendency to judge all else in terms of himself.

The Identity of the Opposites

Whereby is the Tao vitiated that there should be a distinction of true and false? Whereby is speech vitiated that there should be a distinction of right and wrong? How could the Tao depart and be not there? And could there be speech and yet it be not appropriate? The Tao is vitiated by petty virtues. Speech is vitiated by flowery eloquence. So it is that we have the contentions between the Confucianists and the Mo-ists, each affirming what the other denies and denying what the other affirms. But if we are to decide on their several affirmations and denials, there is nothing better than to employ the light of reason.

Everything is its own self; everything is something else's other. Things do not know that they are other things' other; they only know that they are themselves. Thus it is said, the other arises out of the self, just as the self arises out of the other. This is the theory that self and others give rise to each other. Besides, where there is life, there is death; and where there is death, there is life. Where there is impossibility, there is possibility; and where there is possibility, there is impossibility. It is because there is right, that there is wrong; it is because there is wrong, that there is right. This being the situation, the sages do not approach things at this level, but reflect the light of nature. Thereupon the self is also the other; the other is also the self. According to the other, there is one kind of right and wrong. According to the self there is another kind of right and wrong. But really are there such distinctions as the self and the other, or are there no such distinctions? When the self and the other [or the this and the that] lose their contrariety, there we have the very essence of the Tao. Only the essence of the Tao may occupy the centre of the circle, and respond therefrom to the endless opinions from all directions. Affirmation [of the self] is one of the endless opinions; denials [of the other] is another. Therefore it is said that there is nothing better than to employ the light of reason. . . .

The possible is possible; the impossible is impossible. The Tao operates and things follow. Things are what they are called. What are they? They are what they are. What are they not? They are not what they are not. Everything is what it is, and can be what it can be. There is nothing that is not something, and there is nothing that cannot be something. Therefore, for instance, a stalk and a pillar, the ugly and the beautiful, the common and the peculiar, the deceitful and the strange—by the Tao this great variety is all brought into a single unity. Division to one is construction to another; construction to one is destruction to another. Whether in construction or in destruction, all things are in the end brought into unity. . . .

The Decline of Tao

The knowledge of the ancients was perfect. In what way was it perfect? They were not yet aware that there were things. This is the most perfect knowledge; nothing can be added. Then, some were aware that there were things, but not aware that there were distinctions among them. Then, some were aware that there were distinctions, but not yet aware that there was right and wrong among them. When right and wrong became manifest, the Tao thereby declined. With the decline of the Tao came the growth of love. But was there really a growth and a decline? Or was there no growth or decline?

Now I have something to say [namely, that there is no such thing as right and wrong]. I do not know whether or not what I say agrees with what others say [namely, that there is right and wrong].

Whether or not what I say and what others say agree [in maintaining right and wrong], they at least agree [in assuming that there is right and wrong]. Then there is hardly any difference between what I say and what others say. But though this may be the case, let me try to explain myself. There was a beginning. There was a no-beginning [before the beginning]. There was a no-no-beginning [previous to the no-beginning before the beginning]. There was being. There was nonbeing [before there was being]. There was no-nonbeing [before there was nonbeing]. There was no-no-nonbeing [before there was no-nonbeing]. Suddenly being and nonbeing appeared. And yet, between being and nonbeing, I do not know which is really being and which is really nonbeing. Just now I have said something, and yet I do not know whether what I have said really means something, or does not mean anything at all.

The Great Awakening

Leaning against the sun and the moon and carrying the universe under his arm, the sage blends everything into a harmonious whole. He is unmindful of the confusion and the gloom, and equalizes the humble and the honourable. The multitude strive and toil; the sage is primitive and without knowledge. He comprehends ten thousand years as one unity, whole and simple. All things are what they are, and are thus brought together.

How do I know that the love of life is not a delusion? How do I know that he who is afraid of death is not like a man who left his home as a youth and forgot to return? Lady Li was the daughter of the border warden of Ai. When she was first brought to the state of Chin, she wept until the bosom of her robe was drenched with tears. But when she came to the royal residence, shared with the king his luxurious couch and ate sumptuous food, she regretted that she had wept. How do I know that the dead do not repent of their former craving for life? Those who dream of a merry drinking party may the next morning wail and weep. Those who dream of wailing and weeping may in the morning go off gaily to hunt. While they dream they do not know that they are dreaming. In their dream, they may even try to interpret their dream. Only when they have awakened do they begin to know that they have dreamed. By and by comes the great awakening, and then we shall know that it has all been a great dream. Yet all the while the fools think that they are awake; this they are sure of. With minute nicety, they discriminate between princes and grooms. How stupid! Confucius and you are both in a dream. And when I say that you are in a dream, this is also a dream. This way of talking may be called paradoxical. If after ten thousand generations we could once meet a great sage who knew how to explain the paradox, it would be as though we met him after only one morning or one evening.

Chuang Tzu and the Butterfly

Once upon a time, Chuang Chou [i.e., Chuang Tzu] dreamed that he was a butterfly, a butterfly fluttering about, enjoying itself. It did not know that it was Chuang Chou. Suddenly he awoke with a start and he was Chuang Chou again. But he did not know whether he was Chuang Chou who had dreamed that he was a butterfly, or whether he was a butterfly dreaming that he was Chuang Chou. Between Chuang Chou and the butterfly there must be some distinction. This is what is called the transformation of things.

The Natural and the Artificial

'The Tao is without beginning and without end. Things are born and die, without holding to any permanence. They are now empty, now full, without maintaining a constant form. The years cannot be made to abide; time cannot be arrested. Processes of increase and decrease are in operation and every end is followed by a new beginning. Thus may we speak of the great norm [of the Tao] and the principle pervading all things.

'The life of things passes by like a galloping horse. Every movement brings a change, and every hour makes a difference. What is one to do or what is one not to do? Indeed everything will take its own course. . . .

'Therefore it has been said that the natural abides within, the artificial without, and virtue (te) resides in the natural. If one knows the course of nature and man, taking nature as the fundamental and abiding by virtue, one may feel free either to proceed or retreat, either to contract or extend, for there is always a return to the essential and to the ultimate.'

'What do you mean,' enquired the Earl of the River, 'by the natural and the artificial?'

'Horses and oxen,' answered the spirit of the Ocean, 'have four feet. That is the natural. Putting a halter on a horse's head, a string through a bullock's nose—that is the artificial.

'Therefore it has been said, do not let the artificial obliterate the natural; do not let effort obliterate destiny; do not let enjoyment be sacrificed to fame. Diligently observe these precepts without fail, and thus you will revert to the original innocence.'

'The hard will be crushed . . .'

Lao Tzu said: 'Know the masculine but maintain the feminine; become thereby a ravine for the world. Know purity but endure disgrace; become thereby a valley for the world.' Men all reach for the first; he alone took the last. He said, 'Receive unto yourself the refuse of the world.' Men all seek the substantial; he alone took the empty. Because he did not hoard, he had abundance; indeed great was his abundance. His actions were effortless and without waste. He believed in doing nothing, and laughed at the ingenious. Men all seek for happiness; he alone sought self-preservation through adaptation. He said: 'Let us be free from reproach.' He believed in depth for one's foundation, and simplicity as the rule of outward conduct. He said: 'The hard will be crushed; the sharp will be blunted.' He was always generous and tolerant toward things. He would not exploit others. This may be considered the height of perfection. Kuan Yin and Lao Tan—they belonged with the great and true men of old!

Translation and commentary by Y. P. Mei, in Wm. Theodore de Bary, *et al.* (ed.), *Sources of Chinese Tradition* (Columbia University Press, 1960), pp. 64-5, 70-5, 78-9, 85

E. REFLECTING ON GODS, THE SELF, AND THE GOD

299. NUER CONCEPTION OF GOD

The Nuer word we translate 'God' is *kwoth*, Spirit. Nuer also speak of him more definitely as *kwoth nhial* or *kwoth a nhial*, Spirit of the sky or Spirit who is in the sky. There are other and lesser spirits which they class as *kuth nhial*, spirits of the sky or of the above, and *kuth piny*, spirits of the earth or of the below. I discuss the conception of God first because the other spiritual conceptions are dependent on it and can only be understood in relation to it. . . .

We may certainly say that the Nuer do not regard the sky or any celestial phenomenon as God, and this is clearly shown in the distinction made between God and the sky in the expressions 'Spirit of the sky' and 'Spirit who is in the sky.' Moreover, it would even be a mistake to interpret 'of the sky' and 'in the sky' too literally.

It would equally be a mistake to regard the association of God with the sky as pure metaphor, for though the sky is not God, and though God is everywhere, he is thought of as being particularly in the sky, and Nuer generally think of him in a spatial sense as being on high. Hence anything connected with the firmament has associations with him. Nuer sometimes speak of him as falling in the rain and of being in lightning and thunder. . . .

It would be quite contrary to Nuer thought, as I have remarked, and it would even seem absurd to them, to say that sky, moon, rain, and so forth are in themselves, singly or collectively, God. God is Spirit, which, like wind and air, is invisible and ubiquitous. But though God is not these things he is in them in the sense that he reveals himself through them. In this sense, he is in the sky, falls in the rain, shines in the sun and moon, and blows in the wind. These divine manifestations are to be understood as modes of God and not as his essence, which is Spirit.

God being above, everything above is associated with him. This is why the heavenly bodies and the movements and actions connected with them are associated with him. This is why also the spirits of the air are regarded as *gaat kwoth*, children of God, in a way other spirits are not, for they, unlike other spirits, dwell in the air and are also thought of as being in the clouds, which are nearest to the sky. This is why also the *colwic* spirits are so closely associated with God, for he touched them with his fire from heaven and took them to himself. . . .

Nuer say that God is everywhere, that he is 'like wind' and 'like air.' According to Father Crazzolara, he may be spoken of by the epithets *jiom*, wind, and *ghau*, universe, but these words only stand for God in poems or in an allegorical sense and are illustrations of the liking the Nilotic people show in their poetry for metonymy and synecdoche. God is not wind, but *cere jiom*, like wind; and he is not *ghau*, the universe, but *cak ghaua*, the creator of the universe. Another poetic epithet by which he may be referred to is *tutgar*. This is an ox-name, taken from an ox of the kind Nuer call *wer*, which has wide spreading horns and is the most majestic of their beasts. The name is a combination of two words; *tut*, which has the sense of 'strength' or 'greatness,' and *gar*, which has the sense of 'omnipresent,' as in another of God's titles, *kwoth me gargar*, the omnipresent God (*gargar* can also be translated 'limitless'). But the commonest Nuer way of trying to express their idea of the nature of God is to say that he is like wind or air, a metaphor which seems appropriate to us because it is found throughout the hierological literature of the world and we are particularly familiar with it in the Old Testament. Among the Nuer the metaphor is consistent not only with the absence of any fixed abode of God but also of any places where he is thought particularly to dwell, for air and wind are everywhere. Unlike the other spirits God has no prophets or sanctuaries or earthly forms.

God, Spirit in the heavens who is like wind and air, is the creator and mover of all things. Since he made the world he is addressed in prayers as *kwoth ghaua*, Spirit of the universe, with the sense of creator of the universe. The word *cak*, used as a noun, can mean the creation, that is, all created things, and hence the nature or character proper to a person or thing; it can be used in a very special sense to refer to an abnormality, *cak kwoth*, a freak; and, though I think rarely, it is used as a title of God, the creator, as in the expression *cak nath*, creator of men. As a verb 'to create' it signifies creation *ex nihilo*, and when speaking of things can therefore only be used of God. However, the word can be used of men for imaginative constructions, such as the thinking of a name to give a child, inventing a tale, or composing a poem, in the same figurative sense as when we say that an actor creates a part. The word therefore means not only creation from nothing but also creation by thought or imagination, so that 'God created the universe' has the sense of 'God thought of the universe' or 'God imagined the universe.'. . .

Whether they are speaking about events which happened *ne walka*, in the beginning or long ago, or about happenings of yesterday or today, God, creative Spirit, is the final Nuer explanation of everything. When asked how things began or how they have come to be what they are they answer that God made them or that it was his will that they have come to be what they are. The heavens and the earth and the waters on the earth, and the beasts and birds and reptiles and fish were made by him, and he is the author of custom and tradition. The Nuer herd cattle and cultivate millet and spear fish because God gave them these things for their sustenance. He instituted their marriage prohibitions. He gave ritual powers to some men and not to others. He decreed that the Nuer should raid the Dinka and that Europeans should conquer the Nuer. He made one man black and another white (according to one account our white skins are a punishment by God for incest committed by our ancestor with his mother), one man fleet and another slow, one strong and another weak. Everything in nature, in culture, in society, and in men is as it is because God made or willed it so. . . .

In the Nuer conception of God he is thus creative Spirit. He is also a *ran*, a living person, whose *yiegh*, breath or life, sustains man. I have never heard Nuer suggest that he has human form, but though he is himself ubiquitous and invisible, he sees and hears all that happens and he can be angry and can love. . . . Man's relation to him is, as it is among other peoples, on the model of a human social relationship. He is the father of men. . . .

A very common mode of address to the Deity is 'gwandong,' a word which means 'grandfather' or 'ancestor,' and literally 'old father,' but in a religious context 'father' or 'our father' would convey the Nuer sense better; and 'gwara' and 'gwandan,' 'our father,' and the respectful form of address 'gwadin,' 'father,' are also often used in speaking to or about God. God is the father of men in two respects. He is their creator and he is their protector. . . .

But though God is sometimes felt to be present here and now, he is also felt to be far away in the sky. If he hears a whispered prayer, it is spoken with eyes and hands raised to the distant heavens. However, heaven and earth, that is, God and man, for we are justified here in treating the dichotomy anagogically, are not entirely separated. There are comings and goings. God takes the souls of those he destroys by lightning to dwell with him and in him they protect their kinsmen;

he participates in the affairs of men through divers spirits which haunt the atmosphere between heaven and earth and may be regarded as hypostasizations of his modes and attributes; and he is also everywhere present in a way which can only be symbolized, as his ubiquitous presence is symbolized by the Nuer, by the metaphor of wind and air. Also he can be communicated with through prayer and sacrifice, and a certain kind of contact with him is maintained through the social order he is said to have instituted and of which he is the guardian. . . .

E. E. Evans-Pritchard, *Nuer Religion* (London: Oxford University Press, 1957), pp. 1-10

See also nos. 2-7, 51, 67, 91, 126, 127

300. WISDOM, LIBERATION, IMMORTALITY

('Shvetāshvatara Upanishad,' III, V, VI, *selections)*

III, 7. Higher than this is *Brahman*, the supreme, the great hidden in all creatures according to their bodies, the one who envelopes the universe, knowing Him, the Lord, (men) become immortal.

8. I know the Supreme Person of sunlike colour (lustre) beyond the darkness. Only by knowing Him does one pass over death. There is no other path for going there.

9. Than whom there is naught else higher, than whom there is naught smaller, naught greater, (the) one stands like a tree established in heaven, by Him, the Person, is the whole universe filled.

10. That which is beyond this world is without form and without suffering. Those who know that become immortal, but others go only to sorrow.

11. He who is in the faces, heads and necks of all, who dwells in the cave (of the heart) of all beings, who is all-pervading, He is the Lord and therefore the omnipresent *Shiva*.

12. That person indeed is the great lord, the impeller of the highest being. (He has the power of) reaching the purest attainment, the imperishable light.

13. A person of the measure of a thumb is the inner self, ever dwelling in the heart of men. He is the lord of the knowledge framed by the heart and the mind. They who know that become immortal.

14. The person has a thousand heads, a thousand eyes, a thousand feet. He surrounds the earth on all sides and stands ten fingers' breadth beyond.

15. The person is truly this whole world, whatever has been and whatever will be. He is also the lord of immortality, and whatever grows up by food. . . .

19. Without foot or hand, (yet) swift and grasping, he sees without eye, he hears without ear. He knows whatever is to be known; of him there is none who knows. They call him the Primeval, the Supreme Person.

20. Subtler than the subtle, greater than the great is the Self that is set in the cave of the (heart) of the creature. One beholds Him as being actionless and becomes freed from sorrow, when through the grace of the Creator he sees the Lord and His majesty.

21. I know this undecaying, ancient (primeval) Self of all, present in everything on account of infinity. Of whom they declare, there is stoppage of birth. The expounders of *Brahman* proclaim Him to be eternal.

v, 9. This living self is to be known as a part of the hundredth part of the point of a hair divided a hundredfold, yet it is capable of infinity. . . .

11. By means of thought, touch, sight and passions and by the abundance of food and drink there are the birth and development of the (embodied) self. According to his deeds, the embodied self assumes successively various forms in various conditions.

12. The embodied self, according to his own qualities, chooses (assumes) many shapes, gross and subtle. Having himself caused his union with them, through the qualities of his acts and through the qualities of his body, he is seen as another.

13. Him who is without beginning and without end, in the midst of chaos, the creator of all, of manifold form, who alone embraces the universe, he who knows God is freed from all fetters.

14. Him who is to be grasped by the mind, who is called incorporeal, who makes existence and non-existence, the kindly (the auspicious), the maker of creation and its parts, the Divine, they who know Him have left the body behind.

vi, 1. Some wise men speak of inherent nature, others likewise of time (as the first cause), being deluded. But it is the greatness of God in the world, by which this Brahma-wheel is made to turn.

2. He by whom this whole world is always enveloped, the knower, the author of time, the possessor of qualities and all knowledge. Controlled by Him (this) work (of creation) unfolds itself, that which is regarded as earth, water, fire, air and ether. . . .

6. Higher and other than the forms of the world-tree and time is he from whom this world revolves, who brings good and removes evil, the lord of prosperity, having known Him as in one's own self, the immortal, the support of all (he attains *Brahman*).

7. He in whom is the Supreme Lord of lords, who is the highest deity of deities, the supreme master of masters, transcendent, him let us know as God, the lord of the world, the adorable.

8. There is no action and no organ of his to be found. There is not seen his equal or his better. His high power is revealed to be various indeed. The working of his intelligence and strength is inherent (in him). . . .

10. The one God who, according to his own nature, covers himself like a spider with threads produced from *pradhāna* (unmanifested matter), may He grant us entrance into *Brahman*.

11. The one God hidden in all beings, all-pervading, the inner self of all beings, the ordainer of all deeds, who dwells in all beings, the witness, the knower, the only one, devoid of qualities.

12. The one controller of the many, inactive, who makes the one seed manifold, the wise who perceive Him as abiding in their self, to them belongs eternal happiness, not to others.

13. He is the eternal among the eternals, the intelligent among the intelligences, the one among many, who grants desires. That cause which is to be apprehended by discrimination (of *sāmkhya*) and discipline (*yoga*)—by knowing God, one is freed from all fetters. . . .

16. He is the maker of all, the knower of all, the self-caused, the knower, the author of time, the possessor of qualities, the knower of everything, the ruler of nature and of the spirit, the lord of qualities, the cause of worldly existence, and of liberation, of continuance and of bondage.

17. Becoming that, immortal, existing as the lord, the knower, the omnipresent, the guardian of this world is He who rules this world for ever, for no other cause is found for the ruling.

18. To Him who, of old, creates Brahmā and who, verily, delivers to him the Vedas, to that God who is lighted by His own intelligence, do I, eager for liberation, resort for refuge.

19. To Him who is without parts, without activity, tranquil, irreproachable, without blemish, the highest bridge to immortality like a fire with its fuel burnt.

S. Radhakrishnan (editor and translator), *The Principal Upanishads* (New York: Harper & Row, 1953), pp. 727 ff.

301. SHANKARA ON THE NATURE OF BRAHMAN

Shankara (ca. 788-820), founder of the standard system of philosophical Hinduism, was an orthodox Shaivite Brāhman who left his native South India to establish monasteries and to teach throughout India his philosophy of Advaita (Nonduality). Shankara derived his nonsectarian doctrines from the Upanishads, emphasizing salvation (moksha) as the realization through meditation of the identity of the individual soul (ātman) with the Absolute (Brahman). As Brahman is impersonal the phenomenal world is understood by Advaita Vedānta to be appearance or illusion (māyā), altogether outside the ultimate reality of absolute Being-Consciousness-Bliss.

But, it may be asked, is Brahman known or not known (previously to the enquiry into its nature)? If it is known we need not enter on an enquiry concerning it; if it is not known we can not enter on such an enquiry.

We reply that Brahman is known. Brahman, which is all-knowing and endowed with all powers, whose essential nature is eternal purity, intelligence, and freedom, exists. For if we consider the derivation of the word 'Brahman,' from the root brih, 'to be great,' we at once understand that eternal purity, and so on, belong to Brahman. Moreover the existence of Brahman is known on the ground of its being the Self of every one. For every one is conscious of the existence of (his) Self, never thinks 'I am not.' If the existence of the Self were not known, everyone would think 'I am not.' And this Self (of whose existence all are conscious) is Brahman. But if Brahman is generally known as the Self, there is no room for an enquiry into it! Not so, we reply; for there is a conflict of opinions as to its special nature. Unlearned people and the Lokāyatikas are of opinion that the mere body endowed with the quality of intelligence is the Self; others that the organs endowed with intelligence are the Self; others maintain that the internal organ is the Self; others, again, that the Self is a mere momentary idea; others, again, that it is the Void. Others, again (to proceed to the opinion of such as acknowledge the authority of the Veda), maintain that there is a transmigrating being different from the body, and so on, which is both agent and enjoyer (of the fruits of action); others teach that being is enjoying only, not acting; others believe that in addition to the individual souls, there is an all-knowing, all-powerful Lord. Others, finally (i.e., the Vedāntins), maintain that the Lord is the Self of the enjoyer (i.e., of the individual soul whose individual existence is apparent only, the produce of Nescience).

Thus there are many various opinions, basing part of them on sound arguments and scriptural texts, part of them on fallacious arguments and scriptural texts misunderstood. If therefore a man would embrace some one of these opinions without previous consideration, he would bar himself from the highest beatitude and incur grievous loss [1, 1, 1.]

'He knows the highest Brahman becomes even Brahman'

That same highest Brahman constitutes—as we know from passages such as 'that art thou'—the real nature of the individual soul [i.e., *ātman*], while its second nature, i.e., that aspect of it which depends on fictitious limiting conditions, is not its real nature. For as long as the individual soul does not free itself from Nescience in the form of duality—which Nescience may be compared to the mistake of him who in the twilight mistakes a post for a man—and who does not rise to the knowledge of the Self, whose nature is unchangeable, eternal Cognition—which expresses itself in the form 'I am Brahman'—so long it remains the individual soul. But when, discarding the aggregate of body, sense-organs and mind, it arrives, by means of Scripture, at the knowledge that it is not itself that aggregate, that it does not form part of transmigratory existence, but is the True, the Real, the Self, whose nature is pure intelligence; then knowing itself to be of the nature of unchangeable, eternal Cognition, it lifts itself above the vain conceit of being one with this body, and itself becomes the Self, whose nature is unchanging, eternal Cognition. As is declared in such scriptural passages as 'He who knows the highest Brahman becomes even Brahman' (*Mundaka Upanishad*, III, 2, 9). And this is the real nature of the individual soul by means of which it arises from the body and appears in its own form. [1, 3, 19.]

There is only one highest Lord ever unchanging, whose substance is cognition [i.e., of whom cognition is not a mere attribute], and who, by means of Nescience, manifests himself in various ways, just as a thaumaturg appears in different shapes by means of his magical power. . . . To the highest Self which is eternally pure, intelligent and free, which is never changing, one only, not in contact with anything, devoid of form, the opposite characteristics of the individual soul are erroneously ascribed; just as ignorant men ascribe blue colour to the colourless ether. [1, 3, 19.]

Gods, the Self, and the God

The Serpent and the Rope

A man may, in the dark, mistake a piece of rope lying on the ground for a snake and run away from it, frightened and trembling; thereon another man may tell him, 'Do not be afraid, it is only a rope, not a snake'; and he may then dismiss the fear caused by the imagined snake, and stop running. But all the while the presence and subsequent absence of his erroneous notion, as to the rope being a snake, make no difference whatever in the rope itself. Exactly analogous is the case of the individual soul which is in reality one with the highest soul, although Nescience makes it appear different. [I, 4, 6.]

As therefore the individual soul and the highest Self differ in name only, it being a settled matter that perfect knowledge has for its object the absolute oneness of the two; it is senseless to insist (as some do) on a plurality of Selfs, and to maintain that the individual soul is different from the highest Self, and the highest Self from the individual soul. For the Self is indeed called by many different names, but it is one only. Nor does the passage, 'He knows Brahman which is real, knowledge, infinite, as hidden in the cave' (*Taittirīya Upanishad*, II, 1), refer to some one cave (different from the abode of the individual soul). And that nobody else but Brahman is hidden in the cave we know from a subsequent passage, viz. 'Having sent forth he entered into it' (*Taittirīya Upanishad*, II, 6) according to which the creator only entered into the created beings.—Those who insist on the ·distinction of the individual and the highest Self oppose themselves to the true sense of the Vedānta-texts, stand thereby in the way of perfect knowledge, which is the door to perfect beatitude, and groundlessly assume release to be something effected, and therefore non-eternal. (And if they attempt to show that *moksha*, although effected, is eternal) they involve themselves in a conflict with sound logic. [I, 4, 22.]

Brahman and the World

That Brahman is at the same time the operative cause of the world, we have to conclude from the circumstance that there is no other guiding being. Ordinarily material causes, indeed, such as lumps of clay and pieces of gold, are dependent, in order to shape themselves into vessels and ornaments, on extraneous operative causes such as potters and goldsmiths; but outside Brahman as material cause there is no other operative cause to which the material cause could look; for Scripture says that previously to creation Brahman was one without a second.—

The absence of a guiding principle other than the material cause can moreover be established by means of the argument made use of in the Sūtra, viz. accordance with the promissory statements and the illustrative examples. If there were admitted a guiding principle different from the material cause, it would follow that everything cannot be known through one thing, and thereby the promissory statements as well as the illustrative instances would be stultified.—The Self is thus the operative cause, because there is no other ruling principle, and the material cause because there is no other substance from which the world could originate. [I, 4, 23.]

'When the sleeper wakes . . .'

The entire complex of phenomenal existence is considered as true as long as the knowledge of Brahman being the Self of all has not arisen; just as the phantoms of a dream are considered to be true until the sleeper wakes. For as long as a person has not reached the true knowledge of the unity of the Self, so long as it does not enter his mind that the world of effects with its means and objects of right knowledge and its results of actions is untrue; he rather, in consequence of his ignorance, looks on mere effects (such as body, offspring, wealth, etc.) as forming part of and belonging to his Self, forgetful of Brahman being in reality the Self of all. Hence, as long as true knowledge does not present itself, there is no reason why the ordinary course of secular and religious activity should not hold on undisturbed. The case is analogous to that of a dreaming man who in his dream sees manifold things, and, up to the moment of waking, is convinced that his ideas are produced by real perception without suspecting the perception to be a merely apparent one. [II, 7, 14.]

Shankara's *Commentary on Vedānta Sūtra*, as translated by George Thibaut, vol. I, in *Sacred Books of the East*, XXXIV (Oxford, 1890), pp. 14-15, 185-6, 190. 251, 282-3, 285-6, 324

302. RĀMĀNUJA ON BRAHMAN: 'BRAHMAN IS TO BE MEDITATED UPON AS CONSTITUTING THE SELF OF THE MEDITATING DEVOTEE'

Rāmānuja (ca. 1017-1137), a South-Indian Vaishnavite teacher who provided the initial philosophical framework for the new forms of devotional Hinduism (bhakti) which had emerged and spread north from Tamilnad since the ninth century, taught, as did Shankara, in various parts of India and wrote numerous commentaries. His system, Vishishtādvaita (Qualified Nonduality), deriving some of its doctrines from the Pāncarātras, differed from Advaita by emphasizing the reality of the phenomenal world and the essential distinction between the individual soul and a personal God (Vishnu). Salvation, by intense devotion or by abandonment of self (prapatti) to God's grace, returns the ātman to a state neither of annihilation nor of absorption but of love in the eternal presence of God.

But how can the Devotees claim that Brahman which is a different being is their 'Ego'?—Because the texts enable them to apprehend this relation as one free from contradiction. 'He who dwelling within the Self is different from the Self, whom the Self does not know, of whom the Self is the body, who rules the Self from within; he is thy Self, the inner ruler, the immortal one' (Brihad-āranyaka Upanishad, III, 7, 3); 'In the True all these beings have their root, they dwell in the True, they rest in the True; in that all that exists has its Self' (Khata Upanishad, VI, 8); 'All this indeed is Brahman' (Khata Upanishad, III, 14, 1)—all these texts teach that all sentient and nonsentient beings spring from Brahman, are merged in him, breathe through him, are ruled by him, constitute his body; so that he is the Self of all of them. In the same way therefore as, on the basis of the fact that the individual soul occupies with regard to the body the position of a Self, we form such judgments of co-ordination as 'I am a god—I am a man'; the fact of the individual Self being of the nature of Self justifies us in viewing our own Ego as belonging to the highest Self. On the presupposition of all ideas being finally based on Brahman and hence all words also finally denoting Brahman, the texts therefore make such statements of mutual implication as 'I am thou, O holy divinity, and thou art me.' On this view of the relation of individual soul and highest Self there is no real contradiction between two, apparently contradictory, sets of texts, viz., those on the one hand which negative the view of the soul being different from the highest Self, 'Now if a man meditates upon another divinity, thinking "the divinity is one and I another," he does not know'; 'He is incomplete, let him meditate upon Him as the Self; 'Everything abandons him who views anything apart from the Self' (Brihad-āranyaka Upanishad, I, 4, 10; II, 4, 6); and on the other hand those texts which set forth the view of the soul and the highest Self being different entities. 'Thinking of the (individual) Self and the Mover as different' (Shvetāshvatara Upani-

shad, 1, 6). For our view implies a denial of difference in so far as the individual 'I' is of the nature of the Self; and it implies an acknowledgment of difference in so far as it allows the highest Self to differ from the individual soul in the same way as the latter differs from its body. The clause 'he is incomplete' (in one of the texts quoted above) refers to the fact that Brahman which is different from the soul constitutes the Self of the soul, while the soul constitutes the body of Brahman. It thus remains a settled conclusion that Brahman is to be meditated upon as constituting the Self of the meditating Devotee.

Rāmānuja, *Commentary on Vedānta-Sūtras*, IV, 1, 3, as translated by George Thibaut, in *Sacred Books of the East*, XLVIII (Oxford, 1904), pp. 717-18

303. ZOROASTRIAN DUALISM: A SYSTEMATIC PRESENTATION

('Shikand Gumānī Vazār,' chapter VIII)

Mardān-Farrukh, the author of Shikand Gumānī Vazār, an 'Analytical Treatise for the Dispelling of Doubts,' lived in the ninth century A.D. According to R. C. Zaehner, his work is 'in some ways the most interesting of all the Zoroastrian books since it presents a philosophical justification of Zoroastrian dualism in a more or less coherent form; and it further contains a detailed critique of the monotheistic creeds, Islam, Judaism and Christianity as well as an attack on Zoroastrianism's dualistic rival, Manichaeanism.' The great merit of Zoroastrian dualism is that it absolves God from any breath of evil and explains why creation was actually necessary.

(1) Another proof that a contrary principle exists is (2) that good and evil are observable in the world, (3) and more particularly in so far as both good [and bad] conduct are defineable as such, (4) as are darkness and light, (5) right knowledge and wrong knowledge, (6) fragrance and stench, (7) life and death, (8) sickness and health, (9) justice and injustice, (10) slavery and freedom, (11) and all the other contrary activities which indisputably exist and are visible in every country and land at all times; (12) for no country or land exists, has existed, or ever will exist (13) in which the name of good and evil and what that name signifies has not existed or does not exist. (14) Nor can any time or

place be mentioned in which good and evil change their nature essentially.

(15) There are also other contraries whose antagonism is not [one of essence but] one of function, species, or nature. (16) Such is the mutual antagonism of things of like nature as (for example) male and female, (17) (the different) scents, tastes and colours; the Sun, Moon and stars whose dissimilarity is not one of substance but one of function, nature, and constitution, each being adapted to its own particular work. (18) But the dissimilarity of good and evil, light, darkness, and other contrary substances is not one of function but one of substance. (19) This can be seen from the fact that their natures cannot combine and are mutually destructive. (20) For where there is good, there cannot possibly be evil. (21) Where light is admitted, darkness is driven away. (22) Similarly with other contraries, the fact that they cannot combine and are mutually destructive is caused by their dissimilarity in substance. (23) This substantial dissimilarity and mutual destructiveness is observable in phenomena in the material world.

(24) That material world is the effect of the spiritual, and the spiritual is its cause, (25) for the effect is understood through the cause. (26) That the former gives testimony of the latter is obvious to any expert in these matters. (27) That the material is an effect and the spiritual the cause can be proved by the fact that (28) every visible and tangible thing emerges from an unmanifest to a manifest state. . . .

(35) Since we have seen that in the material world contrary substances exist and that they are sometimes mutually co-operative and sometimes mutually destructive, so (must it also be) in the spiritual world (36) which is the cause of the material, (37) and material things are its effects. That this is so is not open to doubt (38) and follows from the very nature of contrary substances. (39-40) I have shown above that the reason and occasion for the wise activity of the Creator which is exemplified in the creative act is the existence of an Adversary. . . .

(57) Now the goodness of the wise Creator can be inferred from the act of creation and from the fact that he cherishes and protects (his creatures), that he ordains and teaches a way and method by which evil can be repelled and sin averted, (58-60) and that he repels and wards off the Adversary who attacks the body; (it can be inferred too) from the organs and faculties of the body (afflicted as they are) by pain and sickness (which come to them) from outside and (which also are) inside the body. . . .

(64) It is suffering and death that destroy the body, not the Creator whose will is good and who preserves and maintains the body. (65) This is clearly so because a wise Creator does not regret or repent of what he has done, (66) nor does he destroy his creatures or make them of no effect, (67) for he is wise and omniscient. (68) It is only possible to attribute regret and repentance for what one has done to one whose knowledge is defective, whose reason is imperfect, and who is ignorant of the final outcome, (69) for knowing and wise persons do not commit actions without cause or occasion. (70) Similarily the actions of ignorant men of perverted intelligence who are ignorant of the final outcome will be haphazard, without cause or occasion.

(71) But the wise (Creator) will dispose wisely and act in accordance with discrimination in warding off from his creatures (the Adversary) whose actions are haphazard and who does not know the final outcome. (72) He, the (demon) whose actions are haphazard, is walled up and circumscribed within a trap and a snare; (73) for it is plain that a moving and living substance cannot be warded off or destroyed in an infinite void, nor is there any security against his harmfulness (74) unless he is circumscribed, uprooted, and made captive. (75) When he is circumscribed and made captive, he is susceptible to suffering and heavy chastisement. (76) But until he is completely conscious of his suffering and fully aware that his actions are based on a wrong knowledge, he continues to have utterly false views of what has befallen him. (77) His experience of suffering (is due to) the complete power of the omnipotent Creator.

(78) When once he has reached full realization of what he suffers at the hands of omnipotence, the wise Creator puts him out of action and hurls him into the infinite Void. (79) Then the good creation will have no fear of him; it will be immortal and free from adversity. (80) Perfect is the wisdom and discrimination of the omniscient Creator of the good and (perfect is) his foreknowledge of what needs to be done. . . .

(103) From this we must infer (104) that what is perfect and complete in its goodness cannot produce evil. (105) If it could, then it would not be perfect, (106) for when a thing is described as perfect, there is no room for anything else (in it); (107) and if there is no room for anything else, nothing else can proceed from it. (108) If God is perfect in goodness and knowledge, plainly ignorance and evil cannot proceed from Him; (109) or if it can, then he is not perfect; (110) and if he is not perfect, then he should not be worshipped as God or as perfectly good.

(111) If (on the other hand) both good and evil originate in God, then he is imperfect so far as goodness is concerned. (112) If he is imperfect in respect of goodness, then he is imperfect in respect of right knowledge. (113) And if he is imperfect in respect of right knowledge, then he is imperfect in respect of reason, consciousness, knowledge, wit, and in all the faculties of knowing. (114) And if he is imperfect in reason, consciousness, wit, and knowledge, he must be imperfect in respect of health; (115) and if he is imperfect in respect of health, he must be sick; (116) and if he must be sick, then he is imperfect in respect of life.

> Translation by R. C. Zaehner, in *The Teachings of the Magi* (London, 1956), pp. 59-66

See also nos. 60, 37-9, 290

304. EPICURUS ON THE GODS

('Letter to Menoeceus,' 123-6)

Epicurus (342?-270 B.C.) was the founder and head of the philosophical school which bears his name. He was born on the island of Samos and taught at Athens from 306 B.C. onward.

First of all believe that God is a being incorruptible [i.e., immortal and unchangeable] and blessed, just as in the common idea of God which is engraved on the mind, and do not assign to him anything contrary to his incorruption or unsuited to his blessedness, and believe about him whatever safeguards his blessedness and incorruption. For gods there certainly are, since the knowledge of them is a matter of immediate perception. But they are not what the majority of men believe them to be, in fact, they do not take care to represent them as they really believe them to be. And the irreligious man is not the one who denies the gods of the majority, but the one who applies to the gods the opinions of the majority. For what the majority say about the gods are not conceptions derived from sensation [*prolepseis*], but false suppositions [*hypolepseis*], according to which the greatest injuries overtake the wicked and the greatest blessings come to [the good] from the gods. For since men are always accustomed to their own virtues, they welcome those who are like themselves, but whatever is not of this sort they regard as alien.

Get accustomed to the idea that death means nothing to us. For all good and evil consist in sensation, and death is only the deprivation of sensation. Hence a real understanding that death means nothing to us makes the mortality of [our] life enjoyable, not by adding to it an unlimited length of time, but by taking away the desire for immortality. For there is nothing dreadful in life for the man who has really grasped the idea that there is nothing dreadful in not living. So that anyone is foolish who says that he is afraid of death, not because it will be painful when it comes, but because it is painful in prospect. For what gives [us] no trouble when it comes is only an empty pain as we look forward to it. So death, the most terrifying of evils, is nothing to us, for as long as we exist death is not present with us, and when death comes then we no longer exist. It is no concern, therefore, either of the living or the dead; for the former it does not exist, while the latter themselves no longer exist.

But the majority at one time flee from death as the greatest of all evils, but at another time [they yearn for it] as a rest from the [evils] in life. [But the wise man neither seeks to escape from life] nor fears to cease living, for neither does life annoy him nor does nonliving seem to be anything evil. Just as in the case of food he does not by any means choose the larger share, but rather the most delicious, so he seeks to enjoy [literally, plucks as fruit], not the longest period of time, but the most pleasant.

Translation by Frederick C. Grant, in his *Hellenistic Religions*, (New York, 1953), pp. 157-8

See also no. 139

305. THE MUSLIM DOCTRINE OF GOD

(Jamāl ad-Dīn al-Qāsimī)

What Muslims believe about the essential nature of the High and Holy One is that He is One God who has no partner. He is from everlasting, having none prior to Him, and He will continue endlessly to exist, having none come after Him. He is eternal, having no ending, continuing without ever being cut off, One who has not ceased and will not cease to be. He is to be described by the attributes of Majesty. For him there is prescribed no consummation or disjunction by the ceasing of perpetuity or the expiration of fixed terms. Nay, rather (LVII, 3): 'He is the First and the Last, the Outward and the Inward, and He knows all things.' Yet He is not a body that has been formed, nor does He resemble any created thing, nor any created thing resemble Him. Space does not encompass Him, nor do the earths[1] and the heavens contain Him, although He is seated on the Throne in that manner of which He speaks and in that sense which He means.[2] He is above the Throne and the heavens, above everything, and yet also beneath the lowest reaches of the watery abyss.[3] His being above does not make Him nearer the Throne and the heaven nor further from the earth and the watery abyss. Nay, rather He is many stages higher than the Throne or the heavens, as He is many stages beyond the earth and the watery abyss, yet in spite of this He is near to every existing thing. He is nearer to man than his jugular vein (I, 16/15), though His being near does not resemble bodily nearness, just as His essential being does not resemble the the essential being of bodily things. He does not come to rest in anything, just as nothing comes to rest in Him. High exalted is He from being included in any space, just as He is far removed from being limited by any time. Nay, indeed, He was before. He created time and space, and He is now as He was.

He is known by the intelligence to be existing in His essential being. As such essential being He will be perceived by the sight in the Lasting Abode,[4] as an act of grace on His part and a kindness to the righteous, in some sort a perfecting of His bounties by letting them look upon His noble face. And He—exalted be He—is living, powerful, mighty, overcoming, free from all shortcomings and any inability. 'Slumber takes Him not nor sleep' (II, 255/256), and no passing away, no death ever comes upon Him. None but He can create and invent, for He stands uniquely alone in producing and innovating. He knows everything that is knowable, is aware of all that is taking place from the lowest depths of the earths to the highest reaches of the heavens, so that not an atom's weight of anything either on earth or in heaven exists apart from His knowledge. He is aware of the crawling of a black ant upon a hard stone in the darkness of the night, and He perceives the movement of each mote in the atmosphere. 'He knows the secret and the most hidden thing' (XX, 7/6). He is acquainted with the promptings of men's consciences, with the movements of their fancies, with their most deeply concealed secrets, [knowing all this] with a knowledge that is from of old and is to eternity, for He will not cease having this attribute for ever and ever.

He—exalted be He—is the One who wills that existing things be, who manages the things that come to pass, so that no affair happens in the world visible or the world invisible[5] except by His determining, His decree, His decision, His will, so that what He wills is, and what He did not will is not, and there is no one who may resist His command or make a change in His decision. He—exalted be He—both hears and sees (XXII, 61/60). There is nothing that may be heard, however faint, that escapes His hearing, and nothing that may be seen, however minute, that is hidden from His vision. Distance does not dim His hearing, nor does darkness hinder His vision, yet His hearing and His seeing have no resemblance to the hearing and seeing of creatures, just as His essential being has no resemblance to that of creatures. He also —exalted be He—speaks, both to bid and to forbid, to promise and to threaten. The Qur'an, the Torah, the Evangel, and the Psalter are Scriptures of His which He sent down to His messengers—on whom be peace. He also—exalted be He—spoke to Moses with the speech which is an attribute of His essence and not a created thing that may perish, nor an attribute of any created thing so that it should be exhausted.

Now He—exalted be He—[is unique in the sense] that there is beside Him no existing thing save that which came into being by His act, proceeding from His equity in the finest and most perfect, in the most complete and equitable way. He is wise in all His actions, just in all His decrees. Everything apart from Him, whether men or jinn or angels, whether heaven or earth, whether animal or plant or mineral, whether perceived of the mind or by the senses, is a new creation which He produced by His power, being brought out from non-existence and produced as a created thing when it had been no thing. Since He was existing in eternity He was alone, and there was no other with Him. Then He brought forth the creation after that, as a demonstration of His power, a fulfillment of that which He had previously willed, and a verification of the word that He had spoken in eternity. It was not that He had any need for it or was in want of it, for it is as a favour that He creates and produces and undertakes things, not out of necessity, and it is as a service that He grants favours and not because He must. So it is He who is the One who grants favours and benefactions, blessings and grace.

Notes

1 Plural because there are seven earths as there are seven heavens.
2 This is the famous problem of the *istiwā'* which so exercised Muslims theologians. Some seven times in the Qu'an it is stated that Allah *istawā* on the Throne, which, if used of some earthly monarch, would mean that he 'sat upon the throne.'
3 *Ath-tharā* in the old cosmology is what is below the lowest depths. Sura xx, 6 '5 says 'To Him belongs what is in the heavens, what is on earth, what is between them both, and what is below the *tharā*.'
4 *Dār al-Qarār* is one of the names of Paradise, so this is a reference to the Muslim doctrine of the beatific vision.
5 *Mulk wa malakūt*, words which both mean 'kingdom,' but refer more particularly to the kingdom of things seen and the kingdom of things unseen.

Translation and notes by Arthur Jeffery, *Islam: Muhammad and His Religion* (New York: Liberal Arts Press, 1958), pp. 90-2

See also nos. 70-3, 231-7, 252, 268, 269

306. THE ESSENCE OF ISLAM

(Al-Malatī, 'Kitāb at-Tanbīh')

Ibn 'Umar has said: Islam is built upon five things: on confessing that that there is no deity save Allah, performing prayers (*salat*), giving the legal alms (*zakat*), going on pilgrimage to the House (i.e., the Ka'ba at Mecca), and fasting during [the month of] Ramadan. Thus did the Apostle of Allah hand it on to us, but beyond that there is holy war (*jihad*), which is an excellent thing. Said Hudaifa: Verily, I know people of two religions among the people of your religion, two religions which are due for hell fire, namely, folk who say that faith is a matter of words [and a man may be a true believer] even though he fornicates and murders, and those who say [that men can be true believers] even if they are patrons of error, claiming that there are not five daily prayers but only two, morning prayer and evening prayer.

'Abdallah al-Yashkuri said: I went to Kufa to procure some mules, and I entered the mosque where there was a man of Qais named Ibn al-Muntafiq who was saying: Someone described to me the Apostle of Allah, and it was pleasing to me, so I went to Mecca to find him, but they said that he was at Muna. So I went to Muna to find him, but they said that he was at 'Arafat. Finally I found him and approached

625

him, getting so close that I could catch the bridle of his mount—or perhaps he said: till I could catch hold of the neck-rein of his mount—so that the necks of our two steeds crossed. I said: 'There are two things about which I want to ask you. What will save me from Hell, and what will assure me entrance to Paradise?' He looked up at the sky, then he turned to face me, and said: 'Even though you have put the matter in short, you are on to something that is immense and really needs a long answer. Nevertheless take this from me: You should worship Allah, associating nothing with Him, perform the prayers that have been prescribed, fast the month of Ramadan, act with people the way you would like them to act with you, do not be averse to folk coming to you but let the people do it, and let go the neck-rein of my riding beast.'

It is related from al-Hasan that the Apostle of Allah said: 'O sons of Adam, prayer prohibits immorality, yet you do not pray.' Ibn 'Abbas quoted the verse (XXXV, 10/11): 'To Him rises up the good word, and the righteous deed He will exalt,' and said: The good word is the making mention of Allah, and the righteous deed is performing the prescribed religious duties (*fara'id*). So whoever makes mention of Allah while performing the prescribed duties is carried on the remembrance of Allah and taken up to the heavens, but he who makes mention of Allah yet does not perform the prescribed duties has his words set in charge of his deeds, which is what he was well entitled to. Said the Apostle of Allah: 'The first thing about which a man will have to give reckoning [at Judgment] will be the fara'id. Should any deficiency be found in them [Allah will say]: "Has my servant any voluntary deeds (*tatawwu'*)?"[1] If such are found He will say: "Fill up [the deficiency in the] *fara'id* from the *tatawwu'*." '

According to Ka'ab the Apostle of Allah said: 'Whoever performs the prayers, and gives the legal alms, and hears and obeys, has a middling sort of faith, but he who loves and hates only for Allah's sake, who gives and withholds only for Allah's sake, has attained a perfect faith.' To the delegation that came from the 'Abd al-Qais, the Apostle of Allah said: 'I command you four things, the first of which is faith in Allah. Do you know what faith in Allah is?' They replied: 'Allah and His Apostle know better.' He said: 'It consists in testifying that there is no deity save Allah, performing the prayers, giving the legal alms, and giving the fifth of the booty.'[2]

Said Ibn 'Umar: 'There are three [necessary things] of which

Gods, the Self, and the God

should a man have two but not have the third [his religion] will not be acceptable. [These three are] prayer, fasting, and the washing one-self pure from that which makes legally impure (janaba).'

Notes

1 I.e., deeds which religiously are good deeds but which are not among the prescribed duties of religion covered by the fara'id. An example would be extra prayers beyond the prescribed five daily prayers.
2 The reference is to the prescription in Sura VIII, 41/42.

Translation and notes by Arthur Jeffery, *Islam: Muhammad and His Religion* (New York: Liberal Arts Press, 1958), pp. 81-3, from Al-Malati's *Kitāb at-Tanbīh*, in Sven Dedering (ed.), 'Die Widerlegung der Irrgläubigen und Neuerer, von Abū'l-Husain al-Malātī, *Bibliotheca Islamica* (Leipzig, 1936), IX, 110-11

ACKNOWLEDGMENTS

Acknowledgment is made to the following for permission to reprint copyrighted material:

THE ADMINISTRATION OF SOUTH WEST AFRICA for extract from 'The Herero' by Heinrich Vedder, in *The Native Tribes of Southwest Africa*; published with the kind permission of the Administration of South West Africa.

GEORGE ALLEN AND UNWIN, LTD for extracts from *The Koran*, translated by A. J. Arberry; *Sufism* by A. J. Arberry; *The Way and its Power* by Arthur Waley; and *The Teachings of the Magi* by R. C. Zaehner.

THE AMERICAN MUSEUM OF NATURAL HISTORY for extract from *The Sun Dance and Other Ceremonies of the Oglala Division of the Teton Dakota* by J. R. Walker, reprinted by courtesy of the American Museum of Natural History.

THE AMERICAN-SCANDINAVIAN FOUNDATION for extracts from *The Poetic Edda*, translated by Henry Adams Bellows.

ANGUS AND ROBERTSON LTD for extracts from *The Australian Aborigines* by A. P. Elkin.

THE ASIATIC SOCIETY OF JAPAN for extract from *Kojiki*, Supplement to Transactions of the Asiatic Society of Japan X (1906), translated by B. H. Chamberlain, reprinted by permission of the Asiatic Society of Japan.

BERNICE P. BISHOP MUSEUM for extracts from *Polynesian Religion* by E. S. Craighill Handy, Honolulu: Bernice P. Bishop Museum (Bulletin 34), 1927, quoted with permission.

BOLLINGEN FOUNDATION for extracts from *Papers from the Eranos Yearbooks*, edited by Joseph Campbell, Bollingen Series XXX, vol. 2 'The Mysteries', p. 25, Pantheon Books; *Hindu Polytheism* by Alain Daniélou, Bollingen Series LXXIII, pp. 367-8 and 377-9, Pantheon Books; and *Monotheism among Primitive Peoples* by Paul Radin, Special Publications of Bollingen Foundation no. 4 (also issued by the Ethnographical Museum Basel Switzerland, 1954), p. 13, 14, 15, Pantheon Books.

GEORGE BRAZILLER, INC for extract from *Islam* by John Alden Williams, copyright © 1961 by John Alden Williams, reprinted by permission of George Braziller, Inc.

CAMBRIDGE UNIVERSITY PRESS for extracts from *The Presocratic Philosophers*, translated by G. S. Kirk and J. E. Raven.

BRUNO CASSIRER (PUBLISHERS) LTD for extracts from *Buddhist Texts Through the Ages* edited by Edward Conze (1954).

CATHOLIC UNIVERSITY OF AMERICA PRESS for extracts from *The Apinaye* by Curt Nimuendaju.

THE CLARENDON PRESS, OXFORD for extracts from *Hymns of the Atharva Veda*, translated by M. Bloomfield; *Nuer Religion* by E. E. Evans-Pritchard; *Jaina Sutras*, parts I and II, translated by H. Jacobi; *Babylonian Wisdom Literature* by

Acknowledgments

W. G. Lambert; A *Vedic Reader for Students* by A. A. Macdonnell; *Zurvan* by R. C. Zaehner; all are reprinted by permission of the Clarendon Press. Oxford.

COLUMBIA UNIVERSITY PRESS for extracts from *Ancient Egyptian Religion* by Henri Frankfort (1948); *The Religion of the Kwakiutl Indians* by Franz Boas, copyright © 1930 by Columbia University Press, New York; *Sources of Chinese Tradition*, edited by William Theodore de Bary, copyright © 1960 by Columbia University Press, New York; *Sources of Indian Tradition*, edited by William Theodore de Bary, copyright © 1958 by Columbia University Press, New York; *Sources of Japanese Tradition*, edited by William Theodore de Bary, copyright © 1958 by Columbia University Press, New York.

COOPER SQUARE PUBLISHERS, INC for extracts from *Latin American Mythology* by H. B. Alexander; *North American Mythology* by H. B. Alexander.

DOUBLEDAY AND COMPANY, INC for extracts from *The Australian Aborigines* by A. P. Elkin.

DOVER PUBLICATIONS, INC for extracts from *Jaina Sutras*, parts I and II, translated by Herman Jacobi.

R. E. DOWNS for extract from *The Religion of the Bare'e-Speaking Toradja of Central Celebes*, published by Uitgeverij Excelsior, 'S-Gravenhage, Netherlands.

EDINBURGH HOUSE PRESS for extracts from *African Ideas of God* by Edwin W. Smith.

THE ESTATE OF WALTER Y. EVANS-WENTZ, DECEASED for extracts from his *Tibet's Great Yogi Milarepa* and *The Tibetan Book of the Dead* (third edition).

FUNK AND WAGNALLS, N.Y. for extract from *The Beginning: Creation Myths around the World*, reprinted by permission of the publishers, Funk and Wagnalls, N.Y.

GOEMAERE PUBLISHERS for extract from *Etudes Bakongo* by S. J. Van Wing, as translated by Edwin W. Smith, *African Ideas of God*.

HARVARD UNIVERSITY PRESS for extracts from *Bhagavad Gītā*, vol. I, Oriental Series, vol. 38, translated and interpreted by Franklin Edgerton (1944); *Nichiren: the Buddhist Prophet*, reprinted by permission of the publishers.

HARVARD UNIVERSITY PRESS and THE LOEB CLASSICAL LIBRARY for extracts from Apollodorus, *The Library*, vol. I, translated by Sir James G. Frazer; Apollonius Rhodius, *The Argonautica*, translated by R. C. Seaton; Herodotus, vol. II, translated by A. D. Godley; Hesiod, *The Homeric Hymns and Homerica*, translated by Hugh G. Evelyn-White; Homer, *The Odyssey*, vols. I and II, translated by A. T. Murray; Plato, *Republic*, translated by Paul Shorey; all are reprinted by permission of the publishers and The Loeb Classical Library.

ÅKE HULTKRANTZ for extracts from his *Conceptions of the Soul among North American Indians*, Ethnographical Museum of Sweden, Stockholm Monograph Series 1.

THE INTERNATIONAL AFRICAN INSTITUTE and Jomo Kenyatta, for extract from 'Kikuyu Religion, Ancestor-Worship and Sacrificial Practices', *Africa*, vol. X (1937); Lorna Marshall, for extract from 'Kung Bushman Religions', *Africa*, vol. XXXII (1962); James W. Telch, for extract from 'The Isoko Tribe', *Africa*, vol. III (1934).

J. PRYTZ JOHANSEN for extracts from his *The Maori and his Religion in its Non-Ritualistic Aspects*, published by Ejnar Munksgaard, Copenhagen (1954).

KONINKLIJK INSTITUUT VOOR TAAL-, LAND- EN VOLKENKUNDE (Royal Institute of Linguistics and Anthropology, The Hague) for extracts for *Ngagu Religion* by Hans Schärer.

Acknowledgments

LIBERAL ARTS DIVISION OF THE BOBBS-MERRILL COMPANY INC for extracts from *Ancient Roman Religion*, Frederick C. Grant, editor, copyright © 1957 by the Liberal Arts Press; *Hellenistic Religions*, edited by Frederick C. Grant, copyright © 1953 by the Liberal Arts Press; *Hesiod's Theogony*, translated by Norman O. Brown, copyright © 1953 by the Liberal Arts Press; *Islam: Muhammad and his Religion*, edited by Arthur Jeffery, copyright © 1958 by the Liberal Arts Press.

MACGIBBON AND KEE, LONDON for extracts from *The Trumpet Shall Sound* by Peter Worseley, MacGibbon and Kee, London (1957).

THE MACMILLAN COMPANY for extracts from *The Koran*, translated by A. J. Arberry; *The Teachings of the Magi* by R. C. Zaehner.

MACMILLAN AND CO. LTD, LONDON for extract from *The Ila-Speaking People of Northern Rhodesia* by E. W. Smith and A. M. Dale. Copyright © 1955 by Allen & Unwin, Ltd.

METHUEN AND COMPANY LTD for extracts from *The Greeks and Their Gods* by W. C. K. Guthrie; *Orpheus and the Greek Religion* by W. C. K. Guthrie.

JOHN MURRAY for extracts from *The Mystery Religions and Christianity* by S. Angus; *The Hymns of Zarathustra*, translated by J. Duchesne-Guillemin; *Buddhist Scriptures* by E. J. Thomas; *The Buddha's Way of Virtue* by W. D. C. Wagiswara and K. S. Saunders.

MUSEUM OF THE AMERICAN INDIAN for extract from *Religion and Ceremonies of the Lenape* by M. R. Harrington.

MONICA WILSON for extracts from her *Communal Rituals of the Nyakusa*, published by the Oxford University Press under the auspices of the International African Institute.

THOMAS NELSON & SONS LTD for extracts from *Documents from Old Testament Times* edited by D. Winton Thomas (1958).

OXFORD UNIVERSITY PRESS, LONDON for extracts from *The Religion of the Rigveda* by H. D. Griswold; *The Bavenda* by H. A. Stayt (as quoted in Edwin W. Smith, *African Ideas of God*), published by the Oxford University Press under the auspices of the International African Institute.

THE PALI TEXT SOCIETY for extracts from *Further Dialogues of the Buddha*, vol. I, translated by Lord Robert Chalmers.

PENGUIN BOOKS LTD, BALTIMORE, MARYLAND for extracts from *Buddhist Scriptures*, translated by Edward Conze.

PENGUIN BOOKS LTD, MIDDLESEX, ENGLAND for extract from *Plato: Protagoras and Meno*, translated by W. C. K. Guthrie.

PENNSYLVANIA HISTORICAL AND MUSEUM COMMISSION for extract from *A Study of the Delaware Indians' Big House Ceremony* by Frank G. Speck, Publications of the Pennsylvania Historical Commission, vol. II, (1931).

THE POLYNESIAN SOCIETY (INC), WELLINGTON, NEW ZEALAND for extracts from 'A Maori Cosmogony' by Hare Hongi, *Journal of the Polynesian Society*, vol. XVI, 1907; 'Maori Personifications' by Elsdon Best, *Journal of the Polynesian Society*, vol. XXXII, (1923); 'Naked Cult in Central West Santo' by Graham Miller, *Journal of the Polynesian Society*, vol. LVII, (1948).

PRINCETON UNIVERSITY PRESS for extracts from *Eleusis and the Eleusinian Mysteries* by George E. Mylonas, reprinted by permission of the Princeton University Press, Copyright 1961; *Ancient Near Eastern Texts Relating to the Old*

Acknowledgments

Testament, edited by James B. Pritchard, reprinted by permission of the Princeton University Press, Copyright 1950.

ROUTLEDGE AND KEGAN PAUL LTD for extracts from *Life of Gotama the Buddha* by Earl Brewster; 'Meaning of the Eleusinian Mysteries' by W. Otto, in *The Mysteries*, edited by Joseph Campbell; *Early Buddhist Scriptures*, translated by E. J. Thomas.

SIDGWICK AND JACKSON LTD for extracts from *The Wonder that Was India* by A. L. Basham, reprinted by permission of the author's representatives and of the publishers Sidgwick and Jackson Ltd.

S.P.C.K., LONDON for extracts from *Muslim Devotion* by Constance E. Padwick, (1961), and *The New Testament Background* edited by Charles K. Barret (1956).

T.G.H. STREHLOW for extract from his *Aranda Traditions*, published by Melbourne University Press.

THAMES AND HUDSON LTD for extracts from *Myth and Symbol in Ancient Egypt* by R. T. Rundle Clark; *Burning Water* by Laurette Séjourné.

UNIVERSITY OF CALIFORNIA PRESS for extracts from *Indian Myths of South Central California* by A. L. Kroeber (University of California Publications in American Archaeology, vol. IV, no. 4, 1906-1907).

THE UNIVERSITY OF CHICAGO PRESS for extracts from Euripedes' 'The Bacchae', translated by William Arrowsmith and Aeschylus' 'Agamemnon', translated by Richmond Lattimore in *The Complete Greek Tragedies*, edited by David Grene and Richmond Lattimore; *The Sumerians* by Samuel N. Kramer; *The Iliad*, translated by Richmond Lattimore; and *The Edicts of Asoka*, translated and edited by N. A. Nikam and Richard McKeon.

THE UNIVERSITY OF NEBRASKA PRESS, for extracts reprinted from *The World's Rim* by Hartley Burr Alexander by permission of University of Nebraska Press, copyright 1953, University of Nebraska Press, Lincoln, Nebraska.

THE UNIVERSITY OF OKLAHOMA PRESS for extracts from *Naskapi: the Savage Hunters of the Labrador Peninsula*, by Frank G. Speck, copyright 1935 by the University of Oklahoma Press.

VANGUARD PRESS, INC for extracts reprinted by permission of the publishers, The Vanguard Press, from *Burning Water* by Laurette Séjourné.

TRINITY COLLEGE, CAMBRIDGE for extracts from *The Belief in Immortality*, vol. I by James G. Frazer, published by Macmillan and Co. Ltd and *Folklore in the Old Testament* by James G. Frazer, published by Macmillan and Co Ltd.

BIBLIOGRAPHY

Chapter 1: *Gods, Goddesses, and Supernatural Beings*

No. 1. On the 'primitive' Supreme Beings and High Gods, see the bibliographies listed in M. Eliade, *Patterns in Comparative Religion*, trans. Rosemary Sheed (London and New York: Sheed and Ward, 1958; Meridian paperbook, 1963), pp. 112-16. On the Australian materials, see Raffaele Pettazzoni, *Dio*, vol. I, titled *L'essere celeste nelle credenze dei popoli primitivi* (Rome, 1922), pp. 1-40; Raffaele Pettazzoni, *The All-Knowing God*, trans. H. J. Rose (London, 1955), chap. XXI; Wilhelm Schmidt, *Der Ursprung der Gottesidee*, vol. III (Münster, 1931), passim; A. P. Elkin, *The Australian Aborigines*, 3rd ed.; (Sydney, 1959; Doubleday Anchor Book, 1964). pp. 196 ff.; W. E. A. Stanner, 'On Aboriginal Religion,' *Oceania*, XXX (1959), nos. 2 and 4; XXXI (1960), nos. 2 and 4; XXXII (1961), no. 20.

Nos. 1ff. On African materials, see Raffaele Pettazzoni, *Dio*, op. cit., pp. 186-259; Raffaele Pettazzoni, *Miti e Leggende*, vol. I (Africa, Australia), pp. 3-401; Raffaele Pettazzoni, *The All-Knowing God* (London, 1955), chap. I; Wilhelm Schmidt, *Ursprung der Gottesidee*, vol. IV (Münster, 1933), vol. VII (Münster, 1941), and vol. VIII (Münster, 1949); J. G. Frazer, *The Worship of Nature* (London, 1926), pp. 89-315; Edwin W. Smith (ed.), *African Ideas of God: A Symposium* (London, 1950); and the bibliographies listed in M. Eliade, *Patterns in Comparative Religion*, trans. Rosemary Sheed (New York and London: Sheed and Ward, 1958), pp. 113-14.

Nos. 8ff. On North and South America, see bibliographies in M. Eliade, *Patterns in Comparative Religion*, pp. 114-15; Wilhelm Schmidt, *Ursprung der Gottesidee*, vols II and V (Münster, 1937); Wilhelm Schmidt, *High Gods in North America* (Oxford, 1933); Raffaele Pettazzoni, *Dio*, pp. 260-348; Raffaele Pettazzoni, *The All-Knowing God*, chaps. XXII-XXIV; Raffaele Pettazzoni, *Miti e Leggende*, vol. III (North America), IV (Central and South America).

No. 13. On the Sun Gods, see bibliographies in M. Eliade, *Patterns in Comparative Religion*, op. cit., pp. 152-3; J. G. Frazer, *The Worship of Nature* (London, 1926), pp. 441-667.

No. 14. On the master of animals, see Raffaele Pettazzoni, *The All-Knowing God* (London 1955), pp. 440 ff.; John M. Cooper, *The Northern Algonquian Supreme Being* (Washington D.C., 1934); Otto Zerries, *Wild-und-Buschgeister in Südamerika* (Stuttgart, 1954); Åke Hultkrantz, 'The Owner of the Animals in the Religion of the North American Indians,' *The Supernatural Owners of Nature*, ed. A. Hultkrantz (Stockholm, 1961), pp. 53-64; Ivar Paulson, *Schultzgeister und Gottheiten des Wildes (Der Jagdtiere und Fische) in Nordeurasien* (Stockholm, 1961); I. Paulson, 'The Animal Guardian: A Critical and Synthetic Review, *History of Religions*, III (1964), pp. 202-19.

Bibliography

No. 15. On Hainuwele and the Dema-deities, see A. E. Jensen, Hainuwele: Volkserzählungen von der Molukkeninsel Ceram (Frankfurt, 1939); A. E. Jensen, Das religiöse Weltbild einer frühen Kultur (Stuttgart, 1948); A. E. Jensen, Myth and Cult among Primitive Peoples, trans. Marianna Tax Choldin and Wolfgang Weissleder (Chicago, 1963); Joseph Campbell, The Masks of God: Primitive Mythology (New York, 1959), pp. 173 ff., 188 ff.

No. 17. On Egyptian religions, see the bibliographies in Jacques Vandier, La Religion Egyptienne (Paris, 1944), pp. 1-9; also Hans Bonnet, Reallexikon der Ägyptischen Religionsgeschichte (Berlin, 1952); Henri Frankfort, Ancient Egyptian Religion (New York, Harper Torchbook, 1961); R. T. Rundle Clark, Myth and Symbol in Ancient Egypt (London, 1959; New York, 1960); Wolfgang Helkck, Die Mythologie de alten Ägypter (in Wörterbuch der Mythologie, ed. H. W. Hausig, vol. I, Die Alten Kulturvölker), pp. 315-406.

Nos. 21 ff. On the Indian (Vedic and Brahmanic) religious texts available in English translations see the bibliographies compiled by Norwin J. Hein, 'Hinduism,' in Charles J. Adams (ed.), A Reader's Guide to the Great Religions, op. cit., pp. 46-53. On the Bhagavad Gītā and Krishna worship, Adams (ed.), pp. 62 ff. A considerable number of texts are translated by Alain Daniélou, Hindu Polytheism (New York, 1964).

For a bibliography of the English translations of Buddhist texts, see Richard A. Gard, 'Buddhism,' in Adams (ed.), A Reader's Guide to the Great Religions, op. cit., pp. 111 ff. A select list in Edward Conze, Buddhism: Its Essence and Development (Oxford, 1951; Harper Torchbook, 1959), pp. 225-6.

No. 29. Cf. The Lotus of the Wonderful Law, translated by W. Soothill (1930).

No. 30. Har Dayal, The Boddhisattva Doctrine in Buddhist Sanskrit Literature (London, 1932); cf. Adams (ed.), A Reader's Guide to the Great Religions, op. cit., p. 148.

No. 31. On the Japanese gods, see the bibliographies compiled by Joseph M. Kitagawa, 'The Religions of Japan,' in Adams (ed.), A Reader's Guide to the Great Religions, op. cit., pp. 168-9.

Nos. 32 ff. On the Greek Gods, see W. K. C. Guthrie, The Greeks and Their Gods (London, 1950; Beacon paperbook, 1955); Walter F. Otto, The Homeric Gods, trans. Moses Hadas (1954; Beacon paperbook, 1964).

No. 36. On Zalmoxis, see Carl Clement, 'Zalmoxis,' Zalmoxis. Revue des Etudes Religieuses, II (Paris-Bucharest, 1939), pp. 53-62; Karl Meuli, 'Scythica,' Hermes, LXX (1935), pp. 127-76, esp. pp. 162 ff.; R. Pettazzoni, 'Il "monoteismo" dei Geti,' Studia in Honorem Acad. D. Decev (Sofia, 1958), pp. 649-55.

Nos. 37-9. On the translations of the Gathas, see R. C. Zaehner, The Dawn and Twilight of Zoroastrianism (London, 1961), pp. 340-1. We made use of J. Duchesne-Guillemin's translation, The Hymns of Zoroaster (London, 1952; Beacon Paperbook, 1963). A critical bibliography of the texts and their interpretations by various scholars, in J. Duchesne-Guillemin, La Religion de l'Iran ancien (Paris, 1962), pp. 17-70. Cf. also Georges Dumézil, Naissance d'archanges (Paris, 1945); G. Dumézil, Les dieux des Indo-Européens (Paris, 1952); G. Dumézil, L'idéologie tripartie des Indo-Européens (Bruxelles, 1958).

On Iranian religions in general, see R. C. Zaehner, The Dawn and Twilight, op. cit.; R. C. Zaehner Zurvan,: A Zoroastrian Dilemma (Oxford, 1955); J. Duchesne-Guillemin, La Religion de l'Iran ancien, op. cit.; J. Duchesne-Guillemin, Symbols and Values in Zoroastrianism (New York, 1966); George

Bibliography

Widengren, *Die Religionen Irans* (Stuttgart, 1965), pp. 360-75, bibliography; G. Widengren, *Iranische Geisteswelt* (Baden-Baden, 1961).

Nos. 40 ff. On the Prophet Muhammad and his biographies, see the critical bibliographies in Charles J. Adams, 'Islam,' in his *A Reader's Guide to the Great Religions*, pp. 293-9. On the translations of the Koran, see Adams (ed.), *op. cit.*, pp. 300-1. On the critical works on the Koran, see Adams (ed.), *op. cit.*, pp. 302-5.

The most readable biography in English is Tor Andrae's *Mohammed: The Man and His Faith* (trans. Theophil Menze, New York, 1935; Harper Torchbook, 1960). For a more meticulous study, cf. W. Montgomery Watt, *Muhammad at Mecca* (Oxford, 1953) and *Muhammad at Medina* (Oxford, 1956).

Chapter 11: Myths of Creation and of Origin

Nos. 44 ff. On the different types of cosmogonical myths, see Charles H. Long, *Alpha: The Myths of Creation* (New York, 1963) and the bibliography listed on pp. 248-51; S. G. F. Brandon, *Creation Legends of the Ancient Near East* (London, 1963); *La naissance du monde* (Collection 'Sources Orientales' [Paris, 1959]; translations of cosmogonic texts from the Ancient Near East, India, Iran, Tibet, China, Laos, Siam); cf. F. Lukas, *Die Grundbegriffe in den Kosmogonien der alten Völker* (Leipzig, 1893); A. Kuhn, *Berichte über den Weltanfang bei den Indochinesen und ihren Nachbarvölkern* (Leipzig, 1935); W. Münsterberger, *Ethnologische Studien an Indonesischen Schöpfungsmythen* (The Hague, 1939); H. Baumann, *Das doppelte Geschlecht* (Berlin, 1955), pp. 164 ff., 184 ff., 268 ff.; Anna-Britta Helbom, 'The Creation Egg,' *Ethnos*, XXVIII (1963), pp. 63-105. See also Raffaele Pettazzoni, *Essays on the History of Religions* (Leiden, 1954), pp. 24 ff. On 'Myths of Beginnings and Creation-Myths'; M. Eliade, *Myth and Reality* (New York, 1963), pp. 1-74.

No. 49. On the earth-diver motif, see M. Eliade, 'Le plongeon cosmogonique,' *Revue de l'Histoire des Religions*, CIX (1961), pp. 157-212.

No. 53. On Japanese mythological and cosmological traditions, see the bibliography of Joseph M. Kitagawa, 'The Religions of Japan' in Adams (ed.), *A Reader's Guide to the Great Religions*, *op. cit.*, pp. 175 ff. For a comparative study, cf. F. K. Numazawa, *Die Weltanfänge in der japanischen Mythologie* (Paris-Luzern, 1946).

No. 54. On Egyptian creation myths, see the bibliography listed in Serge Sauneron and Jean Yoyotte, 'La naissance du monde selon l'Egypte Ancienne,' *La naissance du monde*, *op. cit.*, pp. 88 ff.

No. 55. On Babylonian cosmogony, see Alexander Heidel, *The Babylonian Genesis* (Chicago, 1954).

No. 59. On Hesiod's cosmogonic myth, see introduction (pp. 7-48) and bibliography (p. 49) of *Hesiod's Theogony*, trans. Norman O. Brown (New York, 1953). Cf. also W. Staudacher, *Die Trennung von Himmel und Erde. Ein vorgriechischer Schöpfungsmythus bei Hesiod und die Orphikern* (Tübingen, 1942).

No. 60. On Iranian cosmogony, cf. Jacques Duchesne-Guillemin, *La Religion de l'Iran ancien* (Paris, 1962), pp. 207 ff.

Bibliography

No. 61. On the Völuspá, see Jan de Vries, Altgermanische Religionsgeschichte, vol. II (2nd ed.; Berlin, 1957), pp. 359 ff.

Nos. 62 ff. On the creation of man, see the materials collected by J. G. Frazer, Folklore in the Old Testament, vol. I (London, 1919), pp. 3-44.

Nos. 68 ff. On myths of the origin of death, see J. G. Frazer, Folklore in the Old Testament, op. cit., vol. I, pp. 45-77; Hans Abrahamsson, The Origin of Death: Studies in African Mythology, Studia Ethnographica Upsaliensia, III (Uppsala, 1951).

Nos. 73-4. On the Flood narrative from the Gilgamesh Epic, see Alexander Heidel, The Gilgamesh Epic and Old Testament Parallels (Chicago, 1946). On myths of the Great Flood, see J. G. Frazer, Folklore in the Old Testament, op. cit., vol. I, pp. 104-361.

Chapter III: Man and the Sacred

Nos. 75-7. On the sacred world and cosmic symbolism, see M. Eliade, Cosmos and History (New York, Harper Torchbook, 1959; originally published as The Myth of the Eternal Return), chap. I; M. Eliade, The Sacred and the Profane (New York, Harper Torchbook, 1961), chap. I and the bibliography, pp. 236-8. Also, Lewis Mumford, The City in History (New York, 1961); Werner Müller, Die heilige Stadt (Stuttgart, 1961).

Nos. 78-9. On Australian religions, see R. M. and C. H. Berndt, The World of the First Australian (Chicago, 1964), pp. 185-278.

Nos. 80-1. On sacred life and sacred time, see M. Eliade, The Sacred and the Profane, op. cit., chap. II, and the bibliography, pp. 238-9.

Nos. 85 ff. On E. B. Tylor's theory of animism, see Robert H. Lowie, The History of Ethnological Theory (New York, 1937), pp. 68 ff.; A. E. Jensen, Myth and Cult among Primitive Peoples (Chicago, 1963), pp. 265 ff. On the divine soul, Jensen, Myth and Cult, op. cit., pp. 273 ff.

No. 89. On mana, see the bibliography in M. Eliade, Patterns in Comparative Religion, op. cit., pp. 19 ff.

Nos. 91 ff. On the different types of sacrifice, see Henri Hubert and Manuel Mauss, Sacrifice: Its Nature and Function, trans. W. D. Halls (Chicago, 1964); E. O. James, Sacrifice and Sacrament (New York, 1962); Georges Gusdorf, L'expérience humaine du sacrifice (Paris, 1948); Alfred Loisy, Essai historique sur le Sacrifice (Paris, 1920); Anton Vorblicher, s.v.d., Das Opfer, auf den uns heute noch erreichbaren ältesten Stufen der Menschheitsgeschichte (Mödling bei Wien, 1956).

No. 93. For a historical-comparative study on horse sacrifice, see Wilhelm Koppers, 'Pferdeopfer und Pferdekult der Indogermanen,' Weiner Beiträge zur Kulturgeschichte und Linguistik, IV (1936), pp. 279-411.

Nos. 101 ff. On myth and ritual cf. Henri Frankfort, The Problem of Similarity in Ancient Near Eastern Religion (London, 1951); S. H. Hooke, 'Myth and Ritual: Past and Present,' in his Myth, Ritual and Kingship (Oxford, 1958), pp. 1-21; S. G. F. Brandon, 'The Myth and Ritual Position Critically Considered,' in Hooke (ed.), Myth, Ritual and Kingship, op. cit., pp. 261-91.

No. 119. On pūjā, see bibliography in Adams (ed.), A Reader's Guide to the Great Religions, op. cit., pp. 53-4.

Bibliography

No. 121. On the devotion to Buddha see Henri de Lubac, *Amida* (Paris, 1954).

No. 124. On pilgrimages, see the comparative studies (Israel, Islam, India, China, Japan, etc.) in the volume: *Les Pèlerinages* ('Sources Orientales,' vol. III [Paris, 1960]). Cf. also Agehananda Bharati, 'Pilgrimage in the Indian Tradition,' *History of Religions*, III (1963), pp. 135-67.

Nos. 134 ff. On the Vedic religion, see the bibliography in Adams (ed.), *A Reader's Guide to the Great Religions*, op. cit., pp. 49-50.

Nos. 142 ff. On the patterns of initiation, see M. Eliade, *Rites and Symbols of Initiation* (New York, Harper Torchbook, 1965, originally published as *Birth and Rebirth*); C. J. Bleeker (ed.), *Initiation* (Leiden, 1965).

Nos. 148 ff. On Eleusinian and Hellenistic mysteries, cf. the bibliographies in George E. Mylonas, *Eleusis and the Eleusinian Mysteries* (Princeton, 1961), S. Angus, *The Mystery Religions and Christianity* (London, 1925), and M. Eliade, *Rites and Symbols of Initiation*, pp. 162 ff.

No. 156. On personal piety in Hellenistic times, see A.-T. Festugière, *Personal Religion among the Greeks* (Berkeley-Los Angeles, 1954; 1960) and the bibliographies in Frederick C. Grant, *Ancient Roman Religion* (New York, 1957), pp. 215 ff.; Frederick C. Grant, *Hellenistic Religions: The Age of Syncretism* (New York, 1953), pp. 105 ff.

No. 157. For the esoteric Buddhism of Japan, see the bibliography in Adams (ed.), *A Reader's Guide to the Great Religions*, op. cit., p. 178.

Chapter IV: *Death, Afterlife, Eschatology*

General

On death and disposal of the dead, cf. the bibliographies compiled by J. Wach, *Sociology of Religion* (Chicago, 1944), pp. 66 ff. (nn. 73-88) and by Friedrich Heiler, *Erscheinungsformen und Wesen der Religion* (Stuttgart, 1961), pp. 515-17. Cf. also E. Brendann, *Death Customs* (London, 1930); B. Y. Jouin, *La mort et la tombe* (Paris, 1949); J. N. Schofield, *Archaeology and the After-life* (London, 1951); G. Pfannmüller, *Tod, Jenseits und Unsterblichkeit* (München-Basel, 1953).

On the primitive conception and beliefs related to death and afterlife, cf. Felix Shercke, *Über das Verhalten der Primitiven zum Tode* (Langensalza, 1923); J. G. Frazer, *The Belief in Immortality and the Worship of the Dead* (3 vols.; London, 1913-24); J. G. Frazer, *The Fear of the Dead in Primitive Religion* (3 vols.; London, 1933-6); Rosalind Moss, *The Life after Death in Oceania and the Malay Archipelago* (London, 1925); Theo. Körner, *Totenkult u. Lebensglauben bei den Völkern Ost-Indonesiens* (Leipzig, 1936); H. J. Sell, *Der schlimme Tod bei den Völkern Indonesiens* (The Hague, 1955); Olof Pettersson, *Jabmek and Jabmeaino: A Comparative Study of the Dead and the Realm of the Dead in Lappish Religion* (Lund, 1957).

Nos. 158-9. On the myth of the descent of Ishtar and the Babylonian conception of death and afterlife, see Alexander Heidel, *The Gilgamesh Epic and Old Testament Parallels* (Chicago, 1946), pp. 119 ff.; Erich Ebeling, *Tod und Leben nach den Vorstellungen der Babylonier* (Berlin-Leipzig, 1931).

Nos. 160 ff. On the Indo-Aryan conceptions of death, see E. Arbmann, 'Tod und Unsterblichkeit in vedischen Glauben,' *Archiv für Religionswissenschaft*, XXV-XXVI (1927-28), pp. 339-87, 187-240; A. B. Keith, *Religion and Philosophy of*

Bibliography

the Veda, Harvard Oriental Series, XXXI-XXXII (Cambridge, Mass., 1925), pp. 413-32; cf. also Kurt Ranke, *Indogermanische Totenverehrung*, I, FF Communications, no. 140 (Helsinki, 1951); Hans Hartmann, *Der Totenkult in Irland* (Heidelberg, 1952).

No. 165. On the Oceanian beliefs, see the works of J. G. Frazer and Rosalind Moss, cited at the beginning of this section, under 'General.'

Nos. 166 ff. On the Egyptian funerary ritual and conceptions of the afterlife, see Hans Bonnet, *Reallexikon der ägyptischen Religionsgeschichte* (Berlin, 1952), pp. 828 ff.; C. E. Sander-Hansen, *Der Begriff des Todes bei den Ägyptern* (Copenhagen, 1942); J. Zande, *Death as an Enemy, according to Ancient Egyptian Conceptions* (Leiden, 1960).

No. 171. On the gold plates, cf. Jane Harrison, *Prolegomena to the Study of Greek Religion* (Cambridge, England, 1903), pp. 583 ff.; W. K. C. Guthrie, *Orpheus and the Greek Religion* (London, 1935), pp. 171 ff.

No. 172. On the Iranian conceptions of a future life, cf. N. Söderblom, *La vie future d'après le Mazdéisme* (Paris, 1901); J. D. C. Pavry, *The Zoroastrian Doctrine of a Future Life* (2nd ed.; New York, 1929).

On the judgment of the dead in the Ancient Near East, India, China, Japan, etc., see *Le jugement des morts* ('Sources Orientales,' vol. IV [Paris, 1961]).

No. 173. On the shaman as the guide of the soul, see M. Eliade, *Shamanism: Aechaic Techniques of Ecstasy* (New York and London, 1964).

Nos. 178 ff. On the Greek and Roman conceptions of death and afterlife, see Erwin Rohde, *Psyche: The Cult of Souls and Belief in Immortality among the Greeks* (New York and London, 1925); Franz Cumont, *After-Life in Roman Paganism* (New Haven, 1923); F. Cumont, *Lux perpetua* (Paris, 1949); C. H. Moore, *Ancient Beliefs in the Immortality of the Soul: Our Debt to Greece and Rome* (New York, 1931).

On the Oriental and early Christian representations of the nether world, see André Parrot, *Le 'Refrigerium' dans l'au-delà* (Paris, 1937).

Nos. 184-5. On the Polynesian 'Orpheus' myths, see M. Eliade, *Shamanism*, op. cit., pp. 368 ff. On the North American 'Orpheus' myths, see ibid., pp. 311 ff., and Åke Hultkrantz, *The North American Indian Orpheus Tradition* (Stockholm, 1957).

No. 186. On messianic ideologies in India, see E. Abegg, *Der Messiasglaube in Indien und Iran* (Berlin, 1928).

No. 187. On the Islamic conceptions of Paradise, see Miguel Asin Palacios, *La escatologia musulmana en la Divina Comedia* (2nd ed.; Madrid-Granada, 1943).

Nos. 188 ff. On the myths describing the end of the world, see W. Bousset, *The Antichrist Legend* (London, 1896); Alex Olrik, *Ragnorök, die Sagen vom Weltuntergang* (Berlin, 1922); Jan de Vries, *Altgermanische Religionsgeschichte*, vol. II (2nd ed.; Berlin, 1957), pp. 392-405; M. Eliade, *Myth and Reality*, op. cit., pp. 54ff., chap. IV, 'Eschatology and Cosmogony'.

No. 189. E. Lamotte, 'Prophéties relatives à la disparition de la Bonne Loi,' in René de Berval (ed.), *Présence du Bouddhisme* (Saigon, 1959), pp. 657-68.

No. 190. On Zoroastrian ideas concerning the end of the world, see R. C. Zaehner, *The Dawn and Twilight of Zoroastrianism* (London, 1961), pp. 312 ff.

Nos. 191 ff. On the Islamic beliefs, see Regnar Eklund, *Life between Death and Resurrection according to Islam* (Uppsala, 1941).

Bibliography

Nos. 194 *ff*. On cargo cults and modern messianic movements, cf. P. Worsley, *The Trumpet Shall Sound* (London, 1957); K. O. L. Burridge, *Mambu: A Melanesian Millennium* (London, 1960); G. Guariglia, *Prophetismus und Heilserwartungsbewegungen als völkerkundliches und religionsgeschichtliches Problem* (Horn Wien, 1953); Sylvia L. Thrupp (ed.), *Millennial Dreams in Action: Essays in Comparative Study* (The Hague, 1962); Vittorio Lanternari, *The Religions of the Oppressed: A Study of Modern Messianic Cults* (New York and London, 1963); Wilhelm E. Mühlmann, *Chiliasmus und Nativismus* (Berlin, 1961); I. C. Jarvie, 'Theories of Cargo Cults: A Critical Analysis,' *Oceania*, XXXIV (1963), pp. 1-31, 108-36; M. Eliade, *Mephistopheles and the Androgyne* (New York, 1966, British ed. *The Two and the One*, London, 1965), pp. 125-59; 'Cosmic and Eschatological Renewal.'

Nos. 194-5. For a bibliography of some major writings on the Ghost Dance published after 1896, see Anthony F. C. Wallace Introduction to the new edition (Chicago, 1965), pp. VIII *ff*.

Chapter V: Specialists of the Sacred: From Medicine Men to Mystics and Founders of Religions

Nos. 198 *ff*. On the initiation of the Australian medicine men, see A. P. Elkin, *Aboriginal Men of High Degree* (Sydney, 1945).

No. 202. On North American shamanism, see Willard Z. Park, *Shamanism in Western North America: A Study in Cultural Relationships* (Evanston-Chicago, 1938); Marcelle Bouteiller, *Chamanisme et guérison magique* (Paris, 1950); M. Eliade, *Shamanism: Arihaic Techniques of Ecstasy* (New York and London, 1964), pp. 297 *ff*.

Nos. 203 *ff*. On the different types of shamanistic initiations and seances, see M. Eliade, *Shamanism*, op. cit., pp. 33 *ff*., 181 *ff*., and *passim*.

No. 210. On black magic, see E. E. Evans-Pritchard, *Witchcraft, Oracles and Magic among the Azande* (Oxford, 1937); see also the bibliography listed in M. Eliade, *Patterns in Comparative Religion*, op. cit., pp. 36-7.

No. 211. On the African divine kingship, see the bibliography of Charles H. Long, 'Primitive Religion,' in Adams (ed.), *A Reader's Guide to the Great Religions*, op. cit., p. 19.

No. 214. On *Flamen dialis*, see the numerous works of Georges Dumézil, summarized in his *L'Idéologie tripartie des Indo-Européens* (Bruxelles, 1955).

Nos. 218 *ff*. On different forms of asceticism, cf. O. Hardmann, *The Ideals of Ascetism. An Essay in the Comparative Study of Religion* (London, 1924); P. V. Kane, *History of Dharmashāstra*, vol. II, part 2 (Poona, 1941), pp. 917-75; and the bibliographies listed in M. Eliade, *Yoga: Immortality and Freedom* (New York and London, 1958), pp. 381-5, 391-2, 404-5, 409-10, 419-20, 423-5.

No. 224. On Zarathustra, cf. the bibliography listed above, nos. 37-9.

Nos. 225 ff. On Buddha and Buddhism, cf. the bibliography listed above, nos. 21 *ff*., 29, 30.

Nos. 231 *ff*. On Muhammad and Islam, cf. the bibliographies listed above, nos. 40 *ff*.

No. 238. On the arts and effects of ecstasy in Hellenistic times, see the bibliographies in Frederick C. Grant, *Hellenistic Religions: The Age of Syncretism* (New York, 1953), pp. 151, 169.

Bibliography

Nos. 239-42. On the techniques of Yoga, cf. M. Eliade, *Yoga: Immortality and Freedom*, op. cit., passim, and the bibliography listed p. 372.

Nos. 243 ff. On the Pure Land Buddhism, see the bibliographies listed by Joseph M. Kitagawa, in Adams (ed.), *A Reader's Guide to the Great Religions*, op. cit., pp. 170, 178-9.

Nos. 247 ff. On Zen Buddhism, see D. T. Suzuki, *Manual of Zen Buddhism* (Kyoto, 1935); D. T. Suzuki, *Essays in Zen Buddhism*, 3 vols. (London, 1927, 1933, 1934); Heinrich Dumoulin, *A History of Zen Buddhism*, trans. Paul Peachey (New York, 1963).

No. 251. On Muhammad's ascension, cf. Miguel Asin Palacios, *La escatologia musulmana en la Divina Comedia* (2nd ed.; Madrid-Granada, 1943); George Widengren, *Muhammad, the Apostle of God, and His Ascension* (Uppsala, 1951).

Nos. 252 ff. On Islamic mysticism, see the bibliography of Charles J. Adams, 'Islam,' in his *A Reader's Guide to the Great Religions*, op. cit., pp. 326 ff.

Chapter VI: Speculations on Man and God

Nos. 260, 262, 272-3. On Egyptian religious speculation, see J. H. Breasted, *Development of Religion and Thought in Ancient Egypt* (London, 1912; Harper Torchbook, 1959); John A. Wilson, *The Culture of Ancient Egypt* (Chicago, 1951; Phoenix Books, 1958). Henri Frankfort, John A. Wilson, Thorkild Jacobsen, *Before Philosophy* (Chicago, 1946; Pelican Books, 1949), discuss and compare Egyptian and Mesopotamian myths and theoretical speculations. See also Henri Frankfort, *Kingship and the Gods* (Chicago, 1948); Henri Frankfort, *Ancient Egyptian Religion* (New York: Harper Torchbook, 1961); pp. 59 ff., 88 ff.; S. G. F. Brandon, *Man and His Destiny in the Great Religions* (Manchester, 1962), chap. II.

Nos. 264 ff. On Indian religious thought, see Franklin Edgerton, *The Beginnings of Indian Philosophy: Selections from the Rig Veda, Atharva Veda, Upanishads and Mahabhârata* (Cambridge, Mass., 1965); J. N. Farquhar, *An Outline of the Religious Literature of India* (Oxford, 1920); Louis Renou, *Religions of Ancient India* (London, 1953); S. Radhakrishnan and Charles A. Moore (eds.), *Source Book in Indian Philosophy* (Princeton, 1957); Wm. Theodore de Bary (ed.), *Sources of Indian Tradition* (New York, 1958); Surendranath Dasgupta, *A History of Indian Philosophy*, 5 vols. (Cambridge, England, 1922-55); S. Radhakrishnan, *Indian Philosophy*, 2 vols. (London, 1927); H. Zimmer, *Philosophies of India*, ed. J. Campbell (New York, 1951). See also the bibliographies compiled by Norvin J. Heris, 'Hinduism,' in Adams (ed.), *A Reader's Guide to the Great Religions*, op. cit., pp. 56 ff., 68 ff.

On the interpretation of the Bhagavad Gītā, see Franklin Edgerton, *The Bhagavad Gītā* (New York: Harper Torchbook, 1964), pp. 105-94.

No. 265. On myth, religion and philosophy in ancient Greece, see W. K. C. Guthrie, *The Greeks and Their Gods*, chaps. X-XII; W. K. C. Guthrie, *The Greek Philosophers, from Thales to Aristotle* (London, 1950; Harper Torchbook, 1960); R. B. Onians, *The Origins of European Thought about the Body, the Mind, the Soul, the World, Time and Fate* (2nd ed.; Cambridge, England, 1954); Bruno Snell, *The Discovery of the Mind: The Greek Origins of European*